The Ukrainian Intelligentsia and Genocide

The Ukrainian Intelligentsia and Genocide

The Struggle for History, Language, and Culture in the 1920s and 1930s

Victoria A. Malko

LEXINGTON BOOKS
Lanham • Boulder • New York • London

Published by Lexington Books
An imprint of The Rowman & Littlefield Publishing Group, Inc.
4501 Forbes Boulevard, Suite 200, Lanham, Maryland 20706
www.rowman.com

86-90 Paul Street, London EC2A 4NE

Copyright © 2021 by The Rowman & Littlefield Publishing Group, Inc.

All rights reserved. No part of this book may be reproduced in any form or by any electronic or mechanical means, including information storage and retrieval systems, without written permission from the publisher, except by a reviewer who may quote passages in a review.

British Library Cataloguing in Publication Information Available

Library of Congress Cataloging-in-Publication Data

Names: Malko, Victoria A., 1965- author.
Title: The Ukrainian intelligentsia and genocide : the struggle for history, language, and culture in the 1920s and 1930s / Victoria A. Malko.
Other titles: Struggle for history, language, and culture in the 1920s and 1930s
Description: Lanham : Lexington Books, [2021] | Includes bibliographical references and index.
Identifiers: LCCN 2021036058 (print) | LCCN 2021036059 (ebook) | ISBN 9781498596787 (cloth) | ISBN 9781498596800 (paperback) | ISBN 9781498596794 (ebook)
Subjects: LCSH: Genocide—Ukraine—History—20th century. | Ukraine—History—Famine, 1932-1933. | Famines—Ukraine—History—20th century. | Famines—Soviet Union—History—20th century. | Intellectuals—Ukraine—History—20th century. | Ukraine—History—1921-1944. | National characteristics, Ukrainian.
Classification: LCC DK508.8377 .M295 2021 (print) | LCC DK508.8377 (ebook) | DDC 947.708/4—dc23
LC record available at https://lccn.loc.gov/2021036058
LC ebook record available at https://lccn.loc.gov/2021036059

Contents

List of Figures and Tables — vii

Acknowledgments — ix

Notes on Transliteration and Administrative Divisions — xiii

Introduction: Soviet Genocide against Ukrainians — xv

1 Preconditions — 1

2 Leadership — 47

3 Trial — 87

4 Extermination — 135

5 Denial — 183

Conclusion: Aftermath — 229

Biographical Sketches and Terminology — 269

Bibliography — 305

Index — 341

About the Author — 361

List of Figures and Tables

FIGURES

Figure 1.1	A choir of the Kyïv Labor School No. 1 named after Taras Shevchenko, with school principal Volodymyr Durdukivs'kyi, 1920s	14
Figure 1.2	Poster "Only the Red Army will give us bread" by N. Pomansky (Moscow, 1919)	21
Figure 1.3	Famished children, Berdians'k, Ukraine, 1922	31
Figure 2.1	A group of delegates from the Kharkiv region at the First All-Ukrainian Congress of Teachers, Kharkiv, 1925	55
Figure 2.2	A formation of pioneers of the F. E. Dzerzhinsky Commune, headed by A. S. Makarenko, at a ceremony dedicated to the launching of the reconstructed machine-building factory named after S. Ordzhonikidze in Kramators'k, Kramators'k district, 1931	59
Figure 2.3	Schoolchildren attending lessons in a German seven-year school, Sinel'nykivs'kyi district, Dnipropetrovs'k region, 1933	68
Figure 2.4	Pioneer of Bolshevism in Ukraine and Shums'kyi's successor as the People's Commissar of Education, comrade Mykola Skrypnyk, speaks at a meeting of the Communist Children's Movement (Young Pioneers), Kharkiv, 1930	73
Figure 3.1	An overhead view of the courtroom in the Kharkiv Opera House during the trial of the Union for the Liberation of Ukraine (SVU), 1930	98

viii *List of Figures and Tables*

Figure 3.2 Defendants teacher Nina Tokarivs'ka (first row), writer Liudmyla Cherniakhivs'ka (second row), the former prime minister of the Ukrainian National Republic and leader of the Ukrainian Autocephalous Orthodox Church Prof. V. M. Chekhivs'kyi, and student Borys Matushevs'kyi, during the SVU show trial, 1930 100

Figure 3.3 Defendant Mykola Pavlushkov, student of the Kyïv Institute of People's Education, talks with defense counsel Semen Ratner during the court proceedings in the SVU trial, Kharkiv, 1930 101

Figure 3.4 *Study, New York, 1934* by John Marin (1870–1953) 120

Figure 4.1 Propaganda cartoon in the *Chervonyi perets'* (Red Pepper) satirical biweekly magazine, 1930 (front, see over back) 139

Figure 4.2 Propaganda cartoon in the *Chervonyi perets'* (Red Pepper) satirical biweekly magazine, 1930 (back) 140

Figure 4.3 Mass uprisings in the Ukrainian SSR in 1930 141

Figure 4.4 Schoolchildren from the village of Rakovychi, Radomysl' district, Kyïv region (hot breakfast), 1934 157

Figure 4.5 Vasyl' Ivchuk, school principal in the village Dudarkiv, Boryspil' district (second row, second on the left) with his colleagues and fifth-grade students, 1937 160

Figure 4.6 "Hungernde und verwahrloste Kinder, die sogenannten 'Besprisornyje'" (Starving and neglected children, the so-called *bezprytul'ni*) by Alexander Wienerberger, 1933 161

Figure 5.1 Mortality from the Great Famine in 1932–1933 in the Ukrainian SSR 195

TABLES

Table 4.1 Primary schools, teachers, and students (grades 1 through 4) in Ukraine, 1914–1934 163

Acknowledgments

This book is a result of a long-term study of complex and devastating effects of the Holodomor—genocide against the Ukrainian nation—perpetrated in the 1920s and 1930s. Its first target were members of Ukrainian intelligentsia, the "brain of the nation," in the words of Raphael Lemkin, the father of the U.N. Convention on the Prevention and Punishment of the Crime of Genocide. Ukrainian intelligentsia faced existential threats, resisted, but ultimately were forced to make the "right choice" and serve the Soviet regime in order to survive. The resurgence of Stalinism in Russia and the hybrid war against Ukraine that has commenced since the Revolution of Dignity, 2013–2014, demonstrate the continuity between Stalinist and neo-Stalinist attempts to prevent the crystallization of the nation and subvert Ukraine from within by nonlethal and lethal means. Thus, the struggle for history, language, and culture continues. This book examines how and why this genocide occurred and what role intellectuals, especially teachers, played and continue to play in shaping, contesting, and inculcating history.

Views expressed in this book were informed by conversations with colleagues at a series of conferences and symposia: the International Forum "Ukraine Remembers, World Acknowledges" on the eighty-fifth anniversary of the Holodomor–Genocide; the International Conference "Problem of Existential Choice during the Holodomor–Genocide" at Taras Shevchenko National University in Kyïv, Ukraine; the Association for the Study of Nationalities Annual Convention in New York; and Annual Conventions of the Association for Slavic, East European, and Eurasian Studies in Boston and San Francisco. Observations and insights offered by Professors Myroslava Antonovych, Jars Balan, Halyna Hryn, Iaroslav Kalakura, Nataliia Levchuk, Lubomyr Luciuk, Vasyl' Marochko, Daria Mattingly, Volodymyr Serhiichuk, and Iurii Shapoval shaped research on this topic. The novel coronavirus pandemic interrupted already-scheduled presentations in Washington, D.C., and Berlin, Germany, yet allowed to complete revisions while sheltering in place in Fresno, California.

I am beholden to Dr. Olga Bertelsen, who generously shared her own perspective on the role and fate of the Ukrainian intelligentsia in the 1920s and 1930s, bravely read, and extensively commented on the entire manuscript in very rough form. Professor Hiroaki Kuromiya provided helpful critique on the final draft. Professor Emeritus Roman Serbyn sharpened the author's understanding of Raphael Lemkin's concept of Soviet genocide against the Ukrainian nation. They gave the author additional sources to read and new perspectives to include. I am indebted to Marta Baziuk, Dale A. Bertelsen, Mary and Dan Comelli, Lubow Jowa, Mykola Kotcherha, and Cheryl Madden who read various chapters and the entire manuscript for their thoughtful and enlightening suggestions. I alone am responsible for the views that are expressed in this book.

This work could not have been completed without the archivists and librarians in Ukraine who generously assisted the author in collecting materials. Deep gratitude goes to Andrii Kohut, director of the Sectoral State Archive of the Security Service of Ukraine (*HDA SBU*), who assisted with locating diaries, written by teachers Oleksandra Radchenko and Iurii Sambros, and unearthing hitherto hidden facts from Felix Dzerzhinsky's autobiography that shed light on the use of intelligentsia as forced labor. Ol′ha Bazhan, director of the Central State Archive of Civic Organizations of Ukraine (*TsDAHOU*), and her staff, Larysa Patrak and Ol′ha Dyvnych, assisted with navigating files of the former Communist Party archives. Natalia Makovs′ka, director of the Central State Archive of the Supreme Organs of Administration of Ukraine (*TsDAVOU*), and her staff assisted with locating materials documenting the role of school personnel and activities of the Commissariat of Education in Soviet Ukraine. Archivists Dmytro Stasiuk, Oleksandr Tykhenko, and Maria Dendebera at the Central State Cinephotophono Archive of Ukraine named after H. Pshenychnyi (*TsDKFFAU*) aided the author in searching catalogs of photo illustrations. Most of the photos taken at the time were propagandistic, featuring staged groups of teachers attending conferences or students laboring in workshops. Few authentic photographs of the conditions in 1932–1933 have survived censorship. Propaganda cartoons have been preserved in the National Library of Ukraine named after V. I. Vernads′kyi, and two cartoons from the 1930 satirical magazine will make their first appearance in print in this book thanks to Iana Hrinko and Mykhailo Kostiv. Cartographers at the State Scientific Enterprise "Kartohrafiia" in Ukraine created two maps specifically for this edition.

The staff at museums and libraries in Ukraine and the United States have helped the author chase down sources. Oleksandr Mikhno, director of the

Pedagogical Museum of Ukraine of the National Academy of Pedagogical Sciences of Ukraine, and his research assistant, Tetiana Poliukhovych, deserve special mention for allowing unlimited access to digital collections of educational periodicals published between 1923 and 1933 in Soviet Ukraine. Ol'ha Rokyts'ka of the Kyïv Regional Institute of Advanced Pedagogical Studies in Bila Tserkva shared unique photographs and biographical sketches of the school principal, Vasyl' Ivchuk, the victim of Stalinism and the hero of Ukraine. At the National University "Kyïv-Mohyla Academy," Taïsiia Sydorchuk, director of James E. Mace Museum, kindly guided the author through a vast personal archive of James E. Mace. In Simi Valley, California, Ira G. Pimstein and Jennifer Newby of the Ronald Reagan Presidential Library and Museum facilitated access to boxes of documents pertaining to the work of the U.S. Commission on the Ukraine Famine, directed by James E. Mace. Jurij Dobczansky of the Library of Congress selflessly donated bibliographical rarities, copies of first editions of Ukrainian-language publications on the topic. The author is most grateful for their help.

At Lexington Books, I am extremely grateful to Eric Kuntzman, who acquired this book and gave me encouragement, and to assistant editor Mikayla Mislak, who ably guided me through the process of completing revisions. The suggestions of an anonymous reviewer made the manuscript much more readable and useful. Any shortcomings of this work are my own. I have benefited from support from the Department of History in the College of Social Sciences at California State University, Fresno. Matt Doyle of our university's Henry Madden Library patiently assisted with locating interlibrary loan materials, especially Soviet-era propaganda posters in the New York Public Library.

My deepest thanks go to my family, to my mother, Tamara Chernihovets', and father, Anatoly Mal'ko, who have shared their life stories, humor, and wisdom that sustained the author spiritually throughout the COVID-19 pandemic. In world history courses, students have diligently examined cases of genocide from a comparative perspective, wondering why the Holodomor has been excluded from school and college curricula. Ideas and questions raised during our discussions have made their way to the pages of this book. This work is dedicated with gratitude to them.

Notes on Transliteration and Administrative Divisions

To ensure precision and readability, the author followed the standard Library of Congress system in the text and documents for transliterating Ukrainian names and terms into English. Additionally, the author used Ukrainian abbreviations for republic's branches of government, but transliterated the names of Communist Party and security police (e.g., Politburo, OGPU) from Russian because these variants are more familiar to English-language readers. Names of ethnic Russians and non-Ukrainian party leaders have been rendered in their transliteration from Russian. Last names are rendered with -yi (Ukrainian) and -ii (Russian). The names of cities and administrative divisions in the Ukrainian SSR reflect their Ukrainian pronunciation (e.g., Kyïv, Odesa, Kharkiv), but Russian pronunciation has been preserved in quotes from original documents (e.g., Kiev, Odessa, Kharkov). The spelling of Ukrainian letter ï has been used following the Harvard Ukrainian Research Institute publication guidelines. Ligatures are omitted, but the soft sign (ь) is rendered with a prime (') to reflect the Cyrillic original. The Russian hard sign (ъ) is rendered with two primes ("). English translations of quoted materials are the author's unless otherwise noted.

The Ukrainian SSR went through three administrative changes during the 1930s. Initially, Soviet authorities preserved the tsarist-era *gubernii* (gubernia), known by their Russian spelling, transliterated from Ukrainian as *hubernii*. From 1923 to 1925, they were replaced with smaller *okruhy* (regions) and *raiony* (districts) through the merger and repartition of tsarist-era *volosti* (counties). There were fifty-three *okruhy* in Soviet Ukraine, but this number decreased to forty-one through division and the transfer of territory to the Russian SFSR. The term *krai* (territory), introduced in 1924, designated the North Caucasus, one of the six regions of the Russian SFSR inhabited by Ukrainian ethnic minority. Within the territory of the Ukrainian SSR, Soviet officials created the Moldovan Autonomous SSR and districts for ethnic minorities, including Russian, German, Polish, Jewish, and others. Beginning in 1930, the *okruhy* were abolished. By 1932, they had been replaced by seven large *oblasti* (regions), further subdivided into *raiony* (districts). In 1933, there were 392 administrative districts in Soviet Ukraine. Districts could be rural or urban, roughly equivalent to counties or boroughs. Cities had separate administrations that fell between district and region levels. Within the republic, regions and districts each had party committees, party control commissions, and state bodies. In 1934, the capital of the Ukrainian SSR was transferred from Kharkiv to Kyïv. The number of regions increased through the 1930s to a total of fifteen, including the Moldovan ASSR, by the early 1940s. Throughout this period, the territory and names of districts shifted. Names of cities also changed after the creation of a new Ukrainian orthography in 1928 and its formal adoption by the Soviet Ukrainian Academy of Sciences in 1929. To complicate matters further, the orthography was reformed in 1933 because of its alleged embrace of "nationalist deviation." After the adoption of the Soviet constitution of 1936, the official name of the republic also changed: Socialist Ukraine became Soviet Ukraine.

Introduction

Soviet Genocide against Ukrainians

Radomysl', the town of "happy thought," 1934. Pictured on the cover photo are the teachers and student leaders of School No. 1 named after Taras Shevchenko.[1] The Ukrainian literary specialist George Grabowicz called him "Bard and Prophet, the inspired voice of the people, and the spiritual father of the reborn nation."[2] In his "Testament" (*Zapovit*, 1845), Shevchenko foretold that through struggle his people would break the chains of slavery and tyranny to attain freedom and independence: "Bury me thus I pray, and rise! From chains set yourselves free! And with your foes' unholy blood, baptize your liberty!"[3] Between 1932 and 1933, the Radomysl' district lost 21,705 out of 67,000, or one-third, of its population.[4] In 1913, when my maternal grandfather was just seventeen years old, a bustling industrial district center had a population of 15,165.[5] It had nineteen factories, a water tower, and electric street lights. World War I, the national liberation struggle of 1917–1921, the famine of 1921–1923, and the Great Famine of 1932–1933, the apogee of the Holodomor, devastated the town. Out of six schools established by 1927, only two were still functioning in 1934.[6] Even today, the town's population has not recovered (14,109 as of 2020).[7] In one generation, the survivors lost their national culture, language, and history.

This study is the first of its kind examining existential threats and ideological choices Ukrainian intelligentsia faced as the first group targeted during the genocide known as the Holodomor. To legal scholars, the genocide is an extreme form of collective violence and a crime against humanity. To criminologists, it is a state, organizational, and political crime.[8] To sociologists, it represents violent social or armed conflict between state authorities and civilian groups resisting annihilation.[9] When historians engage in analysis of archival sources, oral histories, and memoirs to reflect on causes and consequences of past genocides, familiar categories of victims and perpetrators are inadequate to account for injustices.[10] Instead, scholars argue the ethics of remembrance requires a shift in our analytical lens from a dichotomy of guilt versus innocence to that of accepting responsibility and accountability. Paraphrasing Michael Rothberg, teachers, doctors, and lawyers were "implicated subjects."[11] Scholars argue that despite being forced to carry out Bolshevik policies,[12] professional elites were able to make individual choices.[13]

Freedom of choice is the cornerstone of philosophy known as Existentialism, which is antithetical to Marxism.[14] Existentialists believe individuals are free and must take personal responsibility for their actions and decision-making. They further contend that individuals must arrive at their own truth and decide which situations are moral. Existentialists, whether religious or atheist, were criticized by Marxists, who called their philosophy "bourgeois" because only bourgeoisie ostensibly have the "luxury" to make individual choices by engaging in contemplation. Marxists believed in economic determinism and action as opposed to contemplation. What choices, if any, could teachers and other members of Ukrainian intelligentsia make in the circumstances of immense coercion, forced deportations, summary incarcerations, and extrajudicial executions?

The core argument of this book is based on a broad definition of the Holodomor as genocide against Ukrainians as a national group in Ukraine and ethnically Ukrainian areas within the borders of the Soviet Union during the 1920s–1930s. The etymology of the term points to one of the tools used to perpetrate genocide. The word *holodomor* is derived from *holod* (hunger) and *mor* (Latin root *mort*-death), meaning "death caused by hunger." The Ukrainian word *holodomor*, spelled with small-h, has been in use to refer to mass deaths as in a plague since 1898, when it appeared in an article describing destitute population suffering from starvation.[15] On August 17, 1933, newspaper *Večerník P. L.* in Prague used it in a headline, "Hladomor v SSSR."[16] Press reports worldwide used neutral linguistic terms "hunger," "famine," and "głod" to depict extreme deficit of food in certain regions of the Soviet Union. German diplomats used such terms as *Hungerkatastrophe* (hunger catastrophe), *Hungersterbens* (death from hunger), and *Planierung der Hungersnot* (planned hunger) in dispatches during 1932–1933.[17] Some of these terms were borrowed by Ukrainian émigré organizations in Europe and North America in the 1930s and used by journalists and publicists in the 1940s through the 1950s. As early as 1933, Ukrainian émigré organizations appealed to the League of Nations and demanded recognition of the famine in Soviet Ukraine, but they secured only six votes.[18] The Soviet Union was not a member of the League at that time. The General Secretariat dismissed the matter considering it an internal affair because Soviet authorities did not admit there was famine in the Ukrainian SSR. In 1949, Ukrainian publicist and civic leader Michael Mischenko introduced the concept of "hunger as a method of terror and rule in the Soviet Union."[19] On May 31, 1953, the newspaper *Ukraïns'ki visti* published an appeal stating, "Let's remind the free world about Moscow's genocide."[20] Appeals from émigré Ukrainian organizations were drowned by disinformation campaigns unleashed from the Kremlin at the onset of the Cold War.

In 1953, Raphael Lemkin defined Soviet policy against the Ukrainian nation as genocide. Lemkin used the specific term "Soviet genocide," based on criteria listed in the U.N. Convention on the Prevention and Punishment of the Crime of Genocide, adopted on December 9, 1948. In his speech on September 20, 1953,[21] addressed to the Ukrainian community in New York on the twentieth anniversary of the 1933 famine, Lemkin went beyond the extermination of people by hunger to what he called the "classic example of Soviet genocide, its longest and broadest experiment in Russification." In his typewritten notes, Lemkin characterized Kremlin's policy toward Ukraine in the first half of the twentieth century as "not simply a case of mass murder, [but as] a case of genocide, of destruction, not of individuals only, but of a culture and a nation."[22] Further, Lemkin defined Stalin's policy in "the Ukraine," as he referred to the Soviet republic at that time, as a four-pronged attack. The first blow was aimed against Ukrainian intelligentsia (the "brain" of the nation), the second against clergy (the "soul" of the nation), and the third at farmers (the "repository of the tradition, folklore and music, the national language and literature," in short, the "national spirit"). The aim of the fourth prong of attack was to change the demographic composition of the population in Ukraine by resettling Red Army veterans and Russian loyalists together with their families into areas depopulated by the genocidal famine.[23] A linguist and lawyer by training, Lemkin proposed an innovative interpretation beyond the etymology of the term "death caused by hunger," combining the intent and fact of physical eradication of Ukrainians as a nation via Russification, political repressions, deportations, and executions.

Until the late 1980s, the term "genocide" in reference to the Holodomor was rarely used; more often historians referred to it as the Great Famine. Emphatic, yet misleading, terms were used by Wasyl Hryshko, who described it as the "Ukrainian holocaust"[24] in 1978, and by Robert Conquest, who called it "terror-famine" in the subtitle of his book in 1986. Already in 1965, Vasyl' Pliushch defined the repressions of the 1920s and 1930s as moral and physical genocide. However, Pliushch used the term genocide for the first time a decade later in the English translation of his book *Genocide of the Ukrainian People*, published in 1973.[25]

Precedent for legal recognition of the Holodomor as genocide was established by the International Commission of Inquiry into the 1932–1933 Famine in Ukraine, when it published its report in 1990.[26] While the Soviet

Union was still in denial, a commission established by the U.S. Congress published its report in April 1988 and, in 1990, published three volumes of oral history interviews with over 200 witnesses.[27] Findings were unequivocal: "Joseph Stalin and those around him committed genocide against Ukrainians in 1932–1933."[28] Soon periodicals began to use the term "famine-genocide."

Raphael Lemkin, who conceptualized genocide in 1942, saw it enshrined in the U.N. Convention on the Prevention and Punishment of the Crime of Genocide in 1948.[29] Article I of the Convention addresses responsibility, confirming that signatories will undertake to prevent and punish genocide, whether committed in time of peace or war. Article II of the Convention specifically defines genocide as "any of the following acts committed with intent to destroy, in whole or in part, a national, ethnical, racial or religious group, as such:

(a) Killing members of the group;
(b) Causing serious bodily or mental harm to members of the group;
(c) Deliberately inflicting on the group conditions of life calculated to bring about its physical destruction in whole or in part;
(d) Imposing measures intended to prevent births within the group;
(e) Forcibly transferring children of the group to another group."[30]

It is worth noting that according to Lemkin, genocide does not necessarily mean the immediate destruction of a nation, rather, a coordinated plan of different actions aimed at destroying essential foundations of life in national groups.

It took more than half a century for a historiographic shift to occur in 2006, when the Parliament of Ukraine recognized the Holodomor as genocide against the Ukrainian national group in accordance with articles of the U.N. Convention on the Prevention and Punishment of the Crime of Genocide.[31] The Genocide Convention "lacked the teeth to condemn the true and only perpetrator of genocide, Russia."[32] It failed to prevent genocides from occurring throughout the twentieth century.

Thus, after the Rwandan genocide, Gregory H. Stanton, professor of Genocide Studies and Prevention at the School for Conflict Analysis and Resolution at George Mason University in Arlington, Virginia, briefed U.S. Department of State officials in 1996 about measures on how to prevent genocidal violence from occurring. Stanton emphasized that prevention has to start early to deescalate cycles of violence that proceed in stages:

(1) classification,
(2) symbolization,
(3) discrimination,

(4) dehumanization,
(5) organization,
(6) polarization,
(7) preparation,
(8) persecution,
(9) extermination, and
(10) denial.[33]

Stanton's model has allowed historians to broaden the theoretical base for studying the Holodomor as a multistage process.[34]

After half a century of Soviet disinformation, which succeeded in deleting the Holodomor from history textbooks and academic discussions, scholars in the West and in Ukraine find it challenging to apply the broad definition proposed by Lemkin to study this case of genocide. Roman Serbyn, professor emeritus of Russian and East European history at the University of Quebec at Montreal, has underscored that Lemkin's analysis offered a novel interpretation beyond *a* famine or *the* famine.[35] Legal scholars and some historians in Ukraine and in the Ukrainian diaspora have embraced it.[36] However, narrow interpretation of the Holodomor as the famine of 1932–1933 has dominated the discourse for so long that some Ukrainian and Western scholars argue broadening the chronological scope dilutes the definition.[37]

Many Russian and pro-Russian or Soviet specialists deny Stalin used the famine of 1932–1933 deliberately to starve Ukrainians and view it as an "all-Union" famine, a tragedy of Soviet countryside.[38] The latter focused on Soviet agricultural policy, thus obscuring the role of Soviet nationality policy. Soviet historian Stanislav Kul′chyts′kyi has recently reinterpreted it as a famine within the famine, which must be analyzed at the intersection of the Kremlin's economic and nationality policies.[39] Yet, focus on economic causes of the famine, continuously promoted as part of disinformation warfare, diverts attention from the targeted group in this instance of genocide.

The case of Ukraine follows a pattern of genocidal violence in early twentieth-century Europe against nations having no states or being on the periphery of empires. Several scholars have examined this case through the imperialist or colonialist paradigm.[40] The first Ukrainian scholar who used the term "colonialism" to define the relationship between Russia and its Ukrainian provinces was Mykola Stasiuk in 1911. His contemporary Max Weber compared non-Russian colonies in the Russian Empire to the British colonies of Ireland and India.[41] Unlike Britain's overseas colonies, Russia's colonies were contiguous. Contemporary scholars argue that experiences of Ukrainians as colonial subjects paralleled the experiences of Armenians during World War I and of Jews during World War II. In the latter two cases, wars legitimized violence against civilian populations singled out as scapegoats of imperial rulers, Ottomans, and the Third Reich. What makes the Ukrainian case unique is that violence was perpetrated during peacetime between two world wars, both of which were fought on Ukrainian blood-soaked lands.[42]

After dissolution of the Soviet Union and opening of archives in Ukraine, historians began to study political repressions against intelligentsia, one of the first groups targeted during the genocide.[43] Two schools of thought, totalitarian and revisionist, continue to dominate the discussion. Sheila Fitzpatrick and J. Arch Getty rejected Robert Conquest's "totalitarian" portrayal of the structure and operations of the Soviet government. Two revisionist historians, R. W. Davies and Stephen Wheatcroft, argued that the famine of 1932–1933 was not intentional, but a result of mismanaged policies and natural disasters, and that negligence and environmental circumstances were the causes of the famine rather than Stalin himself.[44] Anne Applebaum resurrected the "totalitarian" model by contending that Stalin personally planned and executed the famine.[45] Political scientists Carl J. Friedrich of Harvard University and Zbigniew K. Brzezinski of Columbia University analyzed the essence of Stalinism through the prism of totalitarianism.[46] The four basic features or traits that distinguish totalitarian dictatorships from constitutional systems are as follows:

(1) an ideology, to which everyone living in that society is supposed to adhere;
(2) a single mass party typically led by one man, the "dictator";
(3) a system or terror, both physical and psychic, effected through party and secret-police control; and
(4) a mass communications monopoly in the hands of the party.[47]

Significantly, the Soviet system continued to maintain itself after Stalin's death. It was institutionalized through an elaborate bureaucratic network. Political lieutenants of the dictator wielded the levers of control that held the system together because they derived considerable benefits for themselves.

Historiography of political terror has initially centered on Stalin's personality cult along with political and security apparatchiks who sustained their boss in power.[48] Institutional analysis further exposed the nature and functioning of organs of repression, focusing on the organization and carrying out of special operations, yet leaving out ideological aspects of Soviet repressive policies.[49] Scholars have documented deportations of Ukrainian intelligentsia in the 1920s[50] soon after the Union of Soviet Socialist Republics emerged as a unitary state and continued repressions and eventual extermination of nationally conscious intelligentsia, including teachers, in the 1930s.[51] While documenting victims' experiences, these authors overlooked the role that conformists played in carrying out Soviet propaganda, collectivization, and grain-requisition campaigns, including silencing the truth about the famine.

Important archival sources that have shed light on the role of the Soviet security police in persecutions of Ukrainian intelligentsia appeared in a series of articles published in a periodical *Z arkhiviv VUChK, GPU, NKVD, KGB* in the 1990s.[52] The use of the Russian abbreviation GPU rather than the Ukrainian translation DPU has been proposed by Iurii Shapoval, who has published a considerable body of works on the history of the Soviet state security services, as is evident from the title of the documentary collection, *Rozsekrechena pam'iat': Holodomor 1932–1933 rokiv v Ukraïni v dokumentakh GPU-NKVD.*[53] This highlights the fact that the Ukrainian branch was an affiliate subordinated to the OGPU of the USSR in Moscow and followed Soviet leadership directives to implement "special operations" that led to mass deaths of Ukrainians.

Scholars have compiled hitherto unpublished documents related to surveillance of "old" (prerevolution) Ukrainian intelligentsia in preparation for a case fabricated by the GPU against the "counterrevolutionary" and "anti-Soviet" organization, the Union for the Liberation of Ukraine (known by its Ukrainian acronym SVU or *Spilka vyzvolennia Ukraïny*).[54] They have yet to foreground the prominent role of the SVU trial in deliberate destruction of the Ukrainian intelligentsia.[55] In 1929, when thousands of rebellions in Ukrainian villages threatened to topple the Soviet government, a scapegoat had to be found to crush the opposition to the communist[56] regime. Arrests started in May 1929 and, following the staged SVU public hearings in early 1930, repressions touched all educational institutions in Soviet Ukraine. Scholars have studied the trial proceedings and fate of individual defendants extensively in the 1990s and early 2000s.[57] Several eyewitness accounts have been published.[58] Authors of these publications challenged the official version that the SVU was a "plot" and argued against it being a real organization.[59] Scholars have treated the trial as a "prelude to the Holodomor" rather than a continuation of the first prong of attack in Soviet genocide against Ukrainians.

Soviet education policy has been thoroughly studied by American historians, yet their narratives contain gaps because access to sensitive archival sources has been limited. In her monograph *Education and Social Mobility in the Soviet Union, 1921–1934*, Sheila Fitzpatrick delineated the historical period as the "cultural revolution," lauding Soviet achievements.[60] This revisionist American historian of Australian origin examined the implementation of the education policy in all Soviet republics. However, Fitzpatrick had limited access to archives in Moscow and Smolensk in the late 1970s; so her historical account of discrimination and purges of teachers and professors focused mostly on the Russian republic. Fitzpatrick referred to the Ukrainian language issue several times, but failed to explain what happened in Soviet Ukraine in

1932 and 1933. In two out of three statistical tables, the author included data from 1932 to 1933 to illustrate increased enrollment in secondary schools but missed data on the decreased enrollment in primary grades. Intentionally or unintentionally, Fitzpatrick missed the crucial evidence that several million children were unaccounted for.[61] Primary schools were obligatory at the time, so missing statistical data in the Russian archives further highlights the regime's attempt to cover up the crime perpetrated in Soviet Ukraine.

Another Russia-focused study by Larry F. Holmes *The Kremlin and the Schoolhouse: Reforming Education in Soviet Russia, 1917–1931* left no page of the Soviet teachers' newspapers and archival documents unturned to corroborate the scholarship of Roberta Manning, J. Arch Getty, and Lynne Viola who pointed to limits of the regime's power over society.[62] Very few historians have claimed that Bolsheviks had successfully introduced their utopian schemes, except Marxist historians in the former Soviet Union. Holmes failed to contemplate how the battle over educational issues related to the life-and-death struggle for power taking place at the same time in Soviet Ukraine.

To overcome shortcomings of his predecessors, E. Thomas Ewing in his monograph, a methodological tour-de-force, *The Teachers of Stalinism: Policy, Practice and Power in Soviet Schools of the 1930s* compared classroom conditions in Soviet vis-à-vis American, French, British, and German schools. Ewing provided insight into ethnicity, social mobility, gender, state power, and grassroots resistance.[63] However, the author failed to mention purges of educators in 1930 and collapse of schools during 1932–1933 in the Ukrainian SSR.

One of the first studies in English focusing specifically on teachers and schools in Soviet Ukraine in the 1930s was *Breaking the Tongue: Language, Education, and Power in Soviet Ukraine, 1923–1934* by Matthew D. Pauly of Michigan State University.[64] The monograph on the implementation of language policy in Soviet Ukraine from 1923 to 1934 includes biographical sketches of the Ukrainian teachers and academicians as defendants in the SVU trial. Pauly's frequent trips to Ukrainian archives make it an authoritative study of local history. The famine of 1932–1933 is mentioned because it was centered on the Ukrainian republic. Pauly has argued that Bolshevik anxiety about Ukrainian nationalism influenced the tenor of purges. Although Pauly told the story of the SVU trial, he provided no insight into its possible connection to the genocide known as the Holodomor.

Scholars who have studied the fate of the Ukrainian intelligentsia in the 1920s,[65] 1930s,[66] and from the October Socialist Revolution of 1917 to the Great Terror of 1937[67] have noted that the intelligentsia did not fit into Bolshevik social class structure; yet intellectuals, as members of professional unions, had certain ethno-cultural, social, psychological characteristics and followed a code of ethical behavior.[68] A teacher's professional mission was to enlighten the masses and lead them in the struggle for national liberation. Yet many turned into "best friends" of the Communist Party,[69] who under duress "enthusiastically" carried out propaganda, collectivization, and even grain-requisition campaigns. We must analyze if Ukrainian intelligentsia, particularly teachers, could truly make existential choices in circumstances of collective violence.

This book seeks to examine why and how the so-called "cultural revolution" occurred and its impact on society in Soviet Ukraine, especially the role that intelligentsia, the "brain" of the nation, played. Samuel Huntington postulated that great divisions among nations occur along traditional fault lines of culture; thus, he titled his essay provocatively: "The Clash of Civilizations?" Huntington has suggested that cultural conflicts are harder to resolve than political or economic. In ideological conflicts, the question is, "Which side are you on?" and people do choose sides. In conflicts between civilizations, the question is, "What are you?" and the wrong answer to that question means a bullet in the head.[70] Although Russian and Ukrainian cultures seem to have Eastern Orthodox religion as their faith and Cyrillic script as their writing system, branching from the Balto-Slavic language family, they have mutually unintelligible spoken languages[71] and distinct differences in values and beliefs that govern their respective societies. Historically, Western ideas of constitutionalism, human rights, liberty, rule of law, and democracy have penetrated the Russian autocratic state via Ukraine. The historic and historiographic differences[72] need to be considered when analyzing causes and consequences of the Holodomor in Ukraine and the denial of the Holodomor as genocide in Russia.

A systematic complex analysis requires multiple lenses on which to focus in order to avoid a trap of one's discipline bias. Therefore, some of the issues explored in this book include the following:

- Philosophical: Marxism, Leninism, Stalinism, Existentialism.
- Political: modernity, imperialism, colonialism, nationalism, role of government, role of the international community.
- Economic: industrialization, collectivization of agriculture, the use of forced labor.
- Legal: justice, moral versus natural law, suspension of morality and law (bystanders, rescuers), human rights.
- Psychological: thought control, perpetrator psyche, victim behavior, post-traumatic stress disorder, guilt, shame, sacrifice to help the sufferers, denial.
- Social: Social Darwinism, membership in communities ("us" versus "them"), resistance.
- Cultural: values, beliefs, perception of death and dying, coping with grievance, surviving humiliation, memorializing.

The history of the Holodomor as genocide is complex, and a brief survey will not resolve the big question: What is it about human nature that makes some people want to inflict death on others? Nevertheless, this book will attempt to address more specific questions about the history of the Holodomor: Who was involved and in what way? What motivated those people to behave the way they did? What role did the intelligentsia, especially teachers, play? How can study of the past help us understand why brutality and suffering continue in our present world? Thus, the goal of this book is to provide a cautionary tale for present and future generations to become cognizant of the signs of state violence, and to stand in defense of human rights and social justice.

Chronological, statistical, and comparative analytical approaches were used to examine social changes in Ukraine over a decade from the 1920s through the 1930s. Historical research methodology was used to collect primary and secondary sources. Recognizing limitations of storytelling and the politics of memory, a narrative analysis of published witness accounts,[73] and diaries, written by teachers or those who personally knew teachers,[74] was triangulated with governmental documents and official reports that have been preserved in archives of central and regional Communist Party organizations,[75] Ukraine's security service,[76] pedagogical museums,[77] and private libraries.[78] Dissolution of the Soviet Union made access to archives possible for research. Top secret resolutions and case files of repressed teachers hidden for decades shed new light on historical events. Facts gleaned from periodicals fill gaps in archival materials to reveal a complex picture.

Chronologically, this book is divided into five periods discussed in each chapter, respectively. Chapter 1 examines preconditions of the atrocity, from 1917 to 1922, when Ukraine lost its struggle for national liberation and Bolsheviks established their presence, equipped with Marxist ideology and a repressive security police to enforce it. Ideological roots of Soviet genocide against Ukrainians are traced to writings of the fathers of scientific communism, Karl Marx and Friedrich Engels, and the founding father of the first socialist state, Vladimir Lenin. Bolshevik policies toward non-Russian nations and ownership of land were preconditions for establishing the dictatorship of the proletariat following the October Socialist Revolution of 1917. Efforts to rebuild the national education system by "old" (prerevolution) intelligentsia in Ukraine ran into conflict with demand for training new Soviet elite.

Chapter 2 focuses on the period from 1923 to 1927, when Soviet policy toward non-Russian nations was introduced and violence against nationally conscious intelligentsia became institutionalized while giving rise to new "red" intelligentsia. Teachers in Soviet Ukraine became instrumental by serving as propagandists of Bolshevik policies. On the eve of the tenth anniversary of the October Socialist Revolution, Ukrainian separatism was proclaimed a great threat to Soviet power, and authorities set out methods of eliminating this tendency.

Chapter 3 analyzes events between 1928 and 1931, when Soviet policy of secrecy was instituted ahead of the first show trial of the nationally conscious intelligentsia along with a simultaneous suppression of uprisings against the Bolshevik policy of total collectivization leading to the rise of "corrective labor" camps. It foregrounds deportations of nationally conscious intelligentsia in the 1920s and one of the first show trials of participants in the fabricated Union for the Liberation of Ukraine, dubbed the SVU, and subsequent purges of thousands of teachers and the liquidation of the Commissariat of Education in Ukraine. Remaining teaching cadres were intimidated into becoming "enthusiasts" in carrying out Bolshevik propaganda, collectivization, and grain-requisition campaigns. Recalcitrant members of Ukrainian intelligentsia were exiled to labor camps, managed by the GPU in the Russian North, Far East, and Siberia, where they froze, starved to death, or were executed.

Chapter 4 zeros in on the ultimate phase of the genocide: extermination by man-made famine and other means in 1932–1933. Along with beheading the intelligentsia, Stalin and those around him used a variety of tools to put Ukrainian land tillers on their "knees," including requisitions, blacklists, and blockades. Concurrent curtailment of Ukrainization spelled out death to farmers who were carriers of national tradition, culture, and language in Ukraine and beyond its borders in areas populated by ethnic Ukrainians in Russian SFSR. To survive meant to submit to the repressive regime.

Chapter 5 uncovers strategies of denial employed by perpetrators of the genocide. The denial of the Holodomor started with covering up the crime, and continues to this day. Enablers and bystanders contributed to silencing truth about the Holodomor. Silence and secrecy, although not unique, were hallmarks of the Soviet state. Two belts of silence existed: internal, inside the Soviet Union, and external, on the world stage. Bystanders included Western journalists and intellectuals, diplomats, and leaders of great powers who failed to prevent genocidal violence against Ukrainians in the 1930s.

The concluding chapter addresses issues of legal responsibility, as well as economic, social, cultural, and psychological effects of the Holodomor on subsequent generations of Ukrainians. It examines representation of the topic in historical writing and memorials. Spanish-born American philosopher and professor at Harvard George Santayana, known for his aphorisms, warned, "Those who cannot remember the past are condemned to repeat it."[79] This warning is a lesson for our generation to discern the seeds of genocide in Russia's hybrid warfare against Ukraine.[80]

NOTES

1. Taras Shevchenko (1814–1861), Ukraine's leading poet and artist, was born a serf. His patriotic poetry has influenced generations of Ukrainians and inspired their struggle for liberation. Shevchenko was arrested in 1847 and banished from his native land for decades. His works were banned. Not until 1907, they were published in complete form in Ukrainian in the Russian Empire. See Robert Conquest, *The Harvest of Sorrow: Soviet Collectivization and the Terror–Famine* (New York: Oxford University Press, 1986), 28.

2. George G. Grabowicz, *The Poet as Mythmaker: A Study of Symbolic Meaning in Taras Ševčenko* (Cambridge: Harvard Ukrainian Research Institute, 1982), 1.

3. *Zapovit* by Taras Shevchenko, Pereiaslav, December 25, 1845. The translation is from *The Ukrainian Poets, 1189–1962*, eds. Constantine Henry Andrusyshen and Watson Kirkconnell (Toronto: University of Toronto Press, 1963). For additional English versions by various translators, see https://taras-shevchenko.storinka.org/my-testament-poem-of-taras-shevchenko-english-translation-by-various-translators.html. The selected stanza comes from a program of the event honoring Taras Shevchenko, "Ukraine's Greatest Poet, Teacher, and Spiritual Leader," in San Francisco, California, March 2021 (courtesy of Maria Tscherepenko, president of the Ukrainian American Coordinating Council, personal communication, March 16, 2021).

4. *Dovidnyk z osnovnykh statystychno-ekonomichnykh pokaznykiv hospodarstva raioniv Kyïvs'koï oblasti USRR* (Kharkiv, 1933), 6–8; *Derzhavnyi arkhiv Kyïvs'koï oblasti* (hereafter, *DAKO*), f. R-235, op. 1, spr. 21, ark. 1–108; quoted in Volodymyr Serhiychuk, "To Honor All Innocent Victims of the Holodomor," in *Women and the Holodomor-Genocide: Victims, Survivors, Perpetrators*, ed. Victoria A. Malko (Fresno: The Press at California State University, 2019), 125.

5. My maternal grandfather Mykola Chernihovets' was born in Chornobyl', Radomysl's'kyi *povit*, Kyïv *huberniia* in 1896 in a family of grain growers. Special thanks to Ia. M. Bul'boniuk for locating a church record in *Tsentral'nyi derzhavnyi istorychnyi arkhiv Ukraïny, Kyïv* (*TsDIAKU*), f. 127, op. 1078, spr. 2519, ark. 115 zv.

6. "Radomyshl'," in *Istoriia mist i sil Ukraïns'koï RSR: Zhytomyrs'ka oblast'* (Kyïv: Ukraïns'ka Radians'ka Entsyklopediia AN URSR, 1973), http://imsu-zhytomyr.com/mista-i-sela-zhytomyrskoi-oblasti/radomyshlskyj-rajon-/radomyshl-.html.

7. See Table 5 in *Number of Existing Population of Ukraine as of 1 January 2020: Statistical Publication*, ed. Olena Vyshnevska (Kyïv: State Statistics Service of Ukraine, 2020), 30.

8. Alette Smeulers, "Perpetrators of International Crimes: Towards a Typology," in *Supranational Criminology: Towards a Criminology of International Crimes*, eds. Alette Smeulers and Roelof Haveman (Antwer: Intersentia, 2008), 233, 235.

9. Frank Chalk and Kurt Jonassohn, *The History and Sociology of Genocide: Analyses and Case Studies* (New Haven: Yale University Press, 1990). The authors defined genocide and ethnocide as the intent to kill *a part* of a group "in order to terrorize the remainder into giving up their separate identity or their opposition to the perpetrator group or both" (26). The authors proposed a fourfold typology of

genocide, based on the motives of the perpetrator: "(1) to eliminate a real or potential threat; (2) to spread terror among real and potential enemies; (3) to acquire economic wealth; or (4) to implement a belief, a theory, or an ideology" (29). In any given case, more than one of these motives are present. See also British political scientist and sociologist Martin Shaw, who adopts a broad definition of the concept in his book, *What Is Genocide?* (Cambridge: Polity, 2007).

10. Vasyl′ Marochko and Götz Hillig, *Represovani pedahohy Ukraïny: zhertvy politychnoho teroru, 1929–1941* (Kyïv: "Naukovyi svit," 2003); O. Drach, "Spivrobitnyky Cherkas′koho pedahohichnoho instytutu – zhertvy stalins′kykh represii," in *Osvitiany Cherkashchyny – zhertvy radians′koho totalitarnoho rezhymu: dokumental′ne vydannia*, ed. V. Masnenko (Cherkasy: Brama-Ukraïny, 2009), 213–18; Daria Mattingly, "[Extra]ordinary Women: Female Perpetrators of the Holodomor," in *Women and the Holodomor-Genocide*, ed. Victoria A. Malko (Fresno: The Press at California State University, 2019), 51–89.

11. Michael Rothberg, *The Implicated Subject: Beyond Victims and Perpetrators* (Redwood City: Stanford University Press, 2019).

12. Hennadii Iefimenko, "Sotsial′ne oblychchia vchytel′stva USRR v konteksti transformatsiï suspil′stva (1920-ti roky)," *Problemy istoriï Ukraïny: fakty, sudzhennia, poshuky*, no. 17 (2007): 138–61.

13. Ol′ha Koliastruk, *Intelihentsiia USRR u 1920-ti roky: povsiakdenne zhyttia* (Kharkiv: "Rarytety Ukraïny," 2010).

14. Thomas Flynn, *Existentialism: A Very Short Introduction* (New York: Oxford University Press, 2006).

15. *Literaturno-naukovyi vistnyk* 3, no. 7 (1898); quoted in *Vil′nyi tlumachnyi slovnyk*, 2018, http://sum.in.ua/f/Gholodomor. The derivative verb *moryty* is used in Ukrainian colloquial speech to figuratively mean "exhaust" or "torment."

16. "Hladomor v SSSR," *Večerník P. L.*, August 17, 1933. See Iaroslav Hrytsak, "Khto i koly vpershe vzhyv slovo "Holodomor"? *Ukraïna Moderna*, November 24, 2017, http://uamoderna.com/blogy/yaroslav-griczak/etymology-holodomor.

17. Vasyl′ Marochko, "Holodomor–henotsyd," in *Entsyklopediia Holodomoru 1932–1933 rokiv v Ukraïni* (Drohobych: "Kolo," 2018), 91–93.

18. Pavlo Shtepa, *Moskovstvo: Ioho pokhodzhennia, zmist, formy i istorychna tiahlist′*, vol. 2 (Toronto: Semen Stasyshyn, 1968), 362.

19. Michael Mischenko, "Hunger as a Method of Terror and Rule in the Soviet Union," *Ukrainian Quarterly* 5, no. 2 (1949): 219–25.

20. "Nahadaiemo shche vil′nomu svitovi pro moskovs′kyi henotsyd," *Ukraïns′ki visti*, May 31, 1953.

21. "Ukrainians March in Protest Parade. 10,000 Here Mark Anniversary of the 1933 Famine – Clergy Join in the Procession," *New York Times*, September 21, 1953; "Over 154,000 N.Y. Ukrainian Americans March in Protest Parade Marking Anniversary of Soviet Fostered 1932–1933 Famine in Ukraine," *Ukrainian Weekly*, September 26, 1953. Both newspapers mentioned that Raphael Lemkin spoke about "the millions of Ukrainians who died victims to the Soviet Russian plan to exterminate as many of them as possible in order to break the heroic Ukrainian national resistance to Soviet Russian rule and occupation and to Communism." Per personal

communication with Roman Serbyn on September 20, 2019, most probably Lemkin had little time to deliver the entire speech; thus, his concept of Soviet genocide against Ukrainians as the four-pronged attack was not mentioned in the newspaper reports and remained obscured throughout the twentieth century.

22. Raphael Lemkin, "Soviet Genocide in the Ukraine" (typewritten notes), folder 16, box 2, reel 3, ZL-273, "The Raphael Lemkin Papers, 1947–1959," Rare Books and Manuscripts Division, New York Public Library. Steven Jacobs, Roman Serbyn, and Marko Suprun located the text of the speech in the New York Public Library. The manuscript was first quoted in Jean-Louis Panné, "Rafaël Lemkin ou le pouvoir d'un sans-pouvoir," introduction to Rafaël Lemkin, *Qu'est-ce qu'un génocide?* (Monaco: Édition du Rocher, 2008), 7–66. The full text of the speech was first published as an appendix in *Holodomor: Reflections on the Great Famine of 1932–1933 in Soviet Ukraine*, eds. Lubomyr Y. Luciuk and Lisa Grekul (Kingston: Kashtan Press, 2008), 235–42. It was translated into six official languages of the United Nations and twenty-nine other languages and edited by Roman Serbyn and Olesia Stasiuk, *Raphael Lemkin: Soviet Genocide in Ukraine (Article in 28 Languages)* (Kyïv: Maisternia knyhy, 2009), available from https://holodomormuseum.org.ua/wp-content/uploads/2019/04/978-966-2260-15-1.pdf. For a complete text with a facsimile of the manuscript and an introduction by Douglas Irvin-Erickson, see Raphael Lemkin, *Soviet Genocide in the Ukraine*, ed. Lubomyr Y. Lucuk (Kingston: Kashtan Press, 2014).

23. Witnesses testified that trainloads with new settlers from Russian provinces started to arrive during the peak of the famine in Soviet Ukraine in spring 1933. Tugboat brigades that previously requisitioned grain in villages were put in charge of greeting the colonizers. Just at one train station in the village Svatove, such brigades unloaded seventy-five train transports. See *Svoboda*, no. 164, June 17, 1951. Over a million Russian colonists resettled in the areas depopulated by the famine in Soviet Ukraine. See Dmytro Solovey, *Golgota Ukraïny* (Drohobych: "Vidrodzhennia," 1993), 197, 204, 211. The book was first published in English under the title *Golgotha of Ukraine*, Part I, *The Moscow-Bolshevik Occupation Terror in Ukrainian SSR between First and Second World War* (Winnipeg: "Ukrainian Voice," 1953).

24. Wasyl Hryshko, *The Ukrainian holocaust of 1933*, ed. Marco Carynnyk (Toronto: Bahriany Foundation, SUZHERO, DOBRUS, 1983). The original Ukrainian version was published in 1978. At the time, American dictionaries defined the word "holocaust" to mean "a mass slaughter of people." Dictionary definitions did not include "the Holocaust," meaning "the murder by the Nazis of over six million Jews." It appeared in 1980.

25. Vasyl Pliushch, *Genocide of the Ukrainian People: The Artificial Famine in the Years 1932–1933* (München: Ukrainisches Institut für Bildungspolitik, 1973), http://diasporiana.org.ua/wp-content/uploads/books/10887/file.pdf.

26. *International Commission of Inquiry into the 1932–33 Famine in Ukraine: The Final Report* (Stockholm: Stockholm Institute of Public and International Law, No. 109, 1990), https://web.archive.org/web/20081001225745/http://www.ukrainianworldcongress.org/Holodomor/Holodomor-Commission.pdf.

27. Commission on the Ukraine Famine, *Investigation of the Ukrainian Famine, 1932–1933: Report to Congress* (Washington, D.C.: U.S. Government Printing Office, 1988; hereafter: *Report to Congress*), https://catalog.hathitrust.org/Record/007398237; James E. Mace and Leonid Heretz, eds., *Investigation of the Ukrainian Famine, 1932–1933: Oral History Project of the Commission on the Ukraine Famine*, vols. 1–3 (Washington, D.C.: U.S. Government Printing Office, 1990; hereafter: *Oral History Project*), https://catalog.hathitrust.org/Record/009145045.

28. *Report to Congress*, vii.

29. Lemkin wrote, "Generally speaking, genocide does not necessarily mean the immediate destruction of a nation, except when accompanied by mass killings of all members of a nation. It is intended rather to signify a coordinated plan of different actions aiming at the destruction of essential foundations of the life of national groups, with the aim of annihilating the groups themselves. The objectives of such a plan would be disintegration of the political and social institutions, of culture, language, national feelings, religion, and the economic existence of national groups, and the destruction of the personal security, liberty, health, dignity, and even the lives of the individuals belonging to such groups." Raphael Lemkin, *Axis Rule in Occupied Europe: Laws of Occupation, Analysis of Government, Proposals for Redress* (Washington, DC: Carnegie Endowment for International Peace, Division of International Law, 1944), 79.

30. United Nations, Treaty Series, *Convention on the Prevention and Punishment of the Crime of Genocide, adopted by the General Assembly of the United Nations on December 9, 1948*, vol. 78 (1951), 280, https://treaties.un.org/doc/publication/unts/volume%2078/volume-78-i-1021-english.pdf.

31. "Zakon Ukraïny 'Pro Holodomor 1932–1933 v Ukraïni' No. 376-V (Vidomosti Verkhovnoï Rady Ukraïny 2006, No. 50, 504), 28 November 2006," in *The Holodomor of 1932–1933 in Ukraine as a Crime of Genocide under International Law*, eds. Volodymyr Vasylenko and Myroslava Antonovych (Kyïv: Kyïv-Mohyla Academy, 2016), 226–28, https://zakon.rada.gov.ua/laws/show/376-16.

32. This was the position of the American Bar Association articulated in their arguments against U.S. ratification of the treaty. See Anton Weiss-Wendt, *The Soviet Union and the Gutting of the U.N. Genocide Convention* (Madison: University of Wisconsin Press, 2017), 8. It took the U.S. Senate forty years to consent to ratify it on February 19, 1986, and on November 4, 1988, President Ronald Reagan finally signed a bill ratifying the U.N. Convention on Genocide.

33. Gregory H. Stanton, "The Ten Stages of Genocide," *Genocide Watch*, 2020, https://www.genocidewatch.com/ten-stages-of-genocide. Professor Gregory H. Stanton served as a legal advisor to Rukh, the Ukrainian Independence Movement, work for which he was named the Ukrainian Congress Committee of America 1992 Man of the Year.

34. The framework for analysis is reproduced with permission of Dr. Gregory H. Stanton, president of the *Genocide Watch*, per email communication with the author on October 2, 2019. The model was applied to the analysis of the Holodomor in the paper, "A Paradigm Shift in Studying History of the Holodomor as Genocide,"

presented at the International Forum "Ukraine Remembers, the World Acknowledges" on the 85th anniversary of the Holodomor 1932–1933—Genocide of the Ukrainian People, Kyïv, Ukraine, November 22, 2018.

35. Roman Serbyn, "*Holodomor*: The Ukrainian Genocide," in *Rafał Lemkin: A Hero of Humankind*, eds. Agnieszka Bieńczyk-Missala and Sławomir Dębski (Warsaw: Polish Institute of International Affairs, 2010), 205–30. See also Douglas Irvin-Erickson, "Foreword: The Four Pronged Attack—Raphael Lemkin's Theory of Genocide and the Destruction of the Ukrainian Nation," in *Soviet Genocide in the Ukraine*, ed. Luciuk, iv.

36. Wasyl Hryshko, "The Origins of Soviet Genocide," in *The Ukrainian holocaust of 1933*, ed. Marco Carynnyk (Toronto: Bahriany Foundation, SUZHERO, DOBRUS, 1983), 8–68; Volodymyr Vasylenko, "Metodolohiia pravovoï otsinky Holodomoru 1932–1933 rr. v Ukraïni iak zlochynu henotsydu," in *Holodomor 1932–1933 rokiv v Ukraïni iak zlochyn henotsydu zhidno z mizhnarodnym pravom*, eds. Volodymyr Vasylenko and Myroslava Antonovych (Kyïv: Vydavnychyi dim "Kyievo-Mohylians'ka akademiia," 2016), 63–65; Volodymyr Serhiychuk, *Genocide-Holodomor of Ukrainians, 1932–1933* (Vyshgorod: PP Serhiychuk M. I., 2018), 145–46; Myroslava Antonovych, "Individual and Collective Intent in the Crime of Genocide (on the Example of the Holodomor-Genocide against the Ukrainian Nation)," *Actual Problems of International Relations*, no. 145 (2020): 54–61.

37. Michael Ellman, "Stalin and the Soviet Famine of 1932–33 Revisited," *Europe-Asia Studies* 59, no. 4 (2007): 663–93. See also Lesia Onyshko, "Poshyrennia informatsiï pro Holodomor v nezalezhnii Ukraïni: imidzhevi vtraty," *Holodomor 1932–1933 rokiv: vtraty ukraïns'koï natsiï: Materialy Mizhnarodnoï naukovo-praktychnoï konferentsiï (Kyïv, 4 zhovtnia 2016)*, ed. Olesia Stasiuk et al. (Kyïv: Vyd. Oleh Filiuk, 2017), 193–97.

38. Alec Nove, *An Economic History of the USSR, 1917–1991* (New York: Penguin, 1992); N. A. Ivnitskii, "Golod 1932–1933-kh godov: Kto vinovat?," in *Sud'by rossiiskogo krest'ianstva*, ed. I. Afanas'iev (Moscow: Rossiia XX vek, 1996), 333–63; R. W. Davies and S. G. Wheatcroft, *The Years of Hunger: Soviet Agriculture, 1931–1933* (London: Palgrave MacMillan, 2004).

39. Stanislav Kulchytsky, *The Famine of 1932–1933 in Ukraine: An Anatomy of the Holodomor*, trans. Ali Kinsella (Edmonton: Canadian Institute of Ukrainian Studies, 2018), xxiii–xxvi.

40. Pliushch, *Genocide of the Ukrainian People*; Hryshko, *The Ukrainian holocaust of 1933*; Andrea Graziosi, "Viewing the Twentieth Century through the Prism of Ukraine: Reflections on the Heuristic Potential of Ukrainian History," *Harvard Ukrainian Studies* 34, no. 1–4 (2015–2016): 107–28.

41. Stephen Velychenko, *Painting Imperialism and Nationalism Red: The Ukrainian Marxist Critique of Russian Communist Rule in Ukraine, 1918–1925* (Toronto: University of Toronto Press, 2015).

42. Timothy Snyder, "The Soviet Famines," in *Bloodlands: Europe between Hitler and Stalin* (New York: Basic Books, 2010), 21–58.

43. V. Iershov, "Politychni represiï v Zhytomyrs'komu pedinstytuti 1933–1941 rr.," *Volyn'-Zhytomyrshchyna: istorychno-filolohichnyi zbirnyk*, vyp. 3 (1998):

37–71; V. Kondrashov, "'Z korinniam vyrvaty natsional'no-kontrrevoliutsiini elementy z N.P.I.' (Pohrom u Nizhyns'kii vyshchii shkoli na pochatku 30-kh rokiv)," *Siverians'kyi litopys: vseukraïns'kyi naukovyi zhurnal*, no. 2 (20) (1998): 13–15; L. Babenko, "Polityczni represiï 1920–1930-kh rokiv u Poltavs'komu pedahohichnomu instytuti," *Al'manakh Poltavs'koho derzhavnoho pedahohichnoho universytetu "Ridnyi krai,"* no. 2 (21) (2009): 196–209; A. Lysyi, "Represiï proty studentstva ta vykladachiv istorychnoho fakul'tetu Vinnyts'koho uchytel's'koho instytutu v 30-kh rr. XX st.," *Visnyk instytutu istoriï, etnolohiï i prava: zbirnyk naukovykh prats'*, vyp. 8 (2010): 42–45.

44. For a revisionist critique of Conquest, see Sheila Fitzpatrick, "People and Martians," review of *The Great Terror*, by Robert Conquest, and *The Harvest of Sorrow*, by Robert Conquest, *London Review of Books* 41, no. 2 (January 24, 2019): 13–15. See also J. Arch Getty and Roberta Thompson Manning, *Stalinist Terror: New Perspectives* (New York: Cambridge University Press, 1993); Davies and Wheatcroft, *The Years of Hunger*.

45. Anne Applebaum, *Red Famine: Stalin's War on Ukraine* (New York: Doubleday, 2017).

46. Carl J. Friedrich and Zbigniew K. Brzezinski, *Totalitarian Dictatorship and Autocracy*, rev. ed. (Cambridge: Harvard University Press, 1965).

47. Carl J. Friedrich and Zbigniew K. Brzezinski, "The Model of Totalitarianism," in *The Stalin Revolution: Foundations of Soviet Totalitarianism*, ed. Robert V. Daniels (Lexington and Toronto: D. C. Heath and Company, 1972), 198–213, esp. 200–201.

48. Roy A. Medvedev, *Let History Judge*, eds. David Joravsky and Georges Haupt, trans. Colleen Taylor (New York: Alfred A. Knopf, 1971); Roy A. Medvedev, *On Stalin and Stalinism*, trans. Ellen De Kadt (New York: Oxford University Press, 1979); Dmitrii Volkogonov, *Triumf i tragediia: Politicheskii portret I. V. Stalina*, 2 vols. (Moscow: Izv-vo Agentstva pechati Novosti, 1989).

49. Ivan Bilas, *Represyvno-karal'na systema v Ukraïni, 1917–1953: Suspil'no-politychnyi ta istoryko-pravovyi analiz*, 2 vols. (Kyïv: "Lybid'" – "Viis'ko Ukraïny," 1994); Serhii Bilokin', *Masovyi teror iak zasib derzhavnoho upravlinnia v SRSR, 1917–1941 rr.: dzhereloznavche doslidzhennia*, 2nd ed. (Kyïv: Penman, 2017); Viktor Chentsov, *Polityczni represiï v radians'kii Ukraïni v 20-ti roky* (Ternopil': Zbruch, 2000).

50. Serhii Kokin, "Stanovlennia totalitarnoï systemy ta pochatok masovykh politychnykh represii v URSR (1920–1922 rr.)," in *Totalitarna derzhava i politychni represiï v Ukraïni u 20 – 80-ti roky: Materialy Mizhnarodnoï naukovoï konferentsiï (15–16 veresnia 1994 r.)*, eds. P. Panchenko and Ie. Proniuk et al. (Kyïv: NAN Ukraïny, 1998), 224–26; Valentyn Gusiev, "Pro deportatsiiu hrupy ukraïns'koï intelihentsiï za kordon u 1922 r.," in Ibid., 180–82; Mykhailo Kuz'menko, "Naukovo-pedahohichna intelihentsiia USRR 20 – 30-kh rokiv XX st.: evoliutsiia sotsial'no-istorychnoho typu" (doctoral diss., Kharkivs'kyi natsional'nyi universytet im. V. N. Karazina, 2005); Viktor Adamsky, "The Deportation of the Ukrainian Intelligentsia," in *Genocide in Ukraine*, ed. P. Kardash (Melbourne: Fortuna Publishing, 2007), 178–81.

51. For a discussion about the Soviet repressions against Ukrainian intellectuals in the 1930s and their eventual extermination, see Olga Bertelsen and Myroslav Shkandrij, "The Secret Police and the Campaign against Galicians in Soviet Ukraine, 1929–34," *Nationalities Papers: The Journal of Nationalism and Ethnicity* 42, no. 1 (2014): 37–62; Myroslav Shkandrij and Olga Bertelsen, "The Soviet Regime's National Operations in Ukraine, 1929–1934," *Canadian Slavonic Papers* 55, no. 3–4 (2013): 417–47. For biographical portraits of repressed teachers in Ukraine, see Marochko and Hillig, *Represovani pedahohy Ukraïny*.

52. Volodymyr Prystaiko, "Zhertvy terroru: Iak DPU borolysia z ukraïns′koiu akademichnoiu naukoiu (Politychni protsesy 20–30-kh rr.)," *Z arkhiviv VUChK, GPU, NKVD, KGB*, no. 1 (1994): 70–78; Viktor Ocheretianko, "Peresliduvannia ukraïns′koï inteligentsiï v pershii polovyni 20-kh rr. (za materialamy fondiv "Rosiis′koho zarubizhnoho arkhivu" Derzhavnoho arkhivu Rosiis′koï Federatsiï," *Z arkhiviv VUChK, GPU, NKVD, KGB*, no. 1–2 (1997): 240–52; Dmytro Arkhireis′kyi and Viktor Chentsov, "Antyradians′ka natsional′na opozytsiia v USRR v 20-ti rr.: pohliad na problemu kriz′ arkhivni dzherela," *Z arkhiviv VUChK, GPU, NKVD, KGB*, no. 2–4 (2000): 16–55.

53. Valentyna Borysenko, Vasyl′ Danylenko, Serhii Kokin, Olesia Stasiuk, and Iurii Shapoval, *Rozsekrechena pam'iat': Holodomor 1932–1933 rokiv v Ukraïni v dokumentakh GPU-NKVD* (Kyïv: Stylos, 2007).

54. Vasyl′ Danylenko, ed., *Ukraïns'ka intelihentsiia i vlada: Zvedennia sekretnoho viddilu DPU USRR 1927–1929 rr.* (Kyïv: Tempora, 2012), 21, 25, 27, 29.

55. Bilokin′, *Masovyi teror iak zasib derzhavnoho upravlinnia v SRSR*, 2nd ed., 620.

56. I borrow the distinction between capital-c Communism (meaning Soviet-endorsed) and small-c communism (meaning Marxist) from John Dewey; see "Why I Am Not a Communist," *Modern Monthly* 8 (April 1934): 135–37.

57. Serhii Bilokin′, "Repetytsiia bezzakon′: sudovyi protses nad 'Spilkoiu vyzvolennia Ukraïny'," *Ukraïna*, no. 37 (1701), September 10, 1989, 13–15 and no. 38 (1702), September 17, 1989, 20–21; V. Kyryliuk, "Protses SVU – stalins′ka fal′shyvka," *Literaturna Ukraïna*, December 7, 1989; V. Savtsov, "Zlochyn, iakoho ne bulo," *Radians'ka Ukraïna*, September 12, 13, 16, 19, 26, and 27, 1989; H. Kas′ianov, "Dolia akademika Iefremova," *Pid praporom leninizmu*, no. 19 (1989): 75–78; Helii Sniehir′ov, *Naboï dlia rozstrilu (Nen'ko moia, nen'ko . . .): liryko-publitsystychna rozvidka* (Kyïv: Dnipro, 1990); O. Sydorenko,"'Pidlishoho chasu ne bulo . . .': iak i chomu bulo sfabrykovano spravu tak zvanoï Spilky vyzvolennia Ukraïny," *Vechirnii Kyïv*, May 15, 1991; Iurii Shapoval, *Ukraïna 20–50-kh rokiv: storinky nenapysanoï istoriï* (Kyïv: Naukova dumka, 1993), 64–81; Anatolii Bolabol′chenko, *SVU – sud nad perekonanniamy* (Kyïv: UKSP "Kobza," 1994); Hiroaki Kuromiya, "Stalinskii 'velikii perelom' i protsess nad 'Soiuzom osvobozhdeniia Ukrainy'," *Otechestvennaia istoriia*, no. 1 (1994): 190–97; Volodymyr Prystaiko and Iurii Shapoval, *Sprava "Spilky vyzvolennia Ukraïny": nevidomi dokumenty i fakty; naukovo-dokumental′ne vydannia*, ed. Ivan Il′ienko (Kyïv: INTEL, 1995); Iurii Shapoval, "Nevidomi dokumenty pro UAPTs u zv'iazku iz spravoiu 'Spilky vyzvolennia Ukraïny,'" *Liudyna i svit*, nos. 11–12 (1996), 13–17; S. H. Vodotyka,

Akademik Mykhailo Ielyseiovych Slabchenko: narys zhyttia ta tvorchosti (Kyïv: Kherson, 1998); Viktor Danylenko, "Odyn z 45-ty: V. Durdukivs'kyi," *Z arkhiviv VUChK-GPU-NKVD-KGB*, nos. 1–2 (1998): 253–62, http://memorial.kiev.ua/zhurna l/pdf/01-02_1998/253.pdf; Fedir Shepel', "'Zapliamovani' tr'oma bukvamy: 'Sprava SVU' – tse trahediia ne til'ky intelihentsiï," *Den'*, August 1, 2003, http://incognita.day .kyiv.ua/zaplyamovani-troma-bukvami.html; Iurii Shapoval, "Teatral'na istoriia," in *Dolia iak istoriia* (Kyïv: Geneza, 2006), 16–34, https://ipiend.gov.ua/wp-content/up loads/2018/07/shapoval_dolya.pdf.

58. See for instance, *Opera SVU – muzyka GPU: spohady svidkiv; zbirka*, ed. Iurii Khorunzhyi (Kam'ians'k-Shakhtyns'kyi: Stanitsa, 1992); Borys Antonenko-Davydovych, "SVU," *Neopalyma kupyna: narodoznavstvo, istoriia, arkhivy*, no. 1 (1994): 31–66; Hryhorii Kostiuk, *Stalinizm v Ukraïni: heneza i naslidky; doslidzhennia i sposterezhennia suchasnyka* (Kyïv: Smoloskyp, 1995); S. O. Iefremov, *Shchodennyky, 1923–1929* (Kyïv: Hazeta "Rada," 1997).

59. Yuri Shapoval, "The Case of the 'Union for the Liberation of Ukraine': A Prelude to the Holodomor?" *Holodomor Studies* 2, no. 2 (2010): 154.

60. Sheila Fitzpatrick, *Education and Social Mobility in the Soviet Union, 1921–1934* (Cambridge: Cambridge University Press, 1979).

61. Vasyl' Marochko, "Shkoly bez ditei ta vchyteliv," in *Holodomor 1932–1933 rr.* (Kyïv, 2007), 53; Volodymyr Serhiichuk, "Shkil'na statystyka iak vazhlyve dzherelo dlia vstanovlennia kil'kosti vtrat pid chas Holodomoru-henotsydu 1932–1933 rokiv," *Narodna tvorchist' i etnolohiia*, no. 5 (2018): 5–15; Serhiychuk, "To Honor All Innocent Victims of the Holodomor," 119–44.

62. Larry F. Holmes, *The Kremlin and the Schoolhouse: Reforming Education in Soviet Russia, 1917–1931* (Bloomington: Indiana University Press, 1991).

63. E. Thomas Ewing, *The Teachers of Stalinism: Policy, Practice and Power in Soviet Schools of the 1930s* (New York: Peter Lang, 2002).

64. Matthew D. Pauly, *Breaking the Tongue: Language, Education, and Power in Soviet Ukraine, 1923–1934* (Toronto: University of Toronto Press, 2014).

65. P. Bondarchuk, *Natsional'no-kul'turna polityka bil'shovykiv v Ukraïni na pochatku 1920-kh rokiv* (Kyïv: Instytut istoriï Ukraïny NAN Ukraïny, 1998); V. Hrechenko and O. Iarmysh, *Ukraïna v dobu "rann'ioho" totalityzmu (20-ti roky XX st.)* (Kharkiv: Natsional'nyi universytet vnutrishnikh sprav, 2001); Iefimenko, "Sotsial'ne oblychchia vchytel'stva," 138–39.

66. H. V. Kas'ianov, "Ukraïns'ka intelihentsiia v 1933 r.," *Problemy istoriï Ukraïny: fakty, sudzhennia, poshuky*, no. 2 (1992): 92–98; V. M. Danylenko and M. M. Kuz'menko, "Naukovo-pedahohichna intelihentsiia v roky holodu," *Ukraïns'kyi istorychnyi zhurnal*, no. 5 (2003): 145–55.

67. Heorhii Kas'ianov, "Intelihentsiia radians'koï Ukraïny 1920-kh – 30-kh rokiv: sotsial'no-istorychnyi analiz" (doctoral diss., Instytut istoriï Ukraïny, 1993); Heorhii Kas'ianov, *Ukraïns'ka intelihentsiia 1920-kh – 30-kh rokiv: sotsial'nyi portret ta istorychna dolia* (Kyïv: Globus-Vik; Edmonton: Canadian Institute of Ukrainian Studies, University of Alberta, 1992); Heorhii Kas'ianov and Vasyl' Danylenko, *Stalinizm i ukraïns'ka intelihentsiia (20–30-ti rr.)* (Kyïv: Naukova dumka, 1991); Vasyl' Danylenko, Heorhii Kas'ianov, and Stanislav Kul'chyts'kyi, *Stalinizm na Ukraïni,*

1920–30-ti roky (Kyïv: Lybid′, 1991); I. O. Klitsakov, *Pedahohichni kadry Ukraïny (1917–1937 rr.)* (Donets′k: Iugo-Vostok, 1997).

68. Iu. V. Teliachyi, "Ukraïns′ke natsional′no-kul′turne vidrodzhennia v 1917–1921 rr.: do metodolohichnoho kontekstu problemy," *Osvita, nauka i kul′tura na Podilli* 24 (2017): 10. For a definition of the term "intelligentsia" as a sociopsychological concept and an overview of the historical development of intelligentsia in Ukraine, see M. Shlemkevych, in *Entsyklopediia ukraïnoznavstva*, ed. Volodymyr Kubijovyč (Paris; New York: Molode Zhyttia Press, 1959), vol. 3, 877–79.

69. The phrase comes from the title of a monograph by O. V. Luk′ianenko, which examines everyday life of students and faculty of pedagogical institutes in Soviet Ukraine from the 1920s to the 1960s, *"Naiblyzhchi druzi partiï": kolektyvy vyshiv Ukraïny v obrazakh shchodennia 1920-kh – pershoï polovyny 1960-kh rokiv* (Poltava: Vyd-vo "Simon," 2019).

70. Samuel P. Huntington, "The Clash of Civilizations?" *Foreign Affairs* 72, no. 3 (1993): 27.

71. According to Russian linguist Oleg Trubachev, *Etimologicheskii slovar′ russkogo iazyka* (An Etymological Dictionary of Russian), compiled by Max Vasmer, contains around 11,000 words, of which two-thirds are late borrowings (6,300 or 57 percent) and words of unknown origin (1,119 or 10 percent). Common Indo-European lexemes account for 3,191 words. As to the common East Slavic words, there are only seventy-two listed in this dictionary; thus, Ukrainian and Russian languages share 0.6 percent of their vocabulary. See Ilko Maidachevsky, "Linguistic Insights into Ukrainian History: Professor Kostiantyn Tyshchenko speaks about the role of modern linguistics in our identity and the rebuttal of the cradle-of-three-brotherly-peoples theory," *Ukrainian Week*, November 16, 2012, https://ukrainianweek.com/Culture/65223. Ukrainian vocabulary was shaped mostly by European influences, especially by Latin and German (both directly and via Polish), whereas Russian borrowed a sizable part of its vocabulary from Turkic languages.

72. Russian and Ukrainian historiographies differ in their interpretation of six issues: (1) Ukrainian national identity; (2) the national liberation struggle of 1917–1921 and the establishment of the Ukrainian National Republic as an independent state in 1918; (3) the genocidal famine of 1932–1933, perpetrated by Stalin and his accomplices to denationalize Ukraine; (4) the double colonization and exploitation of Ukraine's natural resources by Hitler's Third Reich and Stalin's Soviet Union; (5) the legitimacy of the transfer of the Crimea; and (6) the indigenous origins of the Ukrainian population in the Donbas. See Volodymyr Serhiichuk, "I cherez sto rokiv – odyn na odnoho: Pro rozvytok rosiis′ko-ukraïns′kykh vidnosyn u XX stolitti," *Natsiia i derzhava*, no. 3 (646), March 2017, 8–10, https://ia800901.us.archive.org/25/items/NiD_newspaper/646--31--03--2017--03.pdf.

73. Over 200 witnesses testified before the U.S. Commission on the Ukraine Famine, established in 1985 to conduct a study of the 1932–1933 famine in order to provide the American public with a better understanding of the Soviet system. Although there was no question about schools in a questionnaire developed for oral interviews, dozens of witnesses, some of them teachers, provided detailed accounts

about schools during the Holodomor. See *Report to Congress* and *Oral History Project*. Witness accounts about teachers and schools can also be found in S. O. Pidhainy, ed., *The Black Deeds of the Kremlin: A White Book* (Toronto: Ukrainian Association of Victims of Russian Communist Terror, 1953–1955), 2 vols. In the 2000s, oral histories were collected by an Orthodox priest and his students in all regions of Ukraine, see Iurii Mytsyk, ed., *Ukraïns'kyi holokost 1932–1933: svidchennia tykh, khto vyzhyv* (Kyïv: Vydavnychyi dim "Kyievo-Mohylians'ka akademiia," 2003–2013), vols. 1–9. Witness accounts about schools and teachers have also been published in *Holodomor 1932–1933 rokiv v Ukraïni: dokumenty i materialy*, ed. Ruslan Pyrih (Kyïv: Kyievo-Mohylians'ka akademiia, 2007).

74. See titles of memoirs written by teachers in Oleksandr Komarnits'kyi, *Studenty-pedahohy u modernizatsiï vyshchoï osvity radians'koï Ukraïny u 1920–1930-kh rr.* (Kam'ianets'-Podil's'kyi: TOV Drukarnia "Ruta," 2017).

75. Collections of documents that contain information related to the functioning of educational institutions in Soviet Ukraine between 1923 and 1934 are located in several archives. Specifically, Fond 166 contains documents of the People's Commissariat of Education of the Ukrainian SSR (*Narodnyi komisarisat osvity*, or NKO) and is housed in the Central State Archive of the Supreme Organs of Administration of Ukraine (*Tsentral'nyi derzhavnyi arkhiv vyshchykh orhaniv vlady i upravlinnia Ukraïny*; hereafter: *TsDAVOU*). Unfortunately, the most important year 1933 contains the least evidence. Materials about political and economic campaigns, propaganda and agitation activities, instructions, and circulars that deal with matters of education can be located in Fond 1 Central Committee of the Communist Party (Bolsheviks) of Ukraine (*Tsentral'nyi komitet KP(b)U*) in the Central State Archive of Civic Organizations of Ukraine (*Tsentral'nyi derzhavnyi arkhiv hromads'kykh ob'iednan' Ukraïny*, or *TsDAHOU*).

76. Diaries of repressed teachers can be located in Fond 6 of the Sectoral State Archive of the Security Service of Ukraine (*Haluzevyi derzhavnyi arkhiv Sluzhby bezpeky Ukraïny*; hereafter: *HDA SBU*). These diaries were compiled, edited, and published by Iaroslav Faizulin, *"Represovani" shchodennyky: Holodomor 1932–1933 rokiv v Ukraïni* (Kyïv: Feniks, 2018). Photographs of schools and teachers as well as images of collective farms, show trials, and the famine can be found in the Central State Cinephotophono Archive of Ukraine named after H. Pshenychnyi (abbreviated as *TsDKFFAU* or *Tsentral'nyi derzhavnyi kinofotofonoarkhiv Ukraïny*).

77. Archival collections of the Pedagogical Museum of Ukraine of the Academy of Pedagogical Sciences of Ukraine (*Pedahohichnyi muzei Ukraïny*) contain publications, bulletins, and educational periodicals published in Ukraine in the 1920s and 1930s as well as biographical sketches of leading educational theorists and teachers, available online at http://pmu.in.ua/actual-info/istoria_museiy/.

78. Private archive of Dr. James E. Mace, Executive Director of the U.S. Commission on the Ukraine Famine, contains rare publications in English and Ukrainian that deal with intellectual and cultural history of Ukraine, personal correspondence with scholars, and documents that shed light on Soviet nationality policy. The archive is housed in the James E. Mace Museum at the National University

"Kyïv-Mohyla Academy" in Kyïv, Ukraine. Another part of Dr. James E. Mace's archive as well as documents related to the work of the Commission can be found in the Ronald Reagan Presidential Library and Museum in Simi Valley, California.

79. George Santayana, *The Life of Reason or, The Phases of Human Progress*, 5 vols, vol. 1, *Reason in Common Sense* (Scribner's, 1905), 284. A complete text of the five-volume magnum opus is available online via Project Gutenberg at http://www.gutenberg.org/files/15000/15000-h/15000-h.htm.

80. For an analysis of Stanton's model by an astute Kremlin watcher, Michael MacKay, see his article "The Seeds of Genocide in Russia's Invasion of Ukraine," *Radio Lemberg*, April 17, 2018, http://radiolemberg.com/ua-articles/ua-allarticles/the-seeds-of-genocide-in-russia-s-invasion-of-ukraine.

Chapter 1

Preconditions

World War I and the Bolshevik revolution were precursor events to genocide.[1] Historians trace the ideological roots of Soviet genocide against Ukrainians to writings of the fathers of scientific communism, Karl Marx and Friedrich Engels, and the founding father of the first communist state, Vladimir Lenin. Bolshevik policies toward non-Russian nations and land ownership were two preconditions for establishing the "dictatorship of proletariat." Marx used the expression casually without explanation; Lenin interpreted it to mean a reign of the party incarnated in one leader, "based entirely on violence and not limited by law."[2] Ukraine's leaders attempted to stave off interference from the Entente and the Central Powers. Yet, mobilizing a national army out of remnants of the former imperial army to fight for Ukraine's independence proved to be challenging. Efforts to establish a democratic republic in the Ukrainian ethnographic boundaries and rebuild its educational system evolved under several successive national governments, influenced by competing ideologies, but eventually succumbed to the demand from Moscow to train new "red" elite once Bolsheviks cemented their rule over Ukraine. The aim of totalitarian Soviet education became not to instill convictions but to destroy the capacity to form any. Actions were to be guided by ideology. The famine of 1921–1923, which ensued after a series of Bolshevik onslaughts on Ukraine, dispensed with human will to resist.

MARXIST-LENINIST ROOTS OF SOVIET GENOCIDE

Throughout the final year of World War I, and the lengthy peace process, Ukraine became the battleground of ideas. A panoply of ideologies emerged: socialist (the Central Rada and later the Ukrainian National Republic), monarchist (Pavlo Skoropads′kyi), anarchist (Nestor Makhno[3]), national-communist (Borot′bists[4]), and imperialist (the Russian Whites).[5] On their third attempt, Bolsheviks prevailed. Their ideology, aimed at eliminating the alleged privileged classes (such as the old intelligentsia) or groups blamed for sabotaging state policies (such as the kulaks, in Ukrainian *kurkuli*), provided legitimacy for violence. In situations characterized by collective violence, social engineering is inevitable. It is prudent to examine the foundations of Bolshevik ideology to uncover Marxist-Leninist roots of Soviet genocide against Ukrainians.

Marx's Anti-national Bias

All students of history are required to study Marx's theory. It has been influential in countries all over the world: in the West as a critique of capitalism, often disguised as the critical theory,[6] and in the East as a blueprint for revolutionary change in the struggle against colonial oppression. In his introduction to the essential writings of Karl Marx, Frederic Bender argued that "his role in shaping many of the problems and movements of the industrial era distinguish him as the outstanding social philosopher of his (and our) time," calling it the "Age of Marx."[7] In their theory of communism, German philosophers Karl Marx and Friedrich Engels used the labels "reactionary" and "counterrevolutionary" to denote national and social groups that held adverse views to "progressive" communist goals. The language of the *Manifesto of the Communist Party*, written for the Communist League Congress held in London in 1847, left no doubt as to their anti-national bias.

Ukrainian writer Wasyl Hryshko pointed out that Soviet genocide was rooted in both Soviet-endorsed ideology of scientific communism and anti-Ukrainian policy.[8] In Marxist canon, nationality as a concept is a bourgeois idea. Marx had foreseen the coming of socialism in countries where the industrial working class was in the majority. In the Russian Empire, there was no working class of this kind. Therefore, for Bolsheviks, who ruled over a largely agricultural population, there was an obvious problem. Besides, in the case of Ukraine, farmers were independent smallholders, hardworking, and nationally conscious; they overwhelmingly spoke Ukrainian, the language that Bolsheviks did not understand.

As to the question whether national differences would continue to exist under a new social order, Marx stated in the *Communist Manifesto*:

> The working men have no country. . . . National differences, and antagonisms between peoples, are daily more and more vanishing, owing to the development of the bourgeoisie. . . . The supremacy of the proletariat will cause them to vanish still faster.[9]

A worldwide communist international goal meant liquidation of many nationalities by way of their amalgamation and transformation into a few large supranational complexes. The nationless amalgamation could be only achieved by assimilation to the language and culture of a certain "great" ("first among equals") imperial nation on the road to the "internationally united" communist world.

The fate of nationality in the communist doctrine was subordinated to the way the problem of private property (and the social class of private property owners) was projected to be solved. Engels clarified his program at the First Congress of the Communist League in London, in 1847, as follows:

> The nationalities of the peoples who join together according to the principle of community will be just as much compelled by this union to merge with one another and thereby supersede themselves as the various differences between estates and classes disappear through the superseding of their base—private property.[10]

The proclaimed goal of the communist movement was the abolition of private property and liquidation of classes based on it. The *Communist Manifesto* praised bourgeois achievements in the destruction of the traditional rural way of life, contemptuously called "idiocy of rural life."[11] Marx and Engels proclaimed their aversion to the small proprietors as "petty bourgeois," considered to be a "conservative" and "reactionary" social force.[12] In addition to the labels created for them as a class of small landowners marked for liquidation, the authors described measures and methods that the victorious proletariat would use to consolidate their position as the ruling class. Their theory of action became a blueprint for politically justified genocidal violence. Here is an excerpt from the *Communist Manifesto* on this matter:

> [T]he theory of the Communists may be summed up in the single sentence: Abolition of private property. . . . The Communist revolution is the most radical rupture with traditional property relations. . . . The proletariat will use its political supremacy to wrest, by degrees, all capital from the bourgeoisie, to centralize all means of production in the hands of the State, i.e., of the proletariat organized as the ruling class. . . . Of course, in the beginning, this cannot be effected except by means of despotic inroads on the rights of property . . . by means of measures . . . which . . . are unavoidable as a means of entirely revolutionizing the mode of production. . . . These measures: Abolition of property in land and application of all rents of land to public purposes. . . . Combination of agriculture with manufacturing industries; gradual abolition of the distinction between town and country.

> Political power, properly so-called, is merely the organized violence of one class for suppressing another. . . . If the proletariat . . . , by means of a revolution, makes itself the ruling class, and, as such, sweeps away by force the old conditions of production, then it will, along with these conditions, have swept away the conditions for the existence of class antagonisms, and of classes generally.[13]

In addition to the definition of political power as "the organized violence," several of the key terms from this quotation were actually used by Vladimir Ill'ich Ul'ianov (Lenin)[14] and later his successor Iosif Vissarionovich Dzhugashvili (Stalin)[15] in speeches and resolutions: "sweeping away by force the old conditions of production" and liquidation of the "petty bourgeois" class took the form of liquidation of kulaks as a class and "total collectivization" (combination of agriculture with industry or merging of town and country). Robert Tucker referred to Stalin as "a teacher" and "propagandist," who had mastery of his subject matter and could explain fundamentals of Marxism to ordinary workers.[16] Stalin's fellow revolutionary Simeon Vereshchak remembered him as someone who enjoyed the reputation of being "a second Lenin" and "the best authority on Marxism."[17]

Whether intentionally or not, the founding fathers of the Soviet state ignored that Marx and Engels openly revealed their aversion to "small backward nations"—Austrian Czechs, Slovaks, Croats, Serbs, Slovenes, and Ukrainians—because they did not fit into their scheme of "bourgeois revolution" as a necessary step toward the "proletarian revolution." According to Hryshko, the ideological motivation of Marx and Engels's negative attitude toward Slavs coincided with the great-state nationalism of Germans, Hungarians, and Poles who dominated over Slavs in the Austrian Empire: "Marx and Engels sided with dominant 'big nations' against awakened subjugated nations and ideologically rationalized this as siding with the 'progressive' and therefore 'revolutionary' nations against those that were 'conservative' and 'counterrevolutionary.'" Hryshko found a striking resemblance between the way Marx and Engels combined communist ideology with German great-power nationalism and the way Lenin and Stalin subsequently combined communism with Russian chauvinism. Furthermore, Hryshko has argued that the great-state-nationalist aspect of Marx's concept of "internationalism" in revolutionary practice has been used by all apologists for aggressive expansionism and racism, including German and Russian imperialism and, later, German Nazism and Russian Communism.[18]

To have total economic and social control over Ukraine, especially its grain, Marxist doctrine had to be adapted to fit the needs of Bolshevik colonizing ideology. The self-styled leader of the world proletariat, Lenin himself declared in a speech in Switzerland in 1914 (which is not included in Soviet editions of his works) that "it [Ukraine] has become for Russia what Ireland was for England: exploited in the extreme and receiving nothing in return."[19] Lenin's use of the term "internal colony" in reference to Ukraine was put on a back burner until Ukrainian communists, especially historian Matvii Iavors'kyi, raised the issue of Ukraine's colonial exploitation by the Russian Empire and its successor, the Soviet Union.[20]

Soviet editions excluded inconvenient passages from Marx's classics. For instance, Ukrainian writer Anatolii Dimarov in his last interview in 2014, at the age of ninety-two, intimated that when the Soviet troops "liberated" Luts'k, in Western Ukraine, the Soviet secret police came on the heels of the army:

> What did they occupy themselves with at first? Libraries. They began to remove all the books that were published in Western Ukraine and bring them to the church to burn them later. They even threw out Marx's *Capital* because under the Soviet regime the *Capital* was published without the last chapter, in which the author revised his views and concluded that dictatorship of the proletariat would necessarily lead to dictatorship of a few and arbitrary terror.[21]

Dimarov quietly stole the volume and took notes of the last chapter. For seventy years, the abridged Soviet version of Marxism thrived until it faded away, first from the consciousness of the people following the dissolution of the Soviet Union in 1991, then banned from parks, streets, and other public spaces in Ukraine following the adoption of decommunization laws in April 2015.[22] The decontamination of minds from the communist past might take as long as decomposition of radioactive elements after the Chornobyl explosion in April 1986. Both built on lies, both highly contagious.

During the 1930s, the relationship between Marxism and nationalism in Soviet interpretation was reflected in a speech by Pavel Postyshev, who in late 1933 reportedly stated that "any attempt to harmonize proletarian internationalism with nationalism must make it an instrument of the nationalist counterrevolution."[23] To an outside observer, Ewald Ammende, secretary general of the European Congress of Nationalities, Postyshev's (and Bolshevik's) program appeared as "war to the knife on all the national movements."[24] This "war" was meted against Ukrainians as members of a national group rather than a mere "class," which was an ideological disguise. All means of production had to be in the hands of the state. The *Communist Manifesto*, a programmatic document, clearly outlined a way of achieving the ultimate goal of the new society: the "expropriation of property in land" by exercising political power as "the organized violence."

The "Double Task" of Lenin's Policies

The goals and guidance provided by the *Communist Manifesto* were taken over as an inheritance from the fathers of scientific communism by Lenin, who was half German on his mother's side, and who exhibited a striking affinity for Germany and Marx's teaching.[25] In a historical paradox, Lenin was transported from Germany to Russia in a sealed train[26] and implemented Marx's theory in a country that was last to industrialize. The Russian Empire he attempted to transform was largely non-Russian and thrived on economically exploiting its inner non-Russian colonies. For these reasons, policies that Lenin's minority faction, which referred to themselves euphemistically as Bolsheviks (the majority), had to rely on deception, coercion, and brute force to gain and maintain their power. An analysis of Lenin's writings on the Bolshevik formulation of nationality and land policies provides key to understanding the origins of Soviet genocide.

Regarding Bolshevik nationality policy, its main feature was a dialectical tension between opposites: the proclamation of the "right of every nation to self-determination and even to secession" and the openly declared denial of this right because it clashed with "international" interests of the proletariat. The duplicity of this policy was cynically explained by Lenin himself. Following is a compilation of Lenin's writings on this matter in a logical rather than chronological order from Bolshevik publications:

> In Russia, where the oppressed nations account for 57 percent of the population, where they occupy mostly the border regions, where some of them are more highly cultured than the Great Russians . . . there, in Russia, recognition of the right of nations oppressed by Tsarism to free secession from Russia is absolutely obligatory for Russian Social-Democrats, for the furtherance of their democratic and socialist aims.
>
> . . .
>
> The right to self-determination is one thing, of course, and the expedience of self-determination, the secession of a given nation under given circumstances, is another. This is elementary.
>
> We are in favor of the right to secession (and not in favor of everyone's seceding!) . . . Secession is not what we plan at all. We do not advocate secession. In general, we are opposed to secession. But we stand for the right to secede.
>
> The right to self-determination is an exception in our general premise of centralism. This exception is absolutely essential in view of reactionary Great Russian nationalism . . . but exception must not be too broadly interpreted. In this case, there is not, and must not be anything more than the right to secede.[27]

These pronouncements were part of the Bolshevik official program, *Theses on the National Question*, adopted in 1913 and effective up to the revolution of 1917.[28]

Lenin adopted Engels's thesis about the mission of the proletariat to "destroy nationality" through the "merging with one another" within a large multinational "community" and adapted it to conditions of the Russian Empire. Using Marxist "internationalist" language, Lenin endorsed assimilation, which implied Russification. The following excerpt from Lenin's writings illustrates how he used Marxist arguments in support of his concept of state centralism based on Russian great-power nationalism:

> Marxists are, of course, opposed to federation and decentralization, for the simple reason that capitalism requires for its development the largest and most centralized possible states.... The great centralized state is a tremendous historical step forward from medieval disunity to the socialist unity of the whole world, and only via such a state (inseparably connected with capitalism) can there be any road to socialism.
> ...
> We are certainly in favor of democratic centralism. We are opposed to federation.... Federation means the association of equals, an association that demands common agreement.... We are opposed to the federation in principle, it loosens economic ties and is unsuitable for a single state.[29]

Lenin never defined "democratic centralism"; rather, the regime that he established was better known as the "dictatorship of the proletariat" with his party as the "proletarian vanguard." The rule was centralized without any trace of democracy.

The assimilation of nations in Lenin's mind meant to be nonvoluntary because it involved the supremacy of one nation over another. In Lenin's view the dominant nation was Russia; thus, he welcomed the process of assimilation in Ukraine as a "progressive" factor. The Bolshevik policy was disguised as a process of "getting together" of Russians and Ukrainians. Lenin explained this process as follows:

> For several decades a well-defined process of accelerated economic development has been going on in the South, i.e., Ukraine, attracting hundreds of thousands of peasants and workers from Great Russia to capitalist farms, mines and cities. The "assimilation" [quotation marks by Lenin]—within these limits—of Great Russian and Ukrainian proletariat is an indisputable fact. And this fact is undoubtedly progressive. Capitalism is replacing the ignorant, conservative, settled *muzhik* of the Great Russian or Ukrainian backwoods with a mobile proletariat whose conditions of life break down specifically national narrow-mindedness, both Great Russian and Ukrainian.[30]

Any form of resistance to assimilatory Russification was labeled "bourgeois nationalism" because it posed danger to "international" unity of the proletariat. Lenin condemned the idea of "national culture" and coined an indefinable concept, "international culture of the proletariat," instead. This "internationalization" was a fine substitute for Russification as an instrument of establishing power in the Bolshevik multinational state. Here are some excerpts from Lenin's writings on this matter:

> We do not support "national culture" but international culture. . . . We are against national culture as one of the slogans of bourgeois nationalism. . . . We are in favor of the international culture of the fully democratic and socialist proletariat. . . . Down with the deceptive bourgeois, compromise slogan of "cultural-national autonomy"! . . . The slogan is incorrect, because already under capitalism all economic, political and spiritual life is becoming more and more international. Socialism will make it completely international.[31]

Notable in Lenin's writings is his view on education for national minorities:

> The interests of the working class demand amalgamation of the workers of all nationalities in a given state in united proletarian organizations—political, trade unions, co-operative, educational. . . . The essence of the plan, or program, of what is called "cultural-national autonomy" is separate schools for each nationality. . . . This is absolutely impermissible! As long as different nations live in a single state they are bound to one another by millions and thousands of millions of economic, legal and social bonds. How can education be extricated from these bonds? . . . On the contrary, efforts should be made to unite the nations in educational matters, so that school should be a preparation for what is actually done in real life. . . . We must strive to secure the mixing of the children of all nationalities in uniform pursuit of proletarian educational policy. . . . To preach the establishment of special schools for every "national culture" is reactionary.[32]

Lenin attacked the idea of "national-cultural autonomy" because, at the time, this demand was most prominent in programs of the Jewish Social Democratic Bund and the Ukrainian Social Democratic Workers' Party. For the former, it kept the extraterritorial Jewish nationality alive under pressure of assimilatory factors of the Russian state policy of anti-Semitism. For the latter, it established a legal basis for resistance to Russification and organized struggle for territorial and political autonomy. These two parties evoked Lenin's fury after their refusal to accept a "one and indivisible" Russian "party of the proletariat" of all nations. Leading spokesmen of these parties, F. Liebman and Lev Yurkevych, accused Lenin of being an "assimilator."[33] In his polemic with Yurkevych, leader of the Ukrainian Social Democrats, Lenin argued,

> A Marxist who heaps abuse upon a Marxist of another nation for being an "assimilator" is simply a nationalist philistine. In this unhandsome category

of people are the Bundists and Ukrainian nationalist-socialists such as L. Yurkevych, D. Dontsov and Co. . . . It would be a downright betrayal of socialism, and a silly policy even from the standpoint of the bourgeois "national aims" of the Ukrainians to weaken the ties and the alliance between the Ukrainian and Great Russian proletariat that now exist within the confines of a single state. . . . The Great Russian and Ukrainian workers must work together, and, as long as they live in a single state, act in the closest organizational unity and concert, toward a common or international culture of the proletarian movement, displaying absolute tolerance in the question of language. . . . This is the imperative demand of Marxism. All advocacy of the segregation of the workers of one nation from those of another, all attacks upon Marxist "assimilation," where the proletariat is concerned, to contrapose one national culture as a whole to another allegedly integral national culture, and so forth is bourgeois nationalism, against which it is essential to wage a ruthless struggle.[34]

Lenin's call for a "ruthless struggle" against the "bourgeois nationalism" of Ukrainian Marxists, according to Wasyl Hryshko, was reminiscent of Marx and Engels's threat to employ "ruthless terror" against those "counter-revolutionary nations" which refused to submit their national interests to the great-power interests of Germans, Magyars, and Poles during the European revolutions of 1848.[35] From his study of Marx and Engels, Lenin drew the lesson: "the interests of the liberation of a number of big and very big nations in Europe rate higher than the interests of the movement for liberation of small nations."[36] When Lenin was engaging in this polemic, he was still in exile in Western Europe.

Lenin's treatment of the "Ukrainian question" was closely tied to his hostile attitude toward the "petty bourgeois" class of small proprietors because their aspirations ran contrary to the idea of abolishing private property. To transform a primarily agrarian "bourgeois-democratic" revolution into the "socialist revolution" of the proletariat, he proposed a tactical plan to equitably distribute the land (part of which was held by landlords).[37] In the process, he destroyed not only the autocracy but along with it the economy. At the time, the slogan for "land and freedom" was very appealing. The plan became more urgent during World War I. Bolsheviks seized the opportunity to win the trust of land tillers. The cynicism behind their plan was explained by Lenin as follows:

There is not a word in the resolution about the party undertaking to support transfer of the confiscated land to petty-bourgeois proprietors. The resolution states: we support . . . "up to and including confiscation," i.e. including expropriation without compensation; however, the resolution does not in any way decide to whom the expropriated land is to be given. It was not by chance that

> the question was left open. . . . We must help the peasant uprising in every way, up to and including confiscation of the land, but certainly not including all sorts of petty-bourgeois schemes. We support the peasant movement to the extent that it is revolutionary-democratic. We are making ready (doing so now, at once) to fight it when, and to the extent that, it becomes reactionary and anti-proletarian. The essence of Marxism lies in that double task, which only those who do not understand Marxism can vulgarize or compress into a single and simple task.[38]

The Bolshevik plan was to nationalize all land, making it property of the state, more precisely of the proletariat represented by the party. This plan was in compliance with Marxist doctrine, but for propaganda purposes, the transfer of land was the party's "double task." Hryshko summed up the advantage of such a political "double task": it made it easy to switch from "pro" to "contra" and vice versa at any given time, "depending on tactical or propagandistic expediency."[39]

Both the nationality and land questions became intertwined in Lenin's treatise, *Imperialism, the Highest Stage of Capitalism* (1916). His theses, on the substance of national liberation movements of peoples living under colonial oppression of imperialist states, spell out practical activities formulated as follows:

> It is beyond any doubt that any national movement can only be the bourgeois-democratic movement, since the overwhelming mass of the population of the backward countries consists of peasants who represent bourgeois-capitalist relationships. . . . We, as Communists, should, and will support bourgeois-democratic movements in colonial countries only when they are genuinely revolutionary and when their exponents do not hinder our work of educating and organizing in a revolutionary spirit the peasantry and the masses of the exploited.[40]

Under the pretense of being champions of the "right to self-determination" for oppressed nations and of "land and freedom" for tillers, Bolsheviks established their rule in Ukraine.[41]

INTELLIGENTSIA DURING THE NATIONAL LIBERATION STRUGGLE, 1917–1921

Lenin believed the goal of Soviet schools was "to give youth basic knowledge, to give them skills to develop their own communist views, and to make them into educated people."[42] Other Bolshevik leaders also stressed the political significance of schooling. Stalin formulated his views on the importance of school very candidly: "Education is a weapon, the effect of which depends on the hands that keep it."[43]

In Soviet historiography, Lenin's nationality policy is given credit for giving an opportunity to the working people of Ukraine to create "truly free, sovereign socialist state." A historical narrative was constructed to present educational, economic, cultural, scientific, and technological achievements of the Ukrainian SSR as being possible only in a "brotherly family of nations." Authors of a history of education in the Soviet Union, published in Moscow on the fiftieth anniversary of the October Socialist Revolution of 1917, quoted the 1897 census, according to which 76 percent of the Ukrainian population was illiterate, with illiteracy rate in rural areas almost 80 percent, and 90 percent among women. In 1914–1915, most of the children in Ukraine did not have a chance to attend even a primary school. The authors blamed high illiteracy among Ukrainians on "centuries of suffering under foreign yoke."[44]

How could a vast illiterate mass appear in Ukraine, the cradle of European scholarship? Monasteries in medieval Kyïvan Rus' in the eleventh through thirteenth centuries were the centers of learning; women of the clerical order, in particular, enjoyed a comparatively high level of literacy and were founders of schools for girls.[45] Institutions of higher education appeared in Ukraine early—Ostroh Academy, founded in 1576, and Kyïv-Mohyla Academy, established in 1615—which prompted David Saunders to write a monograph about the Ukrainian impact on Russian culture in the seventeenth and eighteenth centuries.[46] The answer is several hundred years of Russian imperial policies.[47] Peter the Great appropriated the name of Rus' for Muscovy and established a hierarchy of Muscovites as Great Russians, Ukrainians as Little Russians, and Belarussians as White Russians. He banished thousands of Ukrainian Cossacks to dig a canal to the White Sea.[48] The staggering illiteracy rate in Ukraine was also a contribution of Catherine the Great: the "enlightened" ruler's decision to put serfs in bondage to their masters and liquidate all Ukrainian-language schools so that her imperial subjects would speak one common language of the empire, Russian.[49] In the Russian Empire, Ukrainian language was forbidden in schools, in the press, and in public life.[50] It was necessitated by the Russian economic colonization of Ukraine rather than a result of "foreign yoke."[51]

"Without its own national school, the genius of the nation stagnates, it wears off toward denationalization, its spirituality withers away. Foreign culture and education imposed from outside hurt the subjugated nation," wrote Symon Petliura, a teacher-turned-journalist, in an opinion piece in 1907.[52] To Petliura, the first step toward social liberation was through national schooling in Ukraine. He knew intimately the situation in his native Poltava province, where one-third of school-age children (36.9 percent) attended 870 public schools (918 classrooms). Out of 2.9 million people in the province, 204,575 were school-age children who needed as many as 3,409 classrooms.⁵³ The percentage of schoolgirls was extremely low (14 percent in 1899). It did not escape the author's attention that budget allocations for schools declined from 606,959 in 1899 to 592,000 *karbovantsi* in 1900, all the while the province collected 15.2 million in taxes for the imperial Russian government, but spent only 8.8 million *karbovantsi* on its own needs. Influenced by Marxism, Petliura at first advocated Ukrainian autonomy within Russia, but soon he became an ardent advocate for Ukraine's independence.

While battles between Russia and Germany raged on the fields of Ukraine during World War I, successive governments in Ukraine embarked on a project of reconstructing the educational system. This project meant universal, free, mandatory, secular primary education, proportionate representation of national minorities in schools, and a right to open private schools. The school system was envisioned as integrated and accessible, with seven years of mandatory schooling.⁵⁴

Rebuilding the educational system underwent several phases aligned with challenging and rapidly changing political circumstances. During the first phase, from March 1917 to April 1918, centrist political forces in Ukraine supported the Provisional Government in Petrograd and its policies. Together with national and socialist forces, they established the Central Rada (Council), the first modern Ukrainian government. However, it was the Provisional Government in Petrograd that controlled the situation in Ukraine via local self-government (*zemstvo*) agencies. The Provisional Government was in no hurry to allocate financial resources to reform the educational system in Ukraine, but allowed to establish departments of Ukrainian language and literature, history and law.⁵⁵ Therefore, in April 1917, nationally conscious members of intelligentsia formed an All-Ukrainian Teachers' Union to implement the Central Rada's policies. On the eve of the First All-Ukrainian Teachers' Congress, held on April 5–6, 1917, Mykhailo Hrushevs'kyi appealed to Ukrainian professors and lecturers scattered all over Russia to return to Ukraine to help establish national universities.⁵⁶ In the summer of 1917, the All-Ukrainian Teachers' Union organized short-term courses for teachers, worked out new terminology for textbooks, and revised the orthography.⁵⁷

After Central Rada issued its First Universal in June 1917, local governments not only recognized its authority but also collected funds to support it financially. Central Rada established an office in charge of education, with Ivan Steshenko as its general secretary.⁵⁸ In November 1917, Steshenko appealed to all regional and district administrations to organize a conference to discuss the organization of people's education in Ukraine. The conference was held on December 15–20, 1917, and topics of discussion focused on establishing schools and institutes and training cadres. Representatives from district and regional councils were given voice and a seat at the helm of the republic's educational administration. They were entrusted with establishing a network of schools, preschool and after-school programs, drafting budgets, and coordinating activities with cultural and community organizations. They were also in charge of hiring and training teachers, opening libraries, and supplying textbooks to schools. Steshenko praised school administrators: "The organization of a new, liberal, democratic school, which is loved and supported by the people, depends on local self-governing agencies."[59]

Reform of the educational system in Ukraine started. Parish schools were transferred from religious authorities to local self-governing agencies. Most of these schools were primary. Ukrainian language was mandatory in all schools, including those with Russian as the language of instruction. To intensify this transition, the Second All-Ukrainian Teachers' Congress in August 1917 passed a resolution, stating, "From 1 September 1917 all primary schools shall use the Ukrainian language for instruction." The resolution also mandated the use of Ukrainian language in secondary schools and teacher training institutes in accordance with resolutions of the First All-Ukrainian Teachers' Congress.[60] A total of fifty-three new Ukrainian secondary schools, including three Ukrainian gymnasiums in Kyïv, had been established by September 1917.[61] Often, they lacked new buildings to house these schools. At times, the newly established Ukrainian schools had to share buildings with Russian-language schools or conduct classes during evening shifts. For instance, Gymnasium No. 1 named after Taras Shevchenko (see Figure 1.1), later renamed Kyïv Labor School No. 1, operated without a permanent building, whereas the First Kyïv Russian Gymnasium occupied a former palace.[62]

Alongside creating new schools, Ukrainian authorities turned to establishing a system of after-school education. As periodical *Vil'na ukraïns'ka shkola* (Free Ukrainian School) reported in 1918, local school authorities in villages as well as towns had to tackle a monumental task because 80 percent of the people in Ukraine were illiterate. Considering that most of these illiterates were adults beyond school age, local authorities had to organize after-school education. To implement this task, regional and district authorities established educational sections. Scores of instructors were recruited to teach adult courses in the evening or on Sunday morning.[63] Local *zemstvos* also organized three-month courses to train instructors and offered scholarships to attract attendees. The first of such courses for instructors was taught in November 1917, and in 1918 recommendations for organizing after-school education were published in Kyïv.[64]

On January 22, 1918, the Fourth Universal of the Ukrainian National Republic (*Ukraïns'ka narodnia respublika*, or UNR) declared Ukraine independent, breaking away from the federation with the Russian republic.[65] This was done to the sound of the firing of Russian guns across the Dnipro. The

Figure 1.1 A choir of the Kyïv Labor School No. 1 named after Taras Shevchenko, with school principal Volodymyr Durdukivs'kyi, 1920s. *Source*: From TsDKFFAU, od. obl. 0-I 86088.

Central Rada decided to make peace with the Central Powers. On February 7, 1918, the Germans, Austrians, and the delegates of the Central Rada signed the first of the treaties made at Brest-Litovsk. The Central Powers recognized the independence of the Ukrainian National Republic in return for 1 million tons of grain. Also the Central Powers promised to return the Ukrainian prisoners of war and to arm the Ukrainian army to fight against Bolsheviks.[66]

As the educational system became independent from Petrograd's supervision, new commissariats of education for national minority groups (Jewish, Polish, and Russian) as well as school boards were established. The general secretary of education Ivan Steshenko[67] became minister of education. His agenda included establishing free primary seven-year schools, with four-year lower-level and three-year upper-level grades. The Ministry of Education coordinated activities of newly created national minority education councils and established schools in areas of compact settlement of the respective minorities. The goal was to decentralize and democratize education.[68] To overcome the shortage of teachers, Ukrainian authorities organized Institutes of People's Education (*Instytuty narodnoï osvity*, or INOs, which replaced universities) and one-year courses to train cadres for after-school programs. They planned to raise a teacher's salary from 840 to 1,800 *karbovansti*.

However, dire financial circumstances at the time did not allow them to satisfy teachers' needs.[69]

A parallel system of education was established in Kharkiv, when Bolsheviks launched their military aggression against Ukraine on December 17, 1917. Lenin used a disinformation tactic to mislead the public by seemingly granting independence to Ukraine while preparing the Red Army to cross the border. His ultimatum was deliberately worded: "On the Recognition of the Ukrainian National Republic by the Council of People's Commissars and on the Presentation of the Central Rada with an Ultimatum in Response to its Counterrevolutionary Activity."[70] The "counterrevolutionary activity" meant that the Ukrainian Central Rada refused to recognize the Soviets. The Bolsheviks' goal was to discredit the UNR government that began setting up diplomatic missions in Germany, Poland, Austria, and Czechoslovakia.[71] When Bolsheviks set up their own government in Kharkiv and proclaimed formation of the Ukrainian Socialist Soviet Republic, they appointed Volodymyr Zatons′kyi as Commissar of Education. The Soviet government embarked on a path toward vocational polytechnic education already established in neighboring Russia. This first Soviet government was short-lived.[72]

Preceding the confrontation with Bolsheviks, Central Rada received diplomatic recognition by Great Britain and France and engaged in preliminary talks with the Central Powers aimed at concluding a separate peace treaty.[73] These efforts did not result in any military assistance that could stop the Bolshevik invasion. The only victory that Central Rada achieved was at the ballot box. It gained two-thirds of votes in the Ukrainian elections to the All-Russian Constituent Assembly, mostly among the rural delegates.[74] Ukrainian parties secured 53 percent, whereas Bolsheviks obtained only 10 percent of all votes cast in Ukraine.[75] The popularity of the Central Rada did not mean the majority of those who voted for it were also willing to fight for it. This was particularly true of land tillers, "whose sympathies were then lukewarm toward any government."[76]

In January 1918, Central Rada further alienated farmers by outdoing the Bolsheviks in their populism, and abolishing private property on land.[77] Although the slogan of "socialization of land" was popular among poorer farmers, it did not mean they desired a collectivist organization of agriculture. A contemporary observer, who knew the conditions in the Ukrainian countryside, noted that socialization was understood as "taking over the land from the landowners without compensation."[78] Russian repartition of land by the village commune[79] was alien to highly individualist Ukrainian smallholders. Central Rada's decision to overturn the principle of private land ownership caused a disturbance in the life of the village.

Central Rada's decision to sign a peace treaty with the Central Powers on February 9, 1918, gave credence to accusations of Ukrainian Germanophilism.[80]

Opponents painted the Ukrainian national movement as weak. Critics failed to note that the fateful decision was made in a futile attempt to stop the Bolsheviks from subjugating Ukraine. Bolsheviks subverted Central Rada's efforts to recruit an army. Bolsheviks disbanded military regiments; all ranks and uniforms became obsolete. The masses were weary of the war and longed to return home to their land.[81] Neither Germans nor Austrians had interest or sympathy for the Ukrainian national movement. Despite assertions by Soviet historians that from the mid-nineteenth century, Germany worked actively to break up the Russian Empire and create independent Ukraine, evidence suggests otherwise. Before World War I, Germany's investment in Russia totaled 441.5 million rubles, or 19.7 percent of the country's foreign capital.[82] The Reich's policies were aimed at colonizing the black earth belt, the fertile lands of Ukraine.[83] A claim that the German *Drang nach Osten* and the Ukrainian national movement were in some kind of alliance had no basis in fact. The Ukrainian struggle for national liberation was an independent development in which neither the Allies nor the Central Powers played any significant part.[84]

In March 1918, after signing the Treaty of Brest-Litovsk separately with German and Austrian governments, Ukraine, rather than being independent, became a de facto zone of occupation by German and Austrian troops, and a transit station for a large number of refugees. The Central Rada failed to gather 1 million tons of grain to satisfy German military authorities. This provided an excuse for occupying powers to appoint Hetman Pavlo Skoropads'kyi as Ukraine's ruler in April 1918.[85] His rule was short-lived and marked by a health crisis caused by multiple epidemic diseases such as typhus, chicken pox, dysentery, and cholera plus the Spanish flu pandemic that swept through Ukraine in the summer and fall of 1918.[86] By October 1918, nearly 50 percent of the population in urban and rural areas of Ukraine had been infected with the new strain of flu, on top of concurrently running slew of other infectious diseases. Temporary closure of schools, public health education campaigns, and prophylactic measures were implemented.

Amid this health crisis and economic ruin, Ukraine's system of education underwent a second phase in its development. Although Hetman's administration reversed the tendency and attempted to centralize power and dismantle national minority education councils, it continued the Ukrainian language policy in schools initiated by its predecessors.[87] The newly appointed minister of education Professor Mykola Vasylenko appealed to school boards:

> In 1917 children enrolled in primary schools to study in Ukrainian. Now the children in these and other schools need an opportunity to continue their education in Ukrainian, especially in the environment where their national language and motherland are valued and respected.[88]

The Ministry of Education further mandated the establishment of primary schools throughout the republic in 1918–1919 with the teaching of all subjects in Ukrainian. Newly introduced mandatory subjects included history and geography of Ukraine. The press reported that during 1918–1919, nearly 800 primary schools taught mostly in Ukrainian.[89] By that time, all rural schools had already switched to Ukrainian. Skoropads'kyi, in the presence of his Education Minister Vasylenko, assured delegates at teachers' courses that the situation with secondary schools would improve. In the summer of 1918, sixty-four courses for teachers were offered, of these, fifty-nine in Ukrainian and five in Polish and Hebrew.[90] Those secondary schools that continued to use Russian as the language of instruction were required to offer courses in Ukrainian language, literature, history, and geography of Ukraine.[91] Local administrations also financially contributed to developing teaching materials and publishing textbooks in Ukrainian. By the end of 1918, Ukraine boasted 1,073 educational institutions, including boys' and girls' gymnasiums, institutes, commercial and trade schools, seminaries, and clerical schools.[92]

During this period, the first Ukrainian national universities were established, one in Kyïv on October 9, 1918, and another in Kam'ianets'-Podil's'kyi on October 22, 1918.[93] Also at this time, the All-Ukrainian Academy of Sciences was founded. Its president was Volodymyr Vernads'kyi and secretary Ahatanhel Kryms'kyi, both world-known scholars.[94]

Not long after German and Austrian collapse, Hetman's conservative rule was overthrown by national socialist forces in December 1918. A Directory with Volodymyr Vynnychenko and Symon Petliura inaugurated the third period in the history of the Ukrainian National Republic. The Directory, a collective governing body, and its minister of education Petro Kholodnyi, while on the road in an armored train, retreating from city to city, continued the work started by Central Rada on developing compulsory education. A separate department within the Ministry of Education laid out plans for higher education in Ukraine. In 1918 alone, nine teacher training institutes were established, as well as teacher training courses. The most significant achievement of the Directory was the law of January 1919; it recognized Ukrainian as a state language and required its use in all educational institutions as well as the All-Ukrainian Academy of Sciences. Simultaneously, the Ministry of Education approved a new orthography that spurred publication of textbooks and instructional materials. The Directory raised teachers' salaries several times and worked closely with the All-Ukrainian Teacher's Union on solving urgent problems.[95]

The Directory's achievements on the educational front were not matched on the military front. By mid-December 1918, a month after World War I ended in armistice, when Skoropads'kyi fled from Kyïv, the army of the Directory embraced nearly 100,000, while new recruits continued to pour in, both from cities and outlying areas.[96] Cossack chiefs (*otamans*) at all levels, sergeants, self-made captains, colonels, school teachers, and citizens of every rank rushed to support the independence movement.[97] The Directory's army appeared strong to prevent Russia's Bolsheviks from invading from the north, as well as to fight off Russian Monarchist troops of the White General Anton Denikin, who threatened Ukraine from the southeast. Despite the Directory's initial successes and the enthusiasm of its Ukrainian followers, the army began to melt away, and within several months had shrunk to 21,000.[98] The Directory faltered in its implementation of new programs.[99] The Bolsheviks' slogan "land to the tillers" was much more appealing to Ukrainian farmers who were unsuspecting of the Bolshevik's "double task" regarding the land policy.

Prior to the Paris Peace Conference, there was not a single attempt to come to grips with the possible menace of Bolshevism to European security. Ukraine's struggle for national liberation from oppressive policies of German imperialists and Russian Bolsheviks went unnoticed by the Big Four.[100] Although during the Red Scare in the 1920s, Edmund Gale of the *Los Angeles Times* in his cartoon "On the Threshold!" represented Bolshevism not as a pathetic Russian bear but as the bearded Cossack who presses a bloody hand on the door of "Civilization," Bolshevism was viewed in America and Europe as "a temporary, abnormal condition."[101] It was assumed that a democratic constitutional government would be established in Russia.[102]

As of January 21, 1919, the Woodrow Wilson administration was aware that if the Bolshevik regime continued in power, then "there seems to be no alternative to accepting the independence and tracing the frontiers of all the non-Russian nationalities."[103] The authors of the Inquiry report presented to Wilson further recommended the formation of an independent Ukrainian state. The Crimea, too, was to be included in the proposed Ukrainian state. Nevertheless, Wilson's decision was formed by his top Russian adviser Frank A. Golder, who urged the president: "For the sake of peace of the world, for the sake of Russia and Ukraine, for the sake of the Central Powers themselves, Great Russia and Little Russia must be united into a strong and free nation."[104]

President Wilson's Fourteen Points included his commitment to preserve the territorial integrity of what was referred to as "Russia."[105] The Ukrainian delegation at the Paris Peace Conference presented a map of Ukraine, with a prospectus outlining geographic and ethnographic boundaries of territories historically settled by Ukrainians, including Kuban' in the North Caucasus.[106] However, their bid was ultimately rejected, which led to the incorporation of Ukraine into the Soviet Union.

In his examination of American–Ukrainian relations in the 1920s, Constantine Warvariv noted that the official attitude of the United States was further reiterated by the Department of State, when it ordered the Liquidation Commission not to extend credit sales of surplus stocks—clothing, medical supplies, and motor equipment stored by American Forces in France—to Ukraine.[107] As evidence he cited a telegraphic report from the U.S. Commission to Negotiate Peace to the Secretary of State: "The recognized Ukrainian Mission in Paris, which has purchased large quantities of American Army supplies, represents the Petliura Government."[108] In response to the State Department's inquiry, Frank Polk, American plenipotentiary at the Peace Conference, cabled on October 17, 1919:

> The acting President of the mission is Count Tyszkevych and the Vice President is Dr. Paneyko. . . . Paneyko confirms reported purchase by Ukrainian mission of war stocks from American Army but states they have been unable to ship them out of France. Do not know who American army authorities consulted in connection with the sale but it would seem to have been an extraordinary action for them to take without getting views of the Department.[109]

Secretary of State Lansing ordered a thorough investigation of the transaction between the Ukrainian Mission in Paris and American military authorities. The investigation revealed that in April 1919, the chairman of the Liquidation Commission, Judge Edwin Parker, was approached by representatives of the Ukrainian National Republic for the purchase of supplies. Although the United States did not recognize Ukraine at the time, the proposal for the purchase of supplies valued in excess of $11,500,000 was accepted and the contract signed in June. In September 1919, at a meeting with Brig. General Edgar Jadwin, United States' observer in Ukraine, Petliura protested the nondelivery of clothing and equipment bought from the Liquidation Commission. General Jadwin also reported to the State Department that Petliura "requested that Ukrainians in America be permitted to join his army."[110]

When the Liquidation Commission stopped deliveries in early 1920, property valued at approximately $8,000,000 had already been sold (transfer effected on November 11, 1919). The payment was signed by three representatives of the Ukrainian National Republic at the Peace Conference. The materials comprised $6,500,000 worth of articles of clothing, blankets; $1,000,000 worth of medical supplies; and $300,000 worth of motor material including seventy-five Cadillac automobiles. All these were still stored in warehouses in France near Bordeaux and Marseilles during the months of investigation. An additional 600,000 francs were sold to corporations in France in order to defray the expenses of transportation, storage, and handling of supplies. The apparent collapse of the Petliura Government influenced the U.S. State Department's considerations on the matter. The contract was annulled on January 16, 1920, no motive or reason given.[111]

On January 17, 1920, Petliura sent a note to Allied and U.S. commanders in Paris, stating that for two years since December 3, 1918, "Ukraine alone has been fighting against the third Bolshevik onslaught and attempt to bring Communist experiment to Ukraine."[112] He requested free transit through Europe of medical supplies purchased by the Ukrainian representatives in France to help the army and people of Ukraine to withstand existential dual threats from Russian occupation and epidemics of infectious diseases. However, his calls to restore Ukraine's physical well-being to resolve the problem on the Eastern Front went unheeded.

To understand the U.S. State Department's policy toward Ukraine, it is worthwhile to quote the message addressed to the Commission to Negotiate Peace in Paris:

> On the basis of past investigations, the Department is disposed to regard the Ukrainian separatist movement as largely the result of Austrian and German propaganda seeking the disruption of Russia. It is unable to perceive an adequate ethnical basis for erecting a separate state and is not convinced that there is a real popular demand for anything more than such greater measure of local autonomy as will naturally result from the establishment in Russia of a modern democratic government, whether federative or not. The Department feels, accordingly, that the policy of the United States, while leaving to future events the determination of the exact character of the relations that exist between Great and Little Russia, should tend in the meantime, rather to sustain the principle of essential Russian unity than to encourage separatism.[113]

Without internal and external support, the Directory collapsed, and the Red Army marched into Kharkiv.[114] Lenin appointed Christian Rakovsky as head of the new Soviet government in Ukraine. With an utter lack of sensitivity to Ukrainian national aspirations, a French-educated physician of Bulgarian origin, and Rumanian subject who had become a Russian Bolshevik, made derogatory remarks at the Third Ukrainian Congress of Soviets about Ukrainian as the official language of the republic.[115] He was quoted as saying, in February 1919, that recognition of Ukrainian as the national language would be a "reactionary" measure, benefiting the nationalist intelligentsia.[116]

During their second occupation of Ukraine, Bolsheviks were using the same tactics as in previous years. They tried to establish agricultural communes and state farms on the former estates. They also continued their practice of requisitioning grain from Ukrainian farmers. In January 1919, Lenin sent Aleksandr Shlikhter to Ukraine as commissar of supply. He needed 50 million *puds* of grain by June in order to feed Russia's cities and the Red Army.[117] A poster published by the propaganda department in Moscow touted, "Only the Red Army will give us bread" (see Figure 1.2). The artist, N. Pomansky, told the

Figure 1.2 Poster "Only the Red Army will give us bread" by N. Pomansky (Moscow, 1919). *Source*: From Harold M. Fleming Papers, 1917–1971: Russian Revolutionary Era Propaganda Posters, Manuscripts and Archives Division, New York Public Library.

story in two parts. The top half presents the problem: "Denikin has occupied Kharkov and Ekaterinoslav. There is no bread in Moscow and Petrograd." The bottom half presents the solution: "The Red Army is advancing—bread is coming to Soviet Russia." The scales in the center illustrate an increase in bread ration from one-eighth of a pound (top) to a pound and a half (bottom). A note on the bottom warns, "Anyone who tears off this poster or covers it with a flier—commits a counter-revolutionary act!"

As many as 2,700 activists from Petrograd and Moscow arrived to assist Shlikhter with grain expropriation.[118] He later reported that "blood was spilled for every pound of grain collected."[119] From April to June 1919, nearly 328 anti-Bolshevik rebellions swept through Ukraine (in one month from April 1 to May 1—93, in two weeks from May 1 to May 15—28, and from June 1 to June 19—207 rebellions).[120] Bolsheviks held the big cities, but had lost the countryside. Bands of Ukrainian farmers cut telegraph lines, seized sections of railroads, and prevented Bolshevik officials from functioning.[121] By summer, anti-Bolshevik uprisings had cleared the path for Denikin's White Army to move into Ukraine from the southeast. The Directory retreated toward Kyïv. The Ukrainian communists had fled to Russia as Denikin proceeded to threaten Moscow itself.[122]

Anton Denikin's policy overturned all the achievements of the Central Rada, Hetman, and the Directory in the sphere of education. He restored attributes of the imperial school administration that were in existence prior to 1917. School boards lost their right to elect board members and hire teachers. Local self-governing administrations could no longer establish schools and finance education. Most drastically, Ukrainian language was banned. Russian language was proclaimed the official language on the territory of Russia, as well as "Little Russia," as Denikin referred to Ukraine in his decree "To the People of Little Russia" and his Order No. 22 in regard to Ukrainian schools.[123] The latter, in particular, reversed the policy of mandatory use of Ukrainian language in schools that conducted classes in Russian and banned the teaching of history and geography of Ukraine. Ukrainian language teaching became optional. A clarification was added on September 20, 1919, which allowed primary school teachers in early grades to use their students' "native language as a supplementary tool to improve comprehension" in the classroom.[124]

Educational leaders protested against Denikin's policy. Ukrainian cultural and educational associations were formed to support local self-governing administrations. In the midst of political and social upheaval, enthusiasm and selfless efforts of a citizenry arose, dedicated to the idea of Ukrainian statehood. Musicians like Kyrylo Stetsenko, the student of Mykola Lysenko, arranged Ukrainian folk songs and composed liturgical works, including the *Panakhyda*, the first canonical national requiem.[125] In 1919, Stetsenko together with Oleksandr Koshyts' founded the Ukrainian National Chorus to demonstrate the achievements of Ukrainian national music to the world.[126] To finance schools, Poltava intelligentsia created a cooperative Educational Association, "Ukrainian Culture," and raised several million *karbovantsi*. Other cooperatives emerged, the largest of them Dniprosoiuz and Ukrainbank, to support functioning of schools and printing of textbooks.[127] Teachers' conferences passed resolutions condemning Denikin's policy. In the absence of the central government, Ukraine's territory was divided and controlled not only by Denikin's White Army but also a score of warlords, including Nestor Makhno, and the Bolsheviks.

Warlords, who led anarchist bands in central and eastern Ukraine, did very much as they wished.[128] They represented "a single wave in the great sea of rebellion."[129] They were outside of the Directory's control, and did no justice to the national liberation movement. As Henry Abramson pointed out, despite the fact that atrocities, including pogroms in Jewish settlements, were perpetrated by warlords, the Red and White Armies, Soviet historiography blamed Petliura and his command for the 1919 pogroms.[130]

Despite the betrayal of the Galician division, which at a critical moment switched sides and joined Denikin's army, and the indifference of Western powers to the plight of the Ukrainian people, Petliura achieved symbolic victory when on August 8, 1919, the World Socialist Conference in Lucerne recognized the Ukrainian National Republic's independence. Summing up this period of struggle for national liberation, Petliura wrote with a sense of disillusionment and dark foreboding:

> The territory of Ukraine has been considered [by the great powers] as a booty if they can support their claim to it with the military force, but not as a home for the Ukrainian people and minorities who enjoy the right to freedom and equality.[131]

He condemned Russian communists who sought to bolster their own republic's claim to greatness by extracting resources from Ukraine. In hindsight, he realized that Russian Bolsheviks used Marx's anti-capitalist rhetoric as an instrument to "leapfrog into the ranks of great powers."[132]

After assuming leadership at the first congress of the Third International (*Comintern*), launched in March 1919, Bolsheviks prevailed on their third attempt to take over Ukraine. When the Red Army reoccupied Ukraine following the defeat of Denikin, the Politburo meeting, held on November 21, 1919, adopted Lenin's theses concerning the Russian Communist Party's policy toward Ukraine. It is worthwhile to study the entire document:

1. Greatest caution regarding nationalist traditions, strictest observance of equality of the Ukrainian language and culture, all officials to be required to study the Ukrainian language and so forth.
2. Temporary bloc with the Borot′bists to form a center before the convocation of the Congress of Soviets, with the concurrent launching of a propaganda campaign for the complete merger [of the Ukraine] with the RSFSR. For the time being, an independent Ukrainian Soviet Socialist Republic, in close federation with the RSFSR, on the basis of 1 June 1919.
3. In connection with the advance of Red Army troops into the Ukraine, intensified work on the [class] differentiation of the village; singling out three groups; recruiting poor peasants (+ middle peasants) into the administration. Rendering the kulaks completely harmless.
4. Immediately and without fail admit to all revolutionary committees and local soviets no fewer than half of the local peasants, first from among the poorest and second from the middle ones. The strictest requirement of accounting for the implementation of this demand by all nonlocal [party] workers, by all those sent from the center, by all members of the intelligentsia. Detailed working out of procedures for this accounting, and oversight of their actual implementation.
5. The countryside must be disarmed without fail and at all costs.
6. Food work in the Ukraine:

first, give priority to feeding Kharkov and the Donets Basin;¹³³

   second, delay extraction of the surpluses from the Ukraine to Russia, stretching it out as much as possible (that is, getting by in Russia with our [own] surpluses;

   third, use *any* extraction of surpluses to feed the local poor peasants no matter what, giving them without fail a share [of what is] taken from the kulaks;

   fourth, in general, conduct the food policy more cautiously than in Russia, sparing the middle peasant more, taking fewer surpluses.

7. Treat the Jews and urban inhabitants in the Ukraine with an iron rod, transferring them to the front, not letting them into government agencies (except in an insignificant percentage, in particularly exceptional circumstances, under class control).
8. [Place] the teachers' union [*spilka*], the cooperatives, and other such petty bourgeois organizations in the Ukraine under special surveillance, with special measures for their disintegration, for the singling out of Communists.
9. Initiate immediately especially energetic training of a special cadre of [party] workers for the Ukraine with specially reinforced surveillance and screening. Quickly carry out such preparations both through all the individual people's commissariats and through the Orgburo.¹³⁴

First, Lenin cautioned his comrades about Ukrainian "nationalist" rather than "national" traditions. The requirement for all Bolshevik officials to use the Ukrainian language behind the veneer of "equality" disguised the instrumental purpose of Bolshevik elite to indoctrinate cadres loyal to the occupying regime rather than to guarantee language rights of the local population. Second, Lenin proposed to launch a propaganda campaign as a tool to alter mass consciousness in the desired direction: to merge Ukraine with Russia. Third, Lenin admits that the colonial regime would have to be backed by military force. Notable is Lenin's guidance on class differentiation, without a clear definition of who belonged to either a "poor" or "middle peasant" or "kulak" category. This document illustrates that the classification started as early as 1919, establishing categories for social divisions that would mark certain groups as enemies of the occupying regime, subject to eventual extermination. Kulaks as a distinct group for the time being were rendered "harmless." Further down the list, Lenin singled out the All-Ukrainian Teachers' Union (*spilka*) for "special surveillance" with subsequent disintegration. It was liquidated in 1920, when teachers were forced to join a new professional union for educational employees.¹³⁵ Immediately, and "without fail," recruiting half of the local population into soviets to support the regime as stated in the fourth thesis clearly sets the mechanism for genocidal violence that these "ordinary" people would perpetrate a decade later. In anticipation of potential resistance, Lenin directed the Politburo to disarm the countryside. The sixth thesis became a blueprint for the Bolshevik food policy in Ukraine.

Particularly interesting in Lenin's theses is his call for excluding Jews from Soviet government in Ukraine. Richard Pipes noted that this exclusion followed the practice of the White Armies during their 1919 occupation of Ukraine.[136] If Jews were excluded from the Soviet government, where did the perception come that they overwhelmingly supported Bolshevism? Rarely discussed issue appears to have been the migration of Jews from what, until 1914, had been the Pale of Settlement to the cities. Myroslav Shkandrij has noted that Jews were desperate for any kind of employment; for this reason, they were available and prepared to serve the new regime, in the organs of repression, specifically the GPU. The low number of Ukrainians among leading cadres of the republic's security police, according to Vadym Zolotar'iov, "can be explained only by the hidden anti-Ukrainian politics of the Soviet leadership at the time."[137] Jews and Ukrainians were played off against each other: sometimes leaders of Jewish origin were replaced by Ukrainians, sometimes the reverse.[138]

In his fourth thesis, Lenin singled out "all members of the intelligentsia" along with other main enforcers of the policy, who are largely nonlocal party and central apparat authorities. Ukrainian intelligentsia varied in ideological orientations and attitudes toward Bolsheviks. Teachers, many of whom came from the families of nobles, urban industrialists, small proprietors, village clergy, and to a lesser extent proletariat, remained distrustful and refused to recognize the Soviet government, but showed obedience out of fear to lose a job or freedom.[139] Some focused on their narrow teaching duties. To keep a pulse on teachers' sentiments, Bolsheviks gathered teachers at conferences and meetings. Recognizing the challenge of winning teachers onto their side, Bolsheviks initiated a policy of electing teachers to fill vacancies. On May 10, 1919, Volodymyr Zatons'kyi signed a resolution "On the Election of School Personnel," which stated that teachers "had to be trusted by the people." Teachers were selected based on their public performance and had to be recommended by a committee that usually included Communist Party members and union representatives loyal to the Soviet regime. Scholars refer to this policy as the beginning of the purges in teachers' ranks.[140]

Under military control of the Red Army, Bolsheviks formed a new People's Commissariat of Education in Ukraine (*Narodnyi komisariat osvity* or NKO). It established a network of labor schools modeled on already existing ones in neighboring Russia. All other types of schools were eliminated. The labor school was mandatory, free, and secular. The emphasis on the labor component meant to closely align education with practical application of skills demanded by the economy. The labor was meant to be motivated by inner desire rather than forced. It had to be purposeful and useful to the society. Being socialists first, Ukrainian Bolsheviks initially had common ground with their Russian comrades; they envisioned free labor as an educational rather than exploitative tool. In 1919, the NKO in Soviet Ukraine supported the idea of polytechnic education.

In March 1920, the First All-Ukrainian Conference on People's Education refocused the goal toward social protection of children. It was dictated by devastating circumstances of the war and a sharp increase in the number of children who lost parents and homes. Discussions at the conference focused on establishing a new system of education in Soviet Ukraine. The first unified type of seven-year school was created with two levels: primary (grades 1 through 4) and secondary (grades 5 through 7). The seven-year school gave access to professional training in technical colleges. Institutes of higher education also underwent transformation.[141]

Soviet Ukraine's Commissar of Education Hryhorii Hryn'ko and his deputy Ian Riappo did not adhere strictly to the principle of polytechnic school, and delayed its implementation in the republic. This new course, which was approved by the delegates of the Second All-Ukrainian Conference on People's Education in August 1920, was harshly criticized by Lenin. The party recalled Hryn'ko to Moscow to appear before a committee hearing and, unexpectedly, seconded the position of the Ukrainian delegation that the republic needed a different type of school system to meet its needs. Encouraged by the support from the central authorities, Ukrainian Bolsheviks believed that they could combine two incompatible ideologies, national and communist, in creating a unique system of education suitable for future citizens of Ukraine.[142]

The system of education in Soviet Ukraine reflected the need to take over the function of families broken by war, and not only educate children, but also shelter them, organize activities of daily living, and teach social skills.[143] In the midst of the devastation wrecked by war, in 1920, the NKO issued a "Declaration on the Social Upbringing of Children," which refocused emphasis from the labor school toward a "children's house." At first, it was a necessary measure to house all orphaned children. Ultimately, the goal was to take children from the "harmful influence" of their individualistic parents and raise them in a spirit of collectivism. The then Soviet Ukraine's Commissar of Education Hryn'ko explained:

> The social upbringing in its full extent is the structuring of childhood as a whole, developing a collective life for the entire population of children. This is not a starting point, but the final goal of social upbringing. This means the end of individualistic upbringing of children in their families, which would not be possible without establishing socialist economy and restructuring society.[144]

In practice, this meant registering all children under the age of fifteen, distributing them among shelters, developing a network of kindergartens and after-school clubs, opening orphanages, uniting these institutions into children's communities, protecting the rights of children in need of social assistance, especially children with disabilities, labeled at the time "defective" children. The result of the declared program was a total control of the child's individuality by the newly established regime.[145]

A total control of the person's individuality also applied to teachers. Bolsheviks used a variety of forms of ideological pressure to fulfill Lenin's dictum that schools cannot be outside politics or be separate from the state. Chief among these forms was the participation of Communist Party representatives in all teachers' conferences and congresses. Libraries with political propaganda, short summer courses to train social science teachers, guest lectures to acquaint teachers with political theory, and political literacy tests were instituted on a permanent basis.

In March 1920, after liquidation of the Borot'bists,[146] the All-Ukrainian Teachers' Union was dissolved. In August, a new union was established for teachers in Soviet Ukraine, Robos (a blend from *robitnyky osvity* or educational employees).[147] Toward the end of 1920, the Bolsheviks succeeded in enforcing teachers' cooperation with the Soviet government, and Communist Party cells were established in all branches of the Robos in Soviet Ukraine.[148]

From 1921 on, with a temporary liberalization that came along with the New Economic Policy (NEP), the intellectual atmosphere was conducive to educational innovation and experimentation. Communist Party planners expressed no preference for a specific scientific paradigm, and most scholars disagreed on how to interpret Marx's philosophy. No unity existed among educational theorists either. However, they agreed that the prerevolution system of schooling, with its classical gymnasium, had to give way to a school that integrated students from all strata of society. In Ukraine, the struggle for national liberation from 1917 to 1921 spurred efforts to create its national school. The social and political circumstances of the interrupted national struggle led to a search for new methods and approaches to schooling.[149]

New methods had, as their scientific basis, developments in physiology and psychology of the late nineteenth to early twentieth century. One influence on educational theory came from Ivan Pavlov's experimental work on conditional reflexes.[150] Ivan Sokolians'kyi believed that it would bring "a true paradigm shift in pedagogy."[151] Another influence on educational theory came from psychologist Vladimir Bekhterev, author of the *Basic Principles of Objective Psychology and Psycho-reflexology* (1910), who found that human behavior, from rudimentary organic reactions to complex acts of creativity, is essentially reflexive.[152] Educational reflexology was established as a field of study, focusing on child anatomy and physiology based on conditional and unconditional reflexes. In sum, the child's life and education had to be structured and controlled.

All future teachers were required to study Charles Darwin's theory of evolution, the origin of species, anatomy and physiology of the human body, as well as the sympathetic and parasympathetic nervous systems, and endocrine system function, and their effects on the formation of a child's character. Psychological testing became popular, and measurements of sensory organs, motor functions, will, and aesthetic feelings were used to select intellectually gifted children and direct their choice of future profession.[153] Teachers, however, were hardly aware of Engels's compliment to Marx's achievements as the "Darwin of history."[154] Hannah Arendt drew parallels between the two theories: "The 'natural' law of the survival of the fittest is just as much a historical law and could be used as such by racism as Marx's law of the survival of the most progressive class."[155] Teachers were unsuspecting that forces of nature and history let loose by these theories would not permit free action or opposition, or even sympathy, to interfere with the struggle to eliminate "enemies of the people," based on race or class.

The Ukrainian educators in their search for a new scientific theory turned to the West. Despite frequent visits to German universities on scholarly exchanges, they mostly followed Moscow's lead. Nevertheless, the pro-Western orientation in the early 1920s is evident from a programmatic speech presented by Soviet Ukraine's Commissar of Education, Hryn′ko, appropriately titled "Our Path Westward" (*Nash shlyakh na Zakhid*). He stated that Europe had a rich tradition of scientific research in psychology, psychophysiology, psychological techniques, as well as trained specialists in the field of education. In contrast, in Soviet Ukraine, social and political upheaval led to a "chaotic-revolutionary pedagogical activity," which required scientific grounding. Soviet education historian Ol′ha Sukhomlyns′ka characterized Hryn′ko's speech not as a declaration, but "an approach to creating a new pedagogical theory in Ukraine."[156]

THE FAMINE OF 1921–1923 IN SOVIET UKRAINE

Once Lenin and his "red" disciples consolidated their power, they attempted to realize Marx's economic doctrine. Bolsheviks replaced trade with barter and abolished commodity-money relations and the free market.[157] To run the state, they brought about total appropriation of the economy under the guise of nationalization of industrial enterprises and the collectivization of agriculture. The first attempt to build utopia led to a crisis that verged on economic collapse and culminated in the catastrophic famine of 1921–1923 (masked by droughts). According to Soviet historian Stanislav Kul′chyts′kyi, Lenin got out of the crisis by "canceling the prohibition on private enterprise, forgoing the collectivization of agriculture, and restoring free trade between town and country."[158] From the policy of "War Communism," a set of extraordinary measures that had nothing to do with Marx's doctrine, Lenin transitioned to the NEP.

The NEP began in 1921, when *prodrazverstka* was suspended.[159] From 1921 to 1927, the state obtained grain for cities, the army, and a new export fund from farmers either by levying fixed taxes in kind or by purchasing their produce on the free market.[160] The legalization of the market forced Bolshevik leaders to allow entrepreneurial activity. Nationalized industry was organized in trusts based on principles of cost accounting, which required the generation of revenue to fund production costs. Restoration of the credit and banking systems, the introduction of a stable currency, and the promotion of private enterprise revived production.[161] However, teachers' financial situation worsened because, due to the shortage of cash, funding for people's education was transferred to local authorities.[162] The situation with teachers' salaries throughout Soviet Ukraine was dire. In 1922, in the Kyïv region, a teacher could hardly survive on the wage earnings equivalent to one-seventh of the cost of living.[163]

In Soviet Ukraine, famine lasted until the summer of 1923. It was caused by droughts, postwar devastation, the policy of grain expropriation, and excessive export of grain outside the Soviet Union.[164] In 1921, 20 percent of the harvest was lost due to droughts. In Soviet Ukraine, the three regions that were affected most included Donets'k (40 percent), Zaporizhzhia (63 percent), and Katerynoslav (64 percent). To avoid interrupting transport of grain from Soviet Ukraine to Russia, the Council of People's Commissars of the Russian SFSR did not acknowledge the existence of famine in southeastern regions of the Ukrainian SSR until early 1922, when mass mortality began. Once the famine was recognized, the head of the Council of People's Commissars of the Ukrainian SSR, Christian Rakovsky,[165] appealed for aid.[166] The American Relief Administration (ARA), which had been working in the Volga region, the second largest grain-producing area, since August 1921, gave starving Ukrainians 180.9 million emergency rations, only after the Russian SFSR agreed to it on January 10, 1922. The Fridtjof Nansen charitable mission gave 12.2 million in emergency rations. Workers' International Relief, created by the Communist International, gave Soviet Ukraine 383,000 emergency rations. In the fall of 1922, the Soviet government announced that the new harvest had ended the famine; however, in Soviet Ukraine famine lasted till the summer of the following year.[167]

By January 1922, about 1.9 million people had starved in the five famine-struck provinces in Soviet Ukraine's south, but by April their number increased to 3.2 million, and by June peaked at 3.8 million, or 40 percent of the population in affected areas. Diseases, including typhus and cholera, were rampant, and by August, took over half a million more lives. In one governorate, Mykolaïv, from January to October 1922, as many as 37,331 died of hunger, and 50,600 more suffered in various stages of disease due to starvation. Overall, according to the official census data,[168] Ukraine lost between 5.5 and 7.5 million people as a result of World War I, the war for national liberation, and the famine.[169]

The famine of 1921–1923 paralyzed the most rebellious areas of Ukraine's countryside. When physical survival became the most immediate problem, partisan resistance in the villages became impossible. Thus, according to Wasyl Hryshko, "the famine became the ultimate weapon in the Soviet pacification of Ukraine and a proven method of genocide." Hryshko further noted:

> Whether it was planned and executed by the Soviet regime as a genocidal action cannot be positively proved, but the thing is clear: it was used by the Soviet regime as an effective tool in the final stage of subjugation inside Ukraine. The Soviet Russian authorities at first denied the famine in Ukraine, and then hindered all attempts by Western European and American relief organizations to develop full scale action for rescuing the Ukrainian people from mass starvation, while at the same time welcoming relief actions in the Volga region.[170]

Some contemporary Ukrainian scholars, along with diaspora scholars, have noted that the Soviet authorities used the famine instrumentally to put an end to the opposition.[171] However, in her *Red Famine*, Anne Applebaum has argued that this thesis cannot be proven as there is no evidence of a premeditated plan.[172] Yet in the following paragraph, Applebaum quoted Lenin's letter to Viacheslav Molotov, arguing that the famine offered a unique opportunity to seize church property and "not hesitate to put down the least opposition."[173]

The standard of living of intellectual elites declined precipitously. They lost social security and pensions, suffered from arbitrary evictions or requisitions of "surplus" property, and became isolated from their European colleagues due to severed academic ties. Many leading members of the intelligentsia became demoralized, suffering acute material and intellectual deprivations. In 1920, authorities in Moscow established a Central Commission for Food Supply in Russia.[174] Soviet Ukraine had not received any support from the central government, even in the provinces hard hit by famine until October 1921. By then only limited food assistance trickled down to Kharkiv and Kyïv. The leading research centers in these two cities received 170 and 120 food assistance rations.[175] Only 25 percent of scientists and 4 percent of artists in Kharkiv, then capital of Soviet Ukraine, received food assistance.[176] This policy of "divide and rule," typical of imperial control, became evident to M. M. Berezhkov, professor at Nizhyn Institute of People's Education, who recorded in his diary:

Vulgarity, stupidity, ignorance, brutality have become entrenched, consuming everyone, even noble and honest people. We have descended into the sneaky, petty calculation, the mercantilism, the procurement of food rations . . . Civil servants received a food supplement, or a handout (I don't know what to call it) of half a pound of pastry cookies, half a pound of jam and a pound of salt, for a total of 90 *krb*. (Enjoy yourself, indulge like children. . ., but then pay for the indulgence). . . . Without faith, without hope, without active love, there is no authentic, true life, but only existence, animalistic, slavish.[177]

This Bolshevik policy toward the intelligentsia was deliberate. It allowed the ruling regime to control the intelligentsia and force them to compromise. Leon Trotsky admitted bluntly: "We will use hunger to force the intelligentsia to work for us."[178]

Although Bolshevik leaders appealed for international relief, it was too little too late to save children in Soviet Ukraine. By the fall of 1922, nearly 2 million children were starving in Soviet Ukraine's southeastern provinces. Less than half of them (943,500) received food relief.[179] Parents could apply for food assistance for their starving children through TsK Dophol VUTsVK, a special commission of the All-Ukrainian Central Executive Committee to assist the starving, or through foreign charitable organizations. International relief missions took photographs of children partially or fully unclothed to show the effects of famine (see children swollen from starvation in Figure 1.3).[180]

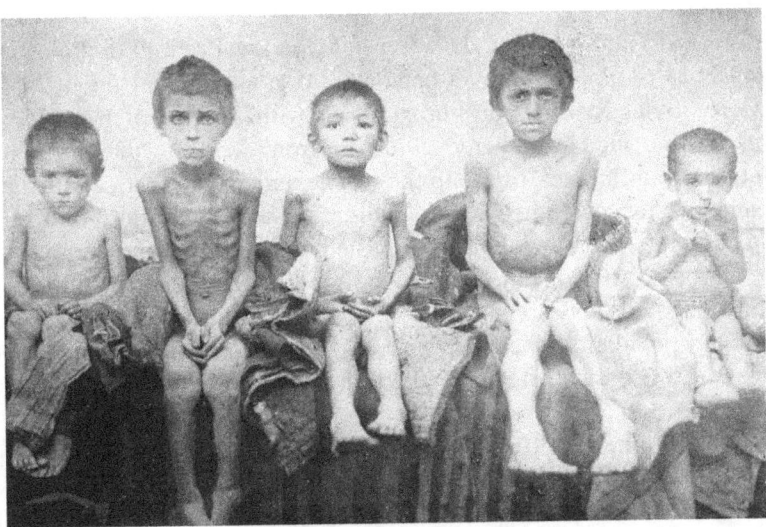

Figure 1.3 Famished children, Berdians'k, Ukraine, 1922. *Source*: From the Photographic Archives of the International Committee of the Red Cross, V-P-HIST-02591-07A.

In January 1923, the Ukrainian Red Cross opened free kitchens to feed 63,000 of the starving children; by February their capacity grew to 100,000, but subsequently no more than 70,000 children received assistance.[181] In April 1923, foreign charitable organizations, including the ARA, Nansen mission, American Baptists (Mennonites), and the Swiss Red Cross, among others, provided food assistance to 360,000 children in Soviet Ukraine.[182] But foreign assistance dwindled once the Soviet Union started shipping grain to sell on the world market. Foreign missions could not fathom that the Soviet government could sell grain overseas as a source of revenue while its own people were dying of hunger.

Homeless children were placed in orphanages, but due to intermittent supply shortages those children were malnourished. Orphanages turned into hot spots for epidemics and mass deaths among children. Even in the better off province of Poltava, half of schoolchildren suffered from tuberculosis and the remaining were emaciated and anemic.[183] Orphanages were severely overcrowded because 56,000 children from famine struck areas in Soviet Russia were evacuated to Soviet Ukraine, and in 1922, they constituted 75 percent of all children in Ukraine's orphanages.[184] In his speech at the Seventh All-Ukrainian Congress of Soviets, held in December 1922, Hryhorii Petrovs′kyi reported that Ukraine accommodated 80,000 children, most of them evacuated from the Volga region (obligated to take care of only 25,000).[185] This organized evacuation plus uncontrolled migration of starving children from Russia aggravated the famine situation in Soviet Ukraine. Along with the evacuation and migration, came a wave of cruelty and child prostitution.

In his classic study, *Man and Society in Calamity*, Pitirim Sorokin assessed the impact of famine on human behavior. As a survivor of the 1921–1922 famine in Soviet Russia, Sorokin came up with a range of behaviors that victims engage in. He gathered evidence from world's calamities—wars, revolutions, and famines—to help the reader understand that cannibalism in non-cannibalistic societies is extremely rare (less than one-third of 1 percent of population), whereas violations of basic honesty and fairness in pursuit of food, such as misuse of rationing cards, hoarding, and taking unfair advantage of others, are widespread (from 20 to 99 percent), but highly variable. Half of the population succumb to pressure of starvation, surrendering or disengaging from most of the aesthetic activities irreconcilable with food-seeking activities.[186]

For the first time in 300 years, cases of cannibalism were reported in areas affected by the famine in Soviet Ukraine's south.[187] Based on Sorokin's observation, more than 99 percent of the population avoided such behavior. As a result of the war, revolution, and famine, human life lost value. Along with physical degradation, morality and dignity vanished. This famine of 1921–1923 became a "dress rehearsal"[188] for the Great Famine of 1932–1933, the apex of the Holodomor, perpetrated with greater ruthlessness by Bolshevik henchmen with support of "devils in military uniforms" (the GPU), who created conditions incompatible with life, causing physical and mental suffering among millions of their victims.

Seeds of genocidal violence, sown in the 1920s, took many years to ripen before reaching the apogee in the 1930s. The main stages of its growth are well-known now. If the whole of human history is to be conceived in class terms, as spelled out in Marx's writings, then "it does follow that the new society must start by a violent break in cultural continuity from the old one."[189] After World War I, Ukraine's struggle to establish itself as a national republic, with a representative democratic government, was curtailed. Using both lethal and nonlethal means, such as vicious propaganda against the weak national government, Bolsheviks subjugated Ukraine, banned all political parties and trade unions, and established a monopoly rule of the Leninist party, the only legitimate mouthpiece of the "toiling masses," equipped with an ideology which justified their power. Economic and nationality policies, conceived as temporary at the time, became permanent components of the new society. After the seizure of power, education became the task of the vanguard of society; the creation of the new Soviet species was the product of sheer coercion.

NOTES

1. Smeulers, "Perpetrators of International Crimes," 233, 235.

2. Leszek Kołakowski, "The Marxist Roots of Stalinism," in *The Great Lie: Classic and Recent Appraisals of Ideology and Totalitarianism*, ed. F. Flagg Taylor IV (Wilmington: Intercollegiate Studies Institute, 2011), 171. The article first appeared in *My Correct Views on Everything* (St. Augustine's Press, 1977).

3. For a special study of Makhno's role in the Ukrainian struggle for liberation, see Frank Sysyn, "Nestor Makhno and the Ukrainian Revolution," in *The Ukraine, 1917–1921: A Study in Revolution*, ed. Taras Hunczak (Cambridge: Harvard Ukrainian Research Institute, 1977), 271–304.

4. S. V. Kul'chyts'kyi, "Borot'bysty," in *Encyclopedia of Modern Ukraine*, ed. I. M. Dziuba et al. (Kyïv: Instytut entsyklopedychnykh doslidzhen' NAN Ukraïny, 2004), http://esu.com.ua/search_articles.php?id=37346.

5. Andrea Graziosi, "Viewing the Twentieth Century through the Prism of Ukraine: Reflections on the Heuristic Potential of Ukrainian History," *Harvard Ukrainian Studies* 34, no. 1–4 (2015–2016): 118.

6. Stephen Bronner, *Critical Theory: A Very Short Introduction* (New York: Oxford University Press, 2011); see also James Bohman, "Critical Theory," *Stanford*

Encyclopedia of Philosophy (Winter 2019 Edition), ed. Edward N. Zalta, https://plato.stanford.edu/archives/win2019/entries/critical-theory/.

7. *Karl Marx: Essential Writings*, ed. Frederic L. Bender (New York: Harper & Row, Publishers, 1972), ix–x.

8. Wasyl Hryshko, "The Origins of Soviet Genocide," in *The Ukrainian holocaust of 1933*, ed. and trans. Marco Carynnyk (Toronto: Bahriany Foundation, SUZHERO, DOBRUS, 1983), 8.

9. Karl Marx, *Communist Manifesto* (Chicago: Henry Regnery Company for the Great Books Foundation, 1949), 30.

10. Karl Marx and Frederick Engels, *Collected Works* (London: Lawrence & Wishart, 1845–1848), vol. 6, 103.

11. Marx, *Communist Manifesto*, 13.

12. Ibid., 20–21.

13. Ibid., 24, 32–34.

14. Lenin is the nom de guerre of Vladimir Ul'ianov adopted after the place of his exile near the Lena river in Siberia. See James H. Billington, "The Legacy of Russian History," in *The Stalin Revolution: Foundations of Soviet Totalitarianism*, ed. Robert V. Daniels (Lexington and Toronto: D. C. Heath and Company, 1972), 160.

15. In 1910, Dzhugashvili adopted the nom de guerre Stalin, which rhymed with Russian-sounding Lenin, and meant "Man of Steel" from the Russian word *stal'*. His earlier conspiratorial pseudonym was Koba, meaning "the fearless" in Turkish. See Robert C. Tucker, *Stalin as Revolutionary, 1879–1929* (New York: W. W. Norton & Company, Inc., 1973), 132. See also Billington, "The Legacy of Russian History," 160.

16. Tucker, *Stalin as Revolutionary*, 116.

17. S. Vereshchak, "Stalin v tiur'me (Vospominaniia politicheskoho zakliuchennogo)," *Dni*, January 22, 1928; quoted in Tucker, *Stalin as Revolutionary*, 117.

18. Hryshko, "The Origins of Soviet Genocide," 14, 19.

19. Roman Serbyn, "Lénine et la question ukrainienne en 1914: le discours 'séparatiste' de Zurich," *Pluriel*, no. 25 (1981): 83; quoted in Orest Subtelny, *Ukraine: A History*, 4th ed. (Toronto: University of Toronto Press, 2009), 268–69.

20. Vladislav Grinevich, "Podolannia totalitarnoho mynuloho – Chastyna 3: Chy buv SSSR imperiieiu, a Ukraïna – koloniieiu?" *Ukraïna moderna*, August 22, 2019, uamoderna.com/blogy/vladislav-grinevich/totalitarism-part-3.

21. Tetiana Teren, "Neopublikovana rozmova z Anatoliiem Dimarovym: Shkoduiu, shcho v takyi strashnyi chas zhyv, koly ne mozhna bulo pysaty pravdu," *Ukraïns'ka Pravda*, July 7, 2014, https://life.pravda.com.ua/society/2014/07/7/174315/.

22. The decommunization of public space commenced in April 2015 when the government of Ukraine, a year following the Revolution of Dignity of 2013–2014, outlawed communist symbols. See Alexander J. Motyl, "Kiev's Purge: Behind the New Legislation to Decommunize Ukraine," *Foreign Affairs*, April 28, 2015, https://www.foreignaffairs.com/articles/ukraine/2015-04-28/kievs-purge.

23. Ewald Ammende, *Human Life in Russia* (London: George Allen and Unwin, 1936), 142.

24. Ammende, *Human Life in Russia*, 145.

25. Lenin's mother, Maria Ul'ianova (née Blank), was the daughter of Alexandr Blank, a well-to-do physician. Some researchers argue that he was a Jewish convert to Orthodox Christianity, Srul' Blank, also spelled Israil Blank. Others believe she was the descendant of German colonists invited to Russia by Catherine the Great. However, Russian historians argue this was another man by a similar name. Her mother Anna Groschopf was the daughter of a German father Johann Groschopf and Swedish mother Anna Östedt. See Christopher Read, *Lenin: A Revolutionary Life* (New York: Routledge, 2005) and Robert Pein, *Lenin: Zhizn' i smert'* (Moscow: Molodaiia gvardiia, 2008). See also interview with Lenin's biographer E. A. Kotelenets, "Bitva za Lenina: shest' mifov o vozhde revoliutsii," *Komsomol'skaia Pravda*, April 22, 2017, https://www.kp.ru/daily/26670.5/3692043/.

26. See Michael Pearson, *The Sealed Train* (New York: Putnam, 1975) and Edward Crankshaw, "When Lenin Returned," *The Atlantic Monthly*, October 1954, https://www.theatlantic.com/magazine/archive/1954/10/when-lenin-returned/303867/. For a train route from Switzerland to Petrograd via Finland, see Joshua Hammer, "Vladimir Lenin's Return Journey to Russia Changed the World Forever," *Smithsonian Magazine*, March 2017, https://www.smithsonianmag.com/travel/vladimir-lenin-return-journey-russia-changed-world-forever-180962127/.

27. V. I. Lenin, *Collected Works*, 45 vols. (Moscow: Progress Publishers, 1960–1970), vol. 22, 154; vol. 19, 243–44, 500–1, 526; vol. 21, 413; quoted in Hryshko, "The Origins of Soviet Genocide," 24–25.

28. The theses were written in October–December 1913 and published in the journal *Prosveshcheniie* no. 10, 11, and 12. For the English text, see V. I. Lenin, "Critical Remarks on the National Question," in *Collected Works*, trans. Bernard Isaacs and Joe Fineberg, ed. Julius Katzer, vol. 20 (Moscow: Progress Publishers, 1964), 17–51, available from https://www.marxists.org/archive/lenin/works/cw/pdf/lenin-cw-vol-20.pdf.

29. Lenin, *Collected Works*, vol. 20, 28, 30, 45; vol. 21, 419; vol. 19, 500; quoted in Hryshko, 26–28.

30. Ibid., vol. 20, 31–32; quoted in Hryshko, 28–29. The Russian word *muzhik* means a rustic, a country bumpkin.

31. Ibid., vol. 19, 116, 118, 246, 248, 250–51, 380–81, 503–4, 533; vol. 20, 20, 22; quoted in Hryshko, 30.

32. Ibid.

33. Hryshko, 32.

34. Lenin, *Collected Works*, vol. 20, 28, 30–33; quoted in Hryshko, 33.

35. Hryshko, 33.

36. Lenin, *Collected Works*, vol. 22, 340–41; quoted in Hryshko, 33.

37. N. Lenin, "The Soldiers and the Land," *Soldatskaia Pravda*, no. 1, April 15, 1917, reprinted in *Collected Works*, vol. 24, 137–38; "Draft Resolution on the Agrarian Question," first published in May 1917 in the pamphlet *Material on the*

Agrarian Question, reprinted in *Collected Works*, vol. 24, 483–85; "Speech on the Agrarian Question, May 22 (June 4) 1917," published in *Izvestiia*, no. 14, May 25, 1917, reprinted in *Collected Works*, vol. 24, 486–505; quoted in V. I. Lenin, *Between the Two Revolutions: Articles and Speeches of 1917* (Moscow: Progress Publishers, 1971), 132–33, 221–42.

38. Lenin, *Collected Works*, vol. 9, 235–36; quoted in Hryshko, 37.
39. Hryshko, 37.
40. Lenin, *Collected Works*, vol. 31, 242–43; quoted in Hryshko, 40.
41. Hryshko, 40.
42. V. I. Lenin, *Sochineniia*, vol. 30 (Moscow: Partiinoe izd-vo, 1932), 413.
43. I. V. Stalin, *Voprosy leninizma* (Moscow: Gospolitizdat, 1945), 610.
44. "Ukrainskaia SSR," in *Narodnoe obrazovanie v SSSR, 1917–1967*, eds. M. A. Prokofiev, P. V. Zimin, M. N. Kolmakova, M. I. Kondakov, and N. P. Kuzin (Moscow: Prosveshchenie, 1967), 326.
45. Oleksander Luhovyi, *Vyznachne zhinotstvo Ukraïny: istorychni zhyttiepysy v chotyr'okh chastynakh* (Toronto: The Ukrainian Publishing Company, 1942), 30, 37, see Digital Collection of the National University "Kyïv-Mohyla Academy" at https://dlib.ukma.edu.ua/document/87; Natalia Polons'ka-Vasylenko, *Vydatni zhinky Ukraïny* (Winnipeg: Ukrainian Women's Association of Canada, printed by Trident Press, 1969), 37–38, 58–59.
46. David Saunders, *The Ukrainian Impact on Russian Culture, 1750–1850* (Edmonton: Canadian Institute of Ukrainian Studies, University of Alberta, 1985).
47. Solovey, *Golgota Ukraïny*, 17. For a detailed analysis of consistent and long-lasting policy of eradicating all varieties of Ukrainian from social realm (ecclesiastic, administrative, and literary) by imperial Russian rulers, see Andrii Danylenko and Halyna Naienko, "Linguistic Russification in Russian Ukraine: Languages, Imperial Models, and Policies," *Russian Linguistics* 43, no. 1 (2019): 19–39, https://doi.org/10.1007/s11185-018-09207-1.
48. The fact that Peter the Great started building a canal from the While Sea to the Gulf of Finland was reported by a journalist from a pro-Soviet British monthly *Russia Today* at the time when Stalin, like Peter I more than 230 years earlier, sent hundreds of thousands of recalcitrant Ukrainians who opposed his regime to dig the canal in 1932. See Geoffrey Pinnock, "A Great Canal Beats Arctic Ocean," *Russia Today*, December 1932, 16. Thanks to Jars Balan of the Canadian Institute of Ukrainian Studies for bringing this article to my attention.
49. Isabel de Madariaga, "The Foundation of the Russian Educational System by Catherine II," *Slavonic and East European Review* 57, no. 3 (1979): 385, 388, 390; and by the same author, *Russia in the Age of Catherine the Great* (New Haven: Yale University Press, 1981).
50. See Johannes Remy, "Against All Odds: Ukrainian in the Russian Empire in the Second Half of the Nineteenth Century," in *The Battle for Ukrainian: A Comparative Perspective*, eds. Michael S. Flier and Andrea Graziosi (Cambridge: Harvard University Press for the Ukrainian Research Institute, 2017), 43–61.
51. Solovey, *Golgota Ukraïny*, 49.

52. Symon Petliura, "Ukraïns'ki katedry i ukraïns'kyi proletariat," *Slovo* (Kyïv), no. 22, September 22, 1907, reprinted in *Symon Petliura: Statti, lysty, dokumenty* (New York: Ukrainian Academy of Arts and Sciences in the U.S., 1956), 64–66.

53. Symon Putliura, "Stan narodn'oï osvity ta medytsyny v Poltavshshyni v tsyfrakh," *Literaturno-Naukovyi Vistnyk* V, no. XIX (1902): 152–54, reprinted in *Symon Petliura*, 13–15.

54. Ol'ha Sukhomlyns'ka, *Narysy istoriï ukraïns'koho shkil'nytstva (1905–1933)* (Kyïv: Zapovit, 1996), 79.

55. D. Rozovyk, "Stanovlennia natsional'noï vyshchoï osvity i naukovo-doslidnoï pratsi v Ukraïni (1917–1920 rr.)," *Etnichna istoriia narodiv Ievropy: Zbirnyk naukovykh prats'*, vyp. 8 (2001): 55–58.

56. "Do ukraïntsiv-profesoriv i prepodavateliv vyshchykh shkil," *Visti z Ukraïns'koï Tsentral'noï rady u Kyievi*, March 21, 1917; quoted in Viktor Adams'kyi, "Ideia natsional'noho universytetu za doby Tsentral'noï Rady: sproba realizatsiï," *Osvita, nauka i kul'tura na Podilli*, no. 24 (2017): 17.

57. Sukhomlyns'ka, *Narysy*, 80, 110–11; see also Klitsakov, *Pedahohichni kadry Ukraïny*, 55.

58. *TsDAVOU*, f. 2581, op. 1, spr. 15, ark 1.

59. Sukhomlyns'ka, *Narysy*, 111–12.

60. Ibid., 112.

61. Ibid., 80.

62. Ibid., 113.

63. I. Kryzhanovs'kyi, "Dekil'ka uvah do postanovky pozashkil'noï osvity na mistsiakh," *Vil'na ukraïns'ka shkola*, no. 5–6 (1918): 26–30; quoted in Sukhomlyns'ka, *Narysy*, 114.

64. Sukhomlyns'ka, *Narysy*, 114.

65. The Central Rada in its Third Universal proclaimed the UNR in reaction to the Bolshevik coup d'état in Petrograd, in federation with future democratic Russia. It declared complete independence in its Fourth Universal. For English translation of all four universals, see Taras Hunczak, ed., *The Ukraine, 1917–1921: A Study in Revolution* (Cambridge: Harvard Ukrainian Research Institute, 1977).

66. U.S. Congress, House of Representatives, Select Committee on Communist Aggression, *Communist Takeover and Occupation of Ukraine*, Special Report No. 4, 88th Cong., 2nd Sess. (Washington, D.C.: U.S. Government Printing Office, 1954), 9.

67. Ivan Steshenko was murdered by the Bolsheviks in July 1918. See Leonid Bilets'kyi, "Ivan Steshenko," *Vil'na ukraïns'ka shkola*, no. 1 (1918): 1–3; quoted in Serhii Bilokin', "Dolia chleniv Tsentral'noï Rady v SSSR," *Vyzvol'nyi shliakh*, kn. 1 (2000): 14–26, https://web.archive.org/web/20081122004310/http://bilokin.mysl enedrevo.com.ua/terror/dchcr.html.

68. Sukhomlyns'ka, *Narysy*, 81–82.

69. Ibid., 114.

70. *Istoriia Sovetskoi Konstitutsii (v dokumentakh) 1917–1956*, ed. S. S. Studenikin (Moscow: Gosiurizdat, 1957), 74. See also *Communist Takeover and Occupation of Ukraine*, 8.

71. Solovey, *Golgota Ukraïny*, 43.

72. Sukhomlyns′ka, *Narysy*, 82.

73. Regarding British recognition of Ukraine, see "Mérey an das k.u.k. Min. d. Äussern: Über die Ankunft der Delegierten der Kiewer Zentralrada sowie Bedenken gegen ihre Zulassung zur nachträglichen Unterzeichnung des Waffenstillstandsvertrages, Brest-Litovsk, 16 December 1917," H-H-SA/PA, Vienna, Kr. 70/6, in Theophil Hornykiewicz, ed., *Ereignisse in der Ukraine, 1914–1922, deren Bedeutung und historische Hintergründe*, vol. II (Horn: Ferdinand Berger und Söhne, 1966), 3. For the French part in the recognition, see Dmytro Doroshenko, *Istoriia Ukraïny, 1917–1923 rr.*, vol. I, 2nd ed. (New York: Bulava Publishing Corporation, 1954), 230–40, 436–37.

74. "Gautsch an das k.u.k. Min. d. Äussern: Bericht über die erste Besprechung mit den ukrain. Delegierten" (n.d.), H-H-SA/PA, Vienna, Kr. 70/6, in Hornykiewicz, vol. II, 6–7.

75. Jurij Borys, *The Russian Communist Party and the Sovietization of the Ukraine: A Study in the Communist Doctrine of the Self-Determination of Nations* (Stockholm: Norstedt & Soner, 1960), 173; see also Conquest, *The Harvest of Sorrow*, 34.

76. Ihor Kamenetsky, "Hrushevsky and the Central Rada: Internal Politics and Foreign Interventions," in *The Ukraine, 1917–1921: A Study in Revolution*, ed. Taras Hunczak (Cambridge: Harvard Ukrainian Research Institute, 1977), 40.

77. Ivan L. Rudnytsky, "The Fourth Universal and Its Ideological Antecedents," in *The Ukraine, 1917–1921: A Study in Revolution*, ed. Taras Hunczak (Cambridge: Harvard Ukrainian Research Institute, 1977), 209.

78. Illia Vytanovych, *Agrarna polityka ukraïns′kykh uriadiv, 1917–1920* (Munich: Ukraïns′ke istorychne tovarystvo, 1968), 5–60.

79. For more on the Russian repartition, see Conquest, *The Harvest of Sorrow*, 19.

80. Oleh S. Fedyshyn, "The Germans and the Union for the Liberation of the Ukraine, 1914–1917," in *The Ukraine, 1917–1921: A Study in Revolution*, ed. Taras Hunczak (Cambridge: Harvard Ukrainian Research Institute, 1977), 305–6.

81. Isaak Mazepa, *Ukraïna v ohni i buri revoliutsiï, 1917–1921*, Part I (Prague: Vyd-vo "Prometei," 1950), 36–37.

82. Fedyshyn, "The Germans and the Union for the Liberation of the Ukraine," 308.

83. See "Timothy Snyder on Germany's Historical Responsibility towards Ukraine," lecture in the German Bundestag on June 20, 2017, organized by the parliamentary faction of the German Green Party, https://www.youtube.com/watch?v=wDjHw_uXeKU.

84. Fedyshyn, "The Germans and the Union for the Liberation of the Ukraine," 322.

85. *Communist Takeover and Occupation of Ukraine*, 10.

86. Liubov Zhvanko, "Tyf, cholera, 'ispanka': zakhody uriadu Skoropads′koho z podolannia epidemiï," *Ukraïna moderna*, March 20, 2020, http://uamoderna.com/md/zhvanko-skoropadsky-pandemics; see also L. M. Zhvanko, *Sotsial′ni vymiry Ukraïns′koï Derzhavy (kviten′– hruden′ 1918 r.)* (Kharkiv: Prapor, 2007).

87. Sukhomlyns′ka, *Narysy*, 83.

88. "Khronika," *Vil'na ukraïns'ka shkola*, no. 1 (1918–1919): 52.
89. Sukhomlyns'ka, *Narysy*, 115.
90. Ibid., 83.
91. Ibid., 116.
92. Ibid., 83.
93. Solovey, *Golgota Ukraïny*, 40.
94. Sukhomlyns'ka, *Narysy*, 84.
95. Ibid., 84–85.
96. Volodymyr Vynnychenko, *Vidrodzhennia natsiï*, vol. III (Kyïv-Vienna: Vyd. Dzvin, 1920), 244–45.
97. Arthur E. Adams, "The Great Ukrainian Jacquerie," in *The Ukraine, 1917–1921: A Study in Revolution*, ed. Taras Hunczak (Cambridge: Harvard Ukrainian Research Institute, 1977), 255.
98. John S. Reshetar, Jr., *The Ukrainian Revolution, 1917–1920: A Study in Nationalism* (Princeton: Princeton University Press, 1952), 257.
99. Adams, "The Great Ukrainian Jacquerie," 259.
100. For more on Directory's negotiations with the representatives of the Entente and a list of demands, see Mazepa, *Ukraïna v ohni i buri revoliutsiï*, 96–114. Mazepa, an eyewitness of the events, noted that the Ukrainian delegation to the Paris Peace Conference consisted of H. Sydorenko and A. Petrushevych, who arrived in Paris on January 20, 1919. The remaining delegates were stuck in other European countries awaiting visas to France.
101. This cartoon was reprinted in *Americans and the Soviet Experiment, 1917–1933* by Peter G. Filene (Cambridge: Harvard University Press, 1967), 38.
102. "Russia Democratized," *Nation*, vol. CIV (March 22, 1917), 327 (editorial); quoted in *American Views of Soviet Russia, 1917–1965*, ed. Peter G. Filene (Homewood, IL: The Dorsey Press, 1968), 2.
103. An Outline of Tentative Recommendations of January 21, 1919, Inquiry Archives, National Archives; quoted in Constantine Warvariv, "America and the Ukrainian National Cause, 1917–1920," in *The Ukraine, 1917–1921: A Study in Revolution*, ed. Taras Hunczak (Cambridge: Harvard Ukrainian Research Institute, 1977), 371.
104. Inquiry Archives, typewritten document No. 188, National Archives; quoted in Warvariv, "America and the Ukrainian National Cause," 370–71.
105. For more on the impact of Wilson's policies on the modern political structuring of Eastern Europe, see Larry Wolff, *Woodrow Wilson and the Reimagining of Eastern Europe* (Palo Alto: Stanford University Press, 2020).
106. The map of Ukraine was included in *Mémoire sur l'indépendance de l'Ukraine présenté à la Conférence de la paix par la délégation de la république ukrainienne*, an official publication of the joint government of the Ukrainian National Republic and Western Ukrainian National Republic (after January 22, 1919, western and eastern parts of Ukraine were reunited). The map was reproduced in an article posted by Likbez.org at http://likbez.org.ua/ua/ukrainskaya-respublika-karta-dlya-parizhskoj-mirnoj-konferentsii-1919-g.html.

107. The Liquidation Commission was established by an act of Congress as part of the U.S. War Department for the purpose of disposing surplus war stocks of the American Expeditionary Forces in Europe that were held in French warehouses. Such classes of stock as clothing, food, medical equipment, and transportation seemed suitable for relieving hunger and the urgent needs of the peoples and stabilizing the governments of Eastern Europe.

108. *Papers Relating to the Foreign Relations of the United States, 1919: Russia* (Washington, D.C.: U.S. Government Printing Office, 1937), 779; quoted in Warvariv, "America and the Ukrainian National Cause," 373.

109. Ibid., 374.

110. For a digest of General Jadwin's report, see *Foreign Relations of the United States, 1919*, 781–83; quoted in Warvariv, "America and the Ukrainian National Cause," 374–78.

111. *Foreign Relations of the United States, 1919*, 787–88; quoted in ibid., 375–78.

112. Symon Petliura, "Nota do Naivyshchoï Rady Soiuznykh i Spoluchenykh Derzhav u Paryzhi," in Oleksander Dotsenko, *Litopys Ukraïns'koï Revoliutsiï*, vol. II, book 5 (L'viv, 1924), 190–91; reprinted in *Symon Petliura*, 243–44.

113. *Foreign Relations of the United States, 1919*, 783–84; quoted in Warvariv, "America and the Ukrainian National Cause," 378–79.

114. At the peak of the Russian Civil War (1917–1923), the Workers' and Peasants' Red Army, commonly referred to as the Red Army, counted 5.4 million in its ranks, two-thirds of whom fought in the former imperial army during the Great War. See G. F. Krivosheev, *Soviet Casualties and Combat Losses in the Twentieth Century* (London: Greenhill Books, 1997).

115. John S. Reshetar, Jr., "The Communist Party of the Ukraine and Its Role in the Ukrainian Revolution," in *The Ukraine, 1917–1921: A Study in Revolution*, ed. Taras Hunczak (Cambridge: Harvard Ukrainian Research Institute, 1977), 180–81.

116. Conquest, *The Harvest of Sorrow*, 37.

117. Reshetar, "The Communist Party of the Ukraine," 181.

118. A. Shlikhter, "Bor'ba za khleb na Ukraine v 1919 godu," *Litopys revoliutsiï*, no. 2 (29) (1928): 117, 135, https://chtyvo.org.ua/authors/Litopys_revoliutsii/1928_N2_29/.

119. Panas Fedenko, *Ukraïns'kyi hromads'kyi rukh u XX st.* (Podebrady, 1934), 115; quoted in Solovey, *Golgota Ukraïny*, 22.

120. Fedenko, *Ukraïns'kyi hromads'kyi rukh*, 115; quoted in Solovey, *Golgota Ukraïny*, 22.

121. The failure of Bolshevik policy and the various uprisings in Ukraine are discussed in Arthur E. Adams, *Bolsheviks in the Ukraine: The Second Campaign, 1918–1919* (New Haven: Yale University Press, 1963).

122. Reshetar, "The Communist Party of the Ukraine," 181–82.

123. Sukhomlyns'ka, *Narysy*, 117.

124. Ibid., 118.

125. The premiere performance of the requiem took place before the All-Ukrainian Orthodox Church Council in 1918. In October 1921, the Ukrainian Autocephalous

Orthodox Church was established. But by the spring of 1922, famine and epidemics became rampant in the country. Stetsenko contracted typhus from one of his parishioners and died at the age of forty. The first complete volume of his sacred works, *Kyrylo Stetsenko: Dukhovni tvory*, ed. by M. Hobdych, was published in Kyïv in 2013.

126. The Ukrainian National Chorus toured Europe in 1920 and 1921. Their performance of Mykola Leontovych's composition *Shchedryk* (Carol of the Bells) gained worldwide popularity after the Ukrainian National Chorus under the direction of composer Koshyts' sang it in Carnegie Hall, where Peter Wilhousky heard it and published it with the English text. The English text is not a translation of the original Ukrainian. The first recording was made in New York City in October 1922 on the Brunswick label. For more on the history of this Christmas classic, see Lydia Tomkiw, "Toll of the Bells," *Slate*, December 19, 2019, https://slate.com/news-and-politics/2019/12/carol-bells-shchedryk-ukraine-leontovych.html.

127. The Dniprosoiuz cooperative annual trade was estimated at 60 million golden *karbovantsi*, whereas Ukrainbank's credit operations amounted to 2.5 billion golden *karbovantsi*. See Solovey, *Golgota Ukraïny*, 38. The Dniprosoiuz sponsored Ukrainian National Chorus performances and published music scores and school textbooks.

128. Among the *otamans* who played significant roles were Hryhoriiv, in Katerynoslav and Aleksandriia; Struk of Chernihiv province; Anhel and Ihnatiiev-Mysera, in Poltava province; Shepel, in Podillia province; Zelenyi, in Kyïv and Poltava provinces; Shuba, in the Lubny district; Kotsur, a village school teacher; Bozhko, in the territory between Bar and Mohyliv-Podil's'kyi, who proclaimed the restoration of the Zaporozhian Sich; and Nestor Makhno, who was joined in the southeastern steppe by many lesser known men as well as the Bolsheviks. See Adams, *Bolsheviks in the Ukraine*, 256–57.

129. Adams, *Bolsheviks in the Ukraine*, 257.

130. Henry Abramson, *A Prayer for the Government: Ukrainians and Jews in Revolutionary Times, 1917–1920* (Cambridge: Distributed by Harvard University Press for the Harvard Ukrainian Research Institute and Center for Jewish Studies, Harvard University, 1999). See also Applebaum, *Red Famine*, 40–53.

131. "Vid Pravytel'stva Ukraïns'koï Narodnoï Respubliky," in Dotsenko, *Litopys Ukraïns'koï Revoliutsiï*, vol. II, book 4 (Kyïv-L'viv, 1923), 343–46; reprinted in *Symon Petliura*, 240–42.

132. Stephen Kotkin, "The Communist Century," *Wall Street Journal*, November 4–5, 2017, C1.

133. The Donets' River industrial basin in southern Ukraine, north of the Sea of Azov, is the main center of the Donbas. Welsh engineers, among them John James Hughes, constructed a metallurgical plant there in 1870 and a small town for coal mine workers around it. It was the beginning of Iuzivka, named after Hughes (modern day Donets'k). See Serhii Plokhy, *The Gates of Europe: A History of Ukraine* (New York: Basic Books, 2015), 175.

134. "Draft Theses of the Central Committee RKP(b) Concerning Policy in the Ukraine," in *The Unknown Lenin: From the Secret Archive*, ed. Richard Pipes (New Haven: Yale University Press, 1996), 76–77.

135. Solovey, *Golgota Ukraïny*, 41.

136. Pipes, ed., *The Unknown Lenin*, 76.

137. Vadym Zolotar′ov, "Kerivnyi sklad NKVS URSR pid chas 'velykoho teroru' (1936–1938 rr.): sotsial′no-statystychnyi analiz," *Z arkhiviv VUChK-GPU-NKVD-KGB* 2, no. 33 (2009): 103–4, http://resource.history.org.ua/publ/gpu_2009_33_2_86.

138. Myroslav Shkandrij, "Breaking Taboos: The Holodomor and the Holocaust in Ukrainian–Jewish Relations," in *Jews and Ukrainians*, eds. Yohanan Petrovsky-Shtern and Antony Polonsky (Portland: The Littman Library of Jewish Civilization, 2014), 263–64.

139. Koliastruk, *Intelihentsiia USRR u 1920-ti roky*.

140. Klitsakov, *Pedahohichni kadry Ukraïny*, 37–40.

141. "Ukrainskaia SSR," in *Narodnoe obrazovanie v SSSR*, 329; see also Sukhomlyns′ka, *Narysy*, 86, 160.

142. Sukhomlyns′ka, *Narysy*, 87; see also Klitsakov, *Pedahohichni kadry Ukraïny*, 46.

143. Sukhomlyns′ka, *Narysy*, 154.

144. Ibid., 155.

145. Ibid., 155–56.

146. For a unique account about this party, see memoirs written by the last survivor of the Borot′bists and GULAG survivor Ivan Maistrenko, *Borot′bism: A Chapter in the History of the Ukrainian Revolution*, ed. Christopher Ford (Stuttgart: *ibidem*-Verlag, 2018).

147. *TsDAHOU*, f. 1, op. 20, spr. 12, ark. 27.

148. Klitsakov, *Pedahohichni kadry Ukraïny*, 48–50, 57–59.

149. Sukhomlyns′ka, *Narysy*, 121–22.

150. American psychologist William Horsley Gantt of Johns Hopkins University, who served as chief of the Medical Division of the American Relief Administration in 1922–1923, worked for five years with Ivan Pavlov (1924–1929). He visited the Soviet Union in the summer of 1933 and in 1935. His personal relations with doctors enabled him to obtain unofficial estimates of the famine losses, which were in contradiction to the official figures given to him in 1933 and 1935 by officials who did not know that he had first-hand information about the real conditions in the Soviet Union. See William Horsley Gantt, "A Medical Review of Soviet Russia: Results of the First Five-Year Plan," *British Medical Journal* 2, no. 3939 (July 4, 1936): 19.

151. Sukhomlyns′ka, *Narysy*, 123.

152. Pauly, *Breaking the Tongue*, 45.

153. Sukhomlyns′ka, *Narysy*, 124.

154. Hannah Arendt, "Ideology and Terror: A Novel Form of Government," in *The Great Lie: Classic and Recent Appraisals of Ideology and Totalitarianism*, ed. F. Flagg Taylor IV (Wilmington: Intercollegiate Studies Institute, 2011), 130. Originally appeared in *Review of Politics* 15, no. 3 (1953).

155. Arendt, "Ideology and Terror," 130.

156. Sukhomlyns′ka, *Narysy*, 125; Pauly, *Breaking the Tongue*, 45.

157. For a discussion of the Communist onslaught of 1918–1920, see Edward Hallett Carr, *The Bolshevik Revolution, 1917–1923*, 3 vols. (London: Macmillan, 1950–53); see also David Priestland, *The Red Flag: A History of Communism* (New York: Grove Press, 2009).

158. Kulchytsky, *The Famine of 1932–1933 in Ukraine*, 141.

159. Ibid., 154.

160. For an informative study of the continuities between the fiscal practices of the Russian Empire and the Soviet Union and how taxation was simultaneously used as a revenue-raising and a state-building tool, see Yanni Kotsonis, *States of Obligation: Taxes and Citizenship in the Russian Empire and Early Soviet Republic* (Toronto: University of Toronto Press, 2016).

161. Stanislav Kul′chyts′kyi, *Komunizm v Ukraïni: pershe desiatyrichchia (1919–1928)* (Kyïv: Osnovy, 1996).

162. Koliastruk, *Intelihentsiia USRR u 1920-ti roky*, 223.

163. *TsDAVOU*, f. 166, op. 2, spr. 287, ark. 17.

164. *Holod 1921–1923 rokiv v Ukraïni: Zbirnyk dokumentiv i materialiv*, ed. S. V. Kul′chyts′kyi (Kyïv: Naukova dumka, 1993), 5.

165. Francis Conte, *Christian Rakovski: A Political Biography* (Boulder: East European Monographs, 1989).

166. "Dopovidna zapyska Kh. G. Rakovs′koho V. I. Leninu pro organizatsiiu prodovol′choï roboty ta zbyrannia khliba v Ukraïni, 28 sichnia 1922 r.," *TsDAHOU*, f. 1, op. 20, spr. 981, ark. 1–9; reprinted in *Holod 1921–1923 rokiv v Ukraïni*, ed. Kul′chyts′kyi, 75–85.

167. Stanislav Kul′chyts′kyi and Ol′ha Movchan, *Nevidomi storinky holodu 1921–1923 rr. v Ukraïni* (Kyïv: Instytut istoriï Ukraïny NAN Ukraïny, 1993).

168. The first All-Russian Census of 1897 did not collect data on national self-identification. The information about the nationality was based on the mother tongue claimed by the respondents. Inasmuch as national identification and language do not necessarily correspond, the 1897 census underestimated the number of Ukrainians. Nevertheless, because few non-Ukrainians learned Ukrainian and because language use is an identifiable badge, language could represent a minimal approximation to nationality in the Ukrainian provinces in 1897. The nationality information compiled from the 1897 census is not comparable to those figures obtained from the later Soviet censuses, which contained different questions and took place after territorial changes. Sole knowledge of Ukrainian did not coincide with a high degree of national awareness, ethnic cohesion, political assertiveness, or ability to act collectively on the part of the speaker. See George Liber, *Soviet Nationality Policy, Urban Growth, and Identity Change in the Ukrainian SSR, 1923–1934* (Cambridge: Cambridge University Press, 1992), 209–10.

169. *God bor′by s golodom 1921–1922: Cherez delegatov VII Vseukrainskogo s″ezda Sovetov vsem trudiashchimsia. Otchet Tsentral′noi Komissii po bor′be s posledstviiami goloda pri VUTsIKe* (Khakrov, 1923), 28–30; reprinted in *Holod 1921–1923 rokiv v Ukraïni*, 201–3.

170. Hryshko, *The Ukrainian holocaust of 1933*, 55.

171. Halyna Zhurbeliuk, "Metodyka istoryko-pravovykh doslidzhen' problem holodu 1921–1923 rr. v Ukraïni: rozvinchannia mifiv," in *Holod v Ukraïni u pershii polovyni XX stolittia: prychyny ta naslidky (1921–1923, 1932–1933, 1946–1947): Materialy Mizhnarodnoï naukovoï konferentsiï, Kyïv, 20–21 lystopada 2013 r.*, ed. Myroslava Antonovych, Hennadii Boriak, Oleksandr Hladun, and Stanislav Kul'chyts'kyi (Kyïv, 2013), 51–58; see also Stanislav Kul'chyts'kyi, *Holodomor 1932–1933 rr. iak henotsyd: trudnoshchi usvidomlennia* (Kyïv: Nash chas, 2008), 140–70.

172. Applebaum, *Red Famine*, 66.

173. Pipes, ed., *The Unknown Lenin*, 152–53; quoted in Applebaum, *Red Famine*, 67.

174. Koliastruk, *Intelihentsiia USRR u 1920-ti roky*, 207.

175. *TsDAVOU*, f. 331, op. 1, spr. 7, ark. 10.

176. *Derzhavnyi arkhiv Kharkivs'koï oblasti (DAKhO)*, f. R-203, op. 1, spr. 981, ark. 10–11; quoted in Koliastruk, *Intelihentsiia USRR u 1920-ti roky*, 207.

177. Instytut rukopysiv Natsional'noï biblioteky Ukraïny im. V. I. Vernads'koho (IR NBUV), f. XXIII, spr. 48, ark. 24–24zv.

178. Quoted in V. Topolianskii, *Vozhdi v zakone: Ocherki fiziologii vlasti* (Moscow: Izd-vo "Prava cheloveka," 1996), 25.

179. *TsDAVOU*, f. 166, op. 2, spr. 1746, ark. 43; reprinted in *Holod 1921–1923 rokiv v Ukraïni*, 19.

180. The photograph was featured in Ivan Herasymovych, *Holod na Ukraïni* (Berlin: Ukraïns'ke slovo, 1922), 143. It was one of the seventeen photographs mailed by the Ukrainian Red Cross in an official envelop date-stamped as arriving in Geneva on May 5, 1922. According to Roman Serbyn, it is now housed among the documents of the "Union international de secours aux enfants" in the Canton Archives of Geneva, Switzerland. The image was also used in a poster and on a postcard to raise relief funds by the Conference universelle juive de secours (Jewish World Relief Conference) in 1921–1922. The author is indebted to Lana Babij for providing detailed documentation about this photograph. The image can be located in the Holodomor Photo Directory, sponsored by the Holodomor Research and Education Consortium, Canadian Institute of Ukrainian Studies, University of Alberta.

181. *Bil'shovyk* (Kyïv), February 11, 1923; *TsDAVOU*, f. 1, op. 2, spr. 1583, ark. 1; spr. 888, ark. 125.

182. *Holod 1921–1923 rokiv v Ukraïni*, 19.

183. "Z dopovidi holovy Tsentral'noï Komisiï dopomohy holoduiuchym H. I. Petrovs'koho na VII Vseukraïns'komu z'ïzdi Rad pro stanovyshche dytiachoho naselennia, 10–14 hrudnia 1922," *TsDAVOU*, f. 1, op. 2, spr. 487, ark. 217–18; reprinted in *Holod 1921–1923 rokiv v Ukraïni*, 186–87.

184. *Holod 1921–1923 rokiv v Ukraïni*, 13.

185. "Iz zvitu Tsentral'noï Komisiï po borot'bi z naslidkamy holodu pry VUTsVK pro evakuatsiiu ditei z Polovzhia v Ukraïnu, 1923," *God bor'by s golodom 1921–1922*, 31; reprinted in *Holod 1921–1923 rokiv v Ukraïni*, 200.

186. Pitirim A. Sorokin, *Man and Society in Calamity: The Effects of War, Revolution, Famine, Pestilence upon Human Mind, Behavior, Social Organization and Cultural Life* (New York: E. P. Dutton, 1942), 81.

187. "Iz chernetky dopovidi likaria L. Aikhenval'da 'Do kazuïstyky liudozherstva' Odes'kii huberns'kii komisiï po borot'bi z naslidkamy holodu, 1923," *Derzhavnyi arkhiv Odes'koï oblasti (DAOO)*, f. R-702, op. 1, spr. 102a, ark. 28–69; reprinted in *Holod 1921–1923 rokiv v Ukraïni*, 204–16.

188. Vasyl' Marochko, among other Ukrainian historians, considers this famine as the first Soviet *holodomor* because Lenin's policy of "War Communism" had at its core a deliberate attempt to use food as a weapon to create conditions of life that caused mass deaths from forced starvation inflicted on grain growers in Ukraine. See his article "Lenins'kyi liudomor 1921–1923 rr.: 'bratnii' rozpodil smerti," *Slovo Prosvity*, April 19–25, 2018, 3.

189. Kołakowski, "The Marxist Roots of Stalinism," 174.

Chapter 2

Leadership

In post–World War I conditions, collective violence set in. A decisive victory was achieved on the "first front"—military—when GPU detachments, with the support of the Red Army, suppressed anti-Bolshevik resistance in Ukraine. On the "second front"—economy—Bolshevik leaders retreated. The Russian Communist Party formally adopted the New Economic Policy (NEP) at the Tenth Congress in March 1921, but it could not become effective because of the famine that lasted three years. While the outside world provided humanitarian relief and assumed the communists were returning to a civilized policy, the economic recovery was temporary as Moscow began gathering controlling power into its own hands in all branches of life.[1] Bolsheviks engaged in battles on the "third front"—culture. The "cultural revolution" started with restructuring of society in Soviet Ukraine. Teachers were turned into propagandists of Bolshevik policies in towns and especially villages, where they enjoyed considerable respect and trust of the local population. The creation of the Union of Soviet Socialist Republics, during the last year of Lenin's life, meant to showcase to the world the fulfillment of a principle of self-determination for national minorities. From 1923 to 1926, a flood of decrees and activities spurred hopes for a national renaissance not only in Ukraine itself but wherever Ukrainians were living in the entire Soviet Union.[2] Soon after, on the eve of the tenth anniversary of the October Socialist Revolution, Ukrainian separatism was proclaimed a great danger to the Soviet empire, and Bolshevik leaders set out plans to fight this tendency, which resulted in a crisis.

INTELLIGENTSIA IN THE FIGHT FOR SOCIALISM

In his political pamphlet *What Is to Be Done?* Lenin wrote that a revolution could only be achieved by strong leadership of the masses by one person, or by a very select few.[3] The pamphlet, written in 1901 and published in Germany in 1902, helped to precipitate Bolsheviks' split from the Menshevik faction of the Russian Social Democratic Workers' Party at its Second Party Congress in 1903 in Brussels.[4] When the Mensheviks made an alliance with the Jewish Bund, Bolsheviks found themselves in a minority. Bolsheviks were a radical, far-left, Marxist faction. As World War I was raging on, Lenin's Bolsheviks organized an armed uprising involving no more than 10,000 people.[5] They directed their coup d'état not against the Provisional Government but against the main soviet in the capital, which was dominated by more moderate socialists. Once in power in early 1918, Bolsheviks renamed themselves the Communist Party as they attempted to forcefully march to socialism and, eventually, to history's final stage—communism. The putsch by the radical left has been promoted throughout seventy years of Soviet historiography as the Great October Socialist Revolution despite the fact that it had no mass support. Examination of their leadership is essential to our understanding of how a sect of the few, who in the name of the people established a dictatorship, could control vast resources, both human and material, and could manipulate public opinion, using modern technologies of radio, cinema, and press, to do its bidding and gain prestige on the global stage of history.

Although intelligentsia did not fit into a "classless society" of workers and peasants, Bolsheviks realized that they had to rely on teachers for several reasons, not least because teachers carried political and civic weight.[6] First, teachers were instrumental in establishing the "melding between town and country" (so-called *zmychka*) by serving as propagandists of Bolshevik policies in towns and especially villages, where they traditionally enjoyed considerable respect and trust of local populations. Second, teachers were heralds of modernity because they educated the younger generation of builders of a new Soviet civilization. Third, Bolsheviks realized that they could not achieve both purposes, maintaining their political power and modernizing the state, without creating a new social order. Teachers were indispensable for the Bolshevik program of molding a new society because teachers influenced other people's ideas and everyday behavior. A new type of Soviet species and a new culture had to be created. As German historian Stefan Plaggenborg put it, the regime "acted as a teacher,"[7] and, at first, had to "teach" its values to professional educators and, through them, to the masses.[8]

"A teacher," Anatoly Lunacharsky wrote, "is a reliable link with the future generations and thus guarantees for us our tomorrow."[9] To guarantee their tomorrow, Bolsheviks had to win teachers over to their side. Some teachers at first had difficulty understanding social changes and stayed on the sidelines. The process of Soviet ideological indoctrination was a challenging one because of "bad influence" on the teachers' consciousness of competing "bourgeois nationalist" parties and groups. Following Lenin's advice, Bolsheviks had to patiently explain to teachers their role in educating and acculturating new generations for the young Soviet state.

Lenin outlined a program on how to work with teachers in his speech at the First Congress of Internationalist Teachers in 1918:

> The army of teachers must set themselves tremendous tasks in the educational sphere . . . The teachers must not confine themselves to narrow pedagogical duties. They must join forces with the entire body of the embattled working people. The task of the new pedagogy is to link up teaching activities with the socialist organization of society.[10]

The Bolshevik leader understood that teachers who inherited "capitalist" culture could not be communist but could not be alienated either and had to be recruited to carry out educational and political activities because teachers possessed knowledge crucial to achieving the goal of societal transformation. The Communist Party's proclaimed goals included the elimination of national, class, social, religious, and other barriers in education, the separation of church from state and school from church, and the creation of a new school bureaucracy.

In the aftermath of the struggle for national liberation, every village was trying to establish a school and hire a teacher.[11] Bolshevik leader Christian Rakovsky, in one of his speeches in 1920, reported: "People everywhere demand schools. Peasants refurbish former landlords' estates into schools. In one of the districts in the Zhytomyr region villagers collected 3 million *karbovantsi* to build a school."[12] A village teacher's social position remained prominent because beyond classroom teaching, a teacher was a valuable conduit of knowledge and indispensable to the transmission of culture. For this reason, teaching became the only outlet for intellectuals to freely participate in the life of society, when political activities were curtailed following the dissolution of opposition parties and civic organizations that Bolsheviks could not control directly.[13]

Among teachers who took the lead in the revival of Ukrainian culture was Varvara Dibert, the daughter of an Orthodox priest, from the Cherkasy region, birthplace of Ukraine's national poet Taras Shevchenko. At the age of seventeen, after completing seventh grade, Varvara became a teacher. She taught in a school in Kaharlyk, a small town near Kyїv. World War I interrupted her plans to pursue higher education as most universities were evacuated. Varvara was the youngest among eleven teachers in her school, the eldest being twenty-five years old. The school was in the hands of women. Varvara Dibert taught seventy-six pupils in the first grade. Her elder brother and cousin served as guards helping to evacuate Hrushevs'kyi's government from Kyïv. In 1922, she married a school principal, who formerly fought on Petliura's side. Varvara Dibert described Ukrainization of schools as a grassroots effort:

> We elected a school council right there on the spot and decided to Ukrainize the school. We did it without any official directives from Kiev.
>
> At the time we had no other textbooks except [Shevchenko's] *Kobzar* and perhaps a few other small books here and there. But we were determined to Ukrainize the primary school immediately. And we began to copy excerpts from the *Kobzar*.[14]

Varvara Dibert recalled that schools had no paper, pens, or pencils, so the teachers used thick paper, normally used for wrapping sugar cubes, to write. One side of the paper was dark blue and the other white. "We would use it to copy passages from the *Kobzar*, which we would hang up on the walls in the classroom." The lack of Ukrainian-language textbooks that she described was coupled with a pedagogical innovation, "a program for progressive education," borrowed from John Dewey.[15] In the absence of teaching materials, it was innovative as it was child-centered and integrated learning around specific, usually local, themes. Even anti-Russian motives in Shevchenko's poetry were tolerated.

The lack of paper was due to the occupation of western border regions after the armistice was signed at the end of World War I. Before the war, the Russian Empire produced 24 million *puds* of paper; however, the Soviet empire could produce only 11 million.[16] The German occupation of Ukraine during the second year of the war led to a 40 percent loss in paper production. A shipment of cellulose and timber from Finland saved the industry from a catastrophic collapse, but soon the shipments stopped, when in 1918, Finland declared independence from the Russian Empire.[17] The paper industry reached its nadir in 1921, dropping to 2 million *puds*. Ironically, between October 1919 and April 1921, the printing press of the Bolshevik Western Front published 35 million copies of propaganda materials in seven languages. Between April and October of 1920, the First Cavalry, while marching from the North Caucasus to reoccupy Ukraine, was able to print 1,336,960 posters and leaflets as well as 21,000 propaganda brochures.[18] Such incessant propaganda subverted efforts of the Ukrainian national government which lacked resources to inform the masses about its policies.[19]

Teachers like Varvara Dibert were among thousands who, in the harsh conditions of Bolshevik onslaught, survived and maintained their national identity. However, as soon as Ukraine lost its struggle for national liberation, the Communist Party purged all political parties and cultural organizations, appropriated assets of the Ukrainian cooperative unions, and dissolved the "counter-revolutionary bourgeois-nationalist" All-Ukrainian Teachers' Union, obligating teachers to join another professional union controlled by Bolsheviks.[20]

A New Teachers' Union

The new teachers' union was not a voluntary professional organization. It did not protect the interests of the profession, but served as a tool of control by the Bolshevik regime. Between 1922 and 1924, the number of teachers in Ukraine sharply decreased. Statistical sources fail to explain the causes. Historians argue that the famine of 1921–1923 was the reason for a decrease in the number of teachers in southern and eastern regions of Soviet Ukraine. At the same time, in northern and western regions of Soviet Ukraine, teachers were dismissed for political reasons.[21]

Ideological subversion of the population started with a campaign to undermine teachers' economic well-being and social standing in the eyes of the local community. Archival documents reveal that in 1921, a teacher's salary in the Kam'ianets'-Podil's'kyi school district in the Vinnytsia province, bordering Poland, could support only one individual, not the entire family, with 95 percent of the salary spent on food. A representative from the school district described local teachers as "naked" and "barefoot" because during the previous year they had received no cash payments, and half the grain supplement was chaff rather than kernels.[22] Out of desperation, having no means to survive, some teachers from the province crossed the border into Poland in search of provisions. Others vented their frustration on students by increasing the difficulty of class assignments. This way, teachers could earn extra money (or bread) by private tutoring. Instead of relief, a local party committee organized a teachers' conference on May 4–9, 1921, and accused the teachers of "sabotage"; as a "preventive measure," a great number of teachers were arrested for alleged "anti-Soviet propaganda."[23] Despite protests from school district authorities, in June 1922, eighty-two teachers were dismissed from their jobs, including F. Pryimak, the school district's leader, accused of being Petliura's follower.[24]

The prominence of village teachers in the enlightenment among the masses had to be harnessed if Bolsheviks wanted to conquer the countryside and bring it in line with the urban "proletarian culture." All publications, decrees, and instructions emphasized: "The Soviet authorities treat new teachers with special attention and care because they are the providers of not only general education, but communist enlightenment among the masses."[25] Despite lofty pronouncements, until 1923, Bolsheviks allocated a tiny 3 percent of the state budget to education.[26] To put it into perspective, the education budget allocation for Soviet Ukraine in 1922–1923 amounted to 6 million golden rubles, an average of 24 kopeks per citizen, which was twenty-two times less than a comparable allocation in Switzerland in 1904, according to one of the leading educational periodicals.[27]

Lenin's essay "Pages from a Diary" (*Stranichki iz dnevnika*), published in 1923, was the Communist Party's programmatic document that laid foundations for the "cultural revolution" in schools, with an emphasis on the training of new teachers and retraining the old cadres. In response, 300 teachers of the Bila Tserkva region, who gathered at a conference, sent their greetings to Lenin wishing him speedy recovery.[28] They wrote, "We would like to assure you, the leader of the proletariat, that temporary material difficulties experienced by the educators will not weaken their work in the direction dictated by the party."[29] The Ukrainian teachers assured Lenin that his words gave them strength to continue the fight.

A collective letter with an expression of support might have reflected teachers' concerns for the health of the Bolshevik leader, who frequently suffered from strokes that left him paralyzed after an unsuccessful assassination attempt in 1918, by Ukrainian Socialist Revolutionary Fanny Kaplan, rather than an affirmation of his program. Bolsheviks started the program to reeducate teachers with the propaganda campaign in the press, followed by purges of politically unreliable teachers. To stir up enthusiasm, Soviet educational periodicals published theses presented by Nadezhda Krupskaya, Lenin's wife, at the Thirteenth Congress of the Russian Communist Party (Bolsheviks) explaining the role of village teachers as liquidators of illiteracy and as propagandists of Bolshevik policies in the countryside.[30]

When soft tactics failed to produce desirable behaviors, harsher measures were initiated. In the border province of Volyn', in 1923, authorities liquidated a group of 106 teachers: 25 were sentenced to death, 56 sentenced to various terms of imprisonment, and 25 dismissed from the job.[31] Protocols of the regional party conference described village teachers' sentiments as negative, characterizing teachers in the "enemy camp" as "politically illiterate," stating that "such cadres could hardly be relied upon to conduct political and cultural activities in the village."[32] In August of that year, the regional GPU put 128 "unreliable" teachers under surveillance, along with 60 doctors and 48 engineers.[33]

Over the summer of 1923, Bolshevik authorities launched a campaign to test teachers' political literacy. Results of the campaign for political reeducation in Soviet Ukraine revealed that among 40,998 teachers, who were required to take tests for political literacy, 34,718 passed it; among them 57.2 percent in the first category, 38.5 percent in the second, and 4.3 percent in the third category. The first category included politically literate teachers, who understood party policies and goals of labor school. The second category included teachers who needed political reeducation. The third category were undesirables, candidates for laying off with potential physical consequences. The coercive campaign achieved its goal of raising political proficiency and improving teachers' ideological qualification. The sole criterion for one's qualification was loyalty to the Soviet regime.[34]

In early 1924, Mykhailo Myronenko reported on the pages of *Radians'ka osvita* (Soviet Education), a periodical published by the People's Commissariat of Education of the Ukrainian SSR, that results of the ideological reeducation campaign were palpable. For instance, in the Poltava region, teachers gathered informally in groups to study party publications, invited party propagandists to present lectures, traveled to other villages to take part in political discussions, joined local village committees, and participated in setting up libraries. The review of the campaign on political literacy concluded with praise for teachers as "the only cultural force in the village." Village correspondent Myronenko also noted that, in addition to teaching, teachers had to work in a village cooperative, attend meetings of the village soviet, work at the library, and serve as clerks on various committees or executive councils. "Whenever land has to be redistributed, or surplus needs to be requisitioned from the *kurkuli*, or census of the population to be completed, teachers are always called upon."[35]

Bolsheviks needed teachers to educate future fighters for communism. Thus, a new term "red pedagogue" was coined. During the first week of October 1924, addressing 150 delegates of the Third All-Ukrainian Conference on Teacher Education held in Kharkiv, in the presence of guests from Moscow, the commissar of education of the Ukrainian SSR laid out four characteristics required of the "red pedagogues":

1) the theoretical training had to be combined with practicum in labor schools;
2) the focus of education had to be on the study of children as members of a collective so that they become future fighters for communism;
3) teachers had to master the basics of the children's communist movement based on materialism as conceptualized by Marx, and scientific pedagogy as envisioned by Lenin;
4) teachers had to become civic activists who would model new norms of thinking and behaving in the new society.[36]

Beginning in 1924, the reeducation of teachers became systematic. In its resolution of October 10, 1924, the All-Ukrainian Central Executive Committee (*Vseukraïns'kyi tsentral'nyi vykonavchyi komitet* or VUTsVK) reported an "end of the retreat on the school front" as one of its achievements.[37] The trend toward recovery was accompanied by expansion of "reeducation" activities that became institutionalized through short-term courses for improving teachers' qualifications, mainly political rather than methodological. For instance, within one year, the Poltava region trained 85 percent of teachers who were subject to political reeducation, 50 percent of whom satisfied the requirements.[38] At the same time, in a directive issued in August 1923, the Central Committee of the Communist Party (Bolsheviks) of Ukraine (TsK KP(b)U) advised all regional and district party organizations that political reeducation should not be interpreted as a purge; those who failed tests should be demoted but not fired.[39] The political reeducation of teachers reshaped the composition of school cadres. Old (prerevolution) pro-Ukrainian intelligentsia were pushed out of schools or learned to "love" political literacy courses, conferences, and tests out of fear of losing their jobs. School cadres became more proletarian and pro-communist.

From 1925, with a shift in the composition of school cadres, teachers took an increasingly active role in the construction of Soviet society. In addition to teaching, 69 percent of teachers in the republic participated in various political campaigns. For instance, in 1925, in the Kyïv region, the percentage of teachers as members of district and village soviets grew from 19 to 36 and as members of committees of non-wealthy (*Komitety nezamozhnykh selian* or KNS) from 7 to 15, respectively.[40] These were the cadres that Bolsheviks relied on for implementing their propaganda, collectivization, and grain requisition campaigns throughout the 1930s.

The turning point occurred on January 5, 1925, when delegates gathered for the First All-Ukrainian Teachers Congress in Kharkiv (see Figure 2.1). Among the registered, 69.7 percent were teachers from rural schools (267 out of 363 delegates) and 30.3 percent teachers from big and small cities of Ukraine (116 out of 363). Most of them were non-Communist Party members (314 or 82 percent). The largely rural delegates demonstrated their support for Communist Party leadership. In terms of teacher's own educational background, 49.8 percent had primary education, 35 percent had specialized secondary education, and only 15.7 percent attained higher education.[41] At the time, Soviet Ukraine had 16,018 schools with 1,844,863 students.[42]

Congress delegates, during one week of sessions, were presented reports about goals of the Soviet government and the "national question" in schools. Greeting the delegates on opening day, an editorial in the newspaper *Kommunist* declared: "Our people's teachers are foremost village teachers. In distant villages, for millions of people teachers are a rare source of culture and knowledge. It is paramount that village teachers work closely with Soviet authorities and the Communist Party."[43]

In his opening remarks, entitled "On the Third Front," Soviet Ukraine's commissar of education Oleksandr Shums'kyi[44] urged teachers to internalize

Figure 2.1 A group of delegates from the Kharkiv region at the First All-Ukrainian Congress of Teachers, Kharkiv, 1925. In the center of the third row, with the goatee, is the Ukrainian People's commissar of education Oleksandr Shums'kyi. *Source*: From *Pershyi Vseukraïns'kyi uchytel's'kyi z'izd v Kharkovi* (Kharkiv: Derzhavne vydavnytstvo Ukraïny, 1925), xxx. Courtesy of TsDKFFAU, od. obl. 0-171971.

"the philosophy of proletariat—historical materialism" and adopt "a dialectical method of inquiry" to become "passionate propagandists of ideas of communism on the cultural front ... among the toiling masses, and especially the younger generation."[45] Education became the third front, after Bolshevik victories on the first front (military) and the second front (economy). Shums'kyi acknowledged that Bolsheviks were too weak and had no allies among teachers to allow them to succeed in their struggle, but expressed the hope that newly recruited cadres would enable Bolsheviks, with minimum resources and maximum enthusiasm, "to implement a motto of our social education: children belong to the state, and the state has to wrestle the responsibility for their upbringing from the family." Breakthrough on this front was also supposed to free women from their household duties that impeded their active participation in the labor force.

Among speakers at the Congress were Sokolians'kyi, who spoke about the social upbringing of children, and Zatons'kyi, who addressed the national question in schools, whereas Mizernyts'kyi[46] reported about the Union's work on behalf of teachers.[47] Out of 500,000 members in the All-Soviet Teachers' Union, nearly one-fifth, or 98,000 teachers, worked in Soviet Ukraine. Of the Teachers' Union members who worked in Soviet Ukraine, 57.7 percent were ethnically Ukrainian, 24.9 percent Russian, and 12 percent Jewish.[48] The main issue that the Congress focused on was the liquidation of illiteracy because as the Commissar of Education admitted, three-quarters of school-age children remained illiterate seven years after the October Socialist Revolution. Another issue was that adults lacked political literacy. Thus, teachers were mobilized to assist Bolsheviks in achieving victory on the third front (education).

"People's teachers are ours," declared P. Solodub[49] in his speech on the revolution and the role of teachers. He admitted that Bolsheviks had to overcome opposition in Ukraine: "'Historically, Ukraine has had a series of bandit formations, led by people's teachers: Zelenyi, Sokolovs'kyi, Tiutiunnyk,'[50] and numerous others who took up arms against workers and peasants to drown the revolution in blood."[51] Thus, Solodub openly acknowledged that the Soviet regime had no support among the local population. He enumerated "bandit formations" led by "people's teachers," recognizing that teachers were the force to reckon with because they could organize opposition to the Soviet regime, especially in the villages. Hence, Bolsheviks won teachers over with allotments of bread rations during the famine of 1922, firewood, renovations, and supplies for schools in 1923, and salary increases in 1924.[52] At the conclusion of Congress, delegates adopted a resolution and forwarded it to the TsK KP(b)U, stating "a thousand-strong army of teachers in the republic was standing firmly under the banner of the October Revolution."[53]

Teachers' support was echoed in a resolution passed during a teacher conference in Pavlohrad in response to the First All-Ukrainian Teachers' Congress in January 1925: "This Congress drew a red line underneath the past, when teachers did not realize the role of the proletariat in the construction of a new civilization and walked a different path, obstructing its grand project."[54] Thus, 1925 marked a turning point, when teachers "realized" the role of the Communist Party, and their ranks grew in towns as well as villages.

The prolonged fight on all the fronts—military, economic, and cultural—left teachers in poor health. The lack of nutritious food, or outright starvation, and unsanitary working conditions due to intermittent supply of water or heating, led to weakening of the immune system, frequent colds and infections. Wave after wave of mass epidemics of typhus, tuberculosis, the Spanish flu, and cholera swept through Ukraine during and after World War I, the struggle for national liberation, and the famine of 1921–1923. As a result, a general medical checkup of educational employees in Soviet Ukraine in the late fall 1924, through early spring of 1925, revealed that 27 percent of intellectuals older than fifty had cardiovascular diseases and 25 percent had digestive disorders.[55] One-fifth of intellectuals suffered not only from physical exhaustion but from mild to severe nervous system disorders, such as depression, neurasthenia, suicidal tendencies, and phobias. For example, a medical commission in Poltava found that one of four intelligentsia members suffered from headaches, dizziness, obsessive fears, irritability, fatigue, and insomnia.[56] From 1925, the Commissariat of Education in Soviet Ukraine was given the responsibility to take care of the well-being of the intelligentsia by distributing perks, vacations, and bonuses to employees under strict Communist Party control.[57]

In November 1927, the Tenth Congress of the KP(b)U summed up the results of a decade of cultural achievements in Soviet Ukraine. The republic built 1,619 new schools (1,570 of these in rural areas) to accommodate 100,000 children.[58] The face of the teaching profession changed over the decade. Their ranks were renewed by 40–45 percent compared to the prerevolution period.[59]

Industrial modernization and urbanization, however, did not draw teachers into cities in large numbers; most of them still worked in public schools in rural areas. Over 70 percent of teachers in Soviet Ukraine worked in rural schools.[60] Working conditions in rural schools were different from urban schools. Class sizes in rural schools were larger. During 1925–1926, an average ratio was 47 schoolchildren per teacher, but as a result of the purges, which depleted teachers ranks, and with simultaneous increases in enrollments, the ratio reached 70, 90, or even 150 in some schools.[61] Teacher shortages even spurred calls for volunteers to teach in schools.[62] In Luhans'k, unemployed urban teachers were recruited to work in rural schools.[63] Male teachers could also delay their military conscription if they agreed to teach in the classroom. Gender parity in the teaching profession remained relatively constant before, as well as the decade after, World War I: the proportion of women increased slightly from 49.3 percent in 1914 to 55.8 percent in 1927.[64] In 1927, an urban teacher had twenty-seven pupils, whereas a rural teacher thirty-seven. It was an improvement from 1925, when a rural teacher could have as many as forty-seven schoolchildren as compared to an urban teacher who had thirty schoolchildren per class. Not only did rural teachers carry a heavier teaching load, they were also required to engage in various campaigns in the community outside school duties. The head of the Teachers' Union of Soviet Ukraine, Mizernyts'kyi, emphasized this fact in his speech in the spring of 1925.[65] Additionally, the disparity in pay further contributed to the lowering of living standards among teachers in rural areas.[66]

A teachers' ethnic background also influenced their disposition. A school census, conducted in 1927, counted 76.7 percent Ukrainian teachers, with the remaining 10.4 percent Russian, 6 percent Jewish, 2.2 percent German, 1.2 percent Polish, 0.9 percent Greek, 0.6 percent each Belarussian and Bulgarian, 0.4 percent each Moldovan and Tatar, and 1.1 percent other.[67] In primary schools, the number of Ukrainian teachers was higher (79.7 percent), whereas in secondary schools, where each subject required specialty training, their number was lower (65.2 percent). Most of the teachers in primary schools taught in Ukrainian (80.1 percent), whereas only 60.4 percent taught in Ukrainian in secondary schools. In other words, by the end of 1927, the percentage of primary schools (grades 1 through 4) that used Ukrainian reflected the percentage of Ukrainians in the total population in the republic (80.1 percent),[68] the exception being secondary schools (grades 5 through 7).[69] At the time, secondary school was not compulsory. Ukrainians were the majority among teachers in the republic, and Bolsheviks used this fact to coerce teachers into carrying out various propaganda campaigns.

Children's Communes

In 1920, the Soviet government established a benevolent society, Children's Friends, with branches in all cities and villages of the republic, and special orphanages to educate and shelter orphaned children. The Chairman of the Council of People's Commissars of the Ukrainian SSR led the effort.[70] In 1921, there were 806 orphanages and, in 1923, their number increased to 1,928; they housed 114,000 orphans.[71] Often homes confiscated from intelligentsia were converted into orphanages after a decree of 1918 abolished private ownership of real estate property.[72]

In the autumn of 1925, there were still 40,000 homeless children in the Ukrainian SSR, most of them from other republics, who tried to escape from famine-ravaged areas, mostly from Russia.[73] This estimated number shifted from day to day. Approximately half of these homeless traveled on trains from city to city; the remaining half, who lost parents and homes during the famine, were in need of shelter and food.[74] In 1924–1925, the Central Commission to Aid Children, which was established to coordinate the fight against child homelessness, had a budget of 3.5 to 4 million rubles.[75] On November 4, 1925, the KP(b)U urged their counterparts in the Russian SFSR to allocate financial assistance to Ukraine to help return 16,000 children home to the republics they came from (mostly from Russia) and to take 5,000 children off the railroads. Ukrainian authorities requested 1.3 million rubles, but central authorities in Moscow allocated 446,000 rubles instead, and the remaining 854,000 had to come from Ukraine's own budget.[76] As evident from reports and resolutions, hastily drafted throughout October 1925, when a new tax policy was introduced, the matter became urgent in the face of the upcoming winter; yet, funds had to be raised elsewhere because sources of revenue for the Commission were dwindling.[77]

By 1925, the Ukrainian SSR had a shortfall of 2.9 million rubles to take care of existing orphanages and children's shelters.[78] The proposed budget allocation of 2.8 million rubles was apportioned to repatriate 2,595 children (purchase railroad tickets at discounted prices plus food rations), to provide patronage to 6,978 homeless children (accommodate with families or relatives), and to place 10,588 homeless children in orphanages and shelters.[79] Even if urgent calls to expedite the process were heeded, the insufficient funds could cover only half of Ukraine's financial capacity to deal with the problem of child homelessness long after the revolution, war, and famine subsided.

Homeless adolescents were placed in juvenile detention centers (*koloniï* or children's communes), which became experimental laboratories for Soviet upbringing methods. In collaboration with the GPU, Anton Makarenko established several such communes; one named after the chief of the Soviet secret police, Felix Dzerzhinsky, is shown in Figure 2.2.[80] Makarenko's collectivist method of education, combined with labor training, was lauded as a humanistic method of upbringing for children who would otherwise join the ranks of criminals under a capitalist system. He depicted his work with orphans in *Pedagogical Poem* (*Pedagogicheskaia poema*, better known in the West under its English title, *Road to Life*). His autobiographical novel *Flags on the Battlements* (*Flagi na bashniakh*, translated into English as *Learning to Live*) formed the "golden fund" of Soviet pedagogical science.[81] The other side of the story has remained hidden because select teachers who worked in the GPU-run communes and orphanages signed nondisclosure agreements.[82]

Figure 2.2 A formation of pioneers of the F. E. Dzerzhinsky Commune, headed by A. S. Makarenko, at a ceremony dedicated to the launching of the reconstructed machine-building factory named after S. Ordzhonikidze in Kramators'k, Kramators'k district, 1931. *Source*: From TsDKFFAU, od. obl. 2-68381.

Teachers who cooperated with the GPU, like the Russified Ukrainian Anton Makarenko, became heroes and role models. Teachers like Oleksandr Zaluzhnyi,[83] the author of the concept of children's collective upbringing, or Hryhorii Vashchenko,[84] also a proponent of this theory, were either purged or exiled abroad. Vashchenko, who often met Makarenko during conferences, offered a scathing critique of Makarenko's pedagogy. First, he noted that Makarenko had shallow knowledge of pedagogical theory; he was the source of his own pedagogy. Second, Makarenko's methods practiced in his children's communes incorporated purely militaristic elements and disciplinary punishments. Third, Makarenko appeared to be strong-willed, egotistical, and condescending toward his colleagues. He was particularly attracted to communism, either a "fanatic Bolshevik" or a careerist. Vashchenko wrote,

> Seems like in his pedagogical practice he should be guided by feelings, especially compassion toward orphans, toward their privations endured in harsh circumstances of the USSR. But in reality he had none of these. Makarenko was a person with a strong will, and in his work he was guided by his reason rather than passion. Besides, he was extremely egocentric. Such people have difficulty showing sympathy. Their own ego is paramount. Their actions are the realization of their own views, and they are less inclined to compromise their actions because they pose a threat to their self-image. There is no need to view Makarenko as a "dreamer" or compare him to Pestalozzi, who was guided in his work by deep sympathy toward unfortunate orphans.[85]

Makarenko was lionized as a preeminent Soviet pedagogical theorist and teachers, who made a moral choice to serve the Soviet regime, were awarded a medal named after him.[86] In the absence of democratic freedoms, in the atmosphere of fear and suspicion, generations of teachers and students, grew up with a psychological syndrome of a "small person" or being a passive "cog" in the collectivist system.[87]

This upbringing, despite its slogans of proletarian internationalism and class solidarity, was at its core subordinated to the communist doctrine, which did not consider human beings as entitled to certain rights. A human being was the object of Soviet experimentation: a robot, a Soviet patriot, a soldier, an agent, or some other entity useful to the Communist Party.[88] Orphans, who were reared in institutions for homeless children, became ideal recruits for the political police.[89] Soviet educator Anton Makarenko, an authority on communist upbringing, wrote in his *Book for Parents*:

> A lot of rudiments of old lifestyle are still present within us, old relations, old traditional moral principles. Without noticing it, we in our day-to-day life repeat many mistakes and falsehoods of the history of humankind. Many of

us subconsciously exaggerate the importance of so-called love, others are still harboring the faith in so-called freedom.[90]

Bolshevism could not stand "so-called love" and "so-called freedom" because these two humanist notions were incompatible with communist doctrine. Makarenko's principles were in tune with the ideology of one of the leading specialists of the Central Institute of Labor, O. K. Gastev, a proponent of Taylorism in labor education, whose slogan, "We have to create automatons from the nerves and muscles," meant none other than the need to control human behavior.[91] The result of this social engineering was an authoritarian, pedantic type of teacher, who served the interests of the Communist Party and Soviet state.

Political Enlightenment

Teachers were indispensable to Bolsheviks in the struggle to liquidate political illiteracy. On December 26, 1919, Lenin signed a decree requiring all eight- to fifty-year-olds learn how to read and write to be able to fully participate in the political life of the state. In May 1921, the government of the Ukrainian SSR issued a decree on the liquidation of illiteracy. An All-Ukrainian Extraordinary Committee on the Liquidation of Illiteracy was in charge of implementing the decree.[92]

The campaign for the liquidation of illiteracy was launched amid economic devastation and the famine of 1921–1923 that led to a sharp decrease in the number of schools in Soviet Ukraine. Because of economic collapse, the responsibility for school funding was transferred to local communities. A turning point came in 1923.[93] That year, May Day was declared the Day of Literacy. Reading materials included the *ABC of Communism*, with Lenin's motto on the cover: "Education! Education! Education!"[94] Soviet Ukraine's commissar of education Zatons'kyi reported at the Fourth Plenum of the VUTsVK early in 1924, that among eighteen- to thirty-five-year-olds in urban areas, 43 percent were illiterate (36 percent men, 49 percent women), whereas in rural areas 72 percent were illiterate (60 percent men, 82 percent women).[95] The goal of the campaign was to fulfill Lenin's testament: "It would be a shame if by the tenth anniversary of Red October not all of our masses will be able to read its great slogans."[96]

The All-Ukrainian Extraordinary Committee on the Liquidation of Illiteracy engaged volunteers who could teach literacy and established literacy centers and schools. During the 1923–1924 academic year, as many as 3,838 such schools and centers were opened. By 1924–1925, their number tripled to 11,538.[97] They planned to liquidate illiteracy among 4 million of the republic's active workforce, eighteen- to thirty-five-year-olds.[98] The chairman of VUTsVK Hryhorii Petrovs'kyi led a newly created volunteer society under the slogan "Down with Illiteracy!" (*Het' nepys'mennist'!*) which contributed to the success of the campaign. To raise funds, VUTsVK secretary Butsenko called for "voluntary contributions" of produce from farmers and "donations" from soldiers and workers' organizations to pay liquidators' salaries.[99]

Mass mobilization to liquidate illiteracy by the Communist Party and Komsomol (Communist Youth League) bore fruits. By 1929, the campaign for literacy engaged 2.8 million adults, among them 1.6 million women.[100] The percentage of literate adults in the Ukrainian SSR grew to 74 percent in cities and up to 53 percent in villages. However, the 1939 census revealed that every fifth citizen of Soviet Ukraine ten years or older was still illiterate.[101] Despite laudatory reports about the fulfillment of plans, the problem of illiteracy was not solved even after two decades of Soviet rule.

Teachers were also recruited to work in a special type of school created for political enlightenment of the general population with the goal of indoctrinating the illiterate masses to Marxist ideology. The method of indoctrination took the form of clubs. Bolsheviks organized political clubs in factories, industrial plants, shops, and military barracks. Education authorities established traveling railroad libraries filled with propaganda materials and organized lectures to "enlighten" the population. The Commissariat of Education coordinated the activities of these clubs, including libraries, literacy centers and schools, museums, sports clubs, and art centers, with all their local and regional branches.[102] A two-year course of political education was required for training cadres.[103] In Ukraine, 75.8 percent of teachers participated in these political enlightenment activities, with 69.5 percent working as librarians, 56.9 percent as lecturers, and 50 percent as literacy instructors.[104] Participation was not a matter of choice, but a means of survival.

In rural areas, political enlightenment assumed a different shape via the so-called "village house" (*sil's'kyi budynok* or *sil'bud*).[105] It was an information hub, a way station with a repair shop, and more. There rural residents could read newspapers, learn about government decrees, get an address of any government agency, listen to lectures by party propagandists, or watch stage shows. These "village houses" recruited *chettsi* (readers) to read local and regional newspapers to illiterate masses. Comrade Zemlianyi reported that, in 1923 in the Uman' region, about 1,085 such "readers" were recruited, on average from 3 to 40 per village.[106] Their role was to politically enlighten rural masses about Soviet policies.

These Soviet-style *sil'budy* faced strong opposition from "Prosvita" (Enlightenment) societies that had been established by the Ukrainian intelligentsia since 1905 to liquidate illiteracy in rural areas. In 1921–1922, despite harsh conditions of famine, the number of these societies increased from 4,000 to 4,500.[107] In February 1922, Soviet education authorities characterized these societies as "a dangerous enemy of the proletariat."[108] Soviet Ukraine's commissar of education Hryhorii Hryn′ko disparaged these long-established "Prosvita" societies because they had exercised an enormous influence on Ukrainian village life:

> During a long period of their existence, a certain ideology of *prosvitianstvo* and a certain type of a *prosvitianyn* has emerged. The so-called "Ukrainian idea," the petit bourgeois national state—the central axis of this ideology. Intolerance toward everything non-Ukrainian (first and foremost Russian) as foreign—a characteristic psychological feature of the *prosvitianyn*. An inerasable stamp of prosperous village democracy is affixed to this entire movement.[109]

The Ukrainian national aspiration to achieve state sovereignty was incompatible with the Bolshevik intent; thus, "Prosvita" societies had to be subordinated, turned "red," or eliminated. By early 1923, only 573 such societies remained in rural areas throughout the republic.[110] The Soviet policy of *korenizatsiia* was instituted to supplant national-patriotic ideals with the Bolshevik ideology.[111] Teachers in Soviet Ukraine had no choice but to serve the Communist Party as propagandists of Bolshevik policies or face persecution for supporting the national idea. Teachers lost not only their high social standing, due to extreme impoverishment brought by the famine, but also respect of their compatriots, due to a swift metamorphosis in their ideological orientation. In turn, the conscious manipulation of society by Bolsheviks became possible because repressions and total control discouraged critical thinking and opposition, and led to fatalistic acceptance of the new reality among the less educated, who learned to conform and wait for better times to come.

SOVIET NATIONALITY POLICY

The nationality policy toward Ukraine was outlined in resolutions of the Tenth (1921) and Twelfth (1923) Party Congresses of the RKP(b), or Russian Communist Party (Bolsheviks). In between two congresses, formation of the Union of Soviet Socialist Republics was announced by delegates at the First Congress of Soviets in Moscow on December 30, 1922. It was "a voluntary union" of "equal nations," which consolidated Russian takeover of Ukraine and other non-Russian republics. The final text of the declaration and the union agreement, however, took months to negotiate. A proposal by the Ukrainian delegation to establish a bicameral parliament with a Council of Nationalities, that would safeguard rights of constituent national republics, was overruled by Stalin. On July 6, 1923, the Soviet Union was officially born. The day became an official Soviet holiday, celebrated as the Day of the USSR or Constitution Day.[112]

In Ukraine, nationality policy, known as *korenizatsiia*, was given the name "Ukrainization." Ukrainians, however, already spoke their native language, so for whom was the policy designed? A grassroots movement after the revolution led to opening of Ukrainian-language schools for Ukrainian-speaking students and schools for other minorities in Ukraine to afford them education in their mother tongue. Why did the Russian Communist Party concern itself with the nationality policy toward Ukraine? The main thrust of the policy was directed toward Ukrainian titular nationality. It was accompanied by similar policies toward minority populations in Soviet Ukraine and in other republics of the Soviet Union. As James Mace stated, "Ukrainization went much further than the others simply because 40 percent of all non-Russians in the USSR in this period were Ukrainians and they outnumbered the next largest group by 6.5 to 1. So the nationality problem was very largely a Ukrainian problem."[113]

When the national question was discussed at the Tenth Party Congress in March 1921, Stalin, then People's Commissar of Nationalities, clashed with his critics from the national republics. Among them were two Ukrainians: Volodymyr Zatons'kyi, who spoke of the Russian "colonizing element" in Ukraine with its belief in "one indivisible" Russia,[114] and Mykola Skrypnyk, who stated that in Stalin's report the national question "had not been resolved in the least."[115] In August 1921, the Council of People's Commissars (*Rada narodnykh komisariv* or RNK) in Soviet Ukraine signed a decree "On the Introduction of the Ukrainian Language in Schools and Soviet Institutions." It polarized the leadership: some like the Commissar of Education Hryn'ko argued that Soviet schools must educate students, while taking into consideration their national distinctiveness, whereas others opposed the existence of Ukraine as a separate nation. The latter made unsubstantiated accusations that schools were in the hands of "Petliura's intelligentsia" and that employees of the Commissariat of Education were heavily influenced by "national chauvinism."[116]

The position of the republic's leadership on this issue became clear at the October 1922 plenum of the TsK KP(b)U. Whereas Ukraine's Communist Party secretary Lebed' and head of the RNK Rakovsky recognized the equality of Ukrainian and Russian languages, their position was that "without consistent efforts to Sovietize national schools, they will inevitably remain citadels of Ukrainian nationalism." Hence, the decision was made to test teachers for political loyalty. Hryn'ko was dismissed and replaced with Zatons'kyi.[117]

The Twelfth Congress of the Russian Communist Party (Bolsheviks), on June 22, 1923, issued a decree which provided for intensified Ukrainization of all state and party organizations.[118] Another decree by the RNK in Ukraine followed on July 27; it mandated the use of Ukrainian language in schools. It instructed education authorities to train new pedagogical cadres who would be fluent in the Ukrainian language and to train new cohorts of professors who would know the Ukrainian language well enough to conduct scientific research.[119] In August, the VUTsVK in its decree affirmed this policy, requiring Ukrainian-language instruction in primary and secondary schools, and expanded it to all levels of government.[120] In September, the VUTsVK and RNK in Soviet Ukraine outlined measures to assist with the implementation of the decree. One way to strengthen the Ukrainian language was to establish Ukrainian-language schools in proportion to the Ukrainian population in the area. Another way to assure the implementation of the decree was to train teachers of the Ukrainian language.[121]

To implement the nationality policy, special Soviet administrative and educational institutions were set up. On the administrative level, sections that were in charge of implementing the policy were integrated into GPU and Communist Party apparatuses as well as the VUTsVK. As the initial thrust of this policy, a system of village councils was created to promote education and publication of materials in the languages of national minority groups.[122] By 1926–1927, a dozen national minority areas of settlement were established, among them were seven German areas.[123] Within these areas, 872 village councils were created, including 292 Russian, 237 German, 139 Polish, 57 Moldovan, 56 Jewish, 45 Bulgarian, 30 Greek, 13 Czech, 2 Belarusian, and 1 Swedish. Often within one area several ethnic village councils coexisted. For instance, the Pulinsky German ethnic area included two Polish, a Russian, a Jewish, and several Ukrainian village councils. A shared space required a certain political culture of tolerance. In theory, the use of minority languages in daily interaction was promoted, yet in practice the language used in village council offices was Russian.[124]

Soviet Ukrainization, 1923

Although 96 percent of teachers were not Communist Party members (*pozapartiini* in Ukrainian), "all were captives of revolutionary romanticism."[125] The Ukrainian Revolution, more precisely the war for independence of 1917–1921, aimed at establishing a democratic government that would guarantee rights to all national minorities, not just the titular nationality. On December 30, 1922, communist Russia formalized its occupation of Ukraine by creating the USSR. Once the Union was created, Bolsheviks pursued the policy of educating local elites loyal to the regime (*korenizatsiia* in Russian, meaning indigenization). In his study of the Soviet language policy in the Ukrainian SSR from 1923 through 1934, Matthew Pauly of Michigan State University has argued that "the Communist Party meant Ukrainization as a means of integrating the bulk of the rural population into the Soviet order."[126] It was through the national language, promoted by school teachers in Ukraine that the Soviet ideal was to be realized.

Rather than being an "affirmative action"[127] as Matthew Pauly, Terry Martin, and other Western historians argue, the policy was a concession of central authorities in Moscow made under pressure from the republic. Historians in Ukraine and the diaspora, as well as in Russia, challenge the view that Moscow consciously promoted and supported Ukrainian language and culture, and demonstrate that the policy of "Ukrainization" was introduced in 1923 to appease national communists in Ukraine.[128] Like a temporary retreat under the NEP, it was the NEP in the cultural sphere. Ukrainization was not a policy Moscow wanted. Behind the seemingly idyllic façade, allowing Ukrainian statehood within the Soviet Union with trappings of the "Ukrainian Renaissance," Moscow was preparing for an offensive. The beginning of the "offensive" in 1928 was also the end of the NEP.[129] Stalin's hasty termination of the NEP, and elimination of the most active participants of Ukrainization as "counterrevolutionaries," was not a betrayal of Lenin in any sense, but a logical continuation of the political practice of his predecessor.[130]

It is no coincidence that Stalin was appointed People's Commissar of Nationalities under Lenin from 1917 until 1922. Stalin considered himself Russian of Georgian origin. Stalin "had many roots in the Russian past," noted James H. Billington of Princeton University. This American historian of Russian culture further observed,

> His addiction to mass armies overbalanced with artillery follows a long tradition leading back to Ivan the Terrible; his xenophobic and disciplinarian conception of education is reminiscent of ... Nicholas I, and Pobedonostsev . . . ; his passion for material innovation and war-supporting technology echoes Peter the Great.[131]

Robert Tucker, professor of politics at Princeton University, noted, "To identify himself with Russia was to take as his revolutionary arena not simply little Georgia but the whole of a great empire covering a sixth of the world." Tucker further argued that the mental process of Russification of the "future prophet of socialism in one country" exhibited Stalin's penchant for bigness.[132]

To integrate Ukraine under a new guise as a constituent republic within the Soviet Union into its "mother country," Russia, Bolshevik authorities had several policy options: pursue either accommodation or assimilation of local elites. Robert Conquest noted that Stalin clearly understood that "the essence of Ukrainian nationhood was contained in the intelligentsia who articulated it" but also in the rural masses "who had sustained it over the centuries." The "decapitation" of the nation by removing its spokesmen was essential in Stalin's mind once he realized that "only a mass terror throughout the body of the nation"—that is, the land tillers who embodied the traditional culture of Ukraine, "could really reduce the country to submission."[133]

What was the real goal behind the requirement for Ukrainization decreed by the RNK on July 27, 1923, to the Commissariat of Education and its local organs? The requirement to correlate a targeted number of Ukrainian-language schools with a proportion of local Ukrainian population deviated from Lenin's views on education for national minorities. More worrisome, by 1932–1933, the number of Ukrainian-language schools rose to 88 percent, in excess of the ethnic-Ukrainian proportion of the republic's population.[134] Although the RNK decree further required study of the Ukrainian language in all non-Ukrainian schools, Russian remained an obligatory subject. The decree specified that Russian was "a common state language" that "connects the Ukrainian people to the culture of the Union of Soviet Socialist Republics."[135]

The Ukrainization policy seemed to be progressing well. Between 1927 and 1929, the number of schools with instruction in Ukrainian language increased from 79 to 81 percent; in institutes, the use of Ukrainian language also increased from 28 to 30 percent.[136] For Jewish, German, Bulgarian, Belarusian, Moldavian, and Greek minorities in Soviet Ukraine, instruction was in their native tongue. Professors and lecturers in institutions of higher education were required to lecture in Ukrainian. Enrollment in postgraduate studies was open only to individuals who could speak and write in Ukrainian.[137] However, the policy was a mixed success; it was resisted by Russian-speaking parents and government officials, who were not Ukrainian, but appointed by Moscow.[138] While Moscow gradually embraced Ukrainization as policy, its own leaders resisted it because they did not want to learn Ukrainian.

Alongside schools for ethnic Ukrainians, there were 1,214 schools for Russian-speaking minority students, 625 German, 457 Jewish, 337 Polish, and dozens of schools with instruction in languages of other national minority populations. Considering the ratio of eight- to fourteen-year-old children of respective nationality to the number of minority schools, German settlements had four times the number of Polish and six times the number of Jewish language schools.[139] Not only had the German settlements more schools than other national minorities in Ukraine, but they also received substantial financial aid from Mennonites in North America and later Hitler's government during the famine of 1933.[140] The absence of actual famine conditions in many German settlements proved to be significant factors that contributed to the lower tallies of Mennonite deaths due to starvation than those often cited for the Ukrainian population.[141] A photo of a lesson in the German seven-year school in the Sinel'nykivs'kyi district, Dnipropetrovs'k region, was taken during the famine of 1933 (see Figure 2.3). No comparable photos of conditions in Ukrainian rural schools have been preserved in the archives, because in some schools there were no students or teachers as entire villages died out.

Was this a progressive policy or a propaganda campaign to win diverse groups over to the Bolshevik cause? While proclaiming the need to educate children in their native tongue, the Communist Party forbade schooling in minority languages. The "artificially created" national minority areas of settlement and respective village councils, as well as schools in minority languages, were liquidated in 1939 when Russification became the official policy.[142]

The reduction of the use of Russian language in schools was never accepted by the Russian minority. Some continued to regard Ukrainian as a mere dialect and expressed open contempt or hostility. The following dialogue between two officials captures the unpleasant experiences of those who failed to learn the Ukrainian language:

–Is Ukrainian a language or a dialect?
–Neither. It is an excuse to dismiss a person from his position.[143]

Before dark clouds began to gather on the horizon, Skrypnyk intensified the process of introduction of education in the native tongue to Ukrainian children beyond Soviet Ukraine's borders in the Russian SFSR. The Ukrainian national awakening touched all areas where Ukrainians settled over the centuries: Kuban', Central Black Earth, Lower Volga, Western Siberia, and

Figure 2.3 Schoolchildren attending lessons in a German seven-year school, Sinel'nykivs'kyi district, Dnipropetrovs'k region, 1933. *Source*: From TsDKFFAU, od. obl. 2-13577.

the Far East.¹⁴⁴ Territories of Kursk and Voronezh Governorates on the border with Ukraine were incorporated into the republic for a brief period in 1918–1920, but after the establishment of the Soviet Union were transferred to the Russian SFSR.¹⁴⁵ Kuban', with over 3 million Ukrainians, and the Far Eastern Republic, with over 300,000 Ukrainians, enjoyed national-cultural autonomy. However, as of 1924, for over 7 million Ukrainians in the Russian SFSR, there were only 150 schools.¹⁴⁶ These schools had 40 primary and 22 secondary school teachers in urban areas and 1,487 primary and 36 secondary school teachers in rural settlements where ethnic Ukrainians lived.¹⁴⁷ These schools often lacked literature, textbooks, and classrooms.

New Ukrainian-language schools sprang up in the Kuban area in the North Caucasus, where descendants from Cossacks had settled centuries before. One of the first teacher training colleges with Ukrainian-language instruction was established in *stanytsia* Poltavs'ka (a Cossack settlement) in the North Caucasus. On July 15, 1924, it boasted twenty-nine new "red pedagogues," who graduated from the college after completing a three-year course of study.¹⁴⁸ In the Far East, Ukrainian sections were established in local education districts. Two pedagogical technical colleges in Valuis'k and Ostrohrad made Ukrainian studies mandatory. So did pedagogical faculty at the Voronizh University, where a Ukrainian studies department was established.¹⁴⁹ These teachers were a tuning fork for national consciousness. They transmitted knowledge about Ukrainian history and culture, served as guardians of national memory and mythology, and shaped their students' ethnic identity. Precisely for these reasons, the curtailment of Ukrainization started outside Soviet Ukraine first, followed by policies to eradicate Ukrainian "bourgeois nationalism" inside Soviet Ukraine.

Overall, the goal of the ambiguous Soviet policy of Ukrainization was to overcome resistance to Bolshevik economic policy and engage the republic's population in construction of the Soviet state.¹⁵⁰ Another goal, to increase the number of Ukrainians in the Communist Party ranks as well as in government offices, was not meant to give the republic's representatives more power in deciding matters of their concern, but to assure they were loyal servants of the central authorities in Moscow. The use of Ukrainian language in the public sphere was limited; the official language of communication was Ukrainian, but the *de facto* language, spoken in schools, institutes of higher education, and offices, was Russian.

THE CRISIS OF 1926

In 1926, at the Fifteenth Party Congress, Stalin indicated that there would be more emphasis on communist ideals, which meant less autonomy, either economic or cultural.¹⁵¹ To strengthen central authority, Stalin brought all commissariats in Soviet republics under the control of Moscow. The intensive drive against private commerce, coupled with plans to collectivize agriculture, led to a gradual reduction of living standards due to loss of exports as the world economic crisis began to unfold.¹⁵²

The declared goal of the Bolshevik nationality policy in Ukraine was "to raise the cultural development of the nation so it can join workers in the fight for socialism."¹⁵³ To secure leadership of the Communist Party, Bolsheviks began to recruit Ukrainian cadres to local, district, and regional committees rather than increasing the overall number of Ukrainians in the party. Three years after the policy was introduced, in 1926, comrade Fedor Korniushin, secretary of the TsK KP(b)U, reported that "the link between the Communist Party and the Ukrainian workers, peasants, and loyal revolutionary Ukrainian intelligentsia has strengthened." As is evident from his statistics, the growth of party membership in the republic was slow: it increased by only 3.7 percent in 1925 (from 33.3 to 37 percent), and slightly doubled to 6.7 percent in 1926 (from 37 to 43.7 percent).¹⁵⁴ Only after nine years of the formation of the Ukrainian SSR, did ethnic Ukrainians constitute a majority in the republic's Communist Party.¹⁵⁵ A journalist, who worked in Kharkiv in the 1930s, observed that the national composition of rank-and-file members was misleading as a measure of Ukrainization because even Jews and people with Ukrainian names, who did not regard themselves as Ukrainians, were listed as Ukrainians. Also, nearly 70 percent of the candidate members were from urban centers, mostly workers and intelligentsia, mostly Russian-speaking, and very few were engaged in agriculture. Importantly, secretaries of regional Communist Party organizations were not Ukrainian. The recruitment of "Ukrainian cadres" was "a purely formal thing" as it was "just a matter of loyalty to the regime, that was the chief criterion," not the fact of being Ukrainian.¹⁵⁶

Although the number and percentage of Ukrainians among the Communist Party cadres increased, less than a quarter (an average of 23 percent) could speak the Ukrainian language.¹⁵⁷ The percentage was higher in the center (55 percent in the Kyïv region, outside Kyïv), but in the single digits in the east (only 4.5 percent in the Kharkiv region). Korniushin explained that "it was not the fault of the proletariat and its party that have to raise and develop the culture that has been suppressed by tsarism for hundreds of years."¹⁵⁸ Using typical Bolshevik propaganda, he claimed that exploiters, non-Russian foreign capitalist owners, accommodated to the repressive language policy of the imperial Russian regime. Korniushin further argued that, in their mutual struggle against foreign capitalism and Russian tsarism, the exploited Ukrainians joined the Russian proletariat and acquired its culture and language because "the Russian culture was more advanced." After introducing his unifying theory, based on the superiority of the Russian language and culture, Korniushin concluded that the policy of forcing proletariat to learn Ukrainian was "inadmissible."[159]

The struggle between the Great Russian chauvinism and local Ukrainian nationalism became apparent during the Twelfth Congress of the Russian Communist Party (Bolsheviks) on April 17–25, 1923. One of the leading Bolshevik leaders, Nikolai Bukharin, told the audience:

> In Ukraine, for instance, where the party constituency is Russian-Jewish, our main task is to work among Ukrainians, and it is because of this a number of our comrades in Ukraine are fighting against Ukrainian nationalism very energetically, with hatred. To implement this policy correctly they have to be reeducated.[160]

However, neither the first secretary of the KP(b)U Emmanuil Kviring (1888–1937) nor the second secretary Dmitrii Lebed' (1893–1937), the ideologue behind the "theory of two cultures," were willing to be "re-educated." Lebed', in his article on the national question, published in *Kommunist* on March 17, 1926, argued that

> theoretically, the struggle between the two cultures is inevitable. In Ukraine, due to historical circumstances, the culture of the city is Russian, but the culture of the village is Ukrainian. Not a single communist or a real Marxist could say that "I believe in the victory of the Ukrainian culture," if this culture will impede our progressive movement.[161]

Ukrainization of schools did not accelerate until Oleksandr Shums'kyi, a former Borot'bist, who joined the Communist Party in 1920, assumed leadership of the Commissariat of Education. Shums'kyi advocated for rapid and total Ukrainization of all aspects of life and opposed appointments of non-Ukrainians to fill government and party positions. Shums'kyi offered a Marxist critique of comrade Lebed's theory. He argued that "proletariat will never allow any struggle with the peasantry over the cultural expression—language" because this would mean giving the "bourgeois nationalists" a green light to unify the masses under their leadership. Shums'kyi suspected that some communists from the intelligentsia, such as poets, professors, writers, or teachers, might have harbored such views.[162] In response, Lebed' gave Shums'kyi a lesson in eliminating political illiteracy, quoting Lenin's theory from *Imperialism, the Highest Stage of Capitalism*.[163] The two comrades were well versed in Bolshevik propaganda; both became victims of party purges and paid with their lives for their blind faith in the Soviet regime.

Seemingly, the policy of Ukrainization was given a boost with the appointment of a Jew from Ukraine, Lazar Kaganovich, as the KP(b)U secretary general from 1925 to 1928. Kaganovich, who was born in Kyïv Governorate and worked as a tailor, studied the Ukrainian language and promoted its use among "red" bureaucrats. Although the Communist Party became more Ukrainian in terms of numbers, the leaders appointed to the republic were not of Ukrainian heritage and did not speak Ukrainian. Ukrainian language was a requirement to get a government job, yet "red" bureaucrats continued to communicate among themselves in Russian. Officials from other republics, who were dispatched to work in Ukraine, were exempt from learning the language. Language testing among party cadres was postponed several times, and eventually abandoned. Kaganovich ran into conflict with Shums'kyi when, as the secretary general, he used the struggle with "nationalist inclinations" as an effective method to establish his authoritarian rule. Half a year after the appointment of Kaganovich, Shums'kyi approached Stalin and demanded to replace the leader of the KP(b)U with Vlas Chubar, a Ukrainian who had joined the Bolsheviks in 1907.

It was under these circumstances that Stalin wrote a letter to "Comrade Kaganovich and other members of the Politburo of the TsK KP(b)U," warning them about the "national deviationism" (referring to Mykola Khvyl'ovyi's slogan "Away from Moscow!").[164] Mykola Khvyl'ovyi[165] articulated his thesis that the question of Ukrainian literature should be separated from that of Russian literature on the grounds that Ukrainian literature had been more influenced by European culture than by Moscow at a communist faction meeting during the First Congress of Proletarian Writers in 1925. Khvyl'ovyi eventually had to submit to party discipline, but his words did not go unnoticed. Stalin, in a conversation with Shums'kyi, agreed with some of the arguments, but in writing he gave a political "carte blanche" to his emissary in Ukraine. Kaganovich skillfully used Stalin's method of "double-bookkeeping" to deal with the opposition.[166] Kaganovich, supported by Stalin, began a campaign of vilification against his opponents and dismissed Shums'kyi in March 1927.

In his place, a staunch communist Mykola Skrypnyk was appointed, no less a supporter of the Ukrainization policy (see Figure 2.4). Skrypnyk was a man of influence and prestige. In his speech at the Tenth Congress of the KP(b)U in November 1927, Kaganovich referred to Skrypnyk as one of "the best of Old Bolsheviks."[167] The son of a railroad worker Skrypnyk became interested in the revolutionary movement while studying in Kharkiv. He joined the Russian Social Democratic Workers' Party in 1897 and dedicated the rest of his life to the revolutionary movement. Skrypnyk was arrested fifteen times, sentenced to a total of thirty-four years of imprisonment, exiled seven times, and on one occasion was sentenced to death. On Lenin's

Figure 2.4 Pioneer of Bolshevism in Ukraine and Shums'kyi's successor as the People's Commissar of Education, comrade Mykola Skrypnyk, speaks at a meeting of the Communist Children's Movement (Young Pioneers), Kharkiv, 1930. *Source*: From TsDKFFAU, od. obl. 0-97364.

suggestion, Skrypnyk was dispatched to Ukraine as a representative of the Central Committee of the Communist Party. Skrypnyk at various times held the Ukrainian posts of secretary of Workers' and Peasants' Inspection, attorney-general, People's Commissar of Internal Affairs, Justice, and Education, vice-chairman of the Council of People's Commissars, and chairman of the State Planning Commission.[168]

Skrypnyk was also a member of the Central Committee of the Russian Communist Party (Bolsheviks) (TsK RKP(b)) and the Executive Committee of the Communist International, six times a delegate to Communist International congresses and leader of the Ukrainian delegation. In the inner-party struggles, he supported Stalin against the opposition. In recognition of his prolific literary contribution, Skrypnyk was made a member of the Academy of Sciences of the Ukrainian SSR. He also edited one of the leading journals for educators in Ukraine. Skrypnyk, who became a vocal critic of "national deviationism," ended up committing suicide the same year, in 1933, two months after Mykola Khvyl'ovyi, whose death marked the beginning of an era so poignantly described by Polish publicist, Jerzy Giedroyc, in his letter to Ukrainian literature researcher Iurii Lavrinenko, who later used it as the title for a collection of that generation's best literary works—*Executed Renaissance*.[169] Despite being its vocal critic, Skrypnyk became a scapegoat, and the Soviet campaign for Ukrainization was permanently linked to his name.

James Mace related what was achieved during the era of Ukrainization:

> Ukrainian schools were opened. The Ukrainian language was being transformed into a vehicle of sophisticated literary and scientific expression. And there was also a tremendous outburst of literary, scholarly activity. The market was flooded with new books in Ukrainian. It seemed at some times that virtually every peasant wanted to be a poet. The leading Soviet Ukrainian writer, the one who was most read was Mykola Khvyl′ovyi. And Khvyl′ovyi, the most popular writer said: "Let's build a world-class Ukrainian culture. Let's have a Ukrainian culture that is on a par with French literature, with English literature, with German literature. The way to do this is to learn those literatures. We have to face Western Europe and interact directly with European culture; not through the medium of Russian culture as we have hitherto done."[170]

In the 1930s, with the intensification of the struggle against "nationalist deviationism," "anti-Soviet," and "fascist" elements seeping into Ukrainian, German, and Polish schools, ethnic territorial settlements and their educational institutions were gradually restructured, then eliminated altogether.[171]

Antin Lak, who taught in the Donbas during the period of Ukrainization, recalled:

> It was a very interesting period in the cultural development of the Ukrainian people. The Commissar of Education Skrypnyk believed that Ukrainian governmental institutions should use Ukrainian rather than Russian. People also must speak the native language not only in their day-to-day private communication but also in government offices. He believed that the government should introduce this policy in the interests of the people and of the state. But later the process was reversed and the Ukrainization was nipped in the bud and Russification started anew.[172]

The most controversial issue was orthography. In 1926, a proposal was made for a new Ukrainian orthography.[173] It was prepared by the State Commission for the Regulation of Ukrainian Orthography of the People's Commissariat of Education.[174] Known as the Kharkiv orthography, or *Skrypnykivka*, it was formally approved in September 1928 by Skrypnyk. It was the first universally recognized standard Ukrainian orthography. Subsequently it was reformed in 1933 because of its alleged embrace of "nationalist deviation."[175] Skrypnyk's refusal to pattern Ukrainian on the Russian model was one of the chief reasons for his overthrow in 1933.[176] One of the most vehement charges pressed against him was that he had helped introduce new symbols into Ukrainian orthography.[177] This was criticized as bourgeois in 1932, but in 1933 was equated with counterrevolution and "assistance to the annexationist plans of the Polish landlords."[178] Tetiana Kardynalovs'ka in her memoirs, *Persistent Past*, wrote how her husband, Serhii Pylypenko, was upset about the work on this project and the persecution of people who worked on it.[179]

On pages of his émigré journal *Tryzub* (Trident), published in Paris, Symon Petliura, the leader of the Ukrainian national government-in-exile, offered a scathing critique of Skrypnyk and Ukrainian communists, Petrovs'kyi and Zatons'kyi. Petliura wrote that the dictatorship of the proletariat, indeed, had clear class and national characteristics: The Ukrainian majority is ruled by the Russian minority who occupy influential posts in the administrative bureaucracy and the military. Comparing the Bolsheviks to the Conquistadors, Petliura characterized Soviet "Ukrainization" as a typical colonial policy, where colonizers are required to master the indigenous language of the colonized to create an illusion that rapacious extraction of resources is carried out not by the foreign power, but by the "brothers" who "speak our language."[180] Deconstructing Chubar's speech addressed to the Communist Youth League in April 1926, Petliura summed up Soviet nationality policy as a failure. Articulating his idea that the pro-Moscow orientation means political and cultural suicide for Ukraine, Petliura dubbed the Bolsheviks' policy "catching of Ukrainian souls." He warned: "The [Soviet] government can transport trainloads of Ukrainian bread, sugar, coal, all of Ukraine's riches, except her Ukrainian soul."[181] Petliura called Chubar a representative of the illegal occupational regime and his speech aimed at the younger generation of Ukrainians as an attempt to train new Janissaries. The following month, on May 25, 1926, Petliura was assassinated by an agent of the Soviet security police on his way to a meeting of Ukrainian émigré organizations in Paris.

One leader, endowed with limitless power, was implicit in the very foundations of Lenin's Communist Party.[182] The process of achieving an ideal of a unified state organism, cemented by party and security police, meant utter destruction of civil society. All forms of human activity were allowed, and imposed, only if they were at the service of the state. The All-Ukrainian Teachers' Union was dissolved, and the teachers were forced to join a union that guided their actions in the direction aligned with the goals of the Communist Party. The language of the Marxist ideology was a tool of social engineering that shaped the consciousness of the intelligentsia who were at work to bring about an autocratic society. Teachers who resisted or failed to pass political loyalty tests were punished with arrests, dismissals from their jobs, and untimely death. The youth, too, had to become one with the minds of their leaders. Ukrainian communists, after a decade of futile attempts to blend the two ideologies, of nationalism and socialism, weathered a storm in 1926. The calm did not last long. The Bolshevik ideal of a unitary state meant the inevitable destruction of any vestiges of Ukrainian national identity or state sovereignty. Such aspirations clouded the minds of the Ukrainian intelligentsia, the Ukrainian Orthodox clergy, and teachers who were the sons and daughters of the priests, as well as toiling masses who tilled their land that provided them with a sense of dignity and economic security. Thus, the state had devised a multipronged attack on these targeted groups.

NOTES

1. *Communist Takeover and Occupation of Ukraine*, 14.
2. Ibid., 15–16.
3. V. I. Lenin, *Essential Works of Lenin: "What Is to Be Done?" and Other Writings*, ed. Henry M. Christman (New York: Dover Publications, Inc., 1987); Richard Pipes, *A Concise History of the Russian Revolution* (New York: Alfred A. Knopf, 1995), 106.
4. "even such a meaningless and ugly term as 'Bolshevik' will 'pass muster,' although it expresses nothing but purely accidental fact that at the Brussels-London Congress of 1903 we were in the majority," wrote Lenin in his "The State and Revolution"; quoted in *Essential Works of Lenin*, 332.
5. Stephen Kotkin, "Communism: A Global Reckoning," *Wall Street Journal*, November 4–5, 2017, C2.
6. Iefimenko, "Sotsial'ne oblychchia vchytel'stva," 138–39.
7. "By educating the workers' party, Marxism educates the vanguard of the proletariat which is capable of assuming power and of leading the whole people to socialism, of directing and organizing the new order, of being the teacher, guide and leader, of all the toiling and exploited in the task of building up their social life without the bourgeoisie and against the bourgeoisie," wrote Lenin in "The State and Revolution"; quoted in *Essential Works of Lenin*, 288.
8. Stefan Plaggenborg, *Revoliutsiia i kul'tura: Kul'turnye orientiry v period mezhdu Oktiabr'skoi revoliutsyei i epokhoi stalinizma* (St. Petersburg: Zhurnal "Neva," 2000), 29.
9. A. V. Lunacharsky, *O narodnom obrazovanii* (Moscow: Izd-vo Akademii Pedagogicheskikh Nauk RSFSR, 1958), 292.
10. V. I. Lenin, "Speech Delivered at the First All-Russia Congress of Internationalist Teachers," June 5, 1918, a report published on June 6, 1918, in *Izvestiia*, no. 114; reprinted in *Collected Works*, 4th English edition, vol. 27 (Moscow: Progress Publishers, 1972), 445–46, https://www.marxists.org/archive/lenin/works/1918/jun/05.htm.
11. Stepan Siropolko, "Narodnia osvita na ukraïns'kykh zemliakh i v koloniiakh," in *Ukraïns'ka kul'tura: Lektsiï*, ed. D. Antonovych (Kyïv: Lybid', 1993); reprinted in *Izbornyk*, http://izbornyk.org.ua/cultur/cult06.htm.
12. *Sovetskoe stroitel'stvo na Ukraine (po dokladam otdelov Gubispolkomov): Itogi odnoi poezdki* (Kharkov, 1920), 44; cited in Iefimenko, "Sotsial'ne oblychchia vchytel'stva," 148.
13. Solovey, *Golgota Ukraïny*, 49.

14. "Case History SW1: Varvara Dibert, b. 1898, Zvenyhorod, Cherkasy," in *Oral History Project*, vol. 2, 710, 714; English version in *Report to Congress*, 373.
15. Pauly, *Breaking the Tongue*, 45.
16. *Bolezni nashego pechatnogo dela po dannym obsledovanii TsKK i NKRKI* (Moscow, 1924), 38; cited in Plaggenborg, *Revoliutsiia i kul'tura*, 131.
17. A. I. Nazarov, *Oktiabr' i kniga: Sozdanie sovetskikh izdatel'stv i formirovanie massovogo chitatelia, 1917–1923* (Moscow, 1968); quoted in Plaggenborg, 131.
18. A. A. Marinov, *V stroiu zashchitnikov Oktiabria: Voenno-politicheskaia kniga 1918–1925 g.* (Moscow: Nauka, 1982), 29–32.
19. Mazepa, *Ukraïna v ohni i buri revoliutsiï*, 120.
20. Solovey, *Golgota Ukraïny*, 31, 32, 39, 42.
21. Iefimenko, "Sotsial'ne oblychchia vchytel'stva," 145.
22. *Derzhavnyi arkhiv Vinnyts'koï oblasti (DAVO)*, f. R-510, op. 1, spr. 129, ark. 28; quoted in Koliastruk, *Intelihentsiia USRR u 1920-ti roky*, 223.
23. I. I. Nikolina, "Vchytel'stvo Podillia u 1920-kh – 30-kh rr. XX st.," in *Vinnychyna: mynule ta s'ohodennia. Kraieznavchi doslidzhennia*, ed. M. M. Kravets' (Vinnytsia: DP DKF, 2005), 157.
24. V. A. Nesterenko, "Ukraïns'ke vchytel'stvo Podillia v 1920–1930-ti roky: suspil'no-politychnyi portret," in *Osvita, nauka i kul'tura na Podilli: Zbirnyk naukovykh prats'*, no. 3 (2003): 157–58.
25. M. O. Avdiienko, *Narodna osvita na Ukraïni* (Kharkiv: TsSU, 1927), 15.
26. Lunacharsky, *O narodnom obrazovanii*, 227.
27. F. Tagin, "Shkola sotsvosa na Ukraine i perspektivy narodnogo obrazovaniia," *Put' prosveshcheniia*, no. 1 (1924); quoted in *Radians'ka osvita* 2, no. 3–4 (1924): 97.
28. Lenin's health never recovered from an attempt on his life made by a Browning pistol-toting Socialist Revolutionary, Fanny Kaplan (born Feiga Haimovna Roitblat), in August 1918. Four years later he suffered a series of strokes, the last of which killed him on January 21, 1924.
29. G. M. Shevchuk, *Kul'turnoe stroitel'stvo na Ukraine v 1921–1925 gg* (Kiev: Iz-vo AN Ukrainian SSR, 1963), 184.
30. M. Baran, "Rolia i zavdannia sil's'koho vchytelia v osvitlenni XIII-ho partiinoho z'ïzdu," *Radians'ka osvita* 2, no. 7 (1924): 5.
31. O. Loiko, "Intelihentsiia Podillia v umovakh nepu," in *Tezy dopovidei 15-oï Vinnyts'koï oblasnoï istoryko-kraieznavchoï konferentsiï* (Vinnytsia, 1996), 61–62.
32. *DAVO*, f. P-1, op. 1, spr. 3, ark. 23.
33. I. P. Mel'nychuk, V. I. Petrenko, and P. M. Kravchenko, "Dokumenty derzhavnoho arkhivu Vinnyts'koï oblasti pro nastroï sil's'koï intelihestiï Podillia v 1920-h rr.," in *Naukovi zapysky Vinnyts'koho derzhavnoho pedahohichnoho universytetu im. Mykhaila Kotsiubyns'koho*, ed. P. S. Hryhorchuk (Vinnytsia: VDPU im. Mykhaila Kotsiubyns'koho, 2006), vyp. 11, 341.
34. Klitsakov, *Pedahohichni kadry Ukraïny*, 73, 78–79.
35. Mykhailo Myronenko, "Z zhyttia sil's'koï shkoly ta vchytel'stva," *Radians'ka osvita* 2, no. 3–4 (1924): 61.

36. Hr. Ivanytsia, "Tretia Vseukraïns'ka konferentsiia po pedosviti," *Radians'ka osvita* 2, no. 9–10 (1924): 88–89.

37. *Zbirnyk uzakonen' ta rozporiadzhen' robitnycho-selians'koho uriadu Ukraïny*, section 43, no. 272 (Kharkiv: Drukarnia UVO im. M. Frunze, 1924), 795–818, http://irbis-nbuv.gov.ua/dlib/item/0000128.

38. "Iz otcheta Agitpropa Poltavskogo Gubkoma s marta 1923 po mart 1924 g.," *Izvestiia Poltavskogo Gubkoma KP(b)U*, no. 15 (1924), 121–22; quoted in Klitsakov, *Pedahohichni kadry Ukraïny*, 76.

39. *TsDAVOU*, f. 2717, op. 1, spr. 70, ark. 28.

40. V. Nagornyi, "Obshchestvenno-politicheskaia rabota sel'skogo uchitelia," *Proletarskaia pravda*, January 4, 1925.

41. V. V. Protsenko, "Osvitians'ka Profspilka USRR v seredyni 1920-kh rr.: Stanovyshche, zavdannia, problemy (za materialamy Pershoho Vseukraïns'koho vchytel's'koho z'ïzdu v Kharkovi)," *Hileia*, no. 116 (2017): 43.

42. *Narodne hospodarstvo USRR (statystychnyi dovidnyk)*, ed. Oleksandr Asatkin (Kyïv: Narodne hospodarstvo ta oblik, 1935), Table 1, 546–47.

43. "Privet sovetskomu uchiteliu," *Kommunist*, January 4, 1925.

44. For a biography of Oleksandr Shums'kyi, see Iurii Shapoval, "Ne samohubets'!" in *Liudyna i systema: shtrykhy do portreta totalitarnoï doby v Ukraïni* (Kyïv: Instytut natsional'nykh vidnosyn i politolohiï NAN Ukraïny, 1994), 134–52; see also Bilokin', "Dolia chleniv Tsentral'noï Rady."

45. Oleksandr Shums'kyi, "Na tretiomu fronti (do uchytel's'koho z'ïzdu), *Radians'ka osvita* 3, no. 1 (1925): 2–9.

46. For a biography of Oleksandr Mizernyts'kyi, see Marochko and Hillig, *Represovani pedahohy Ukraïny*, 64–69; see also Pauly, *Breaking the Tongue*, 76, 377n39.

47. *Pershyi Vseukraïns'kyi uchytel's'kyi z'ïzd v Kharkovi vid 5 do 11 sichnia 1925 r.: Stenohrafichnyi zvit* (Kharkiv: Derzhavne vydavnytstvo Ukraïny, 1925), 3–4; see also Protsenko, "Osvitians'ka Profspilka," 44.

48. Protsenko, "Osvitians'ka Profspilka," 44.

49. In July 1925, P. Solodub was appointed a member of the state commission to oversee drafting of a new Ukrainian orthography, known as the Kharkiv orthography. The commission was chaired by Oleksandr Shums'kyi, then Commissar of Education in Soviet Ukraine. See *Ukraïns'kyi pravopys (Proiekt)* (Kharkiv: DVU, 1926).

50. For more on how the Bolsheviks lured UNR general Iurii Tiutiunnyk to Soviet Ukraine, used his knowledge and connections, and later executed him as "spent material," see Yaroslav Faizulin, "Unwilling Instrument of the State," *Ukrainian Week*, October 14, 2011, https://ukrainianweek.com/History/33007.

51. P. Solodub, "Revoliutsiia i narodnyi uchytel'," *Radians'ka osvita* 3, no. 1 (January 1925): 10.

52. Solodub, "Revoliutsiia i narodnyi uchytel'," 11.

53. Klitsakov, *Pedahohichni kadry Ukraïny*, 133.

54. *TsDAVOU*, f. 2717, op. 2, spr. 29, ark. 7 (1923); *TsDAVOU*, f. 2717, op. 2, spr. 35, ark. 14 (1925).

55. *TsDAVOU*, f. 539, op. 1, spr. 273, ark. 1.
56. *TsDAVOU*, f. 331, op. 1, spr. 158, ark. 9, 10.
57. *TsDAHOU*, f. 1, op. 6, spr. 121, ark. 99.
58. "Ukrainskaia SSR," in *Narodnoe obrazovanie v SSSR*, 332.
59. V. K. Maiboroda, "Osoblyvosti rozvytku systemy vyshchoï pedahohichnoï osvity v URSR (1917–1941 rr.)," *Ukraïns'kyi istorychnyi zhurnal*, no. 11 (1990): 62.
60. *TsDAVOU*, f. 318, op. 1, spr. 1403, ark. 10–11.
61. "Shkola na seli," *Visti VUTsVK*, October 21, 1925.
62. "7,000 uchyteliv (Peredova)," *Visti VUTsVK*, July 31, 1925.
63. Klitsakov, *Pedahohichni kadry Ukraïny*, 92.
64. *Ukraïna: Statystychnyi shchorichnyk* (Kharkiv: TsSU, 1929), 8; see also Iefimenko, "Sotsial'ne oblychchia vchytel'stva," 153.
65. O. Mizernyts'kyi, "Do II Plenumu VUTsP Robos: Pershyi etap," *Robitnyk osvity* 3–4, no. 5–6 (1925): 4.
66. Comrade Polenko reported at the Third Session of the VUTsVK about a "crocodile jaws" ("scissors") gap in salary increases between urban teachers as being 50 percent higher than that of rural teachers. See "Na bizhuchi temy," *Radians'ka osvita* 2, no. 9–10 (1924): 83.
67. *Ukraïna: Statystychnyi shchorichnyk*, 85.
68. *Korotki pidsumky perepysu naselennia Ukraïny 17 hrudnia roku 1926: Natsional'nyi i vikovyi sklad, ridna mova ta pysemnist' naselennia* (Kharkiv, 1928), 4.
69. Iefimenko, "Sotsial'ne oblychchia vchytel'stva," 153.
70. Sukhomlyns'ka, *Narysy*, 156.
71. "Ukrainskaia SSR," in *Narodnoe obrazovanie v SSSR*, 327.
72. Koliastruk, *Intelihentsiia USRR u 1920-ti roky*, 256.
73. *TsDAHOU*, f. 1, op. 20, spr. 2023, ark. 25, 28.
74. *TsDAHOU*, f. 1, op. 20, spr. 2023, ark. 27.
75. "Pershyi vseukraïns'kyi z'ïzd robitnykiv dopomohy ditiam," *Radians'ka osvita* 2, no. 9–10 (1924): 94.
76. *TsDAHOU*, f. 1, op. 20, spr. 2023, ark. 26.
77. Ibid.
78. *TsDAHOU*, f. 1, op. 20, spr. 2023, ark. 27.
79. *TsDAHOU*, f. 1, op. 20, spr. 2023, ark. 33.
80. From 1920 to 1926, Makarenko was in charge of the children's commune named after Maxim Gorky in the village Kovalivka near Poltava. From May 1926 to September 1928, he was in charge of the labor commune named after Maxim Gorky in the village of Kuriazh near Kharkiv. From October 1927 to June 1935, he was the head of the labor commune named after Felix Dzerzhinsky near Kharkiv under the umbrella of the GPU. Makarenko omitted from his writings how these children were used as forced labor on assembly lines. Makarenko wrote his books in Russian. Archives in Kharkiv can shed light on obscure life in this children's commune. For a reevaluation of Makarenko's legacy as the author of the "pedagogical poem" about the upbringing of the children of the "enemies of the people," see Götz Hillig, "Makarenko and Stalinism: Comments and Reflections," *East/West*

Education 15, no. 2 (1994): 103–16; Götz Hillig, *V poiskakh istinnogo Makarenko: russkoiazychnye publikatsii (1976–2014)* (Poltava: Izdatel' Shevchenko R. V., 2014). See also Dietmar Waterkamp, "Götz Hillig and His Search for the True Makarenko. What Did He Find?" *IDE-Online Journal (International Dialogues on Education: Past and Present)* 5, no. 2 (2018), http://www.ide-journal.org/article/2018-volume-5-number-2-gotz-hillig-and-his-search-for-the-true-makarenko-what-did-he-find/.

81. "Ukrainskaia SSR," 328.

82. From the diary of Iurii Sambros, *HDA SBU*, f. 6, spr. 68805-FP, zoshyt no. 6, ark. 953–1052.

83. For a detailed biography of Oleksandr Zaluzhnyi and a list of publications, see Pedagogical Museum of Ukraine, http://pmu.in.ua/virtual-exhibitions/juvilei_pedagogiv/130_rokiv_zalychnii/.

84. For a detailed biography of Hryhorii Vashchenko and a list of his publications, see Pedagogical Museum of Ukraine, http://pmu.in.ua/virtual-exhibitions/.

85. Götz Hillig, "'Mazepynets'' Vashchenko pro 'ianychara' Makarenka: vzaiemyny vidomykh ukraïns'kykh pedahohiv," *Ridna shkola*, no. 6 (1995): 74.

86. In September 1964, the Central Committee of the Communist Party of the Ukrainian SSR established a medal to commemorate Anton Makarenko. The medal was awarded to several dozen education theorists, school principals, and teachers, among them three women.

87. Klitsakov, *Pedahohichni kadry Ukraïny*, 246.

88. Ibid., 27.

89. Margaret Mead, *Soviet Attitudes Toward Authority: An Interdisciplinary Approach to Problems of Soviet Character* (New York: McGraw Hill, 1951), 92.

90. A. S. Makarenko, *Kniga dlia roditelei* (Moscow: Uchpedgiz, 1950), 358. Out of the four planned books, only the first was published in 1937 in *Krasnaia nov'*, nos. 7–10; full text of the book is available from http://jorigami.ru/PP_corner/Classics/Makarenko/Makarenko_A_Book_for_Parents/Makarenko_A_Book_for_Parents.html#_Toc196398223.

91. Plaggenborg, *Revoliutsiia i kul'tura*, 58.

92. "Ukrainskaia SSR," 328.

93. *Narodnoe obrazovanie v SSSR*, 75.

94. *Het' nepysemnist'*, no. 1 (1924): 1.

95. *Het' nepysemnist'*, no. 1 (1924): 4.

96. A. Butsenko, "Cherhovi zavdannia v spravi likvidatsiï nepys'mennosti," *Radians'ka osvita* 2, no. 9–10 (1924): 22.

97. "Ukrainskaia SSR," 329.

98. "Het' nepys'mennist'!" *Radians'ka osvita* 2, no. 9–10 (1924): 96–97.

99. Butsenko, "Cherhovi zavdannia," 21.

100. "Ukrainskaia SSR," 329.

101. Klitsakov, *Pedahohichni kadry Ukraïny*, 261.

102. Sukhomlyns'ka, *Narysy*, 161.

103. "Organizatsiia dvokhrichnykh politosvitnikh kursiv," *Radians'ka osvita* 2, no. 7 (1924): 104.

104. *Soiuz rabotnikov prosveshcheniia na Ukraine (Otchet Ukrburo TsK Rabotpros I-mu Vseukrainskomu s″ezdu, oktiabr′ 1923—oktiabr′ 1924 gg.)* (Kharkov: Ukrburo TsK Rabotpros, 1924), 119.

105. Sukhomlyns′ka, *Narysy*, 162.

106. Lemar, "Instytut chettsiv," *Radians′ka osvita* 2, no. 3–4 (1924): 58.

107. Kas′ianov, *Ukraïns′ka intelihentsiia 1920-kh – 1930-kh rokiv*, 74.

108. *TsDAHOU*, f. 1, op. 6, spr. 32, ark. 75.

109. G. Grin′ko, "Ocherk istorii i sistemy politprosveta," *Put′ prosveshcheniia*, no. 2 (1922): 26; quoted in Sukhomlyns′ka, *Narysy*, 162.

110. Kas′ianov, *Ukraïns′ka intelihentsiia 1920-kh – 1930-kh rokiv*, 75.

111. Koliastruk, *Intelihentsiia USRR u 1920-ti roky*, 226.

112. Hennadii Iefimenko, "Stvorennia SRSR," *Tsei den′ v istoriï*, July 5, 2018, https://www.jnsm.com.ua/h/0706U/.

113. James Mace's testimony, 26; quoted in *Holodomor*, eds. Luciuk and Grekul, 320.

114. *Desiatyi s″ezd RKP(b), Mart 1921 goda* (stenographic report) (Moscow, 1963), 202, 204; quoted in John Kolasky, *Education in Soviet Ukraine* (Toronto: Peter Martin Associates, 1968), 4. John Kolasky, a Canadian communist of Ukrainian extraction, lived and studied in Ukraine from 1963 to 1965.

115. Ibid., 210; quoted in Kolasky, *Education in Soviet Ukraine*, 4.

116. V. V. Masnenko and I. F. Sharov, "Vchytel′stvo ta stanovlennia radians′koï shkoly na Ukraïni v pershii polovyni 20-kh rokiv," *Ukraïns′kyi istorychnyi zhurnal*, no. 12 (1990): 102.

117. Masnenko and Sharov, "Vchytel′stvo," 103.

118. *Kul′turne budivnytstvo v Ukraïns′kii RSR: Vazhlyvishi rishennia komunistychnoï partiï i radians′koho uriadu, 1917–1959 rr.*, vol. I, 1917– June 1941 (Kiev: Ministerstvo kul′tury URSR, 1959), 229–32; quoted in Kolasky, *Education in Soviet Ukraine*, 13.

119. *Kul′turne budivnytsvo v Ukraïns′kii RSR*, vol. I, 239–41; quoted in Kolasky, *Education in Soviet Ukraine*, 13.

120. Pauly, *Breaking the Tongue*, 64–65.

121. *Kul′turne budivnytstvo v Ukraïns′kii RSR*, vol. I, 240; quoted in Kolasky, *Education in Soviet Ukraine*, 13.

122. According to the 1926 census, the main ethnic groups in Ukraine included 23.2 million Ukrainians, 2.6 million Russians, 1.5 million Jews, 476,000 Poles, 393,000 Germans, 257,000 Moldovans, and 104,000 Greeks among others (Bulgarians, Turks, Czechs, Armenians, Hungarians, Romanians, Serbs, and Swedes).

123. B. V. Chirko, "Nemetskaia natsional′naia gruppa v Ukraine v kontekste gosudarstvennoi etnopolitiki 20–30-kh gg. XX st.," in *Voprosy germanskoi istorii*, ed. S. I. Bobyleva (Dnepropetrovsk: "Porogi," 2007), 205.

124. *TsDAVOU*, f. 1, op. 4, spr. 606, ark. 61, 218.

125. Marochko and Hillig, *Represovani pedahohy Ukraïny*, 251.

126. Pauly, *Breaking the Tongue*, 5.

127. Terry Martin, *The Affirmative Action Empire: Nations and Nationalism in the Soviet Union, 1923–1939* (Ithaca: Cornell University Press, 2001); Yuri Slezkine,

"The USSR as a Communal Apartment, or How a Socialist State Promoted Ethnic Particularism," *Slavic Review* 53, no. 2 (1994): 414–52; Ronald Grigor Suny and Terry Martin, eds., *A State of Nations: Empire and Nation-Making in the Age of Lenin and Stalin* (New York: Oxford University Press, 2001).

128. See Elena Borisenok, *Fenomen sovetskoi ukrainizatsii, 1920–1930-e gody* (Moscow: "Evropa," 2006); Konstantin Drozdov, "Ukrainizatsia v Tsentral'nom Chernozem'ie RSFSR v 1923–1928 gg.: K voprosu ob osobennostiakh natsional'noi politiki bol'shevikov v gody NEPa," *The NEP Era*, no. 4 (2010): 43–59; Hryshko, "The Origins of Soviet Genocide," 56–57; Shkandrij and Bertelsen, "The Soviet Regime's National Operations in Ukraine," 420.

129. Hryshko, "The Origins of Soviet Genocide," 67.

130. Ibid., 68.

131. James H. Billington, *The Icon and the Axe: An Interpretive History of Russian Culture* (New York: Alfred A. Knopf, 1968), 532–40, 544–45.

132. Robert C. Tucker, "The Change of National Identity," in *Stalin as Revolutionary*, 137–43. An employee of the U.S. Embassy, Tucker lived in Moscow from 1945 to 1953 and had a Russian-speaking wife.

133. Conquest, *The Harvest of Sorrow*, 219.

134. Pauly, *Breaking the Tongue*, 4.

135. M. Iu. Vyhovs'kyi, *Nomenklatura systemy osvity v USRR 1920–1930-kh rokiv: sotsial'ne pokhodzhennia, personal'nyi sklad ta funksiï* (Kyïv: Heneza, 2006), 196; quoted in Pauly, *Breaking the Tongue*, 376.

136. Kolasky, *Education in Soviet Ukraine*, 16–17.

137. Ibid., 15.

138. Pauly, *Breaking the Tongue*, 68; see also Mykola Doroshko, *Nomenklatura: kerivna verkhivka radians'koï Ukraïny (1917–1938 rr.)* (Kyïv: Nika-Tsentr, 2012).

139. Chirko, "Nemetskaia natsional'naia gruppa v Ukraine," 206.

140. Colin Peter Neufeldt's presentation on "Hitler, Mennonites, and the Holodomor: Nazi Germany and Its Impact on Life of Mennonites in 1932–1933," at the Holodomor Research and Education Center's international scientific conference "Natsional'ni menshyny Radians'koï Ukraïny v epokhu Holodomoru: vtraty, travma, pam'iat'," December 15, 2020, http://history.org.ua/uk/post/45380.

141. See Colin Peter Neufeldt, "The Fate of Mennonites in Ukraine and the Crimea during Soviet Collectivization and the Famine (1930–1933)" (doctoral thesis, University of Alberta, 1999). This work challenges the applicability of the genocide concept to many of the regions populated by Mennonites in Ukraine.

142. On March 5, 1939, the Central Committee of the Communist Party (Bolsheviks) of Ukraine (TsK KP(b) U) adopted the decree "On the liquidation and reconstruction of the artificially created national minority regions and village councils in Ukraine." It did not touch the Russians in Ukraine; since 1936, propagandists referred to them as the "Great Russian people." See L. D. Iakubova, "National'ne administratyvno-terytorial'ne budivnytstvo v USRR/URSR, 1924–1940" in *Entsyklopediia istoriï Ukraïny*, ed. V. A. Smolii et al., vol. 7 (Kyïv: "Naukova dumka," 2010), http://www.history.org.ua/?termin=Natsionalni_rajony.

143. This is an abridged version of a dialogue, written by Ostap Vyshnia, under the title "(Popular) History of the Ukrainian Language" for a special issue on Ukrainization in a satirical biweekly magazine *Chervonyi perets'* (Red Pepper), no. 3 (February 1927), 3. Ostap Vyshnia was a pen name of Pavlo Hubenko, a satirist and humorist, who was arrested in the 1920s, released, then rearrested in 1933 and spent a decade in concentration camps in the Far North in Russia.

144. Drozdov, "Ukrainizatsiia v Tsentral'nom Chernozem'ie RSFSR," 44–45.

145. From 1.5 to 2 million Ukrainians lived in the Central Black Earth region of the Russian SFSR, but they had only thirteen schools where their children could learn their mother tongue. Approximately 1.1 million Ukrainians lived in the Voronezh region. In 1922, there were nine Ukrainian-language primary schools. To meet the demand for opening additional schools, authorities surveyed teachers to identify those willing to teach in Ukrainian. A further inspection revealed that local education departments were indifferent or ignorant of the directive to identify teachers willing to teach Ukrainians in schools in their mother tongue. About 600,000 Ukrainians lived in the Kursk region. There were only four schools to meet their needs, three government funded and one privately funded. See Drozdov, "Ukrainizatsiia v Tsentral'nom Chernozem'ie RSFSR," 50–52.

146. "Zadovolennia osvitnikh potreb ukraïntsiv RRFSR," *Radians'ka osvita* 2, no. 7 (1924): 104.

147. Klitsakov, *Pedahohichni kadry Ukraïny*, 111.

148. K. Kravchenko, "Dytyna Zhovtnia (Ukraïns'kyi Pedahohichnyi Tekhnikum na Kubanshchyni)," *Radians'ka osvita* 2, no. 9–10 (1924): 64.

149. "Zadovolennia osvitnikh potreb ukraïntsiv RRFSR," 104.

150. V. S. Lozyts'kyi, "Polityka ukraïnizatsiï v 20–30-kh rokakh: istoriia, problemy, uroky," *Ukraïns'kyi istorychnyi zhurnal*, no. 3 (1989): 47.

151. *Communist Takeover and Occupation of Ukraine*, 16.

152. Gantt, "A Medical Review," 19.

153. *TsDAHOU*, f. 1, op. 20, spr. 2255, ark. 1.

154. *TsDAHOU*, f. 1, op. 20, spr. 2255, ark. 1.

155. Jurij Borys, "Political Parties in the Ukraine," in *The Ukraine, 1917–1921: A Study in Revolution*, ed. Taras Hunczak (Cambridge: Harvard Ukrainian Research Institute, 1977), 148.

156. Case 67 (interviewer J. R.), *Harvard Project on the Soviet Social System Online*, Schedule B, vol. 7 (Slavic Division, Widener Library, Harvard University), 22; available at https://library.harvard.edu/sites/default/files/static/collections/hpsss/index.html.

157. *TsDAHOU*, f. 1, op. 20, spr. 2255, ark. 6, 8.

158. *TsDAHOU*, f. 1, op. 20, spr. 2255, ark. 6.

159. *TsDAHOU*, f. 1, op. 20, spr. 2255, ark. 7.

160. Hryhorii Hryn'ko reported that the ethnic composition of the KP(b)U in 1923 was 23 percent Ukrainian, 13 percent Jewish, and 57 percent Russian, whereas commissariats were 12 percent Ukrainian, 26 percent Jewish, and 47 percent Russian. See *Chetvertoe soveshchanie TsK RKP s otvetstvennymi rabotnikami natsional'nykh*

respublik i oblastei v Moskve 9–12 iunia 1923 g.: Stenograficheskii otchet (Moscow, 1923), 221; quoted in Iu. I. Shapoval, "Stalinizm i Ukraïna," *Ukraïns'kyi istorychnyi zhurnal*, no. 4 (1991): 48.

161. *TsDAHOU*, f. 1, op. 20, spr. 2255, ark. 12.
162. *TsDAHOU*, f. 1, op. 20, spr. 2255, ark. 18–19.
163. *TsDAHOU*, f. 1, op. 20, spr. 2255, ark. 20–26.
164. Joseph Stalin, "Tov. Kaganovychu ta inshym chlenam PB TsK KP(b)U," in *Mykola Khvyl'ovyi: Tvory v 5 tomakh*, ed. Hryhorii Kostiuk (New York: "Smoloskyp," 1986), 485–89.
165. For a detailed biography, see O. Han, *Trahediia Mykoly Khvyl'ovoho* (Prague: Vyd-vo "Prometei," 1947), 26.
166. Shapoval, "Stalinizm i Ukraïna," 50.
167. *X z'izd KP(b)U, 20–29 lystopada 1927 r.: Sten. zvit*, 522; quoted in Shapoval, "Stalinizm i Ukraïna," 50.
168. Kolasky, *Education in Soviet Ukraine*, 14.
169. Iurii Lavrinenko, *Rozstriliane vidrodzhennia: Antolohiia, 1917–1933* (Kyïv: Smoloskyp, 2004).
170. James Mace's testimony, 27–29; quoted in *Holodomor*, eds. Luciuk and Grekul, 319.
171. Chirko, "Nemetskaia natsional'naia gruppa v Ukraine," 207.
172. "Case History SW3: Antin Lak, b. 1910, Poltava region," *Oral History Project*, vol. 2, 731.
173. *Ukraïns'kyi pravopys (Proiekt)* (Kharkiv: Derzhavne Vyd-vo Ukraïny, 1926).
174. The chair of the commission was People's Commissar for Education O. Shums'kyi and members of the commission included Comrades P. Solodub, M. Iavors'kyi, A. Kryms'kyi, O. Syniavs'kyi, S. Pylypenko, O. Kurylova (Kurilo), E. Tymchenko, G. Holoskevych, M. Johansen, E. Kasianenko, A. Richyts'kyi, N. Kaliuzhnyi, M. Ialovyi, O. Popov, M. Gruns'kyi, V. Hantsov, M. Sulima, V. Butvin, V. Koriak, M. Khvyl'ovyi, S. Iefremov, T. Sekunda, S. Kyrychenko, I. Sokolians'kyi, and O. Skrypnyk.
175. Serhii Vakulenko, "1933 in History of Ukrainian Language: Current Norm and Spelling Practice (an Example of Editorial Policy of Newspaper *Komunist*)," paper presented at the American Association for Slavic Studies Conference in Philadelphia, PA on November 22, 2008; see Ukrainian version "1933-ii rik v istoriï ukraïns'koï movy: chynna norma ta pravopysna praktyka (na prykladi redaktsiinoï polityky hazety "Komunist"), *Historians*, December 3, 2012, http://www.historians.in.ua/index.php/en/ukrayinska-mova/488-cerhiy-vakulenko-1933-ii-rik-v-istorii-ukrainskoi-movy-chynna-norma-ta-pravopysna-praktyka-na-prykladi-redaktsiinoi-polityky-hazety-komunist.
176. See Pauly, *Breaking the Tongue*, 338, 354.
177. The Ukrainian letter г (hard g) and the phonetic combinations of the palatalized letter l with a soft sign or vowel ль, льо, ля for transliteration of foreign words were eliminated, and Russian etymological forms were reintroduced. The letter г was banned in Soviet Ukraine from 1933 to 1990.
178. *Visti*, June 22, 1933; quoted in Conquest, *The Harvest of Sorrow*, 268.

179. Tetiana Kardynalovs'ka, *Nevidstupne mynule* (Kyïv: Vyd-vo M. P. Kots', 1992).

180. Symon Petliura, "'Rosiis'ka menshist'' na Ukraïni (z pryvodu dyskusiï na ostannii sesiï VTsIK-a)," *Tryzub* 2, no. 30, May 9, 1926; reprinted in *Symon Petliura*, 378–83, esp. 383. Petliura started publishing the *Tryzub* (Trident), named after the heraldic coat of arms of the Ukrainian National Republic, when he settled in Paris in 1924.

181. Symon Petliura, "Lovtsi dush," *Tryzub* 2, no. 26–27, April 18, 1926; reprinted in *Symon Petliura*, 364–74.

182. Kołakowski has argued that Trotsky's often-quoted prophecy of 1903 was soon forgotten by the prophet himself. See Kołakowski, "The Marxist Roots of Stalinism," 163.

Chapter 3

Trial

Bolsheviks started social engineering with repressions and deportations of intelligentsia through GPU special operations in the 1920s, and persecutions and eventual destruction of nationally conscious intelligentsia in the 1930s. According to Raphael Lemkin, teachers as members of intelligentsia were victims of the first prong of attack against the Ukrainian national group. As Lemkin argued, the "brain" of the nation was being removed first to de-intellectualize and demoralize the nation.[1] In this aspect, experiences of teachers in Ukraine paralleled the fate of teachers in Nazi Germany and Nazi-occupied countries of Europe,[2] as well as Armenian teachers[3] in the Ottoman Empire. Intelligentsia were unreliable social partners for Bolsheviks and had to be kept under surveillance, with gradual transitioning from preventive control to annihilation.[4] When it became clear that intellectuals could not be easily silenced, Soviet leaders forced dissenters into desolate places devoid of intelligentsia throughout a vast wintry mineral-rich Soviet terrain. Marx's law of survival of the most progressive class dictated that those who stood in the way of Bolsheviks were "enemies" of history and unfit to live. After a temporary retreat under the cover of the New Economic Policy (NEP), the government quietly grouped "enemies" by category (intellectuals, priests, merchants, those in political disfavor or under suspicion) and deprived them of civil rights (no right to vote, no right to pursue higher education, no right to buy in government shops). Total control of the means of production meant that farmers had to turn over their land and farm animals to collective farms voluntarily or be deported. Opposition to compulsory collectivization aroused a wave of protests in early 1930 that swept Soviet power out of hundreds of villages. Responsibility shifted to the Ukrainian national intelligentsia for organizing these protests. Instigated by the Communist Party, the GPU arrested thousands of intellectuals, teachers, writers, and artists and put them on trial for "plotting" to overthrow the Soviet regime. Terror intensified. Laws were drafted so that, in the words of Hannah Arendt, "before its court, all concerned are subjectively innocent: the murdered because they did nothing against the system, and the murderers because they do not really murder but execute a death sentence pronounced by some higher tribunal."[5]

DEPORTATIONS

Immediately after the introduction of the NEP, which allowed liberty in economic and civic life, in a telegram to TsK KP(b)U, Viacheslav Molotov and the GPU's first chief, Felix Dzerzhinsky, emphasized the need to boost vigilance. The authors of the telegram proposed setting up a "militant apparatus for the struggle against counterrevolution," which would enlist "staunch party comrades with experience in this struggle."[6] In May 1921, on direct orders from the TsK KP(b)U, the GPU fabricated one of the first show trials of the Ukrainian Party of Socialist-Revolutionaries.[7] A correspondent for the newspaper *Kommunist* on May 5, 1921, commented that "after the trial the Ukrainian intelligentsia should feel like after a cold, not very pleasant, but refreshing bath."[8] The sword of Damocles was suspended over their heads.

Political atmosphere in institutes of higher education in Soviet Ukraine, above all the teaching of social sciences, began to be closely monitored by the Communist Party. The focus of the party's attention was professors and lecturers who did not wish to change methods of teaching demanded by Bolshevik rulers. To overcome resistance from the "old" professoriate, Bolsheviks in Ukraine organized a network of research departments in Kharkiv, Kyïv, Odesa, and Katerynoslav[9] to train "red" professors. In 1922, they allocated funds to recruit a thousand graduate students. Deputy Commissar of Education Ian Riappo wrote to the TsK KP(b)U, "It is completely understandable that these candidates should be vetted as thoroughly as possible by Ukrholovprofos (Ukrainian Directorate of Professional Education) and its regional branches; furthermore, it is crucial to mobilize as many Communists as possible to research departments."[10]

Bolsheviks were little disposed to tolerate independence of the "old" professoriate. However, the Soviet government could not crush old cadres immediately because preparing "red" professors would take years. In order to make professors and lecturers compliant, the government installed a position of political commissar in all institutes of higher education. Such innovation was unwelcome. Some professors and lecturers resigned; others protested. In February and March 1922, lecturers in Kyïv went on strike in protest against the reduction in the number of teacher training institutions. The unrest also spread to Kharkiv, Kam'ianets'-Podil's'kyi, and Odesa.[11] In response, Lenin recommended to "lay off 20–40 professors . . . hit hard."[12] Rubach, director of the Katerynoslav regional Communist Party committee's propaganda and agitation department, reported to his leadership that "during lectures on innocent apolitical topics lecturers reveal their political face, with clear traces of Menshovism, Socialist Revolutionarism, or Kadetism," referring to non-communist parties of Mensheviks, SRs, and Constitutional Democrats. The next step was to liquidate all party organizations in institutes of higher education, except communist; otherwise, students would be "falling under petty bourgeois influence of the old professorial staff."[13] On March 17, 1922, the Politburo of the TsK KP(b)U ordered propaganda and agitation departments[14] to circulate a directive banning all open debates because they could provide the opposition with an opportunity to freely challenge the Soviet government.

The Politburo instructed the Commissariat of Education and the GPU to closely monitor the conduct of the professorate. On June 23, 1922, following a speech "On Political Statements of Professorate" by Soviet Ukraine's Commissar of Education Hryhorii Hryn'ko, the Politburo of the TsK KP(b)U passed the following resolution whose text read in part:

> To propose that the People's Commissariat of Education implement a planned deportation of those professors who are introducing the greatest upheaval in academic life. To propose to regional party committees to ensure that local economic organs in no way impede this transfer, which should be implemented with maximum steadfastness. To propose to the People's Commissariat of Education and the State Political Directorate [GPU] to apply deportation outside the borders of the federation, as one of the repressive measures against activist elements of the professorate. To propose to the People's Commissariat of Education and the State Political Directorate to act by mutual agreement . . . by informing the Central Committee in advance.[15]

This resolution was sent as a secret circular to all regional party committees for implementation.

Responsibility for the preparation and implementation of the plan to deport Ukrainian intelligentsia was placed on the GPU. In 1921, the GPU completed a major counterinsurgency operation to suppress the last vestiges of struggle for liberation in Ukraine and disarmed the countryside. From 1919 to 1921, the GPU liquidated 6,000 "bandit" formations and arrested 40,000 insurgents in Ukraine. The Bolshevik secret police confiscated 43 cannons, 1,812 shotguns, 31,788 rifles, 2,312 sabers, and 3,902 revolvers.[16]

Red Terror[17] swept throughout Soviet Ukraine, dissuading any volunteers or sympathizers still willing to join ranks of insurgents. A witness recalled how special detachments of the GPU took fifty hostages in a village, forced them to draw at random "life" or "death" slips, and pitted them against one another:

the fortunate one who drew "life" had to kill the unfortunate other who drew "death."[18] In villages suspected of harboring rebels, hostage taking[19] and summary executions of civilians,[20] signed into law in 1921, were effective methods to suppress opposition to the Soviet regime. Alongside the system of hostage taking (*zaruchnytstvo*), occupying Bolshevik authorities legalized summary executions of civilians (*vidpovidachi*) selected at random and blamed for harboring or aiding "bandits." The decree issued on May 30, 1921, signed by Volodymyr Zatons′kyi, then head of the council on combating bandit activities in the Kyïv military district, provided instructions on how two plenipotentiaries have to select one civilian from every twentieth household in a village or at least one civilian from every independent farmstead to be executed as responsible for carrying out acts of "banditry"; the number of civilians executed doubled if a Soviet government official was murdered. The cynicism of Bolshevik extrajudicial killings was based on forcing civilians to carry out executions of their neighbors. Even the staunchest supporters of Ukrainian liberation movement were left without moral strength and firearms to continue their fight.

In 1922, Soviet security police was reorganized and its functions expanded. New legislation gave the GPU authority to crush "counterrevolutionary actions" and adopt immediate measures aimed at exposing them in a timely fashion; to combat espionage; to guard railway and sea routes; to guard borders, combat contraband, and illegal border crossing; and to carry out special tasks assigned by the Presidium of the VTsIK and the Council of People's Commissars to safeguard the revolutionary order. The GPU as well as plenipotentiary representatives of the Communist Party at the district level were granted rights to conduct searches and arrests. Arrests of suspects could be conducted without a special resolution from the GPU or special orders issued by political departments, but it was mandatory to obtain a sanction from the GPU within forty-eight hours. Within two months of the day of arrest, the GPU was obligated to release detainees or request the Presidium of the VTsIK to prolong the term of arrest, if circumstances so demanded. The GPU did not have a right to hand down sentences. All cases, both political and civilian, were transferred to courts.[21]

In the 1920s, when financial crisis lowered morale of the Soviet security police rank-and-file, many were deserting the profession. Economy was in ruins; industrial enterprises could not transfer money to the state treasury because of the lack of currency in circulation. By April 1922, the number of security police cadres had dropped from 34,000 to 18,000. On July 4, 1922, Felix Dzerzhinsky requested the TsK RKP(b) to ensure that GPU personnel receive appropriate financial remuneration and food. Scholars argue that it was a large-scale deportation of Ukrainian intelligentsia that boosted the sagging reputation and revenues of the GPU.[22] In this case, interests of the GPU coincided with those of the Communist Party.

Within one month, by August 3, 1922, the GPU in Soviet Ukraine had compiled a list of candidates for deportation. Among seventy-seven members of intelligentsia on the list were Serhii Iefremov and Volodymyr Chekhivs′kyi, who served in the government of the Ukrainian National Republic in the 1920s, and a large number of professors and lecturers from institutes of higher education in Kyïv, Kharkiv, Katerynoslav, and other cities of Soviet Ukraine.[23] The order came from the Central Committee at the Twelfth Conference of the Russian Communist Party (Bolsheviks), held on August 4–7, 1922. Grigorii Zinoviev gave a speech about anti-Soviet parties arguing that, under the conditions of the NEP, the Communist Party cannot make political compromises as it did in the economic sphere. Zinoviev argued that repressions were "dictated by revolutionary advisability, with respect to crushing those groups seeking to capture the old positions that were seized from them by the proletariat."[24] The speaker pointed to a targeted group without defining it in ethnic terms.

Legal basis for deportations was established three days after the conference, when the VTsIK issued a decree on August 10, 1922, "On Administrative Exile."[25] This legislative act led to the creation of a special commission to deport "counterrevolutionaries" abroad[26] or to distant locales of the Russian SFSR. It was believed that deportation of the intelligentsia from Soviet Ukraine abroad would consolidate anti-Soviet sentiments among the Ukrainian émigré community in the West; thus, the Russian Far North and Siberia became their destinations. In the second half of August 1922, mass arrests of candidates for deportation began. Soviet Ukrainian leaders had to report to Moscow about the progress of the operation in the republic. For this purpose, a secret commission in charge of political censorship was created within the Commissariat of Education to fight petty bourgeois ideology, first headed by Stanislav Kosior, later by Volodymyr Zatons′kyi.[27]

Scholars argue that the real reason behind deportations of intelligentsia was Bolsheviks' fear of losing control over society after the introduction of a liberal economic policy which, from their perspective, would inevitably lead to political demands for freedom of speech and thought and eventually an overthrow of the government.[28] Deportations of Ukrainian intelligentsia along with suppression of the national liberation struggle, requisitions of church property and gold, purges of Ukrainian Autocephalous Orthodox clergy, and the trial of Socialist-Revolutionaries—all of these were measures to prevent and suppress any opposition to the Bolshevik regime. Meanwhile, the "Moscow Gold," a shorthand for looted church jewelry, was used to subsidize revolution and Communist International and conduct intelligence activities abroad.[29]

Dzerzhinsky's writings provide further insight into the rationale for targeting intelligentsia. His secret directive No. 333/G, signed on March 16, 1923, stated that the Soviet government was hampered by its 99.9 percent reliance on "old" intelligentsia's expertise in most of its administrative functions. He proposed practical measures to create a "truly SOVIET" administrative apparatus by purging "old specialists" and exiling them to "colonize the [Russian] North and sparsely populated and devoid of intelligentsia places (Pechora, Arkhangel'sk, Turukhanka)."[30] This measure was supposed to kill two birds with one stone: to solve the problem by purging undesirable cadres as well as to intimidate and force the rest of intelligentsia to work diligently for the regime.

Although an ambiguous policy of Ukrainization[31] was proclaimed in 1923, the rhetoric behind it masked the real goal of removing those who believed in cultural distinctiveness and national statehood, an approach that Iurii Shapoval called "double book-keeping."[32] In November 1923, a secret circular from Moscow instructed its local GPU offices to establish total control over professors, lecturers, and students, their activities in associations, meetings, and publications, by installing a network of informers to report about public sentiments, private comments, and anti-Soviet clandestine activities in Ukraine.[33] Observers called this policy a "mousetrap"[34] because a good number of Ukrainians who had immigrated abroad came back to Ukraine in 1925 at the invitation of the Soviet government. Moscow dispatched "Ukrainian diplomats" Iurii Kotsiubyns'kyi and Oleksandr Shums'kyi as representatives of Soviet Ukraine to the largest diaspora centers in Vienna and Warsaw, respectively, to lure Ukrainian émigré scholars and writers, as well as to extradite Symon Petliura and his generals under an "amnesty," and eventually to put an end to Ukrainian political activities outside the Soviet borders.[35] Some contemporary scholars disagree with the "mousetrap" argument.[36] They agree, though, that most active members of the nationally conscious intelligentsia lured back to Ukraine later disappeared, were exiled, or executed.

CATEGORIES FOR LIQUIDATION

Classification into categories for liquidation started less than a year after the introduction of the Soviet *korenizatsiia* policy when in February 1924, in preparation for a crackdown on the Ukrainian intelligentsia, in a secret circular, the OGPU provided instructions for keeping records on "suspected counterrevolutionaries" in Ukraine in three broad categories[37]:

Political Parties and Organizations

1) All former members of prerevolutionary bourgeois political parties.
2) All former members of monarchical unions and organizations (Black Hundreds).

3) All former members of the Union of Independent Grain Growers (at the time of the Central Rada in the Ukraine).
4) All former members of the gentry and titled persons of the old aristocracy.
5) All former members of the youth organization (Boy Scouts and others).
6) All nationalists of all shades of opinion.

Officials and Employees in the Active Service of Tsarism

1) Officials of the former Ministry of Internal Affairs: all officials of the *Okhranka* [secret political police], police and gendarmerie, secret agents of the *Okhranka* and police. All members of the frontier corps of gendarmerie.
2) Officials of the former Ministry of Justice: members of the district and provincial courts, jurymen, prosecutors of all ranks, justices of the peace and examining magistrates, court executors, and heads of county courts.
3) All commissioned and non-commissioned officers, without exception, of the former tsarist army and fleet.

Secret Enemies of the Soviet Regime

1) All former commissioned officers, non-commissioned officers, and enlisted men of the White movements and armies, the Ukrainian Petliurist formations, and various rebel units and bands who actively resisted Soviet rule. People amnestied by the Soviet authorities are not excluded.
2) All those employed in a civil capacity in the departments and local offices of White governments, the armies of the Ukrainian Central Rada, and the Hetman's state police.
3) All servants of religious bodies: bishops, Orthodox and Catholic priests, rabbis, deacons, churchwardens, choirmasters, and monks.
4) All former merchants, shopkeepers, and "Nepmen."
5) All former landowners, big land-leasers, well-to-do peasants (who formerly employed hired labor), big craftsmen and proprietors of industrial establishments.
6) All persons having someone among their near relatives who at the present time is in an illegal position or is conducting armed resistance against the Soviet regime in the ranks of anti-Soviet bands.
7) All foreigners, irrespective of nationality.
8) All those with relatives or acquaintances abroad.
9) All members of religious sects and communities (Baptists in particular).
10) All scholars and specialists of the old school, particularly those whose political orientation is undeclared up to this day.
11) All persons previously convicted or suspected of contraband and espionage.

As is evident from these lists, a substantial portion of the population was marked for annihilation. On September 17–25, 1924, the OGPU launched a series of operations, arrested and imprisoned 19,670 opponents of the regime in Soviet Ukraine.[38] A secret OGPU instruction of October 1924 drew attention to the growing influence of the Ukrainian Autocephalous Orthodox Church. The local OGPU officers were instructed to increase the number of secret informers among the faithful and to recruit priests themselves for secret service work in the OGPU.[39]

In his letter to the TsK RKP(b) on the punitive policy of the Soviet state, Dzerzhinsky outlined basic principles of the policy. He particularly stressed, "Repression cannot be merciful toward the accused and cannot be expensive either: they have to cover expenses for their upkeep with their own labor. They have to be exiled into desolate places with no roads, such as Pechora, Obdorsk."[40] These places in the Russian wilderness were to be settled by exiled Ukrainian intelligentsia and expropriated Ukrainian farmers, together with their families in the years to come. By some estimates, by the end of 1932, nearly 2.4 million Ukrainians were exiled to distant places in the Russian Far North and Siberia,[41] but official statistics would not be compiled until 1934, when the VChK–OGPU reappeared in its third incarnation as the NKVD.

Perceived "passivity" of the OGPU during the NEP was temporary. As historian Valentyn Moroz noted, economically prosperous due to the NEP and culturally awakened due to the policy of Ukrainization, the republic presented a threat of political separation from Russia, which would mean a collapse of the communist imperial system.[42] As a secret OGPU circular of June 1925 instructed, the secret police "should therefore not lose a good opportunity to unmask our enemies, in order to deal them a crushing blow when the time comes."[43]

Leading intellectuals, like Hrushevs'kyi, Rudnyts'kyi, Krushel'nyts'kyi, were lured into returning by Bolshevik promises of respectable positions in Soviet Ukraine, whereas TsK KPU(b)U and the OGPU held secret meetings on how to deal with intelligentsia. In May 1925, a closed meeting of the Politburo of TsK KP(b)U heard a report from the OGPU and adopted a resolution to create a commission to examine tactics of dealing with the Ukrainian intelligentsia, especially its Academy of Sciences and Hrushevs'kyi. The OGPU put professor Hrushevs'kyi under surveillance, while focusing on his influential colleague, academician Iefremov, in order to subvert Ukrainian intellectual elites.[44]

In March 1926, a pamphlet "On Ukrainian Society" was circulated among the GPU personnel. In May 1926, Petliura was assassinated in Paris by Samuil (Sholem) Schwartzbard. In August 1926, Metropolitan Vasyl' Lypkivs'kyi, who headed the Ukrainian Autocephalous Orthodox Church, and had been known as "secret propagator of Ukrainian separatism," was arrested.[45] In September 1926, another GPU circular "On Ukrainian Separatism" spelled out motives, goals, forms, and methods of fighting against a "tendency to separate Ukraine from Russia."[46] In October, five months after Petliura's murder, a propaganda film was released under an acronym *PKP*, decoded as "Piłsudski Bought Petliura," aiming to denounce the Ukrainian national leader as a traitor and Piłsudski's agent.[47]

Assassination of Petliura was one of the tactics used by Bolsheviks to deal with leading political opponents of the regime during the 1920s. It was a high-profile case since Petliura, leader of the Ukrainian national liberation movement, enjoyed considerable popularity in Ukraine and among émigré communities in the West. Another tactic was to stage a trial of Schwartzbard, Petliura's assassin, in Paris. Schwartzbard was viewed as an avenger by some and as a Bolshevik agent by others. The trial was meant to mar the reputation of the respected Ukrainian leader in the eyes of the international community and to stir anti-Ukrainian sentiments among the Jewish diaspora.[48] Lawyers presented several hundred documents as evidence that Petliura's government, in circumstances of complete anarchy, discouraged and actively prosecuted those of his troops who succumbed to Bolshevik provocations to "Beat the Jews! Save Russia!" and engaged in pogroms against vulnerable Jewish neighbors. These documents did not convince the jurors of his innocence.[49] Significantly, some Jewish organizations did support the Ukrainian liberation movement, and the Directory did recruit Jewish politicians to work in the government of the short-lived Ukrainian National Republic in accordance with its policy of empowering national minorities in Ukraine.[50] Taras Hunczak[51] of Rutgers University reviewed published sources, written by Ukrainian and Jewish contemporaries, and concluded, "the frequently repeated charge that Petliura was antisemitic is absurd" and "to convict Petliura for the tragedy that befell Ukrainian Jewry is to condemn an innocent man and to distort the record of Ukrainian–Jewish relations."[52] The OGPU disinformation planted during the trial permanently besmirched Petliura's reputation and thwarted the Ukrainian–Jewish cooperation. In Ukrainian folk memory, Petliura's name became synonymous with the fight for freedom from foreign oppression.[53]

Petliura was a marked man. He was sentenced to death during the trial of Socialist-Revolutionaries in 1921. The capital punishment was delayed because Petliura escaped arrest and became a fugitive. His political activities in Paris presented an ideological threat to Moscow. Piłsudski's rise to power in 1926 sealed Petliura's fate. Stalin would not allow a renewed Polish-Ukrainian campaign against Moscow.[54] The trial was skillfully managed by

Schwartzbard's attorney Henri Torrès, a communist. Via their embassy in Paris, Bolsheviks supplied necessary documents and witnesses to steer the process toward the desired outcome. Archival evidence substantiates the revelation that the trial in Paris was orchestrated by the OGPU in Moscow.[55]

THE SVU TRIAL

The Bolshevik regime used an arsenal of tools to "reeducate" Ukrainian intelligentsia: arrests, imprisonment, torture, show trials, censure, and "self-criticism."[56] A combination of overt public pressure via propaganda campaigns in the mass media and covert psychological pressure aimed at remolding or outright destroying the mentality of Ukrainian intellectual elites. Once categories for liquidation were established, the frequency of publications about foiled conspiracies against the Bolshevik regime increased. From 1927 to 1929, old intelligentsia were labeled "saboteurs," "anti-Soviet," and "socially alien elements." The GPU developed a network of informers in all Ukrainian institutions of higher education: 732 were recruited in 1927, and their numbers doubled to 1,409 a year later, in 1928.[57] Iurii Sambros recorded in his diary that some of his colleagues at the teacher training institute lost their morality and honesty, and denounced innocent friends or acquaintances in order to survive the next call into the office by a GPU operative.[58]

At the end of 1928, the first explicit Russian interference in the cultural life of Soviet Ukraine began with an attack by secretary of the All-Union Society of Marxist Historians Pavel Gorin on Marxist historian Matvii Iavors′kyi, representative of the regime's historiography in Soviet Ukraine. Mykola Skrypnyk publicly criticized Iavors′kyi's book. In an article, published in *Pravda* on February 10, 1929, Iavors′kyi was accused of treating the history of Ukraine separately from general historical dynamics.[59] The author, who headed the historical section of the Ukrainian Institute of Marxism-Leninism, was forced to "correct mistakes." However, historian's "self-criticism" was insufficient. Iavors′kyi was expelled from the KP(b)U in 1930, arrested in March 1931 for alleged membership in a fabricated national military organization, and later executed in a labor camp during the Great Terror.

In 1929–1930, parallel to the campaign to suppress rebellions in the countryside, repressions touched all educational institutions. Periodicals manipulated public opinion, planting seeds in the minds of the people that physical annihilation of ideological opponents was justified, thus further intensifying terror. Newspaper headlines, like "Class Enemies in Soviet Schools" or "Enemies Sneaked into Our School," became ubiquitous. Teachers were profiled for political-ideological loyalty. In Khortytsia, a German Mennonite farmers' colony in southern Ukraine, every teacher was given a characteristic as either "a Mennonite," "a teacher of old school," "not a Soviet teacher," or "a loyal Soviet teacher."[60] Disloyal teachers could lose their jobs; and during famine, to lose a job as a teacher or a principal meant to lose shelter and a possibility of finding a job elsewhere. Ultimately, it meant death by starvation.

In 1929, to discredit pro-Ukrainian intelligentsia and garner support for his "revolution from above," Stalin authorized repressions against Ukrainian educational leaders and teachers alleged to be members of a nationalist organization. It became necessary to discredit the Ukrainian "bourgeois" intelligentsia in the eyes of workers, the backbone of the Soviet regime, because this intelligentsia had ties to the countryside, the wellspring of Ukrainian national liberation struggle from 1917 to 1921.[61] In April 1929, the GPU allegedly discovered several cells of an underground organization, the Union for the Liberation of Ukraine (*Spilka vyzvolennia Ukraïny* or SVU).[62] That same year, the Communist Party launched public attacks against historians Mykhailo Hrushevs'kyi and Serhii Iefremov. The press accused both academicians, along with many teachers and their students, of "bourgeois nationalism." In May, Borys Matushevs'kyi,[63] Mykola Pavlushkov,[64] and his sister, as well as several of their friends, all members of the Union of Ukrainian Youth (*Spilka ukraïns'koï molodi* or SUM), were arrested.[65] Among major allegations, the GPU incriminated leaders of the SUM with organizing an "illegal" requiem service in memory of Symon Petliura at St. Sophia Cathedral in 1927, during which 100 leaflets were distributed among attendees.[66] Pavlushkov's uncle, academician Iefremov, recorded in his diary that "infanticide" had already started as arrests and searches swept through major cities.[67]

The SVU show trial was conducted in Kharkiv, then the political capital of Soviet Ukraine. In his report, dated December 1, 1929, the head of the GPU of the Ukrainian SSR, Vsevolod Balyts'kyi, known as "Ukraine's guillotine" among the Ukrainian communists,[68] wrote that the "operation to apprehend SVU collaborators" was carried out in twenty-eight regions, and more than 700 people were arrested.[69] Eventually, the GPU arrested, deported, or executed more than 30,000 people—intellectuals, artists, writers, scientists, and teachers—and publicly tried forty-five of them at the Kharkiv Opera House in spring of 1930 (see Figure 3.1).[70]

The GPU scrupulously selected defendants. Kost' Turkalo, an engineer and associate member of the All-Ukrainian Academy of Sciences, published a list of convicted persons in the SVU trial in the 1950s,[71] long before the Sectoral State Archive of the Security Service of Ukraine allowed scholars access to their case files.[72] Among forty-five defendants, more than half were teachers of Ukrainian language and history, as well as professors of Institutes of People's Education (*Instytut narodnoï osvity* or INO) and their students:

Figure 3.1 An overhead view of the courtroom in the Kharkiv Opera House during the trial of the Union for the Liberation of Ukraine (SVU), 1930. The accused are seated behind the bar to the right of the OGPU guard. *Source*: From TsDKFFAU, od. obl. 2-25997.

Serhii Iefremov, 53, son of a priest, former leader of the Ukrainian Party of Socialists Federalists, full member of the All-Ukrainian Academy of Sciences

Volodymyr Durdukivs'kyi, 55, son of a priest, former member of the Ukrainian Party of Socialists Federalists, principal of the 1st Kyïv Labor School

Oleksandr Hrebenets'kyi, 55, son of a priest, teacher at the 1st Kyïv Labor School

Nina Tokarivs'ka, 41, daughter of a priest, teacher at the 1st Kyïv Labor School, former member of the Ukrainian Social Democratic Party

Iurii Trezvyns'kyi, 43, son of a priest, teacher at the 1st Kyïv Labor School

Andrii Zales'kyi, 44, son of a priest, teacher at the 1st Kyïv Labor School

Iosyp Hermaize, 37, professor at the Kyïv Institute of People's Education (KINO), former member of the Ukrainian Social Democratic Party

Vsevolod Hantsov, 37, professor of philology at the KINO, former member of the Ukrainian Party of Socialists Federalists

Hryhorii Ivanytsia, 37, professor of philology at the KINO, former member of the Ukrainian Social Democratic Party, associate of the All-Ukrainian Academy of Sciences

Vasyl' Doha, 43, of peasant descent, professor of the KINO, former member of the Ukrainian Social Democratic Party, associate of the All-Ukrainian Academy of Sciences

Hryhorii Kholodnyi, 43, son of a high school principal, associate of the All-Ukrainian Academy of Sciences, lecturer at the KINO, director of the Institute of the Ukrainian Language

Borys Matushevs'kyi, 22, student of the KINO

Mykola Pavlushkov, 25, son of a priest, student of the KINO

Mykhailo Slabchenko, 47, graduate of the Military Law Academy, member of the All-Ukrainian Academy of Sciences, former member of the Ukrainian Social Democratic Workers' Party, professor of the Odesa INO

Taras Slabchenko, 25, lecturer at the Odesa Workers' University, secretary of the Odesa Scientific Association of the All-Ukrainian Academy of Sciences (son of Mykhailo Slabchenko)

Kyrylo Panchenko-Chalenko, 42, lecturer at the Industrial Technical Secondary School in Odesa

Kostiantyn Shylo, 50, son of a civil servant, head of the editorial department of the Kyïv branch of the State Publishing House, associate of the All-Ukrainian Academy of Sciences, former member of the Ukrainian Social Democratic Workers' Party, former employee of the Department of Education during the Directory (1919)

Petro Iefremov, 46, son of a priest, professor of the Dnipropetrovs'k INO (brother of Serhii Iefremov, vice-president of the All-Ukrainian Academy of Sciences)

Liubov Bidnova, 47, daughter of an officer, teacher at the 20th Dnipropetrovs'k Labor School

Mykola Bilyi, 32, son of a civil servant, teacher in Dnipropetrovs'k

Mykola Lahuta, 42, former member of the Ukrainian Social Democratic Workers' Party, lecturer at the Mykolaïv INO

Volodymyr Shchepotiev, 49, professor of the Poltava INO

Iosyp Karpovych, 43, son of a presbyter, former member of the Ukrainian Party of Socialists Federalists, teacher at the M. M. Kotsiubyns'kyi School in Chernihiv

Among the defendants were seven teachers, one school principal, two lecturers of technical secondary schools, six professors of INO, and two of their students; among the accused were two women (see Figure 3.2). Most teachers were sons and daughters of the Ukrainian Autocephalous Orthodox Church clergy, who were the educated elite, marked for annihilation. One of the most prominent was Volodymyr Chekhivs'kyi, who had given up politics for theology.[73] A third of defendants were from Kyïv; the rest from Poltava, Odesa, Dnipropetrovs'k, Mykolaïv, and Chernihiv "branches" of a fabricated organization. Only five witnesses were called to testify at the trial. Although the defendants' guilt was never established, the court handed down sentences of three-to-ten years' imprisonment.[74] Most of them were executed during the

Figure 3.2 Defendants teacher Nina Tokarivs'ka (first row), writer Liudmyla Cherniakhivs'ka (second row), the former prime minister of the Ukrainian National Republic and leader of the Ukrainian Autocephalous Orthodox Church Prof. V. M. Chekhivs'kyi, and student Borys Matushevs'kyi, during the SVU show trial, 1930.
Source: From TsDKFFAU, od. obl. 2-25995.

Great Terror or died in labor camps.[75] One defendant, Borys Matushevs'kyi,[76] a student, recalled hearing from his interrogator: "We have to put the Ukrainian intelligentsia on its knees, this is our task—and it will be carried out; those whom we do not [put on their knees] we will shoot!"[77]

Methods of the GPU were brutal.[78] Viktor Petrov recalled:

> Every phrase, every move, gesture, and thought is registered. A person is anatomized. A person's consciousness is anatomized. The anatomized consciousness has become the greatest achievement of Bolshevik justice. . . . It is a frightening system of refined sadism.

After such anatomization, a person during interrogations "maniacally repeated everything that was demanded by the investigator."[79] In a letter to the GPU, dated November 14, 1929, Valentin Otamanovs'kyi wrote that he could lose his mind, succumb to psychological torture, and thus sign any testimony.[80] In his autobiography *Moie kaiattia* (My Confession), Otamanovs'kyi vividly pictured the GPU method of destroying personality and intellect as crucifixion, gruesome, and humiliating.[81]

When Mykola Pavlushkov (pictured in Figure 3.3), a student at the Kyïv INO, was arrested, his uncle Serhii Iefremov noted in his diary, "The Ukrainization of the Narym[82] territory has begun."[83] Western Siberia was the region for resettlement of the second wave of exiled Ukrainian farmers.[84] Pavlushkov's interrogation file contains 260 typed pages. This is a fictitious

Figure 3.3 Defendant Mykola Pavlushkov, student of the Kyïv Institute of People's Education, talks with defense counsel Semen Ratner during the court proceedings in the SVU trial, Kharkiv, 1930. *Source*: From TsDKFFAU, od. obl. 2-25994.

account of his uncle's counterrevolutionary activities, drafted in advance by his interrogators, to which a frightened young man affixed his signature. Misled by promises of freedom, the nephew collaborated with the GPU in compiling a case against his own uncle. Trying to save his skin, Pavlushkov informed the interrogators about links of the organization with centers abroad and their preparation for an armed uprising. He even testified about links of his uncle with warlords during the 1918–1919 struggle for the national liberation of Ukraine, although he was a teenager at the time. Apparent contradictions and insinuations in his testimony were "unnoticed" by his interrogators.[85] His mother believed that he was driven to insanity by interrogators and under hypnosis signed incriminating evidence against others.[86]

Attacks on Serhii Iefremov started in fall of 1928, when in three issues of the newspaper *Kommunist*, party functionary Andrii Khvylia wrote disparaging articles about the academician.[87] In November that year, Iefremov recorded in his diary, "In the academy, fortune tellers are trying to predict whether or not I will be exiled."[88] On New Year's Eve, the presidium of the All-Ukrainian Academy of Sciences, following a resolution of the TsK KP(b)U, censured Iefremov for "counterrevolutionary activities." His portrait was taken off the wall in the secretariat of the academy.[89] In February 1929, *Proletars'ka Pravda* called Iefremov "a protégé of the kulaks."[90] In his diary, Iefremov, the leading Ukrainian academician, recorded instances of a "witch hunt" in schools, where Communist Youth League "cavalry" were spying and denouncing sons and daughters of priests. "Unfortunate proletariat, in whose name all these disgusting things are perpetrated, and unfortunate country, in which spies and informers are ruling. Where it is heading—impossible to guess." Rightfully, Iefremov anticipated the grim future: "famine is being made in front of our eyes. . . . Along with it, all economic life has fallen into decay."[91]

Several generations from one family were put on trial and annihilated.[92] Academician Mykhailo Slabchenko was characterized by one of his students to the investigator as follows: "[he] charmed us with his originality, his energy, talent, love for Ukraine, and his European outlook . . . Slabchenko told us that he wanted to raise us as future Ukrainian professors." His son Taras Slabchenko, a young promising scholar, was as patriotic as his father. According to Ryleiev's testimony, "Taras Slabchenko talked about the colonial dependence of Ukraine and the need to have an independent budget and the right to use all the republic's natural resources."[93] In his lectures, Taras Slabchenko tried to teach his students that "the history of Ukraine is a history of a separate people, with distinctive characteristics." For statements like this, he was charged with "chauvinist indoctrination" because of his expressed desire to instill pride in national history among his students. Defense Attorney Semen Ratner recognized that Ukraine lost some of the best of its intellectual elite, but he crossed this thought out of the final draft of his defense argument.[94]

Public court hearings began on March 9, 1930, Taras Shevchenko's birthday. Choice of the trial's opening day was no coincidence. It was meant to strike fear into hearts of every Ukrainian, for whom the Prophet's call to freedom from tyranny remained sacred. So was the trial's final day, when the sentencing was read on Easter Sunday under the chiming of church bells, soon to be toppled and recast into bullets to blow the "brain" of the nation. Instead of mass celebration, the GPU initiated mass persecution. Restructuring of the nation's brain circuitry began. The renaissance, which was underway since the days of the UNR and sustained by ambiguous policy of indigenization that removed barriers to flourishing of the national language and culture, turned into the dark age of executions.

The prosecution's charges were unbelievable: a small group of well-known intellectuals conspired to topple the Soviet government via an armed uprising. Despite the stamp of "top secret" on the case file, the leading newspaper *Visti* started publishing excerpts from the final sentencing statement even before the trial ended.[95] The disinformation campaign unleashed in the press targeted the population in Soviet Ukraine with such insinuations as the admission by defendant Volodymyr Durdukivs′kyi, former principal of Ukrainian Gymnasium No. 1 (renamed Labor School), that he conspired to assassinate Stalin and other Soviet leaders, including Voroshilov and Skrypnyk among others. Durdukivs′kyi was guilty of calling Stalin the "main enemy of the people," who kept power with "his unconquerable will."[96]

Two contemporaries, Valerian Pidmohyl'nyi and Borys Antonenko-Davydovych, who closely followed press reports, decided to attend one of the hearings because they were convinced that the public was deliberately misled. In his memoirs, Antonenko-Davydovych wrote that his colleague invited him to keep him company on a train to Kharkiv. Their plan of action was to listen to the defendants stoically standing their ground, denying any allegations; then, at an opportune moment in a fit of bravery, the duo would come out on the stage and tell the prosecutors that "the trial is a veiled blow against the Ukrainian intelligentsia" and they would be willing to stand trial alongside their intellectual peers. Antonenko-Davydovych admitted that he and his friend cooled off as soon as they observed how the defendants meekly admitted their guilt, without attempting any vigorous defense.[97] The diarist did not record, but could hardly fail to notice, that armed GPU guards were put on the stage right behind the defendants, piercing the audience with their glassy eyes, ready to extinguish any spark of opposition or protest.

After the trial ended, on April 28, 1930, the Politburo of the TsK KP(b)U awarded eight GPU investigators with orders of Red Banner for exposing the SVU "counterrevolutionary" and "anti-Soviet" plot.[98] The case was reopened in August 1989, before Ukraine declared independence from the Union of Soviet Socialist Republics, and all the defendants were found not guilty. All were innocent of the alleged crimes and rehabilitated, posthumously. After examining the SVU trial proceedings, lawyer Anatolii Bolabol'chenko concluded that not only was the ruling of Stalin's court prejudiced, but the chief justice,[99] four state and four public prosecutors, and thirteen defense attorneys barely had time to finish reading all 237 volumes,[100] over 100,000 pages of case files in total, in the twelve days that court was in session. The defense was not effective due to the lack of time to prepare arguments and the fear of appearing too lenient toward "enemies of the people."[101] The outcome of the trial was determined even before it started; thus, its goal was to give the show trial an unmerited aura of legitimacy.

While the show trial was in progress, authorities also instigated a mass campaign to censure the "enemies of the people." On March 26–31, 1930, Commissar of Education Mykola Skrypnyk announced that, in response to the revelations about the activities of the SVU and the SUM, in many institutes students and professors "demanded the most severe punishment for the fascist agents in Soviet institutes."[102] Party cells in pedagogical institutes mobilized students to gather at meetings and publicly condemn the SVU for attempting to return Soviet Ukraine to the old bourgeois order, profess their loyalty to the dictatorship of the proletariat, the Communist Party, and the GPU as its sentinel. Among them was even Serhii Hrushevs'kyi, professor of the Donets'k INO and a nephew of Mykhailo Hrushevs'kyi, Ukraine's leading historian and head of the government during the national liberation struggle. Both met tragic ends.

Ukrainian publicist Dmytro Solovey, who witnessed the SVU trial and personally knew some of the defendants with whom he shared a prison cell in the 1920s, wrote in his memoirs *Golgotha of Ukraine*: "When I was listening to radio broadcasts of SVU trial proceedings, I became convinced that the process was not real but staged deliberately according to the GPU plan with all attendant 'facts' assembled into a case."[103] According to Solovey, Iefremov signed a self-incriminating verdict to save his students from inevitable arrests. This was how a witness justified his conduct. A personal motive to save his beloved wife by signing everything that was demanded of Iefremov had also been in play.[104] The theatrics of the trial diverted public attention in Soviet Ukraine and abroad from the crude methods used by the GPU to physically annihilate leading members of Ukraine's intelligentsia and to bury aspirations of national liberation once and for all.

The spectacle was staged in the Kharkiv Opera House; thus, in folk wisdom, this show trial was dubbed "opera SVU, libretto GPU." During preliminary investigations, most of the defendants, with the exception of three, denied all allegations of being members of the underground organization and insisted they were loyal Soviet citizens.[105] SVU trial documents contain no statute of the organization; its contents were reconstructed from the deposition of its alleged leader, Serhii Iefremov. For these reasons, researchers believe the case had been totally fabricated.[106]

Shaping of a new elite had to start with blowing out the brain of the old intellectual elite. One of the investigators in the SVU case, Solomon Bruk, cynically told Holoskevych: "How we would love to kill all of the Ukrainians; alas, we can't. But you, the Ukrainian intelligentsia, we will exterminate to the last."[107] Durdukivs'kyi recalled that Bruk in his blue GPU uniform "hypnotizes and instills terror in his victims."[108] Interrogators were relentless. Their victims had to write lengthy "confessions" day after day, often on weekends and holidays. They told their life stories in minute detail, disclosing names and places. When provoked to believe they were betrayed by their comrades, most, including women, withstood the pressure. Eventually, all were forced to sign a verdict dictated to them by their tormentors.

Collectivization, camouflaged under the slogan of class struggle, unraveled in parallel to the SVU trial, because the social basis of the alleged Union for the Liberation of Ukraine was in the countryside. The blueprint for extermination of Ukrainians was set in motion: independent farmers were the social base of the SVU, with the "headquarters" in the Ukrainian Academy of Sciences, supported by a network of "commanders" from the Ukrainian Autocephalous Orthodox Church, and trained "militant terrorists" from the Union of the Ukrainian Youth. Cancerous growth of this process of eradicating Ukraine's intellectual and spiritual potential had gnawed at the body of the Ukrainian nation for decades.[109]

The SVU trial foreshadowed Moscow trials of 1936–1938.[110] The SVU and the SUM were the first among fifteen major "underground counter-revolutionary organizations" the GPU "discovered" in Ukraine from 1930 to 1937.[111] The "discovery" of these organizations led to annihilation of pre-Soviet Ukrainian intelligentsia as a group.[112] Decades of scholarly accomplishments of the All-Ukrainian Academy of Sciences were wiped out, and research staff were purged.[113] The trial in spring of 1930 and discovery of numerous "counterrevolutionary" groups marked the beginning of the end for Ukrainization. These "superfluous" members of the Ukrainian intelligentsia became a free labor force for industrial projects administered by the OGPU in desolate places scattered along the Arctic Circle and in the Russian Klondike.

LABOR CAMPS

As Felix Dzerzhinsky envisioned, to stimulate the Soviet economy and settle remote places devoid of intelligentsia, punitive policies had to be merciless. Leading opponents of the regime had to be ruthlessly dealt with, and then the rest of society could be turned into slaves fed by the hands of their executioners in order to be forced to behave well. For that purpose, a system of concentration camps was established by the GPU in the 1930s. At first they were located in places where Russian tsars held criminals and political prisoners, like the "Iron Felix," who spent more than a decade in exile and escaped three times. It was the February Revolution that propelled him from a prison cell in Moscow to the Central Committee as Lenin's right hand.[114] The "Man of Steel," who became indispensable to Lenin and responsible for the implementation of his directives, known by his nickname as "Comrade Index Card" for his managerial skills, also tasted Siberian exile and knew the informer's craft first hand.[115] The camp system Bolsheviks created would surpass tsarist prisons in scale and cruelty.[116] Following is a list of selected labor camps of the OGPU–NKVD established in the 1930s[117]:

- *Baikal-Amur camp* (Bamlag), Svobodny, Far Eastern territory, Russia (November 1932–May 1938). Number of prisoners: 3,800 (December 12, 1932). Activity: construction of the Baikal-Amur railway.
- *Central Asian camp* (Sazlag), Tashkent, Uzbekistan (1930–1943). Number of prisoners: 2,660 (June 1, 1930). Activity: working on farms specializing in cotton and working in cotton-manufacturing plants.

- *Far Eastern camp* (Dallag), Khabarovsk, Russia (1929–April 1939). Number of prisoners: 9,200 (January 1, 1930). Activities: timber cutting, gold and coal mining, railway construction, fishing and fish processing.
- *Kazakhstan camp*, Alma-Ata, Kazakhstan (organized in 1930; reorganized as Karaganda camps (Karlag), Karaganda, in September 1931). Number of prisoners: 5,000 (July 1, 1930); 15,000 (April 15, 1931). Activities: timber cutting, agriculture.
- *Northeastern camp* (Sevvostlag), Nagaevo Bay, Far Eastern territory; Magadan, Khabarovsk territory, Russia (organized in April 1932; reorganized in the early 1950s). Number of prisoners: 11,100 (December 1932). Activities: serving the Dalstroi trust. Dalstroi trust was created in November 1931 to explore and exploit gold deposits along the Kolyma River. From the late 1930s, also specialized in tin production.
- *Northern Camps of Special Designation (SLON)*, Ust-Sysolsk, Komi ASSR; Solvychegodsk (Syktyvkar), Arkhangelsk province, Russia (organized in June 1929; in June 1931 reorganized into Ukhta-Pechora, Ustvymsky, and Temnikovsky camps and the Vaigach OGPU Expedition on the Vaigach Island in the Arctic Ocean). Number of prisoners: 9,250 (October 1, 1929); 49,716 (January 1, 1931). Activities: oil exploration, timber cutting, and highway construction.
- *Siberian camp* (Siblag), Novosibirsk, Mariinsk, Russia (organized in the fall of 1929; still in operation on 1 January 1960). Number of prisoners: 4,592 (January 1, 1930). Activities: agriculture, timber cutting, road construction.
- *Solovetsky camp*, Arkhangelsk province and Kem', Karel-Finn ASSR, Russia (organized in October 1923; reorganized in December 1931 as the White Sea–Baltic Sea camp; separated and re-created in January 1932; merged finally with the White Sea–Baltic Sea camp in December 1933). Number of prisoners: 3,049 (September 1923); 53,123 (January 1, 1930); 71,800 (January 1, 1931). Activities: timber cutting, fishing, consumer goods manufacturing.
- *Svirsky camp* (Svirlag), Lodeinoe Pole station, Leningrad province, Russia (September 1931–July 1937). Number of prisoners: 47,400 (December 1932). Activities: supplying lumber to Leningrad, producing consumer goods.
- *Temnikovsky camp* (Temlag), Moscow province, Russia; June 1931–November 1948). Number of prisoners: 25,541 (October 1, 1934). Activities: supplying lumber to Moscow, manufacturing consumer goods.
- *Ukhta-Pechora camp* (Ukhtpechlag), Chibiu (Ukhta), Komi ASSR, Russia (June 6, 1931–May 1938). Number of prisoners: 13,400 (December 1932). Activities: oil exploration, serving the Ukhta-Pechora trust. Ukhta-Pechora

trust of the OGPU–NKVD created in November 1932 to explore and exploit mineral deposits in the Pechora basin (mostly oil and coal), and to perform related work (road and house construction, agriculture).

- *White Sea–Baltic Sea camp* (Belbaltlag), Medvezh'egorsk, Karel-Finn ASSR, Russia (December 1931–September 1941). Number of prisoners: 107,900 (December 1932). Activities: construction of the White Sea–Baltic Sea Canal; from 1933, supporting the White Sea–Baltic Sea OGPU–NKVD industrial complex (servicing the waterway, cutting timber, constructing the Segezh pulp and paper chemical complex, Tulomsk hydroelectric power station, and Monchegorsk nickel complex).

By 1923, Bolsheviks had established the Solovetsky Special Purpose Camp in the famous Russian Orthodox Solovetsky Monastery complex.[118] From tsarist times, the Solovetsky Monastery was not only a cloister where Orthodox martyrs sought salvation in prayer and fasting but also a place where "criminals" repented for their violations of Russian laws and beliefs. Prisoners were confined in silent cells of the cold, desolate towers of the Solovetsky kremlin.[119] Especially "incorrigible heretics" were thrown into dungeons and fed only bread and water. In one such hole under Uspensky Cathedral, from 1775 to 1801, the commander-in-chief of the Zaporozhian Sich Cossacks, Petro Kalnyshevs'kyi, spent the remainder of his life. He was exiled to the monastery by the order of Catherine the Great. Even after Alexander I offered him freedom, the 110-year-old Cossack declined. It is said his only wish was that the tsar built a new prison because the old one was unbearable. Brigadier-General and hero of the Russo-Turkish war Kalnyshevs'kyi died in 1803 at the age of 112, and was buried beside the cathedral wall. All Ukrainian prisoners considered it their sacred obligation to bow their heads before his tomb.[120]

Trains ran to the ill-famed railway station Kem', with their cargo of prisoners destined for the Solovetsky camp. While on their way, prisoners already sensed the full impact of what awaited them on these death islands, where "a road is long, the heart is heavy, and terror crushes the soul."[121] Initially, between 1923 and 1927, it was a camp for prisoners of war. They worked mainly for their own upkeep; the terror was moderate as compared to that of the second period. In 1926 and 1927, Ukrainian prisoners were mostly officers of Petliura's armed forces, Ukrainian clergy, and old (prerevolution) intelligentsia.[122]

The Solovetsky Islands on the White Sea became known as the "Soviet Union in miniature,"[123] a symbol of the whole system where forced labor was an organic part of a new society and every individual was considered property of the state. The Solovetsky camp was followed by the White Sea–Baltic Sea Canal camp. Kolyma became the third destination once the system was reaching its maximum expansion, and remained central to it for the next fifteen years.[124] Prisoners were used to construct highways, build railroads, cut timber, clear land for farming, build high-voltage electric power lines, drill for oil, mine radioactive clay used in the production of radium, mine for coal, build temporary ice roads used in winter for transportation, manufacture bricks, build barracks for themselves and homes for paid employees, process tar, rocks, gravel, mine for salt, repair equipment and instruments, load and unload cargo, work as truck drivers, chefs in the kitchen, and perform other services.[125] Thus, devoid of intelligentsia desolate places in the Russian Far North and Siberia became settled, and the use of political prisoners as slave labor was institutionalized in the first socialist state.[126] Students of history are often surprised by this fact and argue "no one could have predicted" such an outcome of Marxist humanist socialism. Actually, anarchists did predict it, long before the socialist revolution: "they thought that a society based on Marx's ideological principles would produce slavery and despotism."[127]

A period of "savage lawlessness" in the Solovetsky camp set in during the First Five-Year Plan, when Stalin consolidated his power and launched campaigns to liquidate "all capitalist elements." Stalin expanded the OGPU apparatus and, with the assistance of a Special Assignment Army of the OGPU, he suppressed rebellions in the villages, dispossessed well-to-do farmers, and exiled them with their families to the Solovetsky Islands. Whereas in 1929, there were six concentration camps in the Soviet Union, by February 1932 their number doubled. In 1929, the nationality and type of prisoners changed; most received ten-year sentences of hard labor. They were nearly all Ukrainian farmers (as "counterrevolutionaries"), Ukrainian clergy, writers, professors, and teachers.[128]

No other camp in Russia had so many songs, verses, and anecdotes composed about it. Songs composed by Hennadii Sadovs'kyi, a graduate of Kyïv University, who used to play them on a *bandura*, were sung illegally all over Solovky, the White Sea–Baltic Sea Canal, and Karelia. One song reflected on his service in the Ukrainian Army under Petliura:

Sleep, you unknown,
In moss covered glades!
Sleep, you tortured slaves!
The Solovky pines are whispering
Over the fighters' graves.[129]

Another of his songs, composed at the White Sea–Baltic Sea Canal construction camp, figured as an example of agitation in a trial of members of an organization which was preparing a mass escape of prisoners, but the OGPU could never find out who the author was.

Sentry boxes are asleep at night,
Primeval pine forests moan,
Fires burn on the canal slopes.
It's we the tortured ones,
Who are sentenced to die,
Crumble the hard granite rock
With our chains.
We are one family,
We've become brothers all:
Turkoman, Uzbek, Chechen,
And a sad Georgian,
Son of Ukraine,
Karelian *kaimen*,*
Udmurt and Czech,
Lithuanian and White Ruthenian
We dig with picks
And pry with crowbars
And send curses
To all torturers . . .
And we the tired ones,
Sentenced to die,
Firmly believe that the time
Of revenge and punishment will come.[130]

* A contemptuous name for Karelians.

Sadovs'kyi spent eight years in the ninth Kem' branch of the White Sea–Baltic Sea Canal camp. Having had a long experience of prison life, he taught others how to behave, how best to obtain a little food, and how to preserve self-respect. But his stoicism had limits: two months after he was put in an isolation cell on the third floor of the ruined Dormition Cathedral, he went insane and was seen pacing behind heavily barred windows of the lunatic ward of Solovetsky hospital.[131]

When Stalin decided to settle the account of the rest of the Ukrainian intelligentsia and to liquidate all "unstable elements" of its Communist Party, he inaugurated his new construction project: The White Sea–Baltic Sea Canal. The idea was conceived in February 1931. When the Solovetsky camp was overflowing with Ukrainian insurgents, intelligentsia, and farmers along with dispossessed Kuban' Cossacks, many prisoners were sent to work on the White Sea–Baltic Sea industrial complex, where over 100,000 of them perished in its construction.[132] Among those banished to build the canal were Slabchenko and Hermaize of the All-Ukrainian Academy of Sciences, as well as the student Pavlushkov. They joined other Ukrainian compatriots who lived among "the despairing, groaning, mocking and crying flotsam of humanity."[133]

Unlike the Panama Canal, 80 kilometers long and taking 28 years to complete, or the Suez Canal, 160 kilometers long and taking 10 years to construct, the Soviet White Sea–Baltic Sea Canal, 227 kilometers long, was completed in 1 year and 9 months with the use of timber, sand, and rocks—all without mechanical tools![134] It was named after the Great Teacher Joseph Stalin and became the "school for forging active constructors of communism" out of the "incorrigible." The construction was immortalized in a collective monograph, penned by dozens of prominent Soviet writers in 1934.[135]

The use of a "labor army" was not Stalin's idea, it was first proposed by Leon Trotsky. The "Man of Steel," as Stalin's panegyric goes, designed the route of the canal from the beginning to the ending point.[136] Was the canal built out of economic necessity to develop Karelian wilderness, overgrown with tall pines, as a potential source of foreign currency on the global timber market? Was it constructed out of necessity to secure the Baltic frontier and open the passage for the Soviet navy to global navigation or trade networks? Local workforce in Karelia was seasonal and unreliable. A possibility of war in the Pacific in 1931 was remote. If the canal was meant as a showcase of Soviet efficiency, the opposite was true. It turned out to be "shallow and narrow" as the designer-in-chief, Stalin, noted.[137] On opening day, all heavy equipment and even engines had to be taken off submarines which were then hauled through locks and gates.[138] Crucially, the canal was not included in the original First Five-Year Plan.[139] Then why was the construction plan pushed through in 1932 and completed in 1933?

The canal project absorbed a new wave of purges following the order, telegraphed on December 14–15, 1932, to Russify all Ukrainian institutions beyond the borders of the Ukrainian SSR and before Postyshev's arrival to Ukraine on a special assignment from Stalin. Postyshev came to destroy nationalism at the root, which, at that time, was represented not just by Hrushevs′kyi and Iefremov of the Ukrainian National Republic but by Ukrainian communists.[140] All of them ended up in OGPU labor camps, except two, Khvyl′ovyi and Skrypnyk, who committed suicide in 1933.

During this period, the OGPU became its own state within a state, having administrative departments, identical with People's Commissariats, trusts, highways and railways, as well as civilian and military public works. Old military style divisions of the "labor army" were changed into "phalanx," "columns," and "brigades." Words like "tempo" and "socialist competition" were added to the vocabulary. New prisoners brought to OGPU-run labor camps were Ukrainian farmers, participants in the uprisings of 1929–1932, teachers, writers, poets, scholars, and even students.[141] These were not hard-core incorrigible criminals, but political opponents of the regime (sentenced for "counterrevolutionary crimes"), starving villagers who gathered stalks of wheat in the fields (charged with "theft of socialist property"), as well as members of the patriotic Ukrainian intelligentsia deemed "socially dangerous elements." They accounted for 52.8 percent combined for the three most frequently used articles of conviction as compared to only 7.5 percent convicted for "abuse of power, economic and military crimes" (Communist Party purges) during this period.[142]

The situation for intellectuals from Ukraine became doubly hard in 1936–1937, when prisoners were deprived of even more "rights." More were thrown into isolation cells. "Fascist" trials were held more often and resulted in longer sentences. All those whose terms had expired were given an additional five to ten years. At the end of 1937, two long trains were convoyed out of the Solovetsky Islands. The first transport was made up of those who formed the major part of political prisoner-slaves, the Ukrainians.[143] They were among 1,111 from the Solovetsky camp executed in October 1937—shot and buried at Sandarmokh.[144] Among 289 Ukrainians were theater director Les' Kurbas, writers Valerian Pidmohyl'nyi, Mykola Kulish, Mykola Zerov, and Antin Krushel'nyts'kyi with his two sons.[145]

Humankind's best were wasted in concentration camps that consisted of wooden barracks, tents, or dug-outs in the ground, surrounded by a board fence, 10-feet high, secured with barbed wire, with sentry boxes at 55-yard intervals. Twice daily, at 5 in the morning and 7 in the evening, guards made routine checkups, assisted by the foremen with overseers from cultural and medical departments. Sick prisoners were forced to stand outside, in severe cold, for one-and-a-half to two hours. Political prisoners were driven by criminal prisoners with clubs. Beatings were accompanied by obscene curses in Russian. Specially trained dogs tore at victims until they died. Once a month, searches were conducted to confiscate warm articles of clothing, money, and pieces of bread weighing over 18 ounces as a precaution against attempted escape.[146]

What historians know about living conditions in these camps can only be gleaned from descriptions and drawings left by camp survivors who managed to escape.[147] Wooden barracks were built to be standard 65 × 22 feet, holding around 150 prisoners. In winter, every prisoner's "bedding" was covered with snow that blew through holes, and every morning their damp clothing or "bedding" was frozen. The bedding consisted of one cotton quilt and a slipcover for stuffing with shavings and sawdust. These "mattresses" were breeding places for bedbugs. Felt trousers and straw sandals (*lychaky*) were folded and used as a pillow. Shirts covered the legs, and jackets were used as extra covers.[148] In the evening, prisoners would crowd around a red hot "stove" to dry their wet clothing and footwear made of coarse felt and rubber. Some would take off their shirts in order to burn out lice. A survivor described the scene as follows:

> The smoke and soot, the stench from the scorched rubber boots, from the old sweat-soaked coarse felt boots, the steaming foot-rags and tattered clothing taken off dead prisoners, the filthy underwear covered with crushed bed bugs and roasted lice, the continuous expulsion of excess stomach gases, from which the prisoners constantly suffered as a result of eating decayed fish, half-baked rye bread and the "balanda" made from meat refuse such as intestines—all this created the most foul and offensive odor imaginable, repulsive and unwholesome.[149]

Clothes were issued to prisoners based on three categories: new garments to heads of different departments, cooks, pantry-keepers, technical workers, engineers, and foremen; clothes in still fair condition to the privileged few; and old clothes, taken off dead prisoners, given exclusively to prisoners assigned to do hard labor. According to OGPU regulations, every prisoner was entitled to a new wardrobe of working clothes every two years: a cotton-lined jacket, an under-jacket and under-trousers, a shirt and trousers, and two sets of underwear. In reality, prisoners wore clothes of the second or third category. The quota for each prisoner to receive footwear included four pairs of straw sandals per year; two pairs of rubber boots a year; and a pair of coarse felt boots every two years. After completing their terms, prisoners were released in the same clothes they worked in. In fact, a jacket and a pair of coarse felt trousers outlasted three or four men.[150] Prisoners wore straw sandals and cheap rubber boots all year round; they often suffered frostbite. Rheumatism and arthritis were prevalent.[151]

The OGPU supplied prisoner manpower for labor camps. The camp administration classified laborers into four groups:

1. Group "A": laborers and technical personnel (85 percent) to work in industries, on construction projects, and transportation.
2. Group "B": concentration camp service personnel (10 percent) to work in camp administration, medical-distribution branch, cultural-educational branch, in the kitchen, laundry, steam bath, stores, and distribution centers.
3. Group "C": unemployed (5 percent) sick prisoners relieved from work by the medical staff, or prisoners on trains being transferred from one concentration camp to another, or prisoners who refused to work or who were placed in isolation cells or detained in the camp jail while their cases were being further investigated.
4. Group "D": invalids unfit for work who were slowly coming to an end.[152]

A survivor recalled that the latter were looked upon as useless because they could not be counted on to complete production quotas. Their appearance instilled fear in other prisoners who saw their own possible fate: amputated arms, legs or fingers, severe frostbites, mosquito bites or burns, rotten gums, and permanent blindness. They were on a starvation ration of seven ounces of bread and received no medical aid.[153] Prisoners daily hauled away half a dozen coffins filled with their skeletons.[154]

On a bunk full of bedbugs in a dark cell, in which the sun never shone, with heavy air permeated by the smell of bad tobacco, wet foot rags, pants, and felt boots hanging around, cold and hungry, lived world famous geographer and academician Stepan Rudnyts'kyi. He was in charge of the Research Institute of Geography in Kharkiv, when he was arrested in 1933 and exiled to the Solovetsky camp.[155] In camp, he could not do any physically demanding job, and as an invalid, he was put on a starvation ration. Other Ukrainian prisoners tried to help him, but to no avail. He talked a lot about his numerous acquaintances among European scientists, especially among Germans, about his books translated into foreign languages. He was forbidden to write or have any contact with the outside world.[156] Rudnyts'kyi was among more than 40,000 Ukrainians[157] who went into an exodus following the unsuccessful struggle for national liberation in the 1920s. Why did Bolsheviks lure Rudnyts'kyi from Prague, Czechoslovakia,[158] to Soviet Ukraine in 1926? Did they really want him to establish a new school of Ukrainian geography? What crime did he commit to deserve such cruel and inhumane punishment seven years later? He put Ukraine on the political map of Europe.[159]

A similar fate awaited Rudnyts'kyi's fellow academician, Ukrainian historian and Marxist, Matvii Iavors'kyi. He became a victim of the "pogrom" of Ukrainian historical scholarship in fall of 1929, after the first conference of Marxist historians in Moscow. He was arrested in 1930 and met other Ukrainian exiles in the Solovetsky camp. In camp, he suffered from hunger psychosis. All his fellow countrymen were helping him out by bringing bits of food which Iavors'kyi ate or hid secretly at the head of his bunk.[160] After six months of such "treatment" he somewhat recovered. He always did the hardest jobs and preferred to be left alone. When asked why he was so diligent, Iavors'kyi would bark, "Because I am mad." When the end of his term was in sight, he wrote a letter to Stalin. This letter was copied and read illegally by all Ukrainian exiles on the Solovky. In his letter, Iavors'kyi declared that he renounced his liberty "as long as Stalin and the Russians are continuing to rule in Ukraine." When the letter reached the camp administration, he was transferred into an isolation cell. Three weeks later he was informed that his term of imprisonment was extended for another three years. In 1937, both Rudnyts'kyi and Iavors'kyi were executed.

Iosip Hermaize, an ethnic Jew, who authored multiple works on Ukraine's social and political history, a professor of the Kyïv Institute of People's Education, secretary of the historical division of the All-Ukrainian Academy of Sciences, and a close collaborator of Mykhailo Hrushevs′kyi, was arrested in 1929 for being a member of the fictional SVU. Despite his declarations that he was a Marxist, he was excluded from the ranks of Marxists at the first historians' conference. Hermaize was sentenced to five years of camps, released in 1934, and then rearrested in 1937.[161] His file contains two protocols of the *troika* decision. One is laconic: "Heard case No. 12727 and sentenced Hermaize to 10 years in a concentration camp." Two days later, in December 1937, the same laconic phrase appeared—with case number and not a word about the substance of his crime. He died in the labor camp. State lawlessness was absolute.[162]

The story of Vsevolod Hantsov, professor of the Kyïv Institute of People's Education, is a reflection of the tragedy of Ukraine's intelligentsia doomed for extermination. His eight-year Odyssey was about to expire in August of 1937, then extended for another year. In April 1938, he received additional eight years of camps, starvation rations, and lawlessness. More than twenty years of life crossed out for a law-abiding citizen, not a criminal, but rather a scholar of the Ukrainian language and editor of the dictionary of the Ukrainian language. He was exiled because, in the words of the OGPU investigator, the scholar was a "socially dangerous element." The system marked Hantsov for annihilation. Desperation and pain are palpable in his letter to the Chairman of the Presidium of the Supreme Soviet of the USSR Kliment Voroshilov: "The sentencing for my association with the organization, of which I was not a member and which did not even exist, has become the cause of my life's catastrophe."[163]

Why is it that in the USSR innocent people get arrested? An answer given to a British reporter, who pulled off an interview with a fairly high-ranking GPU serviceman, was revealing. The man shook with laughter to the point that it was quite a while before he could get his words out to answer the reporter's naïve but fundamental question: "Of course, we arrest innocent people; otherwise, no one would be frightened. If people are only arrested for specific misdemeanor, all the others feel safe, and so are ripe for treason."[164] The reporter had stumbled upon the central doctrine of all dictatorial regimes:

> [b]y making justice subjective and arbitrary, every citizen can be plausibly arrested and charged at any time, with the result that they live in a permanent state of incipient guilt and fear. They really do feel themselves to be miserable offenders, not just in the eyes of God, but of their earthly rulers as well. Hence the so easily procured confessions which do not need to be invented or extorted, but truly come from the heart.[165]

Indeed, totalitarian law had to be vague so that each citizen could be considered a criminal whenever the authorities chose to consider him so.

At the bottom of the social hierarchy, created by the communists, the selection of food on the menu was quite different from a typical intellectual's daily calorie intake. It included rye flour, barley, dehydrated potatoes, beets, hardly edible salted fish, meat refuse (liver, lungs, and intestines), tallow, sugar, and vegetable oil. Cheap grade tobacco (*makhorka*) was plentiful for smoking.[166] Food was stored in the open—freezing in winter and rotting in summer. Fresh vegetables, onion or garlic, considered medicine against scurvy, were never given. The menu was short. Breakfast meal: one tablespoon of porridge, or soup made from ground barley, and a mug of hot water. Lunch consisted of *balanda* (soup made from ground barley or dehydrated potatoes and beets with a little "meat" added) and a small piece of rotten fish, which was kept in open barrels with swarms of maggots. Dinner was a variation of breakfast: soup from barley flour and a mug of hot water. Tallow or vegetable oil, 15 grams per person, was used to cook these meals. Together with *makhorka*, soap, and tea, these cost two rubles and amounted to about 1,200 calories.[167] Kitchen personnel doled portions out according to special standing or "blat" (ability to bribe). Pleas for more soup were answered with whacks over the head with an iron ladle and obscenities, "Ask the prosecutor, you son . . . , he'll give you more!"[168]

Bread was given according to the amount of work done. It accounted for 80 percent of a prisoner's diet. For this reason, the administration established a daily ritual of bread rationing. Every evening, when prisoners returned from work, they were given bread according to the percentage of daily norm completed. Political prisoners who did hard labor and completed 91 to 100 percent of daily norm were entitled to 21 ounces of bread daily. Those working on jobs not regulated by quota received 17 ½ ounces. Prisoners who completed 50–70 percent of their daily norm, were given 10 ½ ounces of bread. Prisoners who could not work received 7 ounces. No one received more than two pounds, or a kilogram of bread. It was baked from moldy flour and, according to regulation, only until it was 54 percent done. It contained 20 percent more moisture than fully baked bread, making it heavy and soggy. As a result of consuming half-baked bread, meat refuse, and salty fish, prisoners developed scurvy; their teeth and gums decayed, their limbs became weak; their bodies broke out in dark blotches.[169]

Under duress, in an environment that was designed to dehumanize, a daily routine became a form of regimented punishment. Labor camp prisoners worked a full ten hours each day. The only rest day was Sunday, but even then they were ordered outside to be searched. Prisoners worked in brigades with a brigadier appointed by the administration, who supervised the brigade during and after work and was paid by the brigade. For instance, if a brigade of 24 tree cutters cut 7,500 cubic feet of trees, this total was divided among 25 prisoners (including the brigadier), and each was credited with 96 percent of the daily norm. Tree cutting demanded double effort because axes and saws, crosscuts, and bow saws were always dull and chipped. Ten trudging prisoners harnessed as a sled pulled logs along icy roads. Dogs were the drivers, and if a prisoner's rope slackened, the dogs bit his legs instantly. All dirt had to be moved by spades, picks, crowbars, or heavy wheelbarrows. Boulders and rocks had to be broken with picks and hammers. Gravel was carried to the surface by hand in special containers.[170] The thousands of explosions and millions of kilograms of blown up rocks from the White Sea–Baltic Sea Canal could have been used to build seven Cheops pyramids.[171]

Prisoner wages were determined on a scale based on the type of work and the percentage of daily quota completed. There were only three denominations in camp currency: 50 kopeks, 1 ruble, and 1.50 rubles. To compare, in timbering, cutting trees with a bow saw and sawing them into two-yard lengths, cutting off all branches and piling them, with a daily quota of 15 cubic yards, could earn 59 kopeks per cubic yard. Loading and unloading small freight from barges and carrying it on workers' backs for a distance of 55 yards, at a daily quota of 17 ½ tons, could earn 47 kopeks per ton. Digging pits in frozen ground, 13-feet deep, with a spade and pick, and hauling it 28–55 yards with a wheelbarrow, 14 ½ cubic yards per day, could earn 61 kopeks per cubic yard. One cubic yard of rocky ground usually weighed 1.15 tons.

To take his thoughts from mindless tasks, Mykola Zerov, a graduate of Kyïv University, professor of literature and founder of the neo-Classicist school, wrote and translated Latin poets into Ukrainian from midnight till 5 in the morning. All his works perished, taken away by overseers during searches. Zerov once was given a shovel and told where and how much ground he should dig up. About noon, the professor was sitting on a rock in a pose of Rhoden's *Thinker*.

– How is today's quota? You have not even started working?
– I tried. Don't you see, I dug about ten times. But, you know, it's not earth here but rock, and it's overgrown with some pesky weed. Then, I, my friend, remembered that Latin proverb, which says "One who was not born a hero should not be too hasty to become one" and I sat down to rest.[172]

He was executed at Sandarmokh in 1937, together with other Ukrainian intellectuals.

No mechanical tools were used for building canals or highways, or for loading or unloading freight. Conditions in these so-called "corrective-labor camps," or "Institutions for the Re-education of the Un-submissive," as the public knew them, were grueling and led to moral debasement and speedy death.[173]

Prisoners could request the administration to withdraw a sum of their earnings accumulated on their accounts. Those who worked a full month, full ten hours daily and fulfilled their quotas, could cash small sums. Those who reached 100 percent of their quota could get only 10 percent of their wages. Those who fulfilled only 70 percent of their daily quota or less received no cash. An average quota was about 87 percent for the strongest prisoners; only a few brigades were eligible to receive cash. The majority of prisoners never received cash. Thus, in "classless" Soviet society, the prisoner engineer was given 7 rubles per month, whereas a professional engineer working alongside the prisoner engineer on oil projects in Ukhta-Pechora near the Arctic Circle received 1,500 rubles per month, plus a 50 percent bonus for the distant location, plus another 50 percent bonus for the severe climate, thus earning 3,000 rubles per month gross.[174]

Construction of the canal was projected to cost 400 million; its actual cost was slightly over 101 million rubles.[175] It was built on the cheap. The difference in pay between a free worker and a slave laborer was at the foundation of socialist economy and the reason behind the success of the Soviet industrialization plan. Some scholars, however, argue that these penal camps always aimed at fulfilling political objectives, but fell short on economic indicators.[176] Such labor camps existed until the collapse of the Soviet Union. Most important, there was no need for the Ukrainian intelligentsia to be "corrected" in these labor camps because they were innocent.

FORCED LABOR

By some estimates, from 1930 to 1938, about 400,000 farmers dispossessed of land and property, clergy deprived of ecclesiastical status, and intelligentsia discharged from employment were deported outside Ukraine, and an additional 530,000 were exiled to "corrective labor" camps—a total of 930,000 forced laborers—563,000 men and 367,000 women.[177] Most of them were killed, starved, or worked to death. George Kitchin, a Finnish businessman who spent four years in OGPU prisons and camps before he was freed from the Solovky with help from the Finnish government, wrote that the rate of mortality for 1929–1930 was 22 percent of the total number of prisoners employed at hard labor in timber camps.[178] In addition to the dead, 20 percent of prisoners became totally disabled and 30 percent partially disabled before completing their terms; the survival rate was 13 percent.[179]

Unlike in the United States, where the exploitation of enslaved Africans and immigrant laborers boosted industrial production and propelled the country into the industrial age,[180] in the Soviet Union, development of the industrial economy was managed by the OGPU in labor camps. The OGPU turned into a "vast industrial organization" that herded an enormous mass of forced labor into the harshest sections of the country, where free labor could not otherwise be lured, particularly in the Russian Far North, the Central Asian wilderness, and the more inhospitable sectors of Siberia. Western observer Eugene Lyons described the nature of the institution in 1937 in his memoir:

> When the civilian economic authorities could not cope with a particularly difficult industrial task . . . it was taken over by the GPU and administered with compulsory labor by "educational" methods which included brutal beatings, a diet of garbage, a fearsome mortality rate, a regime that shriveled the spirit and withered the body of the victim and degraded the masters no less than the slaves.[181]

A lot was known in the West about Soviet concentration camps, established under Lenin's rule in the 1920s, a decade before the first concentration camp appeared in Nazi Germany.[182] Articles about Soviet prisons appeared in the German, French, British, and American press.[183] In 1926, a Georgian White army officer, S. A. Malsagov, who managed to escape from Solovky, published *Island Hell*, an account of his experiences in the Solovetsky Islands. In 1927, a French writer, Raymond Duguet, published another book, *Un Bagne en Russie Rouge* (A Prison in Red Russia), where he accurately described the personalities of guards and the horrors of mosquito torture. A French senator wrote a much-quoted article based on testimony of refugees, comparing the situation in the Soviet Union to the findings of the League of Nation's slavery investigation in Liberia.[184]

After the expansion of camps in 1929 and 1930, however, foreign interest in the camps shifted away from the fate of prisoners, and focused on the economic menace that the camps appeared to pose to Western business interests during the Great Depression. According to the American-Russian Chamber of Commerce's handbook, published in New York in 1936, the USSR claimed first place in the world with regard to timber resources, its vast forest areas in the Far North and Siberia, being estimated at 950 million hectares (2.35 billion acres)—making up one-third of the world's total.[185] But at the beginning of the First Five-Year Plan, only about one-third of this area had been brought under exploitation. Thus, steps were taken to utilize these vast timber regions. Total deliveries of timber for industrial purposes increased from 41.1 million cubic meters in 1927–1928 to 99.4 million cubic meters in 1932—an increase of 142 percent.[186] Overall, in the 1930s, the Soviet Union ranked first in output of timber and second after Canada, in timber exports.[187] In 1931, European countries (England, Holland, Germany, France, and Belgium) took

84 percent of Soviet timber exports; England's share alone ranged from 33 to 40 percent. The only country that prohibited the importation of pulpwood and lumber from the Soviet Union was Canada, on the grounds that Soviet industries employed a forced labor.[188]

The timber industry grew out of domestic necessity. The Soviet paper and publishing industries collapsed when timber from forests in Finland became unavailable after the republic attained independence following World War I. The Soviet paper industry was revived in the 1930s, when virgin forests of the Russian taiga were opened to forced settlement. All the timber cutting production was coordinated by the OGPU in concentration camps, euphemistically called "corrective-labor" camps in order to camouflage their true nature: the exploitation of political prisoners as unpaid industrial slaves. Between 1928 and 1930, as many as nineteen such timber felling camps were established within the jurisdiction of the OGPU.[189] Living on a starvation diet, thousands of exiled Ukrainian intelligentsia and farmers were forced to cut timber at quotas beyond their physical strength.

The recovery of paper production led to a substantial increase in the publishing of school textbooks and reading materials for the liquidation of adult illiteracy, as well as various other educational resources for specialized secondary and higher educational institutions. Sadly, most of these publications were full of political propaganda. "Perhaps, there has never been a regime more voluminous than Bolshevik, when it comes to distributing basic political information about its activities and publicizing speeches of politicians of primary and secondary levels of importance," noted a German scholar of the revolution's impact on Soviet culture.[190]

In Britain and the United States, pressure grew for a boycott of cheaper Soviet goods produced by forced labor. The British Labor Party opposed a ban on Soviet goods because of its concern for their socialist brethren and suspicion of the motives of companies promoting it.[191] In the United States, however, the American Federation of Labor came out in support of a boycott. The United States Tariff Act of 1930 (section 307) prescribed that "All goods ... mined, produced or manufactured ... by convict labor and/or forced labor ... shall not be entitled to entry at any of the ports of the United States."[192] On that basis, the U.S. Treasury Department banned the import of Soviet pulpwood and matches.[193] Although the U.S. State Department failed to support the ban, which lasted only a week, discussion of the issue continued.[194] On May 18, 19, and 20, 1931, *The Times* of London printed a series of articles on forced labor in the Soviet Union, concluding with an editorial condemning the British government's recent decision to grant diplomatic recognition to the Soviet Union.[195]

American Marxists in 1933 argued that surplus value extorted from laborers under capitalism, no matter how much it may seem to be the result of free labor, in essence was no different from forced labor. They quoted Marx, who proclaimed in the first volume of his *Capital* that "hunger is not only a peaceable, silent, unremitted pressure, but, . . . the most natural motive to industry and labor." Comparing capitalism in every country facing financial bankruptcy and speedy industrialization of the socialist USSR under the "stimulus" of the First Five-Year Plan, Walter Wilson concluded,

> The fact that the producers, the workers, are deprived of the means of production, creating the whiplash of hunger, lies at the very basis of capitalism. In the Soviet system of economy there can be no hunger in this sense, as under this system all the means of production belong to the producers themselves. Here the stimulus to labor is to produce goods for the satisfaction of human needs and not for the profit of an exploiting class.
>
> . . .
>
> While the capitalist world is hopelessly stuck in the mud of an international crisis, the Soviet Union has no unemployment and marches ahead.[196]

Walter Wilson's theoretical contemplations on the merits of socialism over capitalism were penned while millions of Ukrainians were starved to death. The "facts" used by Wilson to support his arguments were borrowed from

Figure 3.4 *Study, New York, 1934* by John Marin (1870–1953). Oil on canvas, 22 × 28 in. (55.9 × 71.7 cm). *Source*: From The de Young Museum, American Art Fund, 2002.139.

reports by Walter Duranty, *New York Times* correspondent in Moscow.[197] Wilson, who published his rebuttal to charges of the use of forced labor in the Soviet Union in 1933, like John Marin, the artist who painted *Study, New York, 1934* (see Figure 3.4), expressed his belief in the inevitable failure of capitalism and his hope for a bright future of socialism—just as Stalin predicted.

When Lenin died a decade earlier, in 1924, the communist *Daily Worker* portrayed with almost religious fervor its conviction—and the conviction of most American leftists—that the light of Lenin's revolution, the "Soviet star of hope," would continue to illuminate and inspire the world.[198] "The building of the Russian myth required no Machiavellian propaganda tricks," noted Eugene Lyons in his *Assignment in Utopia*. "The outside world in depression years had need of it as a fixed beacon in the storm of doubt."[199] In the face of Nazism, it indeed seemed like the only hope for humanity. Having observed Stalin's government policies for two years since opening of the U.S. Embassy in Moscow, Ambassador William C. Bullitt wrote a dispatch to the secretary of state, offering his assessment of the future:

> There is genuine admiration in the Soviet Union for American technical efficiency and there is full realization of the fact that the Communist movement in the United States is still completely impotent; but it is believed that the people of the United States will not have sufficient political sense to cope with the problems of the productivity of the modern machine and modern agriculture and that after a series of recoveries and crises the United States too will fall (or rise) into the "heaven" of Communism.
>
> To summarize: The aim of the Soviet Government is and will remain, to produce world revolution. The leaders of the Soviet Union believe that the first step toward this revolution must be to strengthen the defensive and offensive power of the Soviet Union. They believe that within ten years the defense position of the Soviet Union will be absolutely impregnable and that within 15 years the offensive power of the Soviet Union will be sufficient to enable it to consolidate by its assistance any communist government which may be set up in Europe. To maintain peace for the present, to keep the nations of Europe divided, to foster enmity between Japan and the United States, and to gain the blind devotion and obedience of the communists of all countries so that they will act against their own governments at the behest of the Communist Pope in the Kremlin, is the sum of Stalin's policy.[200]

Ambassador Bullitt's insightful predictions were received in Washington on August 2, 1935, two years after the truth about the millions of deaths from the genocidal famine in Soviet Ukraine was swept under the rug and the United States granted diplomatic recognition to the Soviet Union.[201]

Similar to other cases of genocide, Ukrainian intelligentsia became the first target for liquidation. Their trials and tribulations lasted from the 1920s through the 1930s, increasing in scope—until all vestiges of Ukrainian aspirations to achieve sovereignty vanished. In the 1920s, deportations of ideological opponents did not solve the problem. The solution came at the confluence of economic necessity to build the first socialist state and the punitive use of political prisoners as slave laborers. As Leszek Kołakowski noted, the Soviet variety of totalitarianism converted people into slaves, thus, bearing certain marks of egalitarianism.[202] The OGPU operation to liquidate "Ukrainian bourgeois nationalism," which officially started in November 1932 under the guise of yet another "grain procurement campaign," had been a decade in the making. Those intellectuals who were candidates for deportation in 1922 were sitting on the court bench in 1929 as defendants in the SVU trial. The old generation patriotic elites had to give way to Soviet cadres. In 1933, a process of crushing the backbone of Ukrainian society was accomplished by genocidal famine. Support for diplomatic recognition of the Soviet Union grew during the Great Depression, when liberal ideals were challenged by the rise of totalitarian regimes.

NOTES

1. Lemkin, "Soviet Genocide in the Ukraine," 3.
2. "Arrest of Teachers Prompts Nationwide Protests," in *Oath and Opposition: Education under the Third Reich* (Washington, D.C.: U.S. Holocaust Memorial Museum, 2016), 12–14, https://www.ushmm.org/m/pdfs/20160229-Oath-and-Opposition.pdf.
3. Grigoris Palak'ean, *Le Golgotha arménien: de Berlin à Deir-es-Zor* (La Ferté-sous-Jouarre: Le Cerle d'Écrits Caucasiens, 2002), 87–94.
4. Koliastruk, *Intelihentsiia USRR u 1920-ti roky*, 166, 174; Shkandrij and Bertelsen, "The Soviet Regime's National Operations," 420.
5. Arendt, "Ideology and Terror," 131.
6. Adamsky, "The Deportation of the Ukrainian Intelligentsia," 178.
7. Viktor Adams'kyi, "Deportatsiia ukraïns'koï intelihentsiï v konteksti stanovlennia totalitarnoho rezhymu," *Rozbudova derzhavy*, no. 8 (1996): 41.
8. Adamsky, "The Deportation of the Ukrainian Intelligentsia," 178.
9. Katerynoslav was named after Catherine the Great in 1784, when the Russian empress annexed Cossack lands and opened the territory for settlement by German farmers. In 1926, the city was named Dnipropetrovs'k after Hryhorii Petrovs'kyi, chairman of the Central Executive Committee of the Soviet Union. In 2016, the last name of the Soviet Ukrainian leader was dropped. The city is currently named Dnipro

after the largest river in Ukraine. It is the fourth largest city, known as an industrial and "space exploration capital" of Ukraine.

10. Adamsky, "The Deportation of the Ukrainian Intelligentsia," 178.

11. *TsDAHOU*, f. 1, op. 20, spr. 45, ark. 208; spr. 1471, ark. 107.

12. Iurii Fel'shtinskii, ed., *VChK-GPU: Dokumenty i materialy* (Moscow: Izd-vo gumanitarnoi literatury, 1995).

13. Adamsky, "The Deportation of the Ukrainian Intelligentsia," 179.

14. In 1921, the Communist Party in Soviet Ukraine established departments of agitation and propaganda following Lenin's speech at the Tenth Party Congress. Propaganda sections within these departments were in charge of schools and institutes. Regional Communist Party cells strengthened the "headquarters of the cultural revolution" by controlling local education authorities and recruiting communists into teaching and administration. In 1921, the Donets'k regional People's Commissariat of Education had 123 communists, Poltava—87, Chernihiv—56, Katerynoslav—45, Volyn'—37, Mykolaïv—39, and Podil's'kyi—42. See *TsDAVOU*, f. 166, op. 2, spr. 514, ark. 39.

15. *TsDAHOU*, f. 1, op. 6, spr. 29, ark. 98; see English translation in Adamsky, "The Deportation of the Ukrainian Intelligentsia," 179–80.

16. Solovey, *Golgota Ukraïny*, 23.

17. On the Red Terror and the history of the Soviet political police, see George Leggett, *The Cheka: Lenin's Political Police* (New York: Oxford University Press, 1986).

18. Vitalii Iurchenko, *Shliakhamy na Solovky (iz zapysok zaslantsia* (L'viv: Vyd-vo "Chervona kalyna," 1931), 85–87; quoted in Solovey, *Golgota Ukraïny*, 131.

19. On April 9, 1921, a decree issued by the Central Commission to Combat Desertion at the Council of People's Commissars of the Ukrainian SSR, signed by Christian Rakovsky and Mikhail Frunze, military commander of the armed forces of Soviet Ukraine and Crimea at the time, included instructions on taking hostages in districts where insurgents were active and where local population supported rebels. See *DAVO*, f. R-925, op. 8, spr. 56; quoted in L. L. Misinkevych, "Zakonodavchi zasady represyvnoï polityky radians'koï vlady v Ukraïni v 20–30-ti rr. XX stolittia," *Universytets'ki naukovi zapysky*, no. 1 (45) (2013): 6.

20. V. Vasyl'iev, "Politychni represiï na Vinnychyni, 1918–1980-ti roky," in *Reabilitovani istoriieiu. Vinnyts'ka oblast'*, ed. V. Vasyl'iev, P. Kravchenko, and R. Podkur (Vinnytsia: DKF, 2006), 9–92; quoted in Misinkevych, "Zakonodavchi zasady," 6.

21. Adamsky, "The Deportation of the Ukrainian Intelligentsia," 180. For the ideological roots of political repressions and the role of the chief prosecutor Andrey Vyshinsky, see Arkadii Vaksberg, *Tsaritsa dokazatel'stv: Vyshynskii i ego zhertvy* (Moscow: AO "Kniga i biznes," 1992).

22. Adamsky, "The Deportation of the Ukrainian Intelligentsia," 180.

23. *TsDAVOU*, f. 4, op. 1, spr. 50, ark. 262; see also Misinkevych, "Zakonodavchi zasady," 7.

24. Adamsky, "The Deportation of the Ukrainian Intelligentsia," 180–81; Koliastruk, *Intelihentsiia USRR u 1920-ti roky*, 175.

25. "Ob administrativnoi vysylke: Dekret VTsIK ot 10.08.1922 g.," *Izvestiia VTsIK*, August 12, 1922. For a full text of the decree, see http://old.ihst.ru/projects/so hist/document/deport/dekret.htm.

26. For a discussion of the center's attitudes toward Ukrainian intellectuals, see Danylenko, *Ukraïns'ka intelihentsiia i vlada*, 19–20; see also Shkandrij and Bertelsen, "The Soviet Regime's National Operations in Ukraine," 424.

27. Kas'ianov, *Ukraïns'ka intelihentsiia 1920kh–30kh rokiv*, 28.

28. Koliastruk, *Intelihentsiia USRR u 1920-ti roky*, 174–75.

29. Bolsheviks had limited access to world financial markets and used confiscated church gold and jewels as a way to subsidize foreign communists. According to documents reproduced in *The Secret World of American Communism* (New Haven: Yale University Press, 1995), John Reed, one of the founders of the American Communist movement, had been given valuables worth over 1 million rubles. Finnish security police captured him and confiscated a large quantity of diamonds in his possession when he attempted to return secretly from Russia to the United States via Finland in 1920. See John Earl Haynes and Harvey Klehr, *In Denial: Historians, Communism, and Espionage* (San Francisco: Encounter Books, 2003), 72–73.

30. *TsOA KGB*, f. 2, op. 1, ed. kh. 1, l. 10–15; reprinted in *F. E. Dzerzhinsky – rukovoditel' VChK–OGPU: Sbornik dokumentov i materialov (1918–1926 gg.)*, eds. N. S. Zakharov, P. G. Grishin, and A. V. Prokopenko (Moscow: Nauchno-izdatel'skii otdel, 1967), 120–21. The author located the document in *HDA SBU*, f. 13, od. zb. 603 with the assistance of the archive's director Andrii Kohut.

31. Giuseppe Perri, "*Korenizacija*: an Ambiguous and Temporary Strategy of Legitimization of Soviet Power in Ukraine (1923–1933) and Its Legacy," *History of Communism in Europe*, no. 5 (2014): 131–54. Francine Hirsch defined Soviet nationality policy to be "*by its nature* both a creative and a destructive process." See Francine Hirsch, "Race without the Practice of Racial Politics," *Slavic Review* 61, no. 1 (2002): 42.

32. Shapoval, *Ukraïna 20–50-kh rokiv*, 26.

33. Danylenko, *Ukraïns'ka intelihentsiia i vlada*, 21.

34. This observation is supported by contemporaries as intimated by the father of Mykola Kotcherha, who was singing in a folk choir and traveling from villages to towns to perform Ukrainian choral music in concerts (personal communication, September 19, 2019). Mykola Kotcherha is president of the Ukrainian Genocide Famine Foundation in Chicago, Illinois.

35. See V. Naddniprianets', *Ukraïns'ki natsional-komunisty: ïkh rolia u vyzvol'nii borot'bi Ukraïny 1917–1956 rr.* (Munich: Political Section of the Ukrainian National Guard, 1956), 23.

36. Arkhireis'kyi and Chentsov, "Antyradians'ka natsional'na opozytsiia," 30.

37. The top secret circular of February 1924 was signed by the Chief of the Lubny Okruh OGPU Section Dvianinov and Chief of Counterespionage Section Zhukov. The English translation of the circular was published in the *Ukrainian Review* (London) in 1958 (issue 6, 149–50) and reprinted in Conquest, *The Harvest of Sorrow*, 71–72.

38. Arkhireis'kyi and Chentsov, "Antyradians'ka natsional'na opozytsiia," 30.

39. *Ukrainian Review*, no. 6, 153; quoted in Conquest, *The Harvest of Sorrow*, 210.

40. *TsOA KGB*, f. 2, op. 2, ed. kh. 85, l. 56–57; first published in the journal *Istoricheskii arkhiv*, no. 1 (1958): 23–24; reprinted in *F. E. Dzerzhinsky – rukovoditel' VChK–OGPU*, 133. The document is located in *HDA SBU*, f. 13, od. zb. 603.

41. Solovey, *Golgota Ukraïny*, 163.

42. Valentyn Moroz, "Nationalism and Genocide: The Origin of the Artificial Famine of 1932–1933 in Ukraine," *The Journal of Historical Review* 6, no. 2 (1985): 207–20.

43. *Ukrainian Review*, no. 6 (1958): 156; quoted in Conquest, *The Harvest of Sorrow*, 71.

44. Prystaiko and Shapoval, *Mykhailo Hrushevs'kyi i GPU-NKVD*, 131, 133–34.

45. Conquest, *The Harvest of Sorrow*, 210–11.

46. Danylenko, *Ukraïns'ka intelihentsiia i vlada*, 25. For the analysis and the text of the document, see Yuri Shapoval, "'On Ukrainian Separatism': A GPU Circular of 1926," *Harvard Ukrainian Studies* 18, no. 3–4 (1994): 275–302.

47. The transcript for the movie was written by Heorhii Stabovyi and Iakov Livshits in 1926. Balyts'kyi forced to cut the movie, giving as a reason that GPU methods could be revealed. A film poster, designed by A. Finohenov, depicts the Red Cavalry in pursuit of surviving soldiers of Iurko Tiutiunnyk's army. In the center of the poster, Hryhorii Kotovs'kyi crosses off a golden Trident on a blue background with his sword. The image amplifies the concept that Bolsheviks in Ukraine are successors of the Ukrainian National Republic (UNR). See Lubomyr Hosejko, *Ukrainian Film Poster of the 1920s: VUFKU* (Kyïv: Oleksandr Dovzhenko National Center, 2015), 19, 21, 34–35, 39, 58–59. See the film poster at https://vufku.org/lost/p-k-p/.

48. Serhii Lytvyn, "Vbyvstvo S. Petliury i GPU: Do istoriohrafiï problemy," *Z arkhiviv VUChK-GPU-NKVD-KGB*, no. 2/4 (13/15) (2000): 404–7.

49. Arnold Margolin, *The Jews of Eastern Europe* (New York: T. Seltzer, 1929), 139; Iurii Kul'chyts'kyi, "Symon Petliura i pohromy," in *Symon Petliura: Zbirnyk studiino-naukovoï konferentsiï v Paryzhi (traven' 1976)*, ed. Wolodymyr Kosyk (München-Paris: Ukrainian Free University, 1980), 138, 142–44, 151, 155.

50. For a study debunking the myth of Ukrainian government's anti-Semitism during the short-lived existence of the Ukrainian National Republic, see Taras Hunczak, *Symon Petliura and the Jews: A Reappraisal* (Toronto: Ukrainian Historical Association, 1985).

51. Taras Hunczak, professor of Soviet, Russian, and East European history at Rutgers University, is the editor of *Russian Imperialism from Ivan the Great to the Revolution* (New Brunswick, 1974); *The Ukraine, 1917–1921: A Study in Revolution* (Cambridge: Cambridge University Press, 1977); *Ukraine and Poland in Documents, 1918–1922*, 2 vols. (New York, 1984); and others.

52. Hunczak, *Symon Petliura and the Jews*, 32–33.

53. Ethnographers recorded a dozen songs that depict Petliura as a folk hero similar to Robin Hood. An epic poem (*duma*) was composed in memory of Petliura. It became popular among the blind *kobzars* of left-bank Ukraine. See K. Danylevs'kyi,

Petliura v sertsiakh i pisniakh svoho narodu (Regensburg: Filiia Tovarystva ukraïns'kykh politychnykh v'iazniv z Regensburga, 1947), 3, 8.

54. Lytvyn, "Vbyvstvo S. Petliury i GPU," 404–7.

55. Shapoval, *Liudyna i systema*, 96–107.

56. S. I. Drovoziuk, "Bil'shovyts'ki tekhnolohiï 'perevykhovannia' ukraïns'koï intelihentsiï u 20–30-kh rr. XX st.," in *Naukovi zapysky Vinnyts'koho derzhavnoho pedahohichnoho universytetu im. M. Kotsiubyns'koho*, ed. P. S. Hryhorchuk (Vinnytsia: VDPU, 2006), 196.

57. Danylenko, *Ukraïns'ka inteligentsiia i vlada*, 21, 25, 27, 29.

58. *HDA SBU*, f. 6, spr. 68805-FP, zoshyt no. 6, ark. 953–1052.

59. Serhii Plokhy, *Unmaking Imperial Russia: Mykhailo Hrushevsky and the Writing of Ukrainian History* (Toronto: University of Toronto Press, 2005), 383–97.

60. *DAZO*, f. 3666, op. 1, spr. 427, ark. 30–32; quoted in Marochko and Hillig, *Represovani pedahohy Ukraïny*, 247. See also Colin Peter Neufeldt, "Collectivizing the *Mutter Ansiedlungen*: The Role of Mennonites in Organizing Kolkhozy in the Khortytsia and Molochansk German National Districts in Ukraine in the late 1920s and early 1930s," in *Minority Report: Mennonite Identities in Imperial Russia and Soviet Ukraine Reconsidered*, ed. Leonard Friesen (Toronto: University of Toronto Press, 2018), 211–59.

61. Hiroaki Kuromiya, "Stalin's 'Great Breakthrough' and the Trial of the Union for the Liberation of the Ukraine" (paper prepared for the conference, "Ukraine under Stalin, 1928–1939," at the University of Toronto, March 2–4, 1990), 14.

62. Prystaiko and Shapoval, *Sprava "Spilky vyzvolennia Ukraïny."*

63. V. I. Pryluts'kyi, *Molod' Ukraïny v umovakh formuvannia totalitarnoho ladu (1920–1939)* (Kyïv: Instytut istoriï Ukraïny NAN Ukraïny, 2001), 214.

64. Mykola Pavlushkov, a student at Kyïv Institute of People's Education and a nephew of Serhii Iefremov, was denounced in the press for allegedly organizing the SUM in 1925 with the goal to establish an independent democratic Ukrainian republic. See "Pokyd'ky radians'koho studentstva (Zamist' obvynuvachuval'noho slova na protsesi 'SVU' ta 'SUM')," *Student revoliutsiï* no. 9 (1930): 1–7; quoted in Komarnits'kyi, *Studenty-pedahohy*, 552.

65. Danylenko, *Ukraïns'ka intelihentsiia i vlada*, 559.

66. Prystaiko and Shapoval, *Sprava "Spilky vyzvolennia Ukraïny,"* 112.

67. Iefremov, *Shchodennyky*, 752, 765–66.

68. Serhii Bilokin', *Masovyi teror iak zasib derzhavnoho upravlinnia v SRSR (1917–1941 rr.): dzhereloznavche doslidzhennia*, vol. 1 (Kyïv, 1999), 574.

69. Marochko and Hillig, *Represovani pedahohy Ukraïny*, 248; Prystaiko and Shapoval, *Sprava "Spilky vyzvolennia Ukraïny,"* 131.

70. Prystaiko and Shapoval, *Sprava "Spilky vyzvolennia Ukraïny,"* 44; see also Shapoval, "The Case of the 'Union for the Liberation of Ukraine'," 161. Iu. I. Shapoval, "Spilka vyzvolennia Ukraïny" ("SVU"), in *Entsyklopediia istoriï Ukraïny*, ed. V. A. Smolii et al. (Kyïv: Instytut istoriï Ukraïny NAN Ukraïny, 2012), vol. 9, 752, http://history.org.ua/LiberUA/978-966-00-1290-5/978-966-00-1290-5.pdf.

71. Kost' Turkalo, "Sorok p'iat': Spohady z sudovoho protsesu SVU 9.3–20.4.1930 roku," *Novi dni* (Toronto), no. 34 (November 1952), 4–8, 29–30; no. 35 (December 1952), 7–9; no. 38 (March 1953), 9–11; no. 39 (April 1953), 8–9.

72. K. Turkalo, "List of Convicted Persons in the SVU Trial," in *The Black Deeds of the Kremlin*, vol. 1, 316–20. The age of each of the defendants was confirmed by the author with their biographical data from interrogation protocols in *HDA SBU*, fond 6, op. 67098-FP, spr. 215471, vol. 2, ark. 280–88.

73. Conquest, *The Harvest of Sorrow*, 211.

74. Shapoval, "The Case of the 'Union for the Liberation of Ukraine'," 160.

75. After a protest was submitted in connection with the SVU case, a resolution handed down by the Supreme Court of the Ukrainian SSR on August 11, 1989, closed the case because of insufficient evidence of a crime in the actions of the defendants, all of whom were fully rehabilitated. See "Protest," *Literaturna Ukraïna*, August 31, 1989; quoted in Shapoval, "The Case of the 'Union for the Liberation of Ukraine,'" 163.

76. In May, Borys Matushevs'kyi during the first interrogation denied that he was a member of a "counterrevolutionary" organization; he insisted that he had always supported Soviet policies. After Solomon Bruk "worked" with him on the case, in October the student wrote a fifty-six-page "penitent confession" about his "nationalist counterrevolutionary worldview." See Prystaiko and Shapoval, *Sprava "Spilky vyzvolennia Ukraïny,"* 74–75.

77. Sniehir'ov, *Naboï dlia rozstrilu*, 110; quoted in Shapoval, 157–58; see also Applebaum, *Red Famine*, 99.

78. For a detailed discussion of interrogation techniques and the use of torture to confirm nationalist charges, see Shkandrij and Bertelsen, "The Soviet Regime's National Operations in Ukraine," 428–31. See also Solovey, *Golgota Ukraïny*, 119–25.

79. Mykhailo Orest, *"Bezsmertni": Spohady pro M. Zerova, P. Filipovycha i M. Drai-Khmaru* (Munich: Instytut literatury im. M. Oresta, 1963), 310; quoted in Prystaiko and Shapoval, *Sprava "Spilky vyzvolennia Ukraïny,"* 419. See also memoir written by Viktor Petrov, *Ukraïns'ki kul'turni diiachi URSR 1920–1940 – zhertvy bil'shovyts'koho teroru* (New York: Prolog, 1959).

80. Prystaiko and Shapoval, *Sprava "Spilky vyzvolennia Ukraïny,"* 426. For an eyewitness account of the use of mind-altering narcotics during interrogations to induce compliance, see Oleksa Buzhans'kyi, "Za hratamy GPU-NKVD," *Svoboda*, no. 297–98, December 1950; quoted in Solovey, *Golgota Ukraïny*, 127–28.

81. V. D. Otamanovs'kyi, "Moie kaiattia," *Podil's'ka starovyna: naukovyi zbirnyk na poshanu vchenoho i kraieznavtsia V. D. Otamanovs'koho*, ed. V. A. Kosakivs'kyi (Vinnytsia, 1993), 24, 27.

82. In 1930, according to the OGPU circular No. 5, nearly 6,556 Ukrainian families, or a total of 23,985 family members, were resettled in a newly created territory of Western Siberia. See *Gosudarstvennyi arkhiv Rossiiskoi Federatsii (GARF)*, f. R 374, op. 28, spr. 4055, ark. 44. For estimated numbers of Ukrainian farmers and their families forcibly resettled to other regions with harsh climates to mine for gold and work on industrial projects in the Russian Far North, Urals, Siberia, Yakutia, and

Kazakhstan, see I. V. Rybak, "Deportatsiia rozkurkulenykh selian druhoïï katehoriï z Ukraïny u 1930 rotsi: masshtaby, kharakter, naslidky," *Naukovi pratsi Kam'ianets'-Podil's'koho natsional'noho universytetu imeni Ivana Ohienka. Istorychni nauky*, no. 22 (2012): 329–30, http://nbuv.gov.ua/UJRN/Npkpnu_2012_22_31.

83. Prystaiko and Shapoval, *Sprava "Spilky vyzvolennia Ukraïny*," 416.

84. Forced resettlement of Ukrainian dispossessed farmers and their families was conducted in four waves. Children between ages ten and fourteen were separated from their parents and returned to Ukraine, where they were placed in orphanages or joined the ranks of homeless. Children younger than eight or nine, who were not separated from their parents, died of frostbite and hunger on route or in the settlements. See Iu. G.-G. (Gorlis-Gors'kyi), *Ave Dictator* (L'viv: Ukraïns'ke vyd-vo, 1941), 5–6, 30; quoted in Solovey, *Golgota Ukraïny*, 163–64.

85. Prystaiko and Shapoval, *Sprava "Spilky vyzvolennia Ukraïny*," 72.

86. Danylenko, *Ukraïns'ka intelihentsiia i vlada*, 596.

87. A. Khvylia, "Pid akademichnym zabralom," *Komunist*, 1928.

88. Prystaiko and Shapoval, *Sprava "Spilky vyzvolennia Ukraïny*," 418.

89. When a decade earlier, on March 25, 1919, the ChK arrested Serhii Iefremov as the former member of the Central Rada, the general assembly of the All-Ukrainian Academy of Sciences appealed to the People's Commissar of Education Volodymyr Zatons'kyi to set him free. On March 31, 1919, the president of the Academy Volodymyr Vernads'kyi also sent a personal letter of appeal to Zatons'kyi with the request to free Iefremov. In 1929, the atmosphere was different, and Iefremov's colleagues and students shunned him.

90. *Proletars'ka Pravda*, February 6, 1929; cited in Prystaiko and Shapoval, *Sprava "Spilky vyzvolennia Ukraïny*," 418.

91. Prystaiko and Shapoval, *Sprava "Spilky vyzvolennia Ukraïny*," 418–19.

92. For biographical sketches of Ukrainian, Polish, and German teachers in Ukraine as victims of political terror, see Marochko and Hillig, *Represovani pedahohy Ukraïny*.

93. Prystaiko and Shapoval, *Sprava "Spilky vyzvolennia Ukraïny*," 422.

94. Ibid., 423.

95. Ivan Il'ienko, "Oskarzhuie istoriia," in Prystaiko and Shapoval, *Sprava "Spilky vyzvolennia Ukraïny*," 413. *Visti*, a newspaper of the All-Ukrainian Central Executive Committee, started publishing excerpts from the SVU case file on February 21, 1930. That same day the newspaper published a complete text of the speech, "Shkidnytstvo 'chystoï' nauky: Kontrrevoliutsiina robota v Ukraïns'kii Akademiï nauk," presented by O. Rykov, Chairman of the Council of People's Commissars of the USSR, who spoke to engineers and scientists five days earlier in Moscow.

96. *Visti*, March 1, 1930; quoted in Prystaiko and Shapoval, *Sprava "Spilky vyzvolennia Ukraïny*," 413.

97. Antonenko-Davydovych, "SVU," 42, 45.

98. *TsDAHOU*, f. 1, op. 6, spr. 184, ark. 87; see also Prystaiko and Shapoval, *Sprava "Spilky vyzvolennia Ukraïny*," 91; Bilokin', *Masovyi teror*, vol. 1, 583.

99. The Chief Justice presiding over the SVU trial Anton Prykhod'ko (a former Borot'bist), one of the leading public prosecutors Panas Liubchenko (also a former

Borot'bist), Prosecutor General Mykhailo Mykhailyk (real name Iosyp Abramovich), and Prosecutor of the Supreme Court of the Ukrainian SSR Lev Solomonovych Akhmatov were executed a decade later during the Great Terror in 1937–1939. For documentary clips and a summary of the SVU trial proceedings, see "Sprava SVU: iak bil'shovyky nyshchyly ukraïns'ku intelihentsiiu," *Istoriia bez mifiv*, August 5, 2020, https://www.youtube.com/watch?v=tEkUbQ5PQVU.

100. All 237 volumes of case file 67098-FP in Fond 6 are available at the *HDA SBU* for scholars to study. As Serhii Bilokin' pointed out, historians tend to mystify state archives. He cautioned that materials preserved in the archives have been carefully selected to represent historical events; thus, they may or may not reflect the reality objectively. The most sensitive records were never stored. The records have never been complete either; they were purged systematically. See Serhii Bilokin', *Novi studiï z istoriï bol'shevyzmu* (Kyïv: Instytut istoriï Ukraïny NAN Ukraïny, 2006), 339–40.

101. Anatolii Bolabol'chenko, "SVU: sud nad perekonanniamy," *Vitchyzna*, no. 11 (1989); quoted in Prystaiko and Shapoval, *Sprava "Spilky vyzvolennia Ukraïny,"* 414.

102. M. O. Skrypnyk, *Novi liniï v natsional'no-kul'turnomu budivnytstvi* (Kharkiv: Derzhavne vydavnytstvo Ukraïny, 1930), 52.

103. Solovey, *Golgota Ukraïny*, 122–23.

104. In 1992, Tetiana Il'chenko wrote a letter to the newspaper *Rada*, stating that she had known Iefremov when she was a child. At that time, he was living at the home of Volodymyr Durdukivs'kyi, whose sister Onysia was Iefremov's wife. During the Nazi occupation of Kyiv, Il'chenko and her mother paid a visit to Onysia, who told them that Iefremov had been threatened. The investigators threatened that his wife would be arrested if he did not sign the papers that they were demanding. See *Rada*, March 27, 1992; quoted in Shapoval, "The Case of the 'Union for the Liberation of Ukraine,'" 166.

105. *HDA SBU*, spr. 67098-FP, vol. 1A, ark. 425. Those who under pressure admitted their "guilt" included Zinovii Morgulis, a lawyer; Mykhailo Slabchenko, academician, professor of the Odesa INO; and Volodymyr Strashkevych, associate member of the All-Ukrainian Academy of Sciences.

106. Bilokin', *Novi studiï z istoriï bol'shevyzmu*, 600. Pavlushkov's sister, who later married one of the GPU interrogators, claimed on the pages of diaspora periodicals that the SVU did exist as an underground organization. See Natalia Pavlushkova, "Pravda i provokatsiia (do 40-richchia sudu nad SVU-SUM)," *Misiia Ukraïny* (published by the Association for the Liberation of Ukraine in Brooklyn, NY, and Toronto, Canada), no. 3 (26) (1970): 1–4; and "Pravda i provokatsiia," *Misiia Ukraïny*, no. 1 (28) (1971): 10–13.

107. Il'ienko, "Oskarzhuie istoriia," in Prystaiko and Shapoval, *Sprava "Spilky vyzvolennia Ukraïny,"* 415.

108. Ibid.

109. Repressions against nationally conscious Ukrainians continued throughout the 1950s, when nationalist fighters from western Ukraine were exiled to concentration camps. The harassment of dissenters and human rights activists, among them Ukrainian poets, writers, and teachers charged with "anti-Soviet propaganda and

agitation" lasted throughout Khrushchev's "Thaw" in the 1960s and the dissident movement of the 1970s, when the Ukrainian Helsinki Group was established, all the way to Gorbachev's perestroika. The last Ukrainian political prisoners were released from prison camps in 1991. Many died in exile. The survivors were rehabilitated in 1991. See Vasyl' Ovsiienko, *Svitlo liudei: Spohady-narysy pro Vasylia Stusa, Iuriia Lytvyna, Oksanu Meshko* (Kyïv: URP, 1996) and Osyp Zinkewych, ed., *Ukraïns'ka Hel'syns'ka Hrupa, 1978–1982: Dokumenty i materialy* (Toronto: V. Symonenko "Smoloskyp" Publishers, 1983).

110. Liber, *Soviet Nationality Policy*, 160–61.

111. For a list of the organizations, see Hryhory Kostiuk, *Stalinist Rule in the Ukraine: A Study of the Decade of Mass Terror (1929–1939)* (New York: Praeger, 1960), 85–86.

112. Liber, *Soviet Nationality Policy*, 162–63.

113. A catalog of publications of the All-Ukrainian Academy of Sciences (founded in 1918, dissolved in 1929, and absorbed into the Academy of Sciences of the USSR) included 286 pages, listing 300 volumes of scientific studies, and 888 scientific publications compiled by 1,800 research associates. Six volumes of a Russian-Ukrainian dictionary, edited by linguist Serhii Iefremov, were removed from circulation. See Solovey, *Golgota Ukraïny*, 50–51. Academicians and research staff, who were purged, were stripped of their scientific titles and jobs, arrested, and prosecuted. See *TsDAVOU*, f. 166, op. 9, spr. 1459, ark. 18.

114. See Felix Dzerzhinsky's autobiography in *TsOA KGB*, f. 1, op. 6, ed. kh. 45, ll. 94–98; reprinted in *F. E. Dzerzhinsky – rukovoditel' VChK – OGPU*, 8–11.

115. Nigel Blundell, *A Pictorial History of Joseph Stalin* (North Dighton: JG Press, 1996), 28.

116. Robert Conquest, *Kolyma: The Arctic Death Camps* (New York: Viking Press, 1978).

117. Oleg V. Khlevniuk, *The History of the Gulag: From Collectivization to the Great Terror* (New Haven: Yale University Press, 2004), 358–63.

118. For a detailed history of the camp, see a database of Soviet "corrective-labor" camps, compiled by M. B. Smirnov, *Sistema ispravitel'no-trudovykh lagerei v SSSR*, eds. N. G. Okhotin and A. B. Roginskii (Moscow: "Zven'ia," 1998), http://old.memo.ru/history/nkvd/gulag.index.htm.

119. A kremlin or *kreml'* is a major fortified central complex found in historic Russian cities.

120. S. O. Pidhainy, "Solowky Concentration Camp," in *The Black Deeds of the Kremlin*, vol. 1, 21.

121. Pidhainy, "Solowky Concentration Camp," 21.

122. Ibid., 22, 24.

123. Bilokin', "Solovky," in *Masovyi teror iak zasib derzhavnoho upravlinnia*, vol. 2, 268–87, esp. 277.

124. Conquest, *Kolyma*, 17.

125. Pidhainy, "Solowky Concentration Camp," 42–68.

126. Michael Jakobson, *Origins of the GULAG: The Soviet Prison Camp System, 1917–1934* (Lexington: University Press of Kentucky, 1993).

127. Kołakowski, "The Marxist Roots of Stalinism," 175.
128. Pidhainy, "Solowky Concentration Camp," 24, 26–27.
129. Pidhainy, "Portraits of Solowky Exiles," in *The Black Deeds of the Kremlin*, vol. 1, 327.
130. Ibid., 328.
131. Ibid., 326.
132. Pidhainy, *The Black Deeds of the Kremlin*, vol. 1, 22, 34–35.
133. Pidhainy, "Portraits of Solowky Exiles," 326–67.
134. Ivan Chukhin, *Kanalo-armeitsy: Istoriia stroitel'stva Belomorkanala v dokumentakh, tsyfrakh, faktakh, fotografiiakh, svidetel'stvakh uchastnikov i ochevidtsev* (Petrozavodsk: "Kareliia," 1990), 13, 25.
135. Chukhin, *Kanalo-armeitsy*, 14.
136. Ibid., 32.
137. Ibid., 18.
138. "Svidetel'stvo uchastnika: S. I. Kozhevnikov, former commander of BCh 1-4 submarine 'Narodovolets' from Petrozavodsk," in Chukhin, *Kanalo-armeitsy*, 23.
139. Chukhin, *Kanalo-armeitsy*, 17.
140. Pidhainy, "Solowky Concentration Camp," 35.
141. Ibid., 36, 38.
142. Khlevniuk, *The History of the Gulag*, 323.
143. Pidhainy, "Solowky Concentration Camp," 40–41.
144. From August 11, 1937, to December 24, 1938, more than 9,000 victims of Soviet political repressions were executed by shooting and buried in 300 separate burial trenches at Sandarmokh. These included 289 members of the Ukrainian intelligentsia. In 1997, "Memorial" Society located killing fields and burial sites at Sandarmokh near Medvezh'egorsk in Karelia (Northwest Russia). Drawing on information from a KGB archive, Russian historian Iurii Dmitriev identified men and women shot at Sandarmokh as follows: 3,500 were inhabitants of Karelia, whereas 4,500 were prisoners working for the White Sea Canal, and 1,111 were brought there from the Solovky "special" prison. Alongside loggers and fishermen from nearby villages, farmers, writers and poets, artists, scientists and scholars, military leaders, doctors, teachers, engineers, clergy, and statesmen found their final resting place there. The position of the skeletons and other remains suggested that the prisoners had been stripped to their underwear, lined up next to a trench with hands and feet tied, and shot in the back of the head with a pistol. Documents in the regional KGB archive identify among the victims 141 Finnish Americans and 127 Finnish Canadians, all of whom joined communist-sponsored migration to Karelia in the early 1930s. Membership in the Communist Party did not save these radicals from their tragic fate. See Haynes and Klehr, *In Denial*, 117–18. For lists of names of prisoners executed at Sandarmokh, see Yuri Dmitriev's *Mesto rasstrela Sandarmokh* (Petrozavodsk, Russia, 1999) and *Mesto pamiati Sandarmokh* (Petrozavodsk, Russia, 2019).
145. For a list of the Ukrainian prisoners of the Solovetsky camp executed in 1937, see Serhii Bilokin', "Rozstril'nyi spysok Solovkiv," *Literaturna Ukraïna*, no. 27 (4488), July 9, 1992, 8; see also Bilokin', "Solovky," 283.
146. Pidhainy, *The Black Deeds of the Kremlin*, 49.

147. Rostislav Gorelov captured the immortal scene in his painting *V lagernom barake* (In a camp barrack), Moscow, 1970–1979, preserved in the Museum of the GULAG History. Born in the Dnipropetrovs'k region, the artist was a student in Moscow at the time of his arrest in 1933 for his alleged participation in an underground organization. Gorelov served his prison camp term in Temlag, where he was assigned to cut timber. See Rostislav Gorelov's biography and paintings at https://bessmertnybarak.ru/Gorelov_Rostislav_Gavrilovich/.

148. Pidhainy, *The Black Deeds of the Kremlin*, 73.

149. Ibid., 51.

150. Ibid., 52–53.

151. For recent scholarly studies of life in the Gulag, see Nicolas Werth, *Cannibal Island: Death in a Siberian Gulag* (Princeton: Princeton University Press, 2007); Lynne Viola, *The Unknown Gulag: The Lost World of Stalin's Special Settlements* (Oxford: Oxford University Press, 2009); and Golfo Alexopoulos, *Illness and Inhumanity in Stalin's Gulag* (New Haven: Yale University Press, 2017).

152. Pidhainy, *The Black Deeds of the Kremlin*, 59.

153. Recently, Dan Healey has examined the treatment of disabled prisoners in an article "Lives in the Balance: Weak and Disabled Prisoners and the Biopolitics of the Gulag," *Kritika: Explorations in Russian and Eurasian History* 16, no. 3 (2015): 527–56.

154. Pidhainy, *The Black Deeds of the Kremlin*, 60.

155. For more on the life and academic career of Stepan Rudnyts'kyi (1877–1937), the founder of modern geography of Ukraine, see a special issue of *Chasopys spotsial'no-ekonomichnoï heohrafiï*, vyp. 32 (2007): 7–48, file:///C:/Users/Admin/Downloads/Chasopys-32_2007-1.pdf. The journal *Chronicle of Social-Economic Geography* is published by the Kharkiv National University named after V. N. Karazin. See also a special issue of *Istoriia ukraïns'koï heohrafiï*, vyp. 16 (2007): 8–41, file:///C:/Users/Admin/Downloads/IUG_16.pdf. The journal is published by Ternopil' Pedagogical University.

156. Pidhainy, "Portraits of Solowky Exiles," 340–41. For a biographical portrait of Rudnyts'kyi based on archival sources, see Oleksandr Rubl'ov, "Fundator ukraïns'koï heohrafichnoï nauky: Stepan Rudnys'kyi – liudyna i uchenyi," *Rehional'na istoriia Ukraïny: Zbirnyk naukovykh statei*, vyp. 12 (2018): 207–304.

157. According to the official Polish registry, there were 43,000 Ukrainian emigrants in the 1920s, among them members of the UNR government-in-exile, officers and rank-and-file in internment camps, diplomats, writers, and intellectual elites. See V. P. Troshchyns'kyi, *Mizhvoienna ukraïns'ka emihratsiia v Ievropi iak istorychne i sotsial'no-politychne iavyshche* (Kyïv: Intel, 1994), 20.

158. The Prague period was the most prolific time for Rudnyts'kyi. After years of working as a teacher of geography and writing his doctoral thesis, he finally assumed a position of professor at a newly established Ukrainian Free University. He published works on political and military geography of Ukraine in German and Ukrainian in Vienna, Berlin, Munich, and L'viv. His German-language work, *Ukraina und die Ukrainer* (Wien: Verlag des allgemeinen ukr. Nationalrates, 1914), was published in Italian and Hungarian translations in Rome and Budapest in 1914, and in English

translation in New York in 1915. Under a pseudonym Sh. Levenko, he printed several editions of his book, *Chomu my khochemo samostiinoï Ukraïny?* (Why do we want an independent Ukraine?), ed. by M. Zalizniak, first in Vienna in 1915, then in Berlin, L'viv, and Stockholm in 1916–1917. Nearly seventy of his published works have been compiled and reprinted by Oleh Shablii in S. L. Rudnyts'kyi, *Chomu my khochemo samostiinoï Ukraïny?* (L'viv: Svit, 1994).

159. *Ethnographische Übersichtskarte [der] Ukraina*, 1:7 500 000 (Wien: Kartogr. Anstalt G. Freytag & Berndt, Ges. m. b. H., 1915). The ethnographic map of Ukraine first appeared in an appendix to *Ukraina und die Ukrainer* in 1914 and in all foreign language editions in 1915. The first Ukrainian translation of the ethnographic map was published in 1917.

160. See Pitirim Sorokin's study of the effects of hunger on a starving individual in *Man and Society in Calamity*.

161. Pidhainy, "Portraits of Solowky Exiles," 342–43.

162. Prystaiko and Shapoval, *Sprava "Spilky vyzvolennia Ukraïny,"* 422.

163. Ibid., 421–22. For a discussion of the letter, written in March 1957, see Serhii Shevchenko, "Vsevolod Hantsov: zhyttia pislia svyntsevoï zlyvy," *Dzerkalo tyzhnia*, May 22, 2014, https://zn.ua/ukr/HISTORY/vsevolod-gancov-zhittya-pislya-svincevoyi-zlivi-_.html.

164. Malcolm Muggeridge, "Chronicles of Wasted Time," *Esquire*, February 1972, 118.

165. Muggeridge, "Chronicles of Wasted Time," 119.

166. In 1932, a new brand of cigarettes was introduced in the Soviet Union, which featured a map of the Belomorkanal (White Sea Canal) on its cover.

167. Pidhainy, *The Black Deeds of the Kremlin*, 57–58.

168. Ibid., 58.

169. Ibid.

170. Ibid., 61–62, 72.

171. Chukhin, *Kanalo-armeitsy*, 103.

172. Pidhainy, "Portraits of Solowky Exiles," 350–51.

173. Pidhainy, *The Black Deeds of the Kremlin*, 69, 73.

174. Ibid., 67–68.

175. Chukhin, *Kanalo-armeitsy*, 118.

176. Paul R. Gregory and Valery Lazarev, eds., *The Economics of Forced Labor: The Soviet Gulag* (Palo Alto: Stanford University Hoover Institution Press, 2003).

177. Vallin et al., "The Great Famine," in *Holodomor*, eds. Luciuk and Grekul, 40.

178. George Kitchin, *Prisoner of the OGPU* (London: Longmans, Green and Co., 1935), 334.

179. Ibid., 335.

180. Ryan Dearinger, *The Filth of Progress: Immigrants, Americans, and the Building of Canals and Railroads in the West* (Oakland: University of California Press, 2015).

181. Eugene Lyons, *Assignment in Utopia* (New York: Harcourt, Brace and Co., 1937), 426.

182. David Dallin and Boris Nicolaevsky, *Forced Labor in Soviet Russia* (London: Hollis and Carter, 1948), 218–19.

183. Anne Applebaum, *Gulag: A History* (New York: Doubleday, 2003), 58–59.

184. Dallin and Nicolaevsky, *Forced Labor in Soviet Russia*, 219.

185. "Timber and Allied Industries," *Handbook of the Soviet Union* (New York: American-Russian Chamber of Commerce, 1936), 176.

186. *Handbook of the Soviet Union*, 177.

187. Ibid., 40.

188. Ibid., 311, 341.

189. John L. Scherer and Michael Jackobson, "The Collectivization of Agriculture and the Soviet Prison Camp System," *Europe Asia Studies*, no. 45 (1993): 538.

190. Plaggenborg, *Revoliutsiia i kul'tura*, 142.

191. Ibid., 221.

192. Walter Wilson, *Forced Labor in the United States* (New York: International Publishers, 1933), 9.

193. Applebaum, *Gulag*, 60.

194. Dallin and Nicolaevsky, *Forced Labor in Soviet Russia*, 220.

195. Applebaum, *Gulag*, 60.

196. Wilson, *Forced Labor in the United States*, 163, 169.

197. For more on the role of Walter Duranty in distorting the truth about the Holodomor, see S. J. Taylor, *Stalin's Apologist: Walter Duranty: The New York Times's Man in Moscow* (New York: Oxford University Press, 1990) and Agnieszka Holland's thriller *Mr. Jones* (Samuel Goldwyn Films, 2020).

198. "The Soviet Star of Hope," *The Daily Worker*, 1924; quoted in Peter G. Filene, *Americans and the Soviet Experiment, 1917–1933* (Cambridge: Harvard University Press, 1967), 130.

199. Lyons, *Assignment in Utopia*, 435.

200. "The Ambassador in the Soviet Union (William C. Bullitt) to the Secretary of State," Moscow, July 19, 1935, Document 241, *Foreign Relations of the United States: The Soviet Union, 1933–1939*, eds. E. R. Perkins, Rogers Platt Churchill, and John Gilbert Reid (Washington, D.C.: U.S. Government Printing Office, 1952), 227, https://history.state.gov/historicaldocuments/frus1933-39/d241.

201. For a detailed account of the vote in support for recognition, see Filene, *Americans and the Soviet Experiment*, 261, 363.

202. Kołakowski, "The Marxist Roots of Stalinism," 160.

Chapter 4

Extermination

From 1929 to 1932, Stalin attempted to repeat a communist onslaught by curtailing the NEP and consolidating state ownership of the means of production. Modernization of industry at the expense of agriculture had precedents in history. Japan modernized successfully through taxation of agriculture.[1] Soviet leaders in their attempt to become competitive with the West (or East) could choose from a plethora of scientific methods. Seemingly, agricultural research institutes were created in Soviet Ukraine for this purpose to only see their staff executed, imprisoned, or exiled at the peak of the Holodomor.[2] Then, as now, it was evident that small farms could not compete with large farms in their output. After all, in the United States, contemporary supersized family farms with $1 million or more in annual sales are only 4 percent of total farms and produce two-thirds of the country's agricultural output.[3] Not all large farms are profitable; the key to their financial health is efficient management.[4] What was the goal of Soviet managers in the 1930s when the Great Depression hit the world market? What was the goal of collectivizing agriculture at the cost of expropriating private property and forcing grain growers to surrender their entire crop while subsisting on grass? Decisions were made at a confluence of utopia and terror. Under the cover of the First Five-Year Plan, once the "brain" of the nation was blown out as a result of the SVU trial,[5] the next prong of the coordinated attack targeted the body of the nation, its land tillers. The ultimate stage of genocide unfolded, the extermination by starvation of grain growers in Soviet Ukraine and areas inhabited by Ukrainian farmers in other parts of the Soviet Union in 1932–1933. Among the tactics used by Stalin and his henchmen were requisitions, blacklists, and blockades.[6] The concurrent curtailment of Ukrainization spelled out death to carriers of national tradition, culture, and language—in Lemkin's words the "soul" of the nation. To survive meant to accommodate or assimilate to the repressive regime.

REBELLIONS

Unlike Lenin, who retreated from an analogous situation, Stalin mobilized the entire repressive apparatus to realize communist doctrine to its fullest extent, no matter what the cost. Kul'chyts'kyi, a scholar of the Soviet agricultural policy, has argued that total collectivization of agriculture was not "total" because it left farmers with remnants of private ownership of the means of production on their own garden plots. The problem was that "the state's attempt to replace free trade between town and country with barter failed."[7] The state did not generate sufficient industrial output to make exchange between town and country equitable. Consequently, contractual agreements between state and farmers turned into forced requisitioning. Predictably, "surplus appropriation" (in Russia *prodrazverstka*), in fact confiscations, from 1930 to 1932, brought the state to the brink of economic collapse.[8]

Soviet historiography maintains that, after fulfilling their quotas for delivering grain, farmers stopped working on collective farms to focus on their private garden plots as a means of survival. What is often neglected is the fact that a *trudoden'*, a blend of *trud* and *den'* or a "workday" as a form of payment for workers on collective farms, was inadequate because farms often could not compensate for workdays. This form of payment was introduced in 1930 because the state had no functioning banking system for money circulation. By spring 1931, this system of payment was imposed on 84 percent of collective farms in Ukraine. Payments were disbursed twice a year, an advance payment in July or August, and the full payment by the decision of the farm administration at the end of the year. Payments for agricultural work were stratified into five categories, averaging one or two workdays, or 60 kopeks to 1 krb. 20 kopeks. There was no minimum payment; it was determined by a variety of factors: crop sizes, principles of distribution, and grain procurement plans. For instance, ploughing 6 hectares of farm land was equivalent to 1.5 workdays, whereas digging out 600 quintal of potatoes or a ton of sugar beets was equivalent to 1.75 workdays. Distribution of seed grain was forbidden until collective farms fulfilled imposed grain procurement quotas. In fall 1932, collective farmers were stripped of one-third of their earned workdays for not fulfilling grain procurement quotas, and in the blacklisted collective farms, workers were stripped of their grain seed advances. In 1933, 48 percent of collective farms in Ukraine did not pay workers for their earned workdays, leaving 4 million farmers and 14 million of their dependents without means to survive.[9]

By 1932, most farms in Soviet Ukraine had been already collectivized.[10] Survivors and witnesses testify that two-thirds of victims were those who worked on collective farms.[11] There were no farms to collectivize because Ukraine was singled out to be the first republic to comply with the Soviet experiment.[12] In other words, collectivization was not the main cause of the high death toll during the genocidal famine in Soviet Ukraine but rather the confiscations of everything edible—to the last kernel of wheat or potato or a pot of borsch on the stove.

Soviet historians have argued that Stalin saved the collective farm system, as well as his own post of general secretary of the TsK VKP(b), through the use of organized terror. According to Kul′chyts′kyi, Stalin achieved this in two ways: first, by delaying Karl Marx's requirement that trade be replaced with barter from the first phase (socialism in Marxist theory as) to the second utopian phase (communism), in which the distribution of material goods according to need would be established, and second, by masterminding a famine.[13] Yet, the economic argument is insufficient to explain the intent of genocidal killing. The famine was organized on territories where non-Russian inhabitants predominated—all of Soviet Ukraine and ethnically Ukrainian regions in the North Caucasus, even as far as Central Asian republics—the territories under Moscow's economic colonization.[14] Russian writers, among them Sergei Maksimov, wrote that "while Ukrainians are dying from starvation, we are drinking tea with jam, white bread, butter, cheese, and buns."[15]

The height of the drive to liquidate small farm proprietors came in February and March of 1930, concurrently with the trial of the nationally conscious Ukrainian intelligentsia. Thousands of Communist Party and Communist Youth League activists were mobilized for the grain procurement campaign.[16] In his novel *Forever Flowing*, Vasily Grossman included a confession of a Communist Party plenipotentiary Anna Mikhailova, a war widow from southern Russia, who arrived in Soviet Ukraine to answer the party's call for intensification of grain procurement.[17] She finds a soul mate in the protagonist of the novel and confides in him that members of grain procurement brigades fell under the spell of propaganda:

> True, they were under a spell—they had sold themselves on the idea that the so-called "kulaks" were pariahs, untouchables, vermin. They would not sit down at a "parasite's" table; the "kulak" child was loathsome; the young "kulak" girl was lower than a louse. They looked on the so-called "kulaks" as cattle, loathsome, repulsive: they had no souls; they stank; they all had venereal diseases; they were enemies of the people and exploited the labor of others.[18]

Propaganda that instigated hatred against people marked for annihilation was incessant: slogans were repeated at meetings, special instructions were broadcast on the radio, and scenes of kulaks burning grain were shown at movie theaters. Stalin himself called them "parasites" and openly proclaimed they must be destroyed as a class. In the eyes of perpetrators, they were not human. Swayed by propaganda, Communist Party members, local activists, and especially outsiders (*buksyry*, or tugboat brigades dispatched to speed up procurement) showed no sympathy for the accursed, convinced that happy days would instantly ensue once they liquidated "enemies of the people." Tugboat brigades were generally larger than local brigades, and sometimes reached 800 members from various organizations, including Komsomol, Communists and non-Communists, and Young Pioneers.[19] "They would have killed their own fathers and mothers simply in order to carry out instructions." Zealous fanatics, who settled their own accounts with their neighbors or family members, shouted the loudest about "political awareness" while stealing from others.[20]

Bolshevik perpetrators denied the humanity of Ukrainian independent-minded farmers. Targeted members of the group were equated with vermin, insects, or diseases. Dehumanization overcame the normal human revulsion against murder. Hate propaganda in print and on the radio was used to vilify the victim group. Bolshevik leaders taught their followers to regard victims as alien to society. In Soviet Ukraine, farmers, labeled *kurkuli*, were portrayed as spiders, snakes, or vermin in Soviet propaganda posters. Figures 4.1 and 4.2 show propaganda cartoons from the January 1930 issue of the *Chervonyi perets'* (Red Pepper) magazine.

This satirical biweekly magazine, printed in Kharkiv, put on its front cover a trio, who under the cover of night are attempting to sneak over the collective farm fence with a locked gate, casting long shadows. The headline reads: "From the front—'holy men,' but from the rear." B. Fridkin, the cartoonist, prompts the reader: "Collective farmer! Before admitting these three citizens into your collective farm, go to page 4." On the bottom of page 4, the punch line goes: "See?! With a shotgun, an ax, and a can of gasoline, the '*kurkuli* are growing into socialism.'" The top half of the front cover is yellow and the bottom half is blue. Yellow and blue colors were used in Soviet propaganda cartoons, hinting that "saboteurs" were Ukrainian nationalists as yellow and blue are national colors of Ukraine.[21]

In 1930, armed with sticks, pitchforks, axes, and occasionally sawed-off shotguns, Ukrainian farmers threatened the success of Stalin's grain procurement plans. The OGPU recorded the explosion of violence against the Soviet regime. The largest number of mass uprisings (4,098 recorded by the OGPU) erupted in the Ukrainian SSR[22] (see Figure 4.3). The success of Stalin's project depended on Soviet Ukraine; therefore, there were significantly more

Figure 4.1 Propaganda cartoon in the *Chervonyi perets'* (Red Pepper) satirical biweekly magazine, 1930 (front, see over back). *Source:* From the National Library of Ukraine named after V. I. Vernads'kyi.

Figure 4.2 Propaganda cartoon in the *Chervonyi perets'* (Red Pepper) satirical biweekly magazine, 1930 (back). *Source:* From the National Library of Ukraine named after V. I. Vernads'kyi.

disturbances in Soviet Ukraine than in three other grain-growing regions of the Central Black Earth (1,373), the North Caucasus (1,061), and the Lower Volga (1,003),[23] where significant numbers of ethnic Ukrainian farmers lived. Mass uprisings in Ukrainian villages in 1930 undermined the legitimacy of Soviet government authorities.[24]

As shown on the map, two regions Volyn' and Podillia sustained more insurgencies where rioters gained control of district centers. Groups of villagers, ranging from 300 to 500 people, took up handmade weapons to attack

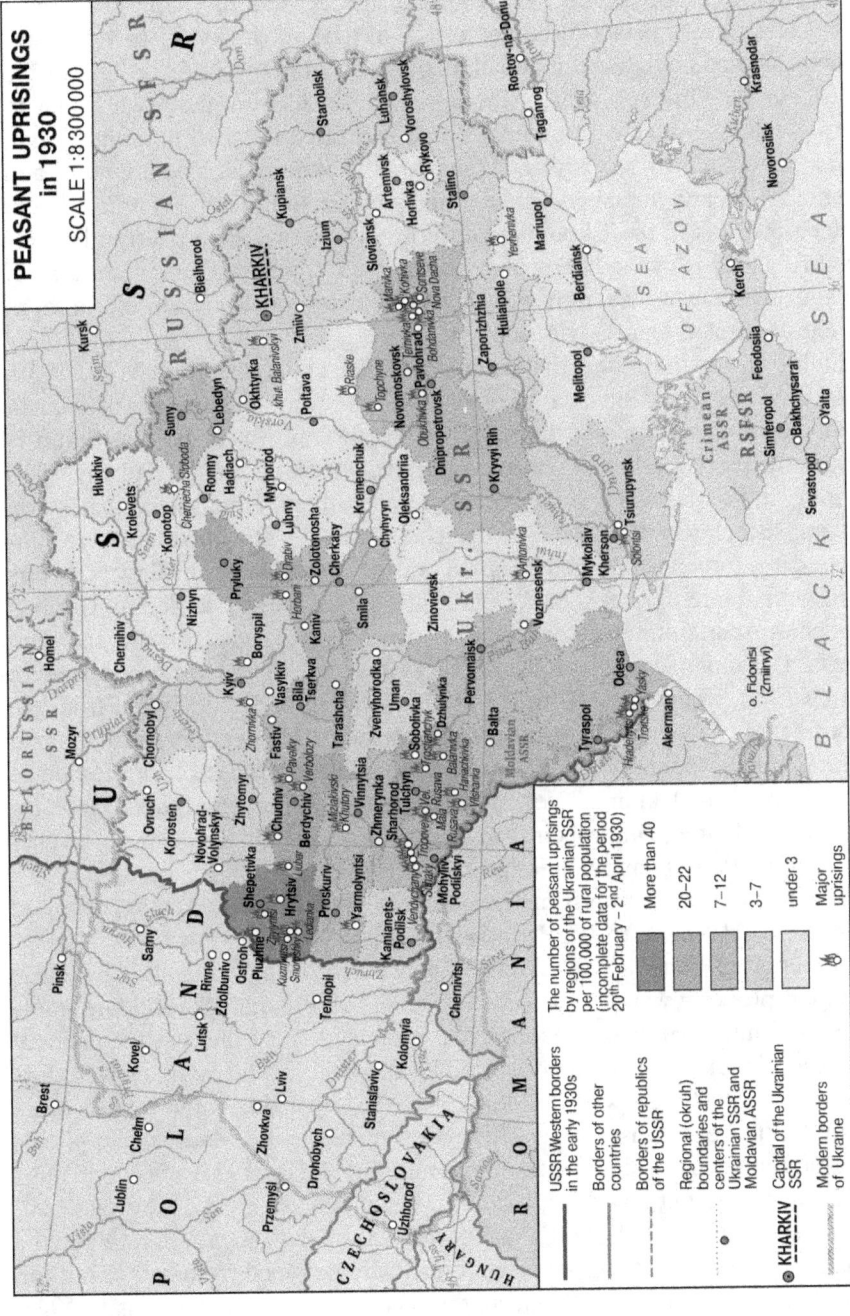

Figure 4.3 Mass uprisings in the Ukrainian SSR in 1930. *Source*: Created by the DNVP "Kartohrafiia," 2019.

Soviet guards who returned fire with machine guns.[25] According to Vsevolod Balyts′kyi, head of the GPU in Ukraine, the Soviets lost control of most villages in the Shepetivs′ka border area.[26] In the Liubars′kyi district, twenty-nine village councils were liquidated and police units were forced out of the district center. In early March, the uprising spread from the town center to nearby villages, where insurgents harnessed horses from the *kolhosp* and, armed with pitchforks or knives, began to kill Communist Youth League and Communist Party members and Soviet plenipotentiaries.[27] By mid-March, sixteen districts in the Ukrainian western border zone were overrun by rioters. In Tul′chyns′kyi and two nearby districts, 340 village committees and 73 village soviets were taken over.[28] New administrations were elected in those villages liberated from Soviet control.

Stalin closely watched the situation in Tul′chyn. On March 19, 1930, Balyts′kyi wrote to Stanislav Kosior, the top Communist Party official in Soviet Ukraine: "Comrade Leplevs′kyi has just informed me that Stalin is proposing the adoption of more aggressive measures in the Tul′chyns′kyi district, and with regard to the repeated unrest there, emphasized that I stop making speeches but instead take decisive action."[29] The uprisings were suppressed by force, with machine guns and in some places artillery.[30] At the same time, more uprisings broke out in the south in areas settled by German Mennonite agricultural colonists, and gradually advanced toward the then Soviet Ukrainian capital of Kharkiv.[31] The peak of the riots occurred in March 1930, when the SVU trial was underway to deflect attention from the coordinated operation to subvert people's struggle for freedom from colonial dependence. Despite the OGPU pronouncement that "peace had returned to practically all of Ukraine," yet another large-scale uprising erupted in early April in Pavlohrad, Dnipropetrovs′k region. It resulted in the deaths of twenty Communist Party plenipotentiaries.[32]

The retribution for uprisings resulted in entire families being deported from Soviet Ukraine to OGPU concentration camps. As many as 150,000 were deported[33] and 170,000 were sentenced for crimes against the state,[34] and their property was confiscated. The rebels used pitchforks and farm tools because hunting rifles or weapons that remained since the war for national liberation in Ukraine were confiscated by the OGPU, and civilians were forbidden to keep firearms of any kind.[35] At the same time Communists were permitted to bear arms; in fact, German semiautomatic Mauser C96 pistols became the status symbol of Soviet commissars.[36] By 1931, mass uprisings in Ukraine were put down, but hardened insurgents engaged in new tactics of small, isolated units.[37] The OGPU reported 288 such "gangs" operating in the republic.[38] The number of protesters drastically declined from over 1 million in 1930 to 75,000 in 1931.[39] During the second wave of repressions in 1931, over 130,000 insurgents were deported from Soviet Ukraine.[40] Nevertheless, by July 1932, the number of mass protests tripled from 319 the year before to 923, with more than 200,000 participants.[41] Stalin, while vacationing in Crimea in August 1932, authorized arrests and executions under the law on "protection of socialist property" to put down resistance in Soviet Ukraine, which was spiraling out of control.

The GPU, militia, and army detachments conducted special operations in Soviet Ukraine to suppress uprisings and resistance to grain and food confiscations in the countryside.[42] Annually between 1929 and 1932, the GPU recorded thousands of incidents of murder, attempted murder, and assault on Communist Party officials and local activists as well as arson and other forms of property damage and labeled them "terrorist acts."[43] "Genocide is always organized, usually by the state, often using militias to provide deniability of state responsibility," noted Gregory Stanton.[44] Often, resistance lasted for several days and nights, at times for weeks. Villages were burned, and participants—men, women, and children—were captured, executed, or exiled to labor camps. A schoolteacher, Volodymyr Benedyk, was one of the Solovky exiles portrayed by Semen Pidhainy in his memoir. Benedyk led the farmer's insurrection, which spread from Kam'ianets'-Podil's'kyi to Vinnytsia and then to Kyïv. The GPU sentenced him to labor camps with the stipulation to never return to Ukraine. Benedyk used to say: "There never was a nation that won its liberation without sacrifice."[45]

BLOCKADES

One of the repressive measures introduced to condemn individuals or collectives for the failure to fulfill grain-requisition target was blacklisting (*chorni doshky*, literally "black boards"). Names of proprietors and collective farms were listed on billboards as well as printed in newspapers for the public to see. One of the initial resolutions to blacklist collective farms was implemented on November 4, 1932, by Stalin's appointee in the North Caucasus, Lazar Kaganovich.[46] As head of the extraordinary grain-procurement commission, Kaganovich went to Ukrainian Cossack farmsteads to convince them into "voluntarily" surrendering surplus grain. Wording in the resolution condemned farmers for "maliciously sabotaging" state grain procurements. Russian historian Nikolai Ivnitskii asserted that Stalin edited the resolution himself.[47]

Blacklisting in Soviet Ukraine was initiated with the resolution adopted by the TsK KP(b)U on November 18, 1932, "On Measures to Strengthen Grain Procurement."[48] According to Soviet historian Stanislav Kul'chyts'kyi, during Molotov's second visit to Kharkiv, then the capital of Soviet Ukraine, he spent two days with Ukrainian communists discussing how to implement Stalin's instructions, specifically the blacklisting piloted in the North Caucasus. Ukrainian historian Heorhii Papakin noted that the Ukrainian resolution was a word-for-word replica of the North Caucasus resolution in its description of blacklisting instructions, with minor variations. The list of repressive measures that created conditions for physical destruction of Ukrainian farmers, with the explicit purpose of "overcoming resistance," included:

a) Immediate suspension of delivery of goods and of cooperative and state trade activities in these villages and the removal of all available goods from cooperative and state stores;
b) Full prohibition of *kolhosp* trade activities among collective farms and collective and private farmers;
c) Suspension of all crediting activities and a demand for preterm collection of credits and other financial obligations;
d) Investigation and purging of collective farms in these villages followed by the removal of counterrevolutionary elements and the organizers of grain-collection disruptions.[49]

Regional executive committees were to carry out the instructions and report to the Communist Party's Central Committee on collective farms being blacklisted. Independent farmers were forced to pay fines in the form of an additional meat procurement (fifteen months) and one-year potato quotas. If independent farmers delivered grain fully by established deadlines, then these fines could be canceled. However, fines could also be doubled in extraordinary circumstances. Moreover, all loans of seed grain issued to independent farmers had to be repaid and credited to collective farm's grain procurement quotas. To enforce these measures, brigades of collective farm activists had to be organized. The November resolution specified that by the first day of December 1932, at least 1,100 of these collective farm brigades had to be dispatched throughout Soviet Ukraine, according to the following regions and numbers[50]:

Kharkiv—350
Kyïv—300
Vinnytsia—200
Chernihiv—100
Odesa—50
Donbas—50
Dnipropetrovs′k—50

Mark Tauger of West Virginia University estimated that if each of these 1,100 brigades searched 100 households, and a household had 5 people, then they took food from 550,000 people, out of 20 million, or about 2 or 3 percent.[51] The crucial point here is that these 3 percent of households produced around 20 percent of the grain.[52] This illustrates that independent farmers were in the minority, but they were the ones squeezed most. This also illustrates, and something Tauger has failed to notice, the repressive nature of the policy.[53] For instance, in two districts in the Poltava region regular search brigades could procure 390,259 *puds* in 67 villages, whereas the tugboat brigade procured 449,000 *puds* in 25 villages.[54] Such tugboat brigades comprised on average from 50 to 200–800 outsiders, whose enforcement tactics contributed to the "impressive results." Tauger belongs to a cohort of revisionist historians who attempt to discredit the view that Soviet totalitarianism was oppressive.[55] Revisionists depict the Soviet Union as not so different from societies in the West, "nothing to fear and even something to admire."[56]

The reasoning behind it was not new; it was a continuation of the Bolshevik policy of grain confiscations. To put down farmers' rebellions, Stalin used methods promulgated by his predecessor, Lenin. The following translation of a letter, signed by Lenin, gives a glimpse into the dictator's thinking in a response to reports from Penza of an uprising there during the first Bolshevik onslaught.[57] Wired via telegraph on August 11, 1918, the letter urged comrades to "mercilessly suppress" the uprising as an example to others. Lenin suggested four extraordinary measures:

1. Hang (hang without fail, so *the people see*) *no fewer than one hundred* known kulaks, rich men, bloodsuckers.
2. Publish their names.
3. Take from them *all* the grain.
4. Designate hostages—as per yesterday's telegram.

Do it in such a way that for hundreds of *versts* around, the people will see, tremble, know, shout: *they are strangling* and will strangle to death the bloodsucker kulaks.

On December 6, 1932, TsK KP(b)U and the Council of People's Commissars of the Ukrainian SSR adopted a joint resolution "On Adding Villages that Maliciously Sabotage Grain Procurements to the Blacklist." This resolution has been thoroughly analyzed by historians.[58] The resolution listed six villages in Dnipropetrovs'k, Odesa, and Kharkiv regions to be added to the All-Ukrainian blacklist. Heorhii Papakin noted that this resolution contradicted the previous one, issued on November 18, because the targets for blacklisting were not collective farms as units of socialist economy or village soviets as administrative units, but entire villages. In other words, all villagers, including farmers, entrepreneurs, workers of machine-tractor stations, and teachers were doomed. "This, beyond doubt, underscores that the goal of the Bolshevik policy was not the fulfillment of a grain procurement plan (it was an excuse), but the creation of conditions incompatible with life for all residents of the village," Papakin concluded.[59] Eventually, as of January 1933, the Ukrainian SSR as a whole was secretly blacklisted.[60]

What was not publicized, and remains the least investigated tactic, was blockading the area at night with military and GPU troops before searching by tugboat brigades (*buksyrni bryhady*) would commence.[61] Official documents do not explicitly list instructions to blockade villages that were added to the blacklist. However, how could a ban on trade and travel of villagers from the zone of organized famine be accomplished without control of population movement? Witnesses provide first-hand accounts of how it felt to be blacklisted—with villages blockaded by troops. Survivors from the village Liutenka, which was blacklisted, recalled:

> All roads and paths around Liutenka were blocked by GPU patrols that did not let anyone in or out of the village. All goods were taken away from stores and the delivery of salt, matches, oil, soap, and medicine seized. They closed schools, the mill, pharmacy, and post office. . . . Special brigades searched for grain in every house but found nothing. In December 1932, villagers died *en masse*. The blockade was not lifted until the beginning of spring [1933] sowing.[62]

Another account of a blockade of blacklisted villages in the Dnipropetrovs'k region was narrated by a village teacher:

> Residents (from Verbky and two neighboring villages Bohdanivka and Ternivka) were not allowed to travel to other villages and to the town of Pavlohrad to procure food. Villages were surrounded by army troops, but people tried to escape at night to the town of Pavlohrad, and sometimes they could at least buy some bread. Anyone caught was severely punished.[63]

Mikhail Frenkin,[64] who taught at a *robfak* school in the Zhytomyr region, recalled how villages were blockaded by special GPU units and how teachers were ordered to assist in implementing this task:

> I remember once all of the teachers who were Komsomol and [Communist] Party members were ordered to surround one of the villages to prevent anyone from escaping while Mobile Units of the GPU (*mangruppy*—in Russian, maneuverable groups) drove the arrested peasants out of the village to the railcars waiting at the train station to deport them. All this was done in secret. The

village would be surrounded during the night to avoid any noise and commotion. That's how it was done. And, the Party apparatus took part. Just let anyone raise their voice in protest and tomorrow that person would be arrested. All of it was part of the Terror . . . it was frightful.[65]

To justify a special GPU operation and give it an aura of legitimacy, the press published a decree issued on November 26, 1932, by the Commissariat of Justice and Prosecutor General of Ukraine.[66] The decree declared that repressive measures were the most effective means to suppress "sabotage" and "class resistance against grain procurement" in 243 districts in Soviet Ukraine.[67] In 1932, the GPU arrested 21,197 "saboteurs," including 1,491 in August; 2,526 in September; 2,850 in October; and 14,330 (or 67.7 percent) in November.[68] The exponential increase in repressions grew in November when Molotov arrived to maximally squeeze out grain from Soviet Ukraine. One-third of the arrested were charged under the new law on protection of socialist property, known as "five ears of wheat" law, adopted in August 1932. Another third were arrested for agitation against the grain-requisition campaign. The remaining third were arrested for speculation, refusal to transport grain, or criticism of authorities. Most of the arrested were independent proprietors; 16.8 percent were labeled *kurkuli*.[69]

Repressions further intensified, when on December 5, 1932, Balyts'kyi issued "Operative Order of the GPU USRR No. 1" that spelled out the main task of the GPU in Soviet Ukraine: to defeat the "counterrevolutionary underground," commonly portrayed as organized by the *kurkuli* and *petliurivtsi* who opposed Soviet policies in the countryside. A special operative group was established with Karl Karlson, deputy head of GPU in Soviet Ukraine, to carry out the order. By mid-December, the operation in the countryside led to arrests of 16,000 "enemies of the people"[70] and expropriation of 11,340 tons of grain.[71] Balyts'kyi reported that the GPU apprehended "bandit formations," organized by the Ukrainian National Republic's government-in-exile, and arrested former members of parties liquidated by Bolsheviks, students and professors of Kyïv institutes, and saboteurs on collective farms, a total of 589 such groups that sabotaged grain procurement.[72] Thus, "grain procurement" was a cover for the organized GPU operation that targeted Ukrainians associated with national aspirations for independence.

IMPLICATED SUBJECTS

Teachers were incrementally turned into accomplices with a carrot-and-stick policy. This phenomenon is not new; it has been observed in other cases of genocide. In his film, *The Look of Silence*, Joshua Oppenheimer documented that mayors and teachers were among killers in villages during the massacres of 1965–1966 in Indonesia.[73] In Soviet Ukraine in the 1930s, schoolteachers were willing and often unwilling members of the *aktyv*—active supporters of the Soviet system, upon whom authorities called to carry out officially sanctioned policies.[74] It is to an activist of this period that the well-known saying is attributed: "Moscow does not believe in tears."[75] The most disturbing fact was that among the activists who helped the GPU in arrests and deportations of dispossessed farmers were teachers who knew their victims.

In her study of rank-and-file perpetrators of the Holodomor, Daria Mattingly of Cambridge University developed a typology based on motivational factors, proposed by Alette Smeulers.[76] Mattingly used the "neutral" Ukrainian term *pryzvidtsi*, which in her view is devoid of any moral or legal qualification, to characterize those whose actions (or inactions) led to starvation of millions of their fellow citizens. Mattingly has argued that the term "perpetrators" (*auctor delicti*) would be apt for Soviet leaders guilty of issuing legislative provisions, whereas the term "executors" (*executor delicti*) would be appropriate to characterize those responsible for deportations and executions of the Ukrainian intelligentsia, clergy, and farmers.[77] The distinction between victims and perpetrators is fluid. As Polish philosopher Leszek Kołakowski noted, application of totalitarian law hinged on arbitrary and changing decisions of executive authorities so that "everyone [was] at the same time an inmate of a concentration camp and a secret police agent."[78] State-sanctioned violence unfolded gradually. Law-abiding citizens, including teachers, were coerced to comply to carry out violence. They joined what Ervin Staub called the "continuum of destruction" and served in institutions created to perpetuate violence, with a predictable reversal of morality.[79] Like the subjects in Stanley Milgram's experiment on obedience, ordinary people subjected their victims to the highest electric shock after a progressive series of smaller shocks.[80] Over a decade, campaign after campaign, citizens in Soviet Ukraine became inured to mass violence perpetrated by the regime with impunity.[81]

Among activists were even family members of the victims. Testifying anonymously, a perpetrator admitted that despite the fact her father was imprisoned during collectivization, she joined grain-requisition campaigns. "Then people lived quietly, didn't talk much about this . . . , but *trymaly iazyk za zubamy*" (in Ukrainian, "kept the tongue behind the teeth," or kept silent).[82] She noted that some activists tried to help victims. When activists recognized that a person was socially valuable, or had special skills, they tried to rescue such a person. However, "there were also those who would denounce, tell lies. Starvation is a terrible thing."[83] Understandably, she did not see herself as guilty and, most probably, did not have an intent to harm victims, but she did nothing to stop abuses. She clearly pointed out that the means of coercion was starvation. This anonymous witness still harbored fear decades after the event and thousands of miles across the Atlantic away from the crime scene. Many teachers mobilized for the "third front" found themselves in a similar situation, tongue tied after years of reeducation, political literacy tests, and guaranteed food ration in exchange for compliance and silence. The alternative was repression, deportation, or worse.

Soviet authorities shaped teachers' behavior with the use of propaganda in newspapers. In the run up to the SVU trial, when arrests of the alleged members of the SVU were underway, in October 1929, a *Pravda* editorial described two categories of teachers. The editorial praised "social enthusiasts" among teachers for giving more than 800 lectures and organizing nearly 2,000 *supryahs* but criticized teachers who had to be forced to fulfill their public duty for their lukewarm attitude to grain requisitions. The editorial reported an incident in a school in the village of Samoilivtsi, Blyznets' district. School authorities ordered children to bring 35 pounds of grain per household (to be included in the school's grain collection plan). One of the teachers in the school was censured for violating a "class approach" by assigning an equal amount to the children of kulaks, middle, and poor farmers. The editorial cited another case in the Meshev district, where a teacher received an anonymous letter: "Better give up work that does not concern you. Stick to teaching or you will be sorry." The editorial stressed that *kurkuli* hate teachers who are "social enthusiasts."[84]

On the eve of the SVU trial, newspapers published a series of reports about murders of teachers by bandits in rural districts of Soviet Ukraine. Chief Prosecutor Lev Akhmatov also issued a statement to the press in November 1929. He announced that two teachers had been murdered for their active participation in collectivization and literacy campaigns. Akhmatov took these murders as evidence that "class struggle" in the village was intensifying. While investigation of "nefarious activities" of the old generation Ukrainian intelligentsia was in progress, Akhmatov emphasized that the majority of teachers were "on the same side of the barricade" with poor and hired laborers.[85] He promised to afford teachers legal protection to defend them against future attacks by their "mortal enemies"—*kurkuli*. The duplicity of the government that prosecuted teachers while simultaneously affording teachers "legal protection" to defend them against attacks by "enemies of the people" was mind boggling.

In January 1930, *Visti* informed its readers that the People's Commissariat of Education had decided to mobilize schools for political and economic assignments in the agricultural campaign. All schools were required to keep a record of their participation in "the social reconstruction of the countryside and the realization of the program mapped by the party and the government."[86] Mikhail Frenkin, who came from Baku, Azerbaijan, to teach in a *robfak* school in the Pulinsky district in Soviet Ukraine, recalled how teachers were taken into villages as plenipotentiaries:

> These were teachers who were [Communist] Party members, Komsomol members. I myself was neither a Komsomol nor Party member. So the teachers would be sent to help with grain requisitioning for a period of two or three weeks, a month or two or three months. One of my colleagues, a man by the name of Vakhnovsky, was a Communist. They would take him, and he would be absent from school for months at a time. He'd spend the whole of that time in the village seeing to the grain requisitions. They continually changed everyone around, so that the entire Party apparatus would take part to one degree or another, although they wouldn't be forced to shoot or kill anyone. They couldn't refuse to take part.[87]

Frenkin noted that schools and institutes in Soviet Ukraine did not function. "The institute where I was working . . . was totally shut down at one point for two months. The teachers and students had been mobilized to take part in all these activities. And then the arrests began."[88]

Teachers who worked in rural schools and depended on the support of local farmers had mixed attitudes toward grain requisitions: some were skeptical, others passive, or "duplicitous" in their attitude toward the policy that would result in death of millions. Realizing that teachers were leaders in the task of building socialism, the state through its press provided a model of normative behavior for teachers to follow: either being honored for their revolutionary activism or risk being vilified for their "bourgeois nationalism." Teachers, who were critical of the Communist Party policy, resisted mobilization, or declined to participate in grain requisitions as assigned, were reprimanded or purged from party ranks.[89] In Dymers'kyi district, a teacher, who was in charge of a requisition brigade and decided to distribute grain to the starving, was arrested for "squandering grain" and prosecuted.[90] As many as 48 teachers in the Chernihiv region were arrested by the GPU for hiding the requisitioned grain and purged from the union.[91]

A vivid account of teachers' quandary was narrated by Oleksander Merkelo, who worked as an accountant on state farms in the village of Kolodiazhna, Dvorichna district, Kharkiv region. As a teenager, he witnessed the famine and was deeply hurt seeing the destruction of hardworking farmers, including his own family. Merkelo befriended teacher Oransky, who was required to participate in all campaigns initiated by Bolsheviks in Soviet Ukraine. The teacher frankly admitted to his friend:

> You are a happy man, after sitting with your abacus for eight hours you go home, and you are not required to join any campaigns. But I have to lie to

farmers and lie to their children that they have a happy childhood in the Soviet Union.

Merkelo ended the story by saying: "That spring he committed suicide."[92] Merkelo explained:

> Teachers were forced, especially young teachers. But let me tell one thing . . . that work, as I told you about Oransky, tormented them. He could not say "no" because that meant being subjected to repression, being arrested. So he had no other choice but to blow his brain. He went to work with great tension in his mind. Obviously, he could not tell the truth to schoolchildren about happy childhood in the Soviet Union advertised in every newspaper and on the radio, when everywhere he saw dead bodies and starving, swollen children.[93]

Unlike commissars, who carried guns, teachers usually did not have access to guns, unless they were subject to conscription. Statistics on suicides are unavailable,[94] so Oransky's story is anecdotal evidence of a mind tormented and ultimately destroyed by the regime.

The mobilization of schoolteachers to take part in the campaign to seize food from households or deport villagers was an extremely traumatizing experience. Mr. Kononenko, who taught in school in the village of Komians'ke in the Dnipropetrovs'k region, felt that teachers were "the most tragic of all figures in the village at that time." In his testimony before members of the U.S. Commission on the Ukraine Famine, Mr. Kononenko stated,

> First of all, one obviously does not become a school teacher out of desire to exert power, or get rich, or to be socially mobile. It is a job that one takes because one wants to teach, one has a real desire to serve those, who particularly children, who want to learn.

The teacher recalled how he was sent out into the fields in the spring of 1933 and forced to read Soviet newspapers, *Visti* VUTsVK or *Komunist*, to villagers during lunch while they were eating:

> It was meant to educate them and the topic was always political. How wonderful was the Soviet political system, how lucky we are to have a leader like Joseph Stalin. And I read them. I know it is the wrong thing to do.
> They hated me because they thought I belonged to that corrupt political system. I tell you honestly, I was hungry because I walked two or three kilometers to that place. I see them eating their beans. I like to eat, but they never asked me, "Maybe you need it." You understand? I was hungry and reading that Soviet official propaganda to convince them of that tragic life.[95]

Another eyewitness Antin Lak, who taught Ukrainian language and literature during the famine in Soviet Ukraine and received 300 grams of bread daily, recalled:

> When I was in Kremenchuk, I walked daily along the streets of the city either to go to the store or to visit my friends, and I saw villagers that flocked to the city to find something to eat. These dressed in rags, emaciated creatures were no longer able to beg for food from people passing by. They stood as if they were on a leash next to the door of special kitchens, designated for the [Communist] Party elite, in hope to get something. Of course, rarely could they get a thing because the *aktyv* did not get much to eat either. Everything was in short supply. And helping the starving was anti-Soviet activity in the eyes of authorities.[96]

The narrator never mentioned whether he had shared his bread with anyone. Making the moral choice to help the starving was equivalent to an "anti-Soviet activity" and punishable. But the narrator went even further, he excused perpetrators by saying that the *aktyv* also starved. The Soviet elite, Communist Party bosses, and GPU officers, as well as their family members, received sufficient food rations. In fact, a teacher was paid about half of what an equivalently senior GPU officer received: but the latter's special ration card for consumer goods at low prices in special shops made his real income twelve times the former's.[97]

Although considered militant atheists, Bolsheviks borrowed a third of their moral code from the Bible. Paraphrasing Apostle Paul, the Constitution of 1918, which governed the Russian Soviet Republic, proclaimed: "those who do not work, do not eat."[98] The bitter irony is that under War Communism and Stalin's collectivization of agriculture, fruits of farmers' labor belonged to the state, so land tillers periodically starved, while the new Soviet elite regularly received their food rations from special stores. By 1931, after the destruction of private trade, the state had assumed responsibility for supplying bread and other foodstuff to the population in cities by creating a centralized hierarchical system of distribution based on the state's perception of each citizen's contribution to the "building of socialism." The four categories included:

1. *City categories.* The "special and first-category list" included Moscow, Leningrad, the republics' capitals, and the main industrial cities and industrial sites of strategically important economic regions, such as the Donbas, the Urals, Western Siberia.
2. *Occupational categories.* Industrial and railroad workers were better treated than other employees, white-collar workers, or members of the

intelligentsia. . . . [S]elf-employed individuals . . . stood at the bottom of this category, while secret-police staff and high- and middle-ranking [Communist] Party members stood at the very top, on a special list.
3. *Status in the family unit.* Employed persons were entitled to higher rations than their dependent children and elderly relatives.
4. *The type of workplace in relation to the "global project of industrialization of the country."* Miners and workers in heavy metallurgical plants and steel mills received higher rations than people working in textile, food, or light-industry factories. Teachers in industrial schools and institutes were better fed than . . . school teachers in rural areas. . . . In addition, enterprises were allowed to set up private plots or "kitchen gardens" for their workers and employees.[99]

In this stratification, which, according to Nicolas Werth, reflected "a new, crude, and cynical relationship between the state and its subjects," two categories languished at the very bottom: (1) the "special resettlers" (*spetspereselentsy*), a majority of whom were stripped of their property and deported to inhospitable areas at the Far North, the Urals, the Narym region in Western Siberia in Soviet Russia, and Kazakhstan; and (2) the forced-labor camp inmates.[100]

In the new food distribution pyramid, teachers were ranked below Communist Party bosses, OGPU apparatchiks, and urban proletariat. Teachers in urban schools and institutes of higher education fared better; teachers in rural districts had to rely on collective farms or private "kitchen gardens" to survive. This put nearly 100,000 teachers in Soviet Ukraine at risk of starving, along with their children and the elderly.[101] Their "kitchen gardens" were insufficient to sustain families, so they often suffered from malnutrition and exhaustion.

COLLAPSE OF SCHOOLS

One of the most moving accounts of the Holodomor was written by Oleksandra Radchenko, a schoolteacher in the Kharkiv region of Soviet Ukraine. In her diary, the thirty-six-year-old teacher of the Russian language recorded not only what she saw around her but also what she thought about the tragedy unfolding before her eyes. On February 19, 1932, Radchenko, who had three young daughters, confided in her diary, "I am so afraid of hunger; I'm afraid for the children." As a deeply religious person, she appealed to higher powers in the face of injustice: "May God protect us and have mercy on us. It would not be so offensive if it were due to a bad harvest, but they have taken away the grain and created an artificial famine."[102]

As a teacher, Radchenko received food rations (*paiki*) that ensured her family's survival, yet she could not be shielded from the horror that was unfolding in her village. Radchenko had to face her pupils in school, and she could not but notice that their numbers dwindled. She risked the wellbeing of her own daughters, but kept writing her observations in her secret diary. On April 5, 1932, four months before harvest, she noted that children were emaciated and infested with parasitic worms because they had nothing left to eat but beet roots. With anger, she reacted to the news printed in *Pravda* the following day about the completion of the dam over the Dnipro. She questioned the wisdom of the fast tempo of this socialist construction project at the expense of children swollen from hunger. On November 20, 1932, Radchenko described how authorities "swept clean" her seventy-year-old neighbor's home of all the stored grain and vegetables which were to last until February. After being dispossessed a couple of years earlier, the old man worked on the farm raising rabbits, but overnight he was turned into a pauper, unable to provide for his sixty-five-year-old wife and crippled daughter.[103]

In a January 9, 1933, entry, Radchenko told a horror story about kidnappings of children, cannibalism, and human meat sold in sausages on the market.[104] On March 23, 1933, on the verge of a nervous breakdown from seeing a dying man on the road to the village and a boy resembling the walking dead wandering in search of food, Oleksanda Radchenko wrote,

> Perhaps, this kind of expression in the eyes is only typical of people who realize that they are going to die but do not want to. But it was a child! . . . Why? Why children? I cried quietly so that my companion would not notice. A thought that I cannot do anything, that millions of children are dying of hunger, that all this is a calamity brought me to the brink of despair.[105]

That spring she was regularly reporting deaths from starvation. "People are dying," wrote Radchenko in a May 16, 1933, entry, "they say that whole villages have died in southern Ukraine."[106]

After World War II, Radchenko was arrested and, following a six-month interrogation, charged with having written "anti-Soviet propaganda."[107] During her trial she told the judges, "I wrote because after 20 years the children won't believe what violent methods were used to build socialism." Radchenko returned to Soviet Ukraine after spending a decade in corrective-labor camps.[108] In 1991, she was posthumously rehabilitated. Her family would have to wait another decade to get access to her diaries in the Sectoral State Archive of the Security Service of Ukraine to learn the truth.[109]

To win teachers to their side, authorities rewarded loyalists well for their cooperation with the regime. Between 1928 and 1932, salaries of primary schoolteachers doubled, not counting periodic bonuses, housing, social security, and pensions.¹¹⁰ During the famine, teachers loyal to the Soviet regime were on a list to receive food rations for themselves and their dependents. Although they were at the bottom of the food distribution hierarchy, teachers in rural schools received flour, grain, and oil.¹¹¹

At the same time, archival documents reveal that in spring of 1932, teachers in rural areas experienced food shortages. In his May 1932 letter, Mayorov, secretary of the Odesa regional bureau of the KP(b)U, reported about the shortage of food in the region and warned authorities that this "negatively affects political sentiments among teachers and leads to cases of teachers abandoning their job." He continued, "There is a real danger that if supplies remain at the current level, certain districts in the region will start a new school year with a significant shortage of teachers. It is necessary to note that mostly young teachers leave their posts, even members of Komsomol."

Writing in Russian, he complained that in his region only 500 teachers had received food rations, whereas "the Kiev region received 9,200, the Vinnitsa region—7,600, and the Kharkov region—2,400." He requested food supply for 80 percent of teachers in rural schools in the Odesa region (9,600 teachers and 9,600 of their dependents) for two months (June and July) to help them survive until a new harvest was gathered: 480 tons of flour, 38.4 tons of grain cereal, and 40.9 tons of sugar.¹¹²

On March 17, 1932, the All-Ukrainian Central Executive Committee newspaper *Visti* shifted the blame for the "irregularities" in supplying teachers and delays in paying teachers' salaries for one or two months on the *kurkuli* and "their agents who have often tried to hamper cultural-educational work."¹¹³ The Executive Committee resolved that the Commissariat of Supply, the Ukrainian Co-operative Association, and the Ukrainian Collective Farm Center "within ten days arrange for supplies from collective farms to be sent to teachers." The Committee also directed the Ukrainian Collective Farm Center, as well as regional and district executive committees, to investigate the payment of teachers' salaries by village soviets. Ten days were too short for three bureaucratic agencies to comply with the directive but too long for teachers to go without bread or salary to buy it.

Cuts in the centralized food supply forced teachers to find salvation elsewhere. In his testimony before the U.S. Commission on the Ukraine Famine, Mikhail Frenkin stated that at the age of twenty-one he was sent to Dovbush, a small town in the Zhytomyr region, to teach in a *robfak* school for adults where he witnessed the famine. He remembered that in 1931, teachers were receiving several *puds* of raw oats so they could share with others in need. In 1932, when he saw corpses in abandoned houses, he ran away from the countryside. He was helped by a friend who arranged a job for him as a lecturer at an institute in the city. He said, "I ran to Kiev because for two weeks I had not a crumb of bread to eat. They stopped giving us *paiki*."¹¹⁴ On the first day of school in 1933, the shortage of teachers reached 98 percent.[115] That year, many schools in rural districts of Soviet Ukraine were without students and teachers.

To survive, teachers taught their pupils how to subsist on food surrogates. Vasyl' Bashtanenko from the Dnipropetrovs'k region remembered how his swollen from starvation teacher, Olena Mykytivna, took her swollen from starvation students outside school into the steppe to dig out gophers' holes in search of food the animals stored for winter. The teacher also took her pupils into a soy field. The teacher distributed beans collected in the field equally among all so that they could carry a handful home to cook. In winter, the teacher took her class to a clay dene where the children could dig some clay and munch on it. The children vandalized sparrows' nests under thatched roofs and hunted all sorts of birds and small animals to stay alive.[116] Bashtanenko portrayed his teacher as a hero. It took courage to avoid patrols in the fields. Children often walked to school in straw sandals or more often barefoot. Only children of village activists or GPU officers could afford to wear chrome boots.

Mariia Panchenko from the Poltava region recalled that in spring time, the *kolhosp* (collective farm) fed those who worked in the fields but gave nothing to children, who began to eat various grasses. When ice melted, children supplemented their diets with fish and little turtles caught in rivers by baking or frying them. The narrator and her brother also went to a nearby forest to gather tree buds, mushrooms, and various weeds. The school was closed in winter, but a teacher was sent in the spring of 1933. All children who were still alive were required to go to school. The narrator recalled how a fellow classmate shared slivers of horse meat. The child's father worked at *salotopka* (fat churning factory), where all dead or dying horses were brought, and took some of the leftovers to school. When lots of people died, authorities sent school children to weed sugar beets. "And how could we weed when we could hardly stand on our feet? But they fed us according to how well we weeded."[117]

If teachers could afford it, they nourished their schoolchildren with a dish called *zatirka*. Vasyl' Mirutenko from the Chopovichne district, Zhytomyr region, recalled a recipe: a little flour was thoroughly stirred into some water, salted, and boiled. As soon as this *zatirka* was taken off the stove, 200–300 grams of it was ladled to each child. When spring came, a little sorrel was added to the *zatirka*, and some potatoes from a new crop, then it could be called borsch.[118] Another survivor L. Pylypenko recalled that salt was hard to get because all trade was deliberately suspended in villages. There was neither animal fat nor oil in this borsch because they were not obtainable anywhere at any price. His colleague Petrushevs'kyi shot sparrows in order to survive. But the gourmandizing did not last long;

Figure 4.4 Schoolchildren from the village of Rakovychi, Radomysl' district, Kyïv region (hot breakfast), 1934. *Source:* From TsDKFFAU, od. obl. 2-3348.

his hunting rifle was confiscated and he was forbidden to keep firearms of any kind. Teachers in his school began to receive a supplement to borsch in the form of "a spoonful of beans cooked in water." The schoolchildren, too, received a spoonful of beans, except children of the "enemies of the people."[119]

In 1932–1933, rural schools began to offer "hot breakfasts."[120] A photo of chubby schoolchildren from the village of Rakovychi, Radomysl' district, Kyïv region, was taken in 1934, a year after the genocidal famine reached its peak (Figure 4.4). They were the survivors from the district that lost one-third of its population between 1932 and 1933. In the first half of 1932, out of 3.5 million children in rural schools in Soviet Ukraine, only 73,000 received such a "hot breakfast" which consisted of 100 grams of bread surrogate and a cup of tea a day.[121] In rural schools, 15–20 percent of schoolchildren and 40 percent of teachers were nourished with "hot breakfasts," typically those who exhibited signs of physical exhaustion or anemia.[122] Two-thirds of children were too malnourished to walk to school. At the time, nearly 10 percent of children in Soviet Ukraine suffered from anemia and 5 percent suffered from tuberculosis.[123] Even if 15–20 percent of 4.4 million schoolchildren in the republic received this free treat,[124] was this all the Soviet government could do to save the children, proclaimed to be "our happiness"?

Two years after millions of children were killed by the genocidal famine, Bolsheviks continued to cover up their crime. The slogan, "Children—our happiness," appeared on the front page of newspaper, *Za bil'shovyts'kyi nastup* (For the Bolshevik Offensive), published by the Markhlevs'kyi district committee of the KP(b)U on September 10, 1935, greeting students and teachers at the beginning of the school year. Portraits of Lenin and "beloved teacher" Stalin adorned the front page as well as a quote from Moscow's emissary in Soviet Ukraine Postyshev, "Work with children—Bolsheviks' pride."[125]

A vivid eyewitness account of the situation with "hot breakfasts" was written by Ivan Koziar, a teacher in the town of Illintsi, Vinnytsia region. Late in 1932, primary school attendance in his town schools dropped by 15 percent, and by early 1933, it declined further by 35 percent. At the peak of the famine, only a third of schoolchildren were able to sit at the desks. Communist Party and local authorities monitored the situation from weekly reports, supplied by school principals. When the attendance dropped precipitously, central authorities cabled a directive from Moscow to all schools in Soviet Ukraine, with the following instructions:

> Considering that the school attendance has declined catastrophically, school principals are required to implement the following measures:
>
> 1. Organize horse drawn wagons to transport children to school every morning and back home in the evening.
> 2. Organize breakfasts for those children who need them the most.
>
> Those who fail to carry out the directive will be prosecuted in courts.[126]

When school principals and teachers were informed about this directive, they thought the Communist Party mercifully meant to save starving children because their parents and teachers could no longer watch their young die on a mass scale. The day after receiving the directive, all school principals walked to Illintsi. They hoped district authorities would allow the sale of produce from state stockpiles to feed the hungry children because trade had seized, leaving all stores empty. The principals were met by communist Mel'nykov, his wife, head of the local education department Kochubei (also a communist), and secretary of the district Communist Party committee Tarashchenko. The principals told authorities they came because, according to the directive, they were obligated to provide breakfasts for starving children in schools. Therefore, they requested that the authorities allow certain amounts of produce to be sold from state stockpiles in order to save the children. The authorities, as if caught by surprise, replied:

We, too, have received the directive as you did, but nowhere does it say that food has to be sold to schools. Thus, we warn you that there will be no sale or distribution of food from state stockpiles; there will be no produce for children and schools, no sale, no trade! You, school principals, have to arrange local food supply or requisition anything edible with the assistance of authorities, if you know where to find it, to provide breakfasts for schoolchildren.[127]

The school principals tried to reason, saying, "You, the local authorities, know full well that the trade is forbidden, no food can be purchased in stores, and even the black market has been closed. Everywhere people are swollen and die because of the famine." The district Communist Party secretary Tarashchenko cut the principals short, shouting, "Shut up!!! Not a single word about the famine. There is no 'famine'; there are 'food shortages'!" The meeting ended, and the school principals left.[128]

When a new school year started in 1933, a teacher walked into his classroom and noticed there were very few children. The teacher started a roll call. Going down the list, he called Vitkovs'kyi (the third letter from the top based on the Cyrillic alphabet). Several hesitant voices answered, "Absent." The teacher asked, "Where is he?" A brave voice answered, "He died." The teacher marked the name with a cross. "Voitko Ol'ha," called the teacher. Several girls answered in a chorus, "She is absent." The teacher asked, "Why?" A girl, in tears, answered, "She died." The teacher lowered his head and marked her name with a cross. Based on the previous year's roster, the teacher expected to see thirty-eight schoolchildren, but after marking names with crosses, he came down to only fourteen still alive. After 1931, lessons in all Soviet schools had to be concluded with a ritual: all children standing at their desks and saying in unison, "Thanks to comrade Stalin for our happy childhood!" The teacher, choking on tears, stood up before the children were required to perform the ritual and rushed out of the classroom.[129]

Not all school principals felt powerless. Vasyl' Ivchuk, a school principal in the village of Dudarkiv, Boryspil' district, Kyïv region, organized meals for children in all grades (see Figure 4.5). To provide additional nutrition, Ivchuk arranged a practicum for his schoolchildren at a local meat processing plant, so that after lessons they could work in exchange for a cup of soup. In this ingenious way, the principal saved all school-age children in his village from starvation. The Soviet government did not forget about his heroic deeds; he was arrested and executed five years after the genocidal famine.[130] The individual moral choice of the school principal to save the starving children ran against Marxist-Leninist "humanist" internationalism.

Figure 4.5 Vasyl' Ivchuk, school principal in the village Dudarkiv, Boryspil' district (second row, second on the left) with his colleagues and fifth-grade students, 1937.
Source: From the Museum of the History of Education of Kyïv Region, od. obl. 3191.

Primary school children suffered the most when food supplies were cut. Students at colleges and institutes were better off because they could "procure" food illegally from farms and fields where they worked or practiced. Even with that loophole, the situation was becoming so dire so that on June 18, 1932, Hryhorii Tkachenko, a Komsomol member from a technical college, wrote a letter to Stanislav Kosior, the first secretary of the TsK KP(b)U. Questioning the wisdom of the Communist Party's agricultural policy, Tkachenko expressed concern that the younger generation "will become sick, infirm and weak, and its numbers will shrink by 50 percent."[131] He was so sure he would receive an answer that he included his home address.

In June 1933, realizing that many classrooms would be empty on the first day of school, Volodymyr Zatons'kyi submitted a proposal to the TsK VKP(b) to lower the age of children admitted to the first grade from eight to seven years. He proposed to introduce this policy at the start of the 1933–1934 school year, using budget allocations for pre-school groups. By doing this schools could boost their enrollment by hundreds of thousands of children. Despite utilizing all available "reserves" and enrolling preschool children younger than eight years in the first grades, the roll call was catastrophic. On September 9, 1933, in the Vinnytsia region alone, only 45 percent of the expected schoolchildren showed up in the Novoushyts'kyi district, 56 percent in the Ianushpil'skyi, 50 percent in the Horodots'kyi, and 66 percent in the Koziatyns'kyi districts.[132] The high mortality rate among children and teachers led to the closing of twenty-eight schools in the Kharkiv region on September 1, 1933.[133] That year, in the Krasnohrad district alone, 62 percent of children in primary grades (1 through 4) and 58 percent in secondary grades (5 through 7) did not show up on the first day of school.[134] Over 90 percent of teachers did not show up either, especially in Varvins'kyi, Bereznians'kyi, and Malo Divyts'kyi districts.[135]

Vasyl' Bashtanenko remembered that children—swollen due to prolonged starvation—were required to go to school, but they hardly learned anything. Out of his twenty-five classmates, 70 percent were swollen.[136] Oles' Derhachov, who in 1933 taught history at a school in the village of Pshenychne, Solonians'kyi district, Dnipropetrovs'k region, recalled that children died in school. A child would recite homework, lose consciousness, and collapse at the desk. Emaciated schoolchildren, who sought medical help in the nearby village of Novopokrovka, died at the doorsteps of the clinic.[137] Others died on the streets. A photo of starving and neglected children was taken by Alexander Wienerberger,[138] an Austrian engineer, who had worked in the then capital of Soviet Ukraine, Kharkiv (see Figure 4.6).

Figure 4.6 "Hungernde und verwahrloste Kinder, die sogenannten 'Besprisornyje'" (Starving and neglected children, the so-called bezprytul'ni) by Alexander Wienerberger, 1933. From *Muss Russland hungern? Menschen- und Völkerschicksale in der Sowjetunion* by Ewald Ammende and Alexander Wienerberger (Wien: W. Braumüller Universitäts-Verlagsbuchhandlung, 1935), Abb. 7. *Source:* Courtesy of TsDKFFAU, od. obl. 0-249172.

In May 1933, in the village of Rudky, Tsarychans'kyi district, Ivan Brovko, seventeen-year-old teacher, witnessed how ten-year-old Mariika Hailo sighed, put her head on the desk, propping it up with her swollen hands, and succumbed to eternal sleep.[139] The class sat silent, struck by what they had just witnessed. Only Lenin smiled from a portrait hanging over the blackboard on the wall. Amid the dead silence in the classroom one could hear a loudspeaker in the school yard, broadcasting a cheerful song: "Our life is joyful today, and will be happier tomorrow!" No one came to take her body and give it a burial: neither her mother who was slowly dying from starvation, nor her sister who had died the prior month, nor her father who had died the day before and whose body was taken to a mass grave. The daughter followed her father, war veteran and amputee, to that same anonymous grave.

"Life in the village ground to a halt: one could no longer hear songs, dogs barking, hens clucking, and weddings stopped," recalled Oleksander Merkelo.[140] Schools became vacant, children emaciated, some were swollen and could no longer go to school. Children even created a new rhyme: "We already have booze, father will bring us more, but it is sad that there is no bread." The survivor added: "I have to say that there was no shortage of moonshine and cigarettes in the so-called USSR. And the moonshine was made, as you know, from grain."[141] Another survivor, V. Savur, from the Kyïv region, remembered that in village cooperative stores moonshine was available in unlimited quantities, for it was a government monopoly in the USSR which brought in exceptional revenues. "That is why, even in those years of famine when masses of people were dying, the distilleries were working at full capacity turning grain into liquor."[142] Scholars argue that Stalin had justified the increase in the production and sale of vodka to find funds for industrialization.[143] Vodka represented up to 40 percent of total rural store sales and provided about 20 percent of state revenues.[144] This fueled the growing addiction rates that occurred during and after the genocidal famine. Many would continue to drink, if only to escape the horrifying reality of their situation.

Regardless of ethnicity, schoolchildren suffered from extreme starvation, most of them in rural areas of Soviet Ukraine. At the beginning of the 1934–1935 school year, all ethnic groups showed similar decreasing enrollment trends, except one. Primary school enrollments of Russian children increased from 8.6 to 11 percent,[145] driven by the resettlement of Red Army veterans and loyalists from Russia into villages depopulated by the genocidal famine. Tugboat brigades that were previously assigned to carry out grain requisitions were dispatched to welcome new settlers. Often local population resented the newcomers, muddied their water wells, and burned their homes (typically new settlers moved into homes left vacant by the famished and diseased Ukrainian farmers).[146]

THE END OF UKRAINIZATION

On August 14, 1931, in his article published on the eve of the first anniversary of introducing compulsory education in the Soviet Union, Mikhail Kalinin boasted that 98 percent of children ages from 8 to 10 in the Ukrainian SSR were enrolled in primary schools compared to 76 percent the year before; graduates of primary schools went on to grades 5–7 in larger numbers (76 percent as opposed 55 percent the year before).[147] More than 15,500 new teachers were recruited, including 3,600 members of Komsomol mobilized to teach in schools.

By 1935, reality had drastically changed. Oleksandr Asatkin, head of the Department of Economic Accounting in Soviet Ukraine, reported an alarming trend. Based on estimates by his statisticians, the number of primary schools, teachers, and students in the Ukrainian SSR dipped below the prerevolution level (see Table 4.1). In 1924–1925, the number dipped as a result of the famine of 1921–1923 in Soviet Ukraine, which affected 3.8 million.[148] A decade later, in 1934–1935, the number dipped further as a result of the genocidal famine of 1932–1933, which claimed 7.1 million.[149] The trend in school statistics has yet to be analyzed by demographers.

Table 4.1 Primary schools, teachers, and students (grades 1 through 4) in Ukraine, 1914–1934

Years	Schools	Teachers	Students
1914–1915	18,386	33,646	1,424,701
1924–1925	14,411	26,849	1,264,341
1925–1926	16,155	32,636	1,463,099
1926–1927	16,720	34,294	1,453,144
1927–1928	17,108	36,665	1,530,026
1928–1929	17,488	39,488	1,585,814
1929–1930	17,944	42,966	1,776,155
1930–1931	17,493	46,655	2,003,371
1931–1932	15,475	43,017	1,795,478
1932–1933	13,354	32,686	1,329,258
1933–1934	12,949	32,146	1,162,354
1934–1935	12,132	29,431	1,074,312

Source: Adapted from *Narodne hospodarstvo USRR (statystychnyi dovidnyk)*, ed. Oleksandr Asatkin (Kyïv: Narodne hospodarstvo ta oblik, 1935), Table 1, 546–47.

In her study of social mobility in Soviet schools, Sheila Fitzpatrick, an American historian of Australian ancestry, argued that achievements during the "cultural revolution" were remarkable.[150] She lauded an increase in the number of Soviet schools, teachers and students, and attributed this achievement to social mobility spurred by the October Socialist Revolution of 1917, while admitting that it plateaued in the late 1930s. Did Fitzpatrick, who had access to archives in Smolensk and Moscow, miss the reverse trend in Soviet Ukraine intentionally or unintentionally? If statistical data for primary schools, mandatory in the Ukrainian SSR at the time, were missing, this indicates an attempt to cover up the crime.

Fitzpatrick also neglected the liquidation of Ukrainization that started outside Soviet Ukraine. On December 15, 1932, Stalin and Molotov signed a resolution to "immediately discontinue Ukrainization" in the North Caucasus, the Central Black Earth, the Far East Region, Kazakhstan, Central Asia, and other areas and "prepare the introduction of Russian language school instruction" in all ethnically Ukrainian areas throughout the Soviet Union.[151] In the North Caucasus region of Kuban', an area settled predominantly by Ukrainian Cossacks in the eighteenth century and Ukrainian farmers from Poltava and Chernihiv regions in the nineteenth century, the large community of *stanytsia* (a Ukrainian Cossack settlement) Poltavs'ka was surrounded by OGPU detachments, and all 30,000 inhabitants were herded together with only few personal belongings and deported to Siberia.[152] The following day the Krasnodar regional paper announced that the "Ukrainian-nationalist-Petliura nest" in Kuban' had been liquidated. The settlement was renamed Krasnoarmeiskaia after the Red Army regiment. Ukrainian language was abolished in schools of Kuban' and teachers were deported.[153]

A Russian witness, Vadim Denisov, an officer of the regional OGPU, recorded how the "Kuban' operation of 1932–1933" was planned and executed in two stages. First, during the preparatory stage, lists of people for liquidation and deportation were drawn in four categories:

(1) Category A: active resisters to be executed;
(2) Category 1: passive resisters to be sentenced to a 10-year or longer exile in labor camps;
(3) Category 2: disloyal to be sentenced to five years of exile and hard labor in concentration camps with subsequent permanent settlement near the Arctic Circle or, if physically fit for labor, into administrative exile in forced settlements in Siberia; and
(4) Category 3: loyalists and supporters of the regime to be spared.[154]

Drawing the lists was arbitrary, completed without investigation. A neighbor could denounce a neighbor to a Communist Party plenipotentiary. Second, once lists were drawn for liquidation in four categories by OGPU operatives, a crackdown operation would commence and additional troops called in. The OGPU and local militias were in charge of the operation. Roads were blocked by patrols. Executions of those listed in Category A were conducted in the fields outside villages, with victims forced to dig their own graves. Reports about these executions with lists of victims were filed by OGPU expeditionary forces. Executions were also carried out in prisons in Rostov and Krasnodar. Those in Category 1 were hoarded to a local train station and transported like cattle to transit camps for subsequent confinement in OGPU-run forced labor camps established for various industrial projects throughout Russia. Children older than sixteen were registered separately from their parents and sentenced to shorter terms. Children younger than ten were left under the guardianship of their close relatives who were not subject to deportation, later placed in orphanages in other cities throughout the Soviet Union. All these crimes were never documented and left no traces in archives. Only lists of people sentenced to be executed, together with reports following the executions, were kept by OGPU field offices. The documentation about people transported by trains to places of forced settlement or exile included instructions and a transport registry; no case files with names, birthdates, length of sentence or reasons for sentencing were ever compiled. Overall, in the Kuban' operation, 2 million people were arrested, as many as 500,000 executed, and the remaining 1.5 million transported to the Russian Arctic Circle and Siberia to mostly perish.[155] The number of executed in the Kuban' operation may seem beyond the realm of possibility as the source quoted by Dmytro Solovey might be pure guesswork of the OGPU operative Denisov. Yet, in a retrospect, Robert Conquest attributed as many as 1 million out of 7 million Ukrainian losses in 1932–1933 to the North Caucasus Territory.[156]

The *stanytsia* Poltavs'ka was given most publicity as an example and served as a prototype for subsequent operations.[157] Soon a pedagogical college in *stanytsia* Umans'ka (a Ukrainian Cossack settlement soon to be renamed Leningradskaia after the cavalry regiment that was stationed there) became the target. Ivan Polezhaiev recorded in his diary entry of February 18, 1933, that upon his arrival as the new college director, he met three instructors and eleven third-year students scheduled to graduate that spring out of fifty that were still alive. Two days later Polezhaiev was summoned by the local OGPU and was ordered to remove all textbooks in Ukrainian and take them to the security police headquarters. Gradually, he realized his mission: to curtail Ukrainization of the college. The task felt "uneasy" and "unpleasant."[158]

Following the SVU trial of 1930, repressions touched all educational institutions in the Ukrainian SSR. According to the 1935 Soviet statistical handbook, in the Ukrainian SSR approximately 46,655 teachers were in primary school classrooms on the first day of September 1930–1931. In 1934–1935, only 29,431 teachers remained in classrooms (see Table 4.1). Within five years of the SVU trial, 17,224 (one-third) of the teachers had been eliminated.[159] Their destiny was never explained by compilers of the statistical handbook. Vasyl' Marochko and Götz Hillig came to a similar conclusion: between 1929 and 1934, from the period of "great purges" of educators in Ukraine that coincided with the launching of the First Five-Year Plan, up to the end of the Holodomor, over 30 percent of teachers perished as a result of repressions and executions.[160] After the SVU trial, the new school year of 1931–1932 started with fewer teachers (3,638 less based on the Soviet statistical source). At the beginning of the next school year, 1932–1933, as many as 10,331 teachers were missing, mostly due to continued arrests, as well as deaths from starvation. That same year, only 5,517 new graduates from 66 teacher training colleges (2,256) and 39 pedagogical institutes (3,261) took over half of vacant jobs.[161]

To relieve chronic shortages of teachers, students were being sent to villages to help with the harvest and to teach in schools. Iryna Medvid' was a third-year student at Kharkiv University when in 1932 she and her classmates were assigned to the Vovchans'k district, in the Kharkiv region, to practice teaching. The situation was a result of teacher arrests in Ukraine. This young student-teacher left a vivid account of her Russian-language lesson for hungry children in Ukraine, which first appeared in the second volume of *The Black Deeds of the Kremlin* in 1955:

The District Department of Education then sent me to "practice" in a school at the village Tsiurupa, which was located on the old estate of General Brusilov.

Even though the children's school was maintained by the government the children were always hungry. The daily ration consisted of two thin slices of soggy bread, a colored liquid in the morning which represented tea, a thin liquid (soup) or a thicker liquid (cereal) for lunch, and again a thin liquid for supper. The children were listless, apathetic, drowsy. They paid no attention and displayed little reaction to anything. The small children suffered most of all because anything they had was stolen from them by the older ones. It was impossible to accomplish anything in such difficult conditions, and finally all our youthful fervor waned amid starvation and hopelessness.

One day, during the Russian language lesson, I had gone through the whole program: checked the pupils' homework, explained the new assignment in the difficult foreign language, and asked some questions. The monosyllabic answers took very little time. The classroom was shrouded in an oppressive stillness. The children sat motionless waiting for the bell, never laughing, talking or asking questions. I racked my brains wondering how to dispel the gloom and awaken some spark of interest in the children.

Then my eyes fell on a new April issue of the "Teacher's Magazine." I leafed nervously through the pages until an article caught my attention, and I began to read. The children sat quietly for some time, then they began to perk up their heads and open their eyes in amazement as they came up and surrounded my desk. I continued to read: "The children finished their lesson and the bell rang. Laughing and playing they skipped downstairs to the dining room where lunch awaited them, among other things, cocoa, white bread and butter. The servant had extra work sweeping up bread crumbs which the boisterous children carelessly scattered."

The children around me, famished and just barely existing, suddenly spoke out. "Where, where was there such food?"

Choking back the tears I answered, "In Moscow."[162]

What moral choice could this young student-teacher make, except crying helplessly? Just like Iryna, many new cadres were young, loyal to the ideals of socialism, but inexperienced. More importantly, the cultural transmission of knowledge was interrupted because the old prerevolution intelligentsia were "hounded" from their posts, and the young "red" cadres were educated under a totalitarian system demanding strict obedience to political dogmas rather than critical thinking.[163] The choices were clear: class consciousness and communist morality were prioritized over national consciousness and humanistic morality.

Varvara Dibert, who taught in Kyïv during the 1930s, despite official sanctions against taking in lodgers, brought two children of one of her colleagues into her own home (the colleague's wife suffered a mental breakdown after his arrest). She recalled that all teachers received porridge at school. "I never dipped a spoon into my portion. I brought it with me back home and divided it between the four children. I treated them for all practical purposes as if they were my own, and we never discriminated against them."[164] Her family kept the two children for one year until their father returned from prison. Perhaps, Dibert was much more mature and could exercise her freedom of choice to help the victims. As a priest's[165] daughter and wife of a school principal who fought on Petliura's side, Dibert was of suspect social origins and had no choice but to flee abroad. She was the oldest witness to testify before the U.S. Commission on the Ukraine Famine about Soviet schools in the 1920s and 1930s.

Social solidarity helped with survival. Bolsheviks, however, discouraged social solidarity. Famine survivor, V. Hrechko, recalled how a teacher was sanctioned for helping the starving "class enemy" in Ukraine in 1932:

A teacher from an incomplete secondary school in Dobrianka, Chernihiv region, P. S-n met a woman with two little children near his house. The woman was begging for food. The teacher, who had his own children, took the beggars to his house and cooked a meal for them. During a table conversation, he found out that the woman was from a neighboring district and her husband, the kulak, was arrested and exiled. S-n tried to help and arrange for the woman to work as a night guard in his school. She, of course, agreed and thanked him. However, when the teacher came to see the school principal, and the chief of the party committee was already in the principal's office, he unexpectedly encountered not only rejection but also a strong reprimand: "Can't you understand that you've made a big political mistake," said the party secretary, "you have demonstrated before your students, – and they have already seen how you were feeding the woman, – your protest against the government and the party." The school principal added: "Had I listened to you, our schoolchildren would have encountered the kulak's offspring and shown sympathy toward them. Is this permissible from the point of view of Communist upbringing?" That was it; a note was added to the teacher's personnel file about his "conciliatory attitude toward hostile elements." And when after celebrating twenty-five years of his teaching career, he was nominated for the position as a school principal, the education committee rejected his candidacy because of the "ties with socially alien elements."[166]

The teacher who made a moral choice to extend humanitarian help to the mother and her children was sanctioned for showing "anti-government" and "anti-party attitudes." Under the slogan of proletarian solidarity, moral foundations of Ukrainian society were shattered.[167]

Another teacher whose diary was repressed, Iurii Sambros, witnessed how an elderly woman was dying, literally illustrating an epitome of one's bitter fate of facing the end of life homeless, forsaken by kin. Sambros, who lost his mother in 1933, recalled how she, in moments of discord or a quarrel with his father, would sentimentally prophesy to her sons through tears that she might end up homeless dying on the street like an old hag. So the agony of a starving woman, whose life was coming to a sorrowful end, struck the diarist's imagination:

> as I was going to the train station every morning, for half a month, day after day, I watched a slow death of an old woman under the fence. . . . With legs swollen from starvation, without any strength left, she was lying near the fence on the path parallel to the railroad tracks.
>
> Surrounded by weeds, heavily covered by dust from the road, with a wooden bowl, placed closer to her head by a charitable soul, for the purpose of collecting alms, all skin-and-bones, translucent, jaundiced, with puffy blue legs and moon-like face, with darkened spots of glassy, empty eyes, she was lying there like a ghost.

At first she was still able to move, to whisper, when someone stopped next to her, but with every other day, she gradually fell silent, lying quietly, only moving her eyes to the right . . . then to the left . . . or staring straight into the blue . . . indifferent sky. Finally, she died. Her corps was lying there for days and nights, engorged with interstitial fluids, then disappeared. Apparently, the police took the corpse away and buried.[168]

Sambros, like other bystanders, reasoned that the woman's agony lasted as long as it did because every passerby was trying to help, but no one could save her from death because everyone did not have enough to eat. Later, Sambros admitted on the pages of his diary that he survived because he bluffed in order to obtain access to a dining hall for Agricultural Academy union members. He befriended a secretary who gave him stamped coupons that he could use to eat in the dining hall for scientific personnel without presenting a membership card. This continued for months until the policy became stricter, and he could not enter the door without a card. Then Sambros cheated shamelessly and obtained access to a dining hall of the Writers' Union with the help of a friend. He frequented the place as a guest of famous writers, but more often not-so-famous journalists. On several occasions he just walked in, assuming his face was familiar to the maître d'hôtel and thus no one would dare to ask if he had a pass. Crispy white tablecloths, napkins, restaurant tableware, polite servants, menus, buffet, vodka, and appetizers—all these were in stark contrast to the swollen starving begging on the streets.[169] Sambros survived; but he had to shed his Ukrainian identity after he moved to Russia to teach.[170]

Summing up "the consequences of the arrested Ukrainization," Valerii Smolii has argued that repressions against Ukrainian nationally conscious intelligentsia, in particular teachers, ultimately robbed the linguistic component of Ukrainization of its vigor and sent a signal to those who might have too enthusiastically taken up charge: "Now the Ukrainian language stopped being the basic means of modernization. Those who wanted to win respected social status and gain entry to new information, to contemporary scientific thought and knowledge, had to resort to the Russian language."[171] The KP(b)U's identification in November 1933 of "local Ukrainian nationalism" as the preeminent danger to Soviet power is seen by some scholars to be the definitive marker of an end to Ukrainization.[172]

By early 1933, when People's Commissariat of Education administrators discussed the Ukrainization of schools, they increasingly talked about it in a negative sense, as a policy that had violated the rights of ethnic Russians and had led to a rise in Ukrainian nationalism.[173] In 1933–1934, when the Communist Party finally declared "local nationalism" the chief danger, Soviet authorities purged the People's Commissariat of Education in the Ukrainian SSR almost entirely of its existing staff.[174] In 1930, none of forty-five members of the Ukrainian intelligentsia sentenced during the SVU trial were from the Commissariat of Education. However, after the show trial ended, all Skrypnyk's deputies and other members of the Commissariat of Education in Soviet Ukraine were purged.[175] In 1933, Mykola Skrypnyk is reported as having defiantly attacked Postyshev before the Central Committee, accusing him of betraying the principles of internationalism. He repeated this at a meeting of the Ukrainian Politburo. Over June and July, Postyshev and other leaders attacked him, and on July 6, 1933, Skrypnyk again defended himself to the Politburo. They demanded his unconditional surrender. That afternoon, instead, he shot himself.[176] On July 10, 1933, *Pravda*, in announcing Skrypnyk's death, blamed him for separatism: "Under the banner of a struggle for Ukrainian culture, the bourgeois nationalist Petliurist elements, well supplied with money by foreign secret service, worked for the separation of the Ukraine from the Soviet Union."[177] Arrests lasted from 1933 to 1934.[178] As scholars noted, "Not only Skrypnyk was on trial, but the Ukrainian intelligentsia, inert, intimidated by terror, fearful of speaking the truth about the famine of 1932–1933."[179]

In the years that followed, the number of Ukrainian schools dropped, and Soviet authorities "no longer consistently compelled the systematic Ukrainization of higher education, opting instead to permit Russian-language predominance."[180] In 1932–1933, nearly 42 percent of schools had Russian-language classrooms; in the following year, the number increased to 94 percent.[181] Although some Ukrainian scholars emphasize that it was too early to speak of Russification as an "organized state policy" in 1933–1934, they cite instances of postsecondary instructors (especially in prestigious educational institutes, administered by all-Union authorities) exclusively using Russian in extracurricular activities.[182]

In December 1934, four lists of banned authors were published, containing works by Ukrainian historians, sociologists, linguists, poets, writers, and anyone else who had been arrested. The authorities decreed that all their books must be removed from libraries, bookstores, and educational institutions. As scholars concluded, "the extermination of the intellectual class was accomplished by the extermination of their words and ideas."[183]

The genocidal famine in Soviet Ukraine turned into an instrument of the nationality policy. This radically distinguished the situation in Ukraine from that in Kazakhstan, where famine-related losses were also very high. On December 14, 1932, Stalin and Molotov signed a resolution of the TsK VKP(b) and the SNK of the USSR, which demanded "correct Ukrainization" in Soviet Ukraine and other regions densely populated by ethnic Ukrainians throughout the Soviet Union. The document also demanded a struggle against Petliurites and other "counterrevolutionary" elements, who this time were accused of organizing the famine.[184] This not only meant the end of the ambiguous policy of "Ukrainization," but marked the decisive phase of the liquidation of the "Ukraine-centered" potential that was never supposed to revive. As scholars rightfully note, the greatest burden of the genocidal famine was placed on Ukrainian land tillers, who were politically most dangerous and resisted collectivization as much as they could. However, for purely organizational reasons, they could not launch an offensive on the city and become dangerous to the regime. The Stalinist regime used the famine and false stories about those who were responsible for it as a concrete pretext for mass-scale repressive campaigns, purges, and the like.[185] The policy of Russification was reversed only in October 1989, when the Ukrainian language was proclaimed the state language of the republic, to lay the foundation for the declaration of state sovereignty and eventual independence of Ukraine in 1991, a reinstatement of independence first proclaimed in 1918 by the Ukrainian National Republic.

NOTES

1. "Japan's Capacity to Modernize," in John K. Fairbank, Edwin O. Reischauer, and Albert M. Craig, *East Asia: The Modern Transformation* (Boston: Houghton Mifflin Company, 1965), 188–91.

2. In spring 1933, to deflect attention from party's responsibility for the man-made famine and to silence the truth, "counterrevolutionary" organizations were "uncovered" by the GPU in leading Ukrainian agricultural institutes. Leading specialists were executed. The ranks of the commissariat of land management in Ukraine down to local machine-tractor stations were purged. See Kas'ianov, "Ukraïns'ka intelihentsiia v 1933 r.," 93–95.

3. Jacob Bunge, "Supersized Family Farms Transform U.S. Agriculture," *Wall Street Journal*, October 24, 2017, A1.

4. Bunge, "Supersized Family Farms," A10.

5. After the SVU trial, from 1930 to 1933, there was a cascade of fabricated cases against Ukrainian intelligentsia, including the Ukrainian National Center (*Ukraïns'kyi natsional'nyi tsentr*, or UNTs), the Ukrainian Military Organization (*Ukraïns'ka viis'kova orhanizatsiia*, or UVO), and the Association of Ukrainian Nationalists (*Ob'iednannia ukraïns'kykh natsionalistiv*, or OUN). See Shkandrij and Bertelsen, "The Soviet Regime's National Operations in Ukraine, 1929–1934," 417–47; Volodymyr Prystaiko and Iurii Shapoval, *Mykhailo Hrushevs'kyi: Sprava "UNTs" i ostanni roky (1931–1934)* (Kyïv: Krytyka, 1999); Iana Prymachenko, "Sprava 'Ob'iednannia ukraïns'kykh natsionalistiv,'" *Tsei den' v istoriï*, December 15, 2017, https://www.jnsm.com.ua/h/1215T/.

6. For a detailed account of famine in 1932–1933, see Applebaum, *Red Famine*, 159–204, 222–61; Conquest, *The Harvest of Sorrow*, 217–82; and Snyder, *Bloodlands*, 40–47.

7. Kulchytsky, *The Famine of 1932–1933 in Ukraine*, 141.
8. Ibid.
9. Marochko et al., *Holodomor-henotsyd*, 56–57.
10. By October 1931, 72 percent of the arable land in Soviet Ukraine had been collectivized. See *Istoriia kolektyvizatsiï sil's'koho hospodarstva Ukraïns'koï RSR, 1917–1937 rr.*, ed. Ivan Hanzha et al., vol. 2 (Kyïv: Naukova dumka, 1965), 554–55.
11. Solovey, *Golgota Ukraïny*, 175–76.
12. In his novel-memoir, Anatolii Dimarov described how collectivization was implemented in a typical Ukrainian village following Stalin's article "The Year of the Great Breakthrough," published on November 7, 1929, the anniversary of the October Socialist Revolution. It announced a radical change in the Soviet economic policy by reversing the NEP of 1921. In Soviet Ukraine, the total collectivization was to be completed in one to two years. See Anatolii Dimarov, "The Hungry Thirties (A Parable about Bread)," In *Stalin's Shadow*, trans. Iurii Tkach (Melbourne: Bayda Books, 1989), 110–75, http://shron1.chtyvo.org.ua/Dimarov_Anatolii/In_Stalins_Shadow_anhl.pdf.
13. Kulchytsky, *The Famine of 1932–1933 in Ukraine*, 141.
14. Solovey, *Golgota Ukraïny*, 177; see also Conquest, *The Harvest of Sorrow*, 274–82, 306.
15. Sergei Maksimov put these words into the mouth of Russian patriot Beletsky, one of the main characters in his novel *Denis Bushuev*, published in 1948; quoted in Ro-i, "Chy odnakovo hnityt' bol'shevyts'kyi rezhym usi narody SSSR?" *Ukraïns'ki visti* (Neu-Ulm), no. 6 (1949); quoted in Solovey, *Golgota Ukraïny*, 177.
16. According to Vasyl' Marochko, in early 1930, nearly 8,451 Communist Party and Communist Youth League activists were recruited and 6,435 dispatched to rural areas in Soviet Ukraine to enforce collectivization; the remaining volunteers were dispatched to the North Caucasus, Lower Volga, and Kazakhstan. Most of them (80 percent) served in village soviets. Their task was accomplished by the end of 1931, when 85 percent of farms in Soviet Ukraine were collectivized. See V. I. Marochko, "Dvadtsiatyp'iatytysiachnyky," *Entsyklopediia istoriï Ukraïny*, ed. V. A. Smolii et al., vol. 2 (Kyïv: Naukova dumka, 2004), 297, http://resource.history.org.ua/item/0001740. For a detailed analysis of backgrounds, motivations, and mentalities of the 25,000ers, see Lynne Viola, *The Best Sons of the Fatherland: Workers in the Vanguard of Soviet Collectivization* (Oxford: Oxford University Press, 1989).
17. Vasily Grossman, *Forever Flowing*, trans. Thomas P. Whitney (New York: Harper & Row, 1972).
18. Grossman, *Forever Flowing*, 141–42. Grossman's daughter Ekaterina Korotkova confirmed to Daria Mattingly that the novel's character Anna was based on Pelageia Semenova. Semenova was born in Likhoslavsk, Tver' region, and after the famine, she returned to Russia. It is unknown how she reflected on being a perpetrator of the genocidal famine in Ukraine or how she explained her motivation. See Mattingly, "[Extra]ordinary Women," in *Women and the Holodomor-Genocide*, ed. Malko, 69–70.
19. Mattingly, "[Extra]ordinary Women," 81.
20. Grossman, *Forever Flowing*, 143.

21. The original issue of the magazine has been preserved in the National Library of Ukraine named after V. I. Vernads'kyi. The author is indebted to Yana Hryn'ko of the National Holodomor-Genocide Museum in Kyïv, Ukraine for her assistance in locating the source of the 1930 propaganda cartoon.

22. V. Danilov, R. Manning, and L. Viola, eds., *Tragediia sovetskoi derevni. Kollektivizatsiia i raskulachivanie. Dokumenty i materialy, 1927–1939*, 5 vols. (Moscow: ROSSPEN, 2000), vol. 2, 791.

23. See *The War Against the Peasantry, 1927–1930: The Tragedy of the Soviet Countryside*, eds. Lynne Viola, V. P. Danilov, N. A. Ivnitskii, and Denis Kozlov (New Haven: Yale University Press, 2005), 320.

24. For more on the 1930 rebellion, see Applebaum, *Red Famine*, 139–58.

25. *TsDAHOU*, f. 1, op. 20, spr. 3191, ark. 37.

26. *TsDAHOU*, f. 1, op. 20, spr. 3184, ark. 95.

27. *TsDAHOU*, f. 1, op. 20, spr. 3191, ark. 41.

28. *TsDAHOU*, f. 1, op. 20, spr. 3154, ark. 11.

29. Ibid.

30. Valerii Vasyl'iev, "Persha hvylia sutsil'noï kolektyvizatsiï i ukraïns'ke selianstvo," in Valerii Vasyl'iev and Linn Viola, *Kolektyvizatsiia i selians'kyi opir na Ukraïni (lystopad 1929 – berezen' 1930 rr.)* (Vinnytsia: Logos, 1997), 233.

31. Bohdan Patryliak, "How Stalin Crushed the Euromaidan of 1930," *Euromaidan Press*, December 1, 2014, http://euromaidanpress.com/2014/12/01/punishment-for-two-maidans-putincrimea-and-stalinholodomor/. For more information about uprisings and their leaders, see Volodymyr Tylishchak, *1930. U.S.R.R. Povstannia: Naukovo-populiarni narysy* (Kyïv: Smoloskyp, 2016).

32. V. M. Danylenko, "Antyradians'ke povstannia selian v Ukraïni naperedodni holodomoru," in *Pavlohrads'ke povstannia 1930 r.: Dokumenty i materialy*, ed. V. M. Danylenko (Kyïv: Ukraïns'kyi pys'mennyk, 2009), 13–27.

33. A. Berelovich and V. Danilov, eds., *Sovetskaia derevnia glazami VChK–OGPU–NKVD, 1918–1939: Dokumenty i materialy*, 4 vols. (Moscow: ROSSPEN, 2003), vol. 3, book 1, 546, 533.

34. *TsDAHOU*, f. 1, op. 20, spr. 6390, ark. 135.

35. L. Pylypenko, "The Starving Schoolteachers' 'Borsch,'" in *The Black Deeds of the Kremlin*, ed. Pidhainy, vol. 2, 578–79.

36. In his memoir, Petro Grigorenko described how in spring 1920 the ChK (forerunner of the GPU) disarmed the Ukrainian countryside. The *chekist* troika read a list of hostages (usually most respected elderly men) and threatened to shoot them if all weapons were not surrendered by the noon of the following day. Overnight, hunting rifles, guns, revolvers, and daggers were thrown in front of the doors of village soviets. Hostages were killed if any sawed-off shotgun or other weapon was found in someone's backyard. See Petro G. Grigorenko, *Memoirs*, trans. Thomas P. Whitney (New York: W. W. Norton, 1982), 17, 40. In 1926, 1928, and 1929, owners of hunting rifles were required to register their firearms. In August 1930, the GPU searched homes of registered owners and confiscated hunting rifles and ammunition.

37. For resistance tactics used by rebel units in Podillia, Chernihiv, and Poltava regions, see Solovey, *Golgota Ukraïny*, 137–39, 141.

38. *HDA SBU*, f. 16, op. 27 (1951 r.), spr. 4, ark. 8.

39. Patryliak, "How Stalin Crushed the Euromaidan of 1930."

40. *Sovetskaia derevnia glazami VChK–OGPU–NKVD*, eds. Berelovich and Danilov, vol. 3, book 1, 708, 710, 711.

41. Patryliak, "How Stalin Crushed the Euromaidan of 1930."

42. Lynne Viola, *Peasant Rebels under Stalin: Collectivization and the Culture of Peasant Resistance* (New York: Oxford University Press, 1996).

43. *The War Against the Peasantry, 1927–1930: The Tragedy of the Soviet Countryside*, eds. Lynne Viola, V. P. Danilov, N. A. Ivnitskii, and Denis Kozlov (New Haven: Yale University Press, 2005), 321.

44. Stanton, "The Ten Stages of Genocide," https://www.genocidewatch.com/ten-stages-of-genocide.

45. Pidhainy, "Portraits of Solowky Exiles," 329.

46. *Tragediia sovetskoi derevni*, eds. Danilov, Manning, and Viola, vol. 3, *Konets 1930–1933*, 367.

47. N. Ivnitskii, "Golod 1932–1933: kto vinovat? (po dokumentam 'Kremlevskogo arkhiva')," in *Holodomor 1932–1933 rr. v Ukraïni: prychyny i naslidky: Mizhnarodna naukova konferentsiia, Kyïv, 9–10 veresnia 1993*, ed. S. Kul'chyts'kyi (Kyïv: Instytut istoriï Ukraïny NAN Ukraïny, 1995), 40.

48. *TsDAHOU*, f. 1, op. 6, spr. 237, ark. 207–216; English translation in "Resolution of the CC CP(b)U Politburo On Measures to Strengthen Grain Procurement (Excerpt), 18 November 1932," in *Holodomor of 1932–33 in Ukraine: Documents and Materials*, ed. Ruslan Pyrih, trans. Stephen Bandera (Kyïv: Kyïv Mohyla Academy Publishing House, 2008), 55–60.

49. *Holodomor of 1932–33 in Ukraine*, ed. Pyrih, 58.

50. Ibid., 59.

51. Mark Tauger, "Review of Anne Applebaum's 'Red Famine: Stalin's War on Ukraine,'" *History News Network* (George Washington University's Columbian College of Arts and Sciences), July 1, 2018, http://historynewsnetwork.org/article/169438.

52. Moshe Lewin, *Political Undercurrents in Soviet Economic Debates: From Bukharin to the Modern Reformers* (Princeton: Princeton University Press, 1974), 176.

53. Mark B. Tauger, "The 1932 Harvest and the Famine of 1933," *Slavic Review* 50, no. 1 (1991): 70–84. In his article, Tauger pointed out that data from Soviet archives demonstrate that the 1932 harvest was considerably lower than official statistics indicate, aggravating the serious food shortage that had struck the country in 1931 and making "famine likely if not inevitable in 1933." His calculations gave a total Soviet harvest of 50 million tons, nearly 30 percent below the official figure of 70 million tons. Tauger exclusively based his thesis that the famine was primarily the result of a genuine shortage on the statistical information from the Soviet publication *Istoriia krest'ianstva SSSR*, vol. 2, *Sovetskoe krest'ianstvo v period sotsialisticheskoi rekonstruktsii narodnogo khoziaistva, 1927–1937* (Moscow: Nauka, 1986).

54. O. Bilous'ko et al., eds., *Natsional'na knyha pam'iati zhertv Holodomoru 1932–1933 rokiv v Ukraïni: Poltavs'ka oblast'* (Poltava: Oriiana, 2008), 944; quoted in Mattingly, "[Extra]ordinary Women," 82.

55. In his paper presented at the Second International Workshop on Lysenkoism on June 22–23, 2012 at the University of Vienna, Austria, Tauger insisted that the drought was the main cause of the famine in 1932–1933, denying rather aggressively Stalin's responsibility for the crime. See "Retrospective for Yale Agrarian Studies," September 2014, https://agrarianstudies.macmillan.yale.edu/sites/default/files/files/papers/TaugerAgrarianStudies.pdf.

56. Haynes and Klehr, "Revising History," *In Denial*, 11–57, esp. 17–18.

57. Document 24, "Letter to V. V. Kuraev, Ye. B. Bosh, A. E. Minkin, 11 August 1918," in *The Unknown Lenin*, ed. Pipes, 50.

58. Kul'chyts'kyi, *Holodomor 1932–1933 rokiv iak henotsyd*, 277; V. Marochko and O. Movchan, *Holodomor 1932–1933 rokiv v Ukraïni: Khronika* (Kyïv: Vydavnychyi dim "Kyievo-Mohylians'ka akademiia," 2008), 166.

59. Heorhii Papakin, *"Chorna doshka": antyselians'ki represiï (1932–1933)* (Kyïv: Instytut istoriï Ukraïny NAN Ukraïny, 2013); Heorhii Papakin, "'Chorna doshka' Holodomoru i liuds'ki vtraty 1932–1933 rokiv," in *Holodomor 1932–1933 rokiv: Vtraty ukraïns'koï natsiï: Materialy mizhnarodnoï naukovo-praktychnoï konferentsiï, Kyïv, 4 zhovtnia 2016 roku*, ed. Olesia Stasiuk et al. (Kyïv: Vyd. Oleh Filiuk, 2017), 160.

60. Kulchytsky, *The Famine of 1932–1933 in Ukraine*, 149.

61. Papakin, "'Chorna doshka' Holodomoru," 162.

62. *Pam'iat' narodu: henotsyd v Ukraïni holodom 1932–1933 rokiv, Svidchennya*, vol. 1, ed. V. Smolii (Kyïv: Vyd. "Kalyta", 2009), 200.

63. *Pam'iat' narodu: henotsyd v Ukraïni holodom 1932–1933 rokiv, Svidchennya*, vol. 2, ed. V. Smolii (Kyïv: Vyd. "Kalyta", 2009), 695.

64. "Case History LH57: Mikhail Frenkin, Baku," in *Oral History Project*, vol. 2, 624; English version in the *Report to Congress*, 363.

65. Ibid., 364.

66. Iurii Shapoval, "Holodomor i ioho zv'iazok iz represiiamy v Ukraïni u 1932–1934 rokah," in *Holod v Ukraïni u pershii polovyni XX stolittia: prychyny ta naslidky (1921–1923, 1932–1933, 1946–1947): Materialy Mizhnarodnoï naukovoï konferentsiï, Kyïv, 20–21 lystopada 2013 r.* (Kyïv, 2013), 154.

67. *HDA SBU*, f. 16, op. 25, spr. 3, ark. 73.

68. Volodymyr Nikol's'kyi, "Represyvna diial'nist' orhaniv GPU pid chas holodomoru v USRR (1932–1933 rr.)," *Z arkhiviv VUChK-GPU-NKVD-KGB*, no. 2 (2001): 484.

69. Nikol's'kyi, "Represyvna diial'nist' orhaniv GPU," 480.

70. *HDA SBU*, f. 42, spr. 9, ark. 83–86.

71. Valerii Vasyl'iev, "Tsina holodnoho khliba," in *Komandyry velykoho holodu: Poïzdky V. Molotova i L. Kaganovycha v Ukraïnu ta na Pivnichnyi Kavkaz, 1932–1933 rr.*, eds. Valerii Vasyl'iev and Iu. Shapoval (Kyïv: Heneza, 2001), 54–55.

72. Vasyl'iev, "Tsina holodnoho khliba," 55.

73. *The Look of Silence*, documentary by Joshua Oppenheimer, 2015; see trailer https://youtu.be/bp1xT302VcY.

74. "Case History LH01: Maria Senyszyn, b. 1925 in the village Mykhailivka, Korosten' district, Zhytomyr region," in *Oral History Project*, vol. 1, 1.

75. Pidhainy, *The Black Deeds of the Kremlin*, vol. 1, 468.
76. Smeulers and Haveman, eds., *Supranational Criminology*, 237. See also Alette Smeulers, "Female Perpetrators: Ordinary and Extra-ordinary Women," *International Criminal Law Review* 15, no. 2 (2015): 207–53.
77. Mattingly, "[Extra]ordinary Women," 57–59.
78. Kołakowski, "The Marxist Roots of Stalinism," 164.
79. Ervin Staub, "The Roots of Evil: Social Conditions, Culture, Personality, and Basic Human Needs," *Personality and Social Psychology Review* 3, no. 3 (1999): 183.
80. Stanley Milgram, "The Dilemma of Obedience," *The Phi Delta Kappan* 55, no. 9 (1974): 604.
81. Kas'ianov, "Ukraïns'ka intelihentsiia v 1933 r.," 98.
82. "Case History LH48: Anonymous female narrator, b. 1910, Kharkiv region," in *Oral History Project*, vol. 1, 570. A proverbial wisdom, *Ïzh borsch z hrybamy, a iazyk trymai za zubamy* (Eat borsch with mushrooms, but keep your tongue behind the teeth), appeared in Ukraine in the 1930s. See *Dozhylasia Ukraïna . . . Narodna tvorchist' chasiv holodomoru i kolektyvizatsiï na Ukraïni*, comp. Ihor Buhaievych (Kyïv: Ukraïns'kyi pys'mennyk, 1993), 23.
83. "Case History LH48," in *Oral History Project*, vol. 1, 567.
84. "A 'Class' Approach to Teachers and Students," *Pravda*, October 27, 1929; quoted in Pidhainy, *The Black Deeds of the Kremlin*, vol. 2, 271–72.
85. "Na zakhyst uchyteliv-aktyvistiv," *Narodnyi uchytel'*, November 13, 1929, 2; quoted in Pauly, *Breaking the Tongue*, 279.
86. "Mobilizing Schools to Help Collectivization," *Visti*, January 15, 1930; quoted in Pidhainy, *The Black Deeds of the Kremlin*, vol. 2, 381.
87. "Case History LH57: Mikhail Frenkin, Baku," in *Oral History Project*, vol. 2, 624; English version in the *Report to Congress*, 363.
88. Ibid., 364. Frenkin, ethnically Jewish, spent ten years in labor camps, followed by seven years of exile, for a total of seventeen years, serving on the trumped up charges for participating first in the Ukrainian Military Organization (UVO) in 1931, then in the Polish Military Organization (POV) in 1933. For more about these GPU operations, see Shkandrij and Bertelsen, "The Soviet Regime's National Operations in Ukraine," 417–47.
89. *Derzhavnyi arkhiv Poltavs'koï oblasti (DAPO)*, f. P-251, op. 1, spr. 4759, ark. 9zv., 21; *DAPO*, f. P-251, op. 1, spr. 4775, ark. 3; quoted in Luk'ianenko, "Nezhodni," in *"Naiblyzhchi druzi partiï,"* 497–99.
90. *TsDAVOU*, f. 2717, op. 2, spr. 1673, ark. 20, 21; quoted in Kas'ianov, "Ukraïns'ka intelihentsiia v 1933 r.," 94.
91. *TsDAVOU*, f. 2717, op. 3, spr. 1689, ark. 15; quoted in Ibid.
92. "Case History SW47: Oleksander Merkelo," in *Oral History Project*, vol. 2, 1038.
93. Ibid., 1040.
94. In 1929, a newspaper correspondent reported about mass suicides as an indicator of passive resistance among teachers in rural areas of Soviet Ukraine. See D. Rozdaibida, "Samohubstva sered osvitian Ukraïny," *Narodnyi uchytel'* (People's

Teacher), September 25, 1929; quoted in Danylenko and Kuz'menko, "Naukovo-pedahohichna intelihentsiia v roku holodu," 151. Teachers who "fled from their personal and professional problems by committing suicide" were mentioned in Holmes, *The Kremlin and the Schoolhouse*, 132–33. For a discussion of the vulnerability of women who taught in rural schools, see Fitzpatrick, *Education and Social Mobility in the Soviet Union*, 161. For a discussion of suicides among women who worked as teachers in Soviet Russia in the 1930s, see E. Thomas Ewing, "Personal Acts with Public Meanings: Suicides by Soviet Women Teachers in the Early Stalin Era," *Gender & History* 14, no. 1 (2002): 117–37.

95. "Mr. Kononenko's Statement before the Commission on the Ukraine Famine Hearing and Meeting, April 30, 1987," Ukraine Famine [Hearing 04/30/1987], box 16921, Gary Bauer Files, Ronald Reagan Presidential Library and Museum.

96. "Case History SW3: Antin Lak, b. 1910, Poltava region," in *Oral History Project*, vol. 2, 731.

97. Alexander Weissberg-Cybulski, *The Accused* (New York: Simon and Schuster, 1951), 189; quoted in Conquest, *The Harvest of Sorrow*, 248.

98. The Second Epistle to the Thessalonians, commonly referred to as Second Thessalonians or 2 Thessalonians is a book from the New Testament of the Bible, traditionally attributed to Paul the Apostle. In its third (and last) chapter, "Warning against Loafers" verse 10 reads: "He who does not work, neither shall he eat" (2 Thess. 3:10). This truism was included into Article 18 of the 1918 Constitution. Although the Moral Code of the Constructors of Communism disappeared from the Communist Party program in 1986, the special system of stores and other privileges, such as vacations at health resorts and travel abroad, lasted until the collapse of the Soviet Union. See Stanislav Kul'chyts'kyi, "Komunisty i moral'," *Ukraïns'kyi tyzhden'*, no. 50 (630), December 12, 2019, https://tyzhden.ua/History/238597.

99. Elena Osokina, *Za fasadom "Stalinskogo izobiliia": Raspredelenie i rynok v snabzhenii naseleniia v gody industrializatsii, 1927–1941* (Moscow: ROSSPEN, 1998), 114–36.

100. Nicolas Werth, "Food Shortages, Hunger, and Famines in the USSR, 1928–33," *East/West: Journal of Ukrainian Studies* III, no. 2 (2016): 43–44.

101. TsDAVOU, f. 4134, op. 1, spr. 180, ark. 7. See also Vasyl' Marochko, "Statystyka zhertv Holodomoru: antropolohichno-demohrafichnyi dyskurs," *Ukraïns'kyi istorychnyi zhurnal*, no. 5 (2017): 118.

102. "Z shchodennyka vchytel'ky O. Radchenko," in *Holodomor 1932–1933 rokiv v Ukraïni*, ed. Pyrih, 1011–26. The original published in P. Slobodianiuk and Iu. Teliachyi, *"Chorna doshka" Ukraïny (podiï 1930-kh rokiv)* (Khmel'nyts'kyi: Podillia, 2001), 38–60.

103. "Z shchodennyka vchytel'ky O. Radchenko," 1011–26.

104. Ibid.

105. Ibid.

106. Ibid.

107. Seven of her thirteen notebooks were confiscated by Stalin's security police during a search of Radchenko's apartment on July 7, 1945, two months after the Soviet victory in World War II. The diary covered the period from 1926 through

1943. Four of the confiscated notebooks were destroyed, but the remaining three contained enough material to convict the author. In her January 8, 1932 entry, the diarist described the celebration of the Orthodox Christmas and grain requisitions, but toward the end of the month, she switched from Ukrainian to Russian. Typically, memoirists use the official language of the state rather than their native language to distance themselves emotionally from the events.

108. Radchenko's eldest daughter Elida (b. 1926) was able to hide six of the notebooks under the pillow, but when she sat down with her father to read the diary, she was horrified by her mother's revelations. The daughter burned the notebooks out of fear that she and other family members could be arrested. See Iryna Musatova, "Desiat' rokiv taboriv za osobysti notatky pro holodomor," *Dzerkalo tyzhnia*, November 25, 2006, no. 45 (624), 20; reprinted in Mytsyk, ed., *Ukraïnskyi holokost*, vol. 4, 373–76. See English version in Volodymyr V'iatrovych, "Oleksandra Radchenko: Persecuted for her Memory," Stichting Totalitaire Regimes en hun Slachtoffers, project of the Platform of European Memory and Conscience; quoted in Applebaum, *Red Famine*, 329.

109. Volodymyr V'iatrovych, "Oleksandra Radchenko – represovana za pam'iat'," *Istorychna Pravda*, November 11, 2013, http://www.istpravda.com.ua/articles/2013/11/22/139903.

110. Klitsakov, *Pedahohichni kadry Ukraïny*, 246.

111. Hanna Didenko (b. 1919), from the village of Naraïvka, Haisyns'kyi district, Vinnytsia region, in Mytsyk, ed., *Ukraïns'kyi holokost*, vol. 7, 15.

112. *TsDAHOU*, f. 1, op. 20, spr. 5258, ark. 39, 36; quoted in *Holodomor 1932–1933 rokiv v Ukraïni*, 181–82.

113. "Supply of Teachers Was Interrupted," *Visti*, March 17, 1932; quoted in Pidhainy, *The Black Deeds of the Kremlin*, vol. 2, 336–37.

114. "Case History LH57: Mikhail Frenkin, b. 1910, Baku," in *Oral History Project*, vol. 2, 619.

115. Marochko and Hillig, *Represovani pedahohy Ukraïny*, 255.

116. Vasyl' Bashtanenko, b. 1924 (interviewed in 1995 by Viktoriia Kul'ko, a philology student from Dnipropetrovs'k State University), in Mytsyk, ed., *Ukraïns'kyi holokost*, vol. 1, 137.

117. "Case History SW35: Mariia Panchenko, b. 1924 in the village of Kunivka, Kobeliaky district, Poltava region," in *Oral History Project*, vol. 2, 927, 929.

118. Vasyl' Mirutenko, "Hot Breakfast at School," in Pidhainy, *The Black Deeds of the Kremlin*, vol. 2, 574.

119. L. Pylypenko, "The Starving Schoolteachers' 'Borsch,'" in Pidhainy, *The Black Deeds of the Kremlin*, vol. 2, 578–79.

120. Danylenko and Kuz'menko, "Naukovo-pedahohichna intelihentsiia v roky holodu," 152.

121. *TsDAHOU*, f. 4134, op. 1, spr. 291, ark. 84.

122. Marochko, "Statystyka zhertv Holodomoru," 118.

123. *TsDAVOU*, f. 4134, op. 1, spr. 820, ark. 14.

124. Vasyl' Marochko, "Hariachi snidanky," in *Entsyklopediia Holodomoru 1932–1933 rokiv v Ukraïni*, 85. For more about "hot breakfasts" in schools and

orphanages, see *Ïdlo 33-ho: Slovnyk Holodomoru* (Odesa: Vyd-vo "Iurydychna literatura," 2003), 31; see also *33-i holod*, eds. Kovalenko and Maniak, 292.

125. See Volodymyr Serhiichuk, *"Holodni, bosi i rozditi": ukraïns′ki dity v 1932–1933 rokakh* (Vyshgorod: PP Serhiichuk M. I., 2020), 58.

126. Ivan Koziar, *Spohady* (Kyïv: Vydavnychyi dim "Kyievo-Mohylians′ka akademiia," 2010), 153–89; reprinted under the title "Zi spohadiv ukraïns′koho emihranta do Kanady Ivana Koziara (1904–1989 rr.)" in Mytsyk, ed., *Ukraïns′kyi holokost*, 535–37.

127. Koziar, *Spohady*, 536.

128. Ibid.

129. Ibid., 537.

130. See H. Okhrimenko, "Dyrektor shkoly riatuvav ditei vid holodnoï smerti," *Ukraïns′ke slovo*, July 20–26, 2005; see also O. Rokyts′ka, "Ivchuk Vasyl′ Iakovych, Heroi Ukraïny: podvyh liudianosti v neliuds′kyi chas," *Narodna osvita* 1, no. 10 (2010), https://www.narodnaosvita.kiev.ua/Narodna_osvita/vupysku/10/statti/rokicka.htm.

131. "Lyst komsomol′tsia H. Tkachenka do sekretaria TsK KP(b)U S. Kosiora pro ekonomichni trudnoshchi na seli ta politychnyi nastrii naselennia," *TsDAHOU*, f. 1, op. 20, spr. 5406, ark. 8–11; reprinted in *Holodomor 1932–1933 rokiv v Ukraïni*, 210–12.

132. Volodymyr Serhiichuk, "Ushanuvaty vsikh nevynno ubiiennykh," *Golos Ukraïny*, May 16, 2018, http://www.golos.com.ua/article/302970.

133. Vasyl′ Marochko, "Shkoly bez ditei ta vchyteliv," in *Holodomor 1932–1933 rr.* (Kyiv, 2007), 50.

134. Marochko, "Shkoly bez ditei ta vchyteliv," 50.

135. Ibid., 51.

136. Vasyl′ Bashtanenko, b. 1924 (interviewed in 1995 by Viktoriia Kul′ko, a philology student from Dnipropetrovs′k State University), in *Ukraïns′kyi holokost*, ed. Mytsyk, vol. 1, 137.

137. Oles′ Derhachov, b. 1902 (interviewed in 1993 by B. Bondarenko, a history student from Dnipropetrovs′k State University), in *Ukraïns′kyi holokost*, ed. Mytsyk, vol. 1, 130–31.

138. An Austrian engineer, Alexander Wienerberger worked at a factory in Kharkiv in 1933 and captured authentic images of the Holodomor for his Red Album titled "The Workers' Paradise. U.S.S.R." The album is in the private collection of Samara Pearce, the photographer's great-granddaughter. See a collection of the original photos in "Holodomor in Kharkiv through the lens of Austrian engineer: photo gallery," *Euromaidan Press*, January 10, 2021, http://euromaidanpress.com/2021/01/10/1933-holodomor-in-kharkiv-through-the-lens-of-austrian-engineer-photo-gallery/. The photo document is archived in the HREC Collection "Alexander Wienerberger: Beyond the Innitzer Album," PD106, http://vitacollections.ca/HREC-holodomor photodirectory/3636214/data.

139. Ivan Brovko (b. 1916), Tsarychans′kyi district; quoted in *Ukraïns′kyi holokost*, ed. Mytsyk, vol. 1, 144–45.

140. "Case History SW47: Oleksander Merkelo," in *Oral History Project*, vol. 2, 1037.

141. Ibid., 1038.

142. V. Savur, "Saved by Whiskey," in Pidhainy, *The Black Deeds of the Kremlin*, vol. 2, 577.

143. Andrea Graziosi, "The Impact of Holodomor Studies on the Understanding of the USSR," in *Contextualizing the Holodomor: The Impact of Thirty Years of Ukrainian Famine Studies*, eds. Andrij Makuch and Frank E. Sysyn (Edmonton: Canadian Institute of Ukrainian Studies Press, 2015), 53.

144. Graziosi, "The Impact of Holodomor Studies," 54.

145. *Narodne hospodarstvo USRR (statystychnyi dovidnyk)*, ed. Asatkin, Table 7, 553.

146. Volodymyr Petrovs'kyi, "Rozhevi okuliary i tverda diisnist'," *Svoboda*, no. 119, May 10, 1952; quoted in Solovey, *Golgota Ukraïny*, 198.

147. "Raporty Ukrainy i RSFSR o vypolnenii plana vseobucha TsK VKP(b) – tov. Staliny, TsK KP(b)U – tov. Kosioru," *Kommunisticheskoe prosveshchenie* 15 (1931): 36–40.

148. *Holod 1921–1923 rokiv v Ukraïni*, ed. Kul'chyts'kyi, 5.

149. V. I. Marochko, "O. M. Asatkin – vyhadanyi 'fal'syfikator' perepysu naselennia 1937 r.," *Ukraïns'kyi istorychnyi zhurnal*, no. 4 (2017): 147, 149. Asatkin was purged for allegedly undermining the Soviet regime by "falsifying" the 1937 population census that demonstrated catastrophic demographic losses in Soviet Ukraine.

150. Fitzpatrick, *Education and Social Mobility in the Soviet Union*.

151. Resolution of the CC AUCP(b) and USSR SNK "On ukrainization in DVK (Far-East Region), Kazakhstan, Central Asia, TsChO (Central Black Earth) and other areas of the USSR" of December 15, 1932; *GARF*, f. 5446, op. 18, d. 466, l. 177; quoted in *Holodomor of 1932–1933 in Ukraine*, ed. Pyrih, 68–69. See also Applebaum, *Red Famine*, 205–7.

152. For an account of the liquidation of *stanytsia* Poltavs'ka, see Fedir Rogiles, "Z nahody 17-richchia znyshchennia stanytsi Poltavs'koï," *Vil'na Kuban'*, no. 2, December 1949; quoted in Solovey, *Golgota Ukraïny*, 165–66.

153. Kolasky, *Education in Soviet Ukraine*, 20–21. For a special study of the destruction of Ukrainian schools and settlements in the North Caucasus in 1932–1933, see Oleksiy Kurinnyi, "Holodomor 1932–1933 rr. na Pivnichnomu Kavkazi iak henotsyd ukraïntsiv," *Materialy Mizhnarodnoï naukovo-praktychnoï konferentsiï "Holodomor 1932–1933 rokiv: vtraty ukraïns'koï natsiï" (Kyïv, 4 zhovtnia 2016 r.)* (Kyïv: Vyd. Oleh Filiuk, 2017), 73–85.

154. Vadim Denisov, "Massovye aktsii KRU i SPU NKVD," *Narodnaia Pravda*, no. 9–10 (September 1950), 29–30; quoted in Solovey, *Golgota Ukraïny*, 167–68.

155. Denisov, "Massovye aktsii KRU i SPU NKVD," 29–30; quoted in Solovey, *Golgota Ukraïny*, 168–70.

156. Conquest, *The Harvest of Sorrow*, 306.

157. Ibid., 277–78.

158. "Dnevniki Ivana Lazarevicha Polezhaeva (30-e gody, stanitsa Umanskaia)," *Rodnaia Kuban'*, no. 3 (2002): 51–60; reprinted in *Ukraïns'kyi holokost*, ed. Mytsyk, vol. 4, 258.

159. *Narodne hospodarstvo USRR (statystychnyi dovidnyk)*, ed. Asatkin, Table 1, 546–47. Thanks to Nataliia Levchuk of the Ptoukha Institute of Demography and Social Studies at the National Academy of Sciences of Ukraine for providing a copy of the statistical handbook.

160. Marochko and Hillig, *Represovani pedahohy Ukraïny*, 255.

161. *Narodne hospodarstvo USRR (statystychnyi dovidnyk)*, Table 37, 578–79; Table 38, 581–82. Soviet Ukraine had two types of postsecondary teacher training institutions: three- to four-year technical colleges (*tekhnikum*) and four- to five-year institutes, which replaced universities. By 1930, thirty-five out of forty-three (81 percent) of these colleges and six out of thirteen (46 percent) institutes in the republic conducted coursework exclusively in Ukrainian. From Stepan Siropolko, *Narodnia osvita na soviets'kii Ukraïni* (Warsaw: Pratsi Ukraïns'koho naukovoho instytutu, 1934), 205.

162. Iryna Medvid', "Lecture on the Russian Language," in Pidhainy, *The Black Deeds of the Kremlin*, vol. 2, 584–85.

163. In a recent study, O. V. Luk'ianenko called teachers "closest allies of the party" to highlight their ideological leaning; however, he listed instances of resistance among students in teacher training institutes and colleges, indicating that most of these isolated cases of resistance ended with the students being dismissed or purged from the Communist Youth League or Communist Party ranks. See Luk'ianenko, "*Naiblyzhchi druzi partiï.*"

164. "Case History SW1: Varvara Dibert," in *Oral History Project*, vol. 2, 710, 718; English version in the *Report to Congress*, 376–78.

165. Priests and clerics were declared, under article 65 of the 1918 Constitution, to be "servants of the bourgeoisie" and disfranchised. This involved their receiving no food ration cards; their children were barred from school beyond the elementary grade. See Conquest, *The Harvest of Sorrow*, 201.

166. V. Grechko, *Kommunisticheskoe vospitanie v SSSR* (Munich: Institute for the Study of the History and Culture of the USSR, 1951), 25.

167. For a study of the deformation of national culture in Ukrainian villages during the Holodomor, see Olesia Stasiuk, "Deformatsiia narodnoï kul'tury v roky henotsydu," *Problemy istoriï Ukraïny: fakty, sudzhennia, poshuky*, no. 18 (2008): 349–61; Olesia Stasiuk, *Henotsyd ukraïnstiv: deformatsiia narodnoï kul'tury* (Kyïv: Stylos, 2008).

168. From part no. 24 of the diary of Iurii Sambros, *HDA SBU*, f. 6, spr. 68805-FP, zoshyt 6, ark. 1015–16; reprinted in *Represovani shchodennyky*, 287–88.

169. Ibid., 291–92.

170. Iurii Sambros, *Shchabli: mii shliakh do komunizmu* (Stages of Life: My Journey Toward Communism) (New York: Suchasnist', 1988).

171. Valerii Smolii, "*Ukraïnizatsiia*" *1920–30-kh rokiv: peredumovy, zdobutky, uroky* (Kyïv: Instytut istoriï Ukraïny NAN Ukraïny, 2003), 183; quoted in Pauly, *Breaking the Tongue*, 344.

172. Pauly, *Breaking the Tongue*, 37.

173. Ibid., 344.

174. In 1928, the People's Commissariat of Education had 202 staff members. During the mass persecution of intelligentsia, 200 of its staff were purged as was reported in their publication *Na fronti kul'tury* (Kyïv: Radians'ka shkola, 1935), 15; quoted in Marochko and Hillig, *Represovani pedahohy Ukraïny*, 7, 10.

175. For studies of the People's Commissariat of Education under Skrypnyk's leadership, see V. M. Danylenko and M. M. Kuz'menko, *Sotsial'nyi typ ta intelektual'no-osvitnii riven' nomenklatury skrypnykivs'koho narkomosu: Biohrafichni narysy* (Sevastopol' and Donets'k: Veber, 2003) and M. Iu. Vyhovs'kyi, *Nomenklatura systemy osvity v USRR 1920–1930-kh rokiv: sotsial'ne pokhodzhennia, personal'nyi sklad ta funktsiï* (Kyïv: Heneza, 2005).

176. Conquest, *The Harvest of Sorrow*, 267–68.

177. "William Strang (Moscow) to Sir Simon on the Suicide of Mykola Skrypnyk, 10 July 1933," in Marco Carynnyk, Lubomyr Y. Luciuk, and Bohdan S. Kordan, eds., *The Foreign Office and the Famine: British Documents on Ukraine and the Great Famine of 1932–1933* (Kingston: Limestone Press, 1988), 253–54.

178. On trials of "nationalists" and Galician teachers, brought by Skrypnyk from Western Ukraine to implement Ukrainization, see Shkandrij and Bertelsen, "The Soviet Regime's National Operations in Ukraine," 423.

179. Marochko and Hillig, *Represovani pedahohy Ukraïny*, 9.

180. Pauly, *Breaking the Tongue*, 344.

181. Marochko and Hillig, *Represovani pedahohy Ukraïny*, 251.

182. Hennadii Iefimenko, *Natsional'na polityka kerivnytstva VKP(b) v Ukraïni 1932–1938 rr. (osvita ta nauka)* (Kyïv: Instytut istoriï Ukraïny, 2000), 36–50; see also Pauly, *Breaking the Tongue*, 410.

183. Bilokin', *Masovyi teror iak zasib derzhavnoho upravlinnia v SRSR*, vol. 2, 519–22; quoted in Applebaum, *Red Famine*, 220.

184. Iurii Shapoval, "Letters from Kharkiv: The Truth about the Holodomor through the Eyes of Italian Diplomats," *Den'*, November 20, 2007; https://day.kyiv.ua/en/article/close/letters-kharkiv.

185. Shapoval, "Letters from Kharkiv."

Chapter 5

Denial

Denial lasts throughout and always follows genocide. If genocide goes unacknowledged, "[it] is among the surest indicators of further genocidal massacres," warned Gregory H. Stanton of George Mason University. According to Stanton, denial includes the following actions typically taken by perpetrators:

> They dig up the mass graves, . . . try to cover up the evidence and intimidate the witnesses. They deny that they committed any crimes, and often blame what happened on the victims. They block investigations of the crimes, and continue to govern until driven from power by force, when they flee into exile. There they remain with impunity . . . unless they are captured and a tribunal is established to try them.[1]

The position of Soviet authorities regarding the man-made nature of the Ukrainian famine and the Kazakh famine, as well as the ultimate destruction of "small" ethnic groups, such as Crimean Tatars or Chechens in the Soviet Union, are examples of denial of genocides against national minorities. Like their Soviet predecessors, Russian officials deny that the Holodomor constitutes a genocide. In 2017, two days before the Holodomor Remembrance Day, Russian Foreign Ministry spokesperson Maria Zakharova informed the international community that the Ukrainian government's position that the 1932–1933 famine in Soviet Ukraine was a genocide "contradict[ed] historical facts" and that claims about the uniqueness of the famine in Soviet Ukraine had been "politically charged."[2] Moreover, Stalin, the key perpetrator of Soviet genocides[3] including the Holodomor, is enjoying renewed popularity in Russia, and systematic denials of Stalin's genocides have become the norm in the Russian Federation. Paula Chertok, a linguist, lawyer, writer, and daughter of Holocaust survivors from Ukraine, Belarus, and Poland, believes that "these denials have taken on a distinctly nasty character" since Ukrainian–Russian relations rapidly deteriorated after Russia's invasion of Ukraine in 2014. She argues that Russian "state-run media have been attempting to use Holodomor denial to boost their campaign against Ukraine and the West," claiming that the calamity had been invented by Ukrainians and "perpetrated by neo-Nazis, who conveniently are also running the coup government in Kyiv."[4]

Ukraine's struggle for the affirmation of the Holodomor as genocide faces the challenge of Russia's denial which protects its self-image.[5] The denial has comprised an array of tactics: challenging the legal definition of the Holodomor as genocide, reinterpreting the genocide against the Ukrainian people as an "all-Union" famine, covering up the true extent of population losses, banning books on the topic, and silencing the truth.

LEGAL CHALLENGE

In its hybrid war[6] against Ukraine, Russia has employed an arsenal of diplomatic and legal instruments.[7] On November 28, 2006, Ukraine adopted the law "On the Holodomor of 1932–1933 in Ukraine," which recognized the cataclysmic historical event that occurred between the two world wars in legal terms as genocide against the Ukrainian national group and criminalized Holodomor denial.[8] In 2007, Ukraine launched a campaign to achieve worldwide recognition of the Holodomor as genocide in the United Nations and other international organizations. In response, in April 2008, when the NATO Summit in Bucharest, Romania, was discussing Ukraine's membership, the Russian State Duma (the lower house of the Federal Assembly) adopted a resolution, stating that "there is no historic evidence that the famine was organized on ethnic grounds."[9] Earlier in March 2008, Valerii Loshchinin, Russia's envoy to the United Nations office in Geneva, told the seventh session of the U.N. Human Rights Council: "We urge against political speculation on subjects related to the general, sometimes tragic, historical past, and against using this for a voluntary interpretation of the rules of international law."[10] The diplomat also argued that Ukraine's Holodomor should not be recognized as genocide under the 1948 U.N. Convention on Genocide.

Deniers assert that Cold War politics shaped the drafting of the U.N. Convention on Genocide, "gutting" many of Raphael Lemkin's original ideas and rendering it "stillborn."[11] They further claim that because the term was coined a decade after the famine, the U.N. Convention of 1948 should not be applied retroactively. This argument has been refuted by legal scholars. The prohibition of genocide is a *jus cogens* norm,[12] to which the general rule of non-retroactivity does not apply. Besides, under the 1968 U.N. Convention on the

Non-Applicability of Statutory Limitations to War Crimes and Crimes Against Humanity, no statutory limitations shall apply to crimes against humanity and the crime of genocide as defined in the U.N. Convention on Genocide, regardless of the dates of their commission, "even if such acts do not constitute a violation of the domestic law of the country in which they were committed."[13] The Convention on Statutory Limitations eliminated any potential domestic barriers to prosecution of persons for acts of genocide as a crime against humanity.

Significantly, the U.N. Convention on Genocide reflects the *génocidaire*[14] Stalin's influence on the process. Both Stalin and his Foreign Minister Viacheslav Molotov read through and commented on a draft of the future Genocide Convention. In bold red pencil, Stalin crossed out the word "political" as a motivation for committing genocide, and Molotov crossed out the entire last paragraph on cultural genocide. They also eliminated the "shortcomings" in the draft theses that they found unacceptable from the Soviet standpoint, crossing out phrases like "forced labor" and "confiscation of property."[15] Clearly, Stalin could not incriminate himself.

Regrettably, Lemkin's conceptualization of Soviet genocide against the Ukrainian nation remained obscured until 2008, when the international community commemorated the sixtieth anniversary of the U.N. Convention on Genocide and his typewritten notes were published. Historian Roman Serbyn first encountered the source cited by French scholar Jean-Louis Panné.[16] A proponent of Lemkin's conceptualization ever since its "discovery" in the New York Public Library, Serbyn concluded that the Holodomor met the criteria set by Article II of the U.N. Convention on Genocide, arguing that the two categories "national" and "ethnic(al)" do apply to the Ukrainian case.[17] The intent was "to destroy in part" the nationally conscious elites and a large portion of the most dynamic element of Ukrainian society, the farmers, so as to reduce Ukrainians to obedient Russified "cogs of the great state mechanism," Stalin's favorite imagery for Soviet citizens. Serbyn has deepened the conceptualization by highlighting two parallel elements in Stalin's strategy to create a single state with a single Soviet people with a uniform consciousness:

> In this way Ukrainians would be destroyed as a national and an ethnic group. To achieve this goal, Stalin used lethal means, starvation imposed on the Ukrainian farming population—the most costly in terms of human lives, but also executions and deportations to Siberia of any Ukrainians opposed or accused of opposition to the regime and its policies. The non-lethal method was "reeducation" of the society into loyal citizens of the [G]reat Russian state that Stalin was building.[18]

Putin's hybrid war resembles Stalin's strategy to subjugate Ukrainians, using both lethal and nonlethal means.

Ukraine's response to the legal challenge was to investigate human rights violations by the Soviet government. On May 22, 2009, the Security Service of Ukraine brought a criminal case for the crime of genocide in Soviet Ukraine in 1932–1933 and initiated court proceedings on the basis of Article 442 of the Criminal Code of Ukraine.[19] After examining the evidence, on January 13, 2010, the Kyïv Court of Appeals in Ukraine ruled that Joseph Stalin and his accomplices were guilty of perpetrating "the genocide of part of a Ukrainian national group by creating conditions of life calculated to bring about its destruction."[20] The legal experts found sufficient precedent to hold the perpetrators accountable, albeit posthumously.

THE "ALL-UNION" FAMINE

The Russian rhetoric behind the façade of the "all-Union" famine as a "tragedy of all the Soviet countryside"[21] points to its economic causes and deflects attention from the national (in Soviet Ukraine) and ethnic (Ukrainian minority in the Russian SFSR) group that was targeted in the genocide. In an attempt to control the narrative, spurred by the recognition of the Holodomor as genocide in Ukraine, Russian historian Viktor Kondrashin of Penza State Pedagogical University, on behalf of the head of the Federal Archival Agency (*Rosarkhiv*) Vladimir Kozlov, issued instructions to Russian scholars and researchers regarding the proper presentation of the famine of 1929–1934 in the USSR. This conceptual framework for discussing the famine, as spelled out in Decree No. 47 of the Federal Archival Agency,[22] issued on October 17, 2007, was conveniently cast in generic terms as "all-Union," a tragedy caused by enforced collectivization and industrialization. Academics were ordered to use a preapproved collection of documents to conform their writing about the famine to the conceptual framework, with the purpose of suppressing anything that would demonstrate the unique situation in Soviet Ukraine.[23]

This collection of archival materials became an instrument in information warfare with the aim to impose Russian political interpretation of the famine on academia and export it to Ukraine. First, on January 17, 2007, the Russian Federal Archival Agency sent a letter to the then head of the State Committee on Archives in Ukraine Olga Ginzburg with Kondrashin's instructions (the only difference being the date range of 1932–1933 in the title), deliberately singling out the "Ukrainian factor" that had to be eliminated from the historical narrative.[24] The following year, the Russian Federal Archival Agency together with the "Historical Memory" Foundation[25] organized an international conference "The Famine in the USSR in the 1930s: Historical and Political Interpretations" in Kharkiv, held on the eve of the Holodomor Remembrance Day on November 21, 2008. Observers noted that it was similar to the Moscow conference of November 17, with the same participants; the only difference was that it was initially planned for Kyïv.[26] The participants included Viktor Kondrashin and Nikolai Ivnitskii, the authorities on famine research in the USSR, as well as Mark Tauger, professor of Russian and Soviet history at West Virginia University,[27] and Stephen G. Wheatcroft, professor of Russian and Soviet history at the University of Melbourne, Australia, who used Russian archives to write his book, *The Years of Hunger*.[28] Experts from Belarus and Kazakhstan were also among the speakers.[29] However, the political agenda of the Ukrainian–Russian relations took precedence over historical research. Speakers at the plenary session included the Russian ambassador to Ukraine Viktor Chernomyrdin and the director of the "Historical Memory" Foundation Aleksandr Diukov among others. The conference hosts were the vice mayor of Kharkiv and the head of the Kharkiv branch of the pro-Russia Party of Regions.[30] The conclusion on the causes, character, and number of victims of the 1929–1934 famine in the USSR had been prepared in advance and distributed on a CD with documents from Russian archives.[31] The Russian position on the famine was repeated in an open letter to the presidents of Russia, Ukraine, Belarus, Kazakhstan, and Kyrgyzstan. The letter accused then President Viktor Yushchenko of using the tragedy of the 1930s for legitimizing his political course aimed at "excluding Ukraine from the common cultural, historical and economic space of the unique East-Slavic civilization."[32] The conference was seen as a provocation and insult to Ukrainian national feelings; the opponents were not allowed to participate or present their arguments in any format because the conference was accessible by invitation only in a remote hotel far away from the city center. The conference had little resonance in the academic community in Ukraine. It served one purpose: to further intensify political polarization in society over the Holodomor.

When Raphael Lemkin's speech, "Soviet Genocide in [the] Ukraine" became public, and the National Holodomor-Genocide Museum opened its exhibitions in Kyïv in 2008, Russia's State Duma went on the offensive, promoting a counternarrative. "There is no historical proof that the famine was organized along ethnic lines. Its victims were millions of citizens of the Soviet Union, representing different peoples and nationalities living largely in agricultural areas of the country," the Russian State Duma resolution stated.[33] This purported ideological motivation is not supported by the facts. The scope and consequences of the "all-Union" famine differed drastically, so much so that based on the 1926 and 1939 population censuses, taken before and after the famine years, the number of Russians in the Soviet Union increased by 28 percent, while the number of Ukrainians decreased by 9.9 percent.[34]

The "all-Union" famine argument is promoted in order to deflect attention from the responsibility of the Communist Party and its sentinel the GPU for the genocide committed in Soviet Ukraine, and to deny that it was perpetrated against nationally conscious Ukrainians. For scholars brought up in the service of the Communist Party, like the Ukrainian historian Stanislav Kul'chyts'kyi, respected by his Russian colleagues, the "all-Union" famine argument became their historiographical credo. Recently, Kul'chyts'kyi has revised his views and proposed the concept of a "famine within the famine," the Holodomor as a unique phenomenon distinct from the "all-Union" famine.[35] To quote Marochko: "If there was the 'all-Union' famine, where was its epicenter?"[36]

Scholars who focus on the economic causes of the famine ignore the fact that "total collectivization" of farms in Soviet Ukraine had been completed by the autumn of 1931 or the spring of 1932 at the latest, much earlier than in Soviet Russia. They dismiss arguments of James Mace, executive director of the U.S. Commission on the Ukraine Famine, who pointed out that the famine ravaged the republic after the harvest was collected in the autumn of 1932 through the winter and spring of 1933. The fact that the 1934 crop, substantially smaller than that of 1932, did not lead to famine (because quotas were lowered and grain was released from state stockpiles), means that in 1932, famine could also have been averted, had the central authorities in Moscow wished to do so.[37] Soviet sources on the grain harvests and state procurements show that the crop was larger in 1932 than in 1931, so crop failure was not the cause of the famine; rather, the reason was excessive state procurements that increased from 1929 on.[38] The climate took its toll in 1931 to a greater extent, and Soviet historiographers had seen 1931 as a worse year than 1932.[39] In the summer of 1932 Molotov, sent to the then Soviet Ukrainian capital of Kharkiv as Stalin's personal emissary, "specifically cited the 1931 drought in the Volga basin, the Southern Urals, Western Siberia, and Kazakhstan as one reason why Ukraine had to meet its obligations to procure grain for the central authorities."[40]

Ukraine's "gold"—grain—was the major commodity for Soviet export, and its deliveries on the world market in millions of tons increased from 2.6 in 1929 to 48.4 in 1930 to 51.8 in 1932 but dropped significantly to 17.6 in 1933 down to 8.4 in 1934.[41] On the global grain market, the Soviet Union faced a difficult situation with a foreign currency exchange due to the Great Depression of 1929–1933. The Soviet Union wanted to beat Canada as a world grain producer, but dumping the grain further depressed market prices. Little effort was made to import industrial equipment and technology on credit mainly because the formal recognition of the Soviet Union by the United States depended on paying off the old debt owed by previous Russian governments in the form of a percentage above the normal rate of interest on a loan granted by the government of the United States.[42]

In the last months of 1932, collective farms, entire villages, and entire regions in Ukraine and the North Caucasus were blacklisted as grain-quota debtors. Blacklisting meant the requisitioning of all produce grown by the farmers on their private plots and stored for the six months to come until the new harvest. Grain was the first item subject to confiscation. This was a draconian measure as there was practically no grain left in the winter months of 1932–1933. Yet, quoting Soviet statistics, Mark Tauger claims that the 1932 harvest was smaller than anticipated or admitted.[43]

The harvest was not bad, as many survivors recalled and scholars, such as Robert Conquest, James Mace, and Stanislav Kul'chyts'kyi, concluded.[44] It would have fed the population in Ukraine. James Mace in his report to U.S. Congress cited "post-Stalinist" statistics to show that this harvest was larger than those of 1931 or 1934 and referred to later Soviet historiography, describing 1931 as a worse year than 1932 because of drought. Mace argued that the 1932 harvest would not have produced mass starvation and

> was not even news when it happened, because at the summer 1932 Third All-Ukrainian Party Conference the Communists in Ukraine were making it as clear as they possibly could that the quotas being imposed on them by Moscow could not possibly be met.[45]

By the third year of requisitioning, the farmers had become convinced that, as in previous two years, the state would confiscate the entire harvest. Although the state tried to promote material interest in collective farming by transitioning in January 1933 from unlimited requisitions to tax obligations (bound by certain limitations) of the collective farms to the state, the farmers saw little incentive to work on collective farm fields and collectively sell produced crops on the market after fulfilling the predetermined obligations. They preferred to work their private garden plots to survive. This was deemed "sabotage." Kul'chyts'kyi has argued that Stalin himself understood this situation perfectly and retreated from unlimited requisitioning, but nonetheless he told the party that he was delivering a "crushing blow" to the farmers.[46]

The "crushing blow" was camouflaged as a winter grain procurement campaign. It is an established fact that it was a planned GPU operation that started in the fall of 1932 and continued in the spring of 1933. The GPU was tasked with suppressing an "armed uprising aimed at overthrowing the Soviet rule and establishing a capitalist order under the so-called Independent Ukrainian Republic."[47] Concurrently, on February 16, 1933, the Communist Party issued directives to ban registration of cases of deaths due to starvation by civilian registries and transferred the registration to the GPU. Village councils were ordered not to list the cause of death. The GPU was also in charge of controlling the population movement and blockaded villages, thus preventing the starving escapees from procuring food elsewhere.

Some Western scholars, along with Tauger, continue to argue that famine was unavoidable and Stalin had no alternative but starve the villages to feed the cities and sell as much grain as possible abroad to pay for his grandiose plans of industrialization. Did Stalin have to take so much food from the countryside after the harvest of 1932 to starve millions of people to death? Did Stalin have to blame the failure to find nonexistent grain on the local Communist Party cells being infiltrated by "Petliurists" and various so-called enemies? Did Stalin have no alternative to building a superior socialist mode of production to compete with exploitative capitalist one by destroying the most prosperous segment of the farming population in Ukraine?

English economist Alec Nove and his followers treat assertions of the genocidal character of the famine in Soviet Ukraine skeptically. An often quoted aphorism penned by Nove, who disagreed with Robert Conquest's claim about Stalin's "crashing blow" having been directed against Ukrainians, is thus, "[Stalin's motive] was surely to strike a 'devastating blow' at peasants in grain-surplus areas, many of whom were Ukrainians, rather than at Ukrainians, many of whom were peasants."[48] Aphorisms like this, which focus narrowly on the agricultural policy, create an impression that Ukraine had no intelligentsia and all Ukrainians were "peasants." In the 1930s, the world was largely rural, with 22 percent of urbanization level.[49] To put it into a global perspective, in the 1930s, in the United States, the percentage of urban was 56 in total population (corresponding to a nationally defined concept), whereas in the Soviet Union the percentage of urban was 19, approximating the world average. No other country in the world, except the Soviet Union, suffered such a drastic loss of population in the 1930s as recorded in the United Nations publication, but the loss was reported in aggregate without providing the percentage of population loss in Soviet Ukraine. Kazakhstan at the time was an autonomous republic within the Russian SFSR, and the mortality from the Kazakh famine in the 1930s skewed statistical trends in the Russian SFSR.[50] The epicenter of the 1932–1933 famine was in Soviet Ukraine as well as the North Caucasus and other grain-producing regions in the Russian SFSR, including Kazakhstan, where Ukrainian farmers settled, voluntarily or involuntarily.

Ukraine became the epicenter of the genocidal famine because it was one of the largest national republics with a strong tradition of national liberation struggle led by its patriotic intelligentsia, strongly rooted in the agricultural population. The Bolshevik slogan of the time was the struggle against "bourgeois nationalism" as the greatest threat.[51] The previous achievements of Ukrainization in the districts of the North Caucasus that aspired to be reunited with Ukraine, as well as in the adjacent districts in the Central Black Earth with the majority Ukrainian population, were curtailed first. The emerging new Ukrainian identity was nipped in the bud, when the Ukrainization campaign was abruptly stopped outside Soviet Ukraine on December 14, 1932, and all leaders of Ukrainian educational and cultural institutions outside the republic in ethnically Ukrainian settlements were arrested, executed, or exiled to concentration camps in the Russian Far North and Siberia.

The crux of the matter is that Stalin employed both nonlethal and lethal means to achieve his goal. The nonlethal means included silencing the truth about the famine, propaganda in the press, and political literacy campaigns designed to ideologically subvert Ukraine's population. The lethal means included special operations of the GPU to eliminate nationally conscious intellectuals[52] and to suppress uprisings in the countryside that threatened to topple the Soviet regime.[53] The elimination of the nationally conscious intelligentsia through GPU special operations in the 1920s and the 1930s, the "brain" of the nation in Lemkin's terms, resulted in thousands of deaths and enormous cultural disruption in Ukraine. In 1929, the GPU arrested 30,000 intellectuals, writers, scientists, and teachers for their alleged participation in the fictitious organization Union for the Liberation of Ukraine (known by its Ukrainian abbreviation as SVU), fabricated by the GPU to intimidate the rest of the population into submission. In the spring of 1930, forty-five of them were put on trial in the Kharkiv Opera House.[54]

Among the arrested were leading Ukrainian historians. Serhii Iefremov, vice president of the All-Ukrainian Academy of Sciences' governing council and secretary of its historical-philological division, was accused of being the leader of the SVU and was sentenced to ten years of imprisonment. Like Iefremov, Iosyp Hermaize (of Jewish ancestry), the secretary of the All-Ukrainian Academy of Sciences' historical division, was vilified in the press ahead of the show trial, and, as soon as the trial ended, was exiled to a labor camp on the Solovetsky Islands in the White Sea in Soviet Russia. Professor Hrushevs'kyi was exiled to Moscow in 1931. In 1934, his body was returned to Soviet Ukraine in a coffin (a lethal outcome of a minor surgery).[55]

While the *crème de la crème* of the old Ukrainian intelligentsia, the living symbols of Ukraine's struggle for independence, were prosecuted at the SVU trial, preparations were made to crack down on the opponents of the regime in the countryside. A secret resolution of January 30, 1930 "On Measures to Liquidate Kulak Households in Districts with Total Collectivization" spelled out methods of destruction in three stages. The first category was comprised of leading opponents of the regime, subject to immediate liquidation by execution or imprisonment in concentration camps. Those assigned to the second category were to be deported from Ukraine to far-off areas in the Russian Far North and Siberia with a stipulation to never return to their homeland.

Clarence A. Manning, professor of Slavic Languages at Columbia University, wrote that by the end of 1932, as many as 2.4 million persons were forcibly removed from Soviet Ukraine to remote places.[56] People who fell into the third category were to be resettled on the worst land outside the collectivized villages.[57] Those who joined uprisings automatically lost their land ownership and citizenship rights.

Additional methods that led to lethal outcomes included special resolutions with instructions, drafted by Stalin, for executive committees on specific measures to put collective farms and independent farmers on blacklists (these included a series of measures, such as the suspension of trade and credit and the removal of all produce from stores).[58] Within a month, the targets for blacklisting became not only collective farms as units of socialist economy or village soviets as administrative units, but entire villages. "This, beyond doubt, underscores that the goal of the Bolshevik policy was not the fulfillment of the grain procurement plan (it was an excuse), but the creation for all the village residents of conditions incompatible with life," noted Heorhii Papakin.[59] Eventually, as of January 1933, the Ukrainian SSR as a whole was secretly blacklisted.[60] As the authorities brutally confiscated all grain and everything edible, they simultaneously sealed the borders of Ukraine and the ethnically Ukrainian Kuban' in the North Caucasus, banning travel to Russian regions (Central Black Earth, the Lower Volga, and Moscow), as well as to Belarus, to procure food.[61] Population movement was controlled by special military detachments and GPU patrols.[62]

By 1934, the last remnants of the Ukrainian Autocephalous Orthodox Church (UAOC) were suppressed. Four successive Metropolitans of the UAOC were arrested and executed during the Great Terror. In addition, thirteen archbishops and bishops were reported dead in Soviet prisons, while in all 1,150 priests and some 20,000 members of parish and district church councils perished in concentration camps.[63] At the end of 1932, over a thousand churches were closed in Soviet Ukraine. Between 1934 and 1936, about 80 percent of the remaining churches in Soviet Ukraine were destroyed.[64]

The assault on Ukrainian intellectuals from the 1920s to 1930s, as well as on Ukrainian clergy and farmers, constituted what Raphael Lemkin later would identify as genocide.[65] The demographic composition of Ukrainian villages was changed when Russian veterans and loyalists with their families were settled in the areas depopulated by the famine.[66] The memories of horrid experiences of starvation, deaths, and displacement haunted those who survived the Holodomor for generations. With the rehabilitation of Stalinism in Putin's Russia, an old mix of lethal and nonlethal means is being redeployed to inspire supporters and fool critics of what analysts dub as a "new generation" warfare.[67]

COVERING UP THE LOSSES

The most effective denial tactic in the Russian disinformation war is diminishing the scale of the population losses. As early as May 31, 1933, Italian Royal Consul in Kharkiv Sergio Gradenigo reported a devastating loss of 10–15 million, commenting that "in my opinion this number will be surpassed and may have already been reached."[68] A month later, in his June 22, 1933, dispatch, Gradenigo reported 9 million deaths in Ukraine alone according to government representatives, adding that "[i]n university circles, however, there is talk of 40–50 percent of the entire Ukrainian population, a figure which I consider to be more accurate (15–16 million)."[69]

Three years after the atrocity, in 1936, American psychologist William Horsley Gantt of Johns Hopkins University published an epidemiological study with results of the First Five-Year Plan in the *British Medical Journal*, quoting 15 million deaths based on estimates of Soviet public health officials.[70] Dr. Gantt served as chief of Medical Division of the American Relief Administration during the famine of 1921–1922, and visited the Soviet Union numerous times, including in the summer of 1933. In a letter to agricultural economist at U.S. Department of Agriculture Dana Dalrymple, dated March 6, 1964, Dr. Gantt confirmed that he "got the maximal figure of fifteen million" dead in the 1932–1933 famine privately from Soviet public health officials and doctors, emphasizing that starvation was complicated by epidemics.[71]

How did we get from the 1930s to the 1990s, from 15 million to just over 3 million deaths in the genocidal famine? In March 1988, the Institute of History of Ukraine received a draft of the Executive Summary of the U.S. Commission on the Ukraine Famine. Soviet historian Stanislav Kul′chyts′kyi was commissioned to write a brochure, *1933: trahediia holodu*, aimed at propagandists and general public, in which he challenged the "irrational idea that the man-made famine was genocide perpetrated against Ukrainians as a national group."[72] Using Cold War rhetoric, Kul′chyts′kyi dismissed the U.S. Commission findings by stating that Congressmen's task was "to help the American people better understand the role of Soviets in organizing the famine" and to create in the minds of the American people an image of the Soviet Union as an "Evil Empire."[73] A historian by training, Kul′chyts′kyi offered his estimate of demographic losses after the 1937 census was declassified in 1987. His formula was simple: 1.7 million (difference between 1933 and 1937) plus 1.8 million (hypothetical natural population increase between 1933 and 1937) equals to 3.5 million.[74]

Thirty years later, in 2018, in a newspaper article, Kul′chyts′kyi argued that "demography, unlike history, where everyone has his own opinion, is a precise science."[75] Kul′chyts′kyi admitted that he was second after Stephen

Wheatcroft of Melbourne University to be granted a privileged access to secret files in the Russian archive in Moscow during his visit in 1990. Kul'chyts'kyi also revealed that using the same census data, Russian dissident demographer Aleksandr Bab'onyshev of Harvard University, who wrote under pseudonym Sergei Maksudov, estimated Ukraine's losses in a range from 4 to 4.8 million.[76]

Russian scholars estimate Holodomor losses in Soviet Ukraine as follows: Elena Osokina[77]—2.7 million, Viktor Danilov and Il'ia Zelenin[78]—3.5 million, Viktor Kondrashin[79]—3.5 million, and Sergei Maksudov[80]—4.5 million. These scholars use the 1926 Soviet census and the repressed 1937 census[81] figures, but ignore the fact that Ukrainians became victims beyond the borders of the republic, in grain-growing regions of the North Caucasus, the Central Black Earth, the Lower Volga, and even Kazakhstan.[82] Based on the 1926 Soviet census, there were 5.8 million Ukrainians in the European part of the Russian SFSR. Of these, 3.1 million lived in the North Caucasus, where they constituted 37 percent of the population. The percentages varied from less than 1 percent in the southern regions to 62 percent in the Kuban' district (Krasnodar region) in the northwest. More than 1 million Ukrainians lived in the Voronezh region (33 percent of the population),[83] the territory which Skrypnyk planned to add to Ukraine through negotiations with Moscow in the 1920s.[84] Although demographers have examined regional differences in demographic losses in Soviet Ukraine and Soviet Russia,[85] so far there is no systematic study providing a breakdown of the population that died from the famine in the Russian SFSR that would allow us to know what number of victims were ethnic Russians, Ukrainians, Germans, Tatars, and other nationalities.

Demographers ignore sources that were compiled during the 1930s in Soviet Ukraine, among them statistical reports from commissariats of health, education, and security police reports, as well as studies conducted by Ukrainian demographers Arsenii Khomenko[86] and Mykhailo Ptukha[87] in the 1930s. For over eighty years, interrogation files of chief demographer Oleksandr Asatkin have been stored in vaults of the Sectoral State Archive of the Security Service of Ukraine, coming to light decades too late.[88] As early as 1935, Asatkin expressed his concern over the peak of mortality observed in 1933.[89] In his note addressed to the leadership of the Communist Party of the Ukrainian SSR, he presented figures on changes in the population of Soviet Ukraine between 1926 and 1934. On September 2, 1937, he was executed for allegedly "falsifying" the census because his staff failed to reach the projected 35 million, reporting instead 27.9 million, a population loss of 7.1 million in Soviet Ukraine.[90] Besides, in November 1942, Ukrainian economist and statistician Stepan Sosnovyi published his article under the evocative title, "Truth about the Famine in Ukraine in 1932–1933," in which he estimated total population losses in Soviet

Denial 195

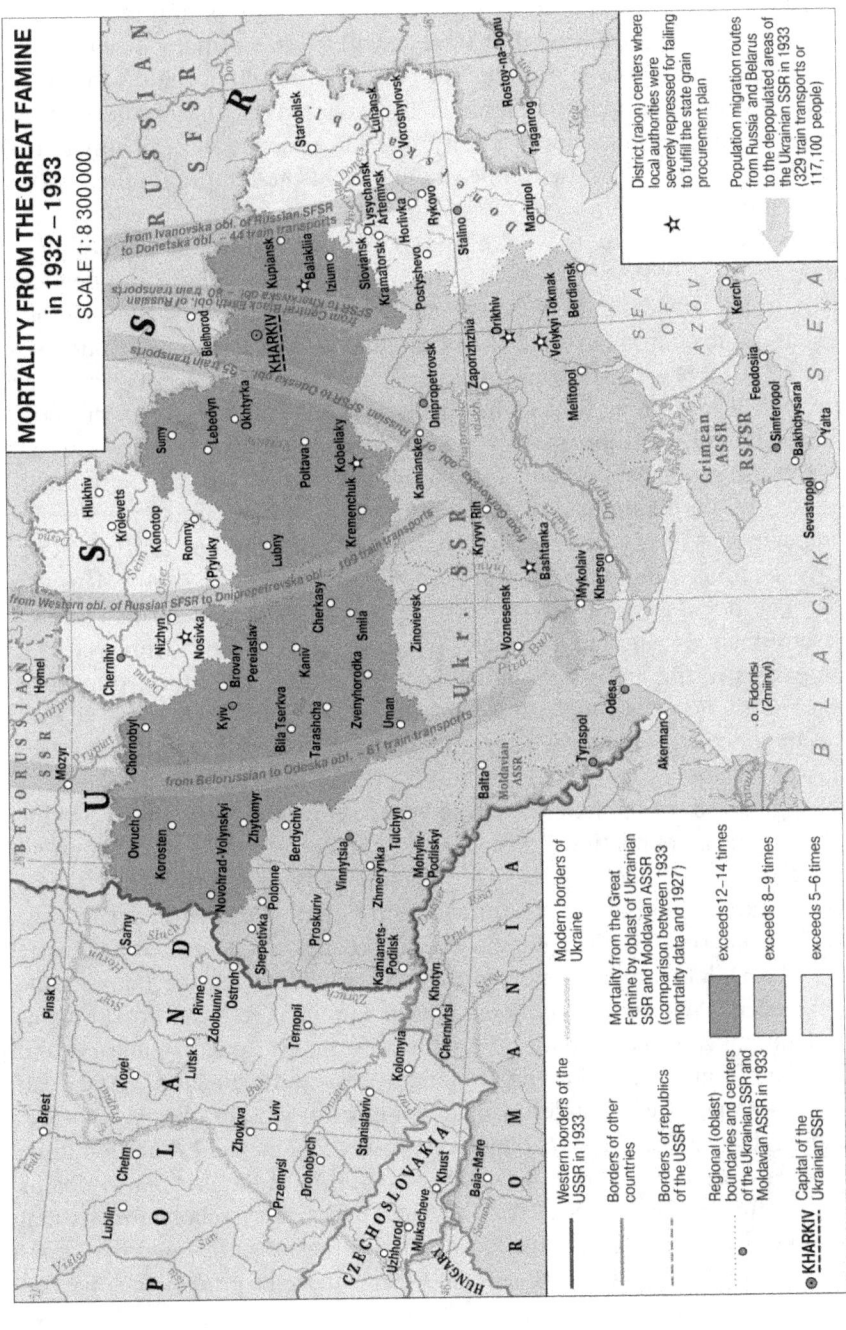

Figure 5.1 Mortality from the Great Famine in 1932–1933 in the Ukrainian SSR. *Source:* Created by the DNVP "Kartohrafiia," 2019.

Ukraine between 1932 and 1938 at 7.5 million, including 4.8 million deaths from 1932 (1.3 million) to 1933 (3.5 million) as a result of enforced starvation.[91] His article was reprinted in *Ukraïns'ki visti* in Germany on February 5, 1950; that is how the Ukrainian diaspora learned about the death toll in Soviet Ukraine. The map in Figure 5.1 shows that in the northern, non-grain-producing regions, the mortality in 1933 exceeded 12–14 times that of 1927, which points to the deliberate nature of the famine used as a tool of genocide.

A few weeks before the unveiling of the U.S. National Holodomor Memorial on November 7, 2015 in Washington, D.C., five leaders of Ukrainian academic institutions and associations in North America appealed to the chairman of the U.S. Committee for Ukrainian Holodomor-Genocide Awareness, Michael Sawkiw, Jr., with a request not to use the figure over 7 million victims as has been known in the Ukrainian diaspora but instead use 3.9 million as a "consensus" figure. Otherwise, they warned, "it will cause protests in certain anti-Ukrainian circles, and will be immediately used by the Kremlin propagandists to discredit Ukrainian science for incompetence."[92] This "consensus" figure includes neither birth deficits, fertility decline, nor ethnic Ukrainian population losses of the Russian SFSR. The population of Soviet Ukraine was inflated and further diluted by resettlement of Russian and Belorussian families of Red Army veterans and loyalists in the areas depopulated by the famine (329 train transports or nearly 117,149 Russian settlers[93] as shown in Figure 5.1). These figures do not include workers recruited from outside the Ukrainian SSR to replace the losses in labor force.[94]

The signatories of the letter dismissed the over 7 million deaths as lacking "methodological foundations" because the number was quoted in "journalistic accounts from the 1930s." They also suggested replacing the "three million children" with a more accurate "one million children under the age of ten." In support of their argument they cited an attack launched by Russia against the Holodomor as genocide, without realizing that the hoax article was posted by *Sputnik International*, the preeminent Russian government-funded propaganda news outlet.[95] In their desire to appear unbiased and fair-minded, a group of Ukrainian demographers and their North American colleagues perpetuate the underestimated number of victims of this genocide. Already in the 1950s, many recognized scholars considered 4.8 million to be a conservative estimate, pointing to up to 8 million as the number of deaths in Ukraine under the Soviets.[96] Yet, twenty-first-century scholars insist that there is no alternative to "serious academic estimates" performed by "reputable demographers" in Ukraine and the West.[97] It seems prudent to offer this letter in its entirety:

Text of the Letter to Michael Sawkiw, Jr., Chairman
U.S. Committee for Ukrainian Holodomor Genocide Awareness
September 1, 2015

Dear Mr. Sawkiw,

We, the presidents or directors of the five major Ukrainian academic institutions and associations in North America, are writing to you and the members of the U.S. Holodomor Commission about a very important matter.

It has come to our attention that the website of the U.S. Holodomor Committee provides the number of Ukrainian deaths in the Holodomor as being 7–10 million. Please be apprised of the fact that this estimate traces back to journalist accounts from the 1930s. All serious academic estimates performed by reputable demographers in Ukraine and the West place the death toll in the 3–5 million range. These figures are accepted by the leading historians in the field, from Andrea Graziosi to Tim Snyder and Stanislav Kulchytsky. The figure of 3.9 million victims of the Holodomor served as the basis for the ruling of the Ukrainian court on the perpetrators of the Holodomor in January 2010, during the last weeks of Viktor Yushchenko's presidency.

Problematic are also figures provided by the website on the dynamics of the Holodomor in Ukraine and the number of children who died in the famine. The website states that "By the end of 1933, nearly 25% of the population of Ukraine, including three million children, had perished." Taking into account the data provided by a group of Ukrainian and U.S. demographers, a much more accurate statement would read as follows. "By the end of 1933, about 17% of the population of Ukraine, including nearly one million children under the age of ten, had perished."

We strongly urge you to change the estimate on the website accordingly. This is vitally important for several reasons:

1) The 4 million estimate, as well as the other two figures, are based on sound demographical and statistical analysis. Such scholarship should not be ignored or treated lightly, as it rests on far more persuasive methodological foundations than journalistic estimates.

2) The 7–10 million figure will elicit a storm of protest from negatively disposed non-Ukrainian sources, with the typical accusation being that it is meant to exceed the death toll in the Holocaust. Such criticism will only divert attention from the tragedy of the Holodomor.

3) The 7–10 million figure will play directly into the hands of Kremlin propagandists, who will claim that, just as the figure is unjustifiably high, so is the treatment of the Ukrainian tragedy as genocide. To provide the Kremlin with such propaganda ammunition at a time of the war in Ukraine strikes us as unwise. The first attack has been already launched:

http://sputniknews.com/politics/20150809/1025560345.html#ixzz3iXdnBIyY

We appreciate and salute your and your colleagues' success in making the U.S. Holodomor Monument a reality, and hope that our arguments will convince you to provide more correct figures on the web site, as well as on the planned plaque for the monument.

Respectfully,

Vitaly Chernetsky, President
American Association for Ukrainian Studies

George Grabowicz, President
Shevchenko Scientific Society

Albert Kipa, President
Ukrainian Academy of Arts and Sciences in the U.S.

Volodymyr Kravchenko, Director
Canadian Institute of Ukrainian Studies

Serhii Plokhii, Director
Harvard Ukrainian Research Institute[98]

Victims on the "territory of the Holodomor" included not only those who starved to death in the fields and villages but also members of various professions who were persecuted, lost jobs and consequently were deprived of any means to survive, the cannibals who suffered extreme mental anguish and turned to beastly behavior to quiet hunger, the innocent prisoners of the GPU labor camps who died from overwork and starvation rations in Russian permafrost, the orphaned children who died from neglect and malnutrition without their names being recorded and the cause of death cynically listed as "Ukrainian."[99] On the documents that were meant to record cause of death, the local offices of ZAGS (Registry of Vital Statistics) were instructed not to list starvation as a cause of death but to substitute any of a number of approved diseases.[100] Hennadii Boriak, then head of the State Committee on Archives in Ukraine, found documents with instructions and a death certificate that had originally listed starvation as cause of death, but later visibly "corrected" to "unknown."[101] Doctors, who were state employees, put down all sorts of diseases as the causes of death, including "sudden illness."[102]

A teacher in Kremenchuk, Antin Lak, who survived on 300 grams of bread a day, recalled how bodies of starved to death victims were picked up by trucks every morning and evening at a medical center. On a visit to the center, where his fellow teacher was hospitalized, he overheard how the doctor Oleksander Ol'shanets'kyi instructed the truck drivers: "There is no famine. People are dying not from starvation but from protein deficiency dropsy." As a Communist Party member he touted the official line not to use the word "famine," but hide the truth from the people and name the cause of death from starvation as death from BBO (*bezbilkovi opukhy* or protein deficiency dropsy).[103] Professors M. D. Strazhesko, M. M. Huberhrits, and V. M. Kohan-Iasnyi conducted clinical trials with patients suffering from protein deficiency dropsy during the genocidal famine.[104]

The mortality rate among children was catastrophic. Historians have used statistics on school enrollments and archival documents to estimate losses among school-aged children. The death toll ranges from 1.7 million[105] to more than 3 million children of preschool and school age in 1932–1933 in Soviet Ukraine.[106] The discrepancy in the numbers might be due to different sets of statistical data used. Such practices became the butt of jokes about "two sets of statistics—one secret set for themselves [the Soviet leaders] and a false set for the public." As one American diplomat who arrived in Moscow in 1934 to work in the newly opened U.S. Embassy recalled, the punch line was that "the Soviet system has two sets of statistics, and both are false."[107]

Scholars have noted that the names of many diseased children were registered just as nicknames, as they were foundlings. Fedir Turchenko and Inna Shuhal'ova, who studied the Zaporizhzhia death registry records, pointed out that often the orphans were given names of famous Ukrainian, Russian, or even foreign writers: Lesia Ukraïnka, Ihor Maiakovs'kyi, Arkadii London, Anna Akhmatova, Maxim Gorky, Karl Libknekht, or Bernard Shaw.[108] In the Mykolaïv State Archives, historian Volodymyr Serhiichuk was able to locate several death certificates issued in 1933 that included nicknames like "Unknown" (*Nevidomyi*) for children in care of the state-funded orphanage named after Hryhorii Petrovs'kyi.[109] Doctors in rural regions avoided the word "starvation" when writing the cause of children's death because it was too risky; they could lose a job, even life. Many orphanages did not compile death records, or their records were incomplete.[110] In some regions, death certificates were not issued for infants, who perished before reaching one year of age.[111]

By the winter of 1932–1933, death certificates no longer appeared. Not only were causes of death altered and death certificates forged, but ZAGS records from the fatal years were sanitized in local offices. A significant part of the documents related to the registration of illnesses and deaths in hospitals and village councils was destroyed "while still hot." A top secret instruction, dated April 13, 1934, from the Odesa Regional Executive Committee (with copies to all lower-level executive committees and inspectors of the National Economic Survey Administration, later the Central Statistical Board) is remarkable evidence of how the crimes against the Ukrainians were covered up by the perpetrators.[112] As a result, according to Boriak, the extant vital statistics registers for the years of 1932–1933 in the state archives contain 3 million deaths,[113] which cover "*a maximum of one-third* of the territory afflicted by the [Great] Famine, and mortality records *directly attributed* to the [Great] Famine constitute *no more than 1.5 percent* of the total mortality records of civil registry offices."[114] Scholars believe that the archival records were purposefully and systematically destroyed by the regime for decades.[115] Thus, erasing the record of memory was a crucial part of Stalin's war against Ukraine then as it is now a crucial part of Putin's disinformation war, in the same battlespace—the mind.

BANNING BOOKS

While targeting Ukraine's information space, Russia is protecting its own by silencing the truth about the past, thus undermining justice. On December 1, 2011, the Meshchanskii district court in Moscow declared books written by Vasyl' Marochko, a Ukrainian historian and president of the Advisory Board of the Association for Holodomor Studies, "extremist" and ordered them to be removed from the shelves of the Ukrainian Library in Moscow.[116] In December 2014, the municipal court in Russian-occupied Feodosia in Crimea charged the director of the library for storing extremist literature (Article 20.20 of the Russian Criminal Code) and imposed a fine in the amount of 2,000 rubles for storing a dozen books in Ukrainian, including Marochko's books on the Holodomor, in two municipal libraries. These books are scholarly publications that were written between 2007 and 2014, based on the analysis of new documentary evidence from the Sectoral State Archive of the Security Service of Ukraine and other state and former Communist Party archives. In the Russian legal system, books about the Holodomor, which is a crime against humanity, are criminalized and erased from history and memory.[117]

Upon hearing the news, Marochko drew parallels to the days of Stalinism in an open letter posted on the Institute of History of Ukraine of the National Academy of Sciences website, saying that "[i]n the 1930s books were banned by entire lists: books were simply repressed, occasionally burned. Looks like this practice is coming back." In his article about the "Russian World" in Feodosiia, Marochko compared book burning to burning of "brother Slavs" on the battlefields of occupied Crimea and Donbas: "all of these are consequences of the rehabilitation of Stalinism, the Holodomor denial, and the revision of the past."[118]

Russia has banned scholarly publications that examined the GPU's role in the Holodomor, deflecting attention from the institution that has perpetrated the crime of genocide but has never been held accountable. Among works included in the list of "extremist" literature is an influential volume on the history of the Soviet security police, *ChK-GPU-NKVD v Ukraïni*. It has been authored by Iurii Shapoval, Volodymyr Prystaiko, and Vadym Zolotar'ov and has been referenced by scholars of Stalinism and Stalin's security apparatus since its publication in 1997. Together with Marochko's books, the 2011

Moscow court verdict criminalized this scholarly publication in an attempt to control the official historical narrative promoted by Russia. Analyzing the interconnectedness of the preceding Soviet and modern Russian methods of control over history writing, Olga Bertelsen pointed out that central to these memory politics are an anti-Ukrainian discourse, ideological subversion, and the cult of *chekists*.[119]

The ban on books was accompanied by an assault on the rights of the Ukrainian minority in Russia. In 2011, the Russian authorities dissolved the Federal Cultural Association of Ukrainians, and in 2012 the Union of Ukrainians, two organizations that represented the interests of all Ukrainians in the Russian Federation. Then in 2018, the Library of Ukrainian Literature in Moscow was closed. The following year, in July 2019, the Office of the Prosecutor General and the Ministry of Justice of the Russian Federation declared the Ukrainian World Congress (UWC) an "undesirable" organization and banned its activities in Russia.[120] More recently, in 2020, the regional structure "Siryi Klyn" of Ukrainians in the Omsk region was dissolved in a quasi-judicial proceeding.[121] The anti-Ukrainian stance of Russian memory politics has emerged as a central feature of the "Russian World"[122] that Putin is promoting.

Current Kremlin's course is anti-Ukrainian and rather aggressive, as it was in the 1930s, when the "crushing blow" to Ukrainian nationalism was piloted in the North Caucasus in November 1932 before it hit the core of the "national spirit" in Soviet Ukraine, synchronized with the grain procurement campaign.[123] On December 15, 1932, Stalin and Molotov signed a resolution to "immediately discontinue Ukrainization" in the Far East Region, Kazakhstan, Central Asia, the Central Black Earth, and other areas and "prepare the introduction of Russian language school instruction" in all ethnically Ukrainian areas throughout the Soviet Union.[124] At the same time the Soviet leaders imposed domestic and international information blockades on the famine in Soviet Ukraine.[125]

The "blockade decree" of January 22, 1933,[126] created a "Stalinist ghetto,"[127] from which starving Ukrainians, young or old, could not escape. Blame for this criminal act was placed on the victims. In November 1933, "local Ukrainian nationalism" was declared to be the preeminent danger to Soviet power in the region.[128] In January 1934, at the Seventeenth Congress of the All-Union Communist Party (Bolsheviks), Pavel Postyshev gloated, "The past year [1933] was the year of defeat of the nationalist counterrevolution."[129] Not incidentally, Postyshev's speech regarding the breakthrough on the grain procurement front that devolved into scapegoating of Ukrainian "bourgeois nationalists," as well as Kosior's speech on the national question, were published in a separate brochure by the International Publishers in New York in English translation with the aim of convincing not only Western observers but even Ukrainians abroad that Bolshevik policies were victorious. Thus, the Soviet disinformation campaign killed two birds with one stone, domestically and internationally. Today, the Russian disinformation war follows the same logic, targeting domestic trust in the governmental institutions and international perceptions of Ukraine and its history.

SILENCING THE TRUTH

"Silence is the think tank of the soul. All religions share and revere silence."[130] Silence can also make the truth unheard of when used as a tool of coercion by the powerful to oppress the powerless.[131] Out of fear of losing a job, school teachers touted the Communist Party line that there was no famine. To suggest that there was a famine was made illegal.[132] A survivor from Stavyshche, a town with about 10,000 people in the Kyïv region, recalled,

> In our schools whenever any of the children mentioned the [Great] Famine, they were corrected by the teachers. They were told that there was no famine, simply a 'year of difficulties.' They confiscated all that we had and designated the year as one of difficulties.[133]

The witness, who was ten at the time of the genocidal famine, further told the U.S. Commission interviewer that they had a very beautiful park in their village, with a stream flowing by. And in all the parks, there were loudspeakers placed as part of the radio network, which was itself linked to the post office. He recited a song that one could always hear in these parks, songs being sung in Russian:

> Swiftly as birds, one after another,
> Fly over our Soviet homeland
> The joyous refrains of town and country:
> Our burdens have lightened—
> Our lives have gladdened!

> They broadcast this song while people were dying in the [Great] Famine. "Our lives have gladdened." I can recall this song from my school years, when they were teaching the children to sing *The Patrolling Pioneer*. What kind of country is this in which children patrol over the fields to keep kernels of grain from the starving peasants for the sake of a "better life"? They themselves sang, "The joyous refrains of town and country." And this song would play every day, ten times a day, and as you were listening to the song, everywhere all around you people are screaming, and dying, while the song was playing on: *"Our burdens have lightened."*[134]

When the interviewer asked the witness what he was thinking during that time, the narrator's answer highlighted the deliberate nature of the famine as a tool of coercion.

> What could I think?! All I could think of was where could I get some food. I didn't think about anything else. They let the Ukrainians have it because they had wanted to separate from Russia. That's what I think. The Ukrainian nation is still paying for that even up to this very day.[135]

School teachers indoctrinated their students about Pavlik Morozov, a young Pioneer hero, who "unmasked" his own father for hiding grain.[136] Students were forbidden to use the word "famine" though food was insufficient even in towns, and in the neighboring village no one was left at all, recalled a lecturer at an agricultural school in Molochans'k, an agricultural Mennonite settlement near Melitopol'.[137] In his novel, *Tema dlia medytatsiï* (Theme for Meditation), Leonid Kononovych symbolically condemned teachers, who chose to participate in Soviet propaganda and grain-requisition campaigns, depicting them as bureaucrats in the realm of education. His protagonist recalls how a teacher instilled "love for the Soviet rule" by beating her student and calling him a "Petliurite puppy" (*petliurivs'ke tsutsenia*).[138]

Teachers, like other Soviet officials, who could see death all around were not permitted—did not permit themselves—to see "starvation." Once a school principal, Kaveev, a Russian, according to a survivor's account, told his colleague, a third-grade teacher Kononenko, to forget it and keep silent. Whether children come [to school] or not, it was the teacher's duty to teach. "Don't involve yourself deeper or be closer. Just do your duty and teach. That's all."[139]

Worst of all, the people were forced to forget. "In 1934, no one talked about the famine as if it had never happened," recalled Vasyl' Nechyporenko. In his village of Bilozir'ia, Cherkasy district, arrests of the enemies of the people continued.

> They continued to remove portraits of the "leaders": Skrypnyk (for some reason in the middle of the lesson), then Kosior, and even 'the friend of children' Postyshev. Quietly, Taras Shevchenko's portrait was taken down but later placed back on the wall.[140]

The survivor further noted,

> When someone mentioned the famine around Komsomol or [Communist] Party members, they pretended they did not hear it. But those who carelessly used their tongue could end up in big trouble. After a while people stopped talking about the famine even among themselves.[141]

The Soviet leaders did not allow even the faintest reference to reality. The refusal to face the truth was applied inside the country and on a world scale. Arthur Koestler, a Hungarian-born British writer and author of the anti-totalitarian book, *The Yogi and the Commissar*, described two "belts of silence" surrounding the famine:

> I spent the winter of 1932–33 mainly in Kharkov, then the capital of Ukraine. . . . Traveling through the countryside was like running the gauntlet: the stations were lined with begging peasants with swollen hands and feet, the women holding up to the carriage windows horrible infants with enormous wobbling heads, sticklike limbs, swollen, pointed bellies. You could swap a loaf of bread for Ukrainian embroidered kerchiefs, national costumes and bedcovers; foreigners could sleep with practically any girl except party members for a pair of shoes or stockings. Under my hotel room window in Kharkov funeral processions marched past all day. The electricity supply in Kharkov had broken down; there was no light in the town, and the trams functioned only for an hour or so a day to take workers to the factories and back. There was also no fuel or petrol in the town and the winter was hard even for Ukraine, with temperatures of 30^0 below zero. Life seemed to come to a standstill, the whole machinery on the verge of collapse.
>
> . . . at the time not the slightest allusion to real conditions was allowed to appear in the Soviet press, including the newspapers of Ukraine itself. Each morning when I read the Kharkov *Kommunist* I learned about plan-figures reached and over-reached, about competitions between factory shock brigades, awards of the Red Banner . . . and so on; the photographs were either of young people, always laughing and always carrying a banner in their hands . . . Not one word about the local famine, epidemics, the dying out of whole villages; even the fact that there was no electricity in Kharkov was not once mentioned in the Kharkov newspaper. It gave one a feeling of dreamlike unreality; the paper seemed to talk about some quite different country which had no point of contact with the daily life we led; and the same applies to the radio.
>
> The consequence of all this was that the vast majority of people in Moscow had no idea of what went on in Kharkov. . . . The enormous land was covered by a blanket of silence and nobody outside the small circle of initiates could form a comprehensive picture of the situation.
>
> A second belt of silence isolated the country from contacts with the outside world. Foreign missions and newspaper correspondents were concentrated in Moscow. . . . To smuggle out news vetoed by the censor meant expulsion; a risk which both journalists and their employers will take only reluctantly, and only when vital issues are at stake. But "vital issues" is an elastic term, and the practical result of continuous pressure was that even conscientious newspapermen evolved a routine of compromise; they cabled no lies, but *nolens volens*

confined themselves to "official dope" . . . The cumulative effect of all this was a picture distorted by half-truths and systematic omissions. This was the foundation on which direct Soviet propaganda could build."[142]

The information blockade was imposed after the Third All-Ukrainian Party Conference in July 1932, when Stalin and Molotov made any mention of the famine punishable as a counterrevolutionary crime.[143] Yet, historians, like Stanislav Kul'chyts'kyi, continued to argue in 1988 on the pages of the *Ukrainian Historical Journal* that the famine was "neither organized, nor man-made, but was an unforeseen outcome of Stalin's economic planning," and that the Communist Party did all it could to alleviate the suffering of the starving population.[144]

Rather than alleviating the suffering of the starving population, the Communist Party was constantly on a look out for "enemies of the people"; purges were conducted periodically. In fact, the Postyshev purge of 1933 followed five previous purges of the Communist Party in 1920, 1921, 1924, 1925, and 1929–1930, in which, as scholars noted, the non-Russian party organizations were hit harder than those in the Russian regions.[145]

In January 1933, Stalin declared that enemies had become increasingly invisible. In eerily familiar language (see the lists of suspected "counterrevolutionaries" in Soviet Ukraine in the 1924 secret OGPU circular in Chapter 3), Stalin declared that

> the last remnants of moribund classes—private manufacturers and their servitors, private traders and their henchmen, former nobles and priests, kulaks and kulak agents, former White Guard officers and police officials, policemen and gendarmes, all sorts of bourgeois intellectuals of a chauvinist type, and all other anti-Soviet elements—have been tossed out.
>
> But tossed out and scattered over the whole face of the USSR, these "have-beens" have wormed their way into our plants and factories, into our government offices and trading organizations, into our railway and water transport enterprises, and, particularly, into the collective farms and state farms. They have crept into these places and taken cover there, donning the mask of "workers" and "peasants," and some have managed to worm their way into the party.
>
> What did they carry with them into these places? They carried with them hatred for the Soviet regime, of course, burning enmity toward new forms of economy, life, and culture.[146]

Like his predecessor Lenin, Stalin called for "revolutionary vigilance." As historian Hiroaki Kuromiya of Indiana University Bloomington noted, "It would appear to be absurd not to fear the ghosts of those who had died *en masse* during the collectivization, industrialization, dekulakization, and famine."[147] Stalin's answer to the unpopular economic and cultural transformation of life was more terror, while keeping it disguised under political vigilance. Attacks on the Ukrainian Communists, intelligentsia, and farmers took place at the apex of the famine in 1933.

The goal of the 1933 purge was to establish an "iron proletarian discipline" within the Communist Party ranks by expelling "foreign" elements. Who conducted the purges and who was purged? Purge commissions made decisions. Their members were "politically literate" cadres who were ideological allies, never worked in the opposition, and had been Communist Party members for over a decade. These criteria excluded most Ukrainians.[148] More Ukrainians were also purged. Of the 104,458 new members and candidate members of the Communist Party since 1931, the KP(b)U purged 37 percent.[149] Between June 1932 and October 1933, approximately three-fourths of the officials of the local soviets and the local party committees were dismissed and replaced by newcomers dispatched from Moscow.

Findings by an investigator in the Chernihiv regional Communist Party organization revealed instances of paying bonuses to the district party bosses, wasting funds on drinking and entertainment, unlawful redirecting of food rations designated for the needy to supply party bureaucrats. "Friends of the Children" Association was left bankrupt, and its regional branch head Pokotilova pocketed 1,669 rubles. District police patronized local gangs, and sold guns and bullets to the gangsters. Instead of guarding the rule of law, local police engaged in sadistic behavior: beating the imprisoned during interrogations, undressing the victims or pushing them off the roof, robbing households at a gunpoint, imposing arbitrary fines on smallholders, locking up owners until they surrender their cows or horses, delaying the distribution of teachers' food rations for more than a month. The author of the report Roizenman noted that every visiting Communist Party secretary, head of the GPU, or police "behaves as if entitled to the money, bread, alcohol, and constantly demands to be fed, but writes off the consumed or confiscated products as compensation for services to the public." "I am from the Center!" was the mantra. Local courts were dysfunctional; people had nowhere to turn for protection. What was the outcome of the purge? Out of 60 names on the list of the regional Communist Party headquarters that counted 179 members and candidate members in its ranks, 16 were purged. The procedure was a public spectacle. The purged party members lost jobs, apartments, food rations, but were released from prisons due to overcrowding. Out of 17,000 regional Communist Party rank-and-file, 4,536 lost their membership (27 percent) and 35 percent more were demoted from members to candidates and from candidates to supporters.[150]

By 1934, before the Great Terror, the Communist Party purged its own ranks to get rid of those who did or did not carry out its programs vigorously enough during the collectivization in 1928–1929 and the grain requisitions in 1932–1933. In many instances, the same activists participated in both campaigns. As archival documents from just one regional Communist Party organization in Chernihiv revealed, the perpetrators purged over 60 percent of their own rank-and-file, including the "inquisitor" Roizenman himself, to cover their tracks.

Silence was imposed on foreign correspondents as early as 1928, when the People's Commissariat of Foreign Affairs in Moscow issued Circular No. 984, which explicitly ordered the Ukrainian authorities to deny any information or assistance to foreign guests and journalists in traveling to the villages. That same year, the OGPU issued the Statute about Secrecy, which narrowed the circle of individuals who could potentially have access to top secret documents. Examining the essence of strategic silence (*polityka zamovchuvannia* in Ukrainian), Olga Bertelsen noted that it was a tool for isolation of the Ukrainian victims and a way to conceal preparations for escalating violence in 1932–1933.[151]

The West kept silent, pretending not to notice. American and British journalists, Louis Fischer of the *Nation*, Eugene Lyons of the *United Press International*, William Henry Chamberlain of the *Manchester Guardian*, and Margaret Bourke-White of *Fortune*, wrote news articles for major dailies and magazines about modernization projects in the Soviet workers and peasants' paradise, obscuring the story about the devastating famine several miles away from the industrial construction sites that they were invited to cover.[152] The irony of the situation is that a 1932 photograph by James Abbe that shows a panoramic opening ceremony of the Dnipro HES (hydroelectric dam) in the background, foregrounded serendipitously a long bread line at the store in its vicinity. Nick Kupensky explained the "blindness" of Western journalists through the prism of "postmodern sublime"[153] as a way to distance themselves, historically or geographically, from the gruesome reality on the ground that did not fit into their modernist narrative about industrialization as progress.

Well-known Western intellectuals participated in the disinformation campaign, among them British playwright and political activist George Bernard Shaw, French prime minister Édouard Herriot, French novelist Romain Rollan, and American novelist Theodore Dreiser.[154] They traveled to the Soviet Union, but they noticed what they were shown on carefully selected and staged routes. After touring these "Potemkin village" settings, they returned home to report that there was no famine in Ukraine. Despite evidence to the contrary, Herriot remained adamant in what he was determined to discover that the Soviet plan of the collectivization of agriculture was successful.[155] The nature of the genocidal famine with its millions of victims did not affect his opinion.

When in 1933, at the peak of the Holodomor, George Bernard Shaw read news about deaths from starvation and cannibalism, he wrote in the preface to his play "On the Rocks" (premiered in November 1933) that he "had not seen people who starved and children were surprisingly chubby."[156] Shaw's fellow Fabian Socialists Lord and Lady (Baroness) Passfield, commonly known as Beatrice and Sydney Webb, traveled to the Soviet Union from late May to late July 1932 and wrote a highly influential 1,000-page account entitled *Soviet Communism: A New Civilization* (1935). George Orwell commented about the British intellectuals: "Huge events like the Ukraine famine of 1933, involving the deaths of millions of people, have actually escaped the attention of the majority of English [R]ussophiles."[157] But as Robert Conquest noted, it was not only a matter of Russophiles "but also of a large and influential body of Western thought."[158] In Conquest's view, "the scandal was not that they justified Soviet actions, but that they refused to hear about them, that they were not prepared to face the evidence."[159]

Among Western journalists who enabled the concealment of truth about the genocidal famine in Soviet Ukraine was Pulitzer Prize winner Walter Duranty. Of British origin, Duranty became the *New York Times* correspondent in Moscow, or rather Moscow's man at the *New York Times*, characterized as "the one-legged Anglo-American granddaddy of fake news."[160] He won personal attention from Stalin and reported the Communist Party line in his articles. On September 14, 1933, he wrote, "But, as far as this writer could learn, there was nothing like famine conditions."[161] Duranty, who downplayed the famine in his dispatches, informed British Embassy staff that he thought it entirely possible that as many as 10 million had perished due to the famine.[162]

Under what conditions Duranty was allowed to work in Moscow is hidden in secret Stalin's archives. On October 27, 1925, a meeting of the TsK RKP(b) discussed the possible deportation of the journalist out of the Soviet Union. Two days later, this issue was discussed again, and the decision was rescinded.[163] In 1932, Duranty won the Pulitzer Prize for his coverage of Soviet Russia the previous year.[164] In one of his dispatches from Moscow on March 31, 1933, he quoted a grotesque cliché, often attributed to genocidal murderer Stalin: "you can't make an omelet without breaking eggs." He shrugged off the Bolshevik leaders' indifference to the casualties of their drive to socialize agriculture as "proper soldierly spirit" because the masterminds were "animated by fanatical conviction."[165]

The most acute observer of the famine was Sergio Gradenigo, Royal Consul of Italy in Kharkiv. On May 31, 1933, in his report to the Italian Embassy in Moscow, he linked the famine and the Ukrainian question, highlighting the role of the international press in perpetuating the world's indifference to the atrocity:

> The famine continues to wreak havoc among the people, and one simply cannot fathom how the world can remain so indifferent to such a catastrophe and how

the international press, which is so quick to bring international condemnation upon Germany for its so-called "atrocious persecution of the Jews," can stand quietly by in the presence of this massacre organized by the Soviet government, in which the Jews play such a major role, albeit not the leading one.

For there is no doubt: 1) that this famine is primarily caused by a contrived scarcity designed "to teach the peasant a lesson," and 2) that there is not one Jew among the famine victims; on the contrary, they are fat and well fed under the fraternal wing of the GPU.

The "ethnographic material" must be changed, cynically stated one Jew who is a high ranking official in the local GPU. One can already foresee the final fate of this "ethnographic material," which is destined for replacement.[166]

Although Gradenigo's views might be reflective of the growing anti-Semitic attitudes in fascist Italy and throughout Europe during the 1930s, it should be also pointed out that the persecution of Jews as active in the Bolshevik repressive apparatus was not a fantasy. There had been a substantial number of Jewish activists within the ChK-GPU-NKVD in Soviet Ukraine from the organization's early years.[167] Mendel Osherowitch, a correspondent of *Forverts* (the *Jewish Daily Forward*), who visited his family in Soviet Ukraine in 1932, dedicated a chapter in his memoir, titled "The Fear of the *GPU* Across the Country," where he noted that the first Yiddish word he heard upon arriving was from the GPU official. His brother served in the GPU, charged with enforcing policies of grain requisitions in the countryside.[168] Such facts are often neglected by contemporary Jewish scholars who write about the Holodomor.[169] The inability to "Ukrainianize" the Cheka appears to have been a long-standing "problem" for the Communist Party in the 1920s.[170] By the late 1930s, anti-Semitism became official state policy, when repressions against Jewish cadres swept through the Communist Party and GPU ranks.[171]

For the Welsh journalist Gareth Jones, who used his connection to David Lloyd George to acquire a diplomatic visa from the Soviet Embassy in Great Britain, the famine was real. Jones crossed the border into the Soviet Union in March 1933 and spent his first week in Moscow interviewing Communist Party officials, Western correspondents, foreign consuls, Soviet literary figures, and ordinary citizens waiting in long bread lines. His handwritten diaries served as the basis for twenty-one articles published between March 31 and April 20, 1933, in the *Evening Standard, Daily Express, Western Mail,* and *Financial News*.[172] Although in his newspaper titles Jones used "Russia" as the generic term to describe areas affected by the famine, he made specific references in the diaries to Ukraine and specific districts in Soviet Ukraine.

As a guest of the German Consulate, Jones secured permission to visit a tractor factory in Kharkiv. On March 10, 1933, he bought a ticket for the overnight train from Moscow. He carried a backpack filled with loaves of bread, butter, cheese, and chocolate bought with foreign currency from Torgsin stores, with an intention to make an unescorted trip into the Ukrainian countryside. Jones got off at a station before reaching Kharkiv and walked 70 kilometers through more than twenty Ukrainian villages. He spent one night of his wanderings with the head of the village soviet and one night with another local family to see for himself the conditions of the countryside. When Jones recorded a starving Ukrainian saying "We have no bread" in his diary, that meant they had no food to eat. Upon leaving the Soviet Union, Jones gave interviews on March 29, 1933, in Berlin, and news of the famine spread quickly, prompting anger from the Soviet officials. Maxim Litvinov blamed consulate staff for issuing visa to Jones and the press department for failing to bring to his attention unfavorable articles. In April 1933, further restrictions on the freedom of movement by foreign correspondents to the areas affected by the famine in Soviet Ukraine were imposed. The Soviet diaries of Jones offer direct eyewitness account of the impact of Stalin's policies on Ukraine's cities and villages.[173] For telling the truth, in 1935, on the eve of his thirtieth birthday, Gareth Jones was assassinated by "bandits," but most probably by Soviet agents, in Inner Mongolia.[174]

Jones was preceded in 1932 by a Canadian journalist of Jewish origin, Rhea Clyman, who traveled thousands of miles through eastern regions of Soviet Ukraine and the North Caucasus, where the OGPU arrested her and deported for a handful of stories that the Kremlin regarded as having slandered the Soviet regime. Given two days to pack her belongings in Moscow, she was briefly visited in her flat by the newly arriving British journalist Malcolm Muggeridge and his wife Katie, and reluctantly left the country under duress on September 24, 1932.[175] Headlines about the Moscow-based correspondent of the *Toronto Evening Telegram* driven from Soviet Union were carried in all major newspapers in Canada and around the Western world. The Politburo of the TsK RKP(b) even issued a formal decree about her expulsion on September 17, 1932.[176]

Clyman was the first to investigate and document stories of forced labor denied by Molotov about the army of prisoners digging the White Sea–Baltic Sea Canal. Her reports from Kem' ("The Town of the Living Dead" in Clyman's words), a way station to the Solovetsky camps, inaccessible to foreign visitors, angered the Soviet officials so that they had to publish a rebuttal titled "New Campaign of Lies Against the Land of Socialist Construction" in the English edition of the *International Press Correspondence* in Berlin to discredit the author.[177] Her honest accounts of how villages in Soviet Ukraine and the North Caucasus were being ravaged by hunger were overlooked by specialists in Soviet and Russian history.[178]

Malcolm Muggeridge, Moscow correspondent for the *Manchester Guardian* during the winter and spring of 1932–1933, was one of the few journalists who were unafraid to tell the truth. In his interview with Marco Carynnyk, a Canadian writer, he recalled how L. B. Golden, the general secretary of the Save the Children Fund, which had been very active during the famine of 1921–1922 in Soviet Russia and Ukraine, approached the British Foreign Office in August 1933 for advice.[179] He had received disturbing information from the press and from private letters about famine in Soviet Ukraine and the North Caucasus. But the first secretary of the Soviet Embassy had assured him that the harvest was a "bumper one," and Golden asked the Foreign Office whether a public appeal should be put out. The Foreign Office told him not to do anything. Muggeridge summed up the attitude of the British government: "The Soviet authorities were not admitting to a famine, and therefore it was agreed that nothing should be said."[180] The silence lasted for so long because it was "the calculated campaign of misinformation that the Soviet authorities mounted to conceal their doings."[181] And the British and the U.S. leaders at the time turned a "blind eye to murder"[182] and "appeased" the Soviet dictator.[183]

To seek international support, the Ukrainian Women's Union in Galicia, then under Polish rule, selected one of its capable and prominent members, Milena Rudnyts'ka, to bring the situation in Soviet Ukraine to the attention of the League of Nations. During 1932–1933, as vice chair of the Public Rescue Committee, she met with politicians, scientists, and educators to raise awareness about the famine. On September 29, 1933, fourteen countries met at the headquarters in the Palais Wilson in Geneva, Switzerland, and Rudnyts'ka along with other members of the Ukrainian delegation presented their findings about mass deaths in Soviet Ukraine and need for international assistance. After several hours of deliberations, the League decided that the famine was an internal problem of the Soviet Union, which was not a member of the League. Then, the delegation turned toward the International Committee of the Red Cross (ICRC) with a plea for help. ICRC officials contacted Soviet officials to gain approval for the Red Cross to organize international aid for Ukraine, but the head of the Soviet Red Crescent Society Avel Enukidze denied that there was any famine in Soviet Ukraine. Rudnyts'ka spoke at another international conference in Vienna in December 1933, urging the international community to pressure the Stalinist regime to admit there was a crisis and allow aid. Denial continued and information about the nature and scope of the famine was suppressed.[184]

In the United States, the Ukrainian National Women's League of America (UNWLA) was one of the most active organizations in the Ukrainian-American community that tried to raise awareness about the famine in Soviet Ukraine. In November 1933, leaders of the UNWLA approached Eleanor

Roosevelt with a request to exert some influence to pressure the Soviet government to allow duty-free admission of relief packages through Torgsin.[185] Mrs. Roosevelt replied that although she realized "that the need was very great, she deeply regretted" that she could do nothing to help.[186] This summary of Mrs. Roosevelt's response comes from a letter preserved in UNWLA archives in New York. The organization's president, Iwanna Rozankowsky, provided this document to Dr. James Mace, Staff Director of the U.S. Commission on the Ukraine Famine.

Eleanor Roosevelt, reflecting on her past life on her seventy-fifth birthday, advised in her *Autobiography*:

> I think that one of the reasons it is so difficult for us, as a people, to understand other areas of the world is that we cannot put ourselves imaginatively in their place. We have no famine. But if we were actually to see people dying of starvation we would care quite a bit.[187]

Yet, the reality of mass starvation in Ukraine, perpetrated by the Soviet government, seemed to require a double standard of blindness from American politicians toward the universality of human suffering. Eleanor Roosevelt took part in the genocide definition discussions at the United Nations, speaking vis-à-vis the Soviet representative Andrei Vyshinsky. The Soviets managed to force a dilution of Lemkin's original and intended broader-scoped definition of genocide. This political tactic worked, because other nations were afraid of not getting any definition at all, if they failed to appease the Soviets on this point.

The UNWLA also published a pamphlet and sent it for comment to the Soviet Embassy on January 3, 1934. A month later it received a letter from Boris Skvirsky, Embassy Counselor, who replied that the idea that the Soviet government was "deliberately killing off the population of the Ukraine" was "wholly grotesque." Claiming that "the Ukrainian population increased at an annual rate of 2% during the past five years," Skvirsky dismissed UNWLA evidence as spurious. The death rate in Ukraine "was the lowest of that of any of the constituent Republics composing the Soviet Union," he stated "and was about 35 percent lower than the pre-war death rate of Tsarist days."[188] The Soviet government denied the famine. The Roosevelt administration sought closer ties with the Soviet government and saw the famine as an internal Soviet affair.

In the context of its time, the sources of hard currency—grain, timber, and gold—kept the Soviet Union as a player in world politics. The Communist International and the Communist Party of the United States of America continued to abide by directives from Stalin and assist in the construction of Soviet workers' paradise.[189]

Eugene Lyons, a member of the Board of Directors of the American Jewish League Against Communism, in his article "American Jews and the Kremlin Purges" in *The New Leader*, March 1953, explained the reasons behind the lack of awareness among American intellectuals of the fact that millions had perished from the man-made famine in the 1930s:

> In the last thirty years, a number of Jews, especially among the educated and the well-to-do, came to defend the Soviet Union and its works. Influenced by Communist propaganda about racial equality and the proscription of anti-Semitism, they found it possible to gloss over assorted Soviet obscenities. In a glow of liberal righteousness, they tended to accept Sovietism "despite everything."[190]

Still another reason was set forth by James Burnham in his review of Peter Viereck's book *Shame and Glory of the Intellectuals*, in March 1953,

> this was the glory of the intellectuals: that in spirit and body they stood firm against Nazi assault. It is the shame of the intellectuals that they stood not firm but servile, deceived and seduced before the equally vicious approach of Nazism's twin, communism. They refused to recognize concentration camps, aggression and terror when, instead of the swastika, there flew the flag of "the revolution" and spoke in the name of "radical slogans."[191]

Soviet disinformation succeeded in silencing the truth about the genocidal famine for over half a century. Domestically, a code of silence was imposed and enforced in preparation for the liquidation of the Ukrainian intellectual elites, who could organize opposition to the regime, as well as their real or alleged supporters, economically self-sufficient farmers, who could potentially wrestle the reins of power from representatives of the colonial Bolshevik regime. Internationally, silencing the truth took the form of controlling access of foreign correspondents to the "crime scene" and staging tours of foreign dignitaries and fellow travelers of the Communist International to showcase industrial construction achievements in Soviet Ukraine, deflecting attention from the famine-ravaged countryside. With the rehabilitation of Stalinism in Russia, the successor to the Soviet Union, the denial took the form of the information war, undermining domestic trust in the governmental institutions and distorting international perceptions of Ukraine and its history.

Stalin singlehandedly edited the U.N. Convention on the Prevention and Punishment of the Crime of Genocide, deleting any incriminating reference to Soviet crimes against humanity. Nevertheless, the remaining text of the U.N. Convention on Genocide has served as the foundation for the legal recognition of the Holodomor as genocide against Ukrainians. Russia has used its veto power in the U.N. Security Council to block Ukraine's demand for the recognition of the Holodomor as genocide by this international organization. When denial could no longer be tenable after the publication of the U.S. governmental report on Communist takeover and occupation of Ukraine, published in the 1950s, which linked "collectivization" with genocide, and a special commission's report on the man-made famine in Soviet Ukraine, published in the late 1980s, Soviet and now Russian scholars have tried to promote a notion of an "all-Union" famine to obscure anti-Ukrainian character of the genocide. The Holodomor death toll ranges from 2 to 15 million.[192] Although the number of victims is not a defining feature of genocide, attempts to cover up the truth and destroy evidence have been well-documented. Ultimately, the topic of the Holodomor has been criminalized in neo-Stalinist Russia.

NOTES

1. Stanton, "The Ten Stages of Genocide," https://www.genocidewatch.com/ten-stages-of-genocide.

2. Ben Johnson, "Russia Still Denies the Holodomor Was 'Genocide,'" *Acton Institute*, November 27, 2017, https://www.acton.org/publications/transatlantic/2017/11/27/russia-still-denies-holodomor-was-genocide.

3. Norman M. Naimark, *Stalin's Genocides* (Princeton: Princeton University Press, 2010).

4. Paula Chertok, "History, Identity and Holodomor Denial: Russia's Continued Assault on Ukraine," *Euromaidan Press*, November 7, 2015, http://euromaidanpress.com/2015/11/07/history-identity-and-holodomor-denial-russia-s-continued-assault-on-ukraine/.

5. Jurij Dobczansky, "Affirmation and Denial: Holodomor-related Resources Recently Acquired by the Library of Congress," *Holodomor Studies* 1, no. 2 (2009): 153–62. On July 1, 2009, the Library of Congress introduced two new subject headings: *Holodomor denial literature* and *Holodomor denial*.

6. Hans Petter Midttun, "Hybrid War in Ukraine—Predictions for 2019 and Beyond," *Euromaidan Press*, April 18, 2019, http://euromaidanpress.com/2019/04/18/hybrid-war-in-ukraine-predictions-for-2019-and-beyond/.

7. The war in the information space is part of a concerted strategy of total war that encompasses the use of economic, political, diplomatic, religious, legal, security, cyber, and military instruments. See Janis Berzins, "Russia's New Generation Warfare in Ukraine: Implications for Latvian Defense Policy" (report from the National Defense Academy of Latvia and the Center for Security and Strategic Research), *Informal Institute for National Security Thinkers and Practitioners Blog*, April 30, 2014, http://maxoki161.blogspot.com/2014/04/russias-new-generation-warfare-in.html.

8. "Zakon Ukraïny 'Pro Holodomor 1932–1933 v Ukraïni' No. 376-V," 226–28.

9. "Duma ne priznala Golodomor 1932–33 godov," *Delo.ua*, April 2, 2008, https://delo.ua/econonomyandpoliticsinukraine/gosduma-ne-priznala-1932-33-go-75225/.

10. "Predstavitel' Rossii nazval politicheskimi spekuliatsiiami popytki kvalifitsirovat' golod 30-kh godov kak genotsid," *Novosti OON*, March 7, 2008, https://news.un.org/ru/story/2008/03/1121751.

11. Weiss-Wendt, *The Soviet Union and the Gutting of the U.N. Genocide Convention*, 280.

12. Bohdan A. Futey, "International Legal Responsibility for Genocide: Justice in the Courts," paper presented at a Conference on Famine-Holodomor, Kyïv, Ukraine, September 25–26, 2008, *Holodomor Education*, 2009, http://www.holodomoreducation.org/index.php/id/178/lang/en. See also *idem*, "Legal Recognition of the Holodomor as Genocide: International Covenants, Agreements, and Court Decisions (Implementing Lemkin's Legacy)," paper presented at the International Forum "Ukraine Remembers, the World Acknowledges!" on the 85th anniversary of the Holodomor 1932–1933—Genocide of the Ukrainian People, Kyïv, Ukraine, November 22, 2018.

13. Kateryna Bondar, "Legal Definition of Genocide: Examining the 1932–1933 Holodomor in Ukraine under the Genocide Convention," in *The Holodomor of 1932–1933 in Ukraine as a Crime of Genocide under International Law*, eds. V. Vasylenko and M. Antonovych (Kyïv: Kyïv-Mohyla Academy, 2016), 99.

14. Naimark, *Stalin's Genocides*, 133.

15. Weiss-Wendt, *The Soviet Union and the Gutting of the U.N. Genocide Convention*, 64–66, 70.

16. Panné, "Rafaël Lemkin ou le pouvoir d'un sans-pouvoir," 7–66.

17. Serbyn, "*Holodomor*," 30.

18. See "Holodomor in the Context of Genocide: A Narrow vs Broad Definition of Genocide," 1–2; a summary of survey findings was distributed by Lana Babij via email to a group of the Holodomor scholars on October 19, 2019.

19. "SBU vozbudila ugolovnoe delo po faktu soversheniia Genotsida," *UNIAN*, May 25, 2009, https://www.unian.net/politics/225116-sbu-vozbudila-ugolovnoe-delo-po-faktu-soversheniya-genotsida-dopolnennaya.html.

20. "Ruling of the Kyiv Court of Appeal Concerning the Commission of the Crime of Genocide Perpetrated by J. V. Stalin (Dzhugashvili), V. M. Molotov (Skriabin), L. N. Kaganovich, P. P. Postyshev, S. V. Kossior, V. Ia. Chubar, and M. M. Khatayevich, 13 January 2010," in *The Holodomor of 1932–1933 in Ukraine as a Crime of Genocide under International Law*, eds. Vasylenko and Antonovych, 356.

21. Viktor Kondrashin, "Hunger in 1932–1933—A Tragedy of the Peoples of the USSR," *Holodomor Studies* 1, no. 2 (2009): 21.

22. A summary of the contents of Decree No. 47 of the Federal Archival Agency, issued on October 17, 2007, with specific instructions on how to use a collection of documents "Famine in the USSR, 1929–1934" is available at *Rosarkhiv* (the Federal Archival Agency), 2008, https://web-archiv.ru/archive/507.

23. In 2007, Viktor Kondrashin was appointed as the editor of a three-volume collection of documents from the Russian central and regional archives that presented

the famine in the USSR as a common tragedy of all the people. In his presentation at the first seminar on July 19, 2010, "Russia-Ukraine: Problems of Interpretation and Assessment of the Holodomor of 1932–33," Kondrashin admitted that his Ukrainian colleagues refused to participate in the joint project. See transcript of Kondrashin's presentation: Viktor Kondrashin, "Golod 1932–33 gg. v nauchnykh issledovaniiakh i istoricheskoi publitsistike," *Uroki istorii: XX vek*, October 4, 2010, https://urokiistorii.ru/article/1185.

24. For a complete text of the letter and seven pages of Kondrashin's "prospectus" for the proposed three-volume collection of documents from the Russian archives with recommendations on how to discuss the famine of 1930–1934 in the USSR, see "Podobrat' ikh [dokumenty] sleduet takim obrazom, chtoby byla vidna tragediia vsego sovetskogo krest'ianstva, bez aktsenta na Ukrainu" [Kondrashin V. Plan-prospekt z rekomendatsiiamy shchodo vidboru dokumentiv dlia zbirnyka 'Golod v SSSR, 1932–1933'. Dodatok do lysta kerivnyka Federal'noho arkhivnoho ahenstva Rosiis'koï Federatsiï V. Kozlova do Holovy Derzhkomarkhivu Ukraïny O. Ginzburg z propozytsiamy pro spivpratsiu. 17 sichnia 2007], from a personal archive of Hennadii Boriak, available on the website of the Institute of History of Ukraine of the National Academy of Sciences of Ukraine since December 5, 2017, at http://resource.history.org.ua/item/0013470. It was first made public by Pavlo Solod'ko in "Iak pysaty pro Holodomor. Instruksiia rosiis'kym istorykam," *Istorychna Pravda*, on November 26, 2012, http://www.istpravda.com.ua/artefacts/2012/11/26/101572/.

25. The "Historical Memory" Foundation (*Fond Istoricheskaiia Pamiat'*) was established in 2008. One of its main goals is to counteract "anti-Russian" interpretation of history in the neighboring countries, as stated on its website http://historyfoundation.ru.

26. Tatiana Zhurzhenko, "'Capital of Despair': Holodomor Memory and Political Conflicts in Kharkiv after the Orange Revolution," *East European Politics and Societies* 25, no. 3 (2011): 631.

27. Mark Tauger's research interest is agrarian history. His publications include *Agriculture in World History* (Routledge Press, 2010) and *Golod, Golodomor, Genotsid?* (Kyïv: Dovira Press, 2008).

28. Davies and Wheatcroft, *The Years of Hunger*.

29. For personal reflections on the Kharkiv conference, its program, and a list of participants, see a blog post by Iurii Shevtsov, "International scientific-practical conference 'Famine in the USSR in the 1930s: historical and political assessments,' Kharkov, 21 November 2008," http://yury-shevtsov.blogspot.com/2008/11/30-21112008.html. Shevtsov, the only invited speaker from Belarus, is the director of the independent Center for European Integration in Minsk, where he teaches International Relations at Belarusian State University. He is the author of *New Ideology: Holodomor* (Moscow: Europe, 2009).

30. The Party of Regions (*Partiia rehioniv*) was a pro-Russia political party of Ukraine created in late 1997. It grew to be the biggest party of Ukraine between 2006 and 2014. As of 2020, the party has disintegrated.

31. Zhurzhenko, "Capital of Despair," 632. A CD with a hundred selected documents from the Russian archives was distributed at the Kharkiv Conference in 2008.

In 2009, an English translation appeared. The two versions differ in the deliberate selection of the documents to fit different audiences. The text of the CD in English includes a preface written by Kondrashin that explains the need to prepare a set of documents to counter a "massive anti-Russian propaganda campaign by the current leaders of Ukraine that had been unleashed both on Ukrainian soil, and abroad, especially in the countries of the European Union, the United States, and Canada, and built around the alleged 'genocide by holodomor' of Ukrainians in 1932–1933" (slide 12). See "Famine in the USSR, 1929–1934: New Documentary Evidence," with Historical Essay by Viktor Kondrashyn; English translation of the documents by Nikita B. Katz; English translation of the Note from the Compilers by Alexandra Dolgova (Moscow: Federal Archival Service, 2009), Compact Disc, http://resource.history.org.ua/item/0008508. The content of the CD has been posted on the Institute of History of Ukraine of the National Academy of Sciences website since March 19, 2013, http://history.org.ua/LiberUA/FamineInUSSR_2009/FamineInUSSR_2009.pdf. No one has paid serious attention or tried to debunk it in academic literature, which further illustrates Russia's success in strategically invading and capturing broader audiences to subvert their opponents.

32. The local newspaper *Kharkovskie izvestiia* devoted a whole page to a report about the conference. See Valerii Tyrnov, "O tragedii bez spekuliatsii: Byl li genotsydom golod 30-kh godov?" *Kharkovskie izvestiia*, November 25, 2008; quoted in Zhurzhenko, 633.

33. For a summary of the announcement, see "Gosduma ne priznala Golodomor 1932–33 godov: Gosudarstvennaia Duma Rossii otritsaet priznaki genotsyda vo vremia goloda 1932–1933 godov na territorii SSSR," *Delo*, April 2, 2008, https://delo.ua/econonomyandpoliticsinukraine/gosduma-ne-priznala-1932-33-go-75225/; see also Steve Gutterman, "Russia: 1930s Famine Was Not Genocide," *Fox News*, April 2, 2008, https://www.foxnews.com/printer_friendly_wires/2008Apr02/0,4675,RussiaUkraineFamine,00.html.

34. *International Commission of Inquiry into the 1932–33 Famine in Ukraine*, 2.

35. Kulchytsky, *The Famine of 1932–1933 in Ukraine*, 140.

36. Vasyl′ Marochko, "Prystrasti dovkola Holodomoru: real′ni mify," *Dzerkalo tyzhnia*, March 24, 2018, https://dt.ua/HISTORY/pristrasti-dovkola-golodomoru-realni-mifi-272997_.html.

37. James Mace, "Research on Documents" (typewritten notes), Ukraine Famine Hearing, April 30, 1987, Box 16921, Gary Bauer Files, Ronald Reagan Presidential Library and Museum.

38. Mace, "Research on Documents," 1.

39. Ibid., 2.

40. James Mace, "Soviet Press Sources on the Famine," in *Report to Congress*, 70.

41. "International Commission of Inquiry into the 1932–33 Famine in Ukraine, 10 March 1990," in *Holodomor*, eds. Luciuk and Grekul, 305.

42. Hugh D. Phillips, "Rapprochement and Estrangement: The United States in Soviet Foreign Policy in the 1930s," in *Soviet–U.S. Relations, 1933–1942* (Moscow: Progress Publishers, 1989), 11–12.

43. Tauger, "The 1932 Harvest and the Famine of 1933," 70–89.

44. Kulchytsky, *The Famine of 1932–1933 in Ukraine*, 142.

45. Letter to the Editor of Ukraine Report 2003, E. Morgan Williams, Ukraine Market Reform Group, Washington, D.C. by Prof. James Mace, Kyiv, Ukraine, June 2, 2003, Concerning the discussion on H-Russia List about Cheryl Madden's "The Ukrainian Famine (Holodomor) of 1932–1933 and Aspects of Stalinism: A Detailed Annotated Bibliography-in-Progress in the English Language." Originally it was published online at http://www.artukraine.com/famineart/mace16.htm. A copy of the text of the letter, saved on November 15, 2016, can be obtained from Cheryl Madden.

46. Kulchytsky, *The Famine of 1932–1933 in Ukraine*, 142.

47. Shapoval, "Holodomor i ioho zv'iazok iz rerpesiiamy v Ukraïni," 155–57.

48. Nove, *An Economic History of the USSR*, 180.

49. U.N. Department of Economic and Social Affairs, *Growth of the World's Urban and Rural Population, 1920–2000*, Population Studies No. 44 (New York: United Nations, 1969), 49.

50. Valentina Zhiromskaia, *Osnovnye tendentsii demograficheskogo razvitiia Rossii v XX veke* (Moscow: Kuchkovo pole, 2012), 109, available at https://www.labirint.ru/books/387399/.

51. Kulchytsky, *The Famine of 1932–1933 in Ukraine*, 148.

52. For a discussion about the Soviet repressions against Ukraine's intellectuals in the 1930s and their eventual extermination, see Bertelsen and Shkandrij, "The Secret Police and the Campaign against Galicians in Soviet Ukraine," 37–62; Shkandrij and Bertelsen, "The Soviet Regime's National Operations in Ukraine," 417–47. For earlier studies of repressions against the Ukrainian intelligentsia, see N. M. Lytvyn, "Polityčni represiï proty naukovoï intelihentsiï v radians'kii Ukraïni v 1920–1930-kh rokakh (ideolohichni aspekty problemy)" (doctoral diss., Kyïv, 2006); O. S. Rubl'ov, *Zakhidnoukraïns'ka intelihentsiia u zahalnonatsional'nykh politychnykh ta kul'turnykh protsesakh (1914–1939)* (Kyïv: Instytut Istoriï Ukraïny NAN Ukraïny, 2004); and O. S. Rubl'ov and Iu. A. Cherchenko, *Stalinshchyna i dolia zakhidnoukraïns'koï intelihentsiï* (Kyïv: Naukova dumka, 1994).

53. In 1930, the GPU recorded 4,098 uprisings in the Ukrainian SSR. There were significantly more disturbances in Ukraine than in three other grain-growing regions of the Central Black Earth (1,373), the North Caucasus (1,061), and the Lower Volga (1,003). See *The War Against the Peasantry*, ed. Viola et al., 320.

54. Prystaiko and Shapoval, *Sprava "Spilky vyzvolennia Ukraïny,"* 44, 413.

55. Professor Iefremov died in a Russian prison in 1939, three months before the end of his prison term. After his release in 1934, Hermaize was rearrested in 1937 and died in a labor camp after his sentence was extended for an additional ten years. See Pauly, *Breaking the Tongue*, 351, 356.

56. Clarence A. Manning, *Ukraine Under the Soviets* (New York: Bookman Associates, 1953), 95; quoted in *The Soviet Empire: Prison House of Nations and Races; A Study in Genocide, Discrimination, and Abuse of Power*, prepared by Joseph G. Whelan, analyst in Eastern European affairs, at the request of the Subcommittee to Investigate the Administration of the Internal Security Act and Other Internal Security Laws of the Committee on the Judiciary, U.S. Senate, 85th Cong., 2nd Sess.,

Document No. 122 (Washington, D.C.: U.S. Government Printing Office, 1958), 15, 19, https://catalog.hathitrust.org/Record/008514963.

57. Kulchytsky, *The Famine of 1932–1933 in Ukraine*, 32.

58. Resolution of the CC CP(B)U Politburo "On Measures to Strengthen Grain Procurement," November 18, 1932, in *Holodomor of 1932–33 in Ukraine*, ed. Pyrih, 55–60.

59. Papakin, "'Chorna doshka' Holodomoru," 160.

60. Kulchytsky, *The Famine of 1932–1933 in Ukraine*, 149.

61. Roman Serbyn, "The Ukrainian Famine of 1932–1933 as Genocide in Light of the U.N. Convention of 1948," *The Ukrainian Quarterly* 62, no. 2 (2006): 187.

62. Papakin, "'Chorna doshka' Holodomoru," 162.

63. Conquest, *The Harvest of Sorrow*, 211–12.

64. Ibid., 212.

65. Lemkin, *Soviet Genocide in the Ukraine*.

66. For the discussion of archival evidence of resettlement of Russian loyalists and their families to villages in southeastern Ukraine depopulated by the 1932–1933 famine, see "Dopryselennia u vymerli ukraïns'ki sela," in Volodymyr Serhiichuk, *Holodomor 1932–1933 rokiv iak henotsyd ukraïnstva* (Vyshgorod: PP Serhiichuk M. I., 2018), 186–206. These settlers received food provisions and farming equipment. Russian language teachers were recruited, which intensified assimilation in schools. On the resettlement of 500,000 Red Army veterans from central Russia to Kuban in the North Caucasus, see P. Polian, *Ne po svoei vole . . . Istoriia i geografiia prinuditel'nykh migratsyi v SSSR* (Moscow: O. G. I. – Memorial, 2001), 78.

67. Nicholas Fedyk, "Russian 'New Generation' Warfare—Theory, Practice, and Lessons for U.S. Strategists," *Small Wars Journal*, August 25, 2016, https://smallwarsjournal.com/jrnl/art/russian-"new-generation"-warfare-theory-practice-and-lessons-for-us-strategists.

68. Mace, *Report to Congress*, 424.

69. Ibid., 434.

70. Gantt, "A Medical Review," 19–22.

71. See appendix to Jaroslaw Sawka, "American Psychiatrist: Fifteen Million Dies in Thirties' Famine," *Ukrainian Quarterly* 38, no. 1 (Spring 1982): 65.

72. S. V. Kul'chyts'kyi, *1933: trahediia holodu*, Seriia 1 "Teoriia i praktyka KPRS. Istoriia," No. 6 (Kyïv: T-vo "Znannia" URSR, 1989), 3.

73. Kul'chyts'kyi, *1933*, 3.

74. Ibid., 47.

75. Stanislav Kul'chyts'kyi, "Mil'ony zahyblykh: skil'ky same?" *Den'*, April 13, 2018, https://day.kyiv.ua/uk/article/istoriya-i-ya/milyony-zagyblyh-skilky-same.

76. Kul'chyts'kyi, "Mil'ony zahyblykh."

77. E. A. Osokina, "Zhertvy goloda 1933 g.: skol'ko ikh? (Analiz demograficheskoi statistiki TsGANKh SSSR)," *Istoriia SSSR*, no. 5 (1991): 18–26; available in *Web Archive*, September 29, 2007, https://web.archive.org/web/20070929204317/http://www.auditorium.ru/books/4522/ch2.pdf.

78. V. P. Danilov and I. Ie. Zelenin, "Organizovannyi golod. K 70-letiiu obshchekrest'ianskoi tragedii," *Otechestvennaia istoriia*, no. 5 (2004): 97–111.

79. V. V. Kondrashin, "Golod 1932–1933 gg. – obshchaia tragediia narodov SSSR: natsional'no-regional'nyi aspect," in *Sovetskiie natsii i natsional'naia politika v 1920–1950-e gody: Materialy VI mezhdunarodnoi nauchnoi konferentsii, Kiev, 10–12 oktiabria 2013 g.*, ed. N. Volynchik (Moscow: ROSSPEN, 2014), 195.

80. Sergei Maksudov (Aleksandr Bab'onyshev), "Byl li golod 1932–33 godov na Ukraine genotsydom?," *Blog Sergeia Maksudova*, September 16, 2016, http://www.maksudovsergei.com/.

81. The 1937 Soviet census was the first census conducted after the famine. It showed the total population of Soviet Ukraine to be lower than it was in 1926. The government declared the census "defective" and executed demographers who conducted it. Some of the documents were destroyed and the remaining results discredited. The 1937 census was declassified in 1987. See F. D. Livshits, "Perepis' naseleniia 1937 goda," in *Demograficheskie protsessy v SSSR*, ed. A. G. Volkov (Moscow: Nauka, 1990), 174–207, and A. G. Volkov, "Perepis' naseleniia 1937 goda: vymysly i pravda," in *Perepis' naseleniia SSSR 1937 goda: istoriia i materialy*, vyp. 3–5 (II) (Moscow: Informtsentr Goskomstata SSSR, 1990), 6–63.

82. For a study of the North Caucasus Ukrainian population as the target of the genocidal famine of 1932–1933, see Oleksii Kurinnyi, "Ukrains'ka spil'nota Pivnichnoho Kavkazu iak ob'iekt Holodomoru 1932–1933 rokiv," in *Holodomor 1932–1933 rokiv v Ukraïni iak zlochyn henotsydu zhidno z mizhnarodnym pravom*, eds. Volodymyr Vasylenko and Myroslava Antonovych (Kyïv: Vydavnychyi dim "Kyievo-Mohylians'ka akademiia," 2016), 161–72. For a study of linguistic genocide of Ukrainians in the Kuban area in the North Caucasus, the Central Black Earth, the Lower Volga, and Kazakhstan, see Serhiichuk, *Holodomor1932–1933 rokiv iak henotsyd ukraïnstva*, 214–61.

83. Tymish Olesevych, *Statystychni tablytsi ukraïns"koho naselennia SSRR za perepysom 17 hrudnia 1926 roku* (Warsaw: Ukraïns'kyi naukovyi instytut, 1930); quoted in Bohdan S. Kordan, "A Note on the Political Geography of the Great Famine of 1932–1933," in *Holodomor*, eds. Luciuk and Grekul, 29.

84. On May 21, 1927, the KP(b)U adopted a resolution proposed by Mykola Skrypnyk to add territories populated by ethnic Ukrainians in neighboring regions to Ukraine based on the principle of self-determination. See *Politychna systema dlia Ukraïny: istorychnyi dosvid i vyklyky suchasnosti*, ed. V. M. Lytvyn (Kyïv: Nika-Tsentr, 2008), 525.

85. Nataliia Levchuk, Oleh Wolowyna, Omelian Rudnytskyi, Alla Kovbasiuk, and Natalia Kulyk, "Regional 1932–1933 Famine Losses: A Comparative Analysis of Ukraine and Russia," *Nationalities Papers* (2020): 1–21, doi:10.1017/nps.2019.55.

86. Arsenii Khomenko, "Liudnist' USRR u perspektyvnomu obchyslenni," *Profilaktychna medytsyna*, no. 11–12 (1932): 47; quoted in Marochko, "Statystyka zhertv Holodomoru," 129.

87. Marochko, "Statystyka zhertv Holodomoru," 130.

88. *HDA SBU*, f. 6, spr. 43187-FP, vol. 1, ark. 19, 91–92.

89. *TsDAHOU*, f. 1, op. 20, spr. 6762, ark. 56; quoted in Marochko, "Statystyka zhertv Holodomoru," 129.

90. Marochko, "O. M. Asatkin – vyhadanyi 'fal′syfikator' perepysu naselennia 1937 r.," 147, 149.

91. Oleksandr Saltan, "Stepan Sosnovyi – pershyi ukraïns′kyi doslidnyk Holodomoru," lecture at the Kharkiv Historical-Philological Association webinar, November 19, 2020, *HistorySumy, Inc. (Sums′kyi istorychnyi portal)*, January 15, 2021, video, 2:32–37:40, http://history.sumy.ua/sources/media-documents/9304-per shyi-doslidnyk-holodomoru.html.

92. See email dated September 1, 2015 re: "Holodomor Memorial" to Michael Sawkiw, Jr., Chairman of the U.S. Committee for Ukrainian Holodomor Genocide Awareness of the Ukrainian Congress Committee of America, signed by Vitaly Chernetsky, American Association for Ukrainian Studies; George Grabowicz, Shevchenko Scientific Society; Albert Kipa, Ukrainian Academy of Arts and Sciences in the United States; Volodymyr Kravchenko, Canadian Institute of Ukrainian Studies; Serhii Plokhii, Harvard Ukrainian Research Institute; quoted in Serhiychuk, "How Millions of Deaths Were Not Included in the Statistics," *Genocide-Holodomor of Ukrainians*, 112.

93. Polian, *Ne po svoei vole*, 78; quoted in Kurinnyi, "Ukraïns′ka spil′nota Pivnichnoho Kavkazu," 165.

94. Serhiychuk, "To Honor All Innocent Victims of the Holodomor," 130–33.

95. Victoria A. Malko, "Russian (Dis)Information Warfare vis-à-vis the Holodomor-Genocide," in *Russian Active Measures: Yesterday, Today, Tomorrow*, ed. Olga Bertelsen (Stuttgart and New York: *ibidem*-Verlag and Columbia University Press, 2021), 215–62.

96. *Communist Takeover and Occupation of Ukraine*, 20; see also Manning, *Ukraine Under the Soviets*, 101.

97. Omelian Rudnytskyi, Nataliia Levchuk, Oleh Wolowyna, Pavlo Shevchuk, and Alla Kovbasiuk, "Demography of a Man-made Human Catastrophe: The Case of Massive Famine in Ukraine, 1932–1933," *Canadian Studies in Population* 42, no. 1–2 (2015): 53–80.

98. The September 1, 2015 collective email to Michael Sawkiw, Jr.; reprinted in Malko, "Russian (Dis)Information," 236–38.

99. Vasyl′ Marochko, *Terytoriia Holodomoru 1932–1933 rr.* (Kyïv: PP Natalia Brekhunenko, 2014); idem, "Statystyka zhertv Holodomoru," 112–32; Volodymyr Serhiichuk, "Istoryko-pravovi aspekty pidrakhunku vtrat vid Holodomoru-henotsydu 1932–1933 rokiv," *Chetverta khvylia*, July 2, 2020, http://4hvylia.com/novyny-usim /7737.html; Solovey, "Skil′ky znyshcheno na Ukraïni liudei," in *Golgota Ukraïny*, 201–16.

100. Hennadii Boriak, *Sources for the Study of the Great Famine in Ukraine* (Cambridge: Harvard University Ukrainian Studies Fund, 2009), 3.

101. *DAKO*, f. 5634, op. 1, spr. 969, ark. 86; quoted in Boriak, *Sources*, 22.

102. Vadym Kohan and Raïsa Nahorna-Persyds′ka, "Medychni aspekty holodu 1932–1933 rr. v Ukraïni," in *Holodomor 1932–1933 rr. v Ukraïni: prychyny i naslidky. Mizhnarodna naukova konferentsiia, Kyïv, 9–10 veresnia 1993 r. Materialy*, ed. S. Kul′chyts′kyi (Kyïv: Instytut istoriï Ukraïny NAN Ukraïny, 1995), 111.

103. "Case History SW3: Antin Lak, b. 1910 in the Poltava region," in *Oral History Project*, 730–31.

104. *DAKhO*, f. 1962, op. 1, spr. 270, ark. 3, 5–6, 9, 15; quoted in Kohan and Nahorna-Persyds'ka, "Medychni aspekty holodu 1932–1933 rr. v Ukraïni," 111–13.

105. Marochko, "Shkoly bez ditei ta vchyteliv," 53.

106. Serhiichuk, "Shkil'na statystyka," 5; *idem*, "*Holodni, bosi i rozditi,*" 92.

107. Charles E. Bohlen, *Witness to History, 1929–1969* (New York: W. W. Norton & Company, 1973), 35.

108. Fedir Turchenko and Inna Shuhal'ova, "Dytiacha smertnist' u roky Holodomoru 1932–1933 rokiv u Zaporizhzhi," in *Holodomor 1932–1933 rokiv: vtraty ukraïns'koï natsiï. Materialy Mizhnarodnoï naukovo-praktychnoï konferentsiï, Kyïv, 4 zhovtnia 2016*, ed. Olesia Stasiuk et al. (Kyïv: Vyd. O. Filiuk, 2017), 113.

109. Death certificate of eight-year-old Vania, whose last name is recorded as *Nevidomyi* (Unknown), dated June 13, 1933, with the cause of death listed as diarrhea, in *DAMO*, od. obl. P1010030; courtesy of Volodymyr Serhiichuk.

110. Inna Shuhal'ova, "Stratehiia vyzhyvannia ditei-ditbudynkivtsiv u roky Holodomoru 1932–1933 v Radians'kii Ukraïni," in *Materialy mizhnarodnoï konferentsiï "Shtuchni holody v Ukraïni XX stolittia," 16 travnia 2018 r.* (Kyïv: Vyd-vo "Kolo," 2018), 360.

111. Volodymyr Serhiychuk, *Genocide-Holodomor of Ukrainians, 1932–1933* (Vyshgorod: PP Serhiychuk M. I., 2020), 175.

112. The top secret circular with instructions regarding withdrawal of death record books for the years of 1932–1933 from the local civil registry (ZAGS) archives of the Odesa *oblast'* into classified storage at the district executive committees, dated April 1934, was located in *DAOO*, f. R-2009, op. 1, spr. 4, ark. 91–92; quoted in Boriak, *Sources*, 28–35.

113. Hennadii Boriak, "Population Losses in the Holodomor and the Destruction of Related Archives: New Archival Evidence," in *After the Holodomor: The Enduring Impact of the Great Famine on Ukraine*, eds. Andrea Graziosi, Lubomyr A. Hajda, and Halyna Hryn (Cambridge: Ukrainian Research Institute of Harvard University, 2013), 204; originally published in *Harvard Ukrainian Studies* 30, nos. 1–4 (2008): 199–215, http://history.org.ua/LiberUA/BoriakPopulationLosses_2008/BoriakPopulationLosses_2008.pdf.

114. Boriak, *Sources*, 21.

115. Niels Erik Rosenfeldt argues that there were three waves of purges of Soviet archival documents: in 1929–1930, 1937–1938, and during the summer of 1941 on the eve of the German invasion of the Soviet Union. See Niels Erik Rosenfeldt, *The "Special" World: Stalin's Power Apparatus and the Soviet System's Secret Structures of Communication*, trans. Sally Laird and John Kendal (Copenhagen: Museum Tusculanum Press, 2009), 1: 88–93. Boriak argues that after the reevacuation of archives in 1945, inventories conducted in 1949, 1955, 1957, 1962, 1965, and 1968 led to thousands of records for the period of 1928–1935 being deliberately destroyed. According to Boriak, "Stalin's regime left just half of the aggregate archives on the Holodomor created at all levels of government." See Boriak, "Population Losses in the Holodomor," 207–12.

116. Vasyl' Marochko, "'Russkii Mir' u Feodosiï: zaborona slova pro Holodomor," *Istorychna Pravda*, January 28, 2015, http://www.istpravda.com.ua/columns/2015/01/28/146975/. On the burning of Ukrainian language books in backyards of municipal libraries in the Kuban' region of the North Caucasus in the spring and summer of 1933, see Jaroslaw Sawka, "Rosiishchennia Kubani – pivdenno-skhidn'oho bastionu Ukraïny," *Rosiishchennia Ukraïny: Naukovo-populiarnyi zbirnyk*, ed. Leonid Poltava (New York: Vydannia ukraïns'koho kongresovoho komitetu Ameryky, 1984), 218, https://shron2.chtyvo.org.ua/Zbirka/Rosiischennia_Ukrainy_naukovo-populiarnyi_zbirnyk.pdf.

117. A list of materials deemed extremist is published on the website of the Ministry of Justice of the Russian Federation. It has expanded from 14 titles in 2007 to 1,271 titles in 2012. See "V Rosiï knyhy pro Holodomor pryrivniuiut'sia do ekstremizmu," *Istorychna Pravda*, June 27, 2012, http://www.istpravda.com.ua/articles/2012/06/27/89363/.

118. Marochko, "'Russkii Mir' u Feodosii."

119. Olga Bertelsen, "A Trial *in Absentia*: Purifying National Historical Narratives in Russia," *Kyiv-Mohyla Humanities Journal*, no. 3 (2016): 57–87.

120. UWC, "UWC Defends Itself against Ban in Russian Federation," *Ukrainian Weekly*, April 26, 2020, 1, 5.

121. Askold S. Lozynskyj, "A New Proposal for the Government of Ukraine," *Ukrainian Weekly*, January 31, 2021, 6.

122. According to Taras Kuzio, Putin's mix of Tsarist and Soviet Russian nationalism gave rise to a "Russian World" doctrine. The visible sign of it is the Russian World Foundation, established in 2007. See Taras Kuzio, "Putin Forever: Ukraine Faces the Prospect of Endless Imperial Aggression," *Atlantic Council*, February 13, 2020, https://www.atlanticcouncil.org/blogs/ukrainealert/putin-forever-ukraine-faces-the-prospect-of-endless-imperial-aggression/.

123. Kurinnyi, "Holodomor 1932–1933 rr. na Pivnichnomu Kavkazi," 73–85.

124. See the December 15, 1932, resolution of the CC AUCP(B) and SNK USSR "On Ukrainization in DVK, Kazakhstan, Central Asia, TsChO and Other Areas of the USSR"; quoted in *Holodomor of 1932–33 in Ukraine*, ed. Pyrih, 68–69.

125. Arthur Koestler, "Soviet Myth and Reality," in *The Yogi and the Commissar and Other Essays* (New York: Macmillan, 1945), 137–39.

126. Credit must be given to Nikolai Ivnitskii from the Institute of Russian History of the Russian Academy of Sciences, who was the first to bring up a detailed analysis of this document from the Russian archives at the 1993 international conference on the occasion of the sixtieth anniversary of the famine. See Ivnitskii, "Golod 1932–1933 gg.," 43.

127. Marochko, *Terytoriia Holodomoru*, 11.

128. P. P. Postyshev, "The Results of the Agricultural Year 1933 and the Immediate Tasks of the Communist Party of the Ukraine" (Speech delivered at the Plenum of the Central Committee of the Communist Party of Ukraine, November 19, 1933), in *Soviet Ukraine Today* (New York: International Publishers, 1934), 95. The English text has been preserved in the National University Kyïv-Mohyla Academy's James E. Mace Library and Museum Archives, od. zb. 819.

129. Pavel Postyshev, "Speech delivered at the Seventeenth Congress of the AUCP(B), 27 January 1934" (excerpts translated by Bohdan Klid), in *The Holodomor Reader: A Sourcebook on the Famine of 1932–1933 in Ukraine*, eds. Bohdan Klid and Alexander J. Motyl (Toronto: Canadian Institute of Ukrainian Studies, 2012), 268.

130. Pete McBride, "The Last Quiet Places: To the End of the Earth in Search of the Healing Power of Silence," *Smithsonian*, October 2020, 51–61.

131. For a strategic use of silence as a tool to marginalize the opposition and cover up mass violence, see Olga Bertelsen, "Starvation and Violence amid the Soviet Politics of Silence: 1928–1929," *Genocide Studies International* 11, no. 1 (2017): 38–67.

132. Conquest, *The Harvest of Sorrow*, 329.

133. "Case History SW34: Anonymous male narrator, b. 1922, Kiev region," in *Oral History Project*, vol. 2, 923; English version in the *Report to Congress*, 387.

134. Ibid., 925; English version in the *Report to Congress*, 392.

135. Ibid.

136. The fourteen-year-old Pavlik Morozov denounced his father, previously head of the village Soviet in the village of Gerasimovka. After the trial and sentence of the father, Morozov was killed by a group of villagers, including his uncle, and is regarded as a martyr. There is now a museum in his village: "In this timbered house was held the court at which Pavlik unmasked his father who sheltered the kulaks." In 1965, the village was additionally adorned with his statue. His name is entered in the Pioneer "Book of Honor." See Conquest, *The Harvest of Sorrow*, 295.

137. Pidhainy, *The Black Deeds of the Kremlin*, vol. 1, 262; quoted in Conquest, *The Harvest of Sorrow*, 259.

138. Leonid Kononovych, *Tema dlia medytasiï* (L'viv: Kal'variia, 2006).

139. "Statement by Mr. Kononenko before the Commission on the Ukraine Famine Hearing and Meeting, April 30, 1987" (typewritten transcript), 43, Ukraine Famine [Hearing 04/30/1987], Box 16921, Gary Bauer Files, Ronald Reagan Presidential Library and Museum.

140. Vasyl' Pavlovych Nechyporenko, b. 1923 in the village of Bilozir'ia, Cherkasky district, Kyïv region, in *Ukraïns'kyi holokost*, ed. Mytsyk, vol. 3, 169.

141. Anastasiia Ivanivna N., b. 1923 in the village of Rodnykivka, Kirovohrad district; in *Ukraïns'kyi holokost*, ed. Mytsyk, vol. 4, 141.

142. Koestler, "Soviet Myth and Reality," 137–39.

143. From a letter written by James Mace to Volodymyr Maniak, editor of the book of memory, January 13, 1989; quoted in *Ukraïns'kyi holokost*, ed. Mytsyk, vol. 5, 294.

144. In his private correspondence with Volodymyr Maniak, James Mace pointed out that Kul'chyts'kyi's disingenuous arguments were criticized even by the Ukrainian scholarly circles. See Mace's letter dated January 13, 1989, in *Ukraïns'kyi holokost*, ed. Mytsyk, vol. 5, 293.

145. T. H. Rigby, *Communist Party Membership in the USSR, 1917–1967* (Princeton: Princeton University Press, 1968), 181; Liber, *Soviet Nationality Policy*, 169.

146. I. V. Stalin, *Sochineniia*, vol. 13 (Moscow, 1951), 207, 212; quoted in Hiroaki Kuromiya, *Freedom and Terror in the Donbas: A Ukrainian-Russian Borderland, 1870s–1990s* (Cambridge: Cambridge University Press, 1998), 184–85.

147. Kuromiya, *Freedom and Terror in the Donbas*, 185.

148. G. Aronshtam, "K chistke natsional'nykh partorganizatsii," *Revoliutsiia i natsional'nosti*, no. 5–6 (1933): 18; quoted in Liber, *Soviet Nationality Policy*, 169.

149. "Dopovid' tov. Sukhomlina," KP(b)U, *XII z'ïzd*, 230; quoted in Liber, *Soviet Nationality Policy*, 169.

150. Volodymyr Shkvarchuk, "Rik 1934: Pokhval'ne slovo tov. Roizenmanu, abo masova chystka Chernihivs'koï oblpartorhanizatsiï," in *Na kazarmennomu stanovyshchi (narysy z istoriï Chernihivshchyny dovoiennykh rokiv)* (Chernihiv: Chernihivs'ki oberehy, 2002), 9–19.

151. Bertelsen, "Starvation and Violence," 39.

152. Nick Kupensky, "Blindness, Hypnosis, Addiction, Fetish: The Language of Holodomor Denial" (paper presented at the Danyliw Seminar on Contemporary Ukraine, University of Ottawa, November 9, 2018).

153. Christine Battersby, *The Sublime, Terror, and Human Difference* (London: Routledge, 2007), 43.

154. Michael David-Fox, *Showcasing the Great Experiment: Cultural Diplomacy and Western Visitors to the Soviet Union, 1921–1941* (New York: Oxford University Press, 2012).

155. *TsDAHOU*, f. 1, op. 20, spr. 6204, ark. 111–12; quoted in Serhiychuk, *Genocide-Holodomor*, 92. See also Snyder, "The Soviet Famines," in *Bloodlands*, 57–58.

156. B. Tsiupyn, "Zapliushchuiuchy ochi: Vydatni zakhidni intelektualy, iaki ne vytrymaly perevirky Holodom," *Tyzhden'*, November 24, 2012, http://tyzhden.ua/History/65731.

157. George Orwell, "Notes on Nationalism," in *The Collected Essays, Journalism, and Letters of George Orwell*, vol. 3 (New York: Harcourt, Brace & World, Inc., 1968), 370.

158. Conquest, *The Harvest of Sorrow*, 321.

159. Ibid.

160. Kyle Smith, "Stalin, Famine, and the *New York Times*: Mr. Jones Tells the Truth about Moscow's Man at the Paper of Record," *National Review*, July 2, 2020, https://www.nationalreview.com/2020/07/movie-review-mr-jones-tells-truth-about-new-york-times-communism/.

161. Walter Duranty, "Abundance Found in North Caucasus," in *New York Times*, September 14, 1933, 14, in James William Crowl, "Angels in Stalin's Paradise: Western Reporters in Soviet Russia, A Case Study of Louis Fischer and Walter Duranty" (doctoral diss., University of Virginia, 1978), 162–67.

162. Mace, "Research on Documents" (typewritten notes).

163. Serhiychuk, *Genocide-Holodomor*, 93.

164. For more on a campaign to revoke Duranty's Pulitzer Prize, see *Not Worthy: Walter Duranty's Pulitzer Prize and the New York Times*, ed. Lubomyr Luciuk (Kingston: Kashtan Press, 2004).

165. For excerpts from Duranty's articles, "Russians Hungry, But Not Starving," March 31, 1933; "Stalin's Mark Is Party Discipline," June 27, 1931; "Stalinism Dominates Russia of Today," June 14, 1931; "Red Army Is Held No Menace to

Peace," June 25, 1931; "Stalinism Solving Minorities Problem," June 26, 1931; "Stalin's Russia Is an Echo of Iron Ivan's," December 20, 1931, see Jacques Steinberg, "Word for Word/Soft Touch; From Our Men in Moscow, In Praise of the Stalinist Future," *New York Times*, October 26, 2003, https://www.nytimes.com/2003/10/26/weekinreview/word-for-word-soft-touch-our-man-moscow-praise-stalinist-future.html?searchResultPosition=2.

166. Report by the Kharkiv Consulate Royal Consul, Sergio Gradenigo, May 31, 1933, "Re: The Famine and the Ukrainian Question," in *Report to Congress*, 424–25, 427; original text in *Lettere da Kharkov*, ed. Graziosi, 168–74; quoted in *The Holodomor Reader*, eds. Klid and Motyl, 280.

167. Iurii Shapoval and Vadym Zolotar′ov have estimated that of the top sixty-eight officials in the Ukrainian security police in 1929–1931, twenty-six were Jews (38 percent), and by 1932–1933, of the top seventy-five *chekists* in the Ukrainian GPU, fifty were Jews (66.6 percent). According to the 1926 census, Jews constituted 6.5 percent of the population in Ukraine. Their dedicated work for the GPU did not shield them from Stalin's Great Terror; most of them were eliminated in the late 1930s. See Iurii Shapoval and Vadym Zolotar′ov, "Ievreï v kerivnytstvi orhaniv DPU–NKVS USRR–URSR u 1920–1930-kh rr.," *Z arkhiviv VUChK-GPU-NKVD-KGB*, no. 34 (2010): 53–93, esp. 56, 58.

168. Mendel Osherowitch, *How People Live in Soviet Russia: Impressions from a Journey*, ed. Lubomyr Y. Luciuk and trans. Sharon Power (Toronto: University of Toronto Chair of Ukrainian Studies and The Kashtan Press, 2020), 187–96.

169. Victoria Khiterer, "The Holodomor and Jews in Kyiv and Ukraine: An Introduction and Observations on a Neglected Topic," *Nationalities Papers* 48, no. 3: Special Issue on the Soviet Famines of 1930–1933 (May 2020): 460–75.

170. Dzerzhinsky, founder and head of Cheka, complained to Lenin in 1920 that "an enormous hindrance in our work is the absence of *chekists* who are Ukrainians" (*V. I. Lenin i VChK: Sbornik dokumentov, 1917–1922 gody*, Moscow, 2001, 200); quoted in Myroslav Shkandrij, "Ukrainianization, Terror and Famine: Coverage in Lviv's *Dilo* and the Nationalist Press of the 1930s," *Nationalities Papers: The Journal of Nationalism and Ethnicity* 40, no. 3 (2012): 451.

171. Liudmyla Hrynevych, "Ievreis′ke natsional′no-kul′turne vidrodzhennia 1920-kh – 1930-kh rr. v USRR u 'prokrustovomu lozhi' bil′shovyts′koï ideolohiï," *Problemy istoriï Ukraïny: fakty, sudzhennia, poshuky*, no. 12 (2004): 232.

172. Ray Gamache, *Gareth Jones: Eyewitness to the Holodomor* (Cardiff: Welsh Academic Press, 2013). For a complete list of Gareth Jones' articles from 1930 to 1935, see garethjones.org.

173. Gareth Jones, *"Tell Them We Are Starving": The 1933 Diaries of Gareth Jones*, with an introduction by Ray Gamache, ed. Lubomyr Luciuk (Kingston: Kashtan Press, 2015), ii–xv. The diaries contain passages in Welsh, Ukrainian, Russian, and German. The pocket diaries have been preserved by Annie Gwen Jones, Gareth's mother. The original diaries are archived at the National Library of Wales in Aberystwyth. A complete set of scalable, color diary pages can be found online at www.garethjones.org/diaries.

174. See a book written by Gareth's niece, Dr. Margaret Siriol Colley and his great nephew, Nigel Linsan Colley, *Gareth Jones: A Manchukuo Incident* (Nottinghamshire: Nigel Linsan Colley, 2001).

175. Jars Balan, "Rhea Clyman: A Forgotten Canadian Eyewitness to the Hunger of 1932," in *Women and the Holodomor-Genocide: Victims, Survivors, Perpetrators*, ed. Victoria A. Malko (Fresno: The Press at California State University, 2019), 113.

176. Balan, "Rhea Clyman," 92.

177. L. Moskwin (Moscow), "New Campaign of Lies Against the Land of Socialist Construction," *International Press Correspondence*, September 29, 1932, 907; thanks to Jars Balan of the Canadian Institute of Ukrainian Studies for bringing this source to my attention.

178. Balan, "Rhea Clyman," 115.

179. "L. B. Golden, General Secretary of the Save the Children Fund, to Sir Robert Vansittart, 24 August 1933, and the Foreign Office to Edward Coote, 7 September, 1933," in *The Foreign Office and the Famine*, eds. Carynnyk, Luciuk, and Kordan, 287–89.

180. Marco Carynnyk, "Malcolm Muggeridge on Stalin's Famine: 'Deliberate' and 'Diabolical' Starvation," in *The Great Famine in Ukraine: The Unknown Holocaust*, eds. Roma Hadzewycz, George B. Zarycky, and Marta Kolomayets (Jersey City: Svoboda Press for Ukrainian National Association, 1983), 50. Originally published in *New Perspectives* (Toronto), February 19, 1983, 4–5.

181. Marco Carynnyk, "Blind Eye to Murder: Britain, the United States and the Ukrainian Famine of 1933," in *Famine in Ukraine, 1932–1933*, eds. Roman Serbyn and Bohdan Krawchenko (Edmonton: Canadian Institute of Ukrainian Studies, 1986), 110; available at https://diasporiana.org.ua/wp-content/uploads/books/16737/file.pdf.

182. Carynnyk, "Blind Eye to Murder," in *Famine in Ukraine,* eds. Serbyn and Krawchenko, 109.

183. Hiroaki Kuromiya, "Democracies and the Holodomor," *Clio World*, no. 1 (2020): 28–35.

184. Lesia Onyshko, "Milena Rudnyts'ka: shtrykhy do portretu," *Nashe slovo*, December 23–30, 2012, 52. In 1958, Rudnyts'ka's book, *Borot'ba za pravdu pro Velykyi Holod* (Fighting for Truth about the Great Famine) took the stance that the famine was a result of organized pressure by the Kremlin to fracture Ukrainian farmers, using collectivization to curb rebellious Ukrainians.

185. Vasyl' Marochko, "'Torgsin': zolota tsina zhyttia ukrains'kykh selian u roky holodu (1932–1933)," *Ukraïns'kyi istorychnyi zhurnal*, no. 3 (2003): 90–91, 100; idem, "Obmin pobutovoho zolota na khlib v Ukraïni v period Holodomoru 1932–1933 rokiv," *Ukraïns'kyi istoryk*, nos. 3–4 (2008): 195–96; idem, "Torgsin," in *Entsyklopediia Holodomoru 1932–1933 rokiv v Ukraïni*, 431–32.

186. Dr. Lubow Margolena Hansen to Dr. Nellie Pelecovich, January 30, 1934, 2–3; Archives of the Ukrainian National Women's League of America, New York, New York; quoted in *Report to Congress*, 167.

187. Eleanor Roosevelt, *The Autobiography of Eleanor Roosevelt* (New York: Harper, 1961), 413.

188. *Famine in Ukraine* (New York: United Ukrainian Organizations, 1934), 6–7; in *Report to Congress*, 176–77.

189. Haynes and Klehr, *In Denial*.

190. Eugene Lyons, "American Jews and the Kremlin Purges," *The New Leader* 36, no. 9 (March 2, 1953): 14–15; quoted in Dmytro Soloviy, "The Golgotha of Ukraine," *Svoboda – Ukrainian Weekly*, June 2, 1953, 2.

191. See James Burnham's review of *Shame and Glory of the Intellectuals* by Peter Viereck, *The New York Times Book Review*, March 15, 1953; quoted in Soloviy, "The Golgotha of Ukraine," 2.

192. Gantt, "A Medical Review," 20; see also Vasylenko, "Metodolohiia pravovoï otsinky Holodomoru," in *Holodomor*, eds. Vasylenko and Antonovych, 54.

Conclusion

Aftermath

In Ukraine, the struggle for international recognition of the Holodomor as genocide is a national issue, symbolic of what Czech novelist Milan Kundera, the survivor of the Soviet occupation, called "the struggle of memory over forgetting."[1] In the 1930s, Stalin's policy of Ukrainization, cloaked in the language of modernization and synchronized with the drive for industrialization and collectivization, led to a shift in Ukrainian national identity.[2] In the words of Victor Rud, a son of Holodomor survivors,

> [i]n number of victims and destruction of a nation's fiber, psychology, sense of self, in terms of coming to the precipice of destroying a nation, in terms of its effects carrying through and being so manifest eighty years afterward, the Holodomor is without parallel in human history.

Rud has further argued that the Holodomor did not become a catalyst for the founding of the Ukrainian state but rather "interred the idea of Ukrainian independence for generations," warning that its reverberations are felt in Ukraine today: "So much so that, though Ukraine is today nominally independent, it is, fundamentally, not a Ukrainian state."[3] This chapter addresses legal responsibility, as well as economic, social, and psychological effects of the Holodomor-genocide on subsequent generations of Ukrainians. It examines the representation of the Holodomor in historical writing and collective memory.

LEGAL RESPONSIBILITY

The Holodomor in a broad sense refers to Soviet genocide against Ukrainians, whereas the famine of 1932–1933 represents the culminating stage of the

Holodomor, and as the act that itself constitutes a crime of genocide.⁴ Legal scholars argue that in accordance with Article II of the U.N. Convention on the Prevention and Punishment of the Crime of Genocide, all enumerated genocidal acts do apply in the case of the Holodomor:

(a) people who resisted were killed;
(b) there was huge bodily and mental harm caused to all victims of the Holodomor (those who died and those who survived);
(c) there were artificially created conditions of life calculated to destroy the Ukrainians;
(d) all those measures prevented births within the Ukrainian national group; and
(e) famine caused transfer of children from their parents.⁵

According to Myroslava Antonovych the list of genocidal acts in Article II of the U.N. Convention on Genocide is exhaustive: (a) through (c) constitute physical genocide, (d) contains a concept of biological genocide, and (e) constitutes cultural genocide. Thus, in the Holodomor, there were acts of physical, biological, and cultural genocide.⁶

The U.N. Convention on Genocide prohibits "deliberately inflicting on the group conditions of life calculated to bring about its physical destruction in whole or in part" and anticipates responsibility for three categories: "constitutionally responsible rulers, public officials, or private individuals." The Convention was ratified by the Russian SFSR and the Ukrainian SSR, on May 3 and November 15, 1954, respectively. The Convention on the Non-Applicability of Statutory Limitations to War Crimes and Crimes Against Humanity, adopted by the United Nations on November 26, 1968, expands the scope of prosecutions for genocide under the U.N. Convention on Genocide by eliminating any domestic barriers to such prosecutions. The Russian SFSR ratified the agreement on April 22 and the Ukrainian SSR on June 19, 1969. The Convention on Statutory Limitations, together with the *jus cogens* (compelling law) status of the prohibition of genocide, eliminates the argument that acts of genocide committed prior to the U.N. Convention on Genocide are not subject to prosecution. The prohibition of genocide is now universally regarded as *jus cogens* (compelling law of preemptory nature), and the duty to punish genocide as an obligation *erga omnes* (against all—states and individuals).⁷

Whereas lawyers refer to genocide as structural or system criminality, criminologists qualify crimes against humanity as state, organizational, or political crimes.⁸ Perpetrators of international crimes usually commit it in a context of mass violence, on behalf of the state, by members of a specific governmental or militarized unit or organization. As Ervin Staub noted, progressive use of violence, or "continuum of destructiveness," toward one specific group, typically the upper class, intellectuals, privileged minorities, or those who represent the old regime, is legitimated by an ideology.[9] On behalf of the state, the Communist Party and its local representatives in Soviet Ukraine, with support of the GPU, set up policies leading to social engineering through extermination.

German sociologist Max Weber argued that the notion of class was insufficient in understanding a complex stratified system of modern societies.[10] While sticking to a definition of class in economic terms, based on ownership of property, he argued that social inequality also arises due to differences in status. Status is a hierarchical ranking of individuals along a dimension of social prestige, which leads to differentials in power and access to scarce goods. Bolsheviks instituted such a system in 1921.[11] Weber noted that Marx may have conflated class and status, and they do coincide in that one's occupation is the source of wealth. Differences in status lead to culturally mandated patterns of deference or avoidance between inferiors and superiors. Bolsheviks realized the most important variable was a decision as to who had the most power in ensuring their interests would be met. Through "dictatorship of proletariat," they placed themselves at the vanguard, displacing clergy and intelligentsia, and forced these strata of society to recognize status entitlements of Soviet commissars and security police, and to give authorities deference to further one's interests and gain desired resources. As Weber foresaw, communism would require an even greater level of detrimental social control and bureaucratization than a capitalist system.

"For a long time, over a quarter of a century since the Twentieth Party Congress, we had deliberated where did Stalin's unlimited cruelty toward his own countrymen originate. We could not even conceive a thought that the father of internal, merciless, and total terror was Lenin," wrote Soviet historian Dmitrii Volkogonov.[12] Likewise, in Vasily Grossman's memoir, *Forever Flowing*, "true believers" did not believe in God. Within them burned another faith—"a faith in the mercilessly vengeful retribution of the great Stalin." They appreciated and respected "the mighty force and its great leaders, Marx, Engels, Lenin, and Stalin."[13] As soldiers of Stalin, perpetrators took his orders. Grossman defined the capital these "true believers" were accumulating—"the trust of the party, more valuable than gold or land."[14] Comparing two Soviet leaders, Grossman observed:

> Seemingly, Stalin built the state Lenin had founded in his, Stalin's, own image. But this is not, of course, the heart of the matter—his image was actually the likeness of the state, and that is precisely why he became its master.
>
> In Stalin, in the Asian despot and the European Marxist combined in his personality and character, the nature of the Soviet state system was expressed precisely and uniquely.

Grossman noted that the despotic Soviet system disguised itself in Western clothing. All those revolutionary categories Lenin considered transitory expedients, such as dictatorship, terror, and the rejection of bourgeois liberties, Stalin transformed into the permanent basis of Soviet life. In his portrait of Stalin, Grossman diagnosed the gendarme:

> In his unimaginable ferocity and cruelty, in his unbelievable falsity and treachery, in his talent for playing the hypocrite, in his cherished resentments and his vengefulness, in his crudeness, rudeness, humor—behold the Asiatic tyrant.
>
> In his knowledge of revolutionary ideas and texts, in his use of the terminology of the progressive West, . . . in his quotations from Gogol and Shchedrin, in his mastery of the most delicate and conspiratorial tricks, in his amorality, he embodied . . . a person for whom any means at all were justified by the ends.
>
> In his faith in administrative documents and police power as the moving force in life, in his secret passion for uniforms and medals, in his unexampled contempt for human dignity, in his deification of a system based on a rigid and autocratic bureaucracy, in his readiness to kill a man on behalf of the holy letter of the law, and immediately thereafter to flout the law with monstrous and capricious violence—in all these respects he embodied the police boss, the gendarme spirit.
>
> In the combination of these three Stalins, the Stalin personality lay.[15]

The underlying principle of the state Stalin built was the absence of freedom. In a state where there is no individual human freedom, there can be no national freedom. Where there is no free intimacy or free antagonism, there is no sense of community. "Dead freedom," writes Grossman, "became the principal figure in a gigantic stage presentation, in a tremendous puppet show on an unbelievable scale. The state, which had no freedom, created a stage set complete with parliament, elections, trade unions, and a whole society and social life."[16] Who actually made the decisions? The decisions were Stalin's. Questions of secondary importance were decided by Stalin's intimates, but they were always decided in his spirit. "Stalin's spirit and the spirit of the state were one and the same."[17] The state without freedom always acted in the name of freedom and democracy. Mistaken is the opinion which maintains that events of collectivization were "meaningless expressions of uncontrolled, unlimited power in the hands of a cruel man." In reality, the state required that blood be shed in the 1930s.

> As Stalin used to express it, it was not shed for nothing: it left its mark. Without it the state would not have survived. After all, non-freedom shed that blood in order to destroy freedom. It was an old, old necessity. It had begun under Lenin.[18]

Polish philosopher Leszek Kołakowski, likewise, traced Stalinist totalitarianism to Lenin, identifying stages of its growth and ripening before reaching its apogee.[19]

Among leaders who used violence as an instrument to stay in power, Alette Smeulers listed the "ruthless dictator" Josef Stalin, as well as the "charismatic almost divine but utterly destructive" Adolf Hitler, the "strict authoritarian" Augusto Pinochet, and the "power hungry careerist" Slobodan Milošević.[20] These perpetrators are typically male, very authoritarian, manipulative, vain, arrogant, harsh, cruel, and merciless, and are referred to as "criminal masterminds."[21] The criminal mastermind type of perpetrator stands apart because he will never submit himself to any authority as he perceives himself to be the ultimate authority. Leaders with criminal masterminds plan and order the crimes, then incite the masses.

The "paper trail" of statutes, decrees, and secret circulars provide a great deal of evidence of Soviet government actions, even though the intent may not be directly spelled out. Professor Chirovsky explained before the International Commission of Inquiry into the 1932–1933 Famine in Ukraine: "The decrees themselves say very little about the reasons, only the policy outlines. But before the decrees were read and pronounced and given to the public knowledge, meetings were held and speeches were delivered to explain the reasons why."[22] Out of a dozen decrees that have been identified as causing the genocidal famine, the law of August 7, 1932, on protecting socialist property, the speculation decree of August 22, 1932, and the internal passport decree of December 27, 1932, are the most important. These three decrees were signed by members of the Politburo. The decree on blacklisting of December 6, 1932, was signed by Vlas Chubar, Chairman of the Council of People's Commissars of the Ukrainian SSR, and by Stanislav Kosior, Secretary of the TsK KP(b)U, who were also Politburo members. The Postyshev decrees, by the very nature of their implementation, hold Postyshev responsible for them, although there is no evidence who signed them. He was also a member of the Politburo.[23]

Historians who studied the Soviet nationality policy in the Ukrainian SSR during the period from 1923 to 1934—Robert Conquest, James Mace, and George Liber among others—have concluded:

> In the Ukraine, this ferocious war against the peasants [independent and collective farm workers] became a war against Ukrainians. Here, the center ruthlessly enforced grain requisitions until starvation began and maintained these quotas as millions starved to death. Forewarned of these tragic consequences by the Ukrainian [Communist] Party leaders, the center did not release grain stores. Instead, it directed a strident campaign against Ukrainian nationalism during this period.[24]

Even scholars who deny that the famine in Ukraine was genocide point out, "Ukrainian nationalism was attacked because it was perceived as a threat to Stalin's procurement policies."[25]

State policies were directed against Ukrainians as a national group throughout the Soviet Union. Stalin asserted the KP(b)U placed the local needs of Ukraine above the needs of the First Five-Year Plan and the construction of socialism in the Soviet Union. Stalin dispatched Pavel Postyshev to Soviet Ukraine because he had worked there from 1923 to 1930 and had been a member of the KP(b)U Politburo from 1926 to 1930. Postyshev was appointed the first secretary of the Kharkiv Communist Party committee to intensify grain confiscations, thus aggravating an already devastating famine. In his new capacity, he came to enforce two resolutions, adopted by the TsK VKP(b) on December 14, 1932, and January 24, 1933. The first resolution accused the leadership of the KP(b)U of tolerating a "nationalist deviation," whereas the second resolution accused Ukrainian Marxist–Leninists of failing to fulfill grain delivery quotas. The language of the resolutions is reflected in a speech Postyshev delivered on November 24, 1933, stating that "any attempt to harmonize proletarian internationalism with nationalism must make it an instrument of the nationalist counterrevolution and therefore must be most vigorously combated in future." He added that the reorganization of forms and methods of Bolshevik leadership in building up Ukrainian culture must consequently imply "a vigorous and consistent struggle for the elimination of nationalist prejudices." Ewald Ammende, who followed Postyshev's path and read reports in *Pravda*, asked,

> What is the meaning of Moscow's program as set out by Postyshev? It means that Moscow has definitely adopted the new course with regard to the nationalities and has abandoned the "rotten compromise" of the first period of Russian nationalism. The new program means war to the knife on all the national movements.[26]

Radical change in the Soviet nationality policy occurred at the Sixteenth Party Congress in 1930. Until then, the official party policy emphasized imperial Russian nationalism as the major threat to the Soviet state. The policy of Ukrainization, conceived as a concession to Ukrainian Bolsheviks, was initiated by the VKP(b) at the Twelfth Congress in 1923 with Lenin's blessings, who warned that Great Russian chauvinism had "deep roots in the past." Between these two congresses, the party interpreted local nationalism as an understandable reaction to Russian chauvinism. Then, in November 1933, Ukrainian "nationalist deviation" was declared the greatest danger to the unity of the Soviet empire. In early January 1933, nearly

15,000 functionaries of various ranks were dispatched to Soviet Ukraine from Moscow to occupy positions as chairmen and secretaries in collective farms, district party secretaries, and chairmen of district executive committees. With the arrival of this contingent, along with Vsevolod Balyts'kyi at the helm of the GPU in Soviet Ukraine, and Pavel Postyshev, new first secretary of the Kharkiv Regional Committee and secretary of the Central Committee of the KP(b)U, "the takeover of Ukraine by the central government was complete."[27]

In accordance with the new policy, Postyshev and Kosior, at the November 1933 plenum of the TsK KP(b)U, announced that "the Ukrainian SSR was no longer a backward Russian colony, but a highly industrialized socialist nation. As such, Ukrainians were no longer an underprivileged nationality. Further efforts to pursue the old Ukrainization policy, therefore, were unnecessary." Although Russian chauvinism was on the rise, the greatest threat to the cause of communism in Ukraine at the moment was Ukrainian nationalism.[28] The use of violence against "Ukrainian nationalists" began on an unprecedented scale. Less than ten months after he arrived in January 1933, Postyshev reported the ousting of over 200 "nationalist elements" from the Soviet Ukraine's Commissariat of Education, over 300 scientific and editorial personnel, 200 who occupied positions as managers of departments and sections in eight central organizations, and nearly 1,000 from cooperative and grain procurement agencies.[29] People were arrested, and after their dismissal were shot or exiled to the distant reaches of the Great Russian Motherland.

In the opinion of Jacob Sundberg, president of the International Commission of Inquiry, the Postyshev decrees should be seen together:

> They clearly link the famine and the reversal in nationality policy and, in my view, the latter element takes preponderance so that the reversal is not incidental to the grain procurement but, rather, the other way around. The famine caused by the grain procurement has been instrumental in implementing the nationalities policy.[30]

How Postyshev viewed his mandate can be established from his own words, quoted in *Chervonyi shliakh* (Red Path), published in Kharkiv in 1934, that "1933 was year the party had conducted the 'Herculean labor' of liquidating nationalist elements in Ukraine."[31] James Mace summarized Postyshev's operation in Soviet Ukraine as follows:

> His house cleaning was extremely thorough. By October 15 in those regions where the ongoing 1933 purge of the Party had been completed, of 120,000

members and candidates of the Communist Party of Ukraine that had been verified, 27,500 had been purged as hostile, vacillating, dissolute elements. Postyshev also revealed later, in November 1933 that he had brought in thousands of new appointees to Ukraine's districts.[32]

Teachers in rural districts constituted two-thirds (51,196) of 75,380 teachers on payroll in 1928–1929,[33] the turning point from the NEP to total state control, and their task was to bring about "socialist transformation" of society. Daria Mattingly has argued that teachers were driven by a variety of motives. Unlike professionals, such as the GPU, militias, and the army, who were trained to enforce policies with the use of violence, teachers recruited to assist authorities did not kill. Among teachers were opportunists (*kar'ierysty*) who used their position of power to benefit financially, settle scores with neighbors, or advance their career through deployment in collectivization, grain procurement, or propaganda campaigns. Fanatics (about 5 percent of perpetrators) were driven by ideology. Young female teachers could have been "compromised" because they were vulnerable; they participated because of explicit or implicit coercion, threats, or aggressive indoctrination.

The majority of perpetrators were conformists, who actively participated in grain procurement campaigns as evident from archival documents. In February 1933, a teacher-activist in the Kaniv district, Kyïv region, locked villagers in a dark room or poured cold water over their heads to force his victims to comply.[34] A member of the Militant Godless Society (*bezbozhniki*), M. K. Serhiïv, reported that teachers assisted authorities by questioning schoolchildren about any concealed grain at home. Typically, such questions were presented during high-stakes tests.[35] Delegates at local conferences reported about unearthing stockpiles of grain "hidden" by the *kurkuli* or by fellow teachers who allegedly "assisted" them.[36] Teachers who opposed grain requisitions in the Chernihiv region in March 1933 were purged from ranks of the Teachers' Union and ended up in GPU prisons, being charged with "counterrevolutionary propaganda" for redistributing grain to the villagers and for helping the *kurkuli* "hide" the grain.[37] As Kas'ianov noted, by 1933, the society had been conditioned to use violence against intelligentsia that did not go along with the totalitarian system.[38] Teachers who survived the purges learned to comply with demands of the ruling elite.[39] Irrespective of their roles, their fate was quite fluid because perpetrators could easily turn into victims. Ultimately, as James Mace noted in his doctoral thesis: "The Ukrainian national intelligentsia, communist and non-communist, was virtually wiped out."[40]

ECONOMIC AFTERMATH

Scholars, who argue that the famine of 1932–1933 was a price to pay for rapid industrialization, fail to notice adverse effects industrialization had on the Ukrainian SSR. Economists have revealed that, as a result of the First Five-Year Plan, the republic, which in 1927 directly or indirectly controlled 81 percent of its industry, by 1932 controlled only 38 percent.[41] Authorities in Moscow deprived the republic of its "economic capital," thus undermining Ukraine's bid to attain independent statehood. Industrialization demanded educated and experienced workers and supervisors, which meant dismissing an employee for not speaking Ukrainian was economically inefficient. Economic centralization necessitated that cadres, technical and political, become mobile and interchangeable from one end of the Soviet Union to another. In view of this need, in a multi-national state, language differences had to be de-emphasized. Language reforms increased Ukrainian divergence from Russian, and, from the point of view of Marxists, were "bourgeois nationalist" and "counterrevolutionary." One common language, Russian, was the language of the Soviet industrial revolution.[42]

Scholars also argue that Stalin faced an overpopulation crisis as Ukrainian provinces, after the emancipation of serfs and land redistribution in the late nineteenth century, had a surplus of 8 million farmers needing additional wages or land to subsist.[43] Migration of these Ukrainian farmers to Siberia and Kazakhstan partially solved the problem in the nineteenth century. However, in the 1920s, settlement of Siberia and Kazakhstan by Ukrainian farmers became involuntary. The Central Executive Committee of the USSR decreed the population transfer on July 30, 1926, and designated the Russian Far East, Siberia, Sakhalin, Murmansk, as well as free lands of the North Caucasus, Lower Volga, and South Urals as places of settlement for the Ukrainian agrarian population. This solution to the "overpopulation" of Ukraine in four years, from 1924 to 1928, forced nearly 142,000 Ukrainian farmers (24 percent of the internal migration) to resettle into grain-producing regions of the Russian republic.[44] They, too, became victims of famine, although demographers do not count them as Ukrainian losses.

Historically, migration to urban centers from Ukrainian provinces increased rapidly and followed the same pattern as in Russian provinces: between 1811 and 1910, population in Ukrainian cities increased by 600 percent[45] and in Russian cities by 800 percent.[46] By the 1930s, nearly 2.9 million Ukrainians were deported or exiled to the Russian republic, where their hard labor fueled industrial progress, while they subsisted on starvation diets in concentration camps and involuntary settlements servicing Soviet industrial projects.[47]

Industrialization and urbanization, as George Liber has pointed out, "delayed the emergence of a mass-based Ukrainian nationalism."[48] Migration to urban centers reoriented Ukrainian farmers' sense of identity: they cut their ties to the countryside as well as to their mother tongue. Increased infusion of Russian speakers to Ukraine's urban centers changed the balance of power in cities and in industrial occupations, as they became, in the words of Mykola Porsh, "cultural agents for de-nationalization."[49] Therefore, attempts of the GPU to prosecute Ukrainian intelligentsia as leaders of the mass-based Ukrainian nationalist movement appear to be baseless. There was no mass-based nationalist movement, but a disorganized political opposition to Soviet policies of the 1930s.

Collectivization of agriculture achieved the opposite of what it was supposed to do; it broke the tie between cities and countryside. The ambiguous policy of *korenizatsiia*, the "rooting" of Soviet power in non-Russian provinces under the leadership of the urban proletariat, became irrelevant once the state initiated the liquidation of independent farmers, the carriers of the national tradition, and pushed them to work in collective farms. Over time, voluntary and involuntary migrants to industrial construction sites cut their bonds with their former villages and succumbed to pressures of Russification in urban centers or exile settlements in Soviet Russia. Defenders of local interests, including Ukrainian Marxist–Leninists, who stopped being unquestioning agents of the Kremlin, became "class enemies" and had to be destroyed. New cadres did not have to know the language of their own national group. S. D. Dimanshtein explained this ideological hegemony of the center as follows:

> We do not need a "non-Russian in general," we do not need an alien class element of any nationality. We need a non-Russian proletarian, a collective farmer, a fighter for socialism, a fighter for the working class. We need a non-Russian who is educated in international assignments of the proletarian revolution.[50]

Scholars note that the conformity to Communist Party leadership in Moscow had to be reestablished in Soviet Ukraine. Periodic purges, coercion, and mass violence were the means to achieve these ends.[51]

Goals of a planned economy were closely linked to repressions. In 1930–1932, the Politburo of the TsK KP(b)U submitted lists to the TsK VKP(b) with the number of dekulakized farmers to be deported. In Moscow, these numbers corresponded to data on the "volume" of labor reserves required for construction projects in the Russian Far North and Siberia. Thus, repressions served as a means of mobilizing a cheap workforce, consisting mainly of forced labor, and covered up under various campaigns against clergy, well-to-do farmers, and "wreckers."[52] Communist leaders consciously deprived innocent people of their freedom, thereby committing crimes against humanity

(Article 174 of the Criminal Code of Ukraine, the deliberate prosecution of an innocent individual).[53] Peter Kardash has reminded that extermination of people on the grounds of their material status constitutes a crime against humanity under Article 6, clause (b) of the International Military Tribunal (IMT) Charter.[54] Executions of "anti-Soviet elements" were executions of people for their anti-communist beliefs. They constitute a crime against humanity under Article 6, clause (c) of the IMT Charter.[55] Indeed, the circulation of Soviet newspapers, posters, and books was paid for with lives of Ukrainians exiled to the Russian Far North to develop the lumber industry. Under pressure of evidence, attested to both by documents of perpetrators and testimonies of survivors, James Mace has noted: "the question ceases to become, How many millions died? One is forced to ask instead, How could so many still survive when literally everything was done to starve them to death? Each account is individual, but taken together their collective accounts of traumatization cannot fail to move even the most 'scientific' of historians."[56]

SOCIAL EFFECTS

Dispatches of foreign diplomats and oral histories of Holodomor survivors bear witness to dramatic shifts in national identity and social roles in Ukrainian society as a result of the historical trauma. In 1933, foreign diplomats openly acknowledged that Bolshevik policies in Ukraine were in part dictated by the necessity of "denationalizing those regions in which Ukrainian or German consciousness have awakened, threatening possible political difficulties in the future, and where, for the sake of the unity of the empire, it is better that a preponderantly Russian population reside." These were observations of Sergio Gradenigo, Royal Consul of Italy, who wrote from the Kharkiv Consulate to the Embassy of Italy in Moscow on May 31, 1933, at the height of the genocidal famine:

> This calamity, which is claiming millions of lives, is destroying the infancy of an entire nation and is really affecting only Ukraine, Kuban, and the Central Volga. Elsewhere it is felt much less or not at all.
>
> In conclusion: The current disaster will bring about a preponderantly Russian colonization of Ukraine. It will transform its ethnographic character. In a future time, perhaps very soon, one will no longer be able to speak of a Ukraine, or a Ukrainian people, and thus not even of a Ukrainian problem, because Ukraine will become a *de facto* Russian region.[57]

After the suicide of Mykola Skrypnyk, Royal Consul Gradenigo sent a confidential report to the Italian Embassy in Moscow on July 19, 1933,

240   Conclusion

describing details of Skrypnyk's death and warning about genocidal capabilities of the regime:

> The dying man was carried to the university clinic, where he regained consciousness during the blood transfusion. He told Postyshev, who had come by, that the real danger for Communism lay in Russian imperialism, which was on the rise.
>   Proceeding at all speed at present is the reform of Ukrainian spelling (it has been stripped of the vocative which Russian, unlike Ukrainian, does not have). In government offices the Russian language is once again being used, in correspondence as well as in verbal dealings between employees.
>   [W]e can only conclude that the Ukrainian people are about to go into an eclipse, which could well turn out to be a night without end, because Russian imperialism, with its present tender mercies (i.e., tender Communist mercies), is capable of wiping a nation—nay, a civilization—right off the face of the earth if we aren't very careful.[58]

The Moscow's intent "to settle the Ukrainian problem once and for all" had been clear to foreign observers for quite some time. The Royal Consul General in Odesa, in a confidential letter to the Italian Ambassador in Moscow on February 19, 1934, wrote:

> The persecutions conducted against the Ukrainian intellectuals, accused of sympathizing with their colleagues and brothers in Galicia and Poland; the suicide of Skrypnyk, the Ukrainian Commissar for Public Education; the incarceration of numerous Germans accused of sympathizing with the Ukrainians; the withholding of the grain reserves from the peasants, which has turned Ukraine over the spring of last year into the site of an unprecedented famine, which according to reliable evidence has sent 7,000,000 people to their deaths; all of these things betoken the Moscow Government's intention to use every means at their disposal to crush every last vestige of Ukrainian nationalism.
>   Ukraine used to be the sole major population center endowed with some degree of ethnic, linguistic and historical cohesiveness that was resisting Moscow's centralization program. This obstacle may now be said to have been overcome.[59]

Three years later, a report based on personal impressions of a German Consulate official in Kharkiv, in May 1936, illustrates the effects of the construction of a "Ukrainian Soviet culture." The German diplomat observed,

> Ukrainian Ukraine has been destroyed. According to approximate estimates, *one-fifth* of its 30-million population, or about 6 million, died from famine in 1932–1933. The people were now sufficiently weak to suffer the final blows

of Moscow's centralism: the elimination of the hitherto obligatory Ukrainian-language examination for officials and administrators, the "reorganization" of the Ukrainian Academy of Sciences, the "purge" of higher education, the destruction of millions of books and other printed materials of the pre-Postyshev era.

What is the situation in Ukraine today, now that Stalin's prefect has already had two and one-half years for the "construction of a Ukrainian Soviet culture"? Here are several examples:

...

I have the opportunity to visit the highest foreign-policy official of Ukraine. He speaks no Ukrainian. In the People's Commissariat of Ukraine, as I learn from him, Russian is spoken.

In the cities one hears almost nothing but Russian. Whoever speaks Ukrainian thereby shows that he is from the countryside and is backward.

Neither in Kiev, nor in Stalino [Donetsk], nor in Kharkov could I acquire a Russian-Ukrainian or Ukrainian-Russian dictionary. "This sort of thing" is no longer available.

The Ukrainian press is rarely bought. . . . There is no Ukrainian literature. There is hardly a Ukrainian book that is not a translation from the Russian. There are no longer any Ukrainian history books.[60]

The German consulate official, returning after a multi-week travel throughout Ukraine, reported his observations as follows:

I visited schools in various places. The impression is everywhere the same. The schools mostly consist of parallel classes. Class A has Russian as the language of instruction; class B has Ukrainian as the language of instruction. Parents may choose the language of instruction for their children. Completely Ukrainian schools are rare, as Ukrainians also frequently send their children to Russian schools. The sections with Russian as language of instruction devote 5 hours per week to Russian-language instruction and 3 to Ukrainian. The Ukrainian section has 5 hours per week of Ukrainian-language instruction and 3 hours of Russian-language instruction. This parallel system is intentionally constructed to enable Russian to dominate as the children's conversational language. Moreover, the teachers in the Ukrainian section are primarily Russians, and in the Russian section they are often Ukrainians. I made this observation in 6 of 8 schools that I visited. The writing abilities of the pupils in the Ukrainian classes are noticeably bad. . . . Hardly a child completes school with adequate knowledge of Ukrainian orthography. . . . That the majority of even the urban Ukrainian population still chooses the Ukrainian language of instruction for their children, despite obvious discrimination against Ukrainian, shows how deeply rooted the consciousness of linguistic and cultural specificity still is in the people. Lectures in the universities of Kiev and Kharkov and in the higher educational institutions of Stalino are almost exclusively in Russian.[61]

In a report on the political situation in Ukraine in 1933, the German Consulate official under the subsection, "The Ukrainian Question," assessed the population's sentiment as follows:

> Characteristic of the population's mood is the widespread view that the Soviet government promoted the expansion of the famine so as to force the Ukrainians to their knees. The frequently heard cynical comment made by individual communists—"We do not fear the hungry; it is the well-fed who are dangerous to us!"—has contributed to strengthening this feeling, even if it hardly corresponds to the view of the party leadership.
>
> Moscow has recognized the tenseness of the situation and has even artificially increased it by the claim of German and Polish attempts at separating Ukraine.[62]

The report was written on January 15, 1934, and Hitler's accession to power and the prospect of Ukraine's liberation appeared politically dangerous to Soviet leaders. Assessing the role of Postyshev, Stalin's confidant, who was sent to Khrakiv with unlimited powers to eliminate the danger of "separatist" tendencies in Ukraine, the report noted that he "produced the preconditions for an assault on the Ukrainian front."[63] The report further described how the assault on the Ukrainian national development unfolded:

> The signal was the removal of Education Commissar [Mykola] Skrypnyk, who had long been a representative of an emphatically Ukrainian Communist orientation. He was followed by high officials in the central apparatus in Kharkov and by leading personalities in the provinces. In the jurisdictional area professors of the Academy of Sciences and of Kiev University, directors of the Institute of Linguistics and the Kiev Film School, school directors, many employees of the "education front," and officials lost their positions and sometimes their freedom. They were all accused of working on behalf of the counterrevolution by promoting Ukrainian chauvinism—be it in language, scholarship, or literature, or be it in administrative regulations. Secret organizations with supposed ties to "German and Polish fascism" were uncovered in ways that enabled the GPU [secret police] to demonstrate once again its talent for constructing highly treasonous intrigues. . . . Revelations of so-called organizations must be regarded with skepticism. They serve above all as a deterrent against *any* Ukrainian tendency and remind the people of the intensified vigilance of the GPU. A new phase in the struggle against Ukrainianism has begun with the well-known November resolutions of the supreme Party leadership in Kharkov.

While they also mention the danger of "Great Russian chauvinism" in addition to "Ukrainian chauvinism," this should be regarded as only a theoretical concession to the Ukrainian masses. In reality, a continually intensifying "Great Russian Communist chauvinism" is the current rule for Soviet policy in Ukraine.[64]

These personal observations of the German Consulate official are corroborated by a Jewish journalist Mendel Osherowitch, who in early 1932 traveled to Ukraine, the land of his birth, to visit his family and write a series of articles under the title, *How People Live in Soviet Russia*.[65] One chapter in his travel notes is devoted to the fear of the GPU across the country. Without the "strongest pillar"—the GPU and many of its overt and covert agents—Stalin's regime would collapse. Osherowitch mused that it would take another writer with Dostoyevsky's talent to evoke a reader's horror and let the world know just how much fear the GPU inspired in the population. Osherowitch's brother served in the GPU.

In June 1934, the capital was transferred back to Kyïv, the historic capital of Ukraine dating from medieval times. In Soviet times, the capital of Ukraine had been Kharkiv, an industrial city, where Bolsheviks established themselves in their first attempt to take over Ukraine. The transfer marked the triumph over Ukrainian nationalism, and the reporter of the *Christian Science Monitor* (Boston) presented the news under the title, "Separatism in Ukraine Suppressed." The reporter observed, "'Symbol of victory over the nationalist elements in Ukraine' is *Izvestiia*'s, the government's newspaper, description of tomorrow's official transfer of the Ukrainian capital from Kharkov to Kiev."[66] The shift in capitals from Kharkiv to Kyïv in 1934 was not the victory of the Ukrainian countryside over the Russified industrial centers. Kyïv did not follow social trends of other industrialized capitals such as Budapest, Prague, or Warsaw. Instead, it was the victory of Soviet power over "nationalistic counterrevolution."[67]

Not only was national identity shifted but also social roles in families. Feminist scholars have identified cultural factors that accounted for gender differences in how men and women experienced the Holodomor. In a patriarchal Ukrainian society, most of the first victims were heads of households. In the absence of their husbands, arrested and exiled to the Russian Far North and Siberia, women had to assume responsibilities of defending themselves and their families. The state eventually took over the role of the "father" figure, thus destroying a traditional social structure and altering gender roles in the Ukrainian family.[68]

State-sanctioned violence not only damaged women's reproductive health but also undermined their role as mothers.[69] Physiological factors accounted for a lower mortality rate among women, a tendency observed in other famines.[70] Yet, there seems to be no physiological protection for those women, who against their biological instinct and socially cultivated image as self-sacrificing mothers, ate their own children in the madness of survivor cannibalism.[71] Although such cases were reported in all regions affected by famine, they were rare (less than one-third of 1 percent of population). Many mothers, overcome by pangs of hunger, were forced to abandon their children on doorsteps of state-run orphanages[72] in desperate hopes, largely futile, that the government would be a better caretaker.[73]

PSYCHOLOGICAL EFFECTS

Historians, who have examined the period from the 1920s to the 1930s, define it as a rupture in the life of Ukrainian society that "affected . . . social psychology, mentality, and culture."[74] Section (b) of Article II of the U.N. Convention on Genocide states that causing serious bodily or mental harm is one of the elements of crime of genocide.[75] Hundreds of Ukraine's intellectuals and thousands of its best farmers endured mental suffering in OGPU labor camps and forced settlements. An estimated 60,000 "counterrevolutionaries" were among the "labor army" building the White Sea–Baltic Sea Canal.[76]

In 1930–1932, an internal investigation by a special commission of the OGPU uncovered abuse of power by a dozen notorious camp guards at the White Sea–Baltic Sea Canal. The guards systematically tortured, humiliated, and killed prisoners to cover up administrative crimes.[77] Besides beatings, bribery and drinking were rampant, women were forced into prostitution or raped, and food rations of the imprisoned were stolen. From the first steps in the Kem' transit station, the imprisoned were greeted by guards and accompanied throughout the day with beatings and Russian expletives, so they internalize that "the power here is not Soviet, but Solovets" and there was no prosecutor with whom to file complaints. The imprisoned were put naked "on the stones" or kept in unheated cells. In summer, they were exposed naked to mosquitoes, or perched on a narrow plank where they were forced to sit still in a crouched position. For a minor violation of the rules, the imprisoned were beaten up by virtually everybody, from overseers to convoys to guards, or locked into "wagons" (unheated isolation log cells) to freeze, or incarcerated into a cube 1 meter in height with all the walls inside covered with sharp wooden slivers, so the condemned would lose their minds and die. When out in the forest on timbering assignments, they were routinely left to freeze. Mock executions were rampant. Mock "leave of absence notes" were given out for failure to complete an assignment, which resulted in carrying a log with a written note on it all the way from the forest a few kilometers back to the camp. The imprisoned were forced to carry water from one ice-hole to another, or to shovel snow from one side of the road to another side, or to cry out "gull one," "gull two" up to 2,000 times. Lawlessness was absolute.[78]

The camp administration pretended not to see these abuses. Violence was institutionalized, so prosecuting a dozen of the most notorious guards did not affect the system. Among the guards were former White and Red Army officers, former Soviet officials, and even former OGPU officers. After the investigation, twelve guards were convicted, three were executed, and the rest were sentenced from three to eight years in various OGPU camps as prisoners.[79] As one notorious guard stated during his testimony:

> This entire system of beatings and torture of prisoners was precisely the system, and not just isolated cases. The civilian administration was well aware of it and condoned it by not taking any measures to stop it. . . . Thus, everyone, who applied beatings, knew it was permitted, and the bosses approved of it.[80]

The thesis that the goal of the camps was to forge criminals into useful members of society does not hold water because the majority of these "criminals" did not commit any crime and were not in need of any "remediation."[81]

The phenomenon of harmful psychological effects, according to Robert Conquest, can be explained by fear and lack of trust.[82] How could this be otherwise in a society with a distorted moral code? The OGPU infiltrated all spheres of life with thousands of secret agents (*seksot*) who overheard conversations and denounced neighbors. In the atmosphere of total terror and suspicion, deliberately stimulated by the ruling regime, denunciations were regarded as an act of civic duty.[83] Olesia Stasiuk has convincingly demonstrated that the genocide led to the breakdown of moral foundations of society. Respect for the elderly, humaneness, kindness, honor, dignity, mercy were sanctioned, whereas denunciations were considered acts of patriotism and "class vigilance."[84] Mass denunciations affected people's psychological well-being, leading to depression, rage, irritability, and doom because the family fabric was torn apart when children denounced their parents and husbands denounced wives or vice versa for a reward of 10–15 percent of confiscated food.[85] The OGPU did not keep records of violations of law, so no traces were left of total lawlessness.[86] Arbitrary executions by *troikas*—a trio of party, OGPU, and a local lumpen activist—without a trial, further led to the deterioration of the sense of justice.[87]

One of the most shocking manifestations of dehumanization during the Holodomor was cannibalism. Scholars have identified a thousand cases of those convicted of cannibalism, and this is a unique indictment of the communist regime.[88] Photographs that documented these cases have survived in the State Archives of the Ministry of Internal Affairs of Soviet Ukraine, but as Hennadii Boriak pointed out, "the public is still not ready today to accept these grisly photo and text records."[89] Examining these cases of ultimate degradation, Olga Bertelsen explained that people's mental activities and cognitive processes became fully subordinated to one obsessive thought: where to obtain food. Due to prolonged starvation and uncertainty about when and where to find food, "the flow of other thoughts and ideas was disrupted, which facilitated intellectual and moral degradation."[90] When people are deprived of food, the human brain functions in a way that cultivates and strengthens the mode of primitive perceptions and limited intellectual strivings.[91] Consequently, memory weakens but memories associated with food or activities related to food sharpen and stay vivid until the death of a starving person.[92] According to Holodomor survivors' memoirs, people no longer engaged in normal daily human activities, such as maintaining proper hygiene, cooking, marrying, sexual relations, and the like.

Starving people committed horrid crimes to survive, and in the process surrendered the ideals of freedom both on individual and collective levels.[93] In the words of the Russian philosopher Nikolai Berdiaev, "freedom is always difficult; slavery is always easy," and a by-product of a hijacked enslaved mentality of "the fallen" is violence.[94] Scholars explain that food deprivation and the threat of dying paralyzes the will for freedom, free speech, and intellectual activities. Struggle for freedom becomes physically and mentally impossible for victims. Slavery appears to them a more attractive option than death. In the case of starving individuals in Soviet Ukraine, their inclination to violence was conditioned physiologically and biochemically. The fabric of society in Soviet Ukraine was transformed: social ties within families were weakened or broken, "altruism, humanism, and self-sacrifice, typical human phenomena in calamity-free times, evaporated and were replaced by extreme egocentrism and animalistic behavior."[95]

Like other historians and medical professionals who studied the effects of extreme starvation, Olga Bertelsen found that the genocidal famine of 1932–1933 had particularly catastrophic effects on the behavior, social conduct, and mentality of women; more women were prosecuted for cannibalism. Psychiatrists believe cannibalism is a symptom of a mental disorder and a delusion maintained despite being contradicted by socially accepted codes of behavior. Women turned to crime because they could not escape from the "double bind"[96] situations that threatened their survival and resulted in dramatic changes in their personality and self-identity. Women turned ovens and gardens into burial places for "unusable" parts of human heads and bones, either from their own child, husband, or passerby. Bolshevik henchmen and "devils in military uniforms" (the OGPU) created conditions incompatible with life causing mental suffering among victims-turned-criminals.

Although cases of cannibalism were limited to rural districts of Ukraine, teachers were aware of this phenomenon and warned their children to be vigilant and stay home instead of risk being kidnapped on the road to school.[97] The ghettoization inside the sealed Ukrainian borders concealed the crime, exacerbating the famine and the people's transgressions. Bertelsen noted that archival documents, oral histories, and written testimonies about human suffering in 1932–1933 place Soviet Ukraine on the "map of moral geography"[98] and in the discourse about the depth of degradation, individual as well as collective provoked and instigated by the state.

Historical trauma of the Holodomor has been analyzed through the psychological prism of individual, collective, and cultural trauma. Historian Vitalii Ohienko pointed out that images of agony and death surrounding victims for prolonged periods of time in their homes, on the streets, or in schools led to stress, depression, dysfunction, and pathological behavior. Using methodology, proposed by psychologists who study post-traumatic stress disorder, Ohienko identified individual and collective characteristics of behavior that affected Holodomor survivors: apathy numbed the living, a defense mechanism survivors developed to distance themselves from painful realities; fear gave way to helplessness; the brutality of fellow human beings led to distrust and slavish passivity; resignation to the inevitability of death deprived victims of the will to live; desensitized witnesses were no longer disturbed by the sight of human skeletons heaped on roadsides or in backyards of railway stations; and burial rituals were no longer performed, and the process of grieving was disrupted.[99]

Scholars studying the social and psychological consequences and long-term effects of the Holodomor concluded that tools of social control used by Bolsheviks included not only concentration camps and prisons to break the will of opponents of the regime but also propaganda campaigns to brainwash and whip up enthusiasm among their supporters. Ideology was used to monopolize collective consciousness. "Sticks-and-carrots" policies rewarded the enthusiasts with food rations, apartments, and promotions, while "rewarding" the objectors with starvation rations, bunkbeds in prisons, and eventually executions by the *troikas*. Some syndromes and symptoms of psychological disorders identified in scholarly literature include:

- fear (hunger psychosis, fear of authority)
- distrust (of neighbors and the world at large)
- degradation (moral and physical)
- misapplication of law (criminalization of society)
- learned helplessness (code of silence)
- loss of expertise (agricultural techniques, entrepreneurship)
- fatalistic disposition
- survivor syndrome

- escapism (living in a dual reality)
- identification with aggressors (the Stockholm syndrome)
- the *Homo Sovieticus* syndrome (inability to think independently, dependence on the state).

One of the durable characteristics of chronic collective trauma is a Stockholm syndrome. Iryna Reva found evidence among Holodomor descendants that suggests the existence of a psychological alliance between the Ukrainian people and the aggressor.[100] The result was an impulse to appear loyal to Soviet rather than national identity and a fear of using the Ukrainian language. Helpless and servile victims of the Holodomor in Ukraine had to identify with their perpetrators.[101] Survivors of OGPU labor camps described how bread was given out ritualistically from the hands of perpetrators to condition their victims into submission. Ohienko noted that this method of disciplining was used on collective farms when food was distributed to those who worked in return for loyalty to the regime but left those jobless, infirmed, and young without means to survive.[102] In her memoir *"Skazhy pro shchaslyve zhyttia..."* (*"Speak of the Happy Life..."*) Anastasiia Lysyvets', who was attending school during the Holodomor, vividly described how food was used as a conditioning tool to punish the recalcitrant and to reward the compliant.[103] Was the underlying goal of the repressive regime to create a new Soviet identity, fostered by fears of re-traumatization, as some scholars argue? The goal was much more mundane: the regime had a large army of Communist Party bureaucrats and OGPU functionaries with their dependents, who did not produce but struggled to survive.[104] An investigation into the distribution of food rations for the privileged Soviet elite and the cost of their vacations at various health resorts is still shrouded in secrecy, and even today, files in the former Communist Party archive with this information are sealed and inaccessible to researchers. Full recovery from the effects of Stockholm syndrome plaguing the Ukrainian psyche might take several generations.

It typically takes more than two generations—Macauley says five—to destroy the memory of earlier times.[105] Outcomes of historical traumas, such as wars, genocides, and famines, are transmitted epigenetically and have a neurobiological impact on mental health of survivors and their descendants.[106] Additional mechanism of trauma transmission, sociocultural, has psychological consequences: changed worldviews, attitudes, and behaviors.[107] Ukrainian psychologists Viktoriia Gorbunova and Vitalii Klymchuk studied the sociocultural transmission of post-traumatic stress disorder among second, third, and fourth generations of Holodomor survivors (721 persons). They found close connection between a pattern of keeping silent about traumatic events that occurred during the Holodomor and the extent of suffering that respondents' families experienced during the Holodomor.

The researchers also found close connection between the avoidance of Holodomor-related topics and a denial and devaluation of Holodomor events within families, especially among individuals who did not know much about the traumatic events during the Holodomor. The most widespread behavioral strategies within families corresponded to trauma-related themes such as eating habits and attitude to food. Researchers suggested that truthful trauma-focused storytelling within families and within communities that have traumatic events in common can decrease the psychological consequences of transgenerational traumas.[108]

HISTORY AND MEMORY

History was not taught as a separate subject in Soviet schools of the 1920s.[109] After a decade of Bolshevik rule in Ukraine, in 1931, the Central Committee issued a resolution "On the Primary and Middle School," which listed history among basic subjects requiring systematic teaching. Fitzpatrick emphasized that drafters of the resolution were simply listing "basic subjects" that they themselves had learned at school rather than making any political or ideological point.[110] In its resolution in 1932, the Central Committee noted that history programs had not been written, and urged a more historical approach to the teaching of social studies. In 1933, another resolution abolished "journal-textbooks" and directed that regular textbooks be prepared for all basic subjects. A year later, on May 15, 1934, the Central Committee and Council of People's Commissars of the Soviet Union jointly issued a decree "On the Teaching of Civil History in Schools."[111] In a follow-up resolution, the Central Committee recommended: "Chronological historical sequence in the setting out of historical events, firmly fixing in the minds of pupils important historical events, historical personages, and dates." It attacked "abstract sociological schemes" and "abstract definition of socio-economic formations."[112] James Mace commented on the teaching of history in post-genocide Soviet Ukraine:

> In November, 1934, a decree on the teaching of history was published. This decree condemned what had hitherto been the official interpretation of Russian history, that czarist Russia had been an empire which oppressed "its colonies and a new ideology of Soviet patriotism was enunciated, rehabilitating Russian imperial history, czars and all."

In late summer of 1935, a decree, signed by Molotov and Stalin, took school administration out of the hands of Soviet republics, placing it under the control of authorities in Moscow. It ordered curricula and textbooks be standardized throughout the Soviet Union and, from January 1936, a school uniform—identical throughout the Soviet Union—be worn by all children.[113]

This uniformity remained decades later. In her autobiography, Eleanor Roosevelt confided that after her second visit to Soviet Russia in the late 1950s, her observations of the conditioning of children in the Soviet Union troubled and alarmed her. She wrote the Soviet youth were conditioned into "disciplined, amenable citizens, prepared to obey any orders given them and incapable of revolt," and two pages later added: "they have little or no desire for freedom." It was a remarkable achievement of the Soviet educational system seen through the eyes of an outside observer:

> "Their conditioning and training has been carefully thought out to prevent deviation of any kind, on any level, from birth to death. . . . This large-scale conditioning of human beings is something so new in the world that we cannot grasp it."[114]

This large-scale conditioning created a new type of Soviet historian. Often referred to as *Homo Sovieticus*, this human being was modern on the outside but a socio-psychological wreck on the inside, with a traumatized consciousness, dependent on ideological myths fed by Communist Party leaders. Not all Soviet historians were alike; there were conformists and non-conformists, national communists, internal opponents, and, of course, dissidents. The trend toward communization of history and historians started not in 1933, but soon after the Bolshevik reconquest of Ukraine in 1919. Soviet Ukrainian historian Iaroslav Kalakura admitted that the "ideology of vulgar Marxism" and stifling "historical materialism" became tools of the struggle for socialism; they constrained Ukrainian historians and teachers of history. Communist Party loyalty, rather than historical truth, served as the principle of objectivity. This led to distortion of the role of historians as social scientists who use primary sources to reconstruct the past and critique narrative constructions of reality. It turned them into "fighters on the ideological front" or servants of the Communist Party catering to the regime, interpreting and justifying its policies. Characteristics of this history writing system were

(1) reliance on one methodology sanctioned by one political party;
(2) commissioned topics for research;
(3) strict censorship and review of manuscripts at all stages of publication;
(4) centralized history curricula;
(5) selection of cadres based on political rather than academic merit; and
(6) privileges for heads of history departments or institutes equivalent to privileges enjoyed by Communist Party *nomenklatura*.[115]

Although Soviet authorities succeeded in editing the Holodomor out of public memory for as long as the regime lasted, memories persisted in families in Ukraine and beyond its borders in the diaspora. Among Ukrainian diaspora organizations in the United States, the Americans for Human Rights in Ukraine (AHRU) played a pivotal role in supporting human rights and establishing historical truth about the genocidal famine in 1932–1933, when Soviet authorities brutally punished any talk about this topic.[116] The AHRU was behind several legislative initiatives bringing international attention to the persecution and imprisonment of Ukrainian human rights activists and establishing a U.S. Congress Commission on the Ukraine Famine to set a historical record some fifty years after the atrocity. The relevant bill was introduced in 1984.[117] Public Law 99-180 authorized the Commission to gather available information on the famine perpetrated by the Soviets, to analyze its causes and effects on the Ukrainian nation, to study the response of the free world to this atrocity, and to provide an insight into the Soviet system of governance to bring about a realistic approach to dealings with the USSR.[118] In 1987, the first report of the Commission circulated in the United States. After the report was sent to first secretary of the Communist Party of Ukraine, Volodymyr Shcherbyts'kyi, he acknowledged the famine in his speech to a party meeting on the seventieth anniversary of the establishment of Soviet rule in Ukraine.[119] Scholars consider this one of the greatest achievements of the AHRU in that it influenced the Soviet policy and moved Ukraine closer to its eventual independence. Eyewitness testimonies were collected through oral history project interviews with more than 200 survivors willing to testify before the U.S. Commission on the Ukraine Famine. The Commission published its report in April 1988, followed by three volumes of eyewitness accounts in 1990. Suppressed memories have spontaneously resurfaced in postindependence Ukraine, stimulated by writers and testimonies of living survivors and their children.[120]

All individual stories told by witnesses have established a narrative of this traumatic historical event. The experience of trauma has left its traces on people's psyches.[121] Psychological reverberations persisting from generation to generation due to the enforced silence need to be further explored. Another direction for further research is the understudied area of deliberate shortages of food supplies to teachers in rural schools. Diaries and memoirs written by teachers and about teachers, educational periodicals, letters, and works of literature about schools during the 1930s need to be further studied to deepen our understanding of this chapter of history. Statistical data compiled by the Commissariat of Education, especially enrollments in primary schools, need to be systematically examined by demographers as an alternative way of estimating the extent of Holodomor losses in Ukraine. Analyzing the curtailment of the Ukrainization policy beyond the borders of Soviet Ukraine in ethnically Ukrainian settlements in Soviet Russia could dispel the myth of "all-Union" famine and shed light on the eradication of language and culture as a defining characteristic of genocide against Ukrainians.

On November 7, 2015, a new monument was unveiled in Washington, D.C. Written on the monument are the words "Holodomor 1932–1933."[122] As James Mace, executive director of the U.S. Commission on the Ukraine Famine, poignantly noted, "It is a unique term that has arisen from the depths of a victimized nation itself."[123] The bronze rectangular sculpture bears an image of a wheat field; stalks progressively fading away from high relief on the left to no relief on the right, as if all wheat has disappeared. It is a symbol of genocide by forced starvation, masterminded by the Communist Party of the Soviet Union with its sentinel, the security police. Symbolically, in 1969, the design architect of the National Holodomor Memorial Larysa Kurylas was a student in the seventh-grade class in Taras Shevchenko School of Ukrainian Studies in Washington, D.C., and her teacher was Varvara Dibert, the oldest witness to testify before the U.S. Commission on the Ukraine Famine twenty years later.[124]

Ahead of a ribbon-cutting ceremony, in August 2015, a Russian news outlet *Sputnik* launched a disinformation[125] campaign, dismissing the Holodomor as a "hoax" created by neo-Nazis in Ukraine with financial support from the West.[126] After the Revolution of Dignity of 2013–2014, toppling pro-Russian corrupt government of Viktor Yanukovych, the Holodomor has become one of the most critical discursive formations for both Ukrainians and Russians, albeit for different reasons.

Putin's history war has become part of his hybrid war against Ukraine. Although definitions can be imprecise and far from universal, Hans Petter Midttun, the Norwegian Defense Attaché in Ukraine from 2014 to 2018, offered his conceptualization of the Russian hybrid war as the parallel and synchronized use of both military and non-military means in an attempt to weaken and subdue Ukraine from within.[127] War in the information space has become part of a concerted strategy of total war encompassing the use of economic, political, diplomatic, religious, legal, security, cyber, and military instruments.[128]

In Ukraine, a "post-genocidal society,"[129] Putin's interpretation of history ignites traumatic memories of Stalin's extermination by hunger in 1932–1933, when a theory of "unified proto-Russian people" was reestablished, jeopardizing the survival of Ukraine's national historical narrative. For fifteen years, until the early 1930s, Mykhailo Hrushevs'kyi's paradigm of Ukrainian national history and other historical accounts of Russia and Kyïvan Rus', including Marxist historical narratives, "existed side by side."[130] Although historians, like Matvei Liubavskii, embraced the statist approach to all-Russian history, "giving greater prominence to the history of Southwestern Rus'," they had not gone as far as Hrushevs'kyi, who completely separated Ukrainian history from that of Russia.[131] Hrushevs'kyi believed that Russians, Ukrainians, and Belarusians each "deserved a history of their own."[132] Yet, after Stalin consolidated his power and subdued Ukraine, Hrushevs'kyi's interpretation was marginalized and replaced by the canon imposed by Moscow. Soviet disinformation succeeded in hiding the truth from the West about the 1932–1933 famine[133] and in rewriting Hrushevs'kyi's history, emphasizing the friendship between the "brotherly nations," Ukrainians and Russians, who together had fought the "enemies" of the Soviet state. Ukrainian teachers, who embraced Hrushevs'kyi's narrative, and for whom their national Bard and Prophet Taras Shevchenko's verses exemplified the national liberation struggle, were harassed and fired. One such teacher, among many, was Pastushko from Artemivs'k, who was denounced and dismissed as a "follower of 'Ukrainian fascists' (!?) Hrushevs'kyi, Iefremov, and Hermaize."[134]

In commemorating the eighty-fifth anniversary of the Holodomor-genocide in 2018, on the last Saturday of November, then President of Ukraine Petro Poroshenko put historical responsibility for the Holodomor on the Russian Federation as the successor to the former Soviet Union.[135] He announced that he proposed to amend the constitution to make permanent a new direction in Ukraine's foreign policy, affirming that Ukraine would be fully integrated into NATO and the European Union: "there will be no future Holodomor, no Great Purge, [and] no Russification."[136] In response, on the following day, Sunday, November 25, 2018, President Putin ordered an attack on Ukrainian vessels in the Black Sea.[137] This action was not only an act of war, it also violated the Freedom of the Sea as enshrined in international law. Poroshenko appealed to Ukraine's partners, the signatories of the Budapest Memorandum, and EU member states to protect Ukraine.[138] At a press conference, when asked about Russia's commitment to protect Ukraine's sovereignty under the Budapest Memorandum, Russian Foreign Minister Sergei Lavrov changed the subject and suggested that Ukraine's leaders are illegitimate. Lavrov went as far as to call Ukrainian people who stood on barricades of the Euromaidan, in 2013–2014, to preserve their freedom and dignity in the face of the corrupt pro-Russian Yanukovych regime "radical nationalists" and "neo-Nazis."[139]

As Russia has rediscovered a sense of geopolitical self-confidence, lost after the Soviet collapse, such conduct has become increasingly frequent. Putin, who was appointed Prime Minister in August 1999 by then ailing Russian President Boris Yeltsin, rose to power with the orchestrated outbreak of the second war in Chechnya, a prelude to Russia's aggressive tactics in its "near abroad."[140] Russia attacked Georgia in August 2008 behind the smokescreen of the Beijing Olympics, and in March 2014 annexed Crimea in southern Ukraine behind the smokescreen of the Sochi Olympics. Russia's occupation of the Donets′k and Luhans′k regions in eastern Ukraine in April 2014 followed. Cease-fire after cease-fire has been violated, resulting in over 13,000 Ukrainian soldiers and volunteers being killed, and over 2 million people internally displaced as airports, schools, hospitals, and roads were shelled to rubble.[141]

Alongside the war for territory, the war for history has emerged as an important feature of Putin's reign, becoming a symbol of the country's bid to reassert its regional as well as global influence. In February 2020, Russian President Vladimir Putin gave a lengthy interview to the Russian state news agency TASS, in which he shared his views of Ukrainian history.[142] This interview revealed his interpretation of the history of Russian–Ukrainian relations based on the idea of Russians and Ukrainians being "one people," sharing a language and cultural traditions, but who had been artificially separated. Persistence of this understanding of history and the process by which Russian nationalists have subordinated and distorted Ukrainian history, emphasizing the narrative of "unification," have been examined in numerous studies.[143] More recently, scholars have observed a new cycle of militarization in Russia,[144] in the tradition of Peter the Great and Joseph Stalin, which might propel Vladimir the (not so) Great[145] to world leadership and regional dominance, sustaining the Soviet historical narrative glorifying the greatness and the exclusivity of Russians, their language, and culture under a new guise—the "Russian World."[146] Rival historical interpretations are both possible and desirable. However, as Oleksiy Goncharenko noted,

> When history is weaponized by an aggressor as part of an attack on the country, there can be no room for ambiguity. The sooner we acknowledge the role of history within Russia's wider hybrid war against Ukraine, the more effectively we will be able to respond to the challenges this creates.[147]

The challenge for Ukraine is Russia's global daily diet of misinformation, disinformation, and outright lies that seek to undermine Ukraine as a viable political state and exploit tensions to destroy society. In Ukraine, ethnic nationalism might not be strong, but civic identity is increasingly consolidated.[148] The danger is that amid the health crisis caused by the novel coronavirus pandemic, which may further exacerbate the economic crisis, pro-Russian forces in Ukraine might engage in hounding of Holodomor scholars and persecuting participants of the Revolution of Dignity while silencing voices of protest.[149] If the current Ukrainian authorities fail to promote a national historical narrative, a foreign and hostile force will attempt to fill the void with a narrative imposed from outside. "Defeat in the history war will automatically mean the loss of national identity. Ultimately, this will lead to the loss of the country itself," warned Ukrainian lawmaker with the European Solidarity party Oleksiy Goncharenko.[150]

When a resolution by Russia's State Duma refused to recognize the Holodomor as genocide, Aleksandr Solzhenitsyn, the author of *The Gulag Archipelago*[151] and Nobel Prize laureate, backed the official Russian line, dismissing the notion that the famine of 1932–1933 in Soviet Ukraine was a genocide by referring to it as a "fable."[152] Ideologically close to Solzhenitsyn and driven by his vision of Russia as a unique "state civilization," Putin openly takes pride in his past as a *chekist*, restoring the old Soviet political police traditions, methods, and values.[153] Since Russia's annexation of Crimea in 2014, there are signs that a "new GULAG is emerging in Russia slowly and insidiously."[154] To quote Robert Conquest,

> [u]ntil this horrible piece of history is openly exposed and denounced by the successors of Stalin it remains a demonstration of the background against which they made their careers, and of the system as a whole. Until they publicly purge themselves of this guilt, until they break with this horror in their past, they remain not only its heirs, but also its accomplices.[155]

Unfortunately, repentance for the crimes of their predecessors called for by Serhii Holovatyi, Minister of Justice of Ukraine, in a foreword to the *ChK in Ukraine*, goes against the principles of the *chekists*' successors who view it as unnecessary and harmful because it might besmirch their reputation.[156]

Putin is attempting to redefine the world order by imposing his own strategic narrative.[157] This new paradigm has been famously described by the Russian political analyst Lilia Shevtsova as "political schizophrenia" or the Kremlin's Triad: "To be with the West; to be inside the West; and to be against the West." In this way, Moscow is pursuing "an exemplary post-postmodern policy comprised of incompatible elements and blurred lines between principles and norms, war and peace, right and wrong, reality and imitation, ally and enemy, law and lawlessness, and internal and external conflict."[158] The Russian political regime is fighting for its survival, using a hybrid war saturated in deceptions, but has little to offer, except Global Order *a la Russe*.

To counter Russian ideological influence, experts suggest that Ukraine has to put its narrative into a broader international context, highlighting its central role in European history from the days of Kyïvan Rus' to the Ukrainian experience at the epicenter of twentieth-century totalitarianism. This approach will debunk the Russian myth about the "all-Union" famine, as well as other myths emanating from the Soviet era (i.e., Ukraine and Russia being "brotherly nations"). As long as the plunder of Ukraine and the mass killing of Ukraine's citizens by forced starvation in 1932–1933 and deportations go unrecognized by Russia and the international community at large, the risk of further violence remains. To stop the war against Ukraine, Russia and partners in the Normandy Four[159] must live up to their global responsibility and restore justice, letting the Ukrainian nation fulfill its historic mission without coercion from Russia, a member of the U.N. Security Council. In order to secure its future, Ukraine must first win the fight for its past.

Scholars have yet to agree on how to characterize the period from 1921 to 1934: historians refer to it as the "cultural revolution," writers call it the "Executed Renaissance," and lawyers define it as Soviet genocide against Ukrainians.[160] Despite disagreement over the chronological delineation, most scholars gravitate toward the broad rather than narrow definition of the Holodomor as genocide in the 1920s–1930s.[161] Popularized by the writer and civic activist Ivan Drach the term "Holodomor" has been carved into the depths of Ukrainian national memory.[162] Teachers as guardians of the historical memory have had professional and individual responsibilities. A sense of responsibility motivated nonconformity among teachers by focusing on preserving national traditions, rather than serving the regime under heightened pressure to conform, and by teaching their students that truth would prevail.[163] This stance echoes Václav Havel's ideas, expressed in his influential essay, "The Power of the Powerless," written in October 1978, when the revisionist historians challenged the totalitarian paradigm. Havel advised his readers that the potential power in counteracting constant and total manipulation of society by the brutal and arbitrary regime lay in being unafraid to make a moral choice and to live as a responsible individual, "in truth."[164]

NOTES

1. Milan Kundera, *The Book of Laughter and Forgetting* (New York: Alfred A. Knopf, 1980), 3.

2. Liber, *Soviet Nationality Policy*, 170.

3. Victor Rud, "Comments Re: Podcast on the Holodomor at The Pursuit," email message to a group of the Holodomor scholars, February 25, 2020. Victor Rud is a board member of the Ukrainian American Bar Association and chairman of its Committee on Foreign Affairs.

4. Antonovych, "Individual and Collective Intent," 59.

5. Ibid.

6. Ibid.

7. See Orna Ben-Naftali and Miri Sharon, "What the ICJ Did Not Say About the Duty to Punish Genocide," *Journal of International Criminal Justice* 5, no. 4 (2007): 859, 869. The International Court of Justice (ICJ) at The Hague in its opinion of

February 26, 2007, recognized an affirmative obligation to prevent genocide, showing that state has an obligation to prevent genocide under Article I. The Court articulated that "responsibility is not incurred simply because genocide occurs, but rather if the State manifestly failed to take all measures to prevent genocide which were within its power, and which might have contributed to preventing genocide." See International Court of Justice, Press Release No. 2007/8, February 26, 2007, www.icj.cij.org. Thanks to Bohdan A. Futey, Senior Judge of the U.S. Court of Federal Claims in Washington, D.C., for bringing this court decision to my attention (personal communication, November 28, 2020).

8. Smeulers, "Perpetrators of International Crimes," 233–65.

9. Ervin Staub, *The Roots of Evil: The Origins of Genocide and Other Group Violence* (Cambridge: Cambridge University Press, 1989).

10. Max Weber, *Wirtschaft und Gesellschaft: Grundriss der verstehenden Soziologie*, ed. Marianne Weber (Tübingen: Mohr, 1922; 5th ed., ed. Johannes Winckelmann, 1980), 531–40.

11. Hennadii Iefimenko, "Kozhnomu – za vyznachenymy partiieiu potrebamy. Iak bil′shovyky maizhe pobuduvaly komunizm," *Dilova stolytsya*, February 28, 2021, https://www.dsnews.ua/ukr/nasha_revolyutsiya_1917/kozhnomu-za-vizna che nimi-partiyeyu-potrebami-yak-bilshoviki-mayzhe-pobuduvali-komunizm-28022021 -417232.

12. Dmitrii Volkogonov, *Lenin: Politicheskii portret*, 2 vols., vol. 1 (Moscow: Novosti, 1994), 186.

13. Grossman, *Forever Flowing*, 74.

14. Ibid.

15. Ibid., 227.

16. Ibid., 228–29.

17. Ibid., 229–30.

18. Ibid., 230.

19. Kołakowski, "The Marxist Roots of Stalinism," 156–76.

20. Smeulers, "Perpetrators of International Crimes," 244.

21. Ibid., 245.

22. *International Commission of Inquiry into the 1932–33 Famine in Ukraine: The Final Report* (Stockholm: Stockholm Institute of Public and International Law, No. 109, 1990). The text of the report is available at https://web.archive.org/web/20081001225745/http://www.ukrainianworldcongress.org/Holodomor/Holodomor -Commission.pdf. See also "International Commission of Inquiry," in *Holodomor*, eds. Luciuk and Grekul, 315.

23. Ibid., 330.

24. Conquest, *The Harvest of Sorrow*, 329–30; *Report to Congress*, 34–35; Liber, *Soviet Nationality Policy*, 166.

25. Barbara B. Green, "Stalinist Terror and the Question of Genocide: The Great Famine," in *Is the Holocaust Unique? Perspectives on Comparative Genocide*, ed. and with an Introduction by Alan S. Rosenbaum with a Foreword by Israel W. Charny (Boulder: Westview Press, 1996), 194.

26. Ammende, 144–45; quoted in *Holodomor*, eds. Luciuk and Grekul, 320.

27. Kolasky, *Education in Soviet Ukraine*, 19.
28. Liber, *Soviet Nationality Policy*, 170.
29. P. P. Postyshev, *Borot'ba za Lenins'ko-Stalins'ku natsional'nu polityku partiï* (Kyïv: Derzhavne vyd-vo Ukraïny, 1935), 64–65.
30. President's Separate Opinion: Professor Jacob Sundberg, "International Commission on Inquiry into the 1932–33 Famine in Ukraine," in *Holodomor*, eds. Luciuk and Grekul, 322.
31. *Chervonyi shliakh* (Kharkiv), nos. 2–3, 1934; quoted in Hryshko, *The Ukrainian holocaust of 1933*, 13; see also *Holodomor*, eds. Luciuk and Grekul, 320.
32. Mace, 66; quoted in *Holodomor*, eds. Luciuk and Grekul, 321.
33. Iefimenko, "Sotsial'ne oblychchia vchytel'stva," 150.
34. *TsDAVOU*, f. 2717, op. 2, spr. 1673, ark. 21.
35. Arkhivni naukovi fondy rukopysiv ta fonozapysiv Instytutu mystetstvoznavstva, folklorystyky ta etnolohiï im. M. Ryl's'koho NAN Ukraïny, fond M. K. Serhiiva, chlena Spilky voiovnychykh bezvirnykiv, f. 30, od. zb. 124, ark. 1 zv.–5.
36. *TsDAVOU*, f. 2717, op. 2, spr. 1689, ark. 11–12.
37. *TsDAVOU*, f. 2717, op. 3, spr. 1689, ark. 15.
38. Kas'ianov, "Ukraïns'ka intelihentsiia v 1933 r.," 98.
39. Mattingly, "[Extra]ordinary Women," 64.
40. Mace, 300; quoted in *Holodomor*, eds. Luciuk and Grekul, 321.
41. Vsevolod Holubnychyi, "History of the Ukrainian Soviet Socialist Republic, 1917–1941," in *Ukraine: A Concise Encyclopedia*, ed. Volodymyr Kubijovyč (Toronto: published for the Ukrainian National Association by University of Toronto Press, 1963–1971, 2 vols.), vol. 1, 818; Liber, *Soviet Nationality Policy*, 171.
42. Liber, *Soviet Nationality Policy*, 171.
43. M. N. Leshchenko, *Klasova borot'ba v ukraïns'komu seli na pochatku XX stolittia* (Kyïv: Politvydav Ukraïny, 1968), 33; Liber, *Soviet Nationality Policy*, 11.
44. B. D. Lanovyk, M. V. Traf'iak, R. M. Mateiko, and Z. M. Matysiakevych, *Ukraïns'ka emihratsiia vid mynuvshyny do s'iohodennia* (Ternopil': Charivnytsia, 1999), 291.
45. I. K. Vologodtsev, *Osobennosti razvitiia gorodov Ukrainy* (Kharkov: Derzhvydav "Gosp-vo Ukrainy," 1930), 49, 51; Liber, *Soviet Nationality Policy*, 11.
46. Thomas S. Fedor, *Patterns of Urban Growth in the Russian Empire during the Nineteenth Century* (Chicago: University of Chicago, Department of Geography Research Paper No. 163, 1975), 40; Liber, *Soviet Nationality Policy*, 12.
47. Lanovyk, Traf'iak, Mateiko, and Matysiakevych, *Ukraïns'ka emihratsiia*, 291–92.
48. Liber, *Soviet Nationality Policy*, 15.
49. Mykola Porsh, "Robitnytstvo Ukraïny: Narys po statystytsi pratsi," *Zapysky Ukraïns'koho naukovoho tovarystva v Kyïvi*, no. 12 (1913): 134–35.
50. Andrew C. Janos, "Ethnicity, Communism, and Political Change in Eastern Europe," *World Politics* 23, no. 3 (1971): 505; Liber, *Soviet Nationality Policy*, 173–74.
51. Janos, "Ethnicity, Communism, and Political Change in Eastern Europe," 519; Liber, *Soviet Nationality Policy*, 174.

52. Chukhin, *Kanalo-armeitsy*, 209–12.

53. Peter Kardash, *Genocide in Ukraine*, trans. Daria Myrna (Melbourne: Fortuna Publishing, 2007), 8.

54. See *Nuremberg Trial Proceedings*, vol. 1, Charter of the International Military Tribunal, The Avalon Project: Documents in Law, History and Diplomacy, Lillian Goldman Law Library, Yale Law School, 2008, https://avalon.law.yale.edu/imt/imtconst.asp#art6.

55. Kardash, *Genocide in Ukraine*, 12.

56. James E. Mace, "Is the Ukrainian Genocide a Myth?" in *Holodomor: Reflections on the Great Famine of 1932–1933 in Soviet Ukraine*, eds. Lubomyr Y. Luciuk and Lisa Grekul (Kingston: Kashtan Press, 2008), 55.

57. Report by the Kharkiv Consulate Royal Consul, Sergio Gradenigo, May 31, 1933, "Re: The Famine and the Ukrainian Question," in *Report to Congress*, 424–25, 427; original text in *Lettere da Kharkov*, ed. Graziosi, 168–74; quoted in *The Holodomor Reader*, eds. Klid and Motyl, 280.

58. Report by the Kharkiv Consulate Royal Consul, Sergio Gradenigo, July 19, 1933, "Re: After the Suicide of Mykola Skrypnyk," in *Report to Congress*, 446–47; quoted in *The Holodomor Reader*, eds. Klid and Motyl, 282.

59. "Letter from the Royal Consul General in Odesa to the Italian Ambassador in Moscow, 19 February 1934," in *Report to Congress*, 475; quoted in *The Holodomor Reader*, eds. Klid and Motyl, 283.

60. German Consulate, Kyïv, May 1936, "Bericht auf Grund von persönlichen Eindrücken bei einer mehrwöchigen Reise durch die Ukraine: Ukrainische Ukraine?," in *Holodomor v Ukraïni 1932–1933 rokiv za dokumentamy politychnoho arkhivu Ministerstva zakordonnykh sprav Federatyvnoï Respubliky Nimechchyny*, ed. A. I. Kudriachenko (Kyïv: Natsional′nyi instytut stratehichnykh doslidzhen′, 2008), 326–28; quoted in *The Holodomor Reader*, eds. Klid and Motyl, 277.

61. Ibid., 278.

62. German Consulate, Kyïv, January 15, 1934, "Politischer Jahresbericht 1933," in *Holodomor v Ukraïni 1932–1933 rokiv*, ed. Kudriachenko, 172–82, 187–88; quoted in *The Holodomor Reader*, eds. Klid and Motyl, 275.

63. Ibid., 276.

64. Ibid.

65. Mendel Osherowitch, "The Fear of the *GPU* Across the Country," in *How People Live in Soviet Russia: Impressions from a Journey*, ed. Lubomyr Y. Luciuk, trans. Sharon Power (Toronto: University of Toronto Chair of Ukrainian Studies and The Kashtan Press, 2020), 187–96.

66. *Holodomor*, eds. Luciuk and Grekul, 322.

67. Liber, *Soviet Nationality Policy*, 170.

68. Oksana Kis, "Defying Death: Women's Experiences of the Holodomor, 1932–1933," *Aspasia*, no. 7 (2013): 42–67.

69. O. Pakhl′ovs′ka, "Maty i antykhryst: vidlunnia holodomoru v literaturi," *Urok ukraïns′koï*, no. 1 (2004): 36–38. See also Oksana Kis, "Women's Experience of the Holodomor: Challenges and Ambiguities of Motherhood," *Journal of Genocide Research*, October 23, 2020, https://doi.org/10.1080/14623528.2020.1834713.

70. Margaret Kelleher, "Woman as Famine Victim: The Figure of Woman in Irish Famine Narratives," in *Gender and Catastrophe*, ed. Ronit Lentin (London: Zed Books, 1997), 241–54; David Fitzpatrick, "Women and the Great Famine," in *Gender Perspectives in Nineteenth-Century Ireland: Public and Private Spheres*, eds. Margaret Kelleher and James H. Murphy (Dublin: Irish Academic Press, 1997), 50–69.

71. Vasyl' Marochko, "Kanibalizm v roky Holodomoru," in *Holod 1932–33 rokiv v Ukraïni: prychyny ta naslidky*, eds. Valerii Smolii et al. (Kyïv: Naukova dumka, 2003), 568–75. See also Snyder, *Bloodlands*, 62–64.

72. Artem Kharchenko, "'. . . potribni bil'sh kvalifikovani robitnyky': kolektyvnyi portret personalu syrotyntsiv naperedodni Holodomoru," *Ukraïna moderna*, January 5, 2019, https://uamoderna.com/md/kharchenko-orphans.

73. Kis, "Defying Death," 55–56; idem, "Women's Experiences of the Holodomor," 12–16.

74. Oleksandr Udod, "Istoriia povsiakdennosti iak skladova istoriï Ukraïny XX st.," *Istoriia ta pravoznavstvo*, nos. 19–21 (2007): 105.

75. *Convention on the Prevention and Punishment of the Crime of Genocide*, 280.

76. Chukhin, *Kanalo-armeitsy*, 219.

77. Known as case No. 877, the investigation found the following to be guilty of "criminal deviation in class approach to correctional policy of the Soviet government": (1) Igor Kurilko, (2) Konstantin Belozerov, (3) Abram Shreider, (4) Vladimir Goncharov, (5) Sergei Belykh, (6) Kuzma Rzhevsky, (7) Valentin Brainin, (8) Aleksander Maisuradzhe, (9) Timofei Gnipp, (10) Leonid Khoruzhik, (11) Wilhelm Kanep, and (12) Aleksander Zubov. See Chukhin, *Kanalo-armeitsy*, 231.

78. Chukhin, *Kanalo-armeitsy*, 232–33.

79. Ibid., 235–37.

80. Ibid., 238.

81. Ibid., 211.

82. Conquest, *The Harvest of Sorrow*, 288.

83. Lidia Kovalenko and Volodymyr Maniak, eds., *33-i holod: Narodna Knyha-Memorial* (Kyïv: Radians'kyi pys'mennyk, 1991), 212–13.

84. Olesia Stasiuk, "Donosy, kradizhky, samosudy v roky Holodomoru iak naslidok represyvnoï polityky," in *Holodomor 1932–1933 rokiv: Vtraty ukraïns'koï natsiï. Materialy mizhnarodnoï naukovo-praktychnoï konferentsiï, Kyïv, 4 zhovtnia 2016*, eds. Olesia Stasiuk et al. (Kyïv: Vyd. Oleh Filiuk, 2017), 178.

85. Svidchennia T. S. Lytveniuk (born 1922), Pryburivka village, Lypovets'kyi district, Vinnytsia region, and Iu. F. Berezny (born 1933), Brovky Pershi village, Andrushivs'kyi district, Zhytomyr region, in Arkhiv Natsional'noho muzeiu "Memorial zhertv Holodomoru"; quoted in Stasiuk, "Donosy, kradizhky, samosudy," 176, 178.

86. Solovey, *Golgota Ukraïny*, 169.

87. Stepan Drovoziuk, "Vysvitlennia dukhovnykh aspektiv henotsydu 1932–1933 rr. v ukraïns'kii istoriohrafiï," in *Henotsyd ukraïns'koho narodu: istorychna pam'iat' ta polityko-pravova otsinka: Mizhnarodna naukovo-teoretychna konferentsiia, Kyïv*,

25 lystopada 2000 r., eds. V. A. Smolii et al. (Kyïv–New York: Vyd-vo M. P. Kots', 2003), 300.

88. Boriak, *Sources*, 27.

89. Ibid., 14.

90. Olga Bertelsen, "Women at Sites of Mass Starvation: Ukraine, 1932–1933," in *Women and the Holodomor-Genocide: Victims, Survivors, Perpetrators*, ed. Victoria A. Malko (Fresno: The Press at California State University, 2019), 36.

91. Ancel Keys, Josef Brožek, Austin Henschel, Olaf Mickelsen, and Henry Longstreet Taylor, *The Biology of Human Starvation*, 2 vols. (Minneapolis: University of Minnesota Press, 1950). Conquest also pointed out to cannibalism as a manifestation of mental disorders caused by starvation. See Conquest, *The Harvest of Sorrow*, 257–58.

92. Sorokin, *Man and Society in Calamity*, 29.

93. Olga Bertelsen, "'Hyphenated' Identities during the Holodomor: Women and Cannibalism," in *Women and Genocide: Survivors, Victims, Perpetrators*, eds. Elissa Bemporad and Joyce W. Warren (Bloomington: Indiana University Press, 2018), 77–96.

94. N. A. Berdiaev, "O rabstve i svobode cheloveka: Opyt personalisticheskoi filosofii," *Biblioteka "Vekhi,"* 2001, http://www.vehi.net/berdyaev/rabstvo/012.html.

95. Bertelsen, "Women at Sites of Mass Starvation," 37.

96. Gregory Bateson, *Steps to an Ecology of Mind* (New York: Ballantine Books, 1972), 206–10; quoted in Bertelsen, "Women at Sites of Mass Starvation," 42–43.

97. Personal communication with Dr. Lubow Jowa, daughter of Holodomor survivors, and president of the Ukrainian Heritage Club of Northern California. Together with her late father, Dr. Jowa played a crucial role in activities of the Americans for Human Rights in Ukraine (AHRU) in support of human rights movement in the Ukrainian SSR.

98. Bertelsen, "Women at Sites of Mass Starvation," 45.

99. Vitalii Ohienko, "Posttravmatychnyi stresovyi syndrom i kolektyvna travma v osobystykh naratyvakh svidkiv Holodomoru," *Ukraïna moderna*, April 6, 2018, http://uamoderna.com/md/ogienko-holodomor-trauma.

100. Iryna Reva, *Po toi bik sebe: sotsial'no-psykholohichni i kul'turni naslidky Holodomoru ta stalins'kykh represii* (Dnipropetrovs'k: A. L. Svidler, 2013).

101. Andrii Bondarchuk, "'Stokhol'ms'kyi syndrom' iak kintseva meta totalitarnoho rezhymu: vid vytokiv do suchasnosti," *Litopys Volyni*, no. 20 (2019): 55–64, http://www.litopys.volyn.ua/index.php/litopys/article/view/153.

102. Vitalii Ohienko, "Holodomor ochyma zhertvy: immobilizatsiia ta upokorennia pratseiu iak stratehiia vyzhyvannia," *Ukraïna Moderna*, January 20, 2020, http://uamoderna.com/md/ogienko-holodomor.

103. Anastasiia Lysyvets', *"Skazhy pro shchaslyve zhyttia . . ."* (Kyïv: KIS, 2019).

104. Stanislav (Taras) Mel'nyk (b. 1929, Kyïv, Ukraine), personal communication, July 15, 2019. In 1933, he was only four years old, when his starving mother, jeopardizing their own lives, sent her child to crawl to steal grain from a state stockpile, located in the vicinity of a railway station in Luk'ianivka. Given his young age

at the time of the event, his memories could be shaped by stories of his mother. After World War II, he was mobilized to serve in the Soviet army. He recalled that soldiers were always hungry and often violated the leave of absence policy to procure bread. The Communist Party recruited cadres aggressively, especially in the army. After his service in the army, he inherited his father's tailor shop. All his life until retirement, he worked as a tailor in a special atelier "Kommunar," a designer bureau for dressing up Ukrainian Communist Party and government officials and members of their families. He headed workers' union and stood in defense of workers' rights. In his last conversation with the author, Stanislav Mel'nyk emphasized that the key to understanding the Soviet food policy was the system of privileges and food rations created by Lenin to feed Bolsheviks. The system had been in place until the collapse of the Soviet Union. It is the system of perks and privileges that the ruling elite of the former Soviet Union cherished the most because they had instant access to delicacies and products that were out of reach to the masses of workers.

105. Conquest, *The Harvest of Sorrow*, 28.

106. Natan P. F. Kellermann, "Epigenetic Transmission of Holocaust Trauma: Can Nightmares Be Inherited," *The Israel Journal of Psychiatry and Related Sciences* 50, no. 1 (2013): 33–39; Kelly Skelton et al., "PTSD and Gene Variants: New Pathways and New Thinking," *Neuropharmacology* 62, no. 2 (2012): 628–37.

107. Brent John Louis Bezo, "The Impact of Intergenerational Transmission of Trauma from the Holodomor Genocide of 1932–1933 in Ukraine" (doctoral diss., Carleton University, 2011); Brent Bezo and Stefania Maggi, "The Intergenerational Impact of the Holodomor Genocide on Gender Roles, Expectations and Performance: The Ukrainian Experience," *Annals of Psychiatry and Mental Health* 3, no. 3 (2015): 1–4; Brent Bezo and Stefania Maggi, "Living in 'Survival Mode': Intergenerational Transmission of Trauma from the Holodomor Genocide of 1932–1933 in Ukraine," *Social Science & Medicine*, no. 134 (2015): 87–94.

108. Viktoriia Gorbunova and Vitalii Klymchuk, "The Psychological Consequences of the Holodomor in Ukraine," *East/West: Journal of Ukrainian Studies* 7, no. 2 (2020): 33–68.

109. Nicholas S. Timasheff, *The Great Retreat: The Growth and Decline of Communism in Russia* (New York: E. P. Dutton & Company, Inc., 1946), 165.

110. Fitzpatrick, *Education and Social Mobility in the Soviet Union*, 230–31.

111. *Narodnoe obrazovanie v SSSR*, 166–67; quoted in Fitzpatrick, *Education and Social Mobility in the Soviet Union*, 231.

112. Fitzpatrick, *Education and Social Mobility in the Soviet Union*, 231.

113. Ammende, 144, note 1; quoted in *Holodomor*, eds. Luciuk and Grekul, 322.

114. Roosevelt, *Autobiography*, 389, 391–92.

115. Iaroslav Kalakura, "Kompleks 'sovkovosti' postradians'koï istoriohrafiï," *Ukraïna – Ievropa – Svit: Mizhnarodnyi zbirnyk naukovykh prats'* (Ternopil': Vyd-vo TNPU named after V. Hnatiuk, 2015), vol. 2, 163–74.

116. For more on the history of the organization, see Tetiana Perga, "Role of Americans for Human Rights in Ukraine in the Support of Human Rights Movement in Ukrainian SSR," *American History and Politics*, no. 5 (2018): 63–71.

117. Ihor Olshaniwsky, head of the AHRU, studied documents of the U.S. Congressional Commission on the Jewish Holocaust and proposed to create an identical commission primarily for research on the Ukrainian famine. New Jersey Congressman James J. Florio and Senator Bill Bradley supported the idea. However, when Florio introduced the bill in 1984, Democratic Party leaders in the House did not agree to submit the bill for consideration, arguing that American taxpayers' money should not be spent on something that happened decades ago. Ukrainian grassroots organizations sent thousands of individual and collective petitions to the White House, Congressional committees and subcommittees, and the House of Representatives. The eventual passage of the bill in the Senate Foreign Affairs Committee was in large part due to personal influence of Dr. Myron Kuropas, deputy head of the AHRU. See "Four to Testify at Senate Hearings on Famine Commission Measure," *Ukrainian Weekly*, July 29, 1984, 1; Perga, "Role of Americans for Human Rights in Ukraine," 67–68.

118. "Bill to Establish a Commission to Study the 1932–1933 Famine Caused by the Soviet Government in Ukraine (H.R. 4459 in the House of Representatives, S. 2456 in the Senate)," *Ukrainian Weekly*, April 1, 1984, http://www.ukrweekly.com/old/archive/1984/148419.shtml.

119. "Shcherbytsky Says Famine Was a Result of Collectivization of Soviet Agriculture," *Ukrainian Weekly*, January 10, 1988, http://www.ukrweekly.com/old/archive/1988/028801.shtml; Stanislav Kulchytsky, "James Mace's Role in Exposing Stalin's Greatest Crime," *Day*, June 15, 2004, https://day.kyiv.ua/en/article/history-and-i/james-maces-role-exposing-stalins-greatest-crime.

120. In 2017, the Holodomor Research and Education Center (HREC) in Ukraine initiated a "Holodomor Family History Global Database" project with the goal to create the world's largest online source of stories of individual people and entire families—Ukrainians, Poles, Jews, Greeks, Russians, Germans, Bulgarians, and others—before, during, and after the Holodomor of 1932–1933 in the Ukrainian SSR. Coordinators of the project are ethnologist and journalist Iaroslava Muzychenko and collector of Holodomor victim testimonies Vira Annusova of Luhans′k. The electronic database has over 3,000 testimonies from family archives and small print-run scholarly publications. Access to the resource was scheduled to open on the eve of the eighty-fifth anniversary of the Holodomor on the portal HREC in Ukraine. See "HREC in Ukraine," *Ukrinform*, April 27, 2018, https://www.ukrinform.net/rubric-society/2450243-we-will-preserve-the-memory-of-the-holodomorgenocide-and-the-fates-of-our-families-and-bring-life-stories-to-the-world-that-will-inspire-people-in-the-future.html.

121. Oksana Kis′, "Kolektyvna pam'iat′ ta istorychna travma: teoretychni refleksiï na tli zhinochykh spohadiv pro Holodomor," in *U poshukakh vlasnoho holosu: Usna istoriia iak teoriia, metod, dzherelo*, eds. Helinada Hrinchenko and Nataliia Khanenko-Friezen (Kharkiv: Skhidnyi Instytut Ukraïnoznavstva im. Koval′s′kykh, 2010), 180–91.

122. Located at the intersection of North Capitol Street, Massachusetts Avenue, and F Streets N.W., the memorial was designed by Larysa Kurylas and built by the National Park Service and the Ukrainian government to honor the victims of

the genocidal famine in Ukraine and educate the American public. See Deborah K. Dietsch, "Local Architect Designs Washington Memorial to Victims of Genocidal Famine in Ukraine," *Washington Post*, July 24, 2014; and "Holodomor Memorial Presented in Washington," *UNIAN*, August 5, 2015, https://www.unian.info/world/1108244-holodomor-memorial-presented-in-washington.html.

123. Mace, "Is the Ukrainian Genocide a Myth?," in *Holodomor*, eds. Luciuk and Grekul, 57.

124. Larysa Kurylas, "With Gratitude to the Sisterhood: Reflections on the Creation of the National Holodomor Memorial," *Our Life* (published by UNWLA), November 2020, 20–21.

125. Ladislav Bittman, *The KGB and Soviet Disinformation: An Insider's View* (Washington: Pergamon-Brassey's International Defense Publishers, 1985) and Martin J. Manning and Herbert Romerstein, "Disinformation," *Historical Dictionary of American Propaganda* (Westwood: Greenwood Press, 2004).

126. Ekaterina Blinova, "Holodomor Hoax: Joseph Stalin's Crime That Never Took Place," *Sputnik News*, August 9, 2015, http://sputniknews.com/politics/20150809/1025560345.html#ixzz3iXdnBIyY.

127. Hans Petter Midttun, "Hybrid War in Ukraine – Predictions for 2019 and Beyond," *Euromaidan Press*, April 18, 2019, http://euromaidanpress.com/2019/04/18/hybrid-war-in-ukraine-predictions-for-2019-and-beyond/.

128. Janis Berzins, "Russia's New Generation Warfare in Ukraine: Implications for Latvian Defense Policy" (report from the National Defence Academy of Latvia and the Center for Security and Strategic Research), *Informal Institute for National Security Thinkers and Practitioners Blog*, April 30, 2014, http://maxoki161.blogspot.com/2014/04/russias-new-generation-warfare-in.html.

129. Mace, "Is the Ukrainian Genocide a Myth?," 57.

130. For a discussion about pre- and post-revolution Russian historical writings, see Plokhy, *Unmaking Imperial Russia*, 346; Panteleimon Kovaliv, *Vstup do istorii skhidn'ioslov'ians'kykh mov* (New York: Shevchenko Scientific Society, 1970), 24–25.

131. Plokhy, *Unmaking Imperial Russia*, 106.

132. Ibid.

133. Taras Kuzio and Paul D'Anieri, "The Soviet Origins of Russian Hybrid Warfare," *E-International Relations*, June 17, 2018, https://www.e-ir.info/2018/06/17/the-soviet-origins-of-russian-hybrid-warfare/.

134. Iurii Mytsyk, "Chystky natsionalistiv u shkolakh 1934 r. (za materialamy kolyshn'oho Dnipropetrovs'koho oblasnoho partarkhivu)," in *Ukraïns'kyi holokost*, ed. Mytsyk, vol. 3, 260.

135. "Poroshenko Blames Russia as USSR Successor for 1930s Famine," *Interfax-Ukraine*, November 24, 2018, https://en.interfax.com.ua/news/general/547761.html.

136. "Poroshenko: Istorychna vidpovidal'nist' za Holodomor – na Rosiis'kii Federatsiï," *Ukraïns'ka Pravda*, November 24, 2018, https://www.pravda.com.ua/ukr/news/2018/11/24/7199187/index.amp.

137. Alex Johnson, "Russia Attacks, Seizes Ukrainian Vessels in Black Sea off Crimea," *NBC News*, November 25, 2018, https://www.nbcnews.com/storyline/ukraine-crisis/russia-attacks-seizes-three-ukrainian-naval-vessels-coast-crimea-black-n939876.

138. The Budapest Memorandum on Security Assurances was signed on December 5, 1994 by the Russian Federation, the United Kingdom, and the United States, guaranteeing Ukraine's sovereignty in return for dismantling its nuclear arsenal. Neither the Russian Federation nor the United Kingdom have recognized the Holodomor as genocide.

139. "Foreign Minister Sergey Lavrov's Remarks and Answers to Media Questions at a News Conference," *Ministry of Foreign Affairs of the Russian Federation*, November 26, 2018, https://www.mid.ru/en/press_service/minister_speeches/-/asset_publisher/7OvQR5KJWVmR/content/id/3420700.

140. Victoria A. Malko, *The Chechen Wars: Responses in Russia and the United States* (Saarbrücken: Lambert Academic Publishing, 2015), v.

141. Catherine Wanner, "Commemoration and the New Frontiers of War in Ukraine," *Slavic Review* 78, no. 2 (2019): 329.

142. See Andrei Vandenko's video interview with President Vladimir Putin, "20 Questions with Vladimir Putin: Putin on Ukraine," *TASS*, February 20, 2020, https://www.youtube.com/watch?v=NG6dxqwxGE4.

143. Among others, see Serguei Ekeltchik, "History, Culture, and Nationhood under High Stalinism: Soviet Ukraine, 1939–1954" (thesis, University of Alberta, 2000), 30–31; Konstantin Sheiko and Stephen Brown, *History as Therapy: Alternative History and Nationalist Imaginings in Russia, 1991–2014* (Stuttgart: *ibidem*-Verlag, 2014). One of the first attempts to remedy Soviet and Russian nationalist historiographical deformations was undertaken in 1981 in the West: see Ivan L. Rudnytsky, ed. (with the assistance of John-Paul Himka), *Rethinking Ukrainian History* (Edmonton: University of Alberta, Canadian Institute of Ukrainian Studies, 1981).

144. See interview with Igor Kliamkin on cycles of militarization and demilitarization in Russian history in Irina Chechel and Aleksandr Markov, "Zatukhaiushchaia tsyklichnost'," *Gefter*, November 6, 2012, http://gefter.ru/archive/6660.

145. Leon Aron, "Vladimir the (not so) Great," *Wall Street Journal*, May 31–June 1, 2014, C1.

146. Kuzio, "Putin Forever."

147. Oleksiy Goncharenko, "Ukraine Cannot Stay Neutral in Putin's History War," *Atlantic Council*, April 21, 2020, https://atlanticcouncil.org/blogs/ukrainealert/ukraine-cannot-stay-neutral-in-putins-history-war/.

148. Hans Petter Midttun, "What If Russia Wins in Ukraine? Consequences of Hybrid War for Europe (Part 2)," *Euromaidan Press*, May 22, 2020, http://euromaidanpress.com/2020/05/22/what-if-russia-wins-in-ukraine-consequences-of-hybrid-war-for-europe-part-2/.

149. In April 2020, the State Bureau of Investigation summoned Volodymyr V'iatrovych, the former director of the Ukrainian Institute of National Remembrance, and charged him with "abuse of power" (conviction carries with it a term of five

to eight years of imprisonment) and "embezzlement of state funds" for organizing a scholarly forum. The International Forum "Ukraine Remembers! World Acknowledges!" was held in November 2018. It brought scholars from fifty countries to the scholarly meeting which raised international awareness about the Holodomor. Criminal charges were also brought against ex-President Poroshenko. The most extraordinary of charges was "action aimed at the violent change or overthrow of the constitutional order or seizing of state power" (Article 109 paragraphs 1, 2 of Ukraine's Criminal Code). The number of criminal investigations against the previous administration, known for its pro-Western stance, has been on the rise. These developments prompted participants of the Revolution of Dignity to publish an open letter warning that under neglect of the authorities, "the pro-Russian forces and agents of the Kremlin" in Ukraine have engaged in revisions of the national historical narrative." The signatories of the letter—some 200 individuals and a dozen organizations—raised their concern that Ukraine's European orientation and chances of EU membership may come to naught. They demanded that the avalanche of fabricated criminal cases against the leaders of the Revolution of Dignity and defenders of Ukraine's freedom cease. See "Zvernennia uchasnykiv Revoliutsiï Hidnosti proty revanshu," *Tyzhden'*, May 6, 2020, https://m.tyzhden.ua/Politics/243374.

150. Goncharenko, "Ukraine Cannot Stay Neutral in Putin's History War."

151. *The Gulag Archipelago: An Experiment in Literary Investigation*, a three-volume, non-fiction text written between 1958 and 1968, was first published in 1973 in the West, followed by an English translation in 1974.

152. Aleksandr Solzhenitsyn, "Possorit' rodnye narody??," *Izvestiia*, April 2, 2008, 2.

153. Julie Fedor, *Russia and the Cult of State Security* (New York: Routledge, 2011), 119.

154. Paul Goble, "A New GULAG Is Emerging Just as Stalin's Did Slowly and Insidiously, Gudkov Warns," *Euromaidan Press*, August 17, 2018, http://euromaidanpress.com/2018/08/17/a-new-gulag-is-emerging-just-as-stalins-did-slowly-and-insidiously-gudkov-warns/; on the consistency of Solzhenitsyn's and Putin's views vis-à-vis Russia and Ukraine, see Taras Kuzio, "Disinformation: Soviet Origins of Contemporary Russian Ukrainophobia," in *Russian Active Measures: Yesterday, Today, Tomorrow*, ed. Olga Bertelsen (Stuttgart and New York: *ibidem*-Verlag and Columbia University Press, 2021), 137–75.

155. Conquest, *Kolyma*, 231.

156. Bertelsen, "A Trial *in Absentia*," 64.

157. Douglas E. Schoen and Evan Roth Smith, *Putin's Master Plan to Destroy Europe, Divide NATO, and Restore Russian Power and Global Influence* (New York: Encounter Books, 2016).

158. Lilia Shevtsova, "The Kremlin's Triad as the Means of Survival," *The American Interest*, April 19, 2016, https://www.the-american-interest.com/2016/04/19/the-kremlins-triad-as-the-means-of-survival/.

159. The Normandy Four is a consultative body of the foreign affairs ministers of Ukraine, Germany, France, and Russia. In October 2019, the Bundestag refused to

recognize the Holodomor as genocide, leaving many convinced that economic profits from the German-Russian joint venture of Nord Stream 2 pipeline traversing the Baltic Sea had taken precedence over the human rights and historical justice.

160. Fitzpatrick, *Education and Social Mobility in the Soviet Union*, 116; Michael David-Fox, "What Is Cultural Revolution?" *The Russian Review* 58, no. 2 (1999): 181–201; Iurii Lavrinenko, *Rozstriliane vidrodzhennia: Antolohiia, 1917–1933* (Kyïv: Smoloskyp, 2004); Lemkin, "Soviet Genocide in the Ukraine," 1–8.

161. "Holodomor in the Context of Genocide: A Narrow vs Broad Definition of Genocide," 3, 9. A summary of survey findings was distributed by Lana Babij via email to members of the Holodomor Educators Network on October 19, 2019.

162. Olga Andriewsky, "Toward a Decentered History: The Study of the Holodomor and Ukrainian Historiography," in *Contextualizing the Holodomor: The Impact of Thirty Years of Ukrainian Famine Studies*, eds. Andrij Makuch and Frank E. Sysyn (Edmonton: Canadian Institute of Ukrainian Studies Press, 2015), 15.

163. Personal communication with Vira Annusova (b. 1956), a school teacher from the village Baranykivka, Bilovods'k district, Luhans'k region, Ukraine, November 20, 2019.

164. Václav Havel, "The Power of the Powerless" (Essay), October 1978, 21. First published in the *International Journal of Politics* in 1979; available from the International Center on Nonviolent Conflict at https://www.nonviolent-conflict.org/resource/the-power-of-the-powerless/.

Biographical Sketches and Terminology

The content for these biographical sketches and definitions of key terms are drawn mostly from Volodymyr Kubijovyč, ed., *Entsyklopediia ukraïnoznavstva*, vols. 1–8 (Paris; New York: Vyd-vo "Molode zhyttia," 1955–1976) and the English translation of these entries in the *Internet Encyclopedia of Ukraine*, hosted by the Canadian Institute of Ukrainian Studies (2001), http://www.encyclopediaofukraine.com/. Terms specific to the Holodomor-genocide are drawn from authoritative and recently completed references: Vasyl' Marochko's *Entsyklopediia Holodomoru 1932–1933 rokiv v Ukraïni* (Drohobych: "Kolo," 2018) and *Holodomor-henotsyd: terminolohiia* (Kyïv: Natsional'nyi muzei Holodomoru-henotsydu, 2019). Other specialized reference sources include *A Dictionary of Scientific Communism* (Moscow: Progress Publishers, 1984); Stanislav Kulchytsky, *The Famine of 1932–1933 in Ukraine: An Anatomy of the Holodomor*, trans. Ali Kinsella (Edmonton: Canadian Institute of Ukrainian Studies, 2018), 149–60; and Matthew D. Pauly, *Breaking the Tongue: Language, Education, and Power in Soviet Ukraine, 1923–1934* (Toronto: University of Toronto Press, 2014), 349–57.

ahitatsiia, or agitation (from Latin *agitatus*, to stir up public feeling), is a political activity, which uses all possible channels of information in order to influence the population behavior.

Agitprop, or agitation and propaganda departments, were tools of the Communist Party to control the minds of the population in the Soviet Union.

aktyv is a term used to describe active supporters of Soviet ideology and economic policy. The term was used in periodicals in the 1930s to laud loyalists of the Communist Party. Among activists were *dvadtsiatyp'iatytysiachnyky*

(25,000ers), or Russian-speaking urban workers, dispatched to Soviet Ukraine. They also included village soviet members, appointed to oversee ten to twenty local households. They served as informers, who helped Bolshevik colonial authorities uncover so-called "anti-Soviet sentiments" among the local population. Activists also served in *buksyrni bryhady* that confiscated grain.

all-Union famine is a term introduced in 2007 by Russian historians to divert attention from the national component of the Holodomor as genocide.

Ewald Ammende (1893–1936) was an Estonian journalist, human rights activist, and politician of Baltic German origin, tapped in 1933 by Cardinal Theodor Innitzer of Vienna to head an Interfaith Relief Committee to aid victims of the Great Famine, known as the Holodomor. In 1935, he published a widely circulated book in German, *Muss Rußland hungern? Menschen und Völkerschicksale in der Sowjetunion* (1935). The following year, a slightly abridged English translation was published, *Human Life in Russia* (1936). His book was the best survey of press accounts of starvation in Soviet Ukraine, the only source at the time that pointed to the link between the genocidal famine and Soviet nationality policy.

ARA, or American Relief Association, was directed by Herbert Hoover, future president of the United States. The U.S. Congress appropriated $20,000,000 under the Russian Famine Relief Act of 1921. The ARA fed approximately 10 million people in Russia, mostly in the Volga region. In late 1922, the ARA extended its operations to Soviet Ukraine. The ARA operations were delayed until anti-Soviet resistance in the Ukrainian countryside was suppressed. The ARA services ended in 1923, when it became known that the Soviet government was exporting grain.

balanda was a low-calorie liquid soup, made from meat refuse, such as intestines, with mixture of flour, ladled to the prisoners of labor camps after the workday.

Vsevolod Balyts'kyi (1892–1937), born in Ukraine, was the first head of the GPU in the Ukrainian SSR from September 1923 to July 1931. Concurrently, he was deputy head of the OGPU in the Soviet Union from July 1930 to July 1934 and specially authorized plenipotentiary representative of the OGPU in the Ukrainian SSR between November 1932 and February 1933. From July 1934 to May 1937, he served as People's Commissar of Internal Affairs (NKVD) in Soviet Ukraine. In 1937, he was arrested and executed during the Great Terror.

bandura is a Ukrainian stringed instrument of the lute family. It has fifty strings, including short auxiliary strings along the body. It evolved from an instrument that appeared in the sixteenth century. Traditionally, it was played by a *kobzar* or minstrel, often a Cossack who had been blinded in captivity. The repertoire consisted primarily of the duma, a type of a folk ballad about Cossack exploits. The duma was an epic song built around historical events and embedded with religious and moralistic elements. Although many themes deal with military action in some form, they impart a moral message in which one should conduct oneself properly in the relationships with the family and community. In December 1934, on Stalin's order, 337 Ukrainian *kobzars* and lyre players were lured to a gathering and later shot, together with the boys who acted as guides for blind musicians, on the outskirts of the village of Kozacha Lopan' near Kharkiv. Their unique Ukrainian *banduras* were burned. See Yuri Mischenko, "Orest Skop: Cossack Mamai," *The Ukrainian Museum*, New York, NY, June 12–September 25, 2016, http://www.ukrainianmuseum.org/ex_160612_SkopCossackMamai.html.

bezbilkovyi nabriak was a typical diagnosis of protein deficiency dropsy that was written in civil registry records that concealed the true cause of death due to severe and prolonged starvation.

bezbozhniki (in Ukrainian *bezvirnyky*) were members of the Union of Militant Atheists of the Soviet Union, established in 1925 to fight against religious way of life. They participated in an anti-religious campaign of 1928–1929 that led to the destruction and confiscation of church property and icons. Their campaign undermined moral foundations of life in the villages guided by Christian values. During 1932–1933, most of the churches, monasteries, and worship houses were closed and destroyed or used for storing confiscated grain. The militant atheists were among members of the *aktyv* and *buksyrni bruhady*.

bezprytul'ni (in Ukrainian) were homeless orphans who lost their parents due to famines or deportations. At first, this anomalous social phenomenon was caused by the famine of 1921–1923, when tens of thousands of orphans traveled from famine-stricken areas to urban centers of Soviet Ukraine. In the 1930s, the causes of a huge influx of orphans in Soviet Ukraine were dekulakization, deportations, and political repressions. In May 1933, the number of homeless children reached 11,000 on the streets of Kharkiv, then the capital of Soviet Ukraine. At the time, orphanages could not accommodate all the homeless children; many were branded on the hand and deported to the outskirts of the city without the right to return, thus deprived of all means of survival.

Borot'bists, a left-nationalist political party of Socialist Revolutionaries in Soviet Ukraine. The party existed for two years. Initially, the Bolsheviks joined forces with the Borot'bists, who controlled the partisan movement in the countryside, but dissolved the party soon after the occupation of Ukraine. Some of the leading members, among them Hryhorii Hryn'ko and Oleksandr Shums'kyi, were coopted by the Bolsheviks and served as commissars of education in Soviet Ukraine.

buksyrni bryhady (in Ukrainian, tugboat brigades) consisted of village activists, teachers, students, inspectors from district control commissions, and Communist Party plenipotentiaries dispatched from Russian urban centers to enforce grain procurement in Soviet Ukraine. They disseminated propaganda, forced villagers to join collective farms, searched houses, and forcibly requisitioned grain, vegetables, cooked food from stoves, millstones, and farm equipment. These activities were often accompanied by violence and destruction of brick stoves or thatched roofs.

Central Rada (in Ukrainian *Tsentral'na Rada*), the first modern Ukrainian government, was founded in Kyïv in March 1917. Mykhailo Hrushevs'kyi was chosen in absentia as its chairman. By its four Universals, the Central Rada led Ukraine from autonomy to independence. In April 1917, a new presidium of the Rada was elected, with Hrushevs'kyi as president and Serhii Iefremov and Volodymyr Vynnychenko as vice presidents. During its existence the Rada held nine plenary sessions. By the end of July 1917, the Rada consisted of 822 deputies, who represented all strata of society, including Ukrainian farmers, soldiers, workers, as well as Ukrainian, Russian, Jewish, and Polish socialist parties, plus professional, educational, economic, and community organizations and the national minorities—Moldavians, Germans, Tatars, Belarusians. Out of the 822 deputies, the 58 members of the Little Rada were chosen, with 18 of these representing the national minorities. Its governments went through multiple changes under the leadership of Volodymyr Vynnychenko from June 1917 to January 1918, and Vsevolod Holubovych from January to April 1918.

Cheka was the All-Russian Extraordinary Commission for Combatting Counterrevolution, Speculation, Sabotage, and Misuse of Authority, colloquially known as *VChK* (*Vserossiiskaia chrezvychainaia komissiia po bor'be s kontrrevoliutsiei i sabotazhem*). Officials of the Cheka were known as *chekists* (in Russian *chekisty*).

chorni doshky (in Ukrainian, literally "black boards," or black lists), a repressive disciplinary measure of blacklisting villages, collective farms, village soviets, and independent farmers for failing to fulfill quotas imposed by central authorities. Stalin first used the term "blacklist" in a speech at the Fourth Conference of the KP(b)U in March 1920 to condemn miners of the Donbas region who were evading conscription in the countryside. The practice of blacklisting returned after the NEP ended in 1928. In November 1932, the measure was implemented in the Kuban (North Caucasus), then replicated on a mass scale in Soviet Ukraine. The December 6, 1932, resolution of the Council of People's Commissars and Central Committee of the Communist Party spelled out the measures. This resolution created "Stalinist ghettos" in rural areas, with all village residents left to starve. Those caught trying to escape were arrested, some executed on the spot, and others forcibly returned to their villages. Blacklists were compiled by regional and district Communist Party representatives and published in newspapers.

Vlas Chubar (1891–1939), an ethnic Ukrainian, was chairman (from July 1923) of the Council of People's Commissars of the Ukrainian SSR and deputy chairman (from 1934) of the Council of People's Commissars of the USSR. He was arrested during the Great Terror in 1938 and executed in 1939. Along with Josef Stalin, Viacheslav Molotov, Lazar Kaganovich, Pavel Postyshev, Stanislav Kosior, and Mendel Khataievich, he was accused of organizing a man-made famine in Soviet Ukraine in 1932–1933 by a Ukrainian Court of Appeal in January 2010, but criminal proceedings against them were quashed due to their deaths.

collectivization (in Ukrainian *kolektyvizatsiia*) was an economic policy of Bolshevik occupation authorities aimed at the liquidation of 5.2 million small farms by stripping owners of their plots of land, farm animals, and farming equipment, while forcing them into 25,000 collective farms owned by the state. Stalin's 1929 article, "The Year of the Great Breakthrough," spelled out the policy. Ukrainian farmers, who resisted the collectivization policy, were forced into labor camps, exiled into forced settlements in the Russian wilderness, or executed on the spot. Soviet Ukraine was one of the first republics subject to total collectivization in one to two years.

Comintern, or Communist International. The First International was founded in London in 1864. The Second International, an organization of socialist and labor parties, was established in Paris in 1889. The Third International (1919–1943) was launched in Moscow in March 1919. It advocated world communism and included representatives from thirty countries, among them the United States, Germany, France, Great Britain, China, Korea, Hungary, Poland, Finland, the three Baltic countries, Sweden, and Persia. The various parties were not independent but national sections of the Communist International, which controlled and monitored their activities.

dekulakization (in Russian *raskulachivanie*), in Ukrainian *rozkurkulennia*, was a form of political terror in the village that targeted well-to-do farmers, so-called *kurkuli*, and aimed at the liquidation of economic self-sufficiency of private and family enterprises. In Soviet Ukraine, the campaign of "eliminating kulaks as a class" camouflaged anti-Ukrainian policy of the Bolsheviks. Under the slogans of building socialism and fulfilling grain procurement plans, well-to-do and later poorer farmers were dispossessed of land, farm animals, equipment, even houses, and banished to forced settlements in Siberia, sentenced to death or decades of forced labor in concentration camps in the Russian Far North and Siberia. The confiscated property served as "capital funds" for collective farms.

dezinformatsiia, or disinformation, is a loan translation from Russian, derived from the title of a propaganda department within security service. The GPU established a "special disinformation office" in 1923 to spread false or misleading information to prevent leaks about forced labor camps for political opponents of the regime and deceive public opinion inside and outside the newly formed Union of Soviet Socialist Republics.

Anatolii Dimarov (real name Harasiuta) (1922–2014) was born near Poltava. His father was a prosperous land owner, who fled persecution. His mother changed her last name and adopted the name of the late village teacher, Dimarov. The mother relocated with her three sons to the Donbas, where she found work as a teacher. Dimarov's adopted name became his pen name. He was one of the first writers who mentioned the events of the Holodomor in his novel *I budut' liudy* (1964). He was spared from persecution due to his popularity as a prose writer and as a handicapped war veteran.

Directory is a collective governing body of the Ukrainian National Republic (in Ukrainian *Dyrektoriia UNR*). It was the state authority created on November 14, 1918, for directing the overthrow of Hetman Pavlo Skoropads'kyi. The uprising against the Hetman was hastened by his declaration of a "federative union" with Russia on that day. The Directory was headed by Volodymyr Vynnychenko (representative of the Ukrainian Social Democratic Workers' Party), and included the following members: the supreme *otaman* Symon Petliura (Ukrainian Social Democratic Workers' Party), Fedir Shvets' (Peasant Association), Opanas Andriievs'kyi (Ukrainian Party of Socialists-Independentists), and Andrii Makarenko (non-partisan member, delegate of the railway workers). The uprising led to Skoropads'kyi's abdication in favor of his council of ministers, which, in turn, yielded power to the Directory. A new government—the Council of National Ministers of the UNR—was established by the

Directory's decree of December 26, 1918. It was chaired by Volodymyr Chekhivs'kyi. The Directory abolished many of the Hetman government's laws and restored the legislation of the Central Rada. The most important of these laws dealt with land distribution, the establishment of Ukrainian as the official language, the autocephaly of the Orthodox Church, and the convening of the Labor Congress. The Labor Congress met in January 1919, and the Directory submitted its powers to the Labor Congress—the legislature of the UNR. In view of the state of war, the Labor Congress invested the Council of National Ministers with executive power. The ministers were appointed by the Directory and were responsible to it between sessions of the Labor Congress. On February 5, 1919, the Directory moved from Kyïv to Vinnytsia on the border with Poland. It frequently changed locations, depending on events at the front. To win the support of the Entente in the Ukrainian-Soviet War, Volodymyr Vynnychenko resigned from the Directory, and Symon Petliura became its head on February 11, 1919. When the talks with the Entente collapsed, a new socialist cabinet was formed by Borys Martos in Rivne on April 9, 1919. At the end of August 1919, it was replaced by Isaak Mazepa's cabinet. Powers in the Directory were not clearly delineated. Besides carrying out their representative and legislative functions, its members sometimes interfered in the affairs of the executive branch and provoked conflicts with the Council of National Ministers. At a meeting of the Directory and the Council of National Ministers on November 15, 1919, at Kam'ianets'-Podil's'kyi, it was decided that in the absence of the two leading members who went abroad on state business, "the supreme authority in the affairs of the Republic [is] invested in the head of the Directory and the supreme *otaman* Symon Petliura, who, in the name of the Directory, will confirm all laws and decrees adopted by the Council of National Ministers." On May 21, 1920, the government of the republic issued an order, confirmed by Petliura, recalling the two members of the Directory for their failure to return from abroad. Thus, the Directory ceased to be a collective body, and all its powers passed to Petliura. After Petliura's death on May 25, 1926, all powers were assumed by the head of the government-in-exile of the Ukrainian National Republic at the time, Andrii Livyts'kyi.

dvadtsiatyp'iatytysiachnyky (25,000ers) were Communist Party and Communist Youth League activists, recruited in 1930 to enforce collectivization. Out of 8,451 activists recruited in Russian urban centers, about 6,435 were dispatched to villages in Soviet Ukraine; the remaining volunteers were dispatched to the North Caucasus, Lower Volga, and Kazakhstan. Most of them (80 percent) served in village soviets. Their task was accomplished by the end of 1931, when 85 percent of farms in Soviet Ukraine were collectivized.

Felix Dzerzhinsky (1877–1926), ethnically Polish, was a professional revolutionary and the head of the Soviet security police, known as *VChK* (GPU, later NKVD, then KGB), from its founding in December 1917 to his sudden death in May 1926. In 1920, Lenin dispatched Dzerzhinsky to Ukraine to pacify the countryside and suppress Makhno and other insurgents, in an "anti-bandit" operation, for which the "Iron Felix" was awarded the Order of the Red Banner. In 1921, he was appointed as Commissar of Transportation in charge of shipping food assistance to the Lower Volga region, affected by famine, and combatting embezzlement and graft on railroads. In February 1924, concurrently with his duties as head of the security police, he was appointed chairman of the Economic Development Committee and tasked with stimulating economic growth through innovation. In May 1926, he criticized the Trotsky-Zinoviev anti-party bloc during a Politburo meeting, and on the last day of the session died of cardiac arrest.

enemy of the people (from Latin *hostis publicus*, dating back to Roman times and meaning "public enemy"). In the Soviet Union under Stalin, "enemy of the people" was a loosely defined term that could implicate anyone, for any reason, at any time. It was a term of denigration slurring the targeted person or group, and was cast against members of all social, political, and civilian classes. The so-called "enemies of the people" found themselves outcasts, without home, hearth, and work; arrested on trumped-up charges, for which no amnesty was granted; and under the threat of execution (immediate or delayed).

genocide, the term coined by Raphael Lemkin in 1944 from the Greek root *genos* (race, tribe) and Latin *-cide* (*caedere*—to kill). It was enshrined in the U.N. Convention on the Prevention and Punishment of the Crime of Genocide in 1948. Article I of the U.N. Convention on Genocide addresses responsibility, confirming that signatories will undertake to prevent and punish genocide, whether committed in time of peace or war. Article II of the U.N. Convention on Genocide specifically defines genocide as any of the following acts committed with intent to destroy, in whole or in part, a national, ethnical, racial or religious group, as such:

(a) Killing members of the group;
(b) Causing serious bodily or mental harm to members of the group;
(c) Deliberately inflicting on the group conditions of life calculated to bring about its physical destruction in whole or in part;
(d) Imposing measures intended to prevent births within the group;

(e) Forcibly transferring children of the group to another group.

GPU (in Russian *Gosudarstvennoe politicheskoe upravlenie*), or State Political Directorate, a successor of *VChK*. From 1922 to 1934, the GPU (Ukrainian abbreviation DPU) was a special organ of the Bolshevik occupational regime in Soviet Ukraine, which carried out political repressions, executions, arrests, and deportations. In 1928, the GPU was granted the right to conduct trials without prosecutor's consent. In 1929, the so-called *triika* (see *troika*) were instituted to expedite the prosecution of legal cases. In 1932–1933, the GPU oversaw the implementation of the law on the "protection of socialist property" (known as the "five ears of wheat" law) and conducted arrests, deportations, and executions of all those who were charged for violating the law by gleaning kernels of wheat in the fields.

GULAG, also spelled Gulag or GULag (Russian acronym for *Glavnoe Upravlenie Lagerei*), or Main Directorate of Camps was the agency in charge of the Soviet network of so-called "corrective-labor" camps set up by order of Lenin in the 1920s, and reaching its peak during Stalin's rule in the 1930s. The first three commandants of Soviet labor camps were Jewish. Fedor (Teodors) Eihmans, a Jew from Latvia, was the commandant of the Solovetsky labor camp from 1924 to 1930, when he became the head of the Soviet prison camp system, known under its acronym GULag. His successor was Lazar Kogan, the son of a wealthy Jewish merchant, who supervised the construction of the White Sea–Baltic Sea Canal in 1932–1933. Between 1932 and 1937, Matvei Berman, the son of a Jewish brickyard owner, was in charge of the GULag. During the Great Terror in 1937–1938, they were arrested and executed. Statistical reports on the number of prisoners and death rates in labor camps prior to 1934, when the GPU was reorganized into the NKVD, were nonexistent or destroyed.

holod (in Ukrainian) hunger, an acute desire for food, malnutrition due to food scarcity.

holodomor (in Ukrainian) means famine, an acute scarcity of food, caused by drought, crop failure, population imbalance, or war, typically accompanied by starvation and epidemics that lead to increased mortality. The word appeared in 1898 in a periodical describing destitute population suffering from extreme starvation. It is derived from *holod* (starvation) and *mor* (Latin root *mort*-death), meaning "death caused by starvation."

Holodomor of 1932–1933 is the ultimate stage of the Holodomor-genocide, the man-made famine in Soviet Ukraine.

Holodomor-genocide is an intentional act of mass extermination of people in Soviet Ukraine and ethnically Ukrainian areas of the Russian SFSR as defined in Article II of the U.N. Convention on the Prevention and Punishment of the Crime of Genocide, adopted in 1948. This crime was perpetrated by the top leadership of the Communist Party and the GPU of the USSR as well as rank-and-file perpetrators on the regional and district levels. This genocide targeted Ukrainians as a national group to thwart the crystallization of the nation and prevent Ukraine's secession from the Soviet Union. In Raphael Lemkin's conceptualization, the first prong of the attack was aimed at Ukrainian intelligentsia, the second against the clergy, and the third against independent farmers. The ethnic composition was diluted by scattering Ukrainians around the USSR and by resettlement of Russian loyalists in the Ukrainian villages depopulated by the famine. According to Article II of the U.N. Convention, all enumerated genocidal acts do apply in the case of the Holodomor:

(a) people who resisted were killed (deported, imprisoned, executed, starved to death);
(b) there was huge bodily and mental harm caused to all Holodomor victims (those who died and those who survived);
(c) there were artificially created conditions of life calculated to destroy the Ukrainians (deportations, blacklisting, confiscations of grain and everything edible, passport regime, ban on travel to procure food, forced labor in concentration camps, forced resettlement outside the borders of Soviet Ukraine in the Russian Far North and Siberia);
(d) all those measures prevented births within the Ukrainian national group; and
(e) children were transferred from their parents (dispossessed, deported, executed) to state-run orphanages and children's communes where they were brought up in obedience to the communist ideology and subservience to the colonial regime.

Among more than 7 million victims of the Holodomor were Ukrainian intelligentsia, clergy, and farmers in Soviet Ukraine as well as the North Caucasus, the Central Black Earth, the Lower Volga, and the Kazakh Autonomous region of the RSFSR, settled by ethnic Ukrainians, who were starved to death during 1932–1933 and who were deported, imprisoned, and executed in labor camps and forced settlements in the Russian Far North and Siberia. So far, sixteen countries have recognized the Holodomor as genocide. The European Parliament and the Parliamentary Assembly of the Council of Europe officially condemned the Stalinist regime's crime against humanity.

Mykhailo Hrushevs'kyi (1866–1934), born to a Ukrainian noble family in the Polish part of the Russian Empire, was a historian and the leader of the Central Rada in 1917–1918. He completed his studies at Kyïv University. In 1894, he was appointed professor of Ukrainian history at L'viv University, then in the Austro-Hungarian Empire. He advanced the idea that the Ukrainian nation had, since the founding of Kyïvan Rus', followed a distinct historical path from that of Russia. In April 1918, he was elected the first president of the Ukrainian National Republic (see *UNR*), but then emigrated after Skoropads'kyi's coup against the UNR. He returned to Soviet Ukraine from Galicia in 1924, attracted by the KP(b)U's promotion of Ukrainization. As the Chair of Modern Ukrainian History at the All-Ukrainian Academy of Sciences, he was the object of GPU surveillance. In 1931, he was arrested and ordered to move to Moscow, where he was kept under house arrest. In 1934, he died in Kislovodsk, North Caucasus, where he was undergoing a minor medical treatment.

Serhii Hrushevs'kyi (1892–1937), a nephew of Mykhailo Hrushevs'kyi, was vice rector of the Donets'k Institute of People's Education. He was exiled to the Solovetsky labor camp and executed at Sandarmokh in Karelia in 1937.

huberniia was the tsarist-era designation for a large administrative area, known by its Russian spelling, *guberniia* (gubernia).

Matvii Iavors'kyi (1885–1937), born in Polish Galicia, then part of the Austro-Hungarian Empire, was a Ukrainian historian and academician. He studied law in L'viv and Vienna Universities. After World War I, he serve in the Ukrainian Galician army. Following the army's withdrawal from central Ukraine in 1919, he joined the KP(b)U in 1920. He used Marxist historiography to write several histories of Ukraine, some of which were used in primary schools in the 1920s. In 1929, he was forced to write a "confession" and dismissed from the Marxist historians ranks for his "nationalist deviation." In 1931, he was arrested and exiled to the Solovetsky Islands. He was executed at Sandarmokh, Karelia, in the Russian SFSR in 1937.

INO (in Ukrainian *Instytuty narodnoï osvity*), or Institutes of People's Education, replaced universities in Soviet Ukraine.

International Commission of Inquiry into the 1932–1933 Famine in Ukraine convened on May 23–27, 1988, in the Europa Hotel in Brussels, Belgium, and on October 31–November 3, 1988, in the United Nations Plaza Hotel in New York City, New York. The idea to organize an international commission was suggested by Toronto lawyer Volodymyr-Iuri Danyliw at the

Fourth Conference of the World Congress of Free Ukrainians in December 1983. The Commission of Inquiry interviewed expert witnesses and issued a report which identified a number of statutory instruments as well as administrative actions characterizing the 1932–1933 famine in Ukraine as genocide. Findings of this commission were delivered to the U.N. Under-Secretary for Human Rights in Geneva on May 9, 1990, and to the president of the Parliamentary Assembly of the Council of Europe on May 10, 1990.

Vasyl' Ivchuk (1902–1938) was a school principal in the village of Dudarkiv, Boryspil' district, Kyïv region. Ivchuk arranged a practicum for schoolchildren at a meat-processing plant so that after lessons they could work in exchange for a cup of soup. In this ingenious way, the principal saved all school-age children in his village from starvation. Ivchuk, who rescued children in 1932–1933, fell victim to the Stalinist totalitarian regime. On May 17, 1938, the *troika* of the Kyïv Regional Directorate of the NKVD arrested Ivchuk and accused him of being a member of the Polish Military Organization. On September 28, 1938, he was executed. He was rehabilitated in 1958. On November 21, 2007, he was awarded a medal of Hero of Ukraine, posthumously.

Lazar Kaganovich (1893–1991), born to Jewish parents in the Radomysl' district, Kyïv Governorate of the Russian Empire (modern Ukraine), was the KP(b)U secretary general from 1925 to 1928 and secretary of the TsK VKP(b) from 1928 to 1939. In October 1932, he headed an extraordinary grain-procurement commission of the TsK VKP(b), which, under the pretext of grain procurement, confiscated all food supplies from farmers in the North Caucasus, especially the Kuban' region, thereby condemning them to death from starvation. Along with Josef Stalin, Viacheslav Molotov, Pavel Postyshev, Stanislav Kosior, Vlas Chubar, and Mendel Khataievich, he was accused of organizing a man-made famine in Soviet Ukraine in 1932–1933 by a Ukrainian Court of Appeal in January 2010, but criminal proceedings against them were quashed due to their deaths.

karbovantsi, abbreviated as krb., equal 100 kopecks, the name of currency before revolution and later in Soviet Ukraine. The first *karbovantsi* banknotes of the Ukrainian National Republic were designed by Heorhii Narbut in December 1917. They were printed in Kyïv and put into circulation in early 1918, prior to the proclamation of independence. The bills were printed with inscriptions in three languages: Ukrainian, Polish, and Yiddish. The design not only emphasized multiethnic populace of Ukraine but also brought together Ukraine's aesthetic Cossack Baroque flourishes and medieval Volodymyr the Great's insignia, the trident. In March 1918, when the

Central Rada returned to Kyïv after subduing the Bolsheviks, the government introduced the new currency the *hryvnia*. In terms of exchange, 1 *karbovanets* = 2 *hryvni*. They went into circulation in September 1918, during the short administration of Hetman Skoropads'kyi, when it was decided to return to the original monetary designation of the *karbovantsi*. The *karbovantsi* were used during the Soviet period. After reinstating its independence in 1991, Ukraine reintroduced the *hryvnia*. See Myroslava M. Mudrak, *The Imaginative World of Heorhii Narbut and the Making of a Ukrainian Brand* (Kyïv: Rodovid Press, 2020), 75–77.

Tetiana Kardynalovs'ka (1899–1993) was a Ukrainian interpreter, language teacher, and writer. She was the daughter of a Russian general of artillery Mykhailo Kardynalovs'kyi. After graduating from a classical gymnasium, she enrolled at the Kyïv Polytechnic Institute, but her education was interrupted by the revolution and war. Her first marriage to Vsevolod Holubovych, the prime minister of the UNR from January to April 1918, ended in divorce. Nevertheless, she continued to work in the editorial office of *Chervonyi Shliakh* (Red Path), managed by her ex-husband. She later married a Ukrainian writer Serhii Pylypenko, who in 1919 joined the Bolsheviks. Pylypenko was murdered during the Stalinist purge in 1934. As a widow of the former "enemy of the people," she lived in Ukraine until World War II, when in 1943 she was deported to Austria. After escaping from a labor camp, she lived in Italy, then Great Britain. After the war, she emigrated to the United States, where she worked at Harvard University teaching Russian and later Ukrainian languages. She wrote memoirs, *Nevidstupne mynule* (Persistent Past).

Petro Kholodnyi (1876–1930) was an avant-garde artist, chemist, and politician. He was one the founders of modern Ukrainian style, called neo-Byzantine. From 1899 to 1917, he worked as professor of chemistry at Kyïv Polytechnic Institute. During the national liberation struggle (1917–1921), he joined the Secretariat of People's Education of the Central Rada. During the Directory he was appointed minister of education. In 1921, Kholodnyi settled in L'viv, then under Polish rule, where he worked on the restoration of icons and painted murals in the Uspensky Cathedral. In 1928, he visited Paris to gather materials for his painting to commemorate Symon Petliura's assassination. The painting was left unfinished, when the artist suddenly died at the age of fifty-four.

Andrii Khvylia [real name Olinter] (1898–1938), born in Bessarabia, was a Communist loyalist and journalist. He joined the KP(b)U in 1918 and was in charge of its Press Section and the Cultural Propaganda Section. In 1933, he was appointed Ukraine's deputy Commissar of Education. As a vocal opponent of Ukrainian nationalism, he was responsible for the death of many Ukrainian cultural leaders. He attacked Mykola Khvyl'ovyi's publications in 1928 and 1930. After Mykola Skrypnyk's suicide in 1933, Khvylia attacked Skrypnyk for introducing orthographic changes to the Ukrainian language in a collection of articles, *Znyshchyty korinnia ukraïns'koho natsionalizmu na movnomu fronti* (To Destroy the Roots of Ukrainian Nationalism on the Linguistic Front, 1933). In 1937, Khvylia was arrested and executed the following year.

Mykola Khvyl'ovyi (1893–1933) was a Ukrainian poet and writer. Born as Mykola Fitil'ov to a family of teachers, Hryhorii Fitil'ov and Elisaveta Tarasenko, in Trostianets', Kharkiv region, he dropped out of classical gymnasium to join Socialist Revolutionaries (SR). In 1915, he enlisted in the army. In 1917, during the February Revolution he headed the soldier's soviet in the Ukrainian Fourteenth Division, where he conducted educational and propaganda activities. After the October Revolution of 1917, his political leaning moved left. In 1918, he briefly served as chief of staff for SR T. Pushkar, who led an uprising against the Bolsheviks in the village of Murakhva, Bohodukhiv district (in 1933, this entire settlement was starved to death). In 1919, he joined the Communist Party. His famous novel, titled *Val'dshnepy* (The Woodsnipes), described as "anti-party" and "counterrevolutionary," remained unfinished and unpublished when he committed suicide in May 1933. His last, and most radical work, "Ukraïna chy Malorosiia?" (Ukraine or Little Russia?), was suppressed by authorities. His vision of Ukraine's historic mission was known as Khvyl'ovism. His followers were physically destroyed during the Stalinist terror or were forced to reconstruct themselves as socialist realists. His works were banned in the Soviet Union.

KNS (from Ukrainian *komitety nezamozhnykh selian*, or *komnezamy*) were committees of "non-wealthy peasants" that existed in the Ukrainian SSR from 1920 to 1933. Together with state security police, they carried out policies of Soviet occupation authorities. They were controlled by the KP(b)U at the county (*povit*) level and, after the administrative and territorial reforms of 1923, at the district (*raion*) level.

kolhosps (in Ukrainian, *kolektyvni hospodarstva*, or collective farms). The Bolsheviks created three kinds of collective farms depending on the degree of the use of means of production: (1) the Association for Joint Cultivation of Land (*Tovarishchestvo po sovmestnoi obrabotke zemli*, in Russian *Tsoz*), (2) the cooperative (in Russian *artel'*), and (3) the commune. Like Lenin in 1919, Stalin in 1930 was unable to force Ukrainian farmers to join the communes, where all means of production were collectivized. The *Tsoz*, which allowed farmers to retain independent control of production, was not acceptable to the authorities. A compromise was found in the cooperative, which allowed farmers to keep their private garden plots.

koloniï, or children's communes, were orphanages, administered by the GPU, where children of the dispossessed farmers, the kulaks, and other "enemies of the people" were indoctrinated in communist ideology and engaged in productive labor in factory workshops. Often, these children became ideal recruits for the state security police.

Komsomol, or Communist Youth League. The All-Union Leninist Communist Youth League (in Russian abbreviated as VLKSM) was founded on October 29, 1918. It was one in a sequence of youth organizations established by the Communist Party to indoctrinate the younger generations from the Octoberists (age 7–9), to the Pioneers (9–14), to the Komsomol (14–28) in communist ideology and loyalty to the ruling regime.

korenizatsiia (in Russian, indigenization), the policy of instituting Soviet power in non-Russian republics. It was an ambiguous policy, initiated in 1923, to overcome resistance to Bolshevik economic policy and engage the population of Soviet Ukraine in construction of the Soviet state. The nationality policy in Ukraine was dubbed "Ukrainization." It was ostensibly designed to promote native language in schools and recruit administrative cadres proficient in the language of the republic. The "Ukrainization" policy was discontinued when the Holodomor-genocide reached its apogee in 1932–1933. Its promoters were prosecuted for "nationalist deviation."

Stanislav Kosior (1889–1939), ethnically Polish, was first secretary of the Central Committee of the Communist Party (Bolsheviks) of Ukraine. He was executed in 1939 during the Great Terror. Along with Josef Stalin, Viacheslav Molotov, Lazar Kaganovich, Pavel Postyshev, Vlas Chubar, and Mendel Khataievich, he was accused of organizing a man-made famine in Soviet Ukraine in 1932–1933 by a Ukrainian Court of Appeal in January 2010, but criminal proceedings against them were quashed due to their deaths.

KP(b)U (in Ukrainian, *Komunistychna partiia (bil'shovykiv) Ukraïny*), or the Communist Party (Bolsheviks) of Ukraine.

krai was the term introduced in 1924 to designate six territories of the Russian SFSR inhabited by ethnic minorities. One of these was the North Caucasus with a large ethnically Ukrainian population. Based on the 1926 census, over 3 million Ukrainians lived in the North Caucasus, where they constituted 37 percent of the population. The percentages varied from 0.1 in the southern regions to 61.5 in the Kuban' district (Krasnodar region) in the Northwest.

Kuban' is a geographic area west of the Crimean Peninsula, bordered by the Kuban' River, the Black Sea, the Don steppe, the Volga delta, and the Caucasus Mountains. The descendants of the Zaporozhian Cossacks relocated to this part of the North Caucasus. A large percentage of the Kuban' population was of Ukrainian ethnicity.

kurkul' (in Russian *kulak*, literally "fist," and figuratively, a greedy, money-grubber, skinflint) was an ideological label, created by the Bolsheviks to brand small proprietors as enemies of the Soviet state and to eliminate them. In 1930, the label was applied to all those who resisted collectivization irrespective of land ownership or wealth. They were dispossessed of property, evicted from their homes, resettled to village outskirts, shot if they resisted, or exiled to Siberia.

Emmanuil Kviring (1888–1937) was a Soviet politician and statesman. Born in the Volga German settlement in the Russian Empire, he joined Socialist Revolutionaries (SRs) in 1906. In 1912, he joined the Bolsheviks. After World War I, he was appointed a leader of the Communist Party (Bolsheviks) of Ukraine from October 1918 to March 1919, and from April 1923 to March 1925. He opposed the "Ukrainization" policy, so he had to leave Kharkiv for Moscow. He worked as an economist in the State Planning Committee. In 1937, he was arrested and executed by the NKVD. In 1956, he was posthumously rehabilitated.

Iurii Lavrinenko (1905–1987) was a literary scholar, critic, and publicist. In 1930, after graduation from the Kharkiv Institute of People's Education, he completed a doctorate at the Institute of Literature of the Academy of Sciences of the Ukrainian SSR. During the Stalinist terror he was arrested several times between 1933 and 1935, and from 1935 to 1939 he was imprisoned in a concentration camp in Noril'sk, Russia. He was exiled after his release. During World War II, he became a refugee in a displaced persons camp in Germany. In 1950, he emigrated to the United States. In 1955–1960, together with Ivan Koshelivets', he edited *Ukraïns'ka literaturna hazeta*. He wrote *Sotsiializm i ukraïns'ka revoliutsiia* (Socialism and the Ukrainian Revolution) in 1949 and *Ukrainian Communism and Soviet-Russian Policy toward the Ukraine: An Annotated Bibliography, 1917–1953* in 1953. He published the anthology *Rozstriliane vidrodzhennia* (Executed Renaissance) in 1959.

Dmitrii Lebed' (1893–1937) was the son of a Russian unskilled worker, who aligned with the Bolsheviks and led a party cell in his native Katerynoslav after the February Revolution. He was second secretary of the TsK KP(b)U from 1920 to 1924, and later held several high-level all-Union and Russian governmental posts. An outspoken opponent of Ukrainization, he was arrested in 1937, accused of Ukrainian nationalism, and executed.

Anatoly Lunacharsky (real name Antonov) (1875–1933) was a Poltava-born author, essayist, and journalist who served as the Commissar of Culture and Education in the first Soviet government until being dismissed by Stalin in 1929. Lunacharsky died in 1933 in Menton, France en route to take up the post of Soviet ambassador to Spain.

lychaky were sandals made from wood bark or straw rope. Since ancient times they had been widely used as footwear in Eastern Europe and Russia, especially in rural areas until the 1930s. They were woven from wood bark (linden, willow, or birch). The sandals were tied to the foot with twisted ropes. This type of footwear was common among the Baltic and Finnish peoples. A similar type of footwear was used by the Japanese (*waraji*), North American Indians, and even Australian aborigines.

Vasyl' Lypkivs'kyi (1864–1937) headed the Ukrainian Autocephalous Orthodox Church (UAOC). In May 1919, he celebrated the first Liturgy in the Ukrainian language—after translating many of the liturgical books into modern Ukrainian—in St. Nicholas's Cathedral in Kyïv. Although this action was opposed by the Russian hierarchy, who defrocked Lypkivs'kyi, it was welcomed by supporters of the emerging Ukrainian national church. In the summer of 1919, Lypkivs'kyi became parish priest of St. Sophia Cathedral in Kyïv. In October 1921, the All-Ukrainian Orthodox Church Council in Kyïv, which had declared the establishment of the UAOC in May 1920, elected Lypkivs'kyi the first metropolitan of the church. Without a traditional episcopal ordination, Lypkivs'kyi was vilified by the Russian church as a non-canonical bishop outside the apostolic succession. Lypkivs'kyi visited more than 500 parishes after his election and oversaw the growth of the UAOC. By 1927, the church claimed 36 bishops and over 2,500 priests. Insisting on the active participation of the laity in church affairs, he propagated many church reforms, and he modified many Orthodox canons and traditions, including the celibacy of bishops, with the result that married men were admitted to episcopal ordination. He was also insistent on preserving the independence of the Ukrainian church vis-à-vis the Moscow Patriarchate. Lypkivs'kyi's popularity soon earned him the enmity of the Soviet authorities, who, after arresting him a few times, had him dismissed by the All-Ukrainian Orthodox Church Council in 1927. From 1927 to 1937 he lived in a Kyïv suburb, under virtual house arrest and in poverty. He was arrested by the NKVD in 1937, charged with anti-Soviet activity, and executed.

Anastasiia Lysyvets' (1922–2011), who witnessed the genocidal famine in Berezan' near Kyïv, lost almost her entire family, including her parents, younger sister, and brother as well as aunts and uncles. In the 1950s, she started working as a teacher of Ukrainian language and literature in the village of Kuianivka, Bilopillia district, Sumy region. Lysyvets' wrote her memoir forty-three years after the events, without hope that it would ever be published. Her memoir, *"Skazhy pro shchaslyve zhyttia . . ."* (Kyïv: KIS, 2019) has been translated into English by Alexander Motyl *"Speak of the Happy Life . . ."* (2021).

James Edward Mace (1952–2004) was of Cherokee origin, born in Muskogee, Oklahoma. He received his doctorate in history from the University of Michigan in 1981. His doctoral dissertation was published as a book, *Communism and the Dilemmas of National Liberation: National Communism in Soviet Ukraine, 1918–1933*. He spent his postdoctoral years at the Harvard Ukrainian Research Institute. From 1985 to 1988, he served as staff director of the U.S. Commission on the Ukraine Famine. In 1993, Dr. Mace moved to Ukraine and became a professor of political science at the National University Kyïv-Mohyla Academy. He died in Kyïv in 2004 at the age of fifty-two. Seven thousand people attended his funeral, and a monument was later constructed over his grave as befitting a national hero.

Nestor Makhno (1889–1934) was an anarchist leader in 1917–1921. He aspired to become a teacher. In 1905, he joined an anarchist party. He was sentenced to life in prison for terrorist activities. In the Butyrki prison in Moscow, he acquired a general and political education. In 1918, he began to mobilize resistance to the Central Powers and Hetman Pavlo Skoropads'kyi, conducting raids on landlords' estates. His volunteer light mobile cavalry units used horse-driven carriages upon which machine guns had been mounted. His forces controlled the entire Huliai-Pole region in Ukraine. In March 1919, the Bolsheviks coopted him into a temporary alliance against Anton Denikin. Makhno's forces concluded a brief pact with Symon Petliura's regular army of the UNR in September 1919, but Makhno continued to operate against Denikin's forces independently. With the defeat of Denikin, Makhno reached the zenith of his influence in Ukraine. His troops, numbering approximately 15,000 to 20,000, controlled about one-third of the present territory of Ukraine (Left-Bank Ukraine and southern Ukraine). In October 1920, Makhno concluded a treaty with Bolsheviks and launched the offensive against Petr Wrangel's army; the Bolsheviks then used this opportunity to deal decisively with the Makhnovites. Makhno was forced to make a dash for the Romanian border, and by way of Poland and Germany, escaped to France, where he remained active in anarchist circles. Nestor Makhno's memoir *Russkaia revoliutsiia na Ukraine* was published in Paris in 1929.

mangruppy (in Russian literally "maneuverable groups"), or mobile units of the GPU that blockaded villages, and carried out arrests, deportations, and executions.

Manifesto of the Communist Party was written by German philosophers Karl Marx and Friedrich Engels and printed a few weeks before the February Revolution in France in 1848. In 1848, the *Communist Manifesto* was translated into several European languages—French, Polish, Italian, Danish, Flemish, and Swedish. First published in German, it was reprinted in twelve different editions in Germany, England, and America. It was first published in English in 1850, and in 1871 in three different translations in America. A Russian translation was published in Geneva in 1869. Marx and Engels wrote a preface to the second Russian edition published in 1882.

Borys Matushevs'kyi (1907–1977) was a son of the former ambassador of the Ukrainian National Republic to Greece and a member of the Ukrainian Party of Socialists-Federalists. From 1923 to 1929, he was a student at the Kyïv Institute of People's Education. As one of the defendants in the SVU trial, he was sentenced to five years of imprisonment. He survived, obtained a passport, left Ukraine, and settled in Khibinogorsk in the Russian SFSR, where he worked at a meteorological station in the vicinity of the Solovetsky camp. He served as a go-between for Ukrainian intelligentsia, forwarding correspondence to their relatives. He was rearrested in 1938, but survived exile in Karelia. During World War II, he served in the Soviet Army. He was unable to obtain release for his mother from a concentration camp. He died in Kyïv of heart failure in 1977.

Mensheviks formed a faction of the Russian Social Democratic Workers' Party (in Russian abbreviated as RSDRP) after the schism at its Second Congress in 1903 in Brussels. Together with the Socialist Revolutionaries (SRs), they played a crucial role in workers' and soldiers' councils. Their activities were outlawed by the Bolsheviks in 1923.

Oleksandr Mizernyts'kyi (1883–1947) was a former Borot'bist, who in the spring of 1924 became head of the Teachers' Union in Soviet Ukraine. He served as the editor of the periodical *Radians'ka osvita* (Soviet Education) and the newspaper *Narodnyi uchytel'* (People's Teacher), published by the Teachers' Union of the Ukrainian SSR. He defended Commissar of Education Oleksandr Shums'kyi in a February 1927 meeting of the Politburo of the KP(b)U. In 1934, he was arrested and spent fourteen years in labor camps in Siberia.

Viacheslav Molotov (né Skryabin) (1890–1986) was a leading figure in the Soviet government from the 1920s, when he rose to power. Skryabin took the pseudonym "Molotov," derived from the Russian word *molot* (hammer) because it had a "proletarian" ring to it. In 1920, he became secretary of the Central Committee of the Ukrainian Communist Party (Bolsheviks). Lenin recalled him to Moscow in 1921, elevating him to full membership of the Central Committee. As a protégé of Joseph Stalin, Molotov became a member of the Politburo in 1926. Molotov served as Chairman of the Council of People's Commissars of the USSR from 1930 to the outbreak of World War II. In this position, he oversaw collectivization of agriculture and the implementation of the First Five-Year Plan. He signed laws that led to mass executions and personally led the commission that confiscated grain from Soviet Ukraine. Along with Josef Stain, Lazar Kaganovich, Pavel Postyshev, Stanislav Kosior, Vlas Chubar, and Mendel Khataievich, he was accused of organizing a manmade famine in Soviet Ukraine by a Ukrainian Court of Appeal in January 2010, but criminal proceedings against them were quashed due to their deaths.

Valentyn Moroz (1936–2019), a leading figure in the Ukrainian national movement, spent thirteen years in Soviet prisons and camps. In 1979, at the JFK airport in New York he, along with four other dissidents, was exchanged for two Soviet KGB agents. For a year, he worked as a Senior Research Fellow at Harvard University's Department of History. In 1997, he moved back to Ukraine, where was a university lecturer until he passed away in April 2019.

NAN (in Ukrainian *Natsional'na akademiia nauk*), or National Academy of Sciences of the Ukrainian SSR. It was founded in 1918, dissolved in 1929, and absorbed into the Academy of Sciences of the USSR. It served as an element of governmental control over the political activities of the intelligentsia.

NEP stands for the New Economic Policy, which was initiated in 1921, when *prodrazverstka* (expropriation of agricultural produce) was suspended and replaced with a fixed tax, giving farmers the opportunity to sell their produce on the free market. The legalization of the market forced the Bolshevik leaders to allow entrepreneurial activity. Industries were nationalized and organized into trusts based on principles of cost accounting. The production was revived after the restoration of the credit and banking system, the introduction of a stable currency, and the promotion of cooperative and private enterprises. The policy was curtailed in 1928.

Nepmen is a derogatory label for those who benefited from the freer economic opportunity of Lenin's New Economic Policy (NEP).

NKO (*Narodnyi komisariat osvity*), or People's Commissariat of Education in Soviet Ukraine.

NKVD (in Russian *Narodnyi komissariat vnutrennikh del*), or People's Commissariat of Internal Affairs, a successor of the GPU. It was reorganized in 1934.

nomenklatura (from Latin *nomenclatura*, meaning a system of names) were a ruling elite in the Soviet Union who held key administrative positions in the government bureaucracy, in media, trade, industry, agriculture, and education. Appointments to these positions were granted only with approval by the Communist Party.

oblasti (regions) were administrative areas, introduced in 1932 (see *okruhy*).

OGPU, or the Joint State Political Directorate, was the security police of the Soviet Union from 1923 to 1934 (see *GPU*). The political police functioned as extrajudicial and punitive organ of the Council of People's Commissars of the USSR. It was established on November 15, 1923, to silence opponents of the Soviet regime. The headquarters in Moscow controlled its sectoral branch in Soviet Ukraine and directed "show trials" that eliminated progressive intelligentsia, clergy, and farmers with the use of "special operations," repressions, and executions.

Okhranka was a secret political police, gendarmerie, in the Russian Empire.

okruhy were administrative areas smaller than *hubernii*, introduced from 1923 to 1925, abolished in 1930, and replaced with *oblasti* in 1932 in Soviet Ukraine.

otaman in Ukrainian Cossack forces was a position of a military leader. The supreme military commander of the Cossack army in Ukrainian was Hetman (a cognate of German *Hauptmann* or "captain," literally "head-man"). *Otamans* were usually elected by the Cossack Host Council or could have been appointed during the military campaigns.

paiok was a special ration card that guaranteed minimum monthly amount of products distributed among Communist Party and state functionaries, security police officers, court judges, prosecutors, military, industrial workers, and intellectual and cultural elites and their dependents due to shortages of products in stores. After 1931, a hierarchical system was instituted for food distribution. Food was also allocated to volunteers who implemented grain expropriation, members of village councils, as well as teachers and village correspondents who assisted in carrying out grain-requisition campaigns. The assortment of products depended on the category. At the beginning of 1933, the supplies were substantially diminished; dependents of industrial workers and intelligentsia were cut off from the lists. In rural areas, all central supplies were cut, except for village activists, plenipotentiaries, and political commissars at tractor stations.

passports were introduced by the Soviet government decree of December 27, 1932. The reason behind introducing the internal passport system was to stop the exodus of starving Ukrainians to procure food in urban areas of Soviet Ukraine, neighboring Russia, and Belarus. Only persons possessing a passport had a right to migrate within the Soviet Union. Passports were not issued to residents of villages, thus limiting their freedom of movement during 1932–1933 to procure food to survive.

Mykola Pavlushkov (1907–1937), born in Tula, Russian Empire, was among the students arrested in 1929 and put on trial with other leading members of the Ukrainian intelligentsia in 1930. As a student at Kyïv Institute of People's Education, he was denounced in the press for allegedly organizing the SUM in 1925 with the goal to establish an independent democratic Ukrainian republic. He was pressured by GPU investigators to implicate his uncle, academician Serhii Iefremov, in organizing the "counterrevolutionary" underground organization, the SVU. He was exiled to the Solovetsky camp, later executed at Sandarmokh in 1937.

Symon Petliura (1879–1926) was a native of Poltava. As a theology student, he joined an underground socialist movement, working as a journalist and editor. For a brief period, he worked as an archivist in the Kuban', studying history of the Ukrainian Cossack settlements in the North Caucasus. He was Secretary of War in the Central Rada (Council), then a member of the Directory and the Commander-in-Chief of the Army of the UNR. He later became the head of the Directory (in May 1919) and head of the Ukrainian government-in-exile (after November 1920). He was assassinated in Paris in May 1926 by a Soviet security police agent.

Petliurite (in Ukrainian *petliurivtsi*), or followers of Symon Petliura, head of the Directory of the UNR. It was a derogatory Soviet term for nationally conscious Ukrainians in general, as well as for real and imagined anti-Soviet elements in Ukraine.

Hryhorii Petrovs'kyi (1878–1958) was a Ukrainian Soviet politician. He was a member of the Russian delegation during signing the Treaty of Brest-Litovsk in 1917. He participated in signing the treaty on the creation of the USSR. As Chairman of Central Executive Committee of the Soviet Union, Petrovs'kyi was one of the officials responsible for implementing Stalin's policy of collectivization.

post-genocidal syndrome is a set of stable psychological and behavioral characteristics caused by the genocidal famine. The term "post-genocidal society" was coined by James Mace to refer to the long-lasting consequences of the Holodomor. The prolonged stress and the "experience" of surviving the Holodomor led to the eradication of distinguishing characteristics of the Ukrainian national group (business entrepreneurship, initiative); the deformation of social relations (denunciations, mob justice); and the erasure of Ukrainian self-identity (avoidance of the use of Ukrainian language, traditions). The forced Russification led to lowering of self-esteem, which impedes the renewal of the national statehood and national historical memory.

Pavel Postyshev (1887–1939), born in Ivanovo in the Vladimir Governorate of the Russian Empire, was a Soviet politician. He had worked in the Ukrainian SSR from 1923 to 1930, and had been a member of the KP(b)U Politburo from 1926 to 1930. In January 1933, he was sent to Soviet Ukraine as Stalin's personal representative. He was elected second secretary of the Central Committee of the Communist Party (Bolsheviks) of Ukraine and first secretary of the Kharkiv city and regional party organizations. Postyshev's mission in Soviet Ukraine was to eliminate any remaining opposition to Stalin by purging all traces of "nationalist deviation" from the Party and to end the policy of Ukrainization. In January 2010, a Ukrainian Court of Appeal accused Pavel Postyshev along with Josef Stalin, Viacheslav Molotov, Lazar Kaganovich, Stanislav Kosior, and Vlas Chubar of organizing a man-made famine in Soviet Ukraine in 1932–1933 but quashed criminal proceedings against them due to their deaths.

propaganda comes from the name of the Catholic organization Congregatio de Propaganda Fide, or Congregation for the Propagation of the Faith, created by Pope Gregory XV in 1622 for missionary work. The dissemination of propaganda aims at spreading ideas to attract supporters.

prodrazverstka (in Russian, expropriation of agricultural produce), a means of requisitioning grain and other food by the Soviet authorities in 1919–1920 and 1930–1932. The state would set the grain quota for agriculture depending on its needs, after which the quota was apportioned to the republics, regions, districts, collective farms, and independent homesteads regardless of the availability of leftover grain on the farms. Failing to fulfill the quota brought on various repressive measures, up to liquidating the farms, and exiling the debtors to the Russian Far North and Siberia to dig canals, build roads, extract ore or gold, or chop timber.

Provisional Government (in Russian *Vremennoie pravitel'stvo*) was established immediately following the abdication of Russian Emperor Nicholas II in March 1917. The Provisional Government lasted approximately eight months, and ceased to exist when Bolsheviks gained power after the so-called "October Revolution" in 1917. It was led first by Prince Georgy Lvov (1861–1925) and then by Alexander Kerensky (1881–1970).

pud is a unit of weight of the Russian Imperial measurement system equivalent to 16 kilograms.

rabfak (in Russian, from *rabochii fakul'tet* in Ukrainian spelled *robfak*), or workers' faculty, was a preparatory school for workers, designed to prepare graduates for entry into institutes of higher education and to produce a technological elite drawn from the proletariat's ranks.

Oleksandra Radchenko (1896–1965) worked as a teacher in a rural school from 1912 to 1936 in the Kharkiv region. She kept a diary, in which she recorded events that unfolded in Soviet Ukraine from 1926 to 1935. Her first entry that described famine was dated February 1930, and the last entry dated February 1935. In her April 5, 1932 entry, she wrote that the famine was manmade. On July 7, 1945, she was arrested and sentenced to ten years of hard labor in Soviet prison camps. She died in 1955, after serving the full term in the prison camps. She was rehabilitated posthumously, on July 23, 1991.

radhosps (in Ukrainian, *radians'ki hospodarstva*), or state farms, were established on the former estates expropriated from landowners and transferred to state control. They were subsidized by the state. They were different from *kolhosps* (collective farms).

raion is a district, an administrative area in an *okruh* or *oblast'*.

Christian Rakovsky (1873–1941) was a French-educated physician of Bulgarian origin, and Rumanian subject, who became a Russian Bolshevik in

1918. He headed the Soviet Ukrainian government from January 1919 to July 1923. Believing in internationalism, he questioned the existence of a distinct Ukrainian nationality. However, by the end of 1921, he had changed his views. He insisted on greater sensitivity with regard to the Ukrainian national question and also sought to expand the political and economic autonomy of the Ukrainian SSR. In April 1923, at the Twelfth Party Congress of the RKP(b) he sharply criticized Joseph Stalin's position on the national question. After being removed from the Ukrainian leadership, he served as Soviet ambassador to Britain (1923–1925) and France (1925–1927). In December 1927, he was expelled from the Communist Party, and a month later he was exiled. In 1929, he joined the opposition. In 1937, he was arrested as a spy, and in 1938 he was sentenced to twenty years of imprisonment. He was shot in a Soviet prison.

Red Terror was a period of repressions and mass killings carried out by the Cheka beginning in 1918, against political enemies of the Bolsheviks. In Soviet Ukraine, the system of Bolshevik extrajudicial killings included two methods: summary executions of randomly selected civilians accused of harboring or aiding "bandits" (see *vidpovidachi*) and hostage taking used to terrorize and disarm the countryside (see *zaruchnytstvo*).

RKP(b) (in Russian *Rosiiskaia Kommunisticheskaia partiia (bol'shevikov)*), or Russian Communist Party (Bolsheviks).

RNK (in Ukrainian *Rada narodnykh komisariv*), or Council of People's Commissars in Soviet Ukraine.

Robos (from Ukrainian, *robitnyky osvity*) was a union for educational employees in Soviet Ukraine, which replaced the All-Ukrainian Teachers' Union, dissolved by Bolsheviks in 1920.

RSFSR abbreviation of the Russian Soviet Federative Socialist Republic.

sabotage is a deliberate action to destroy or obstruct something for political or military advantage. During the Holodomor, the term was used to denote an open resistance to ideological and economic policies of Soviet occupational authorities. The GPU classified the following activities as "acts of sabotage" in reports: agitation against joining collective farms; escape from villages; beating or murder of activists, heads of village soviets, and representatives of security police. Acts of passive sabotage included hiding grain, milling the flour for personal consumption, slaughtering one's farm animals, refusing to surrender seeds for seed funds, delaying fulfillment of planting or harvesting plans. Repressive measures included confiscations of property, arrests, and deportations.

Iurii Sambros (1894–1957?) served as inspector in the Sumy school district in Soviet Ukraine and editor of periodical *Nasha osvita* (Our Education). Sambros taught Ukrainian language and literature for teachers during the 1920s. Together with his friend, Borys Antonenko-Davydovych, Sambros founded an orphanage. He was an advocate of teaching Ukrainian language and culture. In 1930, Sambros published results of his study of language use among students in teacher training institutes. That year, Sambros joined faculty of the reorganized teacher training institute in Sumy, where he taught theory of education and teaching methodology courses. In October 1930, Sambros was apprehended by the GPU during a wave of arrests following the SVU trial. Interrogators pressured him to admit his participation in a military nationalist organization. A meticulous self-defense strategy helped him get out of prison. Fearing further reprisals, Sambros decided to escape from Sumy across the border to Soviet Russia in search of work. He settled in Omsk, then Novosibirsk, and finally Komyshlov in the Sverdlovsk region. In Komyshlov, Sambros taught in a teacher training college from 1946 to 1954. He earned a doctorate and was a recipient of an honorary teacher title in the Russian SFSR. His autobiographical sketches, *Shchabli: Mii shliakh do komunizmu* (Stages of Life: My Journey Toward Communism), written in 1957, were published in 1988 in New York.

scientific communism was one of three major elements of Marxism–Leninism practiced by the Bolsheviks. It is defined in a dictionary as the science dealing with general sociopolitical laws and patterns, ways, forms and methods of changing society along communist lines, according to the historical mission of the proletariat (the socialist revolution). It is the science regarding the working-class struggle and the socialist revolution, about the laws behind the building of socialism and communism, and about the world revolutionary process as a whole.

seksot, the term coined by blending first syllables of two Russian words *sekretnyi sotrudnik*, meaning "secret collaborator." They were recruited by state political police from all strata of society, mainly by threats and blackmail. They were required to inform the GPU about public sentiments, private comments, and anti-Soviet activities in the organizations where they worked and communities where they lived.

Oleksandr Shums'kyi (1890–1946) served as Commissar of Education in the Ukrainian SSR from July to August 1919 and later from September 1924 to February 1927. He was a member of the Ukrainian Party of Socialist Revolutionaries. He pushed for *Borot'bists'* merger with the Bolsheviks. He led the KP(b)U's Agitprop (agitation and propaganda department) from 1923 to 1925. Shums'kyi's protest against Kaganovich's policy in Soviet Ukraine raised Stalin's ire. Shums'kyi was dismissed from his post in 1927 and reassigned to Leningrad, where he was appointed as director of the Institute of National Economy. He was arrested in 1933 and sentenced to ten years of imprisonment. He was poisoned on Stalin's order on the train, when he was returning to Ukraine in 1946.

Pavlo Skoropads'kyi (1873–1945) is a Ukrainian general, statesman, scion of the family of Cossack military leaders dating back to the seventeenth century. Before the revolution, he was a major general and commander of a cavalry regiment in the emperor's House Guard. During World War I, he commanded cavalry divisions and army corps. After the revolution, he oversaw the establishment of the first Ukrainian army corps. He disarmed and demobilized pro-Bolshevik military units returning from the southwestern and Romanian fronts, preventing them from plundering Ukraine. In April 1918, he was proclaimed Hetman of Ukraine. His government overturned all Central Rada policies. The government's social and economic policies were dictated by Germany's imperialistic aims, as well as the interests of Ukraine's large landowners. In December 1918, following Germany's withdrawal from Ukraine, Skoropads'kyi abdicated and fled to Germany. The Directory of the Ukrainian National Republic succeeded in ousting him in a coup. A collection of essays about Skoropads'kyi, edited by his daughter Olena Ott-Skoropads'ka, appeared in 1993 as *Ostannii het'man* (The Last Hetman). His memoirs, edited by Jaroslaw Pelenski, were published in 1995.

Mykola Skrypnyk (1872–1933) was the Old Bolshevik and Ukraine's Commissar of Education from 1927 to 1933. After 1917, he was instrumental in the formation of the first and second Ukrainian Soviet governments. He was a strong defender of cultural autonomy of ethnic Ukrainians beyond the republic's borders in the Russian SFSR. Skrypnyk at various times held the Ukrainian posts of secretary of Workers' and Peasants' Inspection, attorney-general, People's Commissar of Internal Affairs, Justice, and Education, vice-chairman of the Council of People's Commissars, and chairman of the State Planning Commission. He was also a member of the Central Committee of the Russian Communist Party (Bolsheviks) (TsK RKP(b)) and the Executive Committee of the Communist International, six times a delegate to Communist International congresses and leader of the Ukrainian delegation. In the inner party struggles, he supported Stalin against the opposition. In recognition of his prolific literary contribution, Skrypnyk was made a member of the Academy of Sciences of the Ukrainian SSR. He also edited one of the leading journals for educators in Ukraine. In July 1933, he committed suicide.

Skrypnykivka, or the Kharkiv orthography, was prepared in 1926 by the State Commission for the Regulation of Ukrainian Orthography of the People's Commissariat of Education. It was formally approved in September 1928 by

Skrypnyk; thus, the name. It was the first universally recognized standard Ukrainian orthography. Subsequently, it was reformed in 1933 because of its alleged embrace of "nationalist deviation."

SNK (in Russian *Sovet narodnykh komissarov*), or the Council of People's Commissars, was highest executive and administrative authority of the Soviet Union from 1923 to 1946.

Dmytro Solovey (1888–1966) was a Poltava-born historian, economist, and publicist. A graduate of Kharkiv University, he at various times worked at the republic's statistical bureau and the Institute of Ukrainian Culture. In 1944, he escaped to Germany and later immigrated to the United States. He is the author of *Ukraïna v systemi kolonializmu* (Ukraine in the System of Colonialism, 1959) and *Ukraïns'ka nauka v kolonial'nykh putakh* (Ukrainian Science in Colonial Shackles, 1963) that deal with colonial status of Ukraine and its science.

Socialist Revolutionaries (SRs) were members of the Ukrainian Party of Socialist Revolutionaries. In Russia, the party was organized in 1906, and by the summer of 1917 it had more than a million members. The party relied on terrorism in the struggle for political power. In November 1917, the party split, and the Left SRs entered into an alliance with the Bolsheviks. In May 1921, the SRs were put on trial. The Right SRs seized to exist in 1925.

sotsvykh is a blend of the first syllables from two Ukrainian words *sotsial'ne vykhovannia*, meaning social upbringing in preschool and primary schools.

spetspereselentsy (in Russian, "special resettlers") were Ukrainian farmers stripped of their property and deported to inhospitable areas in the Far North, Urals, Western Siberia in Russia, as well as steppes of Kazakhstan. They were at the bottom of the centralized hierarchical system of food distribution in the Soviet Union, one rank above the forced-labor camp inmates.

SRSR (in Ukrainian) stands for the Union of Soviet Socialist Republics (USSR), or the former Soviet Union.

stanytsia (in Ukrainian) was a Cossack settlement in the North Caucasus.

Ivan Steshenko (1873–1918) was a Ukrainian civic and political activist, writer, translator, member of the Ukrainian government, and member of the Shevchenko Scientific Society. He served as the first minister of education of Ukraine. He was murdered by the Bolsheviks in July 1918.

SUM (in Ukrainian *Spilka ukraïns'koï molodi*), or the Union of Ukrainian Youth.

supriah was a joint operation that involved a lot of time and effort. In order to carry on farm work, implements and draught power had to be collected from all over the district and the various pieces of machinery and animals teamed up for the task at hand.

SVU (in Ukrainian *Spilka vyzvolennia Ukraïny*), or Union for the Liberation of Ukraine.

Iurii Tiutiunnyk (1891–1930), born in the Cherkasy region, and a graduate of an agricultural college in Uman, started his military service in the 6th Siberian Regiment in 1913 and was wounded during World War I. In 1917, he became a member of the Central Rada and organized a 20,000-strong force in Zvenyhorod. In 1918, this unit had control over large territories in central and southern Ukraine. In 1919, Tiutiunnyk joined the Army of the UNR. As a brigadier general, he participated in the First Winter Campaign and organized the Second Winter Campaign in 1921. He was lured to Soviet Ukraine in 1923. Tiutiunnyk played himself in *Piłsudski Bought Peliura*, a film that slandered the Ukrainian national liberation movement. In his memoirs, the former *otaman* claimed that he had done everything possible to help people understand that the movie was a lie. A fierce enemy of the communist government, Tiutiunnyk nevertheless taught the tactics of guerrilla warfare in the Kharkiv Red Officer School, where he told about his exploits to those against whom they had been directed. Tiutiunnyk was arrested in 1929 and shot in 1930.

Torgsin is an abbreviation from *Torgovlia s inostrantsami* (in Russian, "trade with foreigners"). This was a chain of special state-run stores, established in 1930. Foreigners who visited the Soviet Union or foreign experts who worked on Soviet construction projects could purchase goods in these stores using hard currency. Beginning in 1931, branch stores expanded to the district level and became accessible to Soviet citizens. During the genocidal famine, the stores extorted gold and anything valuable from the population in exchange for food and foreign-made products. In January 1932, store employees began receiving food rations to stave off stealing and to minimize a turnover of personnel. A store employee was entitled to 1 kg of butter, 1 kg of smoked meat, 3 kg of flour, 2 kg of macaroni, 1 kg of rice, 1 kg of sugar, 1 kg of herring, I kg of cheese, cans of fish in oil, and a bar of soap per month. Often these products were sold on the black market for exorbitant prices. At the time, starving people were bringing valuables (wedding rings, medals, or jewelry) to be weighed in exchange for food. In May 1932, only twenty-six stores functioned in Soviet Ukraine, but by October 1933, the network numbered 263. In 1932–1933, an estimated 66 tons of gold (21 tons in 1932 and 45 tons in 1933) in exchange for food on the territory of the USSR were extorted to pay for imported American and European goods and industrial equipment for Dnipro HES (hydroelectric power station) and Kharkiv tractor factory. In 1933, groceries constituted 90 percent of *Torgsin* sales. Due to shortages of food, thousands of receipts received in exchange for valuables were never redeemed.

troika (in Russian, Ukrainian *triika*) was a trio of party, GPU, and a local lumpen activist who conducted arbitrary executions without a trial.

trudoden' (a blend of *trud* and *den'* or a "workday") was a form of payment for workers on collective farms. This form of payment was introduced in 1930 because the state had no functioning banking system for money circulation. By spring 1931, this system of payment was imposed on 84 percent of collective farms in Soviet Ukraine. In theory, the payment was based on the quantity and quality of work calculated in workdays. In practice, it did not guarantee that collective farmers would be compensated materially for their work on farms. Payments were disbursed twice a year, an advance payment in July or August, and the full payment by the decision of the farm administration at the end of the year. Payments for agricultural work were stratified into five categories, averaging one to two workdays, so the compensation ranged from 60 kopeks to 1 krb. 20 kopeks. There was no minimum guaranteed payment. It was determined by a variety of factors: the crop size, the principle of distribution, and the procurement plan imposed from "above." For instance, ploughing 6 hectares of farm land was equivalent to 1.5 workdays, whereas digging out 600 quintal of potatoes or a ton of sugar beets was equivalent to 1.75 workdays. Distribution of seed grain was forbidden until collective farms fulfilled imposed grain procurement quotas. Often, the collective farms had nothing left over after fulfilling their obligations to the state. In fall 1932, collective farmers were stripped of one-third of their "earned workdays" for failing to fulfill grain procurement quotas, and in the blacklisted collective farms, workers were stripped of their grain seed advances. In 1933, nearly 48 percent of collective farms in Soviet Ukraine did not pay workers for their earned workdays, which means that an estimated 4 million collective farm workers and 14 million of their dependents were deprived of means to survive.

TsChO (in Russian *Tsentral'nyi chernozemnyi okrug*), or the Central Black Earth area of the Russian SFSR (1928–1934), included Voronezh, Kursk, and

Tambov, with a reported population of 11 million in 1931. Based on the 1926 census, from 1.5 to 2 million Ukrainians lived in the Central Black Earth region, including approximately 1.1 million Ukrainians in the Voronezh region and 600,000 in the Kursk region.

TsK (in Russian *Tsentral'nyi komitet*), or the Central Committee.

TsKK (in Russian *Tsentral'naia kontrol'naia komissiia*), or the Central Control Commission.

Kost' Turkalo (1892–1979), son of a priest, graduated from a seminary in Kam'ianets'-Podil's'kyi and later studied engineering at the Kyïv Polytechnic Institute. He was a member of Central Rada (1917–1918). He was one of the leading figures in implementing Ukrainization from 1924 to 1926. He served as editor in a technical section of the Institute of the Ukrainian Language (1926–1929). He was arrested in 1921, rearrested in 1930, and exiled until 1939. After World War II, he immigrated to America. He compiled a list of defendants in the SVU trial, first published in *The Black Deeds of the Kremlin* in the 1950s.

UNR (in Ukrainian *Ukraïns'ka narodnia respublika*), or Ukrainian National Republic. After the Bolshevik seizure of power in Russia, the Central Rada proclaimed the Ukrainian National Republic, designating its territory and its federal relationship with Russia in its Third Universal of November 20, 1917. The Central Rada had the support of the majority of the population of Ukraine. At the end of November 1917, the Bolshevik government of Russia was preparing to seize power in Ukraine, and, on December 17, 1917, sent an ultimatum to Ukraine, which the Central Rada rejected. The Bolshevik army then began its military campaign against Ukraine. The All-Ukrainian Congress of Workers', Soldiers', and Peasants' Deputies met in Kyïv on December 17, 1917, and proclaimed its support for the Central Rada. The Bolshevik deputies left for Kharkiv, where, on December 25, 1917, they established a rival government opposed to the Central Rada. At the same time the Rada sent a delegation to the peace negotiations with the Central Powers in Brest. At the height of the Ukrainian war against Russian Bolsheviks in the mid of the peace negotiations, the Central Rada proclaimed the Fourth Universal on January 25, 1918, which declared the Ukrainian National Republic an independent and sovereign state. The Central Rada passed a series of laws, establishing the eight-hour workday, land reform, and, during its stay in Volyn', laws on the monetary system, a national coat of arms, citizenship in the UNR, and the administrative-territorial division of the territory of Ukraine. The most important legislative act of the Central Rada was the adoption of the Constitution of the UNR on April 29, 1918. After the signing of the Brest-Litovsk Peace Treaty on February 9, 1918, the German army took over the Ukrainian territory that had been occupied by the Bolsheviks, but conflict ensued between the Germans and the UNR because of German interference in the internal affairs of Ukraine. On April 29, 1918, a coup took place with the support of the German army, and General Pavlo Skoropads'kyi was proclaimed Hetman of the Ukrainian State. Hetman Skoropads'kyi dissolved the Central Rada. In December 1918, following Germany's withdrawal from Ukraine, Skoropads'kyi abdicated and fled to Germany. The Directory of the UNR succeeded in ousting him in a coup. The UNR government created a ministry of nationalities with deputy ministers for the Jewish, Polish, and Russian minorities. Minority schools were established in areas of compact settlements of the respective minorities. The government-in-exile of the Ukrainian National Republic continued its existence abroad until 1992, when it formally ceased to exist with the creation of an independent Ukrainian state.

USRR (in Ukrainian *Ukraïns'ka Sotsialistychna Radians'ka Respublika*), or Ukrainian Socialist Soviet Republic (see *URSR*).

URSR (in Ukrainian *Ukraïns'ka Radians'ka Sotsialistychna Respublika*), or Ukrainian Soviet Socialist Republic. After the adoption of the Soviet constitution of 1936, known as Stalin's constitution, the official name was changed by switching two words, Soviet preceding Socialist.

USSR stands for the Union of Soviet Socialist Republics (in Russian *Soiuz Sovetskikh Sotsialisticheskikh Respublik*, abbreviated SSSR), or the former Soviet Union.

Mykola Vasylenko (1866–1935) was Ukrainian historian and minister of education during the Hetman administration. At the invitation of Mykhailo Hrushevs'kyi, Vasylenko joined the Central Rada. Vasylenko was appointed minister of education by Hetman Skoropads'kyi on May 3, 1918, and served in that position until October 25, 1918. During his brief tenure, Vasylenko played a prominent role in founding the All-Ukrainian Academy of Sciences and two universities, one in Kyïv and another in Kam'ianets'-Podil's'kyi. In 1920, Vasylenko headed the All-Ukrainian Academy of Sciences. In 1924, he was arrested and sentenced to ten years of imprisonment for allegedly being a leader of the Kyïv Regional Center, plotting to overthrow the Communist dictatorship and establish democratic people's councils. Under the pressure from the scientific circles, the academician was freed. Due to severe psychological stress, his health condition worsened. In 1929, Vasylenko was dismissed from his post in the academy. His wife, Natalia Polons'ka-Vasylenko, a distinguished historian, wrote a history of the All-Ukrainian Academy of Sciences and a volume on Ukrainian women in history.

Hryhorii Vashchenko (1878–1967) was a teacher and educational theorist from the Poltava region. In 1923, he joined the Poltava Institute of People's Education. As the chair of the pedagogy department, he devoted his work to developing Zaluzhnyi's theory of the collective upbringing. In 1933, he was forced to resign. In search of a job, he moved to Moscow, and after two years without stable employment, he secured a position as a chair of the pedagogy department at the Stalingrad Pedagogical Institute. In 1943, he immigrated to Munich, where he became professor of pedagogy at the Ukrainian Free University. Till the rest of his life, he dedicated his work to the moral and patriotic education of Ukrainian youth in diaspora. In 1957, he authored a draft of the system of education for independent Ukraine. In 1995, a pedagogical society was named after him to popularize his legacy in Ukraine.

VChK (in Russian *Vserossiiskaia chrezvychainaia komissiia*), or All-Russian Extraordinary Commission, commonly spelled as Cheka, was the first of a succession of Soviet security police organizations. Established in December 1917, it was headed by Felix Dzerzhinsky.

versta (in Russian) was approximately one kilometer.

vidpovidachi were civilians selected at random, accused of harboring or aiding "bandits," and executed by the Bolsheviks as part of the system of extra-judicial killings. The decree issued on May 30, 1921, signed by Volodymyr Zatons'kyi, then head of the council on combatting bandit activities in the Kyïv military district, provided instructions on how two plenipotentiaries have to select one civilian from every twentieth household in a village or at least one civilian from every independent farmstead to be executed as responsible for carrying out acts of "banditry"; the number of civilians executed doubled if a Soviet government official was murdered.

VKP(b) (in Russian *Vsesoiuznaia Kommunisticheskaia partiia (bol'shevikov)*) was the All-Union Communist Party (Bolsheviks).

VTsIK (in Russian *Vserossiiskii tsentral'nyi ispolnitel'nyi komitet*), or the All-Russian Central Executive Committee.

VUAN (*Vseukraïns'ka akademiia nauk*), or All-Ukrainian Academy of Sciences. It was founded in 1918, dissolved in 1929, and absorbed into the Academy of Sciences of the USSR. It served as an element of governmental control over the political activities of the intelligentsia.

VUTsVK (in Ukrainian *Vseukraïns'kyi tsentral'nyi vykonavchyi komitet*), or the All-Ukrainian Central Executive Committee.

vykonavtsi perpetrated the genocide known as the Holodomor. They included rank-and-file Communists dispatched from Moscow and other Russian urban centers as well as regional and district branches of the party and repressive security police, the GPU. They were forced to carry out collectivization, grain confiscation, and propaganda campaigns. In addition, teachers were forced to provide the ideological cover for these campaigns. The supply of food for teachers was conditioned on their "participation" in these campaigns as members of *buksyrni bryhady*.

War Communism was the term used by Vladimir Lenin to describe the onslaught of 1918–1920. Lenin claimed that the measures aimed at building communism had been precipitated by wartime conditions. However, the term did not appear until 1921, after the transition to the New Economic Policy (see *NEP*).

ZAGS (in Russian *Zapisi aktov grazhdanskogo sostoianiia*), or Registry of Vital Statistics, for the years of 1932–1933 in the Ukrainian state archives contain 3 million deaths, which cover a maximum of one-third of the territory afflicted by the Holodomor. Mortality records directly attributed to the Holodomor constitute no more than 1.5 percent of the total mortality records of civil registry offices. Soviet archival documents were sanitized in 1929–1930, 1937–1938, and during the summer of 1941 on the eve of the German invasion of the Soviet Union. After the re-evacuation of archives in 1945, inventories conducted in 1949, 1955, 1957, 1962, 1965, and 1968 led to thousands of records for the period of 1928–1935 being deliberately destroyed.

Oleksandr Zaluzhnyi (1886–1938), a teacher and educational theorist from the Dnipropetrovs'k region, published several monographs on the role of the collective in the upbringing of children. Between 1907 and 1910, he studied in Sorbonne, Paris. In 1917, he returned to Ukraine and served in the Central Rada. In 1922, he went to Japan, where he studied its education system. Upon return to Ukraine in 1924, he lectured at the Kharkiv Institute of People's Education. In 1926, he joined the first Ukrainian educational research institute, where he was in charge of the section studying collectivism. His transfer to Moscow in 1935 did not save him from persecution for his experimental work with educational testing and his interest in reflexology. In 1938, he was arrested and imprisoned; rehabilitated posthumously.

zaruchnytstvo was a system of hostage taking, used by occupying Bolshevik authorities.

zatirka, or *zatyrushka*, was a variety of a low-calorie soup made of flour added to water, with a mixture of surrogates, such as grasses, leaves, oat or rye chaff. In August 1932, after the law of "five ears of wheat" was adopted, bread was given out to tractor drivers only, whereas collective farm workers in the fields were fed "hot meals" and had to eat their own bread. In November 1932, public kitchens on collective farms stopped functioning because all grain and food were confiscated due to failure to fulfill grain procurement plans. Mass deaths from starvation and appeals to the government for help in spring of 1933 led to the opening of 22,000 field kitchens on collective farms to feed those who had strength to sow and plant a new crop.

Volodymyr Zatons'kyi (1888–1938) was People's Commissar of Education in the Ukrainian SSR. He was the only Commissar of Education in the 1920s to complete a postsecondary degree, graduating from Kyïv University in 1912. In 1917, he joined Bolsheviks and served twice as Commissar of Education in the first Soviet Ukrainian governments and was instrumental in the formation of the KP(b)U. Zatons'kyi was again appointed the Commissar of Education in October 1922, after Hryhorii Hryn'ko's tenure. Although the reorganization of Ukrainian schools continued under Zatons'kyi's tenure, Ukrainization of schools did not accelerate until Oleksandr Shums'kyi assumed leadership of the People's Commissariat of Education. Zatons'kyi also served as deputy chairman of the Council of People's Commissars from 1927 to 1933 and was elected a member of the Academy of Sciences of the Ukrainian SSR. He reassumed the position of Commissar of Education after Mykola Skrypnyk's dismissal in 1933. He was arrested in 1937 and later executed in 1938.

Bibliography

Abramson, Henry. *A Prayer for the Government: Ukrainians and Jews in Revolutionary Times, 1917–1920*. Cambridge: Distributed by Harvard University Press for the Harvard Ukrainian Research Institute and Center for Jewish Studies, Harvard University, 1999.

Adams, Arthur E. *Bolsheviks in the Ukraine: The Second Campaign, 1918–1919*. New Haven: Yale University Press, 1963.

———. "The Great Ukrainian Jacquerie." In *The Ukraine, 1917–1921: A Study in Revolution*, edited by Taras Hunczak, 247–70. Cambridge: Harvard Ukrainian Research Institute, 1977.

Adams'kyi, Viktor. "Deportatsiia ukraïns'koï intelihentsiï v konteksti stanovlennia totalitarnoho rezhymu." *Rozbudova derzhavy*, no. 8 (1996): 40–44.

———. "Ideia natsional'noho universytetu za doby Tsentral'noï Rady: sproba realizatsiï." *Osvita, nauka i kul'tura na Podilli*, no. 24 (2017), 15–27.

———. "The Deportation of the Ukrainian Intelligentsia." In *Genocide in Ukraine*, edited by Peter Kardash, 178–81. Melbourne: Fortuna Publishing, 2007.

A Dictionary of Scientific Communism. Moscow: Progress Publishers, 1984.

Alexopoulos, Golfo. *Illness and Inhumanity in Stalin's Gulag*. New Haven: Yale University Press, 2017.

Ammende, Ewald. *Human Life in Russia*. Introduction by the Rt. Hon. Lord Dickinson. London: George Allen and Unwin, 1936.

Andriewsky, Olga. "Towards a Decentred History: The Study of the Holodomor and Ukrainian Historiography." In *Contextualizing the Holodomor: The Impact of Thirty Years of Ukrainian Famine Studies*, edited by Andrij Makuch and Frank E. Sysyn, 14–48. Edmonton: Canadian Institute of Ukrainian Studies Press, 2015.

Andrusyshen, Constantine Henry, and Watson Kirkconnell, eds. *The Ukrainian Poets, 1189–1962*. Toronto: University of Toronto Press, 1963.

Antonenko-Davydovych, Borys. "SVU." *Neopalyma kupyna: narodoznavstvo, istoriia, arkhivy*, no. 1 (1994): 31–66.

Antonovych, Myroslava. "Individual and Collective Intent in the Crime of Genocide (on the Example of the Holodomor-Genocide against the Ukrainian Nation)." *Actual Problems of International Relations*, no. 145 (2020): 54–61.

Applebaum, Anne. *Gulag: A History*. New York: Doubleday, 2003.

———. *Red Famine: Stalin's War on Ukraine*. New York: Doubleday, 2017.

Arendt, Hannah. "Ideology and Terror: A Novel Form of Government." In *The Great Lie: Classic and Recent Appraisals of Ideology and Totalitarianism*, edited by F. Flagg Taylor IV, 124–47. Wilmington: Intercollegiate Studies Institute, 2011.

Arkhireis'kyi, Dmytro, and Viktor Chentsov. "Antyradians'ka natsional'na opozytsiia v USRR v 20-ti rr.: pohliad na problemu kriz' arkhivni dzherela." *Z arkhiviv VUChK, GPU, NKVD, KGB*, no. 2–4 (2000): 16–55.

Aron, Leon. "Vladimir the (not so) Great." *Wall Street Journal*, May 31–June 1, 2014.

Asatkin, Oleksandr, ed. *Narodne hospodarstvo USRR (statystychnyi dovidnyk)*. Kyïv: Narodne hospodarstvo ta oblik, 1935.

Avdiienko, M. O. *Narodna osvita na Ukraïni*. Kharkiv: Tsentral'ne Statystychne Upravlinnia, 1927.

Babenko, L. "Politychni represiï 1920–1930-kh rokiv u Poltavs'komu pedahohichnomu instytuti." *Al'manakh Poltavs'koho derzhavnoho pedahohichnoho universytetu "Ridnyi krai*,*"* no. 2 (21) (2009): 196–209.

Balan, Jars. "Rhea Clyman: A Forgotten Canadian Eyewitness to the Hunger of 1932." In *Women and the Holodomor-Genocide: Victims, Survivors, Perpetrators*, edited by Victoria A. Malko, 91–117. Fresno: The Press at California State University, 2019.

Battersby, Christine. *The Sublime, Terror, and Human Difference*. London: Routledge, 2007.

Bender, Frederic L., ed. *Karl Marx: Essential Writings*. New York: Harper & Row, Publishers, 1972.

Ben-Naftali, Orna, and Miri Sharon. "What the ICJ Did Not Say About the Duty to Punish Genocide." *Journal of International Criminal Justice* 5, no. 4 (2007): 859–74.

Berdiaev, N. A. "O rabstve i svobode cheloveka: Opyt personalisticheskoi filosofii." *Biblioteka "Vekhi*,*"* 2001. http://www.vehi.net/berdyaev/rabstvo/012.html.

Berelovich, A., and V. Danilov, eds. *Sovetskaia derevnia glazami VChK–OGPU–NKVD, 1918–1939: Dokumenty i materialy*, 4 vols. Moscow: ROSSPEN, 1998–2012.

Bertelsen, Olga. "A Trial *in Absentia*: Purifying National Historical Narratives in Russia." *Kyiv-Mohyla Humanities Journal*, no. 3 (2016): 57–87.

———. "'Hyphenated' Identities during the Holodomor: Women and Cannibalism." In *Women and Genocide: Survivors, Victims, Perpetrators*, edited by Elissa Bemporad and Joyce W. Warren, 77–96. Bloomington: Indiana University Press, 2018.

———. "Starvation and Violence amid the Soviet Politics of Silence: 1928–1929." *Genocide Studies International* 11, no. 1 (2017): 38–67.

———. "Women at Sites of Mass Starvation: Ukraine, 1932–1933." In *Women and the Holodomor-Genocide: Victims, Survivors, Perpetrators*, edited by Victoria A. Malko, 33–49. Fresno: The Press at California State University, 2019.

———, and Myroslav Shkandrij. "The Secret Police and the Campaign against Galicians in Soviet Ukraine, 1929–34." *Nationalities Papers: The Journal of Nationalism and Ethnicity* 42, no. 1 (2014): 37–62.

Berzins, Janis. "Russia's New Generation Warfare in Ukraine: Implications for Latvian Defense Policy." Report from the National Defence Academy of Latvia and the Center for Security and Strategic Research. *Informal Institute for National Security Thinkers and Practitioners Blog*, April 30, 2014. http://maxoki161.blogspot.com/2014/04/russias-new-generation-warfare-in.html.

Bezo, Brent John Louis. "The Impact of Intergenerational Transmission of Trauma from the Holodomor Genocide of 1932–1933 in Ukraine." Doctoral diss., Carleton University, 2011.

———, and Stefania Maggi. "The Intergenerational Impact of the Holodomor Genocide on Gender Roles, Expectations and Performance: The Ukrainian Experience." *Annals of Psychiatry and Mental Health* 3, no. 3 (2015): 1–4.

———. "Living in 'Survival Mode': Intergenerational Transmission of Trauma from the Holodomor Genocide of 1932–1933 in Ukraine." *Social Science & Medicine*, no. 134 (2015): 87–94.

Bilas, Ivan. *Represyvno-karal'na systema v Ukraïni, 1917–1953: Suspil'no-politychnyi ta istoryko-pravovyi analiz*, 2 vols. Kyïv: "Lybid'" – "Viis'ko Ukraïny," 1994.

"Bill to Establish a Commission to Study the 1932–1933 Famine Caused by the Soviet Government in Ukraine (H.R. 4459 in the House of Representatives, S. 2456 in the Senate)." *Ukrainian Weekly*, April 1, 1984. http://www.ukrweekly.com/old/archive/1984/148419.shtml.

Billington, James H. *The Icon and the Axe: An Interpretive History of Russian Culture*. New York: Alfred A. Knopf, 1968.

———. "The Legacy of Russian History." In *The Stalin Revolution: Foundations of Soviet Totalitarianism*, edited and with an introduction by Robert V. Daniels, 159–68. Lexington and Toronto: D. C. Heath and Company, 1972.

Bilokin', Serhii. "Dolia chleniv Tsentral'noï Rady v SSSR." *Vyzvol'nyi shliakh*, kn. 1 (2000), 14–26. https://web.archive.org/web/20081122004310/http://bilokin.mysl enedrevo.com.ua/terror/dchcr.html.

———. *Masovyi teror iak zasib derzhavnoho upravlinnia v SRSR, 1917–1941 rr.: dzhereloznavche doslidzhennia*, vol 1. Kyïv, 1999.

———. *Masovyi teror iak zasib derzhavnoho upravlinnia v SRSR, 1917–1941 rr.: dzhereloznavche doslidzhennia*, vol. 2. Drohovych: "Kolo," 2013.

———. *Masovyi teror iak zasib derzhavnoho upravlinnia v SRSR, 1917–1941 rr.: dzhereloznavche doslidzhennia*. 2nd ed. Kyïv: Penman, 2017.

———. *Novi studiï z istoriï bol'shevyzmu*. Kyïv: Instytut istoriï Ukraïny NAN Ukraïny, 2006.

———. "Repetytsiia bezzakon': sudovyi protses nad 'Spilkoiu vyzvolennia Ukraïny.'" *Ukraïna*, no. 37 (1701), September 10, 1989, 13–15 and no. 38 (1702), September 17, 1989, 20–21.

———. "Rozstril′nyi spysok Solovkiv." *Literaturna Ukraïna*, no. 27, July 9, 1992.

Bittman, Ladislav. *The KGB and Soviet Disinformation: An Insider's View*. Washington: Pergamon-Brassey's International Defense Publishers, 1985.

Blinova, Ekaterina. "Holodomor Hoax: Joseph Stalin's Crime That Never Took Place." *Sputnik News*, August 9, 2015. http://sputniknews.com/politics/20150809 /1025560345.html#ixzz3iXdnBIyY.

Blundell, Nigel. *A Pictorial History of Joseph Stalin*. North Dighton: JG Press, 1996.

Bohlen, Charles E. *Witness to History, 1929–1969*. New York: W. W. Norton & Company, 1973.

Bohman, James. "Critical Theory." *Stanford Encyclopedia of Philosophy* (Winter 2019 Edition), edited by Edward N. Zalta. https://plato.stanford.edu/archives/win2 019/entries/critical-theory/.

Bolabol′chenko, Anatolii. *SVU – sud nad perekonanniamy*. Kyïv: UKSP "Kobza," 1994.

Bondar, Kateryna. "Legal Definition of Genocide: Examining the 1932–1933 Holodomor in Ukraine under the Genocide Convention." In *The Holodomor of 1932–1933 in Ukraine as a Crime of Genocide under International Law*, edited by Volodymyr Vasylenko and Myroslava Antonovych, 95–119. Kyïv: Kyïv-Mohyla Academy, 2016.

Bondarchuk, Andrii. "'Stokhol′ms′kyi syndrom' iak kintseva meta totalitarnoho rezhymu: vid vytokiv do suchasnosti." *Litopys Volyni*, no. 20 (2019): 55–64.

Bondarchuk, P. *Natsional′no-kul′turna polityka bil′shovykiv v Ukraïni na pochatku 1920-kh rokiv*. Kyïv: Instytut istoriï Ukraïny NAN Ukraïny, 1998.

Boriak, Hennadii. "Population Losses in the Holodomor and the Destruction of Related Archives: New Archival Evidence." In *After the Holodomor: The Enduring Impact of the Great Famine on Ukraine*, edited by Andrea Graziosi, Lubomyr A. Hajda, and Halyna Hryn. Cambridge: Ukrainian Research Institute of Harvard University, 2013. Originally published in *Harvard Ukrainian Studies* 30, nos. 1–4 (2008): 199–215. http://history.org.ua/LiberUA/BoriakPopulationLosses _2008/BoriakPopulationLosses_2008.pdf.

———. *Sources for the Study of the Great Famine in Ukraine*. Cambridge: Harvard University Ukrainian Studies Fund, 2009.

Borisenok, Elena. *Fenomen sovetskoi ukrainizatsii, 1920–1930-e gody*. Moscow: "Evropa," 2006.

Borys, Jurij. "Political Parties in the Ukraine." In *The Ukraine, 1917–1921: A Study in Revolution*, edited by Taras Hunczak, 128–58. Cambridge: Harvard Ukrainian Research Institute, 1977.

———. *The Russian Communist Party and the Sovietization of the Ukraine: A Study in the Communist Doctrine of the Self-Determination of Nations*. Stockholm: Norstedt & Soner, 1960.

Borysenko, Valentyna, Vasyl′ Danylenko, Serhii Kokin, Olesia Stasiuk, and Iurii Shapoval. *Rozsekrechena pam′iat′: Holodomor 1932–1933 rokiv v Ukraïni v dokumentakh GPU-NKVD*. Kyïv: Stylos, 2007.

Bronner, Stephen. *Critical Theory: A Very Short Introduction*. New York: Oxford University Press, 2011.

Buhaievych, Ihor. *Dozhylasia Ukraïna ... Narodna tvorchist' chasiv holodomoru i kolektyvizatsiï na Ukraïni*. Kyïv: Ukraïns'kyi pys'mennyk, 1993.

Bunge, Jacob. "Supersized Family Farms Transform U.S. Agriculture." *Wall Street Journal*, October 24, 2017.

Carr, Edward Hallett. *The Bolshevik Revolution, 1917–1923*, 3 vols. London: Macmillan, 1950–53.

Carynnyk, Marco. "Blind Eye to Murder: Britain, the United States and the Ukrainian Famine of 1933." In *Famine in Ukraine, 1932–1933*, edited by Roman Serbyn and Bohdan Krawchenko, 109–38. Edmonton: Canadian Institute of Ukrainian Studies, 1986.

———, Lubomyr Y. Luciuk, and Bohdan S. Kordan, eds. *The Foreign Office and the Famine: British Documents on Ukraine and the Great Famine of 1932–1933*. Kingston: Limestone Press, 1988.

Chalk, Frank, and Kurt Jonassohn. *The History and Sociology of Genocide: Analyses and Case Studies*. New Haven: Yale University Press, 1990.

Chechel, Irina, and Aleksandr Markov. "Zatukhaiushchaia tsyklichnost'." *Gefter*, November 6, 2012. http://gefter.ru/archive/6660.

Chentsov, Viktor. *Politychni represiï v radians'kii Ukraïni v 20-ti roky*. Ternopil': Zbruch, 2000.

Chertok, Paula. "History, Identity and Holodomor Denial: Russia's Continued Assault on Ukraine." *Euromaidan Press*, November 7, 2015. http://euromaidanpress.com/2015/11/07/history-identity-and-holodomor-denial-russia-s-continued-assault-on-ukraine/.

Chirko, B. V. "Nemetskaia natsional'naia gruppa v Ukraine v kontekste gosudarstvennoi etnopolitiki 20–30-kh gg. XX st." In *Voprosy germanskoi istorii*, edited by S. I. Bobyleva. Dnepropetrovsk: "Porogi," 2007.

Chukhin, Ivan. *Kanalo-armeitsy: Istoriia stroitel'stva Belomorkanala v dokumentakh, tsyfrakh, faktakh, fotografiiakh, svidetel'stvakh uchastnikov i ochevidtsev*. Petrozavodsk: "Kareliia," 1990.

Colley, Margaret Siriol, and Nigel Linsan Colley. *Gareth Jones: A Manchukuo Incident*. Nottinghamshire: Nigel Linsan Colley, 2001.

Conquest, Robert. *Kolyma: The Arctic Death Camps*. New York: Viking Press, 1978.

———. *The Harvest of Sorrow: Soviet Collectivization and the Terror–Famine*. New York: Oxford University Press, 1986.

Conte, Francis. *Christian Rakovski: A Political Biography*. Boulder: East European Monographs, 1989.

Crankshaw, Edward. "When Lenin Returned." *The Atlantic Monthly*, October 1954. https://www.theatlantic.com/magazine/archive/1954/10/when-lenin-returned/303867/.

Crowl, James William. "Angels in Stalin's Paradise: Western Reporters in Soviet Russia, A Case Study of Louis Fischer and Walter Duranty." Doctoral diss., University of Virginia, 1978.

Dallin, David, and Boris Nicolaevsky. *Forced Labor in Soviet Russia*. London: Hollis and Carter, 1948.

Danilov, V., R. Manning, and L. Viola, eds. *Tragediia sovetskoi derevni. Kollektivizatsiia i raskulachivanie. Dokumenty i materialy, 1927–1939*, 5 vols. Moscow: ROSSPEN, 1999–2006.

Danilov, V. P., and I. Ie. Zelenin, "Organizovannyi golod. K 70-letiiu obshchekrest'ianskoi tragedii." *Otechestvennaia istoriia*, no. 5 (2004): 97–111.

Danylenko, Andrii, and Halyna Naienko. "Linguistic Russification in Russian Ukraine: Languages, Imperial Models, and Policies." *Russian Linguistics* 43, no. 1 (2019): 19–39. https://doi.org/10.1007/s11185-018-09207-1.

Danylenko, Viktor. "Odyn z 45-ty: V. Durdukivs'kyi." *Z arkhiviv VUChK-GPU-NKVD-KGB*, nos. 1–2 (1998): 253–62. http://memorial.kiev.ua/zhurnal/pdf/01-0 2_1998/253.pdf.

Danylenko, V. M., ed. *Pavlohrads'ke povstannia 1930 r.: Dokumenty i materialy*. Kyïv: Ukraïns'kyi pys'mennyk, 2009.

———, and M. M. Kuz'menko. "Naukovo-pedahohichna intelihentsiia v roky holodu." *Ukraïns'kyi istorychnyi zhurnal*, no. 5 (2003): 145–55.

———. *Sotsial'nyi typ ta intelektual'no-osvitnii riven' nomenklatury skrypnykivs'koho narkomosu: Biohrafichni narysy*. Sevastopol' and Donets'k: Veber, 2003.

Danylenko, Vasyl', ed. *Ukraïns'ka intelihentsiia i vlada: Zvedennia sekretnoho viddilu DPU USRR 1927–1929 rr.* Kyïv: Tempora, 2012.

Danylenko, Vasyl', Heorhii Kas'ianov, and Stanislav Kul'chyts'kyi. *Stalinizm na Ukraïni, 1920–30-ti roky*. Kyïv: Lybid', 1991.

Danylevs'kyi, K. *Petliura v sertsiakh i pisniakh svoho narodu*. Regensburg: Filiia Tovarystva ukraïns'kykh politychnykh v'iazniv z Regensburga, 1947.

David-Fox, Michael. *Showcasing the Great Experiment: Cultural Diplomacy and Western Visitors to the Soviet Union, 1921–1941*. New York: Oxford University Press, 2012.

———. "What Is Cultural Revolution?" *The Russian Review* 58, no. 2 (1999): 181–201.

Davies, R. W., and S. G. Wheatcroft. *The Years of Hunger: Soviet Agriculture, 1931–1933*, vol. 5 Industrialization of Soviet Russia. London: Palgrave Macmillan, 2004.

Dearinger, Ryan. *The Filth of Progress: Immigrants, Americans, and the Building of Canals and Railroads in the West*. Oakland: University of California Press, 2015.

de Madariaga, Isabel. *Russia in the Age of Catherine the Great*. New Haven: Yale University Press, 1981.

———. "The Foundation of the Russian Educational System by Catherine II." *Slavonic and East European Review* 57, no. 3 (1979): 369–95.

Dewey, John. "Why I Am Not a Communist." *Modern Monthly* 8 (April 1934): 135–37.

Dietsch, Deborah K. "Local Architect Designs Washington Memorial to Victims of Genocidal Famine in Ukraine." *Washington Post*, July 24, 2014.

Dimarov, Anatolii. "The Hungry Thirties (A Parable About Bread)." *In Stalin's Shadow*. Translated from Ukrainian by Iurii Tkach, 110–75. Melbourne: Bayda Books, 1989. http://shron1.chtyvo.org.ua/Dimarov_Anatolii/In_Stalins_Shadow _anhl.pdf.

Dobczansky, Jurij. "Affirmation and Denial: Holodomor-related Resources Recently Acquired by the Library of Congress." *Holodomor Studies* 1, no. 2 (2009): 153–62.
Doroshenko, Dmytro. *Istoriia Ukraïny, 1917–1923 rr*, vol. I. 2nd ed. New York: Bulava Publishing Corporation, 1954.
Doroshko, Mykola. *Nomenklatura: kerivna verkhivka radians′koï Ukraïny (1917–1938 rr.)*. Kyïv: Nika-Tsentr, 2012.
Dovidnyk z osnovnykh statystychno-ekonomichnykh pokaznykiv hospodarstva raioniv Kyïvs′koï oblasti USRR. Kharkiv, 1933.
Drach, O. "Spivrobitnyky Cherkas′koho pedahohichnoho instytutu – zhertvy stalins′kykh represii." In *Osvitiany Cherkashchyny – zhertvy radians′koho totalitarnoho rezhymu: dokumental′ne vydannia*, edited by V. Masnenko, 213–18. Cherkasy: Brama-Ukraïny, 2009.
Drovoziuk, S. I. "Bil′shovyts′ki tekhnolohiï 'perevykhovannia' ukraïns′koï intelihentsiï u 20–30-kh rr. XX st." In *Naukovi zapysky Vinnyts′koho derzhavnoho pedahohichnoho universytetu im. M. Kotsiubyns′koho*, edited by P. S. Hryhorchuk, 193–97. Vinnytsia: VDPU, 2006.
———. "Vysvitlennia dukhovnykh aspektiv henotsydu 1932–1933 rr. v ukraïns′kii istoriohrafiï." In *Henotsyd ukraïns′koho narodu: istorychna pam′iat′ ta polityko-pravova otsinka: Mizhnarodna naukovo-teoretychna konferentsiia, Kyïv, 25 lystopada 2002*, edited by V. A. Smolii et al., 295–304. Kyïv; New York: Vyd-vo M. P. Kots′, 2003.
Drozdov, Konstantin. "Ukrainizatsia v Tsentral′nom Chernozem′ie RSFSR v 1923–1928 gg.: K voprosu ob osobennostiakh natsional′noi politiki bol′shevikov v gody NEPa." *The NEP Era*, no. 4 (2010): 43–59.
"Duma ne priznala Golodomor 1932–33 godov." *Delo.ua*, April 2, 2008. https://delo.ua/econonomyandpoliticsinukraine/gosduma-ne-priznala-1932-33-go-75225/.
Ekeltchik, Serguei. "History, Culture, and Nationhood under High Stalinism: Soviet Ukraine, 1939–1954." Thesis, University of Alberta, 2000.
Ellman, Michael. "Stalin and the Soviet Famine of 1932–33 Revisited." *Europe-Asia Studies* 59, no. 4 (2007): 663–93.
Ewing, E. Thomas. "Personal Acts with Public Meanings: Suicides by Soviet Women Teachers in the Early Stalin Era." *Gender & History* 14, no. 1 (2002): 117–37.
———. *The Teachers of Stalinism: Policy, Practice and Power in Soviet Schools of the 1930s*. New York: Peter Lang, 2002.
Fairbank, John K., Edwin O. Reischauer, and Albert M. Craig. *East Asia: The Modern Transformation*. Boston: Houghton Mifflin Company, 1965.
Faizulin, Iaroslav. *"Represovani" shchodennyky: Holodomor 1932–1933 rokiv v Ukraïni*. Kyïv: Feniks, 2018.
———. "Unwilling Instrument of the State." *Ukrainian Week*, October 14, 2011. https://ukrainianweek.com/History/33007.
"Famine in the USSR, 1929–1934: New Documentary Evidence," with Historical Essay by Viktor Kondrashyn; English translation of the documents by Nikita B. Katz; English translation of the Note from the Compilers by Alexandra Dolgova. Moscow: Federal Archival Service, 2009. Compact Disc. http://resource.history.org.ua/item/0008508.

Fedor, Julie. *Russia and the Cult of State Security*. New York: Routledge, 2011.

Fedor, Thomas S. *Patterns of Urban Growth in the Russian Empire during the Nineteenth Century*. Chicago: University of Chicago, Department of Geography Research Paper No. 163, 1975.

Fedyk, Nicholas. "Russian 'New Generation' Warfare – Theory, Practice, and Lessons for U.S. Strategists." *Small Wars Journal*, August 25, 2016. https://smallwarsjournal.com/jrnl/art/russian-"new-generation"-warfare-theory-practice-and-lessons-for-us-strategists.

Fedyshyn, Oleh S. "The Germans and the Union for the Liberation of the Ukraine, 1914–1917." In *The Ukraine, 1917–1921: A Study in Revolution*, edited by Taras Hunczak, 305–22. Cambridge: Harvard Ukrainian Research Institute, 1977.

Fel′shtinskii, Iurii, ed. *VchK-GPU: Dokumenty i materialy*. Moscow: Izd-vo gumanitarnoi literatury, 1995.

Filene, Peter G. *Americans and the Soviet Experiment, 1917–1933*. Cambridge: Harvard University Press, 1967.

———, ed. *American Views of Soviet Russia, 1917–1965*. Homewood, IL: The Dorsey Press, 1968.

Fitzpatrick, David. "Women and the Great Famine." In *Gender Perspectives in Nineteenth-Century Ireland: Public and Private Spheres*, edited by Margaret Kelleher and James H. Murphy, 50–69. Dublin: Irish Academic Press, 1997.

Fitzpatrick, Sheila. *Education and Social Mobility in the Soviet Union, 1921–1934*. Cambridge: Cambridge University Press, 1979.

———. "People and Martians." Review of *The Great Terror*, by Robert Conquest, and *The Harvest of Sorrow*, by Robert Conquest. *London Review of Books* 41, no. 2 (January 24, 2019): 13–15.

Flynn, Thomas. *Existentialism: A Very Short Introduction*. New York: Oxford University Press, 2006.

"Foreign Minister Sergey Lavrov's Remarks and Answers to Media Questions at a News Conference." *Ministry of Foreign Affairs of the Russian Federation*, November 26, 2018. https://www.mid.ru/en/press_service/minister_speeches/-/asset_publisher/7OvQR5KJWVmR/content/id/3420700.

Foreign Relations of the United States: The Soviet Union, 1933–1939, edited by E. R. Perkins, Rogers Platt Churchill, and John Gilbert Reid. Washington, D.C.: U.S. Government Printing Office, 1952. https://history.state.gov/historicaldocuments/frus1933-39.

"Four to Testify at Senate Hearings on Famine Commission Measure." *Ukrainian Weekly*, July 29, 1984.

Friedrich, Carl J., and Zbigniew K. Brzezinski. "The Model of Totalitarianism." In *The Stalin Revolution: Foundations of Soviet Totalitarianism*, edited by Robert V. Daniels, 198–213. Lexington and Toronto: D. C. Heath and Company, 1972.

———. *Totalitarian Dictatorship and Autocracy*, rev. ed. Cambridge: Harvard University Press, 1965.

Futey, Bohdan A. "International Legal Responsibility for Genocide: Justice in the Courts." Paper presented at a Conference on Famine-Holodomor, Kyïv, Ukraine,

September 25–26, 2008, *Holodomor Education*, 2009. http://www.holodomor education.org/index.php/id/178/lang/en.

———. "Legal Recognition of the Holodomor as Genocide: International Covenants, Agreements, and Court Decisions (Implementing Lemkin's Legacy)." Paper presented at the International Forum "Ukraine Remembers, the World Acknowledges!" on the 85th Anniversary of the Holodomor 1932–1933 – Genocide of the Ukrainian People, Kyïv, Ukraine, November 22, 2018.

Gamache, Ray. *Gareth Jones: Eyewitness to the Holodomor*. Cardiff: Welsh Academic Press, 2013.

Gantt, William Horsley. "A Medical Review of Soviet Russia: Results of the First Five-Year Plan." *British Medical Journal* 2, no. 3939 (July 4, 1936): 19–22.

Getty, J. Arch, and Roberta Thompson Manning. *Stalinist Terror: New Perspectives*. New York: Cambridge University Press, 1993.

Goble, Paul. "A New GULAG Is Emerging Just as Stalin's Did Slowly and Insidiously, Gudkov Warns." *Euromaidan Press*, August 17, 2018. http://euromaid anpress.com/2018/08/17/a-new-gulag-is-emerging-just-as-stalins-did-slowly-and-i nsidiously-gudkov-warns/.

Goncharenko, Oleksiy. "Ukraine Cannot Stay Neutral in Putin's History War." *Atlantic Council*, April 21, 2020. https://atlanticcouncil.org/blogs/ukrainealert/ukr aine-cannot-stay-neutral-in-putins-history-war/.

Gorbunova, Viktoriia, and Vitalii Klymchuk. "The Psychological Consequences of the Holodomor in Ukraine." *East/West: Journal of Ukrainian Studies* 7, no. 2 (2020): 33–68.

"Gosduma ne priznala Golodomor 1932–33 godov: Gosudarstvennaia Duma Rossii otritsaet priznaki genotsyda vo vremia goloda 1932–1933 godov na territorii SSSR." *Delo*, April 2, 2008. https://delo.ua/econonomyandpoliticsinukraine/gosd uma-ne-priznala-1932-33-go-75225/.

Grabowicz, George G. *The Poet as Mythmaker: A Study of Symbolic Meaning in Taras Ševčenko*. Cambridge: Harvard Ukrainian Research Institute, 1982.

Graziosi, Andrea. "The Impact of Holodomor Studies on the Understanding of the USSR." In *Contextualizing the Holodomor: The Impact of Thirty Years of Ukrainian Famine Studies*, edited by Andrij Makuch and Frank E. Sysyn, 49–75. Edmonton: Canadian Institute of Ukrainian Studies Press, 2015.

———. "The Soviet 1931–1933 Famines and the Ukrainian Holodomor: Is a New Interpretation Possible, and What Would Its Consequences Be?" *Harvard Ukrainian Studies* 27, no. 1/4 (2004–2005): 97–115.

———. "Viewing the Twentieth Century through the Prism of Ukraine: Reflections on the Heuristic Potential of Ukrainian History." *Harvard Ukrainian Studies* 34, no. 1–4 (2015–2016): 107–28.

———, ed. *Lettere da Kharkov: La carestia in Ucraina e nel Caucaso del Nord nei rapporti dei diplomatici italiani, 1932–33*. Torino: Einaudi, 1991.

Grechko, V. *Kommunisticheskoe vospitanie v SSSR*. Munich: Institute for the Study of the History and Culture of the USSR, 1951.

Green, Barbara B. "Stalinist Terror and the Question of Genocide: The Great Famine." In *Is the Holocaust Unique? Perspectives on Comparative Genocide*, edited and with an Introduction by Alan S. Rosenbaum with a Foreword by Israel W. Charny, 175–99. Boulder: Westview Press, 1996.

Gregory, Paul R., and Valery Lazarev, eds. *The Economics of Forced Labor: The Soviet Gulag*. Palo Alto: Stanford University Hoover Institution Press, 2003.

Grigorenko, Petro G. *Memoirs*. Translated by Thomas P. Whitney. New York: W. W. Norton, 1982.

Grinevich, Vladislav. "Podolannia totalitarnoho mynuloho – Chastyna 3: Chy buv SSSR imperiieiu, a Ukraïna – koloniieiu?" *Ukraïna moderna*, August 22, 2019. uamoderna.com/blogy/vladislav-grinevich/totalitarism-part-3.

Grossman, Vasily. *Forever Flowing*. Translated by Thomas P. Whitney. New York: Harper & Row, 1972.

Gusiev, Valentyn. "Pro deportatsiiu hrupy ukraïns'koï intelihentsiï za kordon u 1922 r." In *Totalitarna derzhava i politychni represiï v Ukraïni u 20 – 80-ti roky: Materialy Mizhnarodnoï naukovoï konferentsiï (15–16 veresnia 1994 r.)*, edited by P. Panchenko and Ie. Proniuk et al., 180–82. Kyïv: NAN Ukraïny, 1998.

Gutterman, Steve. "Russia: 1930s Famine Was Not Genocide." *Fox News*, April 2, 2008. https://www.foxnews.com/printer_friendly_wires/2008Apr02/0,4675,RussiaUkraineFamine,00.html.

Hadzewycz, Roma, George B. Zarycky, and Marta Kolomayets, eds. *The Great Famine in Ukraine: The Unknown Holocaust*. Jersey City: Svoboda Press for Ukrainian National Association, 1983.

Hammer, Joshua. "Vladimir Lenin's Return Journey to Russia Changed the World Forever." *Smithsonian Magazine*, March 2017. https://www.smithsonianmag.com/travel/vladimir-lenin-return-journey-russia-changed-world-forever-180962127/.

Han, O. *Trahediia Mykoly Khvyl'ovoho*. Prague: Vyd-vo "Prometei," 1947.

Handbook of the Soviet Union. New York: American-Russian Chamber of Commerce, 1936.

Hanzha, Ivan et al., ed. *Istoriia kolektyvizatsiï sil's'koho hospodarstva Ukraïns'koï RSR, 1917–1937 rr*, vol. 2. Kyïv: Naukova dumka, 1965.

Harvard Project on the Soviet Social System Online. Schedule B, vol. 7. Slavic Division, Widener Library, Harvard University. https://library.harvard.edu/sites/default/files/static/collections/hpsss/index.html.

Havel, Václav. "The Power of the Powerless" (Essay). *International Journal of Politics*, 1979. International Center on Nonviolent Conflict. https://www.nonviolent-conflict.org/resource/the-power-of-the-powerless/.

Haynes, John Earl, and Harvey Klehr. *In Denial: Historians, Communism, and Espionage*. San Francisco: Encounter Books, 2003.

Healey, Dan. "Lives in the Balance: Weak and Disabled Prisoners and the Biopolitics of the Gulag." *Kritika: Explorations in Russian and Eurasian History* 16, no. 3 (2015): 527–56.

Hillig, Götz. "Makarenko and Stalinism: Comments and Reflections." *East/West Education* 15, no. 2 (1994): 103–16.

———. "'Mazepynets' Vashchenko pro 'ianychara' Makarenka: vzaiemyny vidomykh ukraïns'kykh pedahohiv." *Ridna shkola*, no. 6 (1995): 74.

———. *V poiskakh istinnogo Makarenko: russkoiazychnye publikatsii (1976–2014)*. Poltava: Izdatel' Shevchenko R. V., 2014.

Hirsch, Francine. "Race without the Practice of Racial Politics." *Slavic Review* 61, no. 1 (2002): 30–43.

"Hladomor v SSSR." *Večerník P. L.*, August 17, 1933.

Holmes, Larry F. *The Kremlin and the Schoolhouse: Reforming Education in Soviet Russia, 1917–1931*. Bloomington: Indiana University Press, 1991.

"Holodomor in Kharkiv through the lens of Austrian engineer: photo gallery." *Euromaidan Press*, 10 January 2021. http://euromaidanpress.com/2021/01/10/1933-holodomor-in-kharkiv-through-the-lens-of-austrian-engineer-photo-gallery/.

"Holodomor Memorial Presented in Washington." *UNIAN*, August 5, 2015. https://www.unian.info/world/1108244-holodomor-memorial-presented-in-washington.html.

Holodomor v Ukraïni 1932–1933 rr.: bibliohrafichnyi pokazhchyk. Edited by S. V. Kul'chyts'kyi. 1st ed. Odesa; Lviv: Vyd-vo M. P. Kots', 2001. http://resource.history.org.ua/item/0008306.

Holodomor v Ukraïni 1932–1933 rr.: bibliohrafichnyi pokazhchyk. Edited by S. V. Kul'chyts'kyi. 2nd ed. Odesa: Vyd-vo Studiia "Negotsiant," 2008. http://resource.history.org.ua/item/0008357.

Holodomor v Ukraïni 1932–1933 rr.: bibliohrafichnyi pokazhchyk. Edited by S. V. Kul'chyts'kyi. 3rd ed. Odesa, 2014. http://resource.history.org.ua/item/0010446.

Hornykiewicz, Theophil, ed. *Ereignisse in der Ukraine, 1914–1922, deren Bedeutung und historische Hintergründe*, vol. II. Horn: Ferdinand Berger und Söhne, 1966.

Hosejko, Lubomyr. *Ukrainian Film Poster of the 1920s: VUFKU*. Kyïv: Oleksandr Dovzhenko National Center, 2015.

"HREC in Ukraine." *Ukrinform*, April 27, 2018. https://www.ukrinform.net/rubric-society/2450243-we-will-preserve-the-memory-of-the-holodomorgenocide-and-the-fates-of-our-families-and-bring-life-stories-to-the-world-that-will-inspire-people-in-the-future.html.

Hrechenko, V., and O. Iarmysh. *Ukraïna v dobu "rann'ioho" totalitaryzmu (20-ti roky XX st.)*. Kharkiv: Natsional'nyi universytet vnutrishnikh sprav, 2001.

Hrynevych, Liudmyla. "Ievreis'ke natsional'no-kul'turne vidrodzhennia 1920-kh – 1930-kh rr. v USRR u 'prokrustovomu lozhi' bil'shovyts'koï ideolohiï." *Problemy istoriï Ukraïny: fakty, sudzhennia, poshuky*, no. 12 (2004): 225–33.

Hryshko, Wasyl. "The Origins of Soviet Genocide." In *The Ukrainian holocaust of 1933*, edited and translated by Marco Carynnyk, 8–68. Toronto: Bahriany Foundation, SUZHERO, DOBRUS, 1983.

Hrytsak, Iaroslav. "Khto i koly vpershe vzhyv slovo "Holodomor"? *Ukraïna Moderna*, November 24, 2017. http://uamoderna.com/blogy/yaroslav-griczak/etymology-holodomor.

Hunczak, Taras. *Symon Petliura and the Jews: A Reappraisal*. Toronto: Ukrainian Historical Association, 1985.

———, ed. *The Ukraine, 1917–1921: A Study in Revolution*. Cambridge: Harvard Ukrainian Research Institute, 1977.

Huntington, Samuel P. "The Clash of Civilizations?" *Foreign Affairs* 72, no. 3 (1993): 22–49.

Iakubova, L. D. "National'ne administratyvno-terytorial'ne budivnytstvo v USRR/URSR, 1924–1940." In *Entsyklopedia istoriï Ukraïny*, edited by V. A. Smolii et al., vol. 7. Kyïv: "Naukova dumka," 2010. http://www.history.org.ua/?termin=Natsionalni_rajony.

Iefimenko, Hennadii. "Kozhnomu – za vyznachenymy partiieiu potrebamy. Iak bil'shovyky maizhe pobuduvaly komunizm." *Dilova stolytsya*, February 28, 2021. https://www.dsnews.ua/ukr/nasha_revolyutsiya_1917/kozhnomu-za-viznachenimi-partiyeyu-potrebami-yak-bilshoviki-mayzhe-pobuduvali-komunizm-28022021-417232.

———. *Natsional'na polityka kerivnytstva VKP(b) v Ukraïni 1932–1938 rr. (osvita ta nauka)*. Kyïv: Instytut istoriï Ukraïny NAN Ukrainy, 2000.

———. "Sotsial'ne oblychchia vchytel'stva USRR v konteksti transformatsiï suspil'stva (1920-ti roky)." *Problemy istoriï Ukraïny: fakty, sudzhennia, poshuky*, no. 17 (2007): 138–61.

———. "Stvorennia SRSR." *Tsei den' v istoriï*, July 5, 2018. https://www.jnsm.com.ua/h/0706U/.

Iefremov, S. O. *Shchodennyky, 1923–1929*. Kyïv: Hazeta "Rada," 1997.

Iershov, V. "Politychni represiï v Zhytomyrs'komu pedinstytuti 1933–1941 rr." *Volyn'-Zhytomyrshchyna: istorychno-filolohichnyi zbirnyk*, vyp. 3 (1998): 37–71.

International Commission of Inquiry into the 1932–33 Famine in Ukraine: The Final Report. Stockholm: Stockholm Institute of Public and International Law, No. 109, 1990. https://web.archive.org/web/20081001225745/http://www.ukrainianworldcongress.org/Holodomor/Holodomor-Commission.pdf.

International Court of Justice. Press Release No. 2007/8, February 26, 2007. www.icj.cij.org.

Internet Encyclopedia of Ukraine. Canadian Institute of Ukrainian Studies, 2001. http://www.encyclopediaofukraine.com/.

Ivnitskii, Nikolai. "Golod 1932–1933 gg.: kto vinovat? (po dokumentam 'Kremlevskogo arkhiva')." In *Holodomor 1932–1933 rr. v Ukraïni: prychyny i naslidky. Mizhnarodna naukova konferentsiia, Kyïv, 9–10 veresnia 1993*, edited by S. Kul'chyts'kyi, 35–44. Kyïv: Instytut istoriï Ukraïny NAN Ukraïny, 1995.

———. "Golod 1932–1933-kh godov: Kto vinovat?" In *Sud'by rossiiskogo krest'ianstva*, edited by I. Afanas'iev, 333–63. Moscow: Rossiia XX vek, 1996.

Ïdlo 33-ho: Slovnyk Holodomoru. Odesa: Vyd-vo "Iurydychna literatura," 2003.

Jakobson, Michael. *Origins of the GULAG: The Soviet Prison Camp System, 1917–1934*. Lexington: University Press of Kentucky, 1993.

Janos, Andrew C. "Ethnicity, Communism, and Political Change in Eastern Europe." *World Politics* 23, no. 3 (1971): 505–19.

Johnson, Alex. "Russia Attacks, Seizes Ukrainian Vessels in Black Sea off Crimea." *NBC News*, November 25, 2018. https://www.nbcnews.com/storyline/ukraine-crisis/russia-attacks-seizes-three-ukrainian-naval-vessels-coast-crimea-black-n939876.

Johnson, Ben. "Russia Still Denies the Holodomor Was 'Genocide'." *Acton Institute*, November 27, 2017. https://www.acton.org/publications/transatlantic/2017/11/27/russia-still-denies-holodomor-was-genocide.

Jones, Gareth. *"Tell Them We Are Starving": The 1933 Diaries of Gareth Jones*, with an introduction by Ray Gamache, edited by Lubomyr Luciuk. Kingston: Kashtan Press, 2015.

Kalakura, Iaroslav. "Kompleks 'sovkovosti' postradians′koï istoriohrafiï." *Ukraïna – Ievropa – Svit: Mizhnarodnyi zbirnyk naukovykh prats′*, vol 2, 163–74. Ternopil′: Vyd-vo TNPU named after V. Hnatiuk, 2015.

Kamenetsky, Ihor. "Hrushevsky and the Central Rada: Internal Politics and Foreign Interventions." In *The Ukraine, 1917–1921: A Study in Revolution*, edited by Taras Hunczak, 33–60. Cambridge: Harvard Ukrainian Research Institute, 1977.

Kardash, Peter. *Genocide in Ukraine*. Translated by Daria Myrna. Melbourne: Fortuna Publishing, 2007.

Kardynalovs′ka, Tetiana. *Nevidstupne mynule*. Kyïv: Vyd-vo M. P. Kots′, 1992.

Kas′ianov, Heorgii. "Dolia akademika Iefremova." *Pid praporom leninizmu*, no. 19 (1989): 75–78.

———. "Intelihentsiia radians′koï Ukraïny 1920-kh – 30-kh rokiv: sotsial′no-istorychnyi analiz." Doctoral diss., Instytut istoriï Ukraïny, 1993.

———. *Ukraïns′ka intelihentsiia 1920-kh – 30-kh rokiv: sotsial′nyi portret ta istorychna dolia*. Kyïv: Globus-Vik; Edmonton: Canadian Institute of Ukrainian Studies, University of Alberta, 1992.

———. "Ukraïns′ka intelihentsia v 1933 r." *Problemy istoriï Ukraïny: fakty, sudzhennia, poshuky*, no. 2 (1992): 92–98.

———, and Vasyl′ Danylenko. *Stalinizm i ukraïns′ka intelihentsiia (20–30-ti rr.)*. Kyïv: Naukova dumka, 1991.

Kelleher, Margaret. "Woman as Famine Victim: The Figure of Woman in Irish Famine Narratives." In *Gender and Catastrophe*, edited by Ronit Lentin, 241–54. London: Zed Books, 1997.

Kellermann, Natan P. F. "Epigenetic Transmission of Holocaust Trauma: Can Nightmares Be Inherited." *The Israel Journal of Psychiatry and Related Sciences* 50, no. 1 (2013): 33–39.

Keys, Ancel, Josef Brožek, Austin Henschel, Olaf Mickelsen, and Henry Longstreet Taylor. *The Biology of Human Starvation*, 2 vols. Minneapolis: University of Minnesota Press, 1950.

Kharchenko, Artem. "'… potribni bil′sh kvalifikovani robitnyky': kolektyvnyi portret personalu syrotyntsiv naperedodni Holodomoru." *Ukraïna moderna*, January 5, 2019. https://uamoderna.com/md/kharchenko-orphans.

Khiterer, Victoria. "The Holodomor and Jews in Kyiv and Ukraine: An Introduction and Observations on a Neglected Topic." *Nationalities Papers* 48, no. 3: Special Issue on the Soviet Famines of 1930–1933 (May 2020): 460–75. https://doi.org/10.1017/nps.2018.79.

Khlevniuk, Oleg V. *The History of the Gulag: From Collectivization to the Great Terror*. New Haven: Yale University Press, 2004.

Khorunzhyi, Iurii, ed. *Opera SVU – muzyka GPU: spohady svidkiv; zbirka*. Kam'ians'k-Shakhtyns'kyi: Stanitsa, 1992.

Kis, Oksana. "Defying Death: Women's Experience of the Holodomor, 1932–1933." *Aspasia* 7 (2013): 42–67.

———. "Kolektyvna pam'iat' ta istorychna travma: teoretychni refleksiï na tli zhinochykh spohadiv pro Holodomor." In *U poshukakh vlasnoho holosu: Usna istoriia iak teoriia, metod, dzherelo*, edited by Helinada Hrinchenko and Nataliia Khanenko-Friezen, 180–91. Kharkiv: Skhidnyi Instytut Ukraïnoznavstva im. Koval's'kykh, 2010.

———. "Women's Experience of the Holodomor: Challenges and Ambiguities of Motherhood." *Journal of Genocide Research*, October 23, 2020. https://doi.org/10.1080/14623528.2020.1834713.

Kitchin, George. *Prisoner of the OGPU*. London: Longmans, Green and Co., 1935.

Klid, Bohdan, and Alexander Motyl, eds. *The Holodomor Reader: A Sourcebook on the Famine of 1932–1933 in Ukraine*. Toronto: Canadian Institute of Ukrainian Studies, 2012.

Klitsakov, I. O. *Pedahohichni kadry Ukraïny (1917–1937 rr.)*. Donets'k: Iugo-Vostok, 1997.

Koestler, Arthur. *The Yogi and the Commissar and Other Essays*. New York: Macmillan, 1945.

Kohan, Vadym, and Raïsa Nahorna-Persyds'ka. "Medychni aspekty holodu 1932–1933 rr. v Ukraïni." In *Holodomor 1932–1933 rr. v Ukraïni: prychyny i naslidky. Mizhnarodna naukova konferentsiia, Kyïv, 9–10 veresnia 1993 r. Materialy*, edited by S. Kul'chyts'kyi, 106–13. Kyïv: Instytut istoriï Ukraïny NAN Ukraïny, 1995.

Kokin, Serhii. "Stanovlennia totalitarnoï systemy ta pochatok masovykh politychnykh represii v URSR (1920–1922 rr.)." In *Totalitarna derzhava i politychni represiï v Ukraïni u 20 – 80-ti roky: Materialy Mizhnarodnoï naukovoï konferentsiï (15–16 veresnia 1994 r.)*, edited by P. Panchenko and Ie. Proniuk et al., 224–26. Kyïv: NAN Ukraïny, 1998.

Kołakowski, Leszek. "The Marxist Roots of Stalinism." In *The Great Lie: Classic and Recent Appraisals of Ideology and Totalitarianism*, edited by F. Flagg Taylor IV, 156–76. Wilmington: Intercollegiate Studies Institute, 2011.

Kolasky, John. *Education in Soviet Ukraine*. Toronto: Peter Martin Associates, 1968.

Koliastruk, Ol'ha. *Intelihentsiia USRR u 1920-ti roky: povsiakdenne zhyttia*. Kharkiv: "Rarytety Ukraïny," 2010.

Komarnits'kyi, O. B. *Studenty-pedahohy u modernizatsiï vyshchoï osvity radians'koï Ukraïny u 1920–1930-kh rr.* Kam'ianets'-Podil's'kyi: "Ruta," 2017.

Kondrashin, Viktor. "Golod 1932–1933 gg. – obshchaia tragediia narodov SSSR: natsional'no-regional'nyi aspekt." In *Sovetskiie natsii i natsional'naia politika v 1920–1950-e gody: Materialy VI mezhdunarodnoi nauchnoi konferentsii, Kiev, 10–12 oktiabria 2013 g.*, edited by N. Volynchik, 187–201. Moscow: ROSSPEN, 2014.

———. "Golod 1932–33 gg. v nauchnykh issledovaniiakh i istoricheskoi publitsistike." Stenogramma vystupleniia V. V. Kondrashina. "Rossiia-Ukraina: problemy ponimaniia i otsenok Golodomora 1932–33 gg." Seminar "Klioterapiia," 19 iiulia 2010 g. *Uroki istorii: XX vek*, October 4, 2010. https://urokiistorii.ru/article/1185.

———. "Hunger in 1932–1933 – A Tragedy of the Peoples of the USSR." *Holodomor Studies* 1, no. 2 (2009): 16–21.

Kondrashov, V. "'Z korinniam vyrvaty natsional'no-kontrrevoliutsiini elementy z N.P.I.' (Pohrom u Nizhyns'kii vyshchii shkoli na pochatku 30-kh rokiv)." *Siverians'kyi litopys: vseukraïns'kyi naukovyi zhurnal*, no. 2 (20) (1998): 13–15.

Kononovych, Leonid. *Tema dlia medytasiï*. L'viv: Kal'variia, 2006.

Kostiuk, Hryhory. *Stalinist Rule in the Ukraine: A Study of the Decade of Mass Terror (1929–1939)*. New York: Praeger, 1960.

———. *Stalinizm v Ukraïni: heneza i naslidky; doslidzhennia i sposterezhennia suchasnyka*. Kyïv: Smoloskyp, 1995.

———, ed. *Mykola Khvyl'ovyi: Tvory v 5 tomakh*. New York: "Smoloskyp," 1986.

Kotelenets, E. A. "Bitva za Lenina: shest' mifov o vozhde revoliutsii." *Komsomol'skaia Pravda*, April 22, 2017. https://www.kp.ru/daily/26670.5/3692043/.

Kotkin, Stephen. "Communism: A Global Reckoning." *Wall Street Journal*, November 4–5, 2017.

———. "The Communist Century." *Wall Street Journal*, November 4–5, 2017.

Kotsonis, Yanni. *States of Obligation: Taxes and Citizenship in the Russian Empire and Early Soviet Republic*. Toronto: University of Toronto Press, 2016.

Kovalenko, Lidia, and Volodymyr Maniak, eds. *33-i holod: Narodna Knyha-Memorial*. Kyïv: Radians'kyi pys'mennyk, 1991.

Kovaliv, Panteleimon. *Vstup do istoriï skhidn'ioslov'ians'kykh mov*. New York: Shevchenko Scientific Society, 1970.

Korotki pidsumky perepysu naselennia Ukraïny 17 hrudnia roku 1926: Natsional'nyi i vikovyi sklad, ridna mova ta pysemnist' naselennia. Kharkiv, 1928.

Krivosheev, G. F. *Soviet Casualties and Combat Losses in the Twentieth Century*. London: Greenhill Books, 1997.

Kubijovyč, Volodymyr, ed. *Ukraine: A Concise Encyclopedia*, 2 vols. Toronto: published for the Ukrainian National Association by University of Toronto Press, 1963–1971.

Kubijovyč, Volodymyr, ed. *Entsyklopediia ukraïnoznavstva*, vols. 1–8. Paris; New York: Vyd-vo "Molode zhyttia," 1955–1976.

Kul'chyts'kyi, Iurii. "Symon Petliura i pohromy." In *Symon Petliura: Zbirnyk studiino-naukovoï konferentsiï v Paryzhi (traven' 1976)*, edited by Wolodymyr Kosyk, 137–59. München; Paris: Ukrainian Free University, 1980.

Kul'chyts'kyi, S. V., ed. *Holod 1921–1923 rokiv v Ukraïni: Zbirnyk dokumentiv i materialiv*. Kyïv: Naukova dumka, 1993.

Kul'chyts'kyi, Stanislav. *1933: trahediia holodu*. Seriia 1 "Teoriia i praktyka KPRS. Istoriia," No. 6. Kyïv: T-vo "Znannia" URSR, 1989.

———. "Borot'bysty." In *Encyclopedia of Modern Ukraine*, edited by I. M. Dziuba et al. Kyïv: Instytut entsyklopedychnykh doslidzhen' NAN Ukraïny, 2004. http://esu.com.ua/search_articles.php?id=37346.

———. *Holod 1932–1933 rr. v Ukraïni iak henotsyd: movoiu dokumentiv, ochyma svidkiv*. Kyïv: Nash chas, 2008.

———. *Holodomor 1932–1933 rr. iak henotsyd: trudnoshchi usvidomlennia.* Kyïv: Nash chas, 2008.

———. "Holodomor u pratsiakh ukraïns'kykh radians'kykh istorykiv 1956–1987 rr." *Istoriia v suchasnii shkoli: naukovo-metodychnyi zhurnal* 10, no. 146 (2013): 29–31.

———. "James Mace's Role in Exposing Stalin's Greatest Crime." *Day*, June 15, 2004. https://day.kyiv.ua/en/article/history-and-i/james-maces-role-exposing-stalins-greatest-crime.

———. "Komunisty i moral'." *Ukraïns'kyi tyzhden'*, no. 50 (630), December 12, 2019. https://tyzhden.ua/History/238597.

———. *Komunizm v Ukraïni: pershe desiatyrichchia (1919–1928).* Kyïv: Osnovy, 1996.

———. "Mil'ony zahyblykh: skil'ky same?" *Den'*, April 13, 2018. https://day.kyiv.ua/uk/article/istoriya-i-ya/milyony-zagyblyh-skilky-same.

———. *The Famine of 1932–1933 in Ukraine: An Anatomy of the Holodomor.* Translated by Ali Kinsella. Edmonton: Canadian Institute of Ukrainian Studies, 2018.

———, and Ol'ha Movchan. *Nevidomi storinky holodu 1921–1923 rr. v Ukraïni.* Kyïv: Instytut istoriï Ukraïny NAN Ukraïny, 1993.

Kundera, Milan. *The Book of Laughter and Forgetting.* New York: Alfred A. Knopf, 1980.

Kupensky, Nick. "Blindness, Hypnosis, Addiction, Fetish: The Language of Holodomor Denial." Paper presented at the Danyliw Seminar on Contemporary Ukraine, University of Ottawa, November 9, 2018.

Kurinnyi, Oleksii. "Holodomor 1932–1933 rr. na Pivnichnomu Kavkazi iak henotsyd ukraïntsiv." In *Materialy Mizhnarodnoï naukovo-praktychnoï konferentsiï "Holodomor 1932–1933 rokiv: vtraty ukrains'koï natsiï" (Kyïv, 4 zhovtnia 2016),* edited by Olesia Stasiuk, Vasyl' Marochko, Volodymyr Serhiichuk et al., 73–85. Kyïv: Vyd. Oleh Filiuk, 2017.

———. "Ukraïns'ka spil'nota Pivnichnoho Kavkazu iak ob'iekt Holodomoru 1932–1933 rokiv." In *Holodomor 1932–1933 rokiv v Ukraïni iak zlochyn henotsydu zhidno z mizhnarodnym pravom,* edited by Volodymyr Vasylenko and Myroslava Antonovych, 161–72. Kyïv: Vydavnychyi dim "Kyievo-Mohylians'ka akademiia," 2016.

Kuromiya, Hiroaki. "Democracies and the Holodomor." *Clio World*, no. 1 (2020): 28–35.

———. *Freedom and Terror in the Donbas: A Ukrainian-Russian Borderland, 1870s–1990s.* Cambridge: Cambridge University Press, 1998.

———. "Stalin's 'Great Breakthrough' and the Trial of the Union for the Liberation of the Ukraine." Paper prepared for the conference, "Ukraine under Stalin, 1928–1939," at the University of Toronto, March 2–4, 1990.

———. "Stalinskii 'velikii perelom' i protsess nad 'Soiuzom osvobozhdeniia Ukrainy'." *Otechestvennaia istoriia*, no. 1 (1994): 190–97.

Kurylas, Larysa. "With Gratitude to the Sisterhood: Reflections on the Creation of the National Holodomor Memorial." *Our Life* (published by UNWLA), November 2020, 20–21.

Kuzio, Taras. "Disinformation: Soviet Origins of Contemporary Russian Ukrainophobia." In *Russian Active Measures: Yesterday, Today, Tomorrow*, edited by Olga Bertelsen, 137–75. Stuttgart and New York: *ibidem*-Verlag and Columbia University Press, 2021.

———. "Putin Forever: Ukraine Faces the Prospect of Endless Imperial Aggression." *Atlantic Council*, February 13, 2020. https://www.atlanticcouncil.org/blogs/ukraine alert/putin-forever-ukraine-faces-the-prospect-of-endless-imperial-aggression/.

———, and Paul D'Anieri. "The Soviet Origins of Russian Hybrid Warfare." *E-International Relations*, June 17, 2018. https://www.e-ir.info/2018/06/17/the-soviet-origins-of-russian-hybrid-warfare/.

Kuz′menko, Mykhailo. "Naukovo-pedahohichna intelihentsiia USRR 20–30-kh rokiv XX st.: evoliutsiia sotsial′no-istorychnoho typu." Doctoral diss., Kharkivs′kyi natsional′nyi universytet im. V. N. Karazina, 2005.

Kyryliuk, V. "Protses SVU–stalins′ka fal′shyvka." *Literaturna Ukraïna*, December 7, 1989.

Lanovyk, B. D., M. V. Traf'iak, R. M. Mateiko, and Z. M. Matysiakevych. *Ukraïns′ka emihratsiia vid mynuvshyny do s'iohodennia*. Ternopil′: Charivnytsia, 1999.

Lavrinenko, Iurii. *Rozstriliane vidrodzhennia: Antolohiia, 1917–1933*. Kyïv: Smoloskyp, 2004.

Leggett, George. *The Cheka: Lenin's Political Police*. New York: Oxford University Press, 1986.

Lemkin, Raphael. *Axis Rule in Occupied Europe: Laws of Occupation, Analysis of Government, Proposals for Redress*. Washington, D.C.: Carnegie Endowment for International Peace, Division of International Law, 1944.

———. "Soviet Genocide in the Ukraine" (typewritten notes). Folder 16. Box 2. Reel 3. ZL-273. "The Raphael Lemkin Papers, 1947–1959." Rare Books and Manuscripts Division. New York Public Library.

———. "Soviet Genocide in the Ukraine." In *Holodomor: Reflections on the Great Famine of 1932–1933 in Soviet Ukraine*, edited by Lubomyr Y. Luciuk and Lisa Grekul, 235–42. Kingston: Kashtan Press, 2008.

———. *Soviet Genocide in the Ukraine*, edited by Lubomyr Y. Luciuk. Kingston: Kashtan Press, 2014.

Lenin, V. I. *Between the Two Revolutions: Articles and Speeches of 1917*. Moscow: Progress Publishers, 1971.

———. "Critical Remarks on the National Question." In *Collected Works*, translated by Bernard Isaacs and Joe Fineberg, edited by Julius Katzer, vol. 20, 17–51. Moscow: Progress Publishers, 1964.

———. *Essential Works of Lenin: "What Is to Be Done?" and Other Writings*, edited with an introduction by Henry M. Christman. New York: Dover Publications, Inc., 1987.

———. *Sochineniia*, vol. 30. Moscow: Partiinoe izd-vo, 1932.

———. "Speech Delivered at the First All-Russia Congress of Internationalist Teachers," June 5, 1918. In *Collected Works*, 4th English edition, vol. 27. Moscow: Progress Publishers, 1972. https://www.marxists.org/archive/lenin/works/1918/jun/05.htm.

Leshchenko, M. N. *Klasova borot'ba v ukraïns'komu seli na pochatku XX stolittia.* Kyïv: Politvydav Ukraïny, 1968.

Levchuk, Nataliia, Oleh Wolowyna, Omelian Rudnytskyi, Alla Kovbasiuk, and Natalia Kulyk. "Regional 1932–1933 Famine Losses: A Comparative Analysis of Ukraine and Russia." *Nationalities Papers* (2020): 1–21. https://doi:10.1017/nps.2019.55.

Lewin, Moshe. *Political Undercurrents in Soviet Economic Debates: From Bukharin to the Modern Reformers.* Princeton: Princeton University Press, 1974.

Liber, George. *Soviet Nationality Policy, Urban Growth, and Identity Change in the Ukrainian SSR, 1923–1934.* Cambridge: Cambridge University Press, 1992.

Livshits, F. D. "Perepis' naseleniia 1937 goda." In *Demograficheskie protsessy v SSSR,* edited by A. G. Volkov, 174–207. Moscow: Nauka, 1990.

Loiko, O. "Intelihentsiia Podillia v umovakh nepu." In *Tezy dopovidei 15-oï Vinnyts'koï oblasnoï istoryko-kraieznavchoï konferentsiï,* 61–62. Vinnytsia, 1996.

Lozynskyj, Askold S. "A New Proposal for the Government of Ukraine." *Ukrainian Weekly,* January 31, 2021.

Lozyts'kyi, V. S. "Polityka ukraïnizatsiï v 20–30-kh rokakh: istoriia, problemy, uroky." *Ukraïns'kyi istorychnyi zhurnal,* no. 3 (1989): 46–55.

Luciuk, Lubomyr, ed. *Not Worthy: Walter Duranty's Pulitzer Prize and the New York Times.* Kingston: Kashtan Press, 2004.

———, and Lisa Grekul, eds. *Holodomor: Reflections on the Great Famine of 1932–1933 in Soviet Ukraine.* Kingston: Kashtan Press, 2008.

Luhovyi, Oleksander. *Vyznachne zhinotstvo Ukraïny: istorychni zhyttiepysy v chotyr'okh chastynakh.* Toronto: The Ukrainian Publishing Company, 1942. Digital Collection of the National University "Kyïv-Mohyla Academy." https://dlib.ukma.edu.ua/document/87.

Luk'ianenko, O. V. *"Naiblyzhchi druzi partiï": kolektyvy vyshiv Ukraïny v obrazakh shchodennia 1920-kh – pershoï polovyny 1960-kh rokiv.* Poltava: Vyd-vo "Simon," 2019.

Lunacharsky, A. V. *O narodnom obrazovanii.* Moscow: Izd-vo Akademii Pedagogicheskikh Nauk RSFSR, 1958.

Lyons, Eugene. "American Jews and the Kremlin Purges." *The New Leader* 36, no. 9 (March 2, 1953): 14–15.

———. *Assignment in Utopia.* New York: Harcourt, Brace and Co., 1937.

Lysyi, A. "Represiï proty studentstva ta vykladachiv istorychnoho fakul'tetu Vinnyts'koho uchytel's'koho instytutu v 30-kh rr. XX st." *Visnyk instytutu istoriï, etnolohiï i prava: zbirnyk naukovykh prats',* vyp. 8 (2010): 42–45.

Lysyvets', Anastasiia. *"Skazhy pro shchaslyve zhyttia ..."* Kyïv: KIS, 2019.

Lytvyn, N. M. "Politychni represiï proty naukovoï intelihentsiï v radians'kii Ukraïni v 1920–1930-kh rokah (ideolohichni aspekty problemy)." Doctoral diss., Kyïv, 2006.

Lytvyn, Serhii. "Vbyvstvo S. Petliury i GPU: Do istoriohrafiï problemy." *Z arkhiviv VUChK-GPU-NKVD-KGB,* no. 2/4 (13/15) (2000): 404–7.

Lytvyn, V. M., ed. *Politychna systema dlia Ukraïny: istorychnyi dosvid i vyklyky suchasnosti.* Kyïv: Nika-Tsentr, 2008.

Mace, James E. "Is the Ukrainian Genocide a Myth?" In *Holodomor: Reflections on the Great Famine of 1932–1933 in Soviet Ukraine*, edited by Lubomyr Y. Luciuk and Lisa Grekul, 49–60. Kingston: Kashtan Press, 2008.

———. "Research on Documents" (typewritten notes). Ukraine Famine Hearing, April 30, 1987. Box 16921. Gary Bauer Files. Ronald Reagan Presidential Library and Museum.

———. "The Komitety Nezamozhnykh Selian and the Structure of Soviet Rule in the Ukrainian Countryside, 1920–1933." *Soviet Studies* 35, no. 4 (October 1983): 487–503.

———, and Leonid Heretz, eds. *Investigation of the Ukrainian Famine, 1932–1933: Oral History Project of the Commission on the Ukraine Famine*, vols. 1–3. Washington, D.C.: U.S. Government Printing Office, 1990. https://catalog.hathitrust.org/Record/009145045.

MacKay, Michael. "The Seeds of Genocide in Russia's Invasion of Ukraine." *Radio Lemberg*, April 17, 2018. http://radiolemberg.com/ua-articles/ua-allarticles/the-seeds-of-genocide-in-russia-s-invasion-of-ukraine.

Maiboroda, V. K. "Osoblyvosti rozvytku systemy vyshchoï pedahohichnoï osvity v URSR (1917–1941 rr.)." *Ukraïns'kyi istorychnyi zhurnal*, no. 11 (1990): 58–64.

Maidachevsky, Ilko. "Linguistic Insights into Ukrainian History: Professor Kostiantyn Tyshchenko speaks about the role of modern linguistics in our identity and the rebuttal of the cradle-of-three-brotherly-peoples theory." *Ukrainian Week*, November 16, 2012. https://ukrainianweek.com/Culture/65223.

Maistrenko, Ivan. *Borot'bism: A Chapter in the History of the Ukrainian Revolution*, edited by Christopher Ford. Stuttgart: *ibidem*-Verlag, 2018.

Makarenko, A. S. *Kniga dlia roditelei*. Moscow: Uchpedgiz, 1950. http://jorigami.ru/PP_corner/Classics/Makarenko/Makarenko_A_Book_for_Parents/Makarenko_A_Book_for_Parents.html#_Toc196398223.

Maksudov, Sergei (Aleksandr Bab'onyshev). "Byl li golod 1932–33 godov na Ukraine genotsydom?" *Blog Sergeia Maksudova*, September 16, 2016. http://www.maksudovsergei.com/.

Malko, Victoria A. "A Paradigm Shift in Studying History of the Holodomor as Genocide." Paper presented at the International Forum "Ukraine Remembers, the World Acknowledges" on the 85th anniversary of the Holodomor 1932–1933 – Genocide of the Ukrainian People, Kyïv, Ukraine, November 22, 2018.

———. "Russian (Dis)Information Warfare vis-à-vis the Holodomor-Genocide." In *Russian Active Measures: Yesterday, Today, Tomorrow*, edited by Olga Bertelsen, 215–62. Stuttgart and New York: *ibidem*-Verlag and Columbia University Press, 2021.

———. *The Chechen Wars: Responses in Russia and the United States*. Saarbrücken: Lambert Academic Publishing, 2015.

Manning, Clarence A. *Ukraine Under the Soviets*. New York: Bookman Associates, 1953.

Manning, Martin J., and Herbert Romerstein. "Disinformation." In *Historical Dictionary of American Propaganda*. Westwood: Greenwood Press, 2004.

Margolin, Arnold. *The Jews of Eastern Europe*. New York: T. Seltzer, 1929.

Marinov, A. A. *V stroiu zashchitnikov Oktiabria: Voenno-politicheskaia kniga 1918–1925 g.* Moscow: Nauka, 1982.

Marochko, Vasyl'. *Entsyklopediia Holodomoru 1932–1933 rokiv v Ukraïni.* Drohobych: "Kolo," 2018.

———. *Holodomor 1932–1933 rr.* Kyïv, 2007.

———. "Kanibalizm v roky Holodomoru." In *Holod 1932–33 rokiv v Ukraïni: prychyny ta naslidky*, edited by Valerii Smolii et al., 568–75. Kyïv: Naukova dumka, 2003.

———. "Lenins'kyi liudomor 1921–1923 rr.: 'bratnii' rozpodil smerti." *Slovo Prosvity*, April 19–25, 2018.

———. "Obmin pobutovoho zolota na khlib v Ukraïni v period Holodomoru 1932–1933 rokiv." *Ukraïns'kyi istoryk*, nos. 3–4 (2008): 194–209.

———. "O. M. Asatkin – vyhadanyi 'fal'syfikator' perepysu naselennia 1937 r." *Ukraïns'kyi istorychnyi zhurnal*, no. 4 (2017): 129–49.

———. "Prystrasti dovkola Holodomoru: real'ni mify." *Dzerkalo tyzhnia*, March 24, 2018. https://dt.ua/HISTORY/pristrasti-dovkola-golodomoru-realni-mifi-272997_.html.

———. "'Russkii Mir' u Feodosiï: zaborona slova pro Holodomor." *Istorychna Pravda*, January 28, 2015. http://www.istpravda.com.ua/columns/2015/01/28/146975/.

———. "Statystyka zhertv Holodomoru: antropolohichno-demohrafichnyi dyskurs." *Ukraïns'kyi istorychnyi zhurnal*, no. 5 (2017): 112–32.

———. *Terytoriia Holodomoru 1932–1933 rr.* Kyïv: PP Natalia Brekhunenko, 2014.

———. "'Torgsin': zolota tsina zhyttia ukrains'kykh selian u roky holodu (1932–1933)." *Ukraïns'kyi istorychnyi zhurnal*, no. 3 (2003): 90–103.

———, et al. *Holodomor-henotsyd: terminolohiia.* Kyïv: Natsional'nyi muzei Holodomoru-henotsydu, 2019.

———, and Götz Hillig. *Represovani pedahohy Ukraïny: zhertvy politychnoho teroru, 1929–1941.* Kyïv: "Naukovyi svit," 2003.

———, and O. Movchan. *Holodomor 1932–1933 rokiv v Ukraïni: Khronika.* Kyïv: Vydavnychyi dim "Kyievo-Mohylians'ka akademiia," 2008.

Martin, Terry. *The Affirmative Action Empire: Nations and Nationalism in the Soviet Union, 1923–1939.* Ithaca: Cornell University Press, 2001.

Marx, Karl. *Communist Manifesto.* Chicago: Henry Regnery Company for the Great Books Foundation, 1949.

———, and Frederick Engels. *Collected Works*, vol. 6. London: Lawrence & Wishart, 1845–1848.

Masnenko, V. V., and I. F. Sharov. "Vchytel'stvo ta stanovlennia radians'koï shkoly na Ukraïni v pershii polovyni 20-kh rokiv." *Ukraïns'kyi istorychnyi zhurnal*, no. 12 (1990): 100–104.

Mattingly, Daria. "[Extra]ordinary Women: Female Perpetrators of the Holodomor." In *Women and the Holodomor-Genocide: Victims, Survivors, Perpetrators*, edited by Victoria A. Malko, 51–89. Fresno: The Press at California State University, 2019.

Mazepa, Isaak. *Ukraïna v ohni i buri revoliutsiï, 1917–1921.* Part I. Prague: Vyd-vo "Prometei," 1950.

McBride, Pete. "The Last Quiet Places: To the End of the Earth in Search of the Healing Power of Silence." *Smithsonian*, October 2020, 51–61.

Mead, Margaret. *Soviet Attitudes Toward Authority: An Interdisciplinary Approach to Problems of Soviet Character.* New York: McGraw Hill, 1951.

Medvedev, Roy A. *Let History Judge.* Edited by David Joravsky and Georges Haupt, translated by Colleen Taylor. New York: Alfred A. Knopf, 1971.

———. *On Stalin and Stalinism.* Translated by Ellen De Kadt. New York: Oxford University Press, 1979.

Mel′nychuk, I. P., V. I. Petrenko, and P. M. Kravchenko. "Dokumenty derzhavnoho arkhivu Vinnyts′koï oblasti pro nastroï sil′s′koï intelihestiï Podillia v 1920-h rr." In *Naukovi zapysky Vinnyts′koho derzhavnoho pedahohichnoho universytetu im. Mykhaila Kotsiubyns′koho,* edited by P. S. Hryhorchuk, 345–48. Vinnytsia: VDPU im. Mykhaila Kotsiubyns′koho, 2006.

Midttun, Hans Petter. "Hybrid War in Ukraine – Predictions for 2019 and Beyond." *Euromaidan Press*, April 18, 2019. http://euromaidanpress.com/2019/04/18/hybrid-war-in-ukraine-predictions-for-2019-and-beyond/.

———. "What If Russia Wins in Ukraine? Consequences of Hybrid War for Europe (Part 2)." *Euromaidan Press*, May 22, 2020. http://euromaidanpress.com/2020/05/22/what-if-russia-wins-in-ukraine-consequences-of-hybrid-war-for-europe-part-2/.

Milgram, Stanley. *Obedience to Authority: Experimental View.* New York: Harper Perennial, Modern Thought, 2009.

———. "The Dilemma of Obedience." *The Phi Delta Kappan* 55, no. 9 (1974): 603–6.

Mischenko, Michael. "Hunger as a Method of Terror and Rule in the Soviet Union." *Ukrainian Quarterly* 5, no. 2 (1949): 219–25.

Misinkevych, L. L. "Zakonodavchi zasady represyvnoï polityky radians′koï vlady v Ukraïni v 20–30-ti rr. XX stolittia." *Universytets′ki naukovi zapysky*, no. 1 (45) (2013): 5–14.

Moroz, Valentyn. "Nationalism and Genocide: The Origin of the Artificial Famine of 1932–1933 in Ukraine." *The Journal of Historical Review* 6, no. 2 (1985): 207–20.

Moskwin, L., "New Campaign of Lies Against the Land of Socialist Construction." *International Press Correspondence*, September 29, 1932.

Motyl, Alexander J. "Kiev's Purge: Behind the New Legislation to Decommunize Ukraine." *Foreign Affairs*, April 28, 2015. https://www.foreignaffairs.com/articles/ukraine/2015-04-28/kievs-purge.

"Mr. Kononenko's Statement before the Commission on the Ukraine Famine Hearing and Meeting, April 30, 1987." Ukraine Famine [Hearing 04/30/1987]. Box 16921. Gary Bauer Files. Ronald Reagan Presidential Library and Museum.

Mudrak, Myroslava M. *The Imaginative World of Heorhii Narbut and the Making of a Ukrainian Brand.* Kyïv: Rodovid Press, 2020.

Muggeridge, Malcolm. "Chronicles of Wasted Time." *Esquire*, February 1972, 114–23, 173.

Mytsyk, Iurii, ed. A. *Ukraïns′kyi holokost 1932–1933: svidchennia tykh, khto vyzhyv*, vols. 1–9. Kyïv: Vydavnychyi dim "Kyievo-Mohylians′ka akademiia," 2003–2013.

Naddniprianets′, V. *Ukraïns′ki natsional-komunisty: ïkh rolia u vyzvol′nii borot′bi Ukraïny 1917–1956 rr.* Munich: Political Section of the Ukrainian National Guard, 1956.

"Nahadaiemo shche vil′nomu svitovi pro moskovs′kyi henotsyd." *Ukraïns′ki visti*, May 31, 1953.

Naimark, Norman M. *Stalin's Genocides*. Princeton: Princeton University Press, 2010.

Nesterenko, V. A. "Ukraïns′ke vchytel′stvo Podillia v 1920–1930-ti roky: suspil′no-politychnyi portret." *Osvita, nauka i kul′tura na Podilli: Zbirnyk naukovykh prats′*, no. 3 (2003): 155–64.

Neufeldt, Colin Peter. "Collectivizing the *Mutter Ansiedlungen*: The Role of Mennonites in Organizing Kolkhozy in the Khortytsia and Molochansk German National Districts in Ukraine in the late 1920s and early 1930s." In *Minority Report: Mennonite Identities in Imperial Russia and Soviet Ukraine Reconsidered*, edited by Leonard Friesen, 211–59. Toronto: University of Toronto Press, 2018.

———. "Hitler, Mennonites, and the Holodomor: Nazi Germany and Its Impact on Life of Mennonites in 1932–1933." Paper presented at the Holodomor Research and Education Center's international scientific conference "Natsional′ni menshyny Radians′koï Ukraïny v epokhu Holodomoru: vtraty, travma, pam'iat′," December 15, 2020. http://history.org.ua/uk/post/45380.

———. "The Fate of Mennonites in Ukraine and the Crimea during Soviet Collectivization and the Famine (1930–1933)." Doctoral thesis, University of Alberta, 1999.

Nikolina, I. I. "Vchytel′stvo Podillia u 1920-kh – 30-kh rr. XX st." In *Vinnychyna: mynule ta s′ohodennia. Kraieznavchi doslidzhennia*, edited by M. M. Kravets′, 156–61. Vinnytsia: DP DKF, 2005.

Nikol′s′kyi, Volodymyr. "Represyvna diial′nist′ orhaniv GPU pid chas holodomoru v USRR (1932–1933 rr.)." *Z arkhiviv VUChK-GPU-NKVD-KGB*, no. 2 (2001): 477–95.

Nove, Alec. *An Economic History of the USSR, 1917–1991*. New York: Penguin, 1992.

Nuremberg Trial Proceedings, vol. 1, Charter of the International Military Tribunal. The Avalon Project: Documents in Law, History and Diplomacy. Lillian Goldman Law Library. Yale Law School, 2008. https://avalon.law.yale.edu/imt/imtconst.asp#art6.

Oath and Opposition: Education under the Third Reich. Washington, D.C.: U.S. Holocaust Memorial Museum, 2016. https://www.ushmm.org/m/pdfs/20160229-Oath-and-Opposition.pdf.

"Ob administrativnoi vysylke: Dekret VTsIK ot 10.08.1922 g." *Izvestiia VTsIK*, August 12, 1922. http://old.ihst.ru/projects/sohist/document/deport/dekret.htm.

Ocheretianko, Viktor. "Peresliduvannia ukraïns′koï inteligentsiï v pershii polovyni 20-kh rr. (za materialamy fondiv "Rosiis′koho zarubizhnoho arkhivu" Derzhavnoho arkhivu Rosiis'koï Federatsiï)." *Z arkhiviv VUChK, GPU, NKVD, KGB*, no. 1–2 (1997): 240–52.

Ohienko, Vitalii. "Holodomor ochyma zhertvy: immobilizatsiia ta upokorennia pratseiu iak stratehiia vyzhyvannia." *Ukraïna Moderna*, January 20, 2020. http://uamoderna.com/md/ogienko-holodomor.

———. "Posttravmatychnyi stresovyi syndrom i kolektyvna travma v osobystykh naratyvakh svidkiv Holodomoru." *Ukraïna moderna*, April 6, 2018. http://uamoderna.com/md/ogienko-holodomor-trauma.

Okhrimenko, H. "Dyrektor shkoly riatuvav ditei vid holodnoï smerti." *Ukraïns'ke slovo*, July 20–26, 2005.

Onyshko, Lesia. "Milena Rudnyts'ka: shtrykhy do portretu." *Nashe slovo*, December 23–30, 2012.

———. "Poshyrennia informatsiï pro Holodomor v nezalezhnii Ukraïni: imidzhevi vtraty." In *Holodomor 1932–1933 rokiv: vtraty ukraïns'koï natsiï: Materialy Mizhnarodnoï naukovo-praktychnoï konferentsiï (Kyïv, 4 zhovtnia 2016)*, edited by Olesia Stasiuk et al., 193–97. Kyïv: Vyd. Oleh Filiuk, 2017.

Orwell, George. *The Collected Essays, Journalism, and Letters of George Orwell*, vol. 3. New York: Harcourt, Brace & World, Inc., 1968.

Osherowitch, Mendel. "The Fear of the *GPU* Across the Country." In *How People Live in Soviet Russia: Impressions from a Journey*, edited by Lubomyr Y. Luciuk, translated from the original Yiddish edition by Sharon Power, 187–96. Toronto: University of Toronto Chair of Ukrainian Studies and The Kashtan Press, 2020.

Osokina, Elena. *Za fasadom "Stalinskogo izobiliia": Raspredelenie i rynok v snabzhenii naseleniia v gody industrializatsii, 1927–1941*. Moscow: ROSSPEN, 1998.

———. "Zhertvy goloda 1933 g.: skol'ko ikh? (Analiz demograficheskoi statistiki TsGANKh SSSR)." *Istoriia SSSR*, no. 5 (1991): 18–26.

Otamanovs'kyi, V. D. "Moie kaiattia." In *Podil's'ka starovyna: naukovyi zbirnyk na poshanu vchenoho i kraieznavtsia V. D. Otamanovs'koho*, edited by V. A. Kosakivs'kyi, 20–29. Vinnytsia, 1993.

"Over 154,000 N.Y. Ukrainian Americans March in Protest Parade Marking Anniversary of Soviet Fostered 1932–1933 Famine in Ukraine." *Ukrainian Weekly*, September 26, 1953.

Ovsiienko, Vasyl'. *Svitlo liudei: Spohady-narysy pro Vasylia Stusa, Iuriia Lytvyna, Oksany Meshko*. Kyïv: URP, 1996.

Pakhl'ovs'ka, O. "Maty i antykhryst: vidlunnia holodomoru v literaturi." *Urok ukraïns'koï*, no. 1 (2004): 36–38.

Palak'ean, Grigoris. *Le Golgotha arménien: de Berlin à Deir-es-Zor*. La Ferté-sous-Jouarre: Le Cerle d'Écrits Caucasiens, 2002.

Panné, Jean-Louis. "Rafaël Lemkin ou le pouvoir d'un sans-pouvoir." Introduction to Rafaël Lemkin, *Qu'est-ce qu'un génocide?*, 7–66. Monaco: Édition du Rocher, 2008.

Papakin, Heorhii. *"Chorna doshka": antyselians'ki represiï (1932–1933)*. Kyïv: Instytut istoriï Ukraïny NAN Ukraïny, 2013.

———. "'Chorna doshka' Holodomoru i liuds'ki vtraty 1932–1933 rokiv." In *Holodomor 1932–1933 rokiv: Vtraty ukraïns'koï natsiï. Materialy mizhnarodnoï naukovo-praktychnoï konferentsiï, Kyïv, 4 zhovtnia 2016 roku*, edited by Olesia Stasiuk et al., 159–64. Kyïv: Vyd. Oleh Filiuk, 2017.

Patryliak, Bohdan. "How Stalin Crushed the Euromaidan of 1930." *Euromaidan Press*, December 1, 2014. http://euromaidanpress.com/2014/12/01/punishment-for-two-maidans-putincrimea-and-stalinholodomor/.

Pauly, Matthew D. *Breaking the Tongue: Language, Education, and Power in Soviet Ukraine, 1923–1934*. Toronto: University of Toronto Press, 2014.

Pavlushkova, Natalia. "Pravda i provokatsiia (do 40-richchia sudu nad SVU-SUM)." *Misiia Ukraïny* (published by the Association for the Liberation of Ukraine in Brooklyn, NY and Toronto, Canada), no. 3 (26) (1970): 1–4.

———. "Pravda i provokatsiia." *Misiia Ukraïny*, no. 1 (28) (1971): 10–13.

Pearson, Michael. *The Sealed Train*. New York: Putnam, 1975.

Pein, Robert. *Lenin: Zhizn' i smert'*. Moscow: Molodaia gvardiia, 2008.

Perga, Tetiana. "Role of Americans for Human Rights in Ukraine in the Support of Human Rights Movement in Ukrainian SSR." *American History and Politics*, no. 5 (2018): 63–71.

Perri, Giuseppe. "*Korenizacija*: An Ambiguous and Temporary Strategy of Legitimization of Soviet Power in Ukraine (1923–1933) and Its Legacy." *History of Communism in Europe*, no. 5 (2014): 131–54.

Pershyi Vseukraïns'kyi uchytel'skyi z'ïzd v Kharkovi vid 5 do 11 sichnia 1925 r. (zi znymkamy uchasnykiv Z'ïzdu). Kharkiv: Derzhavne vydavnytstvo Ukraïny, 1925. https://chtyvo.org.ua/authors/Zbirka/Pershyi_vseukrainskyi_uchytelskyi_zizd_v_Kharkovi_vid_5_do_11_sichnia_1925_r/.

Petrov, Viktor. *Ukraïns'ki kul'turni diiachi URSR 1920–1940 – zhertvy bil'shovyts'koho teroru*. New York: Prolog, 1959.

Phillips, Hugh D. "Rapprochement and Estrangement: The United States in Soviet Foreign Policy in the 1930s." In *Soviet–U.S. Relations, 1933–1942*. Translated from Russian by Kim Pilarski, 9–17. Moscow: Progress Publishers, 1989.

Pidhainy, S. O., ed., *The Black Deeds of the Kremlin: A White Book*, vol. 1, *Book of Testimonies*. Toronto: Ukrainian Association of Victims of Russian Communist Terror, 1953, vol. 2, *The Great Famine in Ukraine in 1932–33*. Detroit: Democratic Organization of Ukrainians Formerly Persecuted by the Soviet Regime, 1955.

Pinnock, Geoffrey. "A Great Canal Beats Arctic Ocean." *Russia Today*, December 1932.

Pipes, Richard. *A Concise History of the Russian Revolution*. New York: Alfred A. Knopf, 1995.

———, ed. *The Unknown Lenin: From the Secret Archive*. New Haven: Yale University Press, 1996.

Plaggenborg, Stefan. *Revoliutsiia i kul'tura: Kul'turnye orientiry v period mezhdu Oktiabr'skoi revoliutsyei i epokhoi stalinizma*. St. Petersburg: Zhurnal "Neva," 2000.

Pliushch, Vasyl. *Genocide of the Ukrainian People: The Artificial Famine in the Years 1932–1933*. München: Ukrainisches Institut für Bildungspolitik, 1973. http://diasporiana.org.ua/wp-content/uploads/books/10887/file.pdf.

Plokhy, Serhii. *The Gates of Europe: A History of Ukraine*. New York: Basic Books, 2015.

———. *Unmaking Imperial Russia: Mykhailo Hrushevsky and the Writing of Ukrainian History*. Toronto: University of Toronto Press, 2005.

"Podobrat′ ikh [dokumenty] sleduet takim obrazom, chtoby byla vidna tragediia vsego sovetskogo krest′ianstva, bez aktsenta na Ukrainu" [Kondrashin V. Plan-prospekt z rekomendatsiiamy shchodo vidboru dokumentiv dlia zbirnyka 'Golod v SSSR, 1932–1933.' Dodatok do lysta kerivnyka Federal′noho arkhivnoho ahenstva Rosiis′koï Federatsiï V. Kozlova do Holovy Derzhkomarkhivu Ukraïny O. Ginzburg z propozytsiamy pro spivpratsiu. 17 sichnia 2007]. Personal Archive of Hennadii Boriak. Institute of History of Ukraine of the National Academy of Sciences of Ukraine, December 5, 2017. http://resource.history.org.ua/item/0013470.

Polian, P. *Ne po svoei vole... Istoriia i geografiia prinuditel′nykh migratsyi v SSSR*. Moscow: O.G.I. – Memorial, 2001.

Polons′ka-Vasylenko, Natalia. *Vydatni zhinky Ukraïny*. Winnipeg: Ukrainian Women's Association of Canada, printed by Trident Press, 1969.

"Poroshenko Blames Russia as USSR Successor for 1930s Famine." *Interfax-Ukraine*, November 24, 2018. https://en.interfax.com.ua/news/general/547761.html.

"Poroshenko: Istorychna vidpovidal′nist′ za Holodomor – na Rosiis′kiï Federatsiï." *Ukraïns′ka Pravda*, November 24, 2018. https://www.pravda.com.ua/ukr/news/2018/11/24/7199187/index.amp.

Porsh, Mykola. "Robitnytstvo Ukraïny: Narys po statystytsi pratsi." *Zapysky Ukraïns′koho naukovoho tovarystva v Kyïvi*, no. 12 (1913): 131–57.

Postyshev, P. P. *Borot′ba za Lenins′ko-Stalins′ku natsional′nu polityku partiï*. Kyïv: Derzhavne vyd-vo Ukraïny, 1935.

———. "The Results of the Agricultural Year 1933 and the Immediate Tasks of the Communist Party of the Ukraine" (Speech delivered at the Plenum of the Central Committee of the Communist Party of Ukraine, November 19, 1933). In *Soviet Ukraine Today*. New York: International Publishers, 1934. Od. zb. 819. James E. Mace Library and Museum Archives. National University Kyïv-Mohyla Academy.

"Predstavitel′ Rossii nazval politicheskimi spekuliatsiiami popytki kvalifitsirovat′ golod 30-kh godov kak genotsid." *Novosti OON*, March 7, 2008. https://news.un.org/ru/story/2008/03/1121751.

Priestland, David. *The Red Flag: A History of Communism*. New York: Grove Press, 2009.

Prokofiev, M. A., P. V. Zimin, M. N. Kolmakova, M. I. Kondakov, and N. P. Kuzin, eds. *Narodnoe obrazovanie v SSSR, 1917–1967*. Moscow: Prosveshchenie, 1967.

Protsenko, V. V. "Osvitians′ka Profspilka USRR v seredyni 1920-kh rr.: Stanovyshche, zavdannia, problemy (za materialamy Pershoho Vseukraïns′koho vchytel′s′koho z′ïzdu v Kharkovi)." *Hileia*, no. 116 (2017): 43–48.

Pryluts′kyi, V. I. *Molod′ Ukraïny v umovakh formuvannia totalitarnoho ladu (1920–1939)*. Kyïv: Instytut istoriï Ukraïny NAN Ukraïny, 2001.

Prymachenko, Iana. "Sprava 'Ob'iednannia ukraïns′kykh natsionalistiv'." *Tsei den' v istoriï*, December 15, 2017. https://www.jnsm.com.ua/h/1215T/.

Prystaiko, Volodymyr. "Zhertvy teroru: Iak DPU borolysia z ukraïns′koiu akademichnoiu naukoiu (Politychni protsesy 20–30-kh rr.)." *Z arkhiviv VUChK, GPU, NKVD, KGB*, no. 1 (1994): 70–78.

Prystaiko, Volodymyr, and Iurii Shapoval. *Mykhailo Hrushevs′kyi i GPU-NKVD: Trahichne desiatylittia, 1924–1934.* Kyïv: "Ukraïna," 1996.

———. *Mykhailo Hrushevs′kyi: Sprava "UNTs" i ostanni roky (1931–1934).* Kyïv: Krytyka, 1999.

———. *Sprava "Spilky vyzvolennia Ukraïny": nevidomi dokumenty i fakty; naukovo-dokumental′ne vydannia*, edited by Ivan Il′ienko. Kyïv: INTEL, 1995.

Pyrih, Ruslan, ed. *Holodomor 1932–1933 rokiv v Ukraïni: dokumenty i materialy.* Kyïv: Kyievo-Mohylians′ka akademiia, 2007.

———. *Holodomor of 1932–33 in Ukraine: Documents and Materials.* Translated by Stephen Bandera. Kyïv: Kyïv Mohyla Academy Publishing House, 2008.

"Radomyshl′." In *Istoriia mist i sil Ukraïns′koï RSR: Zhytomyrs′ka oblast′.* Kyïv: Ukraïns′ka Radians′ka Entsyklopediia AN URSR, 1973. http://imsu-zhytomyr.com/mista-i-sela-zhytomyrskoi-oblasti/radomyshlskyj-rajon-/radomyshl-.html.

Read, Christopher. *Lenin: A Revolutionary Life.* New York: Routledge, 2005.

Remy, Johannes. "Against All Odds: Ukrainian in the Russian Empire in the Second Half of the Nineteenth Century." In *The Battle for Ukrainian: A Comparative Perspective*, edited by Michael S. Flier and Andrea Graziosi, 43–61. Cambridge: Harvard University Press for the Ukrainian Research Institute, 2017.

Reshetar, Jr., John S. "The Communist Party of the Ukraine and Its Role in the Ukrainian Revolution." In *The Ukraine, 1917–1921: A Study in Revolution*, edited by Taras Hunczak, 159–85. Cambridge: Harvard Ukrainian Research Institute, 1977.

———. *The Ukrainian Revolution, 1917–1920: A Study in Nationalism.* Princeton: Princeton University Press, 1952.

Reva, Iryna. *Po toi bik sebe: sotsial′no-psykholohichni ta kul′turni naslidky Holodomoru ta stalins′kykh represii.* Dnipropetrovs′k: A. L. Svidler, 2013.

Rigby, T. H. *Communist Party Membership in the USSR, 1917–1967.* Princeton: Princeton University Press, 1968.

Rokyts′ka, O. "Ivchuk Vasyl′ Iakovych, Heroi Ukraïny: podvyh liudianosti v neliuds′kyi chas." *Narodna osvita* 1, no. 10 (2010). https://www.narodnaosvita.kiev.ua/Narodna_osvita/vupysku/10/statti/rokicka.htm.

Roosevelt, Eleanor. *The Autiobiography of Eleanor Roosevelt.* New York: Harper, 1961.

Rosenfeldt, Niels Erik. *The "Special" World: Stalin's Power Apparatus and the Soviet System's Secret Structures of Communication.* Translated by Sally Laird and John Kendal. Copenhagen: Museum Tusculanum Press, 2009.

Rothberg, Michael. *The Implicated Subject: Beyond Victims and Perpetrators.* Redwood City: Stanford University Press, 2019.

Rozovyk, D. "Stanovlennia natsional′noï vyshchoï osvity i naukovo-doslidnoï pratsi v Ukraïni (1917–1920 rr.)." *Etnichna istoriia narodiv Ievropy: Zbirnyk naukovykh prats'*, vyp. 8 (2001): 55–58.

Rubl'ov, Oleksandr. *Zakhidnoukraïns'ka intelihentsiia u zahalnonatsional'nykh politychnykh ta kul'turnykh protsesakh (1914–1939)*. Kyïv: Instytut istoriï Ukraïny NAN Ukraïny, 2004.

———. "Fundator ukraïns'koï heohrafichnoï nauky: Stepan Rudnys'kyi – liudyna i uchenyi." *Rehional'na istoriia Ukraïny: Zbirnyk naukovykh statei*, vyp. 12 (2018): 207–304.

———, and Iu. A. Cherchenko. *Stalinshchyna i dolia zakhidnoukraïns'koï intelihentsiï*. Kyïv: Naukova dumka, 1994.

Rudnytsky, Ivan L. "The Fourth Universal and Its Ideological Antecedents." In *The Ukraine, 1917–1921: A Study in Revolution*, edited by Taras Hunczak, 186–219. Cambridge: Harvard Ukrainian Research Institute, 1977.

———, ed. (with the assistance of John-Paul Himka). *Rethinking Ukrainian History*. Edmonton: University of Alberta, Canadian Institute of Ukrainian Studies, 1981.

Rudnytskyi, Omelian, Nataliia Levchuk, Oleh Wolowyna, Pavlo Shevchuk, and Alla Kovbasiuk. "Demography of a Man-made Human Catastrophe: The Case of Massive Famine in Ukraine, 1932–1933." *Canadian Studies in Population* 42, no. 1–2 (2015): 53–80.

Rudnyts'kyi, S. L. *Chomu my khochemo samostiinoï Ukraïny?*, edited by Oleh Shablii. L'viv: Svit, 1994.

Rybak, I. V. "Deportatsiia rozkurkulenykh selian druhoï katehoriï z Ukraïny u 1930 rotsi: masshtaby, kharakter, naslidky." *Naukovi pratsi Kam'ianets'-Podil's'koho natsional'noho universytetu imeni Ivana Ohienka. Istorychni nauky*, no. 22 (2012): 327–35.

Saltan, Oleksandr. "Stepan Sosnovyi – pershyi ukraïns'kyi doslidnyk Holodomoru." Lecture at the Kharkiv Historical-Philological Association webinar, November 19, 2020, *HistorySumy, Inc. (Sums'kyi istorychnyi portal)*, January 15, 2021. Video, 2:32–37:40. http://history.sumy.ua/sources/media-documents/9304-pershyi-doslidnyk-holodomoru.html.

Sambros, Iurii. *Shchabli: mii shliakh do komunizmu* (Stages of Life: My Journey Toward Communism). New York: Suchasnist', 1988.

Santayana, George. *The Life of Reason or, The Phases of Human Progress*, 5 vols. Scribner's, 1905. http://www.gutenberg.org/files/15000/15000-h/15000-h.htm.

Saunders, David. *The Ukrainian Impact on Russian Culture, 1750–1850*. Edmonton: Canadian Institute of Ukrainian Studies, University of Alberta, 1985.

Savtsov, V. "Zlochyn, iakoho ne bulo." *Radians'ka Ukraïna*, September 12, 13, 16, 19, 26, and 27, 1989.

Sawka, Jaroslaw. "American Psychiatrist: Fifteen Million Dies in Thirties' Famine." *Ukrainian Quarterly* 38, no. 1 (1982): 61–67.

———. "Rosiishchennia Kubani – pivdenno-skhidn'oho bastionu Ukraïny." *Rosiishchennia Ukraïny: Naukovo-populiarnyi zbirnyk*, edited by Leonid Poltava, 213–19. New York: Vydannia ukraïns'koho kongresovoho komitetu Ameryky, 1984. https://shron2.chtyvo.org.ua/Zbirka/Rosiischennia_Ukrainy_naukovo-populiarnyi_zbirnyk.pdf.

"SBU vozbudila ugolovnoe delo po faktu soversheniia Genotsida." *UNIAN*, May 25, 2009. https://www.unian.net/politics/225116-sbu-vozbudila-ugolovnoe-delo-po-faktu-sovesheniya-genotsida-dopolnennaya.html.

Scherer, John L., and Michael Jackobson. "The Collectivization of Agriculture and the Soviet Prison Camp System." *Europe-Asia Studies* 45, no. 3 (1993): 533–46.

Schoen, Douglas E., and Evan Roth Smith. *Putin's Master Plan to Destroy Europe, Divide NATO, and Restore Russian Power and Global Influence*. New York: Encounter Books, 2016.

Serbyn, Roman. "*Holodomor*: The Ukrainian Genocide." In *Rafał Lemkin: A Hero of Humankind*, edited by Agnieszka Bieńczyk-Missala and Sławomir Dębski, 205–30. Warsaw: Polish Institute of International Affairs, 2010.

———. "The Ukrainian Famine of 1932–1933 as Genocide in Light of the U.N. Convention of 1948." *The Ukrainian Quarterly* 62, no. 2 (2006): 181–94.

———, and Olesia Stasiuk, eds. *Raphael Lemkin: Soviet Genocide in Ukraine (Article in 28 Languages)*. Kyïv: Maisternia knyhy, 2009. https://holodomormuseum.org.ua/wp-content/uploads/2019/04/978-966-2260-15-1.pdf.

Serhiichuk, Volodymyr. *Genocide-Holodomor of Ukrainians, 1932–1933*. Vyshgorod: PP Serhiychuk M. I., 2018.

———. "*Holodni, bosi i rozditi*": *ukraïns'ki dity v 1932–1933 rokakh*. Vyshgorod: PP Serhiichuk M. I., 2020.

———. *Holodomor 1932–1933 rokiv iak henotsyd ukraïnstva*. Vyshgorod: PP Serhiichuk M. I., 2018.

———. "I cherez sto rokiv – odyn na odnoho: Pro rozvytok rosiis'ko-ukraïns'kykh vidnosyn u XX stolitti." *Natsiia i derzhava*, no. 3 (646), March 2017. https://ia800901.us.archive.org/25/items/NiD_newspaper/646--31--03--2017--03.pdf.

———. "Istoryko-pravovi aspekty pidrakhunku vtrat vid Holodomoru-henotsydu 1932–1933 rokiv." *Chetverta khvylia*, July 2, 2020. http://4hvylia.com/novyny-usim/7737.html.

———. "Shkil'na statystyka iak vazhlyve dzherelo dlia vstanovlennia kil'kosti vtrat pid chas Holodomoru-henotsydu 1932–1933 rokiv." *Narodna tvorchist' i etnolohiia*, no. 5 (2018): 5–15.

———. "To Honor All Innocent Victims of the Holodomor." In *Women and the Holodomor-Genocide: Victims, Survivors, Perpetrators*, edited by Victoria A. Malko, 119–44. Fresno: The Press at California State University, 2019.

———. "Ushanuvaty vsikh nevynno ubiiennykh." *Golos Ukraïny*, May 16, 2018. http://www.golos.com.ua/article/302970.

Shapoval, Iurii. "Holodomor i ioho zv'iazok iz represiiamy v Ukraïni u 1932–1934 rokah." In *Holod v Ukraïni u pershii polovyni XX stolittia: prychyny ta naslidky (1921–1923, 1932–1933, 1946–1947): Materialy Mizhnarodnoï naukovoï konferentsiï, Kyïv, 20–21 lystopada 2013 r.*, 153–61. Kyïv, 2013.

———. "Letters from Kharkiv: The Truth about the Holodomor through the Eyes of Italian Diplomats." *Den'*, November 20, 2007. https://day.kyiv.ua/en/article/close/letters-kharkiv.

———. *Liudyna i systema: shtrykhy do portreta totalitarnoï doby v Ukraïni*. Kyïv: Instytut natsional'nykh vidnosyn i politolohiï NAN Ukraïny, 1994.

———. "Nevidomi dokumenty pro UAPTs u zv'iazku iz spravoiu 'Spilky vyzvolennia Ukraïny.'" *Liudyna i svit*, nos. 11–12 (1996), 13–17.

———. "'On Ukrainian Separatism': A GPU Circular of 1926." *Harvard Ukrainian Studies* 18, no. 3–4 (1994): 275–302.

———. "Stalinizm i Ukraïna." *Ukraïns'kyi istorychnyi zhurnal*, no. 4 (1991): 43–54.

———. "Teatral'na istoriia." In *Dolia iak istoriia*, 16–34. Kyïv: Geneza, 2006. https://ipiend.gov.ua/wp-content/uploads/2018/07/shapoval_dolya.pdf.

———. "The Case of the 'Union for the Liberation of Ukraine': A Prelude to the Holodomor?" *Holodomor Studies* 2, no. 2 (2010): 153–82.

———. *Ukraïna 20–50-kh rokiv: storinky nenapysanoï istoriï*. Kyïv: Naukova dumka, 1993.

———, and Vadym Zolotar'ov. "Ievreï v kerivnytstvi orhaniv DPU–NKVS USRR–URSR u 1920–1930-kh rr." *Z arkhiviv VUChK-GPU-NKVD-KGB*, no. 34 (2010): 53–93.

Shaw, Martin. *What Is Genocide?* Cambridge: Polity, 2007.

"Shcherbytsky Says Famine Was a Result of Collectivization of Soviet Agriculture." *Ukrainian Weekly*, January 10, 1988. http://www.ukrweekly.com/old/archive/1988/028801.shtml.

Sheiko, Konstantin, and Stephen Brown. *History as Therapy: Alternative History and Nationalist Imaginings in Russia, 1991–2014*. Stuttgart: *ibidem*-Verlag, 2014.

Shepel', Fedir. "'Zapliamovani' tr'oma bukvamy: 'Sprava SVU' – tse trahediia ne til'ky intelihentsiï." *Den'*, August 1, 2003. http://incognita.day.kyiv.ua/zaplyamovani-troma-bukvami.html.

Shevchenko, Serhii. "Vsevolod Hantsov: zhyttia pislia svyntsevoï zlyvy." *Dzerkalo tyzhnia*, May 22, 2014. https://zn.ua/ukr/HISTORY/vsevolod-gancov-zhittya-pyslya-svincevoyi-zlivi-_.html.

Shevchuk, G. M. *Kul'turnoe stroitel'stvo na Ukraine v 1921–1925 gg*. Kiev: Izd-vo AN Ukrainian SSR, 1963.

Shevtsov, Iurii. "International scientific-practical conference 'Famine in the USSR in the 1930s: historical and political assessments,' Kharkov, 21 November 2008." http://yury-shevtsov.blogspot.com/2008/11/30-21112008.html.

Shevtsova, Lilia. "The Kremlin's Triad as the Means of Survival." *The American Interest*, April 19, 2016. https://www.the-american-interest.com/2016/04/19/the-kremlins-triad-as-the-means-of-survival/.

Shkandrij, Myroslav. "Breaking Taboos: The Holodomor and the Holocaust in Ukrainian–Jewish Relations." In *Jews and Ukrainians*, edited by Yohanan Petrovsky-Shtern and Antony Polonsky, 259–73. Portland: The Littman Library of Jewish Civilization, 2014.

———. "Ukrainianization, Terror and Famine: Coverage in Lviv's *Dilo* and the Nationalist Press of the 1930s." *Nationalities Papers: The Journal of Nationalism and Ethnicity* 40, no. 3 (2012): 431–51.

———, and Olga Bertelsen. "The Soviet Regime's National Operations in Ukraine, 1929–1934." *Canadian Slavonic Papers* 55, nos. 3–4 (2013): 417–47.

Shkvarchuk, Volodymyr. "Rik 1934: Pokhval'ne slovo tov. Roizenmanu, abo masova chystka Chernihivs'koï oblpartorhanizatsiï." In *Na kazarmennomu stanovyshchi (narysy z istoriï Chernihivshchyny dovoiennykh rokiv)*, 9–19. Chernihiv: Chernihivs′ki oberehy, 2002.

Shlikhter, A. "Bor′ba za khleb na Ukraine v 1919 godu." *Litopys revoliutsiï*, no. 2 (29) (1928): 96–135. https://chtyvo.org.ua/authors/Litopys_revoliutsii/1928_N2_29/.

Shtepa, Pavlo. *Moskovstvo: Ioho pokhodzhennia, zmist, formy i istorychna tiahlist′*, vol. 2. Toronto: Semen Stasyshyn, 1968.

Shuhal′ova, Inna. "Stratehiia vyzhyvannia ditei-ditbudynkivtsiv u roky Holodomoru 1932–1933 v Radians′kii Ukraïni." *Materialy mizhnarodnoï konferentsiï "Shtuchni holody v Ukraïni XX stolittia," 16 travnia 2018 r.* Kyïv: Vyd-vo "Kolo," 2018.

Siropolko, Stepan. *Narodnia osvita na soviets′kii Ukraïni*. Warsaw: Pratsi Ukrains′koho naukovoho instytutu, 1934.

———. "Narodnia osvita na ukraïns′kykh zemliakh i v koloniiakh." In *Ukraïns′ka kul′tura: Lektsiï*, edited by D. Antonovych. Kyïv: Lybid′, 1993. Reprinted in *Izbornyk*, http://izbornyk.org.ua/cultur/cult06.htm.

Skelton, Kelly et al. "PTSD and Gene Variants: New Pathways and New Thinking." *Neuropharmacology* 62, no. 2 (2012): 628–37.

Skrypnyk, M. O. *Novi liniï v natsional′no-kul′turnomu budivnytstvi*. Kharkiv: Derzhavne vydavnytstvo Ukraïny, 1930.

Slezkine, Yuri. "The USSR as a Communal Apartment, or How a Socialist State Promoted Ethnic Particularism." *Slavic Review* 53, no. 2 (1994): 414–52.

Slobodianiuk, P., and Iu. Teliachyi. *"Chorna doshka" Ukraïny (podiï 1930-kh rokiv)*. Khmel′nyts′kyi: Podillia, 2001.

Smeulers, Alette. "Female Perpetrators – Ordinary and Extra-ordinary Women." *International Criminal Law Review* 15, no. 2 (2015): 207–53.

———. "Perpetrators of International Crimes: Towards a Typology." In *Supranational Criminology: Towards a Criminology of International Crimes*, edited by Alette Smeulers and Roelof Haveman, 233–65. Antwer: Intersentia, 2008.

———, and Roelof Haveman, eds. *Supranational Criminology: Towards a Criminology of International Crimes*. Antwer: Intersentia, 2008.

Smirnov, M. B. *Sistema ispravitel′no-trudovykh lagerei v SSSR*, edited by N. G. Okhotin and A. B. Roginskii. Moscow: "Zven′ia," 1998. http://old.memo.ru/history/nkvd/gulag.index.htm.

Smith, Kyle. "Stalin, Famine, and the *New York Times*: Mr. Jones Tells the Truth about Moscow's Man at the Paper of Record." *National Review*, July 2, 2020. https://www.nationalreview.com/2020/07/movie-review-mr-jones-tells-truth-about-new-york-times-communism/.

Smolii, V. A. et al., eds. *Entsyklopediia istoriï Ukraïny*, vols. 1–10. Kyïv: Naukova dumka, 2003–2013.

———. *Pam′iat′ narodu: henotsyd v Ukraïni holodom 1932–1933 rokiv, Svidchennya*, 2 vols. Kyïv: Vyd. "Kalyta," 2009.

Sniehir′ov, Helii. *Naboï dlia rozstrilu (Nen′ko moia, nen′ko . . .): liryko-publitsystychna rozvidka*. Kyïv: Dnipro, 1990.

Snyder, Timothy. "The Soviet Famines." In *Bloodlands: Europe between Hitler and Stalin*, 21–58. New York: Basic Books, 2010.

Soiuz rabotnikov prosveshcheniia na Ukraine (Otchet Ukrburo TsK Rabotpros I-mu Vseukrainskomu s"ezdu, oktiabr' 1923 – ortiabr' 1924 gg.). Kharkov: Ukrburo TsK Rabotpros, 1924.

Solod′ko, Pavlo. "Iak pysaty pro Holodomor. Instruktsiia rosiis′kym istorykam." *Istorychna Pravda*, November 26, 2012. http://www.istpravda.com.ua/artefacts/2012/11/26/101572/.

Solovey, Dmytro. *Golgota Ukraïny.* Drohobych: "Vidrodzhennia," 1993.

———. *Golgotha of Ukraine. Part I, The Moscow-Bolshevik Occupation Terror in Ukrainian SSR between First and Second World War.* Winnipeg: "Ukrainian Voice," 1953.

———. "The Golgotha of Ukraine." *Svoboda – Ukrainian Weekly*, June 2, 1953.

Solzhenitsyn, Aleksandr. "Possorit′ rodnye narody??" *Izvestiia*, April 2, 2008.

Sorokin, Pitirim A. *Man and Society in Calamity: The Effects of War, Revolution, Famine, Pestilence upon Human Mind, Behavior, Social Organization and Cultural Life.* New York: E. P. Dutton, 1942.

"Sprava SVU: iak bil′shovyky nyshchyly ukraïns′ku intelihentsiiu." *Istoriia bez mifiv*, August 5, 2020. https://www.youtube.com/watch?v=tEkUbQ5PQVU.

Stalin, I. V. *Sochineniia*, vol. 6. Moscow: OGIZ, 1947.

———. *Voprosy leninizma.* Moscow: Gospolitizdat, 1945.

Stanton, Gregory H. "The Ten Stages of Genocide." *Genocide Watch*, 2020. https://www.genocidewatch.com/ten-stages-of-genocide.

Stasiuk, Olesia. "Deformatsiia narodnoï kul′tury v roky henotsydu." *Problemy istoriï Ukraïny: fakty, sudzhennia, poshuky*, no. 18 (2008): 349–61.

———. "Donosy, kradizhky, samosudy v roky Holodomoru iak naslidok represyvnoï polityky." In *Holodomor 1932–1933 rokiv: Vtraty ukraïns′koï natsiï. Materialy mizhnarodnoï naukovo-praktychnoï konferentsiï, Kyïv, 4 zhovtnia 2016*, edited by Olesia Stasiuk et al., 175–79. Kyïv: Vyd. Oleh Filiuk, 2017.

———. *Henotsyd ukraïnstiv: deformatsiia narodnoï kul′tury.* Kyïv: Stylos, 2008.

Staub, Ervin. "The Roots of Evil: Social Conditions, Culture, Personality, and Basic Human Needs." *Personality and Social Psychology Review* 3, no. 3 (1999): 179–92.

———. *The Roots of Evil: The Origins of Genocide and Other Group Violence.* Cambridge: Cambridge University Press, 1989.

Steinberg, Jacques. "Word for Word/Soft Touch; From Our Men in Moscow, In Praise of the Stalinist Future." *New York Times*, October 26, 2003. https://www.nytimes.com/2003/10/26/weekinreview/word-for-word-soft-touch-our-man-moscow-praise-stalinist-future.html?searchResultPosition=2.

Studenikin, S. S., ed. *Istoriia Sovetskoi Konstitutsii (v dokumentakh) 1917–1956.* Moscow: Gosiurizdat, 1957.

Subtelny, Orest. *Ukraine: A History*, 4th ed. Toronto: University of Toronto Press, 2009.

Sukhomlyns′ka, Ol′ha. *Narysy istoriï ukraïns′koho shkil′nytstva (1905–1933).* Kyïv: Zapovit, 1996.

Suny, Ronald Grigor, and Terry Martin, eds. *A State of Nations: Empire and Nation-Making in the Age of Lenin and Stalin.* New York: Oxford University Press, 2001.

Sydorenko, O. "'Pidlishoho chasu ne bulo . . .': iak i chomu bulo sfabrykovano spravu tak zvanoï Spilky vyzvolennia Ukraïny." *Vechirnii Kyïv*, May 15, 1991.

Symon Petliura: Statti, lysty, dokumenty. New York: Ukrainian Academy of Arts and Sciences in the U.S., 1956.

Sysyn, Frank. "Nestor Makhno and the Ukrainian Revolution." In *The Ukraine, 1917–1921: A Study in Revolution*, edited by Taras Hunczak, 271–304. Cambridge: Harvard Ukrainian Research Institute, 1977.

Taras Shevchenko's poem "My Testament." English translation by various translators. https://taras-shevchenko.storinka.org/my-testament-poem-of-taras-shevc henko-english-translation-by-various-translators.html.

Tarasov, Ruslan, Oleksiy Grytsenko, Vitaliy Panasiuk, and Stuart Greer. "How Ukraine's Holodomor Famine Was Secretly Photographed." *RFE/RL's Ukrainian Service*, November 22, 2018. https://www.rferl.org/a/how-holodomor-famine-was -secretly-documented/29615511.html.

Tauger, Mark B. "Retrospective for Yale Agrarian Studies." September 2014. https:/ /agrarianstudies.macmillan.yale.edu/sites/default/files/files/papers/TaugerAgrarian Studies.pdf.

———. "Review of Anne Applebaum's 'Red Famine: Stalin's War on Ukraine'." *History News Network* (George Washington University's Columbian College of Arts and Sciences), July 1, 2018. http://historynewsnetwork.org/article/169438.

———. "The 1932 Harvest and the Famine of 1933." *Slavic Review* 50, no. 1 (1991): 70–89.

Taylor, S. J. *Stalin's Apologist: Walter Duranty: The New York Times's Man in Moscow*. New York: Oxford University Press, 1990.

Teliachyi, Iu. V. "Ukraïns′ke natsional′no-kul′turne vidrodzhennia v 1917–1921 rr.: do metodolohichnoho kontekstu problemy." *Osvita, nauka i kul′tura na Podilli*, no. 24 (2017): 7–14.

Teren, Tetiana. "Neopublikovana rozmova z Anatoliiem Dimarovym: Shkoduiu, shcho v takyi strashnyi chas zhyv, koly ne mozhna bulo pysaty pravdu." *Ukraïns'ka Pravda*, July 7, 2014. https://life.pravda.com.ua/society/2014/07/7/174315/.

The Soviet Empire: Prison House of Nations and Races; A Study in Genocide, Discrimination, and Abuse of Power, prepared by Joseph G. Whelan, analyst in Eastern European affairs, at the request of the Subcommittee to Investigate the Administration of the Internal Security Act and Other Internal Security Laws of the Committee on the Judiciary. U.S. Senate. 85th Cong., 2nd Sess. Document No. 122. Washington, D.C.: U.S. Government Printing Office, 1958. https://catalog .hathitrust.org/Record/008514963.

Timasheff, Nicholas S. *The Great Retreat: The Growth and Decline of Communism in Russia*. New York: E. P. Dutton & Company, Inc., 1946.

"Timothy Snyder on Germany's Historical Responsibility towards Ukraine." Lecture in the German Bundestag on June 20, 2017, organized by the parliamentary faction of the German Green Party. https://www.youtube.com/watch?v=wDjHw_uXeKU.

Tlumachnyi slovnyk ukraïns′koï movy. 2018. http://sum.in.ua/f/Gholodomor.

Tomkiw, Lydia. "Toll of the Bells." *Slate*, December 19, 2019. https://slate.com/news -and-politics/2019/12/carol-bells-shchedryk-ukraine-leontovych.html.

Topolianskii, V. *Vozhdi v zakone: Ocherki fiziologii vlasti*. Moscow: Izd-vo "Prava cheloveka," 1996.
Troshchyns'kyi, V. P. *Mizhvoienna ukraïns'ka emihratsiia v Ievropi iak istorychne i sotsial'no-politychne iavyshche*. Kyïv: Intel, 1994.
Tsiupyn, B. "Zapliushchuiuchy ochi: Vydatni zakhidni intelektualy, iaki ne vytrymaly perevirky Holodom." *Tyzhden'*, November 24, 2012. http://tyzhden.ua/History/65731.
Tucker, Robert C. *Stalin as Revolutionary, 1879–1929*. New York: W. W. Norton & Company, Inc., 1973.
Turchenko, Fedir, and Inna Shuhal'ova. "Dytiacha smertnist' u roky Holodomoru 1932–1933 rokiv u Zaporizhzhi." In *Holodomor 1932–1933 rokiv: Vtraty ukraïns'koï natsiï. Materialy Mizhnarodnoï naukovo-praktychnoï konferentsiï, Kyïv, 4 zhovtnia 2016*, edited by Olesia Stasiuk et al., 109–15. Kyïv: Vyd. Oleh Filiuk, 2017.
Tylishchak, Volodymyr. *1930. U.S.R.R. Povstannia: Naukovo-populiarni narysy*. Kyïv: Smoloskyp, 2016.
Udod, Oleksandr. "Istoriia povsiakdennosti iak skladova istoriï Ukraïny XX st." *Istoriia ta pravoznavstvo*, nos. 19–21 (2007): 104–17.
Ukraïna: Statystychnyi shchorichnyk. Kharkiv: Tsentral'ne Statystychne Upravlinnia, 1929.
"Ukrainians March in Protest Parade. 10,000 Here Mark Anniversary of the 1933 Famine – Clergy Join in the Procession." *New York Times*, September 21, 1953.
Ukraïns'kyi pravopys (Proiekt). Kharkiv: Derzhavne Vyd-vo Ukraïny, 1926.
U.N. Department of Economic and Social Affairs. *Growth of the World's Urban and Rural Population, 1920–2000*. Population Studies No. 44. New York: United Nations, 1969.
United Nations, Treaty Series. *Convention on the Prevention and Punishment of the Crime of Genocide, adopted by the General Assembly of the United Nations on December 9, 1948*, vol. 78. 1951. https://treaties.un.org/doc/publication/unts/volume%2078/volume-78-i-1021-english.pdf.
U.S. Commission on the Ukraine Famine. *Investigation of the Ukrainian Famine, 1932–1933: Report to Congress*. Washington, D.C.: U.S. Government Printing Office, 1988. https://catalog.hathitrust.org/Record/007398237.
U.S. Congress, House of Representatives, Select Committee on Communist Aggression. *Communist Takeover and Occupation of Ukraine*. Special Report No. 4. 88th Cong., 2nd Sess. Washington, D.C.: U.S. Government Printing Office, 1954. https://catalog.hathitrust.org/Record/001855373.
UWC. "UWC Defends Itself against Ban in Russian Federation." *Ukrainian Weekly*, April 26, 2020.
Vaksberg, Arkadii. *Tsaritsa dokazatel'stv: Vyshynskii i ego zhertvy*. Moscow: AO "Kniga i biznes," 1992.
Vakulenko, Serhii. "1933 in History of Ukrainian Language: Current Norm and Spelling Practice (an Example of Editorial Policy of Newspaper *Komunist*)." Paper presented at the American Association for Slavic Studies Conference in Philadelphia, PA on November 22, 2008. See Ukrainian version "1933-ii rik

v istoriï ukraïns′koï movy: chynna norma ta pravopysna praktyka (na prykladi redaktsiinoï polityky hazety "Komunist"). *Historians*, December 3, 2012. http://www.historians.in.ua/index.php/en/ukrayinska-mova/488-cerhiy-vakulenko-1933-ii-rik-v-istorii-ukrainskoi-movy-chynna-norma-ta-pravopysna-praktyka-na-prykladi-redaktsiinoi-polityky-hazety-komunist.

Vandenko, Andrei. "20 Questions with Vladimir Putin: Putin on Ukraine." *TASS*, February 20, 2020. https://www.youtube.com/watch?v=NG6dxqwxGE4.

Vasylenko, Volodymyr. "Metodolohiia pravovoï otsinky Holodomoru 1932–1933 rr. v Ukraïni iak zlochynu genotsydu." In *Holodomor 1932–1933 rokiv v Ukraïni iak zlochyn henotsydu zhidno z mizhnarodnym pravom*, edited by Volodymyr Vasylenko and Myroslava Antonovych, 13–73. Kyïv: Kyievo-Mohylians′ka akademiia, 2016.

Vasyl′iev, Valerii, and Iurii Shapoval, eds. *Komandyry velykoho holodu: Poïzdky V. Molotova i L. Kaganovycha v Ukraïnu ta na Pivnichnyi Kavkaz, 1932–1933 rr.* Kyïv: Heneza, 2001.

Vasyl′iev, Valerii, and Linn Viola. *Kolektyvizatsiia i selians′kyi opir na Ukraïni (lystopad 1929 – berezen′ 1930 rr.).* Vinnytsia: Logos, 1997.

Velychenko, Stephen. *Painting Imperialism and Nationalism Red: The Ukrainian Marxist Critique of Russian Communist Rule in Ukraine, 1918–1925.* Toronto: University of Toronto Press, 2015.

V'iatrovych, Volodymyr. "Oleksandra Radchenko – represovana za pam'iat′." *Istorychna Pravda*, November 11, 2013. http://www.istpravda.com.ua/articles/2013/11/22/139903.

Viereck, Peter. *Shame and Glory of the Intellectuals: Babbitt Jr. vs. the Rediscovery of Values.* Boston: The Beacon Press, 1953.

Viola, Lynne. *Peasant Rebels under Stalin: Collectivization and the Culture of Peasant Resistance.* New York: Oxford University Press, 1996.

———. *The Best Sons of the Fatherland: Workers in the Vanguard of Soviet Collectivization.* Oxford: Oxford University Press, 1989.

———. *The Unknown Gulag: The Lost World of Stalin's Special Settlements.* Oxford: Oxford University Press, 2009.

———, V. P. Danilov, N. A. Ivnitskii, and Denis Kozlov, eds. *The War Against the Peasantry, 1927–1930: The Tragedy of the Soviet Countryside.* New Haven: Yale University Press, 2005.

Vodotyka, S. H. *Akademik Mykhailo Ielyseiovych Slabchenko: narys zhyttia ta tvorchosti.* Kyïv: Kherson, 1998.

Volkogonov, Dmitrii. *Lenin: Politicheskii portret*, 2 vols. Moscow: Novosti, 1994.

———. *Triumf i tragediia: Politicheskii portret I. V. Stalina*, 2 vols. Moscow: Izv-vo Agentstva pechati Novosti, 1989.

Volkov, A. G. "Perepis′ naseleniia 1937 goda: vymysly i pravda." In *Perepis′ naseleniia SSSR 1937 goda: istoriia i materialy*, vyp. 3–5 (II), 6–63. Moscow: Informtsentr Goskomstata SSSR, 1990.

Vologodtsev, I. K. *Osobennosti razvitiia gorodov Ukrainy.* Kharkov: Derzhvydav "Gosp-vo Ukrainy," 1930.

"V Rosiï knyhy pro Holodomor pryrivniuiut'sia do ekstremizmu." *Istorychna Pravda*, June 27, 2012. http://www.istpravda.com.ua/articles/2012/06/27/89363/.

Vyhovs'kyi, M. Iu. *Nomenklatura systemy osvity v USRR 1920–1930-kh rokiv: sotsial'ne pokhodzhennia, personal'nyi sklad ta funktsiï*. Kyïv: Heneza, 2005.

Vynnychenko, Volodymyr. *Vidrodzhennia natsiï*, vol. III. Kyïv-Vienna: Vyd. Dzvin, 1920. http://exlibris.org.ua/vinnichenko/index.html.

Vyshnevska, Olena, ed. *Number of Existing Population of Ukraine as of 1 January 2020: Statistical Publication*. Kyïv: State Statistics Service of Ukraine, 2020.

Vytanovych, Illia. *Agrarna polityka ukraïns'kykh uriadiv, 1917–1920*. Munich: Ukraïns'ke istorychne tovarystvo, 1968.

Wanner, Catherine. "Commemoration and the New Frontiers of War in Ukraine." *Slavic Review* 78, no. 2 (2019): 328–35.

Warvariv, Constantine. "America and the Ukrainian National Cause, 1917–1920." In *The Ukraine, 1917–1921: A Study in Revolution*, edited by Taras Hunczak, 352–81. Cambridge: Harvard Ukrainian Research Institute, 1977.

Waterkamp, Dietmar. "Götz Hillig and His Search for the True Makarenko. What Did He Find?" *IDE-Online Journal (International Dialogues on Education: Past and Present)* 5, no. 2 (2018). http://www.ide-journal.org/article/2018-volume-5-number-2-gotz-hillig-and-his-search-for-the-true-makarenko-what-did-he-find/.

Weber, Max. *Wirtschaft und Gesellschaft: Grundriss der verstehenden Soziologie*. Edited by Marianne Weber. Tübingen: Mohr, 1922.

Weiss-Wendt, Anton. *The Soviet Union and the Gutting of the U.N. Genocide Convention*. Madison: University of Wisconsin Press, 2017.

Werth, Nicolas. *Cannibal Island: Death in a Siberian Gulag*. Princeton: Princeton University Press, 2007.

———. "Food Shortages, Hunger, and Famines in the USSR, 1928–33." *East/West: Journal of Ukrainian Studies* III, no. 2 (2016): 35–49.

Wilson, Walter. *Forced Labor in the United States*. New York: International Publishers, 1933.

Wolff, Larry. *Woodrow Wilson and the Reimagining of Eastern Europe*. Palo Alto: Stanford University Press, 2020.

"Zakon Ukraïny 'Pro Holodomor 1932–1933 v Ukraïni' No. 376-V (Vidomosti Verkhovnoï Rady Ukraïny 2006, No. 50, 504), 28 November 2006." In *The Holodomor of 1932–1933 in Ukraine as a Crime of Genocide under International Law*, edited by Volodymyr Vasylenko and Myroslava Antonovych, 226–28. Kyïv: Kyïv-Mohyla Academy, 2016. https://zakon.rada.gov.ua/laws/show/376-16.

Zbirnyk uzakonen' ta rozporiadzhen' robitnycho-selians'koho uriadu Ukraïny. Kharkiv: Drukarnia UVO im. M. Frunze, 1924. http://irbis-nbuv.gov.ua/dlib/item/0000128.

Zhiromskaia, Valentina. *Osnovnye tendentsii demograficheskogo razvitiia Rossii v XX veke*. Moscow: Kuchkovo pole, 2012.

Zhurbeliuk, Halyna. "Metodyka istoryko-pravovykh doslidzhen' problem holodu 1921–1923 rr. v Ukraïni: rozvinchannia mifiv." In *Holod v Ukraïni u pershii polovyni XX stolittia: prychyny ta naslidky (1921–1923, 1932–1933, 1946–1947): Materialy Mizhnarodnoï naukovoï konferentsiï, Kyïv, 20–21 lystopada 2013 r.*, edited by Myroslava Antonovych, Hennadii Boriak, Oleksandr Hladun, and Stanislav Kul′chyts′kyi, 51–58. Kyiv, 2013.

Zhurzhenko, Tatiana. "'Capital of Despair': Holodomor Memory and Political Conflicts in Kharkiv after the Orange Revolution." *East European Politics and Societies* 25, no. 3 (2011): 597–639.

Zhvanko, Liubov. *Sotsial′ni vymiry Ukraïns′koï Derzhavy (kviten′ – hruden′ 1918 r.)*. Kharkiv: Prapor, 2007.

———. "Tyf, cholera, 'ispanka': zakhody uriadu Skoropads′koho z podolannia epidemiï." *Ukraïna moderna*, March 20, 2020. http://uamoderna.com/md/zhvanko-skoropadsky-pandemics.

Zinkewych, Osyp, ed. *Ukraïns′ka Hel′syns′ka Hrupa, 1978–1982: Dokumenty i materialy*. Toronto: V. Symonenko "Smoloskyp" Publishers, 1983.

Zolotar′ov, Vadym. "Kerivnyi sklad NKVS URSR pid chas 'velykoho teroru' (1936–1938 rr.): sotsial′no-statystychnyi analiz." *Z arkhiviv VUChK-GPU-NKVD-KGB* 2, no. 33 (2009): 86–115. http://resource.history.org.ua/publ/gpu_2009_33_2_86.

"Zvernennia uchasnykiv Revoliutsiï Hidnosti proty revanshu." *Tyzhden′*, May 6, 2020. https://m.tyzhden.ua/Politics/243374.

Index

Page references for figures are italicized.

activists, 21, 137–38, 144–46, 148, 151–52, 172n16, 236, 245, 269–70, 275. *See also* collectivization; grain confiscations; tugboat brigades
Agitprop, 89, 123n14, 269, 294
agricultural policy. *See* Soviet agriculture
All-Russian Extraordinary Commission for Combatting Counterrevolution, Speculation, Sabotage, and Misuse of Authority. *See* Cheka (VChK)
All-Ukrainian Academy of Sciences, 17, 73, 94, 97–99, 101, 105, 109, 113, 128n89, 130n113, 191, 241, 279, 284, 300–301, 303. *See also* VUAN
"all-Union" famine, xix, 184, 186–92, 214, 252, 255, 270
American Relief Administration (ARA), 29, 31, 42n150, 193, 270
Ammende, Ewald, 5, 161, 234, 270
anti-Semitism, 8, 209, 213
Antonenko-Davydovych, Borys, 103, 294
Arendt, Hannah, 28, 88
Asatkin, Oleksandr, 163, 194

Balyts'kyi, Vsevolod, 97, 142, 147, 235, 270

Bidnova, Liubov, 99
Bilyi, Mykola, 99
Bolsheviks, 1–2; and budget allocations for education, 52; and confiscation of church property and gold, 91, 124n29; first occupation of Ukraine (1918), 15; and food policy in Ukraine, 23–24; and grain confiscations in Ukraine (1919), 21; and intelligentsia, xv, 27, 51–58, 88–89; and Makhno, 41n128, 286–87; and nationality policy, 6–8, 10–11, 63–69, 75; October Socialist Revolution (coup d'état, 1917), xxii, xxiv–xxv, 1, 11, 47–48, 56, 61; and policy toward non-Russian nations, xxiv, 15; and recognition of UNR, 15; second occupation of Ukraine (1919), 20; and status entitlements, 231; third occupation of Ukraine (1920), 20
Borot'bists, 2, 23, 27, 71, 272, 294
Brest-Litovsk, Treaty (1918), 14, 16, 300
British Foreign Office, 211
Bruk, Solomon, 104, 127n76
buksyrni bryhady. *See* tugboat brigades

Bullitt, William C., 121

cannibalism, 32, 154, 207, 245–47
capitalism, 7–8, 10, 119–21, 231
Catherine the Great, 11, 107, 122n9
censuses, 11, 30, 43n168, 53, 81n122, 187, 193–94, 220n81
Central Black Earth, 68, 83n145, 140, 164, 190, 192, 201, 298–99. *See also* TsChO
Central Rada, 1, 12, 14–15, 22, 93; about, 272; and Bolsheviks, 15–16, 37n65, 281, 299; diplomatic recognition in Europe (1918), 15; First Universal (1917), 12; Fourth Universal (1918) declares Ukraine independent, 13, 37n65, 299; persecution of former members of, 93, 297, 299, 300, 302; Secretariat of People's Education, 281; and UNR, 13, 299–300
chauvinism, 4, 64, 71, 234–35, 242–43
Cheka (VChK), 94, 128n89, 200, 209, 272, 293, 301. *See also* GPU (State Political Directorate); NKVD; OGPU (Joint State Political Directorate); Soviet secret police
Chekhivs'kyi, Volodymyr, 91, 99, *100*, 275
chekists, 201, 226n167, 226n170, 255, 272
Cherkasy (region), 49, 203, 297
Chernihiv (city and region), 99, 144, 150, 164, 167, 207, 236
children: Central Commission to Aid (TsK Dophol VUTsVK), 58; communes, 27, 59–61, 283; deportations of, 165; with disabilities, 27; during famine of 1921–1923, *31*, 32; during Holodomor of 1932–1933, 150, 153–63, 197–99, 271; homeless, 58–59, *161*, 271; and "hot breakfasts", 157–59; intellectually gifted, 28; orphanages, 26–27, 32, 58–59, 164, 199; social protection of, 26; social upbringing of, 26–27, 53–55, 59–61, 296, 301
chorni doshky (blacklisting), 135–36, 143–47, 189, 192, 272–73. *See also* Holodomor of 1932–1933
Chubar, Vlas, 233, 273
civilization(s), xxiii, 18, 48, 56, 240, 255
class: categories, 23–24; in communist doctrine, 3–4, 28, 33, 120; consciousness, 167; enemies, 96, 149, 167; and intelligentsia, xxii; liquidation of kulaks as, 138; national group *vs.*, 5; solidarity, 60; and status, 231
Clyman, Rhea, 210
collective farms: about, 282–83; anti-Soviet uprisings and, 138–42; blacklisting of, 143–44; grain confiscations, 144–47; law on theft of socialist property, 143, 147, 233; meat penalties, 144; payment in workdays on, 136–37, 298
collectivization, xxi, xxiii, 87, 186, 206–7, 229; activists during, 137–38, 144–46, 172n16; *dvadtsiatyp'iatytysiachnyky* (25,000ers), 275–76; and Holodomor of 1932–1933, 137, 214; resistance to, 138, 140–43; and Stalin's policy of, 135–36, 229, 232, 273; total, xxv, 4, 136, 172n12, 191
colonialism, xix, xxiii, 5, 10, 24, 64, 75, 137, 235, 239, 249, 296
Comintern (Communist International), 23, 29, 73, 91, 212–13, 273. *See also* Third International
Committees of Non-wealthy Peasants (KNS), 54, 282
communism, 2–4, 48, 53, 60–61, 110, 121, 137, 213, 231
Communist Party: and anti-Semitism, 209; Bolsheviks renamed as, 48; and cultural revolution, 47–49, 52; and education, 47–49, 60–61; and

Index

food rations, 30–31, 152–53, 155; and Holodomor of 1932–1933, 205; and "hot breakfasts" in schools, 157–58; and intelligentsia, 88–90; and Komsomol, 62, 138, 142, 146, 150; and KP(b)U membership, 70–71; and liquidation of illiteracy, 62; and moral code, 152, 177n98; nationality policy, 63, 70–71; *nomenklatura*, 250; and People's Commissariat of Education, 57; and purges of all political parties, 51; and purges of members, 205; and Robos, 27, 51; and Russian language, 70–72; and teachers, xxiii, 25, 47–49, 51–57, 61, 63, 65, 75–76, 150, 202, 294; and teaching of history and social sciences, 249–50; and Ukrainian language, 23–24, 70, 72; and Ukrainization, 64, 75. See also KP(b)U; RKP(b)

Communist Party (Bolsheviks) of Ukraine, 54, 56, 160, 283; and blacklisting, 143–44; ethnic composition of, 70–71, 83n160; and GPU, 88, 94; and intelligentsia, 70, 88; Kaganovich as leader of, 72; Korniushin as secretary of, 70; Kosior as secretary of, 160; Kviring as secretary of, 71; Lebed' as secretary of, 71; and national culture, 242; nationality policy, 64, 70–71; and political reeducation of teachers, 52–56; and Postyshev, 158, 234–36; purges of, 206, 235–36; and Tenth Congress of, 57, 72; and Third All-Ukrainian Party Conference (1932), 205; and Ukrainization, 64, 70–71, 75; and Zatons'kyi, 303. See also KP(b)U

Communist Youth League. See Komsomol (Communist Youth League)

concentration camps. See labor camps

Conquest, Robert, xvii, xx, 66, 165, 190, 208, 233, 245, 255

Cossacks, 11, 18, 69, 107, 109, 122n9, 143, 164–65, 271, 280, 289–90, 295

counterrevolution/-revolutionaries, 2, 15, 74; GPU and, 90, 92–93; and intelligentsia, 88, 91–93, 111; nationalism and, 5, 9, 201, 243; Operative Order No. 1 (1932), 147; SVU as organization of, 103, 105; teachers and, 66, 108, 110; in Ukrainian agricultural institutes, 171n2; Ukrainian farmers as, 108, 110

Crimea, 18, 142, 200, 253

cultural revolution, xxi, xxiii, 47, 52, 123n14, 164, 256

Danyliw, Volodymyr-Iuri, 279
decommunization, 5, 34n22
dekulakization, 205, 238, 274
denationalization, 11, 238
Denikin, Anton, 18, 21–22, 286
Dewey, John, 50
dezinformatsiya. See disinformation
Dibert, Varvara, 49–50, 167, 252
dictatorship, xx, 1, 5, 7, 75, 114, 231–32
Dimarov, Anatolii, 5, 172n12, 274
Directory (of Ukrainian National Republic), 17, 22, 99, 274–75, 300
disinformation, xvii, xix, 15, 200–202, 207, 213, 252, 254, 274
Dnipropetrovs'k (city; former Katerynoslav, now Dnipro), 21, 29, 68, 88, 99, 122n9
Dnipropetrovs'k (region; former Katerynoslav, now Dnipro), 29, 67–68, 142, 144, 146, 151, 156, 161
Doha, Vasyl', 98
Donbas (Donets Basin), 24, 41n133, 74, 144, 152, 200
Donets'k (city; former Stalino), 103, 241–42, 279
Donets'k (region), 29, 254

DPU. *See* GPU (State Political Directorate)
Duranty, Walter, 121, 208
Durdukivs'kyi, Volodymyr, *14*, 98, 102, 129n104
Dzerzhinsky, Felix, 59, 88, 90–92, 105, 226n170, 276, 301

education: *ABC of Communism*, 61; collectivist method of, 59–60; Communist Party and, 47, 49, 60–61; councils for national minorities, 16, 65; cultural revolution and, xxi, 47, 52; decentralization of, 14; labor, 25–26, 53, 61; and language, 13, 16–17; and nationality policy, 65; and national universities, 17; and nation building, 11–14, 16–17; primary, 17, 26; secondary, 26; social, 55; and Soviet political agenda, 1, 48–49; standardization of, 250; Taylorism in, 61; vocational/polytechnic, 15, 26
enemy of the people, 28, 102–3, 137–38, 147, 149, 157, 203, 205, 276
Engels, Friedrich, xxiv, 1, 2, 4, 6, 9, 28, 231, 287
ethnic/national minorities: areas of settlement, 65, 74; commissariats of education for, 14, 16; Germans, 65, 240; Mennonites, 67, 96–97, 142; and native-language schools, 14, 65, 67, 74; and Russian language, 65; Russian language *vs.* languages of, 65, 67, 69; self-determination for, 47; Ukrainian settlements in RSFSR, 68–69, 83n145, 299; Ukrainization and, 67, 169; village councils, 65, 82n142
ethnic/national-minority schools: closures, 74; for ethnic Ukrainian children in FSFSR, 69, 83n145; German, 67, *68*, 74; Jewish, 67; and nationality policy, 10, 65, 67–68; Polish, 67, 74; Russian, 67; and UNR, 300

Euromaidan. *See* Revolution of Dignity (2013–2014)
Existentialism, xvi, xxiii

famine (1921–1923), xv, 1, 51, 56, 62, 193; assistance from international organizations, 29; cannibalism during, 32–33; children during, 31–32, 45n185, 58–59; death statistics, 30, 163; as "dress rehearsal" for Great Famine, 33; as first Soviet *holodomor*, 45n188; grain exports during, 32; schools during, 61; in Soviet Ukraine, 28–33, 61; teachers during, 51, 56, 61; as tool of genocide, 30; Ukrainian intelligentsia during, 30, 56. *See also* American Relief Administration
famine-genocide (1932–1933), xvii–xviii. *See also* Holodomor of 1932–1933
First Five-Year Plan, 108, 110, 118, 120, 135, 166, 193, 237
forced labor, xxiii, 117–20, 238
Frenkin, Mikhail, 146, 149–50, 155, 176n88

Gantt, William Horsley, 42n150, 193
genocide, 135, 143, 212; Armenian, xix, 87; famine as tool of, 30, 196; Holodomor, xv–xviii, xxi, xxiv–xxv, 196, 229–30, 278; Indonesian massacres, 148; Lemkin's creation of term, xviii; xxixn29, 276; linguistic, 220n82; and nationalism, 125n42; perpetrators, 183, 230, 233; prevention, xviii; Rwandan, xviii; Soviet, xv, xvii, xxi, 1–2, 183, 229, 278; stages of, xviii–xix; typology of, xxvin9; against Ukrainians, xv–xviii, xxi, 1–2, 229–30, 252, 256; U.N. definition of, xviii, 276–77
GPU (State Political Directorate), 33, 52, 243; and anti-Soviet uprisings, 138, 140–42, 218n53; arrests,

87–92, 94, 114, 146–47, 191; and assassination of Petliura, 94–96; blockades of blacklisted villages, 146–47; cadres, 25, 90, 94, 209, 226n167, 226n170; deportations, 88–91, 94, 142, 164–65, 191–92; and food rations, 152–53; functions, 90; and KP(b)U, 94; and Kuban' operation (1932–1933), 164–65; and labor camps, 105–107, 112, 117–19; and methods of interrogation, 100–101, 104, 127n76, 127n80; and nationality policy, 65; pamphlet "On Ukrainian Separatism", 95; and People's Commissariat of Education, 89, 123n14; and registry of deaths during Holodomor of 1932–1933, 189; and repressions of Ukrainian intelligentsia, xxi, 88–94, 96, 100–17, 171n5, 191, 242; and Special Assignment Army of, 108; and Statute about Secrecy, 207; and suppression of anti-Bolshevik resistance in Ukraine, 21, 89–90; and suppression of Ukrainian Autocephalous Orthodox Church, 93–95; and SVU show trial, xxi, 97–105; and trial of Ukrainian SRs, 91, 95; and *troika*, 245, 247, 277; and Ukrainization, 65; use of Russian abbreviation, xxi. *See also* Cheka (VChK); NKVD; OGPU (Joint State Political Directorate); Soviet secret police

Gradenigo, Sergio, 193, 208, 239

grain confiscations: activists and, 21, 137, 172n16; Communist Party plenipotentiaries and, 137, 141, 206; as GPU operations to crash Ukrainian opposition to, 142–43; Komsomol and, 137, 146; and KP(b)U, 233–34; and nationality policy, 235; resistance to, 21, 138, 140–44, 146, 150; and "sabotage", 143, 145–47; teachers and, 54, 236; tugboat brigades and, 137–38, 144–46; Young Pioneers and, 138

Great Famine of 1932–1933. *See* Holodomor of 1932–1933

Great Terror, xxii, 96, 100, 192, 206, 277

Grigorenko, Petro, 173n36

Grossman, Vasily, 137, 231–32

GULAG (Main Directorate of Camps), 277; dissident memoirs on, 118; expansion in the 1930s, 107–8; and GPU, 105–7, 112, 117–19; Kolyma, 106–7; labor camps, 105–7; Museum of History of, 132n147; rise in Putin's Russia, 255; Solovetsky Islands, 107–8, 111, 113, 117–18, 131n144, 210, 244, 277, 279; White Sea–Baltic Sea Canal, 106–10, 116–17, 131n144, 133n166, 210, 244, 277

gymnasia, 13, 17, 27

Hantsov, Vsevolod, 84n173, 98, 114, 133n163

Havel, Václav, 256

Hermaize, Iosyp, 98, 109, 114, 191, 218n55, 253

Herriot, Édouard, 207

history: communization of, 250; and first conference of Marxist historians (1929), 113–14; and historiographic differences, xxiii, xxxivn72; and hybrid war, 254; revisionist, 145, 256; teaching of, 249; writing of, 200, 250

holocaust, xvii, xxviiin24

Holocaust, xxviiin24, 183, 197

holod, xvi, 277

holodomor, xvi, 45n188, 277

Holodomor of 1932–1933: as apogee of the Holodomor-genocide, 229–30, 277; blacklisting during, 135–36, 143–47, 189, 192, 272–73; blockades of villages, 146–47, 201; border closures during, 192; cannibalism during, 154, 207, 244–47; children during, 150, 153–63, 197–99, 244, 271; collapse of schools during, 153–62; confiscation of everything edible during, 136–37, 143, 189; cover-up, 158, 193–210; death certificates (ZAGS), 198–99, 222n115; death statistics, 163, 193–94, 196–99, 212, 214; and defeat of Ukrainian nationalism, 201; definition of, 277; economic aftermath, 237–39; end of Ukrainization, 163–66, 169–71; as famine, xix–xx, xxii; foreign diplomatic dispatches about, 239–43; foreign press coverage of, 207–10; Gareth Jones' tour of Ukraine, 209–10; as GPU special operation, 147, 189; grain export during, 188; grain procurement quotas, 144–45, 147, 188; "hot breakfasts" in schools during, 156–59; information blockade, 201, 204; internal passport decree, 233, 290; law on protecting socialist property, 233; as man-made famine, 277; mortality rate, *195*; non-payment for workdays, 298–99; number of victims, 193–200, 214, 240; and Roosevelt administration, 212; silencing in Soviet press, 204–5; Soviet propaganda blaming Ukrainian nationalism, 138–40; and speculation decree, 233; Torgsin hard currency stores during, 210, 212, 297–98; tugboat brigades, xxviiin23, 138, 144–46, 162, 272; vodka addiction rates after, 162

Holodomor-genocide: bystanders, xxv, 169; commemoration of, 253; criminological perspective on, xv; cultural effects, 191, 229, 247–48; definition, 278; deformation of morality during, 168; dehumanization, 138, 245–46; denial, xxiii, 183–200, 202, 214n5, 249, 252; destruction of books, 200–201, 241; epigenetic effects, 248; Great Famine of 1932–1933 as apogee of, xv, 33, 277; hate propaganda during, 138–40; as historical trauma, 239, 247; history of, xix, 251; as instrument of nationality policy, 170, 201; legal perspective on, xv; legal responsibility for, xxv, 184–86, 229–36; memorialization, 251–52; as multi-pronged attack (Lemkin), 278; National Museum, 187; number of victims, 193–200, 240, 278; organization of, 142–47; perpetrators, xv, 148, 186, 236, 278; and post-genocidal society, 249, 252; psychological effects, xxv, 229, 244–49; recognition of, xvii–xviii, 184, 186, 214, 229, 278; remembrance, 183, 186, 251; social effects, xxv, 229, 239–44; sociological perspective on, xv; survivors, 229, 239, 247–49; and SVU show trial of Ukrainian intelligentsia, xxi–xxii, xxv, 97–105; victims, xv, 138, 148, 168, 198, 201, 207, 214, 236–37, 243, 246, 278

Holoskevych, Hryhorii, 84n174, 104
Homo Sovieticus, 248, 250
Hrebenets'kyi, Oleksandr, 98
Hrushevs'kyi, Mykhailo, 12, 50, 94, 97, 103, 110, 114, 191, 252–53, 272, 279
Hrushevs'kyi, Serhii, 103, 279
Hryn'ko, Hryhorii, 26, 28, 63–64, 89, 272
Hryshko, Wasyl, xvii, xxviiin24, 2, 4, 9–10, 30
hunger, xvi–xvii, 31, 113, 119–20, 277
hybrid war, xxv, 184–85, 252, 254

Iavors'kyi, Matvii, 5, 84n173, 96, 113, 279
Iefremov, Petro, 99
Iefremov, Serhii, 84n174, 91, 94, 97–102, 104, 110, 128n89, 129n104, 130n113, 191, 218n55, 253, 272, 290

Index 347

imperialism, xix, xxiii, 4, 10–11, 47, 249
implicated subjects, xvi, 147–48
industrialization, xxiii, 117, 186, 190, 229, 237
Innitzer, Theodor, Cardinal, Archbishop of Vienna, 270
Institute of People's Education (INO), 14; Dnipropetrovs′k (Katerynoslav), 88, 91; Donets′k, 103, 279; GPU and, 96–103; Kam'ianets′-Podil′s′kyi, 88; Kharkiv, 88, 91; Kyïv, 88, 91, 98–99, 101, 113–14; Mykolaïv, 99; Nizhyn, 30; Odesa, 88, 99; Poltava, 99; protests in, 88; and SVU defendants, 97–100; and training of "red" professors, 88
intelligentsia: Bolshevik attitudes toward, xxii, 31, 48; Communist Party and, xxii, 70, 75; cultural revolution and, xxiii, 47; definition of, xxxivn68; and hierarchy of food distribution, 152–53; KP(b)U and, 70, 88; and national consciousness, 75; repression of, xx, 87, 236; standard of living, 30–31; teachers as members of, xvi, 27, 49, 75–76, 87; and Ukrainization, 66, 70–71
International Commission of Inquiry into the 1932–1933 Famine in Ukraine, xvii, 233, 279–80
International Military Tribunal Charter, 239
Ivanytsia, Hryhorii, 98
Ivchuk, Vasyl′, 159, *160*, 280

Jadwin, Edgar, 19
Jews, xix; and KP(b)U membership, 70–71, 83n160; migration from Pale of Settlement, 25; and nationality policy, 67; RKP(b) policy toward, 24–25; and Russian anti-Semitism, 8, 25, 95; and service in GPU, 25, 209, 226n167; and Social Democratic Bund, 8, 48; and Ukrainization, 70; violence against, 22, 95; and work in UNR government, 95
Jones, Gareth, 209, 226n173

Kaganovich, Lazar, 72, 143, 280
Kalnyshevs′kyi, Petro, 107
Kam'ianets′-Podil′s′kyi (city and region), 17, 51, 88, 143, 275
Kardynalovs′ka, Tetiana, 75, 281
Karpovych, Iosyp, 99
Kazakhstan (autonomous region within RSFSR), 106, 153, 164, 170, 172n16, 187–88, 190, 201
Kharkiv (city), 15, 20–21, 24, 72, 142, 161, 186–87, 204, 208–9, 239–43, 271; First All-Ukrainian Teachers Congress in, 54; intelligentsia in, 30; Institute of People's Education, 88, 91, 284; Research Institute of Geography in, 113; SVU show trial in Opera House, *98, 100–101*, 191; Third All-Ukrainian Conference on Teacher Education in, 53; University, 166, 296; orthography, 74, 78n49, 240
Kharkiv (region): blacklisting of villages in, 144; grain confiscations in, 144, 150; KP(b)U membership in, 70; teachers' congress delegates from, *55*; teachers in, 150–51, 153–55, 166; Ukrainian language proficiency in, 70; Ukrainization in, 70
Kholodnyi, Hryhorii, 99
Kholodnyi, Petro, 17, 281
Khomenko, Arsenii, 194
Khvylia, Andrii, 281–82
Khvyl′ovyi, Mykola, 72–74, 84n174, 110, 282
KNS. *See* Committees of Non-wealthy Peasants (KNS)
kobzars, 125n53, 271
Koestler, Arthur, 204

kolhosps. See collective farms

koloniï (children's communes), 27, 58–61, 283. *See also* Makarenko, Anton

Komsomol (Communist Youth League): about, 283; and activist search brigades, 172n16; Chubar's speech addressed to, 75; and grain confiscations, 137–38, 146; informers in institutes of higher education, 101; and liquidation of illiteracy, 62; and teachers, 146, 154, 163, 203; and Young Pioneers, 138

korenizatsiia. See nationality policy

Kosior, Stanislav, 91, 142, 160, 201, 203, 233, 283

KP(b)U. *See* Communist Party (Bolsheviks) of Ukraine

Kremenchuk (city), 152, 198

Krupskaya, Nadezhda (Lenin's wife), 52

Krushel′nyts′kyi, Antin, 94, 111

Kryms′kyi, Ahatanhel, 17, 84n174

Kuban′ (North Caucasus district): blacklisting in, 272–73; deportations from, 164–65; ethic Ukrainian population in, 18, 68–69, 194, 283–84; Poltavs′ka (Cossack settlement), 69, 164–65; Russification in, 223n116; teacher training college in, 69; Ukrainization in, 68–69, 164–65

kulaks, 155, 284; arrests of, 147; children of, 167–68; and collectivization, 137; definition of, 23–24; dekulakization, 274; deportations of, 142–43; exile to labor camps, 142; hate propaganda against, 138–40; liquidation of, 191–92; "sabotage" by, 138, 143, 147; Stalin on, 138, 205; teachers and, 53, 236; Young Pioneers and, 203, 224n136

kurkuli. See kulaks

Kursk (region), 69, 83n145, 298

Kviring, Emmanuil, 71, 284

Kyïvan Rus′ (medieval state), 11, 252, 255, 279

Kyïv (city), 17, 21, 50, 155, 184, 186, 187, 275, 281, 287; Film School, 242; First All-Ukrainian Teachers' Congress in (1917), 12; first national university in, 17; Gymnasium No. 1 named after Taras Shevchenko, 13; Institute of Linguistics, 242; Institute of People's Education in, 88, 91, 98–99, 113–14; intelligentsia in, 30; Labor School No. 1 named after Taras Shevchenko, 13, *14*, 98, 102; National Holodomor-Genocide Museum in, 172, 187; transfer of capital from Kharkiv to, 243; University, 108, 116, 242, 303

Kyïv (region), 49–50, 54, 70, 72, 143–44, 157, 159, 202, 236

labor camps, 100, 105–7, 142, 164, 213; and classification of laborers, 112–13; corrective, xxv, 116, 119, 130n118, 154; food rations in, 115, 153; forced labor in, 117–20, 210, 244; and GPU, 105–7, 112, 117–19; Kem′ transit station to, 106–7, 109, 210, 244; Kolyma, 106–7; living conditions in, 111–12, 131n147; mortality rate in, 117; political prisoners in, 111, 115, 119, 122; prisoner wages in, 116–17; production quotas in, 115; on Solovetsky Islands, 106–8, 111, 113, 117–18, 131n144, 210, 244, 274, 279; timber felling camps, 119; treatment of prisoners in, 111–12, 244–45; Ukrainian intelligentsia in, xxv, 100, 107–17; White Sea–Baltic Sea Canal, 106–10, 116–17, 131n144, 133n166, 210, 244, 277. *See also* GULAG (Main Directorate of Camps)

labor schools, 25–26, 53, 61

Lahuta, Mykola, 99
land: Bolshevik policy toward ownership of, xxiv, 1, 6, 9, 15, 18; Central Rada policy toward, 15; expropriation of, 5, 9, 53; in Marxist doctrine, 3, 10; Russian repartition of, 15; socialization of, 15
language: policy in Soviet Ukraine, xxii, 66; Ukrainian farmers as repository of national, xvii
League of Nations, xvi, 118, 211
Lebed', Dmitrii, 64, 71, 284–85
Lemkin, Raphael, xxviin21, 184, 212; as author of U.N. Convention on Genocide, xvii–xviii; conceptualized Soviet genocide, xvii, xix, 87, 136, 185, 192, 278
Lenin, Vladimir, xxiv, 1, 4–6, 15, 20, 28, 34n14, 35n25, 52, 61, 72, 88–89, 136, 157, 161, 231–33; assassination attempt on, 52, 77n28; and assimilation of nations, 7; creates secret police (Cheka), 105; creates USSR, 47; establishes concentration camps, 118, 277; and First Congress of Internationalist Teachers (1918), 49; as founding father of first socialist state, xxiv; *Imperialism, the Highest Stage of Capitalism*, 10, 71; land policy, 9–10; and liquidation of illiteracy, 61; and Marxism, 6, 10, 76n7; and Molotov, 30; and nationality policy, 11; New Economic Policy, 28–29, 136; and October Socialist Revolution (coup d'état, 1917), 48; and Skrypnyk, 72–73; and Stalin, 4, 66; and suppression of anti-Bolshevik uprisings, 145; theses on RKP(b) policy toward Ukraine, 23–24; and Ukrainian intelligentsia, 25, 88–89; views on role of teachers, 49, 52; views on self-determination of nations and secession, 6, 10, 47; views on use of political power, 4, 75; and War Communism, 29, 45n188, 302; writings on education, 8, 49; writings on national culture, 8–9
Leninism, xxiii, 33
Lower Volga (region), 68, 140, 172n16, 192
Luhans'k (city and region), 254
Lunacharsky, Anatoly, 48, 285
Lyons, Eugene, 207, 213
Lypkivs'kyi, Vasyl', Metropolitan, 94–95, 285
Lysyvets', Anastasiia, 248, 286

Mace, James E., 64, 74, 188–89, 212, 224n144, 233, 235–36, 239, 249, 286
Makarenko, Anton, 59–61, 79n80, 80n86
Makhno, Nestor, 2, 22, 276, 286–87
Manifesto of the Communist Party, 2–3, 5, 287
Marx, Karl, xxiv, 1–6, 23, 27, 231–32, 287; and anti-national bias, 2–4, 9; and anti-peasant attitude, 4, 10; *Capital*, 5, 120; as "Darwin of history", 28; on hunger as motive for labor, 120; and theory of communism, 2, 137
Marxism, xvi, xxiii, 2, 4, 5, 7–8, 12, 62, 75, 76n7, 108, 119, 250
Marxism-Leninism, 1, 159, 294
Matushevs'kyi, Borys, 97, 99, *100*, 127n76, 287
Mennonites, 32, 67, 82n140, 97, 141, 203
Mizernyts'kyi, Oleksandr, 55, 57, 287–88
modernization, 57, 135, 207, 229
Molotov, Viacheslav, 30, 143, 185, 188, 201, 205, 249, 288
Morozov, Pavlik, 203, 224n136
Muggeridge, Malcolm, 210–11
Muscovy (medieval principality), 11
Mykolaïv (city and region), 30, 99, 199

Nansen, Fridtjof, 29, 32
nationalism, xxiii, 4–5, 7–10, 12, 20, 63–64, 75, 92–93, 201
nationality policy, 63–69, 170, 283; Bolsheviks and, 6–11; education and, 65; and grain confiscations, 201, 235; KP(b)U and, 64, 70–71; native languages and, 65; Petliura on Soviet Ukrainization, 75; RKP(b) and, 63–64; schools and, 64; Soviet, 63–69, 75, 233; Ukrainization, 64–75, 283
national liberation struggle (1917–1921), xv, xxiv, 10–23, 49, 56, 65, 89, 297
New Economic Policy (NEP), 27, 29, 66, 87–88, 135, 288
New York (city), xvii, *120*, 121, 185, 201, 212, 279
NKO. *See* People's Commissariat of Education (in Soviet Ukraine)
NKVD. *See* Cheka (VChK); GPU (State Political Directorate); OGPU (Joint State Political Directorate); People's Commissariat of Internal Affairs; Soviet secret police
nomenklatura, 250, 289
North Caucasus, 50, 190, 210–11; and blacklisting, 143–44, 189; and border closure, 192; ethnic Ukrainian population in, 18, 137, 165, 194, 201, 283–84; and grain confiscations, 172n16; Kuban' operation (1932–1933), 164–65; pedagogical college in, 69, 165; resettlement of Red Army veterans to, 219n66; resistance to collectivization, 190; Russification in, 223n116; and Ukrainization, 68–69, 164–65, 190, 201

October Socialist Revolution (coup d'état, 1917), xxii, xxiv–xxv, 1, 11, 47–48, 56, 61, 164, 282
Odesa (city and region), 88, 99, 144–45, 154–55, 199, 240

OGPU (Joint State Political Directorate). *See* Soviet secret police
orthography. *See* Ukrainian language
Otamanovs'kyi, Valentin, 100
otamans (Cossack chieftains), 18, 41n128, 289, 297

paiki (food rations), 31, 152–55, 289–90
Panchenko-Chalenko, Kyrylo, 99
Paris (city), 19–20, 75, 94–96, 281; Ukrainian Mission in, 19
Paris Peace Conference, 18–19, 39n100, 39n106
Pavlohrad (city and district), 56, 142, 146
Pavlov, Ivan, 27, 42n150
Pavlushkov, Mykola, 97, 99–100, *101*, 110, 126n64, 129n106, 290
peasants, 10, 23–24, 71, 74, 93, 190, 204–5, 207, 233
People's Commissariat of Education (in Soviet Ukraine), 25, 123n14, 235, 289, 303–4; Declaration on Social Upbringing of Children, 26; and GPU, 89, 91; and Kharkiv orthography (1926), 74, 78n49, 295–96; and mobilization for agricultural campaign, 149; and political reeducation campaign, 53–56; and purges of, 169–70; and Ukrainization, 67, 169–70. *See also* NKO
People's Commissariat of Internal Affairs, 270, 277, 284, 286, 289. *See also* NKVD
Peter the Great, 11, 36n48, 66, 254
Petliura, Symon, 11–12, 17, 19–20, 23, 75, 92, 94–95, 108, 125n47, 125n53, 274–75, 290
Petliurites (followers of Petliura), 51, 93, 107, 147, 164, 167, 170, 190, 203, 290–91
Petrovs'kyi, Hryhorii, 32, 62, 75, 122n9, 199, 291

Pidmohyl′nyi, Valerian, 103, 111
Piłsudski, Josef, Marshal, 95, 125n47
Podillia (region), 140–42
political enlightenment, 61–63
political police. *See* Cheka (VChK); GPU (State Political Directorate); NKVD; Soviet secret police
Poltava (city and region), 11–12, 22, 32, 53–54, 56–57, 99, 156, 164, 290
polytechnic education. *See* vocational education
post-genocidal syndrome, 252, 291
post-traumatic stress disorder, 247–49
Postyshev, Pavel, 5, 158, 170, 201, 203, 205, 233–36, 242, 291
proletariat, 1–4, 7–9, 25, 51–52, 55–56, 60, 63, 70–71, 75, 76n7, 238. *See also* working class
propaganda, xxi, 24, 33, 50–52, 54, 58, 62, 71, 96, 119, 121, 123n14, 137–38, 154, 193, 197, 247, 291
"Prosvita" (cultural societies), 62–63
Putin, Vladimir, 185, 200–201, 252, 254–55

Radchenko, Oleksandra, 153–54, 177n107, 178n108, 292
Radomysl′ (town and district), xv, 157, 280
Rakovsky, Christian, 20, 29, 49, 64, 123n19, 292–93
Ratner, Semen, *101*, 102
Red Army, 40n114, 164; and first occupation of Ukraine, 15; and grain confiscation detachments, 20–21; and pogroms (1919), 22; and second occupation of Ukraine, 20; suppression of anti-Bolshevik uprisings in Ukraine, 21, 47; and third occupation of Ukraine, 20, 23; veterans resettled in depopulated by famine areas of Ukraine, xvii, 162, *195*, 219n66
Red Cross, 31–32, 44n180, 211

Red October. *See* October Socialist Revolution (coup d'état, 1917)
Red Terror, 89–90, 123n19, 173n36, 293
Roosevelt, Eleanor, 212, 250
Revolution of Dignity (2013–2014), 34n22, 252–54, 266n149
Riappo, Ian, 26, 88
RKP(b). *See* Russian Communist Party (Bolsheviks)
Robos (educational employees union), 24–25, 51–58, 236, 293
Rudnyts′kyi, Stepan, 94, 113, 132n158
rural areas; anti-Soviet uprisings in, 138, 140–43; epidemic diseases in, 16; literacy rate in, 11, 61; political enlightenment in, 61–63; "Prosvita" societies in, 62–63; teachers in, 47–48, 52–58, 155; Ukrainization in, 49–50, 66–69. *See also* village(s)
rural schools: and grain confiscations, 150; enrollment in, 57; teacher shortages in, 57; teachers in, 57, 150; Ukrainian-language instruction, 17; Ukrainization and, 49–50, 67–69; urban schools *vs.*, 57
rural-urban relationship, 48, 71, 136, 237
Russia (in Soviet era): communal farming tradition, 15; and composition of tugboat brigades, 137–38, 172n16; and composition of secret police, 25, 90, 226n167, 226n170; and creation of USSR, 63–64; death statistics for 1932–1933 famine, 194; Duranty's coverage of, 208; education in, xxii; Eleanor Roosevelt's visit to, 250; famine of 1921–1922 in, 29–30, 32; Kondrashin on famine in 1929–1934 in, 186–87, 194, 215n23, 216n24, 217n31; and paper production, 50; and People's Commissariat of Foreign Affairs, 207; as perpetrator

of genocide, xviii; Ukrainian ethnic settlements in, 18, 68–69, 83n145, 137, 140, 163–65, 172n16, 190, 194, 201, 283–84, 298–99; Wilson's Fourteen Points and, 18, 20. See also Central Black Earth; Kazakhstan (autonomous region within RSFSR); Lower Volga (region); North Caucasus

Russian Empire, xix, 2, 5–7, 12; anti-Semitism in, 8; collapse of (1917), 48; Germany's investments in, 16; inner colonies of, xix, 4–6; and Kyïvan Rus', 11; *Okhranka* (imperial secret police), 93, 289; and paper production, 50; suppression of Ukrainian language and culture in, 11, 70

Russian Communist Party (Bolsheviks), 63, 71, 90–91, 293; and Clyman, 210; and Duranty, 208; and GPU, 90; and nationality policy, 63–65, 71; and New Economic Policy, 47; policy toward Ukraine, 23–24; and Skrypnyk, 73; Thirteenth Congress of, 52; and Ukrainization, 64–65, 71. See also RKP(b)

Russian culture: Ukrainian culture *vs.*, xxiii, 11, 70–71, 74

Russian history: Ukrainian history *vs.*, xxxivn72, 253–54

Russian language: Communist Party and, 70, 72; in Donbas, 241; ethnic-minority languages *vs.*, 67; in ethnic Ukrainian areas of USSR, 163; extracurricular use of, 170; and native-language instruction for schoolchildren, 67; in non-Russian schools, 67, 241; privileging of, 22, 67, 69–70, 170, 241; publications in, 241; state employees and, 67, 72; teachers and, 153, 166, 169; Ukrainian language *vs.*, xxiii, xxxivn71, 64, 67, 69–71, 169, 237, 240–41; Ukrainization and, 70–71, 163, 165, 169–70; urban population and, 70; working class and, 7–9, 70

Russian-language instruction: ethnic Russians and, 68; in post-secondary education, 170, 242; in secondary education, 170, 241; Ukrainian *vs.*, 68, 241

Russian-language schools, 13; Ukrainian language in, 17, 241; and Ukrainization, 169–70

Russia, post-Soviet: annexation of Crimea (2014), 200; Federal Archival Agency, 186, 215n22; Federal Cultural Association of Ukrainians in, 201; "Historical Memory" Foundation, 186–87, 216n25; Holodomor denial, 183–84, 255; hybrid war against Ukraine, xxv, 183–85, 254; Library of Ukrainian Literature, 200–201; rehabilitation of Stalinism in, 183, 192, 200; Russian World Foundation, 213, 223n122; *Sputnik International* (propaganda news outlet), 196–97; State Duma, 184, 187, 255; support of Yanukovych, 252; Union of Ukrainians in, 201; war in Donbas, 200

Russification, xvii, 7–8, 36n47, 66–68, 74, 110, 169–71, 238, 253, 291

sabotage, 51, 143, 145–47, 189, 293
Sadovs′kyi, Hennadii, 108–9
Sambros, Iurii, 96, 168–69, 294
Sandarmokh (Karelia, RSFSR), 111, 116, 131n144, 279, 290
Schwartzbard, Samuil (Sholem), 94–96
scientific communism, xxiv, 1–2, 5, 294
secondary education: primary and secondary schools, 13–14, 16–17, 22, 25–26, 49–50, 65, 67–69, 74, 170, 241; and school enrollments in Ukraine (1932–1933), xxii, 160–64, 166
seksot, 94, 96, 245, 294

Shaw, George Bernard, 207
Shchepotiev, Volodymyr, 99
Shevchenko, Taras, xv, 49–50, 102, 203; *Kobzar*, 50; *Zapovit*, xv
Shums'kyi, Oleksandr, 54, *55*, 71–72, 78n49, 84n173, 92, 272, 287, 294–95, 303
Shylo, Kostiantyn, 99
Skoropads'kyi, Pavlo, 2, 16–17, 274, 295
Skrypnyk, Mykola, 64, 68, 72, *73*, 74–75, 102–3, 110, 169–70, 194, 203, 220n84, 239–40, 242, 281, 295–96, 303
Skrypnykivka (Kharkiv orthography), 74, 295–96
Slabchenko, Mykhailo, 99, 102, 109, 129n105
Slabchenko, Taras, 99, 102
social engineering, 2, 61, 75, 87, 231
socialism, 2, 7–9, 48–49, 51–58, 70–75, 108, 119–21, 137–38, 152–54
Sokolians'kyi, Ivan, 27, 55, 84n174
Solovey, Dmytro, 104, 165, 296
Solzhenitsyn, Aleksandr, 255
Sorokin, Pitirim, 32–33
Sosnovyi, Stepan, 194
Soviet agriculture, xix, 135–36, 160, 190
Soviet genocide, xv, xvii, xxi, 1–2, 183, 229, 278
Soviet industry: construction projects managed by GPU, 105–7, 112, 117–19; First Five-Year Plan, 108, 110, 118, 120, 135, 166, 193, 237; food ration cards in cities, 152–53; "Great Breakthrough", 171n12, 273; need for development of natural resources, 276; timber trade, 118–19
Soviet secret police, 5, 59, 75; archival documentation of 1930 rebellions, 138, 140–42, 218n53; campaign in Ukraine (1919–1922), 89–90; and cannibalism cases, 245–46; collaboration with Commissariat of Education, 89, 123n14; Dzerzhinsky as chief of, 59; and Gareth Jones' tour of Ukraine, 209; and GULAG, 105–7, 112, 117–19; and institutions for recruiting cadres for, 60; Jewish cadres in, 25, 90, 94, 226n167, 226n170; Lenin creates, 105; name changes, xxi; patrolling Ukrainian borders (1933), 146–47; recruiting informers, 94, 96, 245, 294; repressions of Ukrainian intelligentsia, xxi, 88–94, 96, 100–19, 129n109, 171n5, 191, 242; and SVU show trial, xxi, 97–105; and trial of Ukrainian SRs, 91, 95; and *troika*, 245, 247, 277. *See also* Cheka (VChK); GPU (State Political Directorate); NKVD; OGPU (Joint State Political Directorate)
Soviet Union: creation of, 63–64; dissolution of, xx, 5; education in, xxi–xxii; as "Evil Empire", 193; incorporation of Ukraine into, 18, 65–66, 69; indigenization policy (*korenizatsiia*), 63–69; labor camps in, 105–19; paper industry in, 119; recognition by the United States, 122; timber industry in, 118–19; vodka monopoly in, 161–62; Western intellectuals visit, 207. *See also* USSR (Union of Soviet Socialist Republics)
Stalin, Joseph, xviii, xx, xxv, 34n15, 63, 69–70, 105, 108, 151, 208; and collectivization of agriculture, 135–36, 229, 273; and Constitution (1936), 300; decisions affecting Ukraine (1932–1933), 137, 145, 170, 189, 192, 201, 205, 234; edict on theft of socialist property (August 1932), 143, 146; ends NEP, 66; and ethnicity, 66; fear of renewed Polish-Ukrainian campaign, 95; as *genocidaire*, xx, 183, 185, 233; and GPU, 108, 243; and "Great

Breakthrough", 171n12, 273; as Great Teacher, 4, 110, 158; and Lenin, 4, 66, 231–32; letter to KP(b)U regarding "national deviationism", 72; liquidation of kulaks, 138; and Marxism, 4, 231; and mass uprisings in Ukraine (1930), 142; and militarization cycles, 254; open letter from Iavors'kyi to, 113; as People's Commissar of Nationalities, 64, 66; personality, 231–32; personality cult, xx; posthumous conviction for genocide, 186, 273; and Postyshev, 242; purges of Ukrainian Communist Party, 205–6; and retribution for uprisings in Ukraine, 142–43; and "revolution from above", 97; and school administration, 249; and schoolchildren, 159; Shums'kyi and, 72; Skrypnyk and, 73; and SVU show trial, 102; and Ukrainization, 66, 170–71, 201, 229; and U.N. Convention on Genocide, 185, 213; view on significance of schooling, 10–11; and White Sea–Baltic Sea Canal, 109–10; and world revolution, 121

Stalinism, xxiii, 200, 213. *See also* totalitarianism

Steshenko, Ivan, 12–14, 296

Stockholm syndrome, 248

Strang, William, 182n177

SUM (Union of Ukrainian Youth), 97, 103, 105, 290, 297

SVU show trial, 135, 142; defendants, xxi, 98–100, 103–4, 122; GPU and, xxi, 97–105; in Kharkiv Opera House, 97, 98, 104, 191; as prelude to Holodomor, xxi; proceedings, 103, 129n99; and public court hearings, 102; public prosecutors during, 103, 128n99; purges of teachers after, 165–66, 294; Ukrainian history and language professors as defendants, 97–99

SVU (Union for the Liberation of Ukraine): as "anti-Soviet" organization, xxi, 103; arrests of members, 97, 148, 191; branches, 99; condemnation of, 103; as "counterrevolutionary" organization, 103; farmers as social base of, 104; GPU and, xxi, 97–105; interrogation files, 103–4, 129n100; as "plot", xxi, 103, 129n106; statute, 104; SUM and, 97, 103–4, 290; Ukrainian intelligentsia and, xxi–xxii, xxv, 97–105; and Ukrainization, 105; and VUAN, 104

teachers: as activists, 148–50, 236; and All-Soviet Teachers' Union, 55; and All-Ukrainian Teachers' Union, 12, 17, 24, 27, 51; arrests of, 52; blacklisting of villages and, 146–47; Bolshevik attitudes toward, 25–26, 31, 51; and children's communes, 58–61; and collectivization campaign, 149–51; Communist Party and, xxiii, 47–49, 51–57, 61, 63, 65, 75–76, 150, 158–59, 202, 250; as conduits of culture, 49, 55; and cultural revolution, 47–49, 52; during famine (1921–1923), 30–31, 51, 56; economic wellbeing of, 14–15, 17, 51, 56–57; educational background of, 54; ethnic background of, 55, 57–58; existential choices of, xvi; extermination of nationally-conscious, xx, 242; First All-Ukrainian Conference on People's Education (1920), 26; First All-Ukrainian Teachers' Congress (1917), 12–13; First All-Ukrainian Teachers' Congress (1925), 54; First Congress of Internationalist Teachers, 49; and food rations, 152–55; and food shortages, 155; and food surrogates, 156; and gender parity, 57; GPU and, 52, 60, 146; as guardians of national memory, 256; and health conditions of, 56–57; ideological orientations of, 27, 53–54, 63, 149–51; as implicated subjects, 147–49; and KNS, 54; and Komsomol, 150, 155; and *kurkuli*, 149; and labor camps, 108–10; Lenin and, 52; and liquidation of illiteracy, 61–63; and Marx's theory, 28, 55; as members of intelligentsia, xvi, 27, 49, 75–76, 87; in minority-language schools, 14, 57–58, 67–69, 83n145; murder of, 149; and national identity, 50–51, 169; and national liberation struggle, 18, 50–51; and opposition to Soviet regime, 56; passivity of, 148, 150; People's Commissariat of Education and, 25, 53, 62; as perpetrators, 236; and political enlightenment, 61–63; political indoctrination of, 27, 49, 52–55, 62; in primary schools, 17, 22, 57–58, 69, 154, 165; progressive pedagogy and, 50; as propagandists of Bolshevik policies, xxiv, 47–48, 52, 55, 63; and "Prosvita" societies, 62–63; protest against Denikin's policy, 22; purges of, xxii, 25, 51–52, 165–66, 236, 242; qualifications, 53; as "red pedagogues", 53, 69; Robos and, 24–25, 27, 51–58, 236, 287–88; rural, 47–48, 51–58, 62–63, 150, 153–57, 166; Second All-Ukrainian Conference on People's Education (1920), 26; Second All-Ukrainian Teachers' Congress (1917), 13; in secondary schools, 17, 58, 69; shortage of, 14, 57, 155; as social enthusiasts, 149; social role of, 48–49, 63; suicides among, 151, 176n94; and SVU show trial, xxii, xxv, 97–105, 149; and teacher training courses, 17; Third All-Ukrainian Conference on Teacher Education (1924), 53; and Ukrainian culture, 69; and Ukrainian history, 17, 69, 97–99, 102; and Ukrainian language, 17, 65–66, 69, 97–99; in Ukrainian-language schools, 17, 67, 170; Ukrainian-language schools in RSFSR, 69; and Ukrainization, 50, 66; and UNR, 17; urban, 47–48, 54, 57

terror, xvii, xx, 67, 147, 205, 231–32, 245

textbooks: All-Ukrainian Teachers' Union and, 12; and history teaching, 249; Holodomor in history, xix; paper shortage and, 50; publishing, 17, 22; shortages of, 50; standardization of, 250; and timber industry, 118–19

Third International. *See Comintern* (Communist International)

Tiutiunnyk, Iurii, 56, 78n50, 125n47, 297

Tokarivs'ka, Nina, 98, *100*

Torgsin (hard currency stores), 210, 212, 297–98

totalitarianism, xx, 1, 115, 122, 233, 255

trade union. *See* Robos (educational employees union)

Trezvyns'kyi, Iurii, 98

troika, 114, 245, 247, 277, 298

Trotsky, Leon, 31, 110

TsChO. *See* Central Black Earth

tugboat brigades, xxviiin23, 138, 144–46, 162, 272

Ukraine, xix–xx, xxii; anti-Bolshevik resistance in, 21, 89–90; anti-Soviet uprisings in, 138, 140, *141*, 142–43, 218n53; ARA admitted to, 29–31; arrests of opponents of Soviet regime, 87–92, 94, 114, 146, 191; Association for Holodomor Studies in, 200; blacklisting, 143–46, 189; blockades of blacklisted villages in, 145–46, 190; Bolshevik budget allocations to education in, 52,

58; Bolshevik food policy in, 24, 152–53; categories for liquidation of "suspected counterrevolutionaries" in, 92–93; children in, 26–27, 31–32, 55–56, 58–61, 150, 153–65, 197–99; collapse of schools in, xxii, 160–62; collectivization imposed on, 136, 171–72, 172n12; death statistics for 1932–1933, 163, 193, 196, 199, 212, 214; declares independence (1991), 171; decommunization laws, 5; delegation at Paris Peace Conference, 18–19; deportations of intelligentsia, 87–93, 117; deportations of kulaks from, 142, 191–92; educational system in, 11–14, 16–17, 24–28, 301; end of Ukrainization, 162–63, 169–70; epidemic diseases in, 16, 20, 30, 32, 56; ethnographic boundaries of, 18, 39n106, 133n159; famine of 1921–1923 in, 28–33, 193; first Bolshevik occupation of, 15; geography of, 17, 113; German occupation of, 16, 50; grain confiscations in, 21, 29, 54, 143–47, 172n16; grain exports from, 188; Holodomor of 1932–1933 in, 135–37, 143–47, 153–63, 169–71, 189, 192–210, 212, 214, 229–30, 239–47; and Hrushevs′kyi's return (1924), 279; Institute of History of Ukraine, 193, 200; internal passport system (from 1932), 233, 290; KP(b)U membership in, 70; Lemkin on Soviet genocide in, xvii, xix, 87, 136, 185, 192, 278; liquidation of illiteracy in, 60–63; mass uprisings (1930), 140, *141*, 142–43; merges with RSFSR, 23; Molotov's visit (1932), 188; mortality from Great Famine (1932–1933), *195*; National Holodomor-Genocide Museum in, 187; nationality policy in, 7, 11, 64, 70; and national liberation struggle, xv, xxiv, 10–23, 30, 49; non-Bolshevik Ukrainization, 12–13, 17, 50; and political enlightenment, 61–63; political literacy of teachers in, 52–55, 62; reports of Western journalists about, 207–10; Revolution of Dignity (2013–2014), 34n22, 252–54, 266n149; Russian hybrid war against, 184–85, 252, 254; Russians in, 82n142; Security Service of, 154, 200; second Bolshevik occupation of, 20, 186, 194; Stalin's decisions affecting, 137, 145, 170, 189, 192, 201, 205, 234; State Committee on Archives in, 186, 198; teachers' union members in, 91; third Bolshevik occupation of, 20

Ukrainian Autocephalous Orthodox Church (UAOC), 40n125, 95, 99, 104, 192, 275, 285

Ukrainian culture: and educational associations, 22; orientation toward European culture, 74; "Prosvita" societies and, 62–63; purges of institutions connected to, 242–43; revival of, 12–15, 17–18, 22, 49–50; Russian culture *vs.*, xxiii, 11–12, 70–71, 74; Soviet, 240–41; and theory of two cultures, 71; and Ukrainization, 70–75

Ukrainian farmers: blacklisting of, 135–36, 143–47, 189, 192, 272–73; and Bolshevik land policy, 9, 15, 18; Borot′bists (left wing party), 23; collectivization imposed on, 136; Committees of Non-wealthy Peasants, 54, 282; exiled to Russian Far North and Siberia, 108, 110–11, 117, 127n82, 128n84; and industrialization and urbanization, 238; labeled as *kurkuli*, 138; mass uprisings (1930), 138, 140–43; and OGPU reports about, 138, 140–41; rejection of communal farming in 1920s, 15; as repository of folklore and music, xvii; as repository of national culture, xxv, 67; resistance to collectivization, 138; resistance to grain confiscations (1919), 20–21; and settlement in grain-growing areas of RSFSR (1924–1928), 237; Soviet propaganda denigrating, 139–40; Stalin's view of, 66–67; as target in Soviet genocide, xvii, 76, 135

Ukrainian history: lack of textbooks, 249; purges of teachers and professors of, 97–102, 113–14, 170; Putin's views on, 252, 254; removal of book on, 170, 241; rewriting of, 252–53; Russian history *vs*., xxxivn72, 253–54; teaching of, 17, 22, 69, 249

Ukrainian intelligentsia: attitudes toward Soviet government, 25; categories for liquidation, 92–93; deportations of, xx, 88–92; executed at Sandarmokh, 131n144; existential choices of, xvi, xxiii; extermination of nationally-conscious, xx, xxv, 100–17, 129n109, 191, 240; GPU and, 94, 100–19, 171n5, 238; ideological orientations of, 25, 54; and national identity, 75, 169; and nationality policy, 70, 75; non-communist, 54, 65, 236; old (prerevolution), xxiv, 54, 91–92, 96, 107, 167; Petliura's, 64; as political prisoners, 111, 115, 119; and "Prosvita" societies, 62–63; "red" elite replacement for, xxiv, 54, 88, 167; and RKP(b) policy toward, 23, 25, 94; and SVU show trial, xxi, xxv, 97–105; as target of Soviet genocide, xv, xvii, 76, 87, 122; and trial of SRs, 91, 95

Ukrainian language: banned by Denikin, 22; Bolshevik policy toward, 23–24; borrowings in, xxxivn71; Central Rada's policy toward, 12; Communist Party cadres and, 23–24, 70, 72; dictionaries, 114, 241; during Directory's rule, 17; higher education institutions and, 17, 65, 67; imperial Russian suppression of, 11, 70; KP(b)U membership and, 70; Mace on, 74; mandated in schools, 13, 17, 64–65; and modernization, 169; moved "closer" to Russian, 84n177; new orthography (1919), 17; orthographic commission (1926), 74, 78n49, 84n174; persecution of scholars of, 98–99, 101–2, 111, 114, 116; and post-famine "Russification", 170–71, 239, 291; recognized as state language (1919), 17, 20; revival during the struggle for national liberation, 13, 17; rural *vs*. urban environments and uses, 57–58; Russian language *vs*., xxiii, xxxivn71, 64, 67, 69–71, 169, 237, 240–41; and Skoropads′kyi's rule, 16–17; state employees and, 67, 72; testing of, 72, 241; teachers and, 17, 65–66, 69, 97–99; and Ukrainization, 63–75, 83n143, 163–65, 169

Ukrainian-language instruction: expansion of, 65; in non-Ukrainian schools, 65, 67; in primary schools, 16–17, 65, 241; in Russian-language schools, 22, 241; in secondary schools, 13, 17, 65, 241; and teacher training, 13, 65, 69

Ukrainian-language literature: lack of, 50, 241; Mace on, 74; textbooks, 17, 50; under tsarism, 11; and Ukrainian-language schools in the Russian SFSR, 69

Ukrainian-language schools: number of, 67, 170; gymnasia, 13; and national identity, 11; overcrowding of, 13; popular pressure for, 49; at post-secondary level, 67, 170; in RSFSR, 68–69, 83n145; in Russian Empire, 11; Russification of, 11, 69, 170; secondary, 13; and Ukrainization, 74, 169

Ukrainian nationalism, xxii, 69, 138, 169, 190, 201, 233–35, 238, 240, 243

Ukrainian National Republic (UNR), 1, 13–14, 17, 125n47, 125n50, 171, 281; about, 299–300; and Bolsheviks, 15; and Chekhivs'kyi, 91, *100*; Directory of, 17, 22, 99, 274–75, 300; Fourth Universal declares Ukraine independent (1918), 13, 37n65, 299; government-in-exile, 300; GPU repression of supporters of, 110, 147, 298–302; and Liquidation Commission, 19; and ministry of nationalities, 300; recognition by Great Britain and France, 15; recognition by World Socialist Conference, 23; and Ukrainian Mission in Paris (1919–1920), 19–20; and Ukrainian National Chorus, 22, 41n126. *See also* Central Rada; Directory (of Ukrainian National Republic)

Ukrainian National Women's League of America (UNWLA), 211–12

Ukrainian Party of Socialist Revolutionaries (SRs), 52, 88, 91, 95, 296

Ukrainian Revolution. *See* national liberation struggle (1917–1921)

Ukrainians: deported and exiled to labor camps, 117; forcibly resettled to Siberia, 127n82, 128n84; in KP(b)U, 70, 206; as Little Russians, 11, 18, 20, 22; as national group targeted in Soviet genocide, xv–xvi, 186, 229; as political prisoners, 111, 129n109; repressions against, 140, 186, 234; in RSFSR, 68–69, 83n145, 299; and Russification, xvii, 7–8, 36n47, 67–68, 74, 110, 169–71, 238, 253, 291; Stalin's "crashing blow" directed against, 190

Ukrainian separatism, 20, 47, 74, 242–43

Ukrainization, xxv; and Cheka, 209; *Chervonyi perets'* special issue on, 83n143; in Donbas, 74; end of, 69, 74, 102, 105, 110, 135, 164–65, 169–70, 190–91, 235; in ethnic Ukrainian areas of RSFSR, 68–69, 83n145, 140, 190, 201; KP(b)U and, 64, 70–71, 75; limits of, 69; Mace on, 64, 74; as NEP in cultural sphere, 66; non-Bolshevik, 12–13, 17, 50; in North Caucasus, 164–65; People's Commissariat of Education and, 67, 72, 74, 169; Petliura on Soviet, 75; political goals of, 69, 92; resistance to, 68; Soviet, 63–75; Stalin and, 63, 70, 164, 201, 229

U.N. Convention on the Non-applicability of Statutory Limitations to War Crimes and Crimes Against Humanity, 185, 230

U.N. Convention on the Prevention and Punishment of the Crime of Genocide, xvii–xviii, 184–85, 230, 244

Union of Militant Atheists (*bezbozhniki*), 236, 271

Union of Ukrainian Youth. *See* SUM (Union of Ukrainian Youth)

Union for the Liberation of Ukraine. *See* SVU (Union for the Liberation of Ukraine)

United Nations, 184, 190, 214

United States, 18, 117, 119, 135, 273, 281, 296; Communist movement in, 121, 124n29, 212; and farm management, 135; and forced labor, 119–20; Jewish intellectuals in, 213; and recognition of USSR, 122, 188; and Tariff Act (1930), 119

urban-rural relationship. *See* rural-urban relationship

U.S. Commission on the Ukraine Famine, xviii, xxxivn73, 151, 155, 167, 188, 193, 202, 212, 251–52, 286

U.S. Department of State, xviii, 19–20, 119, 121

U.S. National Holodomor Memorial, 196, 252
USSR (Union of Soviet Socialist Republics). See Soviet Union

Vasylenko, Mykola, 16–17, 300–301
Vashchenko, Hryhorii, 60, 301
VChK. See Cheka (VChK)
vidpovidachi (system of extrajudicial killing), 89–90, 293, 301. See also Red Terror
village(s): councils in national minority areas, 65, 82n142; demand for schools in, 49; Gareth Jones' tour of Ukrainian, 210; "Prosvita" societies in, 62–63; Rhea Clyman's account of famine in Ukrainian, 210; teachers in, 47–48, 51–58, 62, 65, 150, 153–57, 166. See also rural areas
Vinnytsia (city and region), 51, 140–42, 155, 158–61, 275
violence, xv, xviii, xx, xxiii–xxv, 1–5, 47, 148, 207, 230, 233, 243, 245–46, 256
Volga (region), 29–30, 68, 140, 188, 192, 239, 270
Volyn' (region), 52, 140–42, 299
Voronizh (city and region), 69, 83n145, 194, 298
VUAN. See All-Ukrainian Academy of Sciences
vykonavtsi (perpetrators): about, 302; and collectivization, 137–38, 302; Communist Party Politburo as, 233–35; Communist Party rank-and-file as, 235–36; and grain confiscations, 302; and GPU, 302; and propaganda campaigns, 137–40, 302; teachers' participation as, 148–50, 236, 302; urban proletariat as, 172n16. See also *buksyrni bryhady*
Vynnychenko, Volodymyr, 24, 272, 274–75

Vyshinsky, Andrey, 212

War Communism, 29, 45n188, 152, 302
Washington, D.C. (city), 121; National Holodomor Memorial in, 196, 252, 263n122; Taras Shevchenko School of Ukrainian Studies in, 252
Webb, Beatrice and Sidney, 208
Weber, Max, xix, 231
White Army, 2, 22, 25, 245
Wienerberger, Alexander, 161, 179n138
Wilson, Woodrow, 18
women, 11–12, 55, 61–62, 99, 104, 117, 168, 204, 211–12, 236, 243–44, 246
working class: hierarchy of food distribution, 152–53; intelligentsia and, 49; and nationality, 6; nationality policy and, 8–9, 70; as ruling class, 4; Russian *vs.* Ukrainian, 9; schools (*robfaky*), 292; and socialism, 2; Ukrainization of, 70

Yanukovych, Viktor, 252
Young Pioneers, *59*, *73*, 138, 202
Yurkevych, Lev, 8
Yushchenko, Viktor, 187, 197

ZAGS (registry of vital statistics), 198–99, 302
Zales'kyi, Andrii, 98
Zaluzhnyi, Oleksandr, 60, 302
Zaporizhzhia (region), 29
zaruchnytstvo (system of extrajudicial killings), 89–90, 293, 303. See also Red Terror
zatirka (food surrogate), 156, 303
Zatons'kyi, Volodymyr, 15, 25, 55, 61, 64, 75, 90–91, 128n89, 160, 303
zemstvos (local self-governing administrations), 12–13, 22
Zerov, Mykola, 111, 116
Zhytomyr (region), 49, 146, 155–56

About the Author

Dr. Victoria A. Malko is a faculty member in the Department of History and founding coordinator of Holodomor Studies at California State University, Fresno. She is author of *The Chechen Wars: Responses in Russia and the United States* (2015); editor of *Women and the Holodomor-Genocide: Victims, Survivors, Perpetrators* (2019); contributor to *Russian Active Measures: Yesterday, Today, Tomorrow*, edited by Olga Bertelsen (2021); and member of the editorial board of *American History and Politics*, a bilingual peer-reviewed journal published by the Department of History of Taras Shevchenko National University. She also serves on an Advisory Board of the National Holodomor-Genocide Museum.

www.ingramcontent.com/pod-product-compliance
Lightning Source LLC
Chambersburg PA
CBHW052055300426
44117CB00013B/2133